PCI-X
System
Architecture

PC System Architecture Series

MindShare, Inc.

Please see our web site (http://www.awl.com/cseng/series/mindshare) for more information on these titles.

80486 System Architecture: Third Edition
0-201-40994-1

AGP System Architecture: Second Edition
0-201-70069-7

CardBus System Architecture
0-201-40997-6

EISA System Architecture: Second Edition
0-201-40995-X

FireWire® System Architecture: Second Edition
0-201-48535-4

ISA System Architecture: Third Edition
0-201-40996-8

PCI System Architecture: Fourth Edition
0-201-30974-2

PCI-X System Architecture
0-201-72682-3

PCMCIA System Architecture: Second Edition
0-201-40991-7

Pentium® Pro and Pentium® II System Architecture: Second Edition
0-201-30973-4

Pentium® Processor System Architecture: Second Edition
0-201-40992-5

Plug and Play System Architecture
0-201-41013-3

Power PC System Architecture
0-201-40990-9

Protected Mode Software Architecture
0-201-55447-X

Universal Serial Bus System Architecture
0-201-46137-4

PCI-X
System
Architecture

MindShare, Inc.
Tom Shanley

ADDISON–WESLEY

Boston • San Francisco • New York • Toronto • Montreal
London • Munich • Paris • Madrid
Capetown • Sydney • Tokyo • Singapore • Mexico City

For more information, please contact:
Pearson Education Corporate Sales Division
One Lake Street
Upper Saddle River, NJ 07458
(800) 382-3419
corpsales@pearsontechgroup.com

Library of Congress Cataloging-in-Publication Data
Shanley, Tom.
    PCI-X system architecture / Tom Shanley. -- 1st ed.
        p.cm. -- (PC system architecture series)
    ISBN 0-201-72682-3
        1. Computer architecture. 2. Microcomputers--Buses. I. Title. II. Series

QA76.9.A73 S4543 2001
004.2'2--dc21   00-050418

Set in 10 point Palatino by MindShare, Inc.

1 2 3 4 5 6 7 8 9 10—MA—0403020100
First Printing, November 2000

For my darlin' Nancy

Contents

About This Book

Part 1: Basic Concepts

Chapter 1: PCI Needed Improvement

Contents

Chapter 2: PCI-X Improves on PCI

Contents

Contents

Contents

Chapter 5: PCI-X Is a Registered Bus

Chapter 6: Intro to Commands

Chapter 7: Intro to Transaction Phases

Contents

Chapter 8: Intro to Transaction Termination

Chapter 9: Intro to Split and Immediate Transactions

Contents

Part 2: Transaction Protocol

Chapter 10: Bus Arbitration

Contents

Chapter 11: Detailed Command Description

Contents

Contents

Chapter 12: Latency Rules

Contents

Chapter 13: The Address, Attribute and Response Phases

Contents

Chapter 14: Dword Transactions

Chapter 15: Burst Transactions

Contents

Chapter 16: Transaction Terminations

Contents

Chapter 17: Split Completion Messages

Chapter 18: 64-Bit Transactions

Contents

Contents

Chapter 19: Parity Generation and Checking

Contents

Contents

Part 3: Device Configuration

Chapter 20: Configuration Transactions

Contents

Chapter 21: Non-Bridge Configuration Registers

Contents

Chapter 22: Bridge Configuration Registers

Contents

Contents

Part 4: Load Tuning

Chapter 23: Load Tuning Mechanisms

Part 5: PCI-X Bridges

Chapter 24: PCIX-to-PCIX Bridges

Contents

Contents

Contents

Part 6: Error Detection and Handling

Chapter 26: Error Detection and Handling

Contents

Contents

Contents

Part 7: Electrical Issues

Chapter 27: Electrical Issues

Contents

Figures

Figures

Figures

Figures

Figures

Tables

Acknowledgments

The author would like to extend special thanks to Allen Goodrum and Dwight Riley for their time and insights.

About This Book

The MindShare Architecture Series

The MindShare Architecture book series includes: *ISA System Architecture, EISA System Architecture, 80486 System Architecture, PCI System Architecture, Pentium Processor System Architecture, PCMCIA System Architecture, PowerPC System Architecture, Plug and Play System Architecture, CardBus System Architecture, Protected Mode Software Architecture, Pentium Pro and Pentium II System Architecture, USB System Architecture, FireWire System Architecture, PCI-X System Architecture,* and *AGP System Architecture.* The book series is published by Addison-Wesley.

Rather than duplicating common information in each book, the series uses the building-block approach. *ISA System Architecture* is the core book upon which the others build. Table 1 on page 1 illustrates the relationship of the books to each other.

Table 1: PC Architecture Book Series

Category	Title	Edition	ISBN
Processor Architecture	80486 System Architecture	3rd	0-201-40994-1
	Pentium Processor System Architecture	2nd	0-201-40992-5
	Pentium Pro and Pentium II System Architecture	2nd	0-201-30973-4
	PowerPC System Architecture	1st	0-201-40990-9

Table 1: PC Architecture Book Series (Continued)

Category	Title	Edition	ISBN
Bus Architecture	PCI System Architecture	4th	0-201-30974-2
	EISA System Architecture	Out-of-print	0-201-40995-X
	Firewire System Architecture: IEEE 1394	2nd	0-201-48535-4
	ISA System Architecture	3rd	0-201-40996-8
	Universal Serial Bus System Architecture	1st	0-201-46137-4
	PCI-X System Architecture	1st	0-201-72682-3
Other Architectures	PCMCIA System Architecture: 16-Bit PC Cards	2nd	0-201-40991-7
	CardBus System Architecture	1st	0-201-40997-6
	Plug and Play System Architecture	1st	0-201-41013-3
	Protected Mode Software Architecture	1st	0-201-55447-X
	AGP System Architecture	1st	0-201-37964-3

Cautionary Note

The reader should keep in mind that MindShare's book series often deals with rapidly evolving technologies. This being the case, it should be recognized that the book is a "snapshot" of the state of the targeted technology at the time that the book was completed. We attempt to update each book on a timely basis to reflect changes in the targeted technology, but, due to various factors (waiting for the next version of the spec to be "frozen," the time necessary to make the changes, and the time to produce the books and get them out to the distribution channels), there will always be a delay.

This Book Assumes PCI Background Knowledge

As with all MindShare books, this book assumes that the reader has prior knowledge of PCI (because PCI-X is built on top of PCI). Likewise, the PCI-X spec assumes prior knowledge of PCI and describes only how PCI-X differs from PCI as described in the PCI 2.2 spec and the 1.1 PCI-to-PCI Bridge Architecture spec. The reader may gain this background knowledge by reading the MindShare book entitled *PCI System Architecture, Fourth Edition* (published by Addison-Wesley).

Specifications This Book Is Based On

This book is based on the version 1.0 PCI-X specification and the version "AF" Errata and Clarifications document. Please note the author received the Errata and Clarifications document quite late in the development of the book and every effort was made to integrate this new information. In one or two cases, the amount of time that it would have taken to study and integrate the new information would have delayed the publishing of the book. Rather than delay the book, the author chose to clearly identify the area in question and urges the reader to read the appropriate section of the Errata and Clarifications document.

Organization of This Book

The book is organized as follows:

Part 1: Basic Concepts
    Chapter 1: PCI Needed Improvement
    Chapter 2: PCI-X Improves on PCI
    Chapter 3: Lowest Common Denominator Defines Mode
    Chapter 4: Device Types and Bus Initialization
    Chapter 5: PCI-X Is a Registered Bus
    Chapter 6: Intro to Commands
    Chapter 7: Intro to Transaction Phases
    Chapter 8: Intro to Transaction Termination
    Chapter 9: Intro to Split and Immediate Transactions
Part 2: Transaction Protocol
    Chapter 10: Bus Arbitration
    Chapter 11: Detailed Command Description

PCI-X System Architecture

Who This Book Is For

This book is intended for use by hardware and software design and support personnel. The tutorial approach to the subject may also make the book useful to technical people who are not involved in design or support.

Prerequisite Knowledge

The reader should be familiar with PC and PCI System Architectures. Mind-Share's ISA System Architecture and PCI System Architecture books provide that foundation material. *PCI-X is built upon the PCI bus standard. This book assumes that the reader has a working knowledge of the PCI bus protocol.*

Documentation Conventions

This document contains conventions for numeric values as follows.

Hexadecimal Notation

This section defines the typographical convention used throughout this book. All hex numbers are followed by an "h." Examples:

```
9A4Eh
0100h
```

Binary Notation

All binary numbers are followed by a "b." Examples:

```
0001 0101b
01b
```

Decimal Notation

Numbers without any suffix are decimal. When required for clarity, decimal numbers are followed by a "d." The following examples each represent a decimal number:

```
16
255
256d
128d
```

Bits Versus Bytes Notation

This book employs the standard notation for differentiating bits versus bytes.

All abbreviations for "bits" use lower case. For example:

1.5Mb/s
2Mb

All references to "bytes" are specified in upper case. For example:

10MB/s
1KB

Bit Fields (Logical Groups of Bits or Signals)

All bit fields are designated in little-endian bit ordering:

[X:Y],

where "X" is the most-significant bit and "Y" is the least-significant bit of the field.

Timing Diagram Drawing Convention

In PCI-X, events are synchronized with the rising-edge of the PCI-X clock. For example, if a PCI-X device enables or disables an output driver or changes a driven signal from active to inactive, it will start doing so coincident with the rising-edge of the clock. Timing diagrams in this book are drawn such that signals transition near the middle of the PCI-X clock period, thereby indicating some non-zero (real-world) delay with respect to the PCI-X clocks to which they are referenced.

At some times, a signal is actively driven while at other times it isn't. When a PCI-X device is actively driving a signal, the signal is depicted as a solid line. When a signal is not being actively driven, it may be pulled high or low by a resistor, or may be allowed to float. Whenever a signal is not actively driven, the timing diagram depicts it as a dashed line. If the dashed line is high or low, assume that a pull up or pull down resistor is maintaining the state of that signal. When a signal is in a float state, the dashed line will be midway between the active-high and -low voltage levels.

The turnaround symbol, represented by two curved arrows pointing to each other's tails, indicates that a signal (or a group of signals) is being returned to the float state by its current owner. The current owner is backing off its output driver(s) for this signal (or group of signals) in preparation for another device taking ownership and turning on its output driver(s).

Some of the signal representations shown in Figure 1 on page 7 require further explanation:

- In Figure 1 on page 7, the signals with the annotation "signal driven to an undefined state" have a solid outline and are filled with a hash pattern. This means that the signal owner must drive something on those signals during that clock cycle, but it can be any value.
- The signals with the annotation "signal driven to a defined state" have a solid outline and a white fill pattern. This means that the signal owner must drive a valid value (e.g., an address, or data) on those signals during that clock cycle.
- The signals with the annotation "signal driven to a unspecified state or floated" have a dashed outline and a hash fill pattern. This means that the signal owner may either drive any value on those signals during that clock cycle or may back off its output drivers from those signals.

Figure 1: Signal Documentation Standards

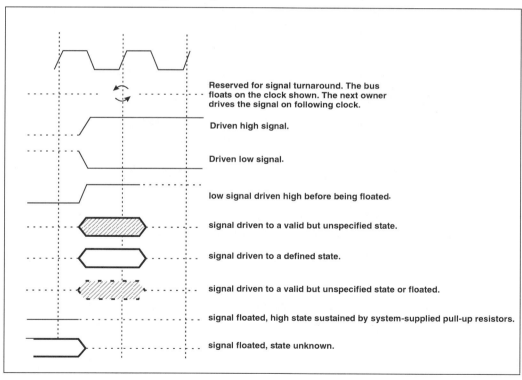

Clock-by-Clock Timing Diagram Description

Each timing diagram is accompanied by a clock-by-clock description. The description of the events that occur in a given clock cycle follows the following format:

CLOCK 1. The clock cycle number is clearly identified by number and is immediately followed by:

ON the rising-edge of clock 1:

- This is the description of an event that occurs on the rising-edge of clock 1.
- This is the description of another event that occurs on the rising-edge of clock 1.

DURING clock cycle 1:

- This is the description of an event that occurs during clock cycle 1.
- This is the description of another event that occurs during clock cycle 1.

CLOCK 2.

Signal Polarity

Any signal name with a pound sign (#) suffix following it is asserted when driven low. Signal names lacking the pound sign suffix are asserted when high.

Visit Our Web Site

Our web site contains a listing of all of our courses and books. In addition, it contains errata for a number of the books, a hot link to our publisher's web site, and course outlines.

www.mindshare.com

Our publisher's web site contains a listing or our currently available books and includes pricing and ordering information. Their home page is accessible at:

www.awl.com/cseng

We Want Your Feedback

MindShare values your comments and suggestions. You can contact us via mail, phone, fax or Internet email.

Phone: (719) 487-1417 and in the U.S. (800) 633-1440
Fax: (719) 487-1434
E-mail: tom@mindshare.com

For information on MindShare seminars, please check our web site.

Mailing Address:

MindShare, Inc.
4285 Slash Pine Drive
Colorado Springs, CO 80908

Part 1:
Basic Concepts

This Part

Part 1 introduces basic concepts and terminology and consists of the following chapters:

- Chapter 1: PCI Needed Improvement
- Chapter 2: PCI-X Improves on PCI
- Chapter 3: Lowest Common Denominator Defines Mode
- Chapter 4: Device Types and Bus Initialization
- Chapter 5: PCI-X Is a Registered Bus
- Chapter 6: Intro to Commands
- Chapter 7: Intro to Transaction Phases
- Chapter 8: Intro to Transaction Termination
- Chapter 9: Intro to Split and Immediate Transactions

The Next Part

Part 2 provides a detailed description of the PCI-X bus protocol and consists of the following chapters:

- Chapter 10: Bus Arbitration
- Chapter 11: Detailed Command Description
- Chapter 12: Latency Rules
- Chapter 13: The Address, Attribute and Response Phases
- Chapter 14: Dword Transactions
- Chapter 15: Burst Transactions
- Chapter 16: Transaction Terminations
- Chapter 17: Split Completion Messages
- Chapter 18: 64-Bit Transactions
- Chapter 19: Parity Generation and Checking

1 *PCI Needed Improvement*

This Chapter

This chapter describes the areas of the PCI bus protocol that the architects of the PCI-X bus protocol identified as needing improvement.

The Next Chapter

The next chapter introduces the primary improvements in PCI-X that targeted deficiencies in the PCI bus protocol. This includes: higher bus speeds, elimination of Wait States, block-oriented transfers, Latency Timer optimization, transfer size specification, Split Transactions, load tuning, Data Phase parity error recovery, bus width indication, MSI capability, Power Management capability, elimination of snoops, widening of memory decoders, and the elimination of stepping and Fast Back-to-Back transactions.

Wait States Yield Poor Performance

A PCI transaction consists of the Address Phase and one or more Data Phases. In each Data Phase, either the Initiator or the target can delay the transfer of the current dword (or, during 64-bit data transfers, qword). According to the rules first established in the PCI 2.1 specification, the initiator can keep its IRDY# signal deasserted for up to seven clocks in each Data Phase. The target can keep TRDY# deasserted for up to 15 clocks from the assertion of FRAME# in the first Data Phase, and for up to seven clocks in each subsequent Data Phase of a burst transaction.

In other words, the PCI spec permits the initiator and target to make poor use of the bus. Obviously, this type of behavior would yield poor performance for the initiator performing the transaction as well as for other bus masters awaiting bus ownership to initiate transfers.

Relatively Slow Clock Speed

PCI buses may be designed to operate in either the 0-33.33MHz range or the 33.33-66.66MHz range. Data items (i.e., dwords or qwords) are transferred on each rising-edge of the clock on which both IRDY# and TRDY# are sampled asserted. This yields a maximum transfer rate of 33.33M transfers per second on a low-speed bus and 66.66M transfers per second on a high-speed bus. The best-case scenario is when the bus is running at 66.66MHz, neither the initiator nor the target inserts any Wait States in the transaction's Data Phases, and both parties are 64-bit devices. This would permit a maximum transfer rate of 66.66M 8-byte transfers per second, or 533.28MB per second.

Transfer Size Unknown

When a PCI master initiates a burst transaction (i.e., a memory transaction), it does not indicate how much data it intends to transfer. The PCI memory access commands are:

- **Memory Read** (MR). Indicates that the master intends to read an unspecified amount of data from memory starting at the indicated dword (or qword if it is performing 64-bit transfers). By using this command, the master is indicating to any bridge that the read may have to traverse either that:
  - it has specific knowledge that the memory region is non-Prefetchable memory, or
  - it doesn't know whether it's prefetchable or not.
- **Memory Read Line** (MRL). Indicates the master intends to read an unspecified amount of data from memory starting at the initial dword (or qword) and that it knows that the area of memory from the start dword (or qword) address up to the end of the current line is Prefetchable memory.
- **Memory Read Multiple Line** (MRM). Indicates the master intends to read an unspecified amount of data from memory starting at the initial dword (or qword) and that it knows that the area of memory from the start dword (or qword) address up to the end of the line after the current line is Prefetchable memory.
- **Memory Write** (MW). Indicates the master intends to write an unspecified amount of data to memory starting at the start dword (or qword) address specified in the Address Phase.
- **Memory Write and Invalidate** (MWI). Indicates that the master has issued a start address aligned on a line boundary and that it intends to write an unspecified number of full lines to memory.

In each of these cases the master issues a dword- or qword-aligned start address and does not specify how much data it intends to read or write. This presents buffer management problems to:

- any bridges that the transaction must traverse.
  - On a read from memory, a bridge does not know how much data will ultimately be read by the originating master. It therefore doesn't know how much data to read from the target when it passes the memory read transaction to the target bus and doesn't know how much buffer space to allocate to hold the returning read data.
  - On a write to memory, the bridge doesn't know how much buffer space to allocate in its posted memory write buffer to absorb the write data into.
- the target that is being read from or written to.
  - On a memory read, the target doesn't know how much data will ultimately be read. It therefore doesn't know how far ahead it can safely read from its internal memory.
  - On a memory write, the target doesn't know how much buffer space to allocate in its inbound posted memory write buffer to absorb the write data into.

PCI Delayed Transactions Are Inefficient

If the target of a PCI transaction cannot transfer the first data item within 16 clocks from the assertion of FRAME#, it memorizes the transaction and issues a Retry to the Initiator. In other words, it treats it as PCI Delayed Transaction.

Initiator Retries Use Up Valuable Bus Time

After receiving a Retry, the initiator is obliged to repeatedly rearbitrate for the bus. The target will continue to respond to each repeat of the transaction request with a Retry until it is ready to start transferring data within 16 clocks from the initiation of the transaction.

Initiator Doesn't Supply Transfer Count

The PCI target memorizes all of the transaction information that the initiator supplies it with:

- The start dword (or qword) address.
- The command.
- The Byte Enable settings issued in the first Data Phase.
- If it's an IO or a Config write transaction, the write data supplied in the first Data Phase.

This is referred to as the Delayed Read or Write Request (DRR or DWR). If the request is a memory read (MR, MRL, or MRM), the initiator has not specified the amount of data to be read. As mentioned earlier, this creates buffer management and read-ahead problems for the target or any bridge in the path to the target.

Delayed Completion

Once the target has obtained the requested read data or has delivered the write data, the request has been transformed from a Delayed Request into a Delayed Completion. The target must then await the originating master's next repeat of the transaction so it can give the completion to it.

Initiator's Transaction ID Is Sketchy at Best

The only information that the target can use to identify the master that is repeating a previously memorized request is the start address, command, Byte Enables issued in the first Data Phase, and the write data (if it's a write). Since it is possible for another master to mimic the request issued earlier by another master, the target may give the completion to the wrong master.

Snoops Hurt Performance

Refer to Figure 1-1 on page 18.

Host/PCIX Bridge Knows AGP's Area of Memory Is Non-Cacheable

The Host/PCIX bridge typically contains the main memory controller. It is also the communication path between PCI masters and main memory. The AGP 2.0 spec dictates that the region of main memory allocated to the AGP graphics adapter must be designated as non-cacheable memory. This means that the processors do not cache copies of memory lines from this region. There is therefore no reason for the Host/PCIX bridge to generate snoop transactions on the processor bus whenever the AGP adapter accesses its designated area of memory.

Memory Used by PCI Masters May or May Not Be Cached

Other than the region of main memory assigned to the AGP adapter, the Host/PCIX bridge does not know what areas of main memory are cached by the processor(s). This means that it must generate a snoop transaction on the processor bus whenever a PCI master attempts to access main memory.

Snoops Slow Down PCI Accesses to Main Memory

When a PCI adapter starts an access to main memory, the Host/PCIX bridge acts as the target of the PCI transaction. Because the master may be addressing a stale line in system memory, the Host/PCIX bridge cannot allow the PCI master to start transferring data with memory until the results of the snoop have been presented to the Host/PCIX bridge by the processor(s). While awaiting the snoop result, the Host/PCIX bridge may insert Wait States into the first Data Phase or may issue a Retry to the PCI master. This delay in the transfer of the first data item certainly impacts the performance of the PCI master.

Snoop Traffic on Processor Bus Can Hurt Processor(s)

Each time that the Host/PCIX bridge generates a snoop transaction on the processor bus, the processor bus is a little less available to the processor(s). If PCI bus masters access main memory frequently, this can have an adverse effect on the performance of the processor.

Main Memory Less Available to Processor(s)

In addition, during periods of time when PCI masters are generating a lot of traffic to main memory, the memory bus is less available for the processors to use.

Figure 1-1: Block Diagram of Example System

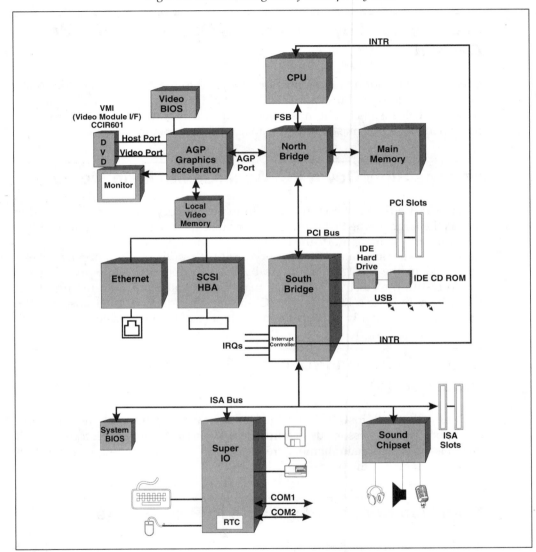

Latency Timer Use Not Optimized in PCI

Refer to Figure 1-2 on page 20. The following two sections describe usage of the Min_Gnt and Latency Timer configuration registers in the PCI (rather than the PCI-X) environment.

Min_Gnt Register: Timeslice Request

Optional for a bus master and not applicable to non-master devices. This read-only register is implemented by bus master devices and not by target devices. The value hardwired into this register indicates how long the master would like to retain PCI bus ownership (in order to attain good performance) whenever it initiates a transaction. The value indicates how long a burst period the device needs (in increments of 1/4 of a microsecond, or 250ns). A value of zero indicates the device has no stringent requirement in this area.

Latency Timer: "Timeslice" Register

The Latency Timer defines the minimum amount of time, in PCI clock cycles, that the bus master can retain ownership of the bus whenever it initiates a new transaction. The bus master decrements its Latency Timer by one on each rising-edge of the clock after it initiates a transaction. It may continue its transaction until either:

- it has completed the overall burst transfer (if it doesn't lose its grant), or
- the target asserts STOP# to prematurely terminate the transaction, or
- it has exhausted its timeslice (LT value) and it has been preempted (lost its GNT# to another PCI master),

whichever comes first.

A master's Latency Timer value is programmed either by the configuration portion of the BIOS or by the OS during setup and/or run-time. Software consults the master's hardwired Min_Gnt register value in order to determine the timeslice desired by the designer of the master.

Insufficient Info to Select a Good Value

Software depends upon the designer telling the truth regarding the master's need for a timeslice of a specified duration. If the Min_Gnt values for all masters on a PCI bus indicate that they need a timeslice of FFh (255 PCI clock cycles), the software has no recourse but to assign equal timeslices to each master on that bus. This may be better than that needed by some masters and worse than that needed by others, resulting in poor performance for some masters that need more bandwidth.

Figure 1-2: Type 0 Configuration Header Registers

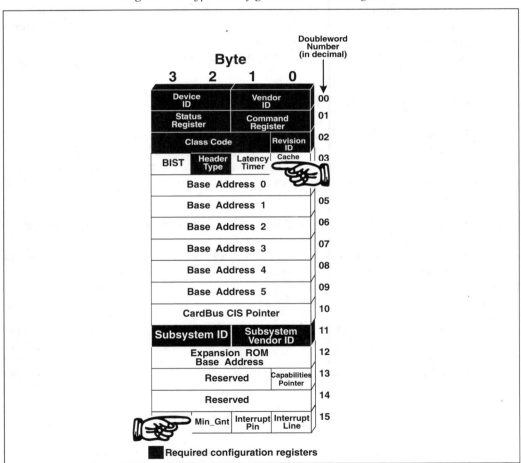

Data Phase Parity Error Recovery Usually Not Possible

PCI Data Parity Error Recovery

The PCI specification permits recovery from Data Phase parity errors but does not require it. The specification recommends that recovery be attempted at the lowest possible level (i.e., by the bus master). Ideally, the master should attempt error recovery without involving software. If the master cannot perform an action or actions to recover from the error, it should report the error to its device driver and possibly the driver can perform error recovery. The error should only be reported to the OS if neither the master nor its driver can recover from the error. How the OS responds to the error is OS-specific.

If the device reports the error by asserting SERR#, error recovery cannot be attempted (because assertion of SERR# causes the chipset to issue a fatal interrupt to the processor and the OS will shut down; see "Important Note Regarding Chipsets That Monitor PERR#" on page 22). Examples of recovery by the master, device driver and the OS are listed below:

- **Recovery by the bus master**. The master may attempt recovery by re-attempting the transaction if it knows that it will have no side effects (e.g., if the target device is a FIFO buffer, the access should not be re-attempted). If the re-attempt of the access completes with no errors, the master does not have to report an error to the system. If the attempt (or, perhaps several attempts) is unsuccessful, then the master must report the error. If there is a device driver associated with the master, the master alerts the driver to the error by generating an interrupt, setting a status bit, or some similar method. If there isn't a device driver associated with the master, the master may report the error by asserting SERR#.
- **Recovery by the device driver**. Assuming that the bus master reported the error to its device driver (e.g., by setting a device-specific status bit and generating an interrupt), the driver may instruct the bus master to re-attempt the transaction (once again, the driver must know that the re-attempt will not cause side effects). If the access completes with no errors, the device driver does not have to report the error to the OS. If the access error cannot be recovered from, the driver must report the error to the OS.
- **Recovery by the operating system**. How the OS responds to the report of a data parity error is OS-specific.

Important Note Regarding Chipsets That Monitor PERR#

In many PCI platform designs (i.e., chipset designs), the chipset logic converts any assertion of PERR# by anyone into an assertion of SERR#. This means that if either the master (on a read) or the target (on a write) asserts PERR#, the chipset may very well either assert SERR# or just take the same action that it normally does when it detects SERR# asserted by another party. Typically, this results in the generation of a fatal interrupt to the processor (such as an NMI or a Machine Check).

No Indication of Device Width

In the PCI environment, software cannot determine the width of a function's connection to the AD bus (32-bits or 64-bits). As a result, software cannot determine that the end-user may have installed a 64-bit capable card in a 32-bit connector.

MSI Feature Optional in PCI Environment

Introduction

A PCI function that generates interrupt requests to request servicing by its device driver can do so using one of **two methods**:

METHOD 1. As described in the earlier parts of this chapter, the device designer can use a **pin** on the device to signal an interrupt request to the processor.

METHOD 2. Alternatively, the designer can implement Message Signaled Interrupt, or **MSI**, capability and use it to signal an interrupt request to the processor. This method eliminates the need for an interrupt pin and trace and is described in this section.

The spec recommends that a function that implements MSI capability also use an interrupt pin to allow usage of the device in a system that doesn't support MSI capability. System configuration software cannot assume that an MSI-capable function has an interrupt pin.

Advantages of MSI Interrupts

The advantages of MSI interrupt generation versus using an interrupt pin are as follows:

- eliminates the need for interrupt traces.
- eliminates multiple PCI functions sharing the same interrupt request input on the interrupt controller.
- eliminates the chaining of device drivers.
- eliminates the need to perform a dummy read from a device in its interrupt service routine to force all posted memory writes to be flushed to memory.

Power Management Optional

Legacy PCI Devices—No Standard PM Method

PCI devices designed before the advent of the *PCI Bus Power Management (PM) Interface Spec* may or may not implement some form of power management. If a legacy device implements some form of power management, the method used to control the device's power state is specific to the device and therefore requires device-specific software to manage it.

PCI devices that do not implement any form of power management logic can only be in one of two possible power states, On (D0) or Off (D3$_{cold}$), and cannot be programmatically switched between the two.

Device Support for PCI PM Optional

It is optional whether or not a PCI device implements power management capability. If it does and was designed after the advent of the PCI Power Management spec, it must be implemented as defined by that spec.

Discovering Function's PM Capability

The New Capabilities registers are essentially a linked list of configuration register sets, each of which controls an optional new capability that the PCI function may implement. The Capability ID of the PM register set is 01h. To determine if a PCI function implements the PM registers:

PCI-X System Architecture

STEP 1. Software **checks** bit 4 (**Capabilities List bit**) of the function's **PCI configuration Status register** (see Figure 1-4 on page 25 and Figure 1-3 on page 24). A one indicates that the Capabilities Pointer register is implemented in the first byte of dword 13d of the function's configuration Header space.

STEP 2. The programmer then **reads** the dword-aligned pointer from the **Capabilities Pointer register** and uses it to read the indicated dword from the function's configuration space. This is the first dword of the first New Capability register set.

STEP 3. Refer to Figure 1-5 on page 26. If the first (i.e., least-significant) byte of the dword read contains **Capability ID 01h**, this identifies it as the PM register set used to control the function's power state. If the ID is something other than 01h, then this is the register set for a New Capability other than PM (e.g., AGP or VPD). The byte immediately following the Capability ID byte is the pointer (within the function's configuration space) to the start of the register set for the next New Capability (if there are any additional New Capabilities). 00h indicates there isn't any, while a non-zero value is a valid pointer. As **software traverses the linked-list** of the function's New Capabilities, its PM register set will hopefully be located.

Figure 1-3: PCI Configuration Status Register

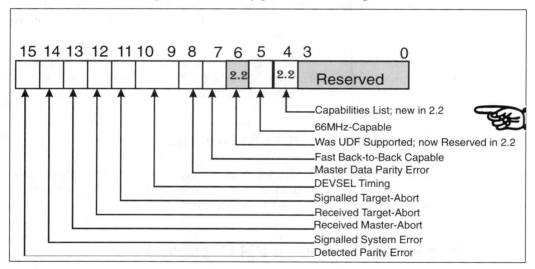

24

Figure 1-4: PCI Type 0 Configuration Header Registers

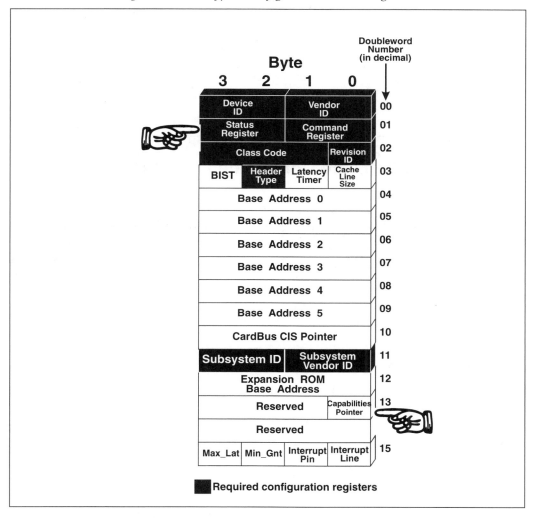

Figure 1-5: PCI Power Management Capability Register Set

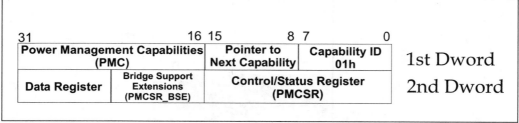

Figure 1-5: PCI Power Management Capability Register Set

Configuration Software Constrained by 32-Bit Memory BARs

Figure 1-6 on page 26 pictures a 32-bit memory BAR, while Figure 1-7 on page 27 pictures a 64-bit memory BAR. When implementing a programmable memory decoder in a PCI function, the designer may implement it as either a 32- or 64-bit BAR. If a 32-bit BAR is implemented, this constrains the configuration software in that it can only assign a 32-bit memory address within the first 4GB of memory space to the decoder. This makes the configuration software's job somewhat more difficult in that a 64-bit BAR would permit it to assign the decoder a memory range either below or above the 4GB address boundary.

Figure 1-6: 32-Bit Memory Base Address Register (BAR)

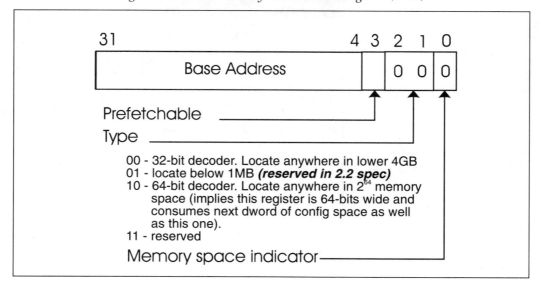

Figure 1-7: 64-Bit Memory Base Address Register (BAR)

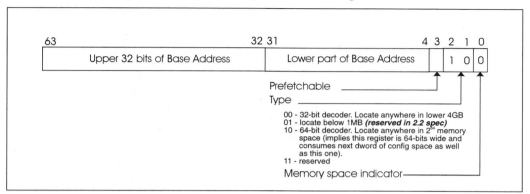

Stepping Yields Poor Performance

A PCI bus master may use Stepping to gradually build the address on the AD bus before it asserts FRAME. During a write transaction, the master may be designed to gradually build the write data on the bus before it asserts IRDY# to indicate the presence of the data to the target. Conversely, during a read transaction, the target may be designed to gradually build the read data on the bus before it asserts TRDY# to indicate the presence of the data to the master.

This gradual building of the address and/or data negatively affects the performance of the master and target involved in the transaction.

2 PCI-X Improves on PCI

The Previous Chapter

The previous chapter described the areas of the PCI bus protocol that the architects of the PCI-X bus protocol identified as needing improvement.

This Chapter

This chapter introduces the primary improvements in PCI-X that targeted deficiencies in the PCI bus protocol. This includes: higher bus speeds, elimination of Wait States, block-oriented transfers, Latency Timer optimization, transfer size specification, Split Transactions, load-tuning, Data Phase parity error recovery, bus width indication, MSI capability, Power Management capability, elimination of snoops, widening of memory decoders, and the elimination of stepping and Fast Back-to-Back transactions.

The Next Chapter

The PCI-X bus is backward-compatible with PCI cards. If the Source Bridge discovers that one or more of the add-in cards on a PCI-X bus are PCI rather than PCI-X cards, it instructs all of the PCI-X capable devices on that bus to use the PCI protocol and also tells them what speed the bus will run at. The next chapter describes how the programmer can determine that a bus is a PCI-X bus and can then determine if any of the devices on the bus are PCI rather than PCI-X devices. Upon detection of a PCI device installed in a PCI-X connector, the programmer almost certainly would inform the end-user of the performance degradation that will result if the card remains installed in the system.

PCI-X Is Backward-Compatible With PCI

One of the primary goals was that PCI-X be backward-compatible with PCI. To achieve that goal, the PCI-X spec dictates the following:

- **PCI-X uses the traditional PCI connector with one pin definition changed.** Pin B38 is a ground plane pin on a conventional PCI card, but is defined as the PCIXCAP pin on a PCI-X capable card. The PCIXCAP signal line is pulled up to a logic one on the system board. A complete description of this pin can be found in "PCIXCAP Indicates Protocol/Frequency Required" on page 58.
- **PCI-X capable devices must be capable of utilizing either the PCI-X or PCI bus protocols.** If any of the add-in cards installed ground the PCIXCAP signal, all devices on that bus must use the PCI protocol and the bus must operate at a frequency that ensures the proper operation of the slowest PCI card installed. As described in "Supplying PCI-X Devices With Protocol and Speed" on page 64, the Source Bridge for a PCI-X bus provides an initialization pattern to the PCI-X capable devices on that bus upon the removal of the reset signal. Based on the pattern provided, a PCI-X device automatically selects the appropriate protocol to utilize, as well as the frequency range its PLLs (phase-locked loops) must lock to.

PCI-X Is More System-Centric Than PCI

The PCI-X spec has a more system-centric focus than the PCI spec. The PCI spec tends to focus more on the design of the PCI function, its configuration and performance. PCI-X on the other hand has as its primary focus the performance of the system as a whole rather than the performance of each function. As examples:

- The spec limits the maximum transfer size of individual transaction requests that may be issued by a master.
- The spec defines a default timeslice that is strongly recommended for PCI-X masters.
- Special status bits are implemented that permit software to detect how well a bridge is handling acceptance of transactions that cross the bridge in either direction.
- After testing the status bits referenced in the previous bullet item, software can adjust how a bridge uses its internal buffer space. This permits software to smooth the flow of transactions across the bridge in either direction.
- Software can clamp the maximum size of memory read burst transactions that may be issued by a master.
- Software can clamp the maximum number of Split Transactions that a master may have outstanding at a given moment in time.

Higher Clock Speeds Possible

While the highest speed a PCI bus may operate at is 66.66MHz, a PCI-X bus may run at anywhere from 50MHz-133.33MHz. As in PCI, a data item can be transferred on each rising-edge of the clock and significantly higher throughput may be obtained over a bus operating in PCI-X mode at a higher clock rate.

Wait States Eliminated

While in PCI both the master and the target can legally insert Wait States during the transfer of individual data items, this is not permitted in PCI-X.

- The master is never permitted to insert Wait States to delay the transfer of any data item.
- The target can insert a limited number of Wait States to delay the transfer of the first data item (because you basically surprised it with the transfer request), but must then keep TRDY# asserted in each subsequent Data Phase.

For a more detailed discussion of the latency rules, refer to Chapter 12, entitled "Latency Rules," on page 189.

Data Transferred in Blocks

In PCI, Data Transferred as a Series of Data Items

In a PCI transaction, data is transferred as a series of individual dwords (or qwords) and both the master and the target can delay the transfer of each data item by deasserting their respective ready signals (IRDY# and TRDY#). In addition, both the master and the target can disconnect (i.e., terminate) the transaction on any dword (or qword) boundary. The master can disconnect the transaction by simply indicating to the target that the current data item is the final one of the transfer (by asserting IRDY# and deasserting FRAME#). The target can issue a disconnect to the master by asserting the STOP# signal in any Data Phase.

In PCI-X, Data Transferred as a Series of Blocks

In PCI-X, data is transferred as a series of blocks, each of which consists of 128 bytes (it should be noted, however, that a PCI-X master can transfer less than a block if it so chooses). A block boundary is one that is divisible by 128 and is referred to as an **Allowable Disconnect Boundary (ADB)**.

Master Cannot Delay Transfer of First Data Block

When starting a transaction, the master must be immediately ready to transfer at least the first data block. If it's not ready to do so, it must not arbitrate for bus ownership.

- On a write, the master must therefore have the first data block buffered up and ready to output at full-speed.
- On a read, the master must have at least one block of buffer space reserved to receive the first data block at full-speed.

Target Can Only Delay Transfer of First Block

The target is permitted to delay the transfer of the first data block (by keeping TRDY# deasserted for a limited number of Wait States), but must either:

- Transfer the remaining data blocks at full-speed (i.e., it is not permitted to deassert TRDY# to delay a data transfer), or
- Assert STOP# to force the master to disconnect on a block boundary.

Master and Target Can Only Disconnect on Block Boundaries

If a transfer consists of more than one data block, the master and the target are only permitted to disconnect the transaction on block boundaries (due to current buffer availability conditions).

But...There Are Two Exceptions

1. The target can issue a Single Data Phase Disconnect (see "Single Data Phase Disconnect" on page 108 for more detail) to the master when transferring the first data item. A target that doesn't support burst transactions uses this method to force the initiator to disconnect the transaction upon completion of the first Data Phase.
2. If the transfer size specified by the master indicates a transfer of less than a block, then the transaction will terminate when the transfer count is exhausted.

Disconnecting on Block Boundaries

Master Disconnection of a Transfer

Assume that a master ultimately intends to write 1024 bytes of data (eight blocks of data) to memory starting on an address divisible by 128 (but note that in PCI-X the start address can be any byte-specific address). It currently has several of the initial data blocks ready to write, but is still accumulating the remainder of the data. Since it has several blocks ready to write, it arbitrates for the bus and initiates a burst memory write transaction stating its intention to write a total of 1024 bytes of data. It writes the first three blocks of data and then begins writing the fourth block. As it approaches the boundary (i.e., ADB) between the fourth and fifth blocks, it signals to the target that it wishes to disconnect the transaction on the upcoming block boundary before the transfer count is exhausted. The target will honor the disconnection and the current burst memory write transaction will terminate on the ADB between the fourth and fifth blocks.

When the master has one or more additional blocks of the remaining data buffered up and ready to write at full-speed, it rearbitrates for the bus and resumes the burst memory write at the start of the next block.

Target Disconnection of a Transfer

Using the previous example, the target may have sufficient buffer space to accept some but not all of the data that the master intends to write. In this case, it accepts the data at full-speed into its buffer until it only has one remaining block (128 bytes) of buffer space remaining. It then asserts STOP# during the transfer of this block, thereby commanding the master to disconnect the transaction on the upcoming block boundary.

The master is then forced to rearbitrate for the bus and will then resume the burst memory write at the point of disconnection.

Latency Timer Usage

As in PCI, each bus master is assigned a timeslice. If it is preempted (i.e., its GNT# signal is deasserted by the arbiter) before it has transferred all of the data it intended to transfer, it may continue the transaction until its timeslice has expired and must then disconnect the transaction on the next block boundary.

A detailed discussion of the Latency Timer can be found in "How the Initiator Deals With Preemption" on page 143.

Requester and Completer

The originator of a transaction is referred to as the **Requester**, while the target addressed by the transaction is referred to as the **Completer**.

Transfer Size Specified

While the transfer size is not specified in a PCI transaction, it is supplied by the bus master in a PCI-X transaction. The transfer size is specified as a **byte transfer count** and can be anywhere from 1-to-4096 bytes (4KB) in size.

Requester ID and Transaction ID Are Specified

In addition to the byte transfer count, the Requester of a PCI-X transaction also supplies its ID in the form of:

- bus number
- device number
- function number

This is referred to as the **Requester ID**.

In addition, the initiator also supplies a transaction ID, referred to as the **transaction tag**.

The combination of the Requester ID and the transaction tag is referred to as the **Sequence ID** and uniquely identifies the transaction request.

Split Transactions Replace Delayed Transactions

Target Cannot Transfer Data Within 16 Clocks From FRAME# Assertion

The following two sections contrast the different methods used by PCI and PCI-X targets to handle long-latency accesses (i.e., it takes more than 16 clocks from the assertion of FRAME# to begin transferring data).

Long-Latency Access Handling in PCI

In PCI, a target that cannot accept write data or supply read data within 16 clocks from the assertion of FRAME# must issue a Retry to the master and memorize what little information the master has supplied it about the transaction request. The master must repeatedly rearbitrate for bus ownership and Retry the transaction. The target treats the transaction as a Delayed Read or Write Request and performs the read or write. Eventually, it has some read data to give to the master or has written the data and is awaiting a Retry of the request by the master. It can then quickly (i.e., within 16 clocks of the repeated transaction's start) start delivering read data or signal acceptance of the write data.

Long-Latency Access Handling in PCI-X

In a PCI-X environment, the Requester supplies the following information to the Completer:

- Transaction type (e.g., memory read).
- Start byte address (while start memory addresses in PCI are dword- or qword-aligned, all start addresses in PCI-X are byte-aligned).
- Byte transfer count.
- Its Requester ID (bus number, device number, function number).
- Its transaction number (i.e., Tag). Together with the Requester ID, this is referred to as the Sequence ID.

If the Completer cannot start supplying read data within 16 clocks from the assertion of FRAME#, it treats the transaction as a Split Request.

1. The Completer memorizes the Sequence ID, command type, start address, and byte transfer count.
2. The Completer issues a Split Response to the Requester (using TRDY#, STOP# and DEVSEL#; for more information, refer to "Target Issues a Split Response" on page 308).
3. The Requester would not have initiated the Request if it didn't have a sufficient amount of free buffer space to accept all of the read data it was requesting.
4. Upon receipt of the Split Response, the Requester must commit the buffer space to hold the read data when the Completer starts returning it at a later time.
5. In addition, upon receipt of the Split Response, the Requester moves the Request to its Split Request Queue and suspends it for completion at a later time.
6. The Completer internally initiates the read of the requested read data.
7. When it has read all of the requested read data into a buffer (or at least a block of the requested read data), the Completer arbitrates for bus ownership and initiates a **Split Completion** transaction. In the transaction's Address Phase, the Completer places the Sequence ID on the address bus (i.e., the AD bus).
8. The Requester latches the transaction type (Split Completion) and the Sequence ID (Requester ID plus transaction Tag). It compares the Requester ID to its Requester ID, has a match, and asserts DEVSEL# to claim the transaction.
9. The Requester uses the supplied transaction Tag to identify which of its currently suspended Split Requests it matches. In this example, it's the previously issued memory read request. The Requester moves the Request from its Split Request Queue and makes it the active transaction.
10. In the Data Phases of the Split Completion transaction, the Completer supplies the requested read data to the Requester.

Split Transactions More Efficient Than Delayed

It should be obvious that the PCI-X Split Transaction mechanism is significantly more efficient than the PCI Delayed transaction method.

- Upon receipt of the Split Response from the Completer, the Requester surrenders the bus, thereby making it available for other masters.
- The Completer has bus master capability, enabling it to attain bus ownership to perform the subsequent Split Completion transaction.

Example: Requester and Completer on Same Bus

Refer to Figure 2-1 on page 37. In this example, the Requester and Completer are on the same bus and the Completer cannot begin transferring data within 16 clocks from the assertion of FRAME#. It therefore handles a Request as a Split Request. This scenario follows the same steps already outlined in "Long-Latency Access Handling in PCI-X" on page 35.

Figure 2-1: Example with Requester and Completer on Same PCI-X Bus

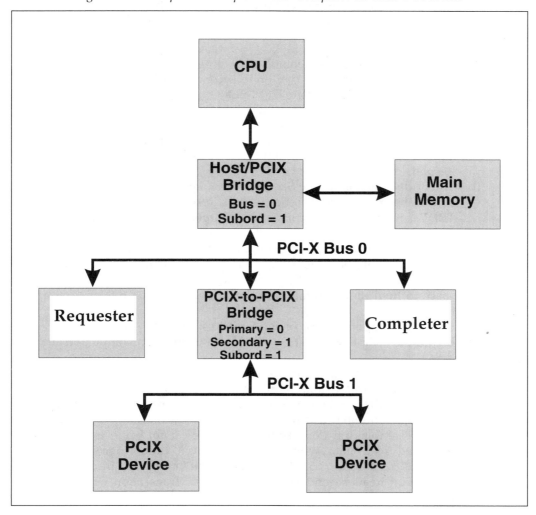

Example: Requester and Completer on Different Buses

Refer to Figure 2-2 on page 40. All transactions other than memory writes that must traverse a PCIX-to-PCIX bridge must be treated as Split Requests. Memory writes are posted within a bridge for later delivery. In this example, the PCI-X Requester on bus zero issues a burst memory read request to a Completer that resides on bus one. It should be obvious that the Request must traverse the PCIX-to-PCIX bridge that guides traffic between the two buses. The steps that follow describe the actions taken by the Requester, the Bridge, and the Completer.

1. The Bridge latches the Request and, recognizing that the memory target resides beyond the bridge (i.e., on its secondary side), it acts as the target of the transaction (i.e., it asserts DEVSEL#).
2. Since the transaction isn't a memory write, the Bridge will have to split it. This is only possible if the Bridge has room in its primary interface Split Transaction Queue to memorize the new Request. In this example, it does have room. If it did not, it would have to issue a Retry rather than a Split Response to the Requester.
3. The Bridge memorizes the Sequence ID, command type, start address, and byte transfer count and issues a Split Response to the Requester (using TRDY#, STOP# and DEVSEL#; see "Target Issues a Split Response" on page 308).
4. The Requester would not have initiated the Request if it didn't have a sufficient amount of free buffer space to accept the read data it was requesting.
5. Upon receipt of the Split Response, the Requester must commit the buffer space to hold the read data that the Bridge will start returning at a later time.
6. In addition, upon receipt of the Split Response the Requester moves the Request to its Split Request Queue and suspends it for completion at a later time.
7. The Bridge arbitrates for ownership of bus one and re-initiates the burst memory read transaction. Acting as the surrogate for the Requester, it uses the same address, command, and Sequence ID (bus number, device number, function number, and transaction tag) that was issued by the Requester.
8. In this example, the Completer on bus one cannot begin transferring the requested read data within 16 clocks from the Bridge's assertion of FRAME#, so it issues a Split Response to the Bridge. The Bridge moves the transaction to its secondary interface's Split Transaction Queue and suspends it.

9. When the Completer has read all of the requested read data into a buffer (or at least a block of the requested read data), the Completer arbitrates for ownership of bus one and initiates a **Split Completion** transaction. In the Split Completion's transaction's Address Phase, the Completer places the Sequence ID (that it received in the Request) on the address bus (i.e., the AD bus).

10. The Bridge's secondary interface latches the transaction type (Split Completion) and the Sequence ID (Requester ID plus transaction Tag). It compares the bus number field of the Requester ID to its Primary Bus Number configuration register's value, has a match, and asserts DEVSEL# to claim the transaction.

11. The Bridge accepts the memory read data into its internal buffers.

12. The Bridge then arbitrates for ownership of bus zero and initiates a Split Completion transaction using the information it received in the Split Completion transaction initiated by the Completer.

13. The Requester latches the transaction type (Split Completion) and the Sequence ID (Requester ID plus transaction Tag). It compares the Requester ID to its Requester ID, has a match, and asserts DEVSEL# to claim the transaction.

14. The Requester uses the supplied transaction Tag to identify which of its currently suspended Split Requests it matches. In this example, it's the previously issued memory read request. The Requester moves the Request from its Split Request Queue and makes it the active transaction.

15. In the Data Phases of the Split Completion transaction, the Bridge supplies the requested read data to the Requester.

Figure 2-2: Example with Requester and Completer on Different PCI-X Buses

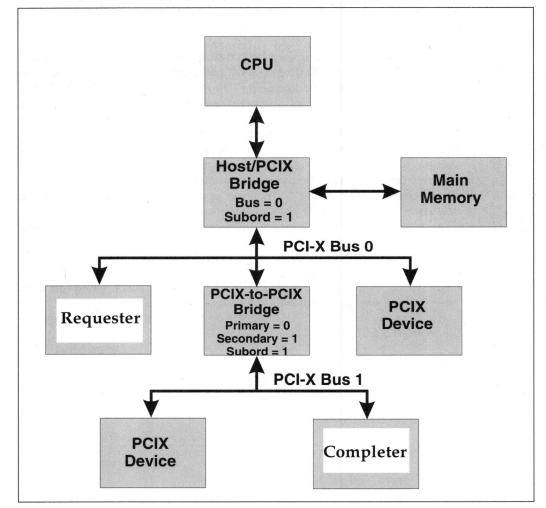

Dynamic Traffic Analysis and Load Tuning

A PCI-X bridge obviously has a primary side (the side closer to main memory) and a secondary side. It incorporates logic that permits traffic analysis software to determine how well the Bridge is handling traffic in both directions across the Bridge. It also contains registers that indicate the size of the Bridge's buffers and defines how it uses those buffers.

- Each interface implements a status bit that indicates if it rejected (i.e., issued a Retry in response to) one or more Split Completion transactions coming back to the respective interface due to insufficient buffer space. Alternatively, although it began to accept previously requested memory read data supplied in a Split Completion transaction, it was forced to issue a Disconnect due to running out of buffer space.
- Each interface implements a status bit that indicates if it delayed passing one more requests through the bridge that would have to be treated as Split Requests. It delayed them because it didn't have sufficient buffer space to accept the Split Completion data that would subsequently be returned on the opposite side of the Bridge.
- Each interface implements a hard-wired, read-only register that indicates the size of its buffer that is used to store Split Completion data.
- Each interface implements a read/write register that permits the load-tuning software to define how the Bridge uses its Split Completion buffer.

A detailed discussion of these status bits and registers can be found in:

- "Bridge Secondary Interface Efficiency Status Bits" on page 501.
- "Bridge Primary Interface Efficiency Status Bits" on page 505.
- "Interpreting the Efficiency Bits" on page 519.

Data Phase Parity Error Recovery

General

The following sections provide a brief overview of Data Phase parity error handling in the PCI-X environment. A more detailed discussion can be found in Chapter 19, entitled "Parity Generation and Checking," on page 383.

Recovery Usually Not Possible in PCI

As described in the previous chapter, recovery from a Data Phase parity error in PCI is problematic. Most PCI chipsets monitor the PERR# signal as an input and issue a fatal hardware interrupt (e.g., NMI in an x86processor environment) if PERR# assertion is detected. This eliminates any possibility of error recovery on the part of a PCI master or its associated driver.

PCI-X Chipset Does Not Monitor PERR#

Unlike a PCI chipset, the PCI-X chipset does not monitor PERR# and generate a fatal hardware interrupt to the processor if some device should assert PERR#. Rather, it only observes SERR# as an input and generates a fatal hardware interrupt (e.g., NMI) to the processor if SERR# is detected asserted.

What the PCI-X Spec Says

The spec states:

"All PCI-X devices in combination with system software and their device drivers are required either to recover from a data parity error or to assert SERR#."

Requester Hardware Doesn't Handle Error Itself

The spec states:

"Devices are allowed to attempt to recover from a data parity error only under control of the software. Only the device driver has the necessary information to determine what is appropriate and necessary to repeat and what is not."

In other words, the Requester hardware does not attempt error recovery on its own, but rather under the guidance of its device driver.

With Appropriate Master and Device Driver Design, Recovery Possible

Each function capable of acting as a Requester contains a Data Parity Error Recover Enable bit in its PCI-X Command register that reset initially clears to zero. This disables the function's ability to recover from Data Phase parity errors. When the OS loads the device driver associated with the Requester, it calls and executes the driver's initialization code. If the driver implements recovery logic, its initialization code will set the Requester's Data Parity Error Recover Enable bit to one.

Chapter 2: PCI-X Improves on PCI

If the Requester detects PERR# asserted during a transaction, it will set a status bit in a device-specific status register to indicate that a Data Phase parity error was detected. In addition, it then generates an interrupt to invoke its device driver's interrupt handler. The handler checks the device's status, sees that a Data Phase parity error was detected and executes the handler's parity error handler routine.

Device Driver With No Recovery Capability = SERR#

If a PCI-X Requester's driver doesn't implement Data Phase parity error recovery, then the driver's initialization code will not set the Requester's Data Parity Error Recover Enable command bit to one. If the Requester encurs a Data Phase parity error, it asserts SERR# (assuming that the SERR# Enable bit in its PCI Command register is set to one). The chipset detects SERR# asserted and generates a fatal hardware error (e.g., NMI) to the processor. In other words, the end result is the same as it would be in a PCI environment.

If Bus in PCI Mode, Bridge Monitors PERR#

If the source Bridge (either the Host/PCIX bridge or a PCIX-to-PCIX bridge) detects the presence of a conventional PCI device installed on a PCI-X bus, it instructs all PCI-X capable devices on the bus that the bus will operate in PCI protocol mode.

Relative to Data Phase parity errors, this implies that the Bridge must handle any assertion of PERR# in the legacy manner: when PERR# is detected asserted, it must generate a fatal hardware interrupt (e.g., NMI) to the processor. If it is the Host/PCIX bridge, it can generate the interrupt directly to the processor. On the other hand, if it is a PCIX-to-PCIX Bridge, it would assert SERR# on its primary side. This will be seen by the Host/PCIX bridge which will, in turn, generate the interrupt to the processor.

It should be stressed that the spec doesn't say this and that the author is extrapolating this from the information actually present in the spec. The rationale is as follows: if the Bridge operated as it normally does when in PCI-X mode, it would pay no attention to the assertion of PERR# and the error would not be delivered to the processor.

64-Bit Connection Indication

Each PCI-X function implements a PCI-X Status register. Within this register is a hardwired, read-only bit that indicates the width of the function's connection to the system board's AD bus (32- or 64-bits). This permits the configuration programmer to detect when a 64-bit card is installed in a 32-bit card connector (or vice versa). The end-user could then be prompted to move the card to a connector of the appropriate width.

MSI Feature Mandatory

As described in the previous chapter, generation of interrupt requests via Message Signaled Interrupt (MSI) rather than using an interrupt pin is quite advantageous. While it is optional whether a PCI function implements the ability to generate interrupt requests via MSI, PCI-X functions that generate interrupt requests must implement MSI capability. Additionally, implementation of an interrupt pin is optional but recommended to ensure interoperability in platforms that don't support MSI capability.

Power Management Mandatory for Add-In Devices

Implementation of the PCI power management register set in a PCI function is optional. Implementation is mandatory for a PCI-X function designed for inclusion on add-on cards, and optional for a function designed to be embedded on the system board.

Snoops Can Be Eliminated

The previous chapter discussed the necessity for generation of snoop transactions by the Host/PCIX bridge whenever a PCI master attempts to access main memory. This causes degradation of the PCI master's performance, as well as using valuable processor front side bus bandwidth.

A PCI-X Requester's device driver requests ownership of a main memory buffer to be used by its associated Requester. The driver may request that the OS memory allocation routine designate the assigned buffer area as non-cacheable. In this case, the driver's initialization routine will set a device-specific bit in one of the Requester's device-specific registers giving it permission to set the No Snoop attribute bit whenever it initiates a memory access to its assigned buffer.

As a result, the Host/PCIX bridge will not generate snoop transactions when the Requester is accessing main memory. Rather, it will give it immediate access to memory, thereby yielding better performance for the Requester's memory accesses.

Memory BARS Must Be 64-Bit Width

While a PCI function's memory BARs (i.e., programmable memory decoders) may be implemented as either 32- or 64-bit BARs, all of a PCI-X function's memory BARs (both non-prefetchable and prefetchable) must be implemented as 64-bit BARs. This gives the configuration software the ability to assign each memory BAR an address range below or above the 4GB address boundary.

Also see the next section for a description of the DAC command.

Bus Masters That Access Memory Must Support DAC Command

The previous section explained why all PCI-X memory BARs must be implemented as 64-bit BARs. It is likewise a rule that all PCI-X Requesters that access memory must be capable of using the Dual-Address Cycle (DAC) command. This stands to reason: if a Requester's driver assigned it a memory buffer above the 4GB boundary but it was incapable of using the DAC command, it would not be able to address its buffer.

For a detailed description of the PCI-X DAC command, refer to "Addressing Memory Above 4GB Boundary" on page 372. For a detailed description of the PCI DAC command, refer to the chapter entitled "The 64-Bit PCI Extension" in the MindShare book entitled *PCI System Architecture* (published by Addison-Wesley).

Stepping Eliminated

Due to the low performance associated with its use, both address and data stepping are forbidden in the PCI-X environment. It should be noted that in one case, a form of address stepping is mandated in the PCI-X environment. This is when a Requester is performing a configuration access, and a detailed description can be found in Chapter 20, entitled "Configuration Transactions," on page 425.

For a detailed description of stepping in the PCI environment, refer to the chapter entitled *Fast Back-to-Back and Stepping* in the MindShare book entitled *PCI System Architecture, Fourth Edition* (published by Addison-Wesley).

Fast Back-to-Back Transactions Eliminated

Due to their complexity and the insignificant increase in performance they may yield, fast back-to-back transactions are not permitted in the PCI-X environment. This also means that the associated bits in a function's PCI Command and Status registers are also not used. For more information on PCI fast back-to-back transactions, refer to the chapter entitled *Fast Back-to-Back and Stepping* in the MindShare book entitled *PCI System Architecture, Fourth Edition* (published by Addison-Wesley). For more information on PCI-X usage of the associated Command and Status register bits refer to Chapter 21, entitled "Non-Bridge Configuration Registers," on page 453.

3 Lowest Common Denominator Defines Mode

The Previous Chapter

The previous chapter introduced the primary improvements in PCI-X that targeted deficiencies in the PCI bus protocol. This includes: higher bus speeds, elimination of Wait States, block-oriented transfers, Latency Timer optimization, transfer size specification, Split Transactions, load tuning, Data Phase parity error recovery, bus width indication, MSI capability, Power Management capability, elimination of snoops, widening of memory decoders, and the elimination of stepping and Fast Back-to-Back transactions.

This Chapter

The PCI-X bus is backward-compatible with PCI cards. If the Source Bridge discovers that one or more of the add-in cards on a PCI-X bus are PCI rather than PCI-X cards, it instructs all of the PCI-X capable devices on that bus to use the PCI protocol and also tells them what speed the bus will run at. This chapter describes how the programmer can determine that a bus is a PCI-X bus and can then determine if any of the devices on the bus are PCI rather than PCI-X devices. Upon detection of a PCI device installed in a PCI-X connector, the programmer almost certainly would inform the end-user of the performance degradation that will result if the card remains installed in the system.

The Next Chapter

As introduced in this chapter (see "Bus Protocol/Speed = Lowest Common Denominator" on page 48), the Source Bridge for a PCI-X bus interrogates two signals at startup time to determine the protocol and bus speed to be used on its secondary bus during this power-up session. The protocol and speed are selected to ensure that the least-capable device functions correctly. The next chapter provides a detailed description of this process.

Bus Protocol/Speed = Lowest Common Denominator

The Source Bridge is the bridge which originates a PCI or a PCI-X bus. In Figure 3-1 on page 51 and Figure 3-2 on page 53, the Host/PCIX bridge is the Source Bridge for the PCI-X bus directly on the other side of it. In Figure 3-3 on page 54, the left-hand Host/PCIX bridge is the Source Bridge for the PCI-X bus, while the right-hand Host/PCIX bridge is the Source Bridge for the PCI bus.

At startup time (during the assertion of reset), the Source Bridge samples two signals to determine the protocol and bus speed supported by the least-capable device installed on the bus. The bridge then tells the PCI-X capable devices on its secondary bus what protocol and bus speed will be used during this power-up session. In other words, the bus protocol and bus clock chosen will ensure that the least-capable device functions correctly. A detailed discussion of this process can be found in Chapter 4, entitled "Device Types and Bus Initialization," on page 55.

It should be obvious that the benefits yielded by the more efficient PCI-X protocol and its higher bus speeds are lost if the end-user is permitted to install a conventional PCI card on a PCI-X bus.

Discovering a PCI-X Bus

The programmer discovers a PCI-X bus in the following manner:

1. Using the Class Code configuration register, discover a North Bridge (i.e., a Host/PCI bridge) or a PCI-to-PCI bridge.
2. Determine if the Capabilities List status bit in the bridge's PCI configuration Status register is hardwired to one. If it is, go to step 3; if it isn't, then it is not a PCI-X bridge.
3. Traverse the bridge's New Capabilities register sets to determine if it implements the PCI-X capability configuration register set. If it does, then the bus on the bridge's secondary side is a PCI-X bus.

A detailed description of the PCI configuration registers can be found in the MindShare book entitled *PCI System Architecture, Fourth Edition* (published by Addison-Wesley). A detailed description of the PCI-X configuration registers can be found in "Function's PCI-X Capability Register Set" on page 470 and in "Bridge's PCI-X Capability Register Set" on page 497.

Chapter 3: Lowest Common Denominator Defines Mode

Discovering PCI Devices on a PCI-X Bus

As mentioned earlier in this chapter, for performance reasons it's advisable to detect PCI cards on a PCI-X bus and then prompt the end-user to either remove them from the machine or to move the cards to a bus intended only for PCI devices.

A PCI function can be detected by checking for the absence of the PCI-X configuration registers:

1. Determine if the Capabilities List status bit in the function's PCI configuration Status register is hardwired to one. If it is, go to step 2; if it isn't, then it is not a PCI-X function.
2. Traverse the function's New Capabilities register sets to determine if it implements the PCI-X capability configuration register set. If it doesn't, then the function is not a PCI-X function.

Some Example Systems

System With No Connectors on PCI-X Bus

If the system pictured in Figure 3-1 on page 51 had no connectors on the PCI-X bus, the PCI-X bus would operate in PCI-X protocol mode and at a speed that ensures the proper operation of the least-capable PCI-X device on the bus.

Single Bus System With Connectors

Figure 3-1 on page 51 illustrates a system with a single PCI-X bus with two connectors. There are a number of possible scenarios:

- Both cards may be PCI-X capable. In this case, the PCI-X bus will operate in PCI-X protocol mode and at a speed that ensures the proper operation of the least-capable PCI-X device.
- One card may be PCI-X capable while the other is a PCI device, or both may be PCI devices. In this case, the PCI-X bus will operate as a PCI bus at a lower speed to ensure that the PCI card functions correctly.

- Either card may incorporate a PCIX-to-PCIX bridge. In this case, the bridge's primary side will operate in PCI-X mode, but there are two possible operational scenarios for its secondary side:
    - All devices on the bridge's secondary bus may be embedded PCI-X capable devices. In this case, the secondary bus operates in PCI-X mode at a speed that ensures proper operation of the least-capable PCI-X device on the secondary bus.
    - The bus on the bridge's secondary side may include one or more connectors. The secondary bus will then operate in the protocol/speed mode that ensures proper operation of the least-capable device on the bus.
- Either card may incorporate a PCI-to-PCI bridge. In this case, both buses will operate in PCI mode, resulting in severe performance degradation on the PCI-X capable bus (because it's operating in PCI mode).

Figure 3-1: Simple System Block Diagram

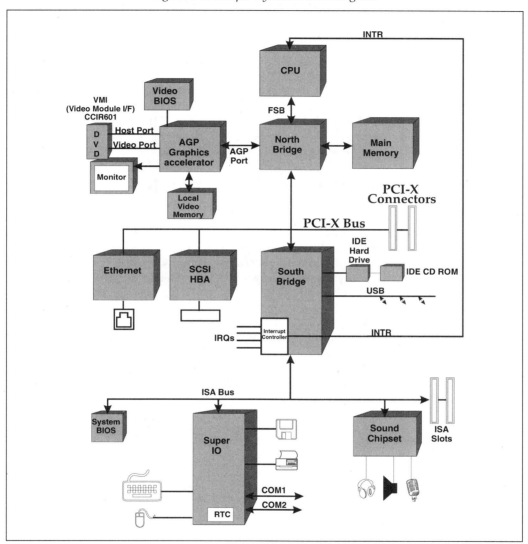

Systems Supporting Both PCI-X and PCI Environments

Introduction

In order to partition the slower PCI devices from the higher-performance PCI-X devices, the system designer may incorporate both a PCI and a PCI-X bus in the system. The following two sections describe some of the possible implementations.

System With Single Host/PCIX Bridge

Refer to Figure 3-2 on page 53. In this platform, the system designer has embedded a PCIX-to-PCIX or a PCIX-to-PCI bridge on PCI-X bus 0. The intention is to compartmentalize the PCI devices on PCI bus 1 on the bridge's secondary side. At startup time, the configuration software scans PCI-X bus 0 looking for any PCI devices and, if any are found, prompts the end-user to move them to connectors located on PCI bus 1.

This permits the PCI-X devices on bus 0 to operate at peak efficiency when performing transfers with main memory or with each other. While it is true that PCI transfers must sometimes cross the PCI-X bus, they are performed using the more efficient PCI-X protocol and speeds because the bridge's primary interface operates in PCI-X mode rather than PCI mode.

Figure 3-2: System With Single Host/PCIX Bridge and a Subordinate PCI Bus

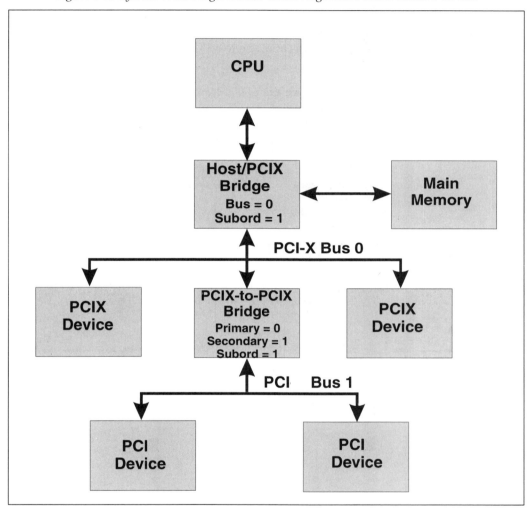

Dual Host/PCIX Bridge System

Refer to Figure 3-3 on page 54. In this platform, the system designer has achieved the compartmentalization of the PCI devices by incorporating dual North Bridges: one to a PCI bus and one to a PCI-X bus.

Figure 3-3: System With Dual North Bridges

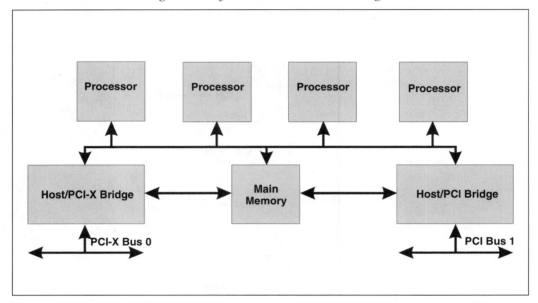

4 *Device Types and Bus Initialization*

The Previous Chapter

The PCI-X bus is backward-compatible with PCI cards. If the Source Bridge discovers that one or more of the add-in cards on a PCI-X bus are PCI rather than PCI-X cards, it instructs all of the PCI-X capable devices on that bus to use the PCI protocol and also tells them what speed the bus will run at. The previous chapter described how the programmer can determine that a bus is a PCI-X bus and can then determine if any of the devices on the bus are PCI rather than PCI-X devices. Upon detection of a PCI device installed in a PCI-X connector, the programmer almost certainly would inform the end-user of the performance degradation that will result if the card remains installed in the system.

This Chapter

As introduced in the previous chapter (see "Bus Protocol/Speed = Lowest Common Denominator" on page 48), the Source Bridge for a PCI-X bus interrogates two signals at startup time to determine the protocol and bus speed to be used on its secondary bus during this power-up session. The protocol and speed are selected to ensure that the least-capable device functions correctly. This chapter provides a detailed description of this process.

The Next Chapter

The next chapter describes the registered nature of the PCI-X bus.

All Devices Support 33MHz PCI

General

All PCI and PCI-X devices support operation on a 33MHz PCI bus, while it's optional whether a PCI or a 66MHz PCI-X device supports operation on a 66MHz PCI bus. Refer to Figure 4-1 on page 57. A device indicates that it will operate correctly on a high-speed PCI bus by not grounding the M66EN pin (pin B49).

133MHz PCI-X Device Must Support 33MHz and 66MHz PCI

A 133MHz-capable PCI-X device must support both 33MHz and 66MHz PCI operation.

When M66EN Is Grounded on a Card

As illustrated in Figure 4-1 on page 57, M66EN on the system board has a required pull-up resistor on it that maintains it in the asserted state unless a card installed in a connector grounds it.

- When a 33MHz PCI card is installed in a connector on a 66MHz PCI bus or a PCI-X bus, it grounds the M66EN signal to the Source Bridge.
- When a 66MHz PCI-X card capable of 33MHz (but not 66MHz) PCI operation is installed in a connector, it grounds M66EN.

Effect of Grounded M66EN on a PCI Source Bridge

This informs the clock generator within the PCI bridge that the clock must be divided by two to ensure proper operation of the 33MHz-capable PCI device.

Effect of Grounded M66EN on a PCI-X Source Bridge

A low on M66EN informs a PCI-X bridge that if the PCI protocol is used, it must use a clock speed of 33MHz or less in order to ensure proper operation of the 33MHz-capable PCI device.

M66EN Usage on a 66MHz PCI Card or a PCI-X Card

On a 66MHz-capable PCI card or on a PCI-X card, M66EN is either:

- not connected to anything on the card. In this case, by not grounding M66EN, the card (either PCI or PCI-X) is indicating that it supports 66MHz PCI operation.
- or may be connected as an input on the card. This is the case if a PCI card can only operate properly on a high-speed PCI bus. It can determine if it's located on a high- or low-speed bus by sampling the state of its M66EN input. If it determines that it is located on a low-speed PCI bus, it could then set a bit in a device-specific status register to inform its device driver that it needs to be relocated to a high-speed PCI bus in order to achieve adequate performance.

Figure 4-1: State of M66EN Defines Clock Frequency

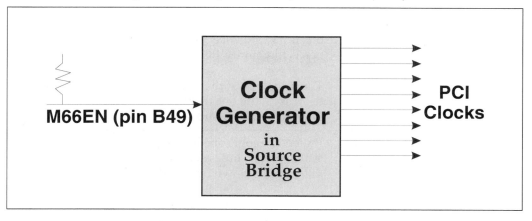

All PCI-X Devices Support 66MHz PCI-X Mode

All PCI-X devices support operation in PCI-X protocol mode from 50MHz through 66MHz. Optionally, a PCI-X device may support operation from 50MHz through 133MHz.

PCIXCAP Indicates Protocol/Frequency Required

General

PCIXCAP (pin B38) is the only new signal defined on the standard PCI connector to support PCI-X. Refer to Figure 4-2 on page 60 and Table 4-1 on page 58. The PCIXCAP signal is tested (along with M66EN) by the Source Bridge at power-up time to determine the least-capable device present on the bus.

Table 4-1: Treatment of PCIXCAP on Add-In Card

Treatment On Card	Effect on PCIXCAP Input to Source Bridge
Grounded on a PCI card.	Grounded, providing a logic low on the Source Bridge's PCIXCAP input. This informs the Source Bridge that at least one card installed on the PCI-X bus is a PCI device. The least-capable device on the bus is therefore a PCI device. The bridge must therefore inform all PCI-X capable devices on the bus that the PCI protocol will be used during this power-up session.
Tied to a decoupling capacitor.	Pulled to a logic one by the pull-up resistor on the system board unless grounded by a PCI card or partially pulled down by a 66MHz-capable PCI-X card. If the bridge detects a logic one on PCIXCAP, the least-capable device on the bus is therefore a 133MHz-capable PCI-X device. The bridge must inform all PCI-X capable devices on the bus that the PCI-X protocol will be used during this power-up session and the clock speed will operate in the range between 66MHz and 133MHz.

Table 4-1: Treatment of PCIXCAP on Add-In Card (Continued)

Treatment On Card	Effect on PCIXCAP Input to Source Bridge
Pulled partially down by a 10K Ohm resistor.	The on-card resistor forms a voltage divider with the pull-up resistor on the system board, yielding a signal level somewhere between a logic high and a logic low (unless PCIXCAP is grounded by a PCI card).
	If the bridge detects a logic level somewhere between a logic high and a logic low on PCIXCAP, the least-capable device on the bus is therefore a 66MHz-capable PCI-X device. The bridge must inform all PCI-X capable devices on the bus that the PCI-X protocol will be used during this power-up session and the clock speed will operate in the range between 50MHz and 66MHz.

Figure 4-2: Treatment of PCIXCAP (pin B38) on Add-In Card

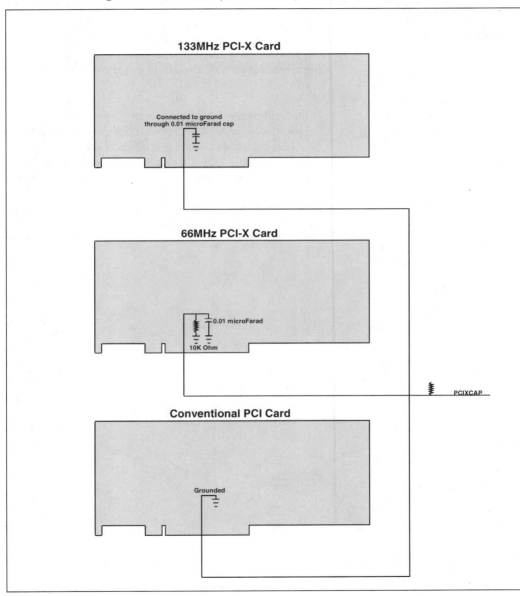

PCIXCAP Indicates Capabilities of Card's First Device

When a non-bridge device is the only device on an add-in card, its connection to the PCIXCAP pin must indicate whether or not every function in the device implements the PCI-X Capability register set. In addition, the state of the 133MHz-capable status bit in each function's PCI-X Status register must also accurately reflect the state of the PCIXCAP pin connection.

If the first device on an add-in card is a PCIX-to-PCIX bridge, the card's connection to the PCIXCAP pin indicates whether or not that bridge implements the PCI-X Capability register set. If the device that contains the bridge is a multi-function device, its connection to the PCIXCAP pin must indicate whether or not every function in the device implements the PCI-X Capability register set. In addition, the state of the 133MHz-capable status bit in each function's PCI-X Status register must also accurately reflect the state of the PCIXCAP pin connection.

Device Not Permitted to Use PCIXCAP as Input or Output

In order to ensure that the appropriate voltage level is indicated to the Source Bridge on the PCIXCAP signal line, devices on cards are not allowed to load down PCIXCAP by connecting on-card inputs or outputs to the signal line.

Bridge's Interpretation of M66EN and PCIXCAP

At power-up time, the bridge asserts RST# to the devices on its secondary bus. To determine the capabilities of the least-capable device residing on its secondary side, the bridge samples the state of its M66EN and PCIXCAP inputs while asserting RST# to the devices on its secondary side. Table 4-2 on page 62 defines the bridge's interpretation of the values viewed on these two inputs.

Table 4-2: Source Bridge's Interpretation of PCIXCAP and M66EN

M66EN	PCIXCAP			Bus Frequency and Protocol
	Logic High	Mid-Range	Logic Low	
1	x			All devices support 133MHz PCI-X (PCIXCAP is high) and 66MHz PCI (M66EN is high). Bus will run at 66-133MHz using the PCI-X protocol.
1		x		Least-capable device(s) is a 66MHz PCI-X device (PCIX-CAP is mid-range), so bus will run at 50-66MHz using the PCI-X protocol. All devices support 66MHz PCI (M66EN is high).
1			x	Least-capable device(s) is a 66MHz (M66EN is high) PCI device (PCIXCAP is low), so bus will run at 66MHz using PCI protocol.
0	x			All devices support 133MHz PCI-X (PCIXCAP is high), and at least one card has grounded M66EN, indicating it only supports 33MHz PCI. Bus will run at 66-133MHz using the PCI-X protocol.

Table 4-2: Source Bridge's Interpretation of PCIXCAP and M66EN (Continued)

M66EN	PCIXCAP			Bus Frequency and Protocol
	Logic High	Mid-Range	Logic Low	
0		x		Least-capable device(s) is a 66MHz PCI-X device (PCIX-CAP is mid-range). At least one card has grounded M66EN, indicating it only supports 33MHz PCI. Bus will run at 50-66MHz using the PCI-X protocol.
0			x	The least-capable card(s) is a 33MHz (M66EN is grounded) PCI device (PCIXCAP is grounded). Bus will run at 33MHz using the PCI protocol.

Maximum Reliable Speed Verified by Design and Testing

Neither the PCI spec nor the PCI-X spec states the maximum number of devices that may be placed on a PCI or PCI-X bus. This is because the system designer must balance the targeted speed at which the bus will be run with the number of embedded devices and connectors to be placed on the bus. The more loads placed on the bus, the slower the bus must be run to ensure reliable operation. A reliable bus population/bus speed combination must be verified by extensive testing. As in PCI, each device is only allowed to place one load on each bus signal line. The mechanics of the pin/connector interface morphs a signal as it traverses the interconnect. Each connector therefore counts as a load on the bus, and the card installed in the connector applies an additional load per signal line. In other words, each populated connector counts as two electrical loads on the bus.

During the development of the PCI-X spec, Compaq Computer performed rigorous testing based on four PCI-X bus topologies. These were considered to be the most popular topologies and are listed in Table 4-3 on page 64.

Table 4-3: Common Topologies Versus Bus Speed

Number of Connectors	Bus Speed
1	133MHz
2	100Mhz
4	66MHz

Supplying PCI-X Devices With Protocol and Speed

General

After sampling the state of M66EN and PCIXCAP while asserting RST# to the devices on its secondary side, the Source Bridge then:

1. Supplies an initialization pattern to the PCI-X capable devices on the bus. This pattern tells the PCI-X capable devices which bus protocol will be used as well as the basic operational range of the bus clock frequency.
2. Deasserts the RST# signal. All of the PCI-X capable devices latch the pattern on the trailing-edge of RST#.
3. Removes the initialization pattern.

The pattern is supplied using the three PCI signals TRDY#, DEVSEL#, and STOP#. Table 4-4 on page 66 defines the encoding of the initialization pattern.

Host/PCIX Bridge Pattern Delivery Sequence

The following sequence is used by a Host/PCIX Bridge when delivering the initialization pattern to PCI-X bus 0:

1. Apply power to all devices on the bus. While the power supply voltages are stabilizing, float pattern delivery signals (as required by the PCI 2.2 spec) and assert RST#. The pull-up resistors on these signals deassert them. The AD and C/BE# buses must be parked in the low logic level during this time (also required by the PCI 2.2 spec). When the power supply indicates that all of the supply voltages are within the proper tolerances, proceed to the next step.

2. Sense the states of PCIXCAP and M66EN for all devices on the bus.
3. Select the mode and clock frequency compatible with the least-capable card present on the bus.
4. If the mode is to be 33MHz PCI, deassert M66EN for all devices on the bus. This requirement is automatically met if M66EN is bused to all devices on the bus.
5. Supply the appropriate PCI-X initialization pattern on the bus.
6. Deassert RST#.
7. Remove the pattern from TRDY#, STOP#, and DEVSEL#.

PCIX-to-PCIX Bridge Pattern Delivery Sequence

The Sequence

The following sequence is used by a PCIX-to-PCIX Bridge when delivering the initialization pattern to PCI-X bus 0:

1. Sense the states of PCIXCAP and M66EN for all devices on the secondary bus.
2. Select the appropriate mode and clock frequency based on the least-capable device present on the bus. The design of the bridge, trace lengths, and the number of loads on the bus determine the actual frequency at which the bus operates in each mode.
3. If the mode is to be 33MHz PCI, deassert M66EN to all devices on the secondary bus. This requirement is automatically met if M66EN is bused to all devices on the secondary bus.
4. Assert the appropriate signals for the PCI-X initialization pattern on the secondary bus. Leave the others floating so the pull-up resistors deassert them. The bridge must not actively deassert the bus control signals while RST# is deasserted, because one of the power supply voltages could be out of range.
5. Deassert RST# on the secondary bus.

But First...

When RST# is asserted to the bridge's primary side by the Source Bridge for the primary side bus, the bridge resets its internal state machines, asserts RST# on the secondary side, floats the secondary bus control signals (including the ones in the PCI-X initialization pattern), and drives the secondary AD and C/BE# buses to the low logic-level state to keep them from floating. When RST# is deasserted on its primary side, the bridge latches the clock frequency and protocol information (i.e., the initialization pattern) and sets up its primary interface accordingly.

Many PCIX-to-PCIX bridges derive the clock for the secondary bus from the clock delivered to its primary interface. These bridges contain a PLL that syncs up to the primary clock and delivers the derived clock (which could be the same as, a multiple of, or slower than the primary clock frequency) to the devices on its secondary side.

In order to correctly set up its PLL that generates the secondary side clock, such a bridge must first latch the initialization pattern on its primary side to determine the frequency range of the primary side clock. It can then correctly generate the clock to the secondary side devices and indicate the appropriate frequency range in the initialization pattern to the secondary side devices.

Bridges that generate the secondary side clock independent of the primary side clock can deliver the initialization pattern to the secondary side devices (see the previous section) before the pattern has been latched on its primary side.

Table 4-4: Initialization Pattern Encoding

Initialization Pattern			Protocol	Clock Frequency Range
DEVSEL#	STOP#	TRDY#		
deasserted	deasserted	deasserted	PCI	Defined by state of M66EN. 0 = not greater than 33MHz. 1 = > 33MHz but not greater than 66MHz.
deasserted	deasserted	asserted	PCI-X	50-66MHz. Exact speed verified by design and rigorous testing. A bridge running its secondary bus at 66MHz uses this pattern.
deasserted	asserted	deasserted	PCI-X	66-100MHz. Exact speed verified by design and rigorous testing. A bridge running its secondary bus at 100MHz uses this pattern.
deasserted	asserted	asserted	PCI-X	100-133MHz. Exact speed verified by design and rigorous testing.
asserted	deasserted	deasserted	Reserved	Reserved

Table 4-4: Initialization Pattern Encoding (Continued)

Initialization Pattern			Protocol	Clock Frequency Range
DEVSEL#	STOP#	TRDY#		
asserted	deasserted	asserted	Reserved	Reserved
asserted	asserted	deasserted	Reserved	Reserved
asserted	asserted	asserted	Reserved	Reserved

Why Bus Must Be Idle When Init Pattern Driven

The Source Bridge must ensure that the bus is Idle (FRAME# and IRDY# deasserted) when the initialization pattern is supplied to the PCI-X capable devices. This is to ensure that PCI devices do not become confused by the assertion of some combination of TRDY#, STOP#, and DEVSEL# when the pattern is presented on the bus and is held for some period of time after RST# is deasserted.

Upon Receipt of Pattern, Device Initializes Itself

Upon receipt of the initialization pattern, all PCI-X capable devices must initialize the following:

- Bus master and target state machines for the correct protocol.
- All internal PLL lock ranges.
- Electrical differences.
- Configuration register default content, usage and bit field interpretation.

Init Pattern Setup and Hold Time

General

Refer to Figure 4-3 on page 68. While the setup time specifies that the pattern must be presented on the bus for at least 10 clocks prior to the deassertion of RST#, the Hold time is specified as a time interval (50ns) rather than a number of clocks. After the rising edge of RST#, the initialization pattern signals (DEVSEL#, TRDY#, and STOP#) must be deasserted by the bridge no later than two clocks before the first assertion of FRAME# by any master and must be floated no later than one clock before FRAME# is asserted.

Relationship With Trhff

The PCI 2.2 spec defines Trhff as five clock cycles in duration. During this period, the bridge must ensure (by not granting bus ownership to any master) that a transaction is not initiated by any master. This guarantees all devices on the bus five clock cycles after RST# removal to prepare to deal with transactions. At a bus speed of 133MHz, each clock cycle is 7.5ns in duration, so five clock cycles is 37.5ns. The bridge must ensure that the maximum pattern hold time does not interfere with this timing parameter.

Figure 4-3: Initialization Pattern Setup and Hold Time

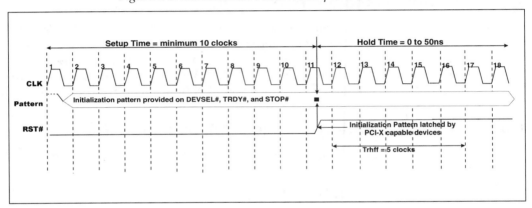

Reassertion of RST# Necessitates Redelivery of Pattern

General

If a bridge should assert RST# to the devices on its secondary side (see the following two sections), it must redrive the initialization pattern to those devices before deasserting RST# to them. This is necessary because PCI-X devices forget the pattern when RST# is asserted, so they must be resupplied with the bus protocol and frequency information.

Secondary Bus RST# Follows RST# on Primary Side

If RST# is asserted by the Source Bridge that controls the bus on the primary side of a PCIX-to-PCIX bridge, the bridge must assert RST# on its secondary side.

Chapter 4: Device Types and Bus Initialization

Secondary Bus RST# Under Software Control

The programmer may force a PCIX-to-PCIX bridge to assert RST# to the devices on its secondary side by writing a one into the Secondary Bus Reset bit (see Figure 4-5 on page 70) in the bridge's Bridge Control configuration register (see Figure 4-4 on page 69).

Figure 4-4: Bridge Configuration Header Registers

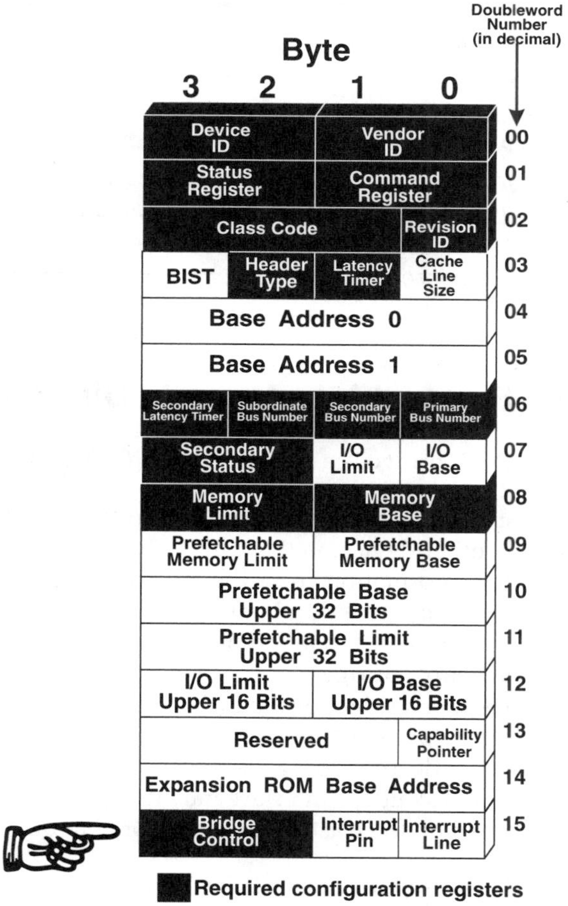

Figure 4-5: Bridge Control Register

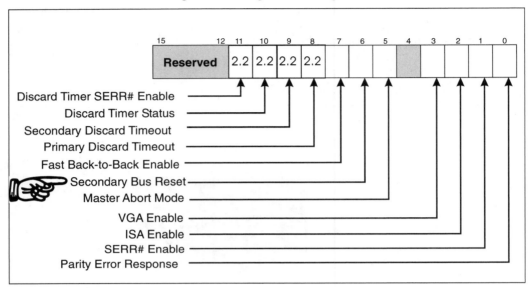

Bridge Must Support Interfaces in Different Modes

A PCIX-to-PCIX bridge is a citizen of two PCI-X buses:

- It is just another device that resides on the PCI-X bus on its primary side. Like any other device on that bus, it therefore receives the protocol and bus frequency information from the Source Bridge for that bus (based on the least-capable card on that bus). Its primary interface may therefore end up in either PCI or PCI-X mode based on the initialization pattern it receives from the Source Bridge.
- It is the Source Bridge for the PCI-X bus on its secondary side and therefore provides the protocol and bus frequency information to the devices on its secondary side (including its secondary side interface). The operational mode of its secondary interface may therefore end up in either PCI or PCI-X mode based on the least-capable card on that bus.

The two interfaces of a PCIX-to-PCIX bridge must therefore be capable of operating with different protocols and different bus frequencies.

Hot-Plug PCI-X Bus Initialization

Some Systems Permit Hot-Plug of PCI-X Cards

This section deals with a PCI-X bus that permits the end-user to install or remove PCI or PCI-X cards while the system and devices on the hot-plug PCI-X bus continue to operate without interruption.

For Background on PCI Hot-Plug...

PCI-X hot-plug is an extension of PCI hot-plug. For background information on PCI hot-plug, refer to:

- The MindShare book entitled *PCI System Architecture, Fourth Edition* or later (published by Addison-Wesley). Refer to the chapter entitled *Hot-Plug PCI*.
- PCI Hot-Plug Spec, available from the PCI SIG. As of this writing, the current spec version is 1.0, but the SIG has a subcommittee working on an update.

Problems Associated With PCI-X Hot-Plug

The following are some of the problems associated with hot-installing cards on a PCI-X bus:

1. **Installation of a PCI card on a PCI-X bus**. If the end-user is permitted to do this, the bridge will be forced to assert RST# to all devices on the bus and reinitialize them in PCI rather than PCI-X mode. This would, of course, result in a precipitous reduction in performance for all devices on the bus.
2. **Installation of a PCI-X card with lesser speed capabilities than the bus's current operational speed**. If the end-user is permitted to do this, the bridge will be forced to assert RST# to all devices on the bus and reinitialize them to operate at a reduced bus speed. This would result in a reduction in performance for all devices on the bus.
3. **Installation of a card with a PCIX-to-PCIX bridge on it**. The configuration software would have to assign a number to the bridge's secondary bus. This could possibly result in a forced renumbering of other buses in the system and would cause a severe disruption in system traffic flow.

4. **Installation of a card with a PCI-to-PCI bridge on it**. This would cause two problems:
   - The configuration software would have to assign a number to the bridge's secondary bus. This could possibly result in a forced renumbering of other buses in the system and would cause a severe disruption in system traffic flow.
   - A PCI-to-PCI bridge is a PCI device rather than a PCI-X capable device. If the end-user is permitted to install this card on a PCI-X bus, the Source Bridge for that bus will be forced to assert RST# to all devices on the bus and reinitialize them in PCI rather than PCI-X mode. This would, of course, result in a precipitous reduction in performance for all devices on the bus.

5. **Driving the initialization pattern to a newly installed card**. The bus must be Idle when this is done, so the bridge must first quiesce bus activity before driving the initialization pattern to the newly installed card. Devices that are already operational must ignore the initialization pattern driven to a newly installed device.
   - The Source Bridge or Hot-Plug Controller must permit the programmer to individually check the state of PCIXCAP from each hot-plug connector without powering on the card.
   - Problems associated with a hot-plug bus that supports 66MHz PCI operation.
   - Conservation of memory and IO address space.
   - Software cannot change a bridge's Secondary Bus Number configuration register while Requesters on the secondary bus have currently outstanding Split Transactions.
   - Possible adjustment of the Maximum Memory Byte Count value assigned to each Requester on the bus may be necessary when a new Requester is hot-installed.

The sections that follow describe each of the above problems and their respective solutions.

Determination of Card Capabilities

General

Before attaching a new card to the bus, the programmer must determine if the new card is of a lesser capability than the current bus operational mode. If it is of limited capability and software attaches it to the bus, the performance of the devices on that bus will be reduced, possibly to a great degree. The following sections discuss how the capabilities of a card may be determined and some possible actions that might be taken.

Determining the Presence of a PCI Card

There are two ways that the programmer can determine the presence of a PCI card installed in a hot-plug PCI-X connector: one is totally unacceptable while the other method makes sense:

Unacceptable Method. The programmer could take the following series of actions:

1. Command all of the drivers associated with Requesters on the bus to quiesce bus activity and wait for all of the drivers to report back that all transactions initiated by their associated Requesters have been completed.
2. Command the Source Bridge to reassert RST# to all devices on the bus, drive the 33MHz PCI pattern, and then deassert RST#.
3. Access the new card's configuration registers to determine if it implements the PCI-X capability configuration registers. If it doesn't, it's a PCI card.

It should be noted that asserting RST# to all devices on the bus causes them to lose their configuration information, necessitating the reconfiguration of all functions in all devices that reside on the bus. Obviously, this method causes a total disruption of system operation and is less than desirable. The method defined in the next section is infinitely preferable.

Acceptable Method. The more acceptable method permits the programmer to read the state of the PCIXCAP signal from the connector in question. This would typically be accomplished through a design-specific status port within the hot-plug controller. There are three possible states for the PCIX-CAP signal:

- A logic low indicates the presence of a PCI card.
- A logic high indicates that only 133MHz-capable PCI-X cards are present.
- A mid-range level indicates that only 66MHz-capable PCI-X cards are present.

If a PCI card is detected, the programmer would likely then urge the end-user to remove the card and either not install it in the machine at all or install it in a connector on a system bus intended for PCI devices. Alternatively, the end-user may override the suggestion and allow the attachment of the card to the bus. In this case, software would take the following actions:

1. Command all of the drivers associated with masters on the bus to quiesce bus activity and wait for all of the drivers to report back that all transactions initiated by their associated Requesters have been completed.
2. Command the Source Bridge to reassert RST# to all devices on the bus, drive either the 33MHz or 66MHz PCI pattern, and then deassert RST#.
   - If one or more devices on the bus do not support 66MHz PCI operation, the bridge would drive the 33MHz PCI pattern.
   - If the bridge determines that all devices on the bus support 66MHz PCI operation (by sampling a logic high on the M66EN signal from each connector), the bridge would drive the 66MHz PCI pattern.

It should be noted that asserting RST# to all devices on the bus causes them to lose their configuration information, necessitating the reconfiguration of all functions in all devices that reside on the bus.

Determining the Presence of a 66MHz PCI Card

A 66MHz PCI card would return a logic low on PCIXCAP and a logic high on M66EN. An alternative method to detect the presence of a 66MHz-capable PCI card would be to downshift the entire bus to 33MHz PCI mode, attach the new card, and read the 66MHz-Capable status bit from the PCI configuration status register of a function on the card. Obviously, this is a more draconian method than reading the state of the connector's M66EN and PCIXCAP signals.

Determining the Presence of a 66MHz-Capable PCI-X Card

As previously discussed, a mid-range level on the PCIXCAP signal from a connector indicates the presence of a 66MHz-capable PCI-X card in the connector.

If the bus is currently operating in 66MHz PCI-X mode, the programmer can safely perform the series of actions necessary to attach the card to the bus. For more information, refer to "Host/PCIX Bridge Pattern Delivery Sequence" on page 64 and "PCIX-to-PCIX Bridge Pattern Delivery Sequence" on page 65.

If the bus is currently operating in 133MHz PCI-X mode, the performance of the bus would have to be downgraded to accommodate the new card. In this case, it is recommended (by the author, not by the spec) that the end-user be forewarned about the degradation of performance and be given the option of installing the card or not. If it is decided to attach the card to the bus, software would have to quiesce the bus, reset all devices, and supply the new initialization pattern to all devices on the bus. It should be noted that asserting RST# to all devices on the bus causes them to lose their configuration information, necessitating the reconfiguration of all functions in all devices that reside on the bus.

Determining the Presence of a 133MHz-Capable PCI-X Card

A logic high on the PCIXCAP signal from a connector indicates the presence of a 133MHz-capable PCI-X card in the connector.

If the bus is currently operating in 133MHz PCI-X mode, the programmer can safely perform the series of actions necessary to attach the card to the bus. For more information, refer to "Host/PCIX Bridge Pattern Delivery Sequence" on page 64 and "PCIX-to-PCIX Bridge Pattern Delivery Sequence" on page 65.

On the other hand, if the bus is currently operating in a lower performance mode, there are a couple of choices:

- If there is a different hot-plug bus that is currently operating in 133MHz PCI-X mode with an unoccupied connector, the end-user could be urged to move the card to that connector.
- If the end-user chooses to leave the card in the current connector, the programmer can perform the series of actions necessary to attach the card to the bus. For more information, refer to "Host/PCIX Bridge Pattern Delivery Sequence" on page 64 and "PCIX-to-PCIX Bridge Pattern Delivery Sequence" on page 65.

Hot-Install of Card With PCIX-to-PCIX Bridge on It

Description. This card would have either a mid-level voltage or a logic high on its PCIXCAP signal line. The configuration software would attach it to the bus and the Source Bridge would supply its primary side interface with the appropriate initialization pattern. When the Source Bridge asserts RST# to the primary interface of the bridge on the card, the bridge on the card will assert RST# on its secondary bus and will drive the appropriate initialization pattern to the community of devices residing on its secondary side (based on the least-capable card discovered on its secondary bus).

Software determines that it is a bridge by reading a class code of 0604h from the upper two bytes of its Class Code configuration register. It further determines that it's a PCIX-to-PCIX bridge (rather than a PCI-to-PCI bridge) by detecting the presence of the PCI-X capability register set.

Before attempting to access any of the configuration registers within functions on the secondary bus, software must first assign a number to the bridge's secondary side bus by writing the assigned bus number into the bridge's Secondary Bus Number configuration register.

Refer to Figure 4-6 on page 77. Assume that the two device positions on PCI-X bus 1 are hot-plug connectors and that the system has already been configured and has been running for a while. Now assume that the end-user hot-installs a card with a PCIX-to-PCIX bridge on it. When the configuration software discovers this, it must then assign a number to the bridge's Secondary Bus Number configuration register. This new bus must be numbered as bus 2, the next sequential bus number. Since this bus number has already been assigned to the bus beneath Bridge B, however, the configuration software must change Bridge B's secondary bus number to 3 and Bridge C's secondary bus number to 4. This requires a quiescing of the entire system, followed by a complete reconfiguration of the system. As explained later in this book, after changing the number of a bus, the configuration software must perform at least one Type 0 configuration write transaction to each PCI-X function on that bus to inform it of the new bus number.

How to Avoid Bus Renumbering During Run-Time. The problem described in the previous section could have been avoided if the original bus numbering had been done as follows:

- Bridge A's secondary bus number set to 1.
- Bridge B's secondary bus number set to 4.
- Bridge C's secondary bus number set to 5.

This numbering takes into account the two hot-swap connectors located on bus 1 and the possibility that the end-user may install a card with a PCIX-to-PCIX or a PCI-to-PCI bridge in either or both of these connectors.

Figure 4-6: System With Multiple PCI-X Buses

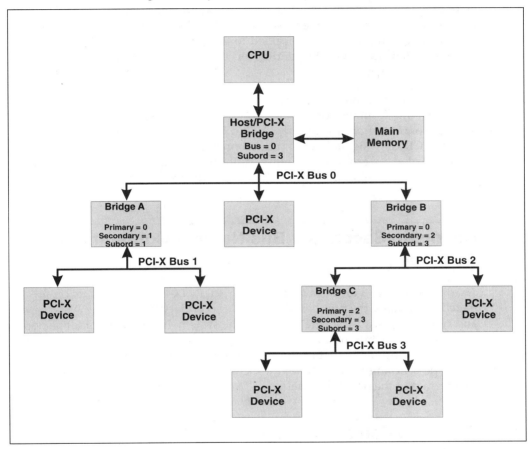

Hot-Install of Card With PCI-to-PCI Bridge on It

This card would have a logic zero on its PCIXCAP signal line. If the end-user decides to leave it in the connector, the entire bus the connector resides on must be downshifted into PCI mode (either 33MHz, or 66MHz if it's supported). In addition, as outlined in the previous section, bus renumbering may have to be performed.

Checking PCIXCAP Without Power Applied to Card

In some systems, the Source Bridge and/or hot-plug controller may check the state of a connector's PCIXCAP signal line before applying power to the card. Although power is not applied to the card, the PCIXCAP logic on the card in no way depends on power being applied to the card. On the system board, PCIX-CAP is pulled up to Vcc. Depending on the type of card installed in the slot, PCIXCAP may be:

* connected to ground on a PCI card, yielding a logic low on the PCIXCAP signal line from the connector.
* not connected on a 133MHz-capable PCI-X card, yielding a logic high on the PCIXCAP signal line from the connector.
* connected to ground through a pull-down resistor on a 66MHz-capable PCI-X card, yielding a mid-range level on the PCIXCAP signal line from the connector.

Changing Secondary Bus Number Configuration Register

As discussed in "Hot-Install of Card With PCIX-to-PCIX Bridge on It" on page 75, changing the number of a bridge's secondary bus after the system is up and running can cause severe trauma to the system. Not only would it be necessary to perform bus renumbering, but as stated in that earlier section, after changing the number of a bus, the configuration software must perform at least one Type 0 Configuration Write transaction to each PCI-X function on that bus to inform it of the new bus number.

Conservation of Address Space

General

Once a system is up and running, the configuration software has already allocated memory and IO address ranges to all devices within the system that have memory and IO decoders. The allocation of additional, non-conflicting blocks of memory and/or IO space to a hot-installed card can be problematic. Basically, the hot-plug spec takes the point of view that a function should be absolutely truthful regarding the size of memory blocks and/or IO blocks that it may need assigned to its decoders (i.e., a function's Base Address Registers, or BARs).

Chapter 4: Device Types and Bus Initialization

While the author is generally resistant to cutting and pasting verbiage from the spec, sometimes the reader is best served by seeing the exact phrasing from the spec.

Requesting Memory Space

The PCI spec states:

> "Devices are free to consume more address space than required, but decoding down to a **4KB space** for memory is **suggested for devices that need less than that amount**. For instance, a device that has 64 bytes of registers to be mapped into Memory Space may consume up to 4KB of address space in order to minimize the number of bits in the address decoder. Devices that do consume more address space than they use are not required to respond to the unused portion of that address space. Devices that map control functions into I/O Space may not consume more than 256 bytes per I/O Base Address register."

The PCI-X spec, however, states:

> "Unlike conventional PCI devices, which were permitted to decode 4KB address ranges even if they did not need that much, PCI-X **devices** that implement Base Address registers are **encouraged to request the minimum address space they need** to support their programming interface. Available address space in some systems is congested. This is particularly true of PCI hot-plug systems in which the addresses available for adding new devices must be partitioned among several slots. Available address space is further fragmented when devices and empty slots appear on the secondary side of a PCI-X bridge. Devices that don't request more address space than they need are preferred in such systems."

In addition, the PCI-X spec states:

> "**Memory address ranges** (including those assigned through Base Address registers) for all devices **must be no smaller than 128 bytes**. System configuration software assigns the memory range of each function of each device (that requests Memory Space) to different ranges aligned to ADBs. No two device-functions respond to addresses between the same two adjacent ADBs."

Requesting IO Space

The PCI-X spec states:

"I/O Space is limited, especially in hot-plug systems, and I/O references are generally slower than memory references. PCI-X **devices are discouraged from using I/O Space. If I/O Space is required, the device must also provide access to the same registers in Memory Space**. In other words, if the device uses a Base Address register (BAR) to request I/O Space, it must also use another BAR to request Memory Space for the same resource. If sufficient I/O Space is not available, system configuration software only assigns Memory Space resources. (PCI 2.2 recommends this mapping of the device into both address spaces.)"

Early Configuration Access to Newly-Installed Device

From the perspective of a newly installed card, RST# has just been removed from it, so it's Initialization Time (the first 2^{26} clock cycles after RST# is deasserted; see "What's Going on During Initialization Time?" on page 191). It therefore can legally ignore the 16-clock target latency rule when software attempts to access its configuration registers. In a hot-plug system wherein other devices on the bus are already operational, insertion of a multitude of Wait States into a configuration access can make the bus unavailable for potentially long periods of time. This must not occur in a high-availability hot-plug system.

To prevent this problem, it is the responsibility of the configuration software to ensure that it does not attempt to access any location within the newly installed device until Initialization Time has elapsed.

Possible Adjustment of Max Memory Read Byte Count Values

The configuration software can regulate the maximum size of a memory read block transaction initiated by a Requester. Limits for the Requesters present on a bus at power-up time are assigned to each Requester's Maximum Memory Read Byte Count register during the initial system configuration.

If a new Requester is hot-installed on a bus, the configuration software may choose to adjust the values assigned to the other Requesters to better accommodate the manner in which the new Requester will use the bus. Additional information can be found in "Adjustable Fields/Registers" on page 516.

Placing Device in Low-Power Mode Requires Quiesce

Before the system power management software places a device in a diminished power-usage state (i.e., D1, D2, D3$_{Hot}$), it must ensure that the device has been quiesced. For more information on quiescing a device, refer to "Hot-Plug Event May Cause Bus Renumbering" on page 494.

5   *PCI-X Is a Registered Bus*

The Previous Chapter

As introduced in an earlier chapter (see "Bus Protocol/Speed = Lowest Common Denominator" on page 48), the Source Bridge for a PCI-X bus interrogates two signals at startup time to determine the protocol and bus speed to be used on its secondary bus during this power-up session. The protocol and speed are selected to ensure that the least-capable device functions correctly. The previous chapter provided a detailed description of this process.

This Chapter

This chapter describes the registered nature of the PCI-X bus.

The Next Chapter

The next chapter introduces the PCI-X commands (i.e., the transaction types). They are divided into three categories:

- The Dword commands.
- The Burst commands.
- The Dual-Address Cycle (DAC) command.

PCI-X Is a Low-Voltage Swing (LVS) Bus

When a bus is designed to run at high clock speeds, the speed at which an output driver can change the state of a signal from one logic state to another becomes very important. While a 5 Volt signaling environment is fine for a PCI bus running at speeds up to 33.33MHz, at 66MHz it would take an output driver too long to change the state of a signal line from one logic state to another. That's why 66MHz PCI must be implemented using 3.3 Volt drivers and receivers. It takes less time to change the state of a signal on a bus that utilizes a low-Voltage swing (LVS). PCI-X devices may also optionally support the 5V signaling environment when operating in 33MHz PCI mode.

Likewise, to ensure proper operation at speeds ranging from 66MHz to 133MHz, PCI-X is implemented as an LVS bus and requires all devices to implement 3.3 Volt drivers and receivers.

Introduction to the Registered Nature of the Bus

Due to the high-speed nature of the PCI-X clock (50-133MHz), the bus protocol dictates that all devices must employ registered inputs and outputs. Refer to the general example illustrated in Figure 5-1 on page 85:

CLOCK 1.

ON the rising-edge of clock one:

- a device's output register clocks out a new state onto a signal line.

CLOCK 2.

ON the rising-edge of clock two:

- Another device (or devices) latches the state of the signal line into its input register.

DURING clock cycle two:

- The registered signal level is examined by the receiving device's logic and the device develops its response to the signal's registered state.

CLOCK 3.

ON the rising-edge of clock three:

- The receiving device clocks its response out of its output register onto the appropriate signal line.

Figure 5-1: General Example of the Bus's Registered Nature

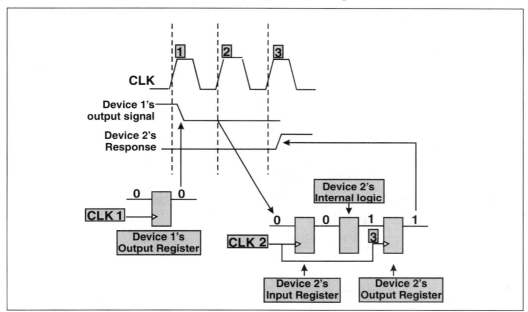

Address/Command Decode Example

Refer to the example pictured in Figure 5-2 on page 86:

CLOCK 3.

ON the rising-edge of clock three:

- All targets clock the address and command presented on AD[31:0] and C/BE#[3:0] into their input registers.

DURING clock cycle three:

- The targets begin the decode. One of the targets has been configured to recognize this address, so its internal decode logic develops an asserted level (low) on its internal version of DEVSEL# (s1_DEVSEL#).

CLOCK 4.

ON the rising-edge of clock four:

- The target clocks an asserted level onto the external DEVSEL# signal.

CLOCK 5.

ON the rising-edge of clock five:

- The initiator clocks DEVSEL# into its input register for the first time.

DURING clock cycle five:

- The initiator's internal logic samples its internal, registered version of DEVSEL# (s1_DEVSEL#) and detects it asserted. This informs the initiator that it has connected with a target.

Figure 5-2: Registered Bus Example Using Command/Address Decode

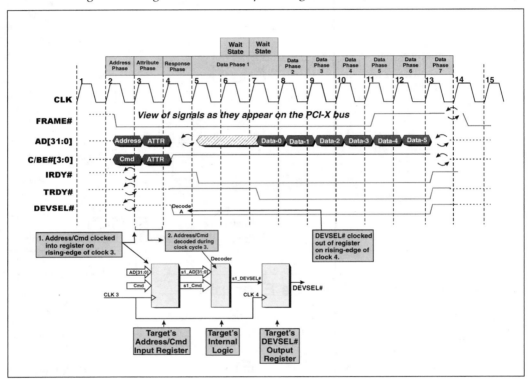

Data Read Example

This example continues that discussed in the previous example. Refer to the example pictured in Figure 5-3 on page 88:

CLOCK 5.

DURING clock cycle five:

- The initiator's internal logic detected that the target had asserted DEVSEL# during clock four. This defines the initiator's first data sampling point as the rising-edge of clock six.

CLOCK 6.

ON the rising-edge of clock six:
- The initiator registers data from AD[31:0] and the state of TRDY#.

DURING clock cycle six:
- The initiator detects the deasserted state of its registered version of TRDY# (s1_TRDY#). As a result, it discards the data that was registered from AD[31:0] on the rising-edge of clock six.

CLOCK 7.

ON the rising-edge of clock seven:
- The initiator once again registers data from AD[31:0] and the state of TRDY#.

DURING clock cycle seven:
- The initiator detects the deasserted state of its registered version of TRDY# (s1_TRDY#). As a result, it discards the data that was registered from AD[31:0] on the rising-edge of clock seven.

CLOCK 8.

ON the rising-edge of clock eight:
- The initiator once again registers data from AD[31:0] and the state of TRDY#.

DURING clock cycle eight:
- The initiator detects the asserted state of its registered version of TRDY# (s1_TRDY#). As a result, it places the data that was registered from AD[31:0] on the rising-edge of clock eight into its internal read buffer.

Figure 5-3: Registered Bus Example Using Data/TRDY# Sampling During a Read

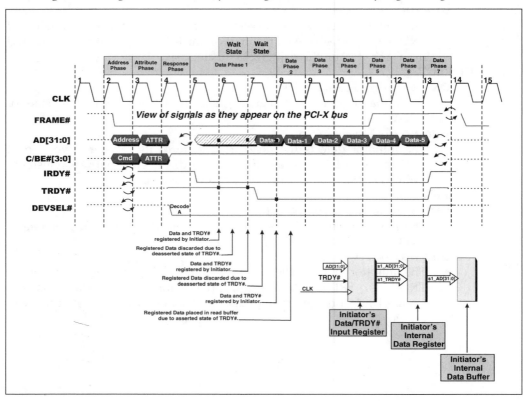

6   *Intro to Commands*

The Previous Chapter

The previous chapter described the registered nature of the PCI-X bus.

This Chapter

This chapter introduces the PCI-X commands (i.e., the transaction types). They are divided into three categories:

- The Dword commands.
- The Burst commands.
- The Dual-Address Cycle (DAC) command.

The Next Chapter

The next chapter introduces the four phases of a PCI-X transaction:

- Address Phase.
- Attribute Phase.
- Response Phase.
- Data Phase(s).

Commands Fall Into Three Categories

PCI-X commands (i.e., transaction types) can be divided into three categories:

- those that only transfer a single dword or a subset thereof;
- those that can be used to transfer blocks of between one byte and 4KB of memory data;
- and the Dual-Address Cycle (DAC) command, which is only used to address memory above the 4GB address boundary.

The following three sections provide an introduction to each of the commands. A detailed discussion of the commands can be found in Chapter 11, entitled "Detailed Command Description," on page 147. A detailed discussion of the DAC command can be found in "Addressing Memory Above 4GB Boundary" on page 372.

Command Encoding

The command and address are issued on C/BE#[3:0] by the initiator in the transaction's Address Phase (see clock two of Figure 6-1 on page 91). Table 6-1 on page 90 lists the Dword command encoding, while Table 6-2 on page 90 lists the Burst transaction command encoding.

Table 6-1: PCI-X Dword Commands

C/BE[3:0]# or C/BE[7:4]# (binary)	PCI-X Command
0000	Interrupt Acknowledge
0001	Special Cycle
0010	IO Read
0011	IO Write
0110	Memory Read Dword
1010	Configuration Read
1011	Configuration Write

Table 6-2: PCI-X Burst Commands

C/BE[3:0]# or C/BE[7:4]# (binary)	PCI-X Command	Byte Enable Usage
0111	Memory Write	Byte Enables define bytes to be transferred within target dword. Any combination of Byte Enables is valid.

Table 6-2: PCI-X Burst Commands (Continued)

C/BE[3:0]# or C/BE[7:4]# (binary)	PCI-X Command	Byte Enable Usage
1000	Alias to Memory Read Block	Byte Enables are reserved during Data Phases and must be driven deasserted (high) by initiator.
1001	Alias to Memory Write Block	
1100	Split Completion	
1110	Memory Read Block	
1111	Memory Write Block	

Figure 6-1: Example PCI-X Transaction

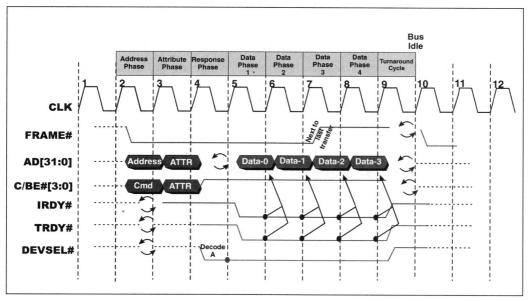

Dword Commands

General

As mentioned earlier, the dword commands are used to transfer a single dword or a subset thereof. The dword commands are:

- IO Read and Write commands
- Memory Read Dword command
- Configuration Read and Write commands
- Interrupt Acknowledge command
- Special Cycle command

The sections that follow introduce each of these commands.

IO Read and Write Commands

The IO Read and IO Write commands are used to access a device's control/status/data registers when they are mapped into IO space rather than memory space. Hypothetically, in PCI the IO Read and Write commands can be used to perform burst IO reads or writes. In reality, however, they have only been implemented to transfer single IO dwords or a subset thereof. The PCI-X spec is therefore just recognizing reality in only permitting single Data Phase IO transactions.

For a detailed description of the IO Read and Write commands, refer to "IO Read and Memory Read Dword" on page 216 and "IO Write" on page 224.

Memory Read Dword Command

The Memory Read Dword command is used to read a single dword or a subset thereof from memory-mapped IO ports (i.e., a device's control/status/data registers when they are mapped into memory space rather than IO space).

For a detailed description of the Memory Read Dword Command, refer to "IO Read and Memory Read Dword" on page 216.

Chapter 6: Intro to Commands

Configuration Read and Write Commands

The Configuration Read and Write commands are used to access a function's configuration registers. Hypothetically, in PCI the Configuration Read and Write commands can be used to perform burst Configuration reads or writes. In reality, however, they have only been implemented to transfer single Configuration dwords or a subset thereof. The PCI-X spec is therefore just recognizing reality in only permitting single Data Phase configuration transactions.

For a detailed description of the Configuration Read and Write commands, refer to:

- "Configuration Read and Write Transactions" on page 234.
- Chapter 20, entitled "Configuration Transactions," on page 425.

Interrupt Acknowledge Command

Refer to Figure 6-2 on page 94. The Interrupt Acknowledge command is issued by the Host/PCIX Bridge (see Figure 6-2 on page 94) to read the interrupt vector from the interrupt controller and deliver it to the processor. The interrupt vector can be between one byte and four bytes in length and can therefore be read in a single Data Phase transaction.

For a detailed description of the Interrupt Acknowledge command, refer to "Interrupt Acknowledge Command" on page 234.

Figure 6-2: Example System Block Diagram

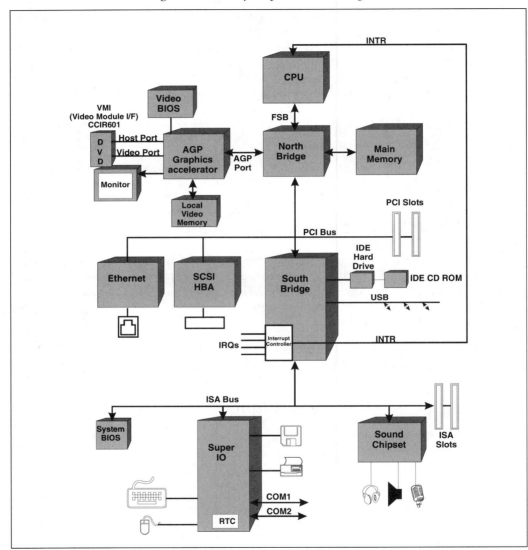

Special Cycle Command

The Special Cycle command is issued by an initiator to broadcast a message of between one and four bytes of information to one or more targets residing on a target PCI-X bus. Each target on the PCI-X bus must examine the message to determine whether the message applies to it (a target may be designed not to recognize any messages or to recognize only specific messages; most targets don't pay any attention to messages delivered via the Special Cycle transaction). As an example of message passing using the Special Cycle transaction, Intel x86 processors use the Special Cycle transaction to indicate when they are going into a Halt or a Shutdown condition.

For a detailed description of the Special Cycle command, refer to "Special Cycle Command" on page 235.

Burst Commands

All Burst-Oriented Commands Are Memory Transfers

The PCI-X burst-oriented commands are used to perform memory transfers of between 1 and 4096 bytes of information. The spec writers constrained the maximum byte transfer count of each transfer request to 4KB in the interest of a fair sharing of bus bandwidth and target resources among multiple masters.

Start Address Is Byte-Aligned

In PCI-X memory-oriented commands, the start address is always byte-aligned and is delivered on AD[31:0].

Transfer Length

In PCI-X burst memory transactions, a byte transfer count is issued by the initiator and it defines the end address. The start byte address + the byte transfer count -1 = the end address.

Linear Addressing Is Implied

Unlike PCI memory addressing, no addressing sequence information is delivered on AD[1:0]. In essence, they've eliminated Cache Line Wrap addressing and all memory addressing is Linear by implication. As the transaction proceeds from Data Phase to Data Phase:

- A 32-bit memory target increments its address counter by four to point to the start address of the next dword.
- Assuming that a 64-bit transfer is in progress, a 64-bit memory target increments its address counter by eight to point to the start address of the next qword.

Memory Read Block Command

The Memory Read Block command is an all-inclusive read starting at the start byte address and encompassing all locations up to and including the end address identified by the byte transfer count issued by the initiator. Since the command type defines this as an all-inclusive read, the Byte Enables are not needed and are reserved and driven high in all Data Phases of the transaction.

For a detailed description of the Memory Read Block command, refer to "Memory Read Block Transaction" on page 241.

Alias To Memory Read Block Command

This command is really a place-holder for a possible future command. Currently, no Requesters are permitted to issue this command. If a target is addressed by this command, it must treat it as if it's a Memory Read Block command.

As an example, this could be used in the future to indicate a double-data rate transfer request wherein a block of data might be transferred using both of the clock edges to double throughput.

Memory Write Block Command

The Memory Write Block command is an all-inclusive write starting at the start byte address and encompassing all locations up to and including the end address identified by the byte transfer count issued by the initiator. Since the command type defines this as an all-inclusive write, the Byte Enables are not needed and are reserved and driven high in all Data Phases of the transaction.

For a detailed description of the Memory Write Block command, refer to "Memory Write Block Transaction" on page 253.

Alias To Memory Write Block Command

This command is really a place-holder for a possible future command. Currently, no Requesters are permitted to issue this command. If a target is addressed by this command, it must treat it as if it's a Memory Write Block command.

As an example, this could be used in the future to indicate a double-data rate transfer request wherein a block of data might be transferred using both of the clock edges to double throughput.

Memory Write Command

An initiator uses the Memory Write command if it wishes to write bytes into some but not all locations within the range defined by the start byte address and the byte transfer count. The Byte Enables issued by the initiator in each Data Phase identify the locations to be written within the current dword (or qword if performing 64-bit transfers).

For a detailed description of the Memory Write command, refer to "Memory Write Transaction" on page 260.

Split Completion Command

This command is used by a Completer to return previously requested read data to the Requester, or a success/failure indication for a previously issued write, or an error on a previously requested read. More information on the Split Completion command can be found in:

- "Split Completion Transaction" on page 274.
- Chapter 9, entitled "Intro to Split and Immediate Transactions," on page 113.
- Chapter 17, entitled "Split Completion Messages," on page 313.

Dual-Address Cycle (DAC) Command

The Dual-Address Cycle command may only be used when issuing a start memory address located above the 4GB address boundary. For a detailed description of the DAC command, refer to "Addressing Memory Above 4GB Boundary" on page 372.

7 *Intro to Transaction Phases*

The Previous Chapter

The previous chapter introduces the PCI-X commands (i.e21., the transction types). They are divided into three categories:

- The Dword commands.
- The Burst commands.
- The Dual-Address Cycle (DAC) command.

This Chapter

This chapter introduces the four phases of a PCI-X transaction:

- Address Phase.
- Attribute Phase.
- Response Phase.
- Data Phase(s).

The Next Chapter

The next chapter introduces the reasons why the initiator or target would terminate a transaction. It also introduces the manner in which a bridge handles transactions that target internal locations within the bridge as well as transactions that must traverse the bridge.

The PCI Transaction Phases

The PCI transaction consists of two phases:

- In the **Address Phase**, the initiator drives out the address and the command and asserts FRAME# to indicate that a transaction has been initiated.
- In each **Data Phase** (the transaction may include one or more Data Phases), the initiator transfers a data item between itself and the target. A data item consists of a dword or a subset thereof (if it's a 32-bit transfer), or a qword or a subset thereof (if it's a 64-bit transfer).

The PCI-X Transaction Phases

Refer to Figure 7-1 on page 102. Each PCI-X transaction consists of four or more phases: the Address Phase, the Attribute Phase, the Response Phase, and the Data Phase(s). The following sections provide a brief description of each phase.

Address Phase

In the **Address Phase** (see clock two of Figure 7-1), the initiator drives out the **start byte address** onto the AD bus, the **command** onto the C/BE# bus, **and** asserts **FRAME#** to indicate that a transaction has been initiated. The Address Phase is one clock in duration (note, however, that if the initiator uses the DAC command, there will be two Address Phases, each of which is one clock in duration). The targets on the bus clock the address, the command, and the state of the FRAME# signal into their respective input registers on the next rising-edge of the clock. A detailed description of the Address Phase can be found in Chapter 13, entitled "The Address, Attribute and Response Phases," on page 197.

Attribute Phase

The **Attribute Phase** (see clock three of Figure 7-1) is one clock in duration and immediately follows the Address Phase. In the Attribute Phase, the initiator outputs the following information onto AD[31:0] and C/BE#[3:0]:

- The byte transfer couht (if it's a memory burst transaction), or the Byte Enables (if it's a dword transaction).

- The identity of the entity that originated the transaction request (the initiator of the current transaction could be the Requester, or a bridge passing the transaction along for a master on the other side of the bridge).
- The transaction ID.
- If it's a memory transaction, the No Snoop and Relaxed Ordering attribute bits.
- If it's a configuration transaction, the number of the bus that the transaction is being performed on.
- If it's a Split Completion transaction, a set of attributes different from those mentioned earlier in the list.

A detailed description of the Attribute Phase can be found in Chapter 13, entitled "The Address, Attribute and Response Phases," on page 197.

Response Phase

In the Response Phase (see clock four of Figure 7-1), the initiator awaits the target's assertion of DEVSEL#. The assertion of DEVSEL# informs the initiator that it has successfully connected with a target. If no target asserts DEVSEL#, the initiator experiences a Master Abort and returns the bus to the Idle state. In all cases other than a Special Cycle transaction, this is an error.

A detailed description of the Response Phase can be found in Chapter 13, entitled "The Address, Attribute and Response Phases," on page 197.

Data Phase(s)

In the Data Phase (or Data Phases; see clocks five through eight of Figure 7-1), a data item (a dword or a qword, or a subset of a dword or a qword) is transferred between the initiator and target on each rising-edge of the clock when both IRDY# and TRDY# are asserted.

A more detailed description can be found in:

- Chapter 12, entitled "Latency Rules," on page 189.
- Chapter 14, entitled "Dword Transactions," on page 215.
- Chapter 15, entitled "Burst Transactions," on page 239.
- Chapter 16, entitled "Transaction Terminations," on page 279.

PCI-X System Architecture

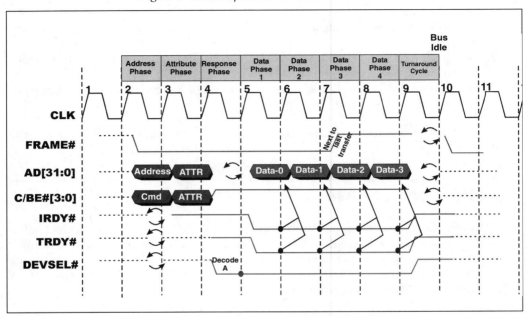

Figure 7-1: Example PCI-X Burst Transaction

8 *Intro to Transaction Termination*

The Previous Chapter

The previous chapter introduced the four phases of a PCI-X transaction:

- Address Phase.
- Attribute Phase.
- Response Phase.
- Data Phase(s).

This Chapter

This chapter introduces the reasons why the initiator or target would terminate a transaction. It also introduces the manner in which a bridge handles transactions that target internal locations within the bridge as well as transactions that must traverse the bridge.

The Next Chapter

In PCI-X, Split Transactions take the place of PCI Delayed transactions. The next chapter introduces the concepts and terminology associated with PCI-X Split Transactions. In addition, it defines PCI-X Immediate transactions.

Introduction

The initiator and the target involved in a transaction have various reasons and methods of terminating a transaction. The primary and best reason is that they have achieved byte count satisfaction. In other words, they're done. The sections that follow introduce the reasons for and the methods used to terminate a transaction.

More detailed descriptions of the various terminations are found in subsequent chapters such as Chapter 16, entitled "Transaction Terminations," on page 279.

Initiator Termination of Transaction

There are four reasons why the initiator would terminate a transaction of its own accord:

- It's completed its transfer and it's happy.
- It's almost full and its wants the target to stop feeding it.
- It's almost empty and it wants to temporarily stop the transaction until it has more data to write.
- It's lonely because nobody responds to its request.

That's a pretty folksy way of stating it, so here's the more technically correct way of stating it:

- It has achieved byte count satisfaction.
- It's approaching a buffer dry or a buffer full condition before the byte transfer count has been satisfied.
- No connection has been established with the addressed target.

Byte Count Satisfaction

As stated earlier, the primary and best reason for terminating a transaction is because the byte transfer count has been exhausted. The initiator issues a byte-specific start address and a byte transfer count at the start of the transaction (in the Address and Attribute Phases, respectively). Both parties decrement the initial byte count and terminate the transaction upon completing the final Data Phase.

A detailed description of this termination type can be found in "Byte Count Satisfaction" on page 280.

Initiator Approaching Buffer Full or Dry Condition

As mentioned in "Data Transferred in Blocks" on page 31, data in PCI-X transactions is transferred in blocks of 128 bytes each. Consider the following example scenario:

Chapter 8: Intro to Transaction Termination

1. A PCI-X device wishes to write 2KB of data into memory, but it currently has only 512 bytes of write data buffered up and ready to blast out to memory.
2. While continuing to accumulate the additional data from a background source (e.g., a disk drive or the network), the device arbitrates for bus ownership and initiates a Memory Write Block transaction specifying the full 2KB to be written.
3. The background data source cannot keep up with the device's transfer rate, so the device will approach a buffer dry condition before it has accumulated the full 2KB of write data to pump out to memory.
4. As the write progresses, the initiator writes several blocks and then starts to transfer the last data block it has available.
5. As it approaches that block boundary, the initiator signals to the target that it needs to disconnect on the upcoming block boundary. This is referred to as a **Disconnect At Next ADB** issued by the initiator. The target will honor it and both of them will back off the bus in the clock immediately following the transfer of the last data item of the block.

A detailed description of initiator issuance of a Disconnect at Next ADB can be found in "Initiator Issues Disconnect at Next ADB" on page 289.

Connection Timeout

As in PCI, the initiator allows a finite amount of time for the addressed target to indicate the establishment of a connection (by asserting DEVSEL#). If the target doesn't respond within the allotted time, the initiator experiences a Master Abort and returns the bus to the Idle state to make the bus available to other initiators. As in PCI, a PCI-X initiator samples DEVSEL# a total of four times and, if it is deasserted all four times, the initiator returns the bus to the Idle state.

In all cases other than the Special Cycle transaction this is an error, while it is the natural end to a Special Cycle transaction (because no target is supposed to respond to the quiet broadcast of a message). In transactions other than Special Cycle, the initiator sets the Received Master Abort bit in its PCI configuration Status register (see Figure 8-1 on page 106) and invokes its driver, typically by generating an interrupt, to come check its status.

A complete description of Master Abort can found in "Initiator Termination Due to Connection Timeout" on page 290.

Figure 8-1: PCI Configuration Status Register

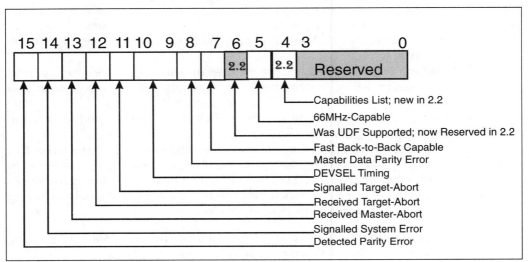

Early Target Termination of Transaction

General

There a number of reasons why a target would terminate a transaction before the requested data transfer has completed:

- It's broken.
- The initiator is addressing locations it doesn't implement.
- It's full and has no room to memorize the initial request or, if it's a memory write, to accept the write data.
- The initiator wants to burst, but it can't handle bursts.
- It's going to take a while to deliver the write data or to fetch the read data requested, so the target memorizes the transaction and breaks the connection. It will reconnect with the request originator (i.e., the Requester) later to give you the result.

Chapter 8: Intro to Transaction Termination

Target Abort

Reasons for a Target Abort

The following are the three reasons why a target might issue a Target Abort to the initiator:

- The target is broken and issues a Target Abort to the initiator, forcing the initiator to terminate the transaction.
- The target of a Split Completion transaction (the Requester) detects an Address Phase parity error.
- Observing the Byte Enable settings in a Data Phase, the target determines that the initiator is addressing one or more unimplemented IO or memory-mapped IO ports within the currently addressed IO dword, or the memory-mapped IO dword. Consequently, the target issues a Target Abort to the initiator.

Target Abort Always Ends a Transaction

The reception of a Target Abort in the first or any other Data Phase always causes the initiator to terminate the transaction.

- The target sets the Signaled Target Abort bit in its PCI configuration Status register (see Figure 8-1 on page 106).
- The initiator sets the Received Target Abort bit in its PCI configuration Status register (see Figure 8-1 on page 106). In addition, the initiator invokes its driver, typically by generating an interrupt, to come check its status.

A detailed description of a Target Abort can be found in "Target Abort" on page 290.

Retry

Reasons for Issuing a Retry

The following are reasons why a target might issue a Retry to the initiator:

- Upon the initiation of a memory write transaction, the target has a temporarily full posted memory write buffer condition and can not accept any data from the initiator. It issues a Retry to the initiator.

- Bridges deal with all transactions other than memory writes that must traverse the bridge by memorizing and then performing them on the destination bus. A bridge that cannot memorize any additional transactions until one or more previously memorized transactions are completed will issue a Retry to the initiator.
- A target that issued a Split Response earlier in time will later initiate a Split Completion transaction to return the previously requested read data or a write completion notification message. A bridge that is acting as the target in the return path to the originator of the request (i.e., the Requester) may not have reserved any buffer space for the data and will issue a Retry to the initiator of the Split Completion transaction.

Initiator's Response to a Retry

Response to a Retry in PCI. When a PCI initiator receives a Retry from a PCI target, the initiator must periodically reattempt the transaction until the target transfers at least the first data item. It is illegal to just "give up" and not repeat the transaction. This means there is no such thing as a purely speculative transaction in the PCI environment.

Response to a Retry in PCI-X. In PCI-X, when an initiator attempts a transaction and receives a Retry from the target, the initiator may choose not to repeat the transaction. This means that PCI-X does support a purely speculative transaction. However, it would almost certainly be a memory read wherein the initiator decides to read some data in case it may need it in the future, but then the need for the read data goes away before the initiator receives any of the data. The idea of a purely speculative write is quite alarming (but the spec appears to permit it).

Detailed Description of Retry

A detailed description of Retry can be found in "Target Issues a Retry" on page 294.

Single Data Phase Disconnect

Assume that an initiator starts a burst memory transaction with a target that doesn't support bursting (i.e., it doesn't implement an address counter). The target issues a Single Data Phase Disconnect to the initiator, forcing the initiator to terminate the transaction upon completion of the first Data Phase.

Chapter 8: Intro to Transaction Termination

A detailed description of target issuance of a Single Data Phase Disconnect can be found in "Single Data Phase Disconnect" on page 108.

Disconnect At Next ADB

The following are reasons why a target might issue a Disconnect At Next ADB to the initiator:

- During a memory write transaction, the Completer accepts one or more blocks of write data, but is then approaching a temporary buffer full condition. It issues a Disconnect At Next ADB to the initiator to force a disconnect on the upcoming block boundary.
- A bridge may begin to accept memory write data into its posted-memory write buffer, but as its buffer approaches a buffer full condition it issues a Disconnect At Next ADB to the initiator. This forces the initiator to disconnect at the upcoming block boundary.
- A target that issued a Split Response earlier in time will later initiate a Split Completion transaction to return the previously requested read data or a write completion notification message. A bridge that is acting as the target in the return path to the request originator (i.e., the Requester) may not have reserved sufficient buffer space for all of the data and, as it approaches a buffer full condition, will issue a Disconnect At Next ADB to the initiator of the Split Completion transaction.

A detailed description of Disconnect At Next ADB can be found in "Target Issues Disconnect At Next ADB" on page 299.

Split Response

Definition

If a target receives a transaction request (other than a memory write) wherein it will take longer than 16 clocks from the assertion of FRAME# before the target can start transferring data, the target memorizes the request and issues a Split Response to the initiator. This instructs the initiator to move the request to its Split Transaction Queue and suspend it. Inherent in the Split Response is the promise that the target will initiate a Split Completion transaction at a later time to pick up the thread of that transaction.

A detailed description of Split Response can be found in "Target Issues a Split Response" on page 308.

Commands That Will Not Receive a Split Response

The target is not permitted to issue a Split Response to the following commands:

- **Memory Write and Memory Write Block commands**. Memory writes must be posted in the function's (or bridge's) posted-memory write buffer. This rule exists for performance reasons: the buffer can accept write data far faster than memory can.
- **Split Completion command**. When a Completer (acting as an initiator) initiates a Split Completion transaction to respond to a request it memorized earlier, the target of the Split Completion (who received a Split Response to the request it issued earlier) is not permitted to respond with a Split Response.
- **Special Cycle command**. As in PCI, it is illegal for any device to respond to a Special Cycle transaction in any way.

Bridge Handling of Memory Writes

When a bridge is acting as the target of a Memory Write or a Memory Write Block transaction, it must post the write data and is not permitted to issue a Split Response. This is true in both of the following cases:

- the data is being written into internal memory within the bridge.
- the data is being written to a Completer that resides on the opposite side of the bridge.

A bridge accumulates memory write sequences in its posted write buffer. When it forwards the contents of its posted write buffer, it is prohibited from combining different write sequences into one sequence. They must each be performed on the destination bus as separate sequences using the same Sequence IDs that were issued by the originators of the memory write sequences (i.e., the Requesters).

Bridge Handling of Transactions Other Than Memory Writes

There are two possible cases:

- The transaction is addressing a location within the bridge itself.
- The transaction is addressing a Completer that resides on the other side of the bridge.

Addressing a Location Within the Bridge

When a transaction is addressing a location within the bridge, the bridge can either:

- Respond immediately (if it can start transferring data within 16 clocks from the assertion of FRAME#), or
- Issue a Split Response if it will take longer than 16 clocks from the assertion of FRAME# to perform the internal IO or Configuration Write, or to obtain the requested read data.

Addressing a Location on the Opposite Side of Bridge

When a transaction is addressing a Completer that resides on the other side of the bridge, the bridge must split the transaction. In other words, it issues a Split Response to the transaction originator, performs the transaction on the destination bus, and then initiates a Split Completion transaction to return the previously requested read data or the write completion notice to the transaction originator (i.e., the Requester).

9 *Intro to Split and Immediate Transactions*

The Previous Chapter

The previous chapter inroduced the reasons why the initiator or target would terminate a transaction. It also introduced the manner in which a bridge handles transactions that target internal locations within the bridge as well as transactions that must traverse the bridge.

This Chapter

In PCI-X, Split Transactions take the place of PCI Delayed transactions. This chapter introduces the concepts and terminology associated with PCI-X Split Transactions. In addition, it defines PCI-X Immediate transactions.

The Next Chapter

The next chapter provides a detailed description of bus arbitration in the PCI-X bus environment. It provides:

* a detailed, step-by-step description of an example arbitration among a number of initiators
* the initiator design rules
* the arbiter design rules
* a discussion of bus parking
* a detailed description of preemption and the initiator's Latency Timer.

Definition of Requester and Completer

The Requester is defined as the originator of a transaction request, while the Completer is the target addressed in the request. They may both be on the same bus or could be on different buses. In that case, the request would have to traverse one or more bridges to arrive at the Completer.

Definition of a Sequence

A Sequence is defined as the series of one or more transactions that satisfy a transaction request issued by a Requester.

Definition of Requester ID, Tag, and Sequence ID

When a Requester issues a transaction request, it issues the following information:

- The start byte address and the command.
- The byte transfer count.
- The Requester ID in the form of its Bus Number, Device Number, and Function Number.
- The Requester assigns a unique transaction ID, referred to as the transaction Tag, to the transaction.

Taken together, the Requester ID plus the Tag form a unique request identifier, referred to as the Sequence ID.

How Does a Device Know Its Requester ID?

In the previous section, it states that a PCI-X initiator supplies the Completer with its Requester ID (Bus Number, Device Number, and Function Number) whenever it issues a transaction. It should be obvious that a PCI-X function explicitly knows what function it is within a PCI-X device, but how would it know which device (i.e., package) it lives in, and what bus it resides on?

Each PCI-X function implements a PCI-X Status register (see Figure 9-1 on page 115) in its configuration space. This register contains the function's Requester ID information. The Function field is hardwired, but the Bus and Device fields are read/writable. On power-up, they do not contain valid information. When the configuration software discovers a function (by reading its Vendor ID register) and causes the Source Bridge that the function resides on to generate one or more Type 0 configuration write transactions to the function's configuration registers, the bridge automatically supplies the function targeted by the configuration write with the bus number (supplied from the bridge's Secondary Bus Number register) and device number (supplied in the address of the configuration write transaction). The function updates its Bus and Device fields each time a Type 0 configuration write is performed to any of its configuration registers.

Detailed descriptions of the PCI-X configuration registers and configuration transactions can be found in:

- Chapter 20, entitled "Configuration Transactions," on page 425.
- Chapter 21, entitled "Non-Bridge Configuration Registers," on page 453.
- Chapter 22, entitled "Bridge Configuration Registers," on page 487.

Figure 9-1: PCI-X Status Register

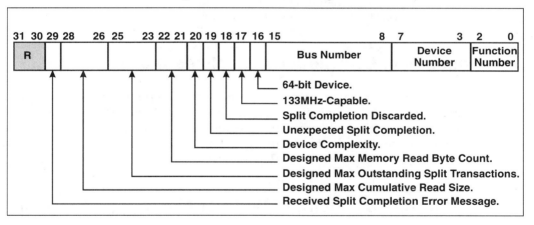

Immediate Transaction

Definition of an Immediate Transaction

An Immediate transaction is defined as:

- A transaction that transfers at least some of the data immediately. This includes:
    - A transaction that receives a Single Data Phase Disconnect.
    - A transaction that transfers some data and then receives a Disconnect At Next ADB.
    - A transaction that immediately transfers all of the data.
- A transaction that terminates due to a Master or Target Abort.

Transactions that do not complete as Immediate transactions are:

- Transactions terminated with Retry.
- Transactions terminated with Split Response.

Immediate Completion Completes the Sequence...

When a Requester experiences immediate completion of a transaction (see the previous section), the Sequence is considered complete and the requester may or may not rearbitrate for the bus to resume the transaction. If it chooses to resume the transaction, it may use the same or a different Tag (because an immediate completion retires the Tag assigned to the current transaction).

...Unless It's a Memory Write or Memory Write Block

The spec contains the following statement (note that the italicized text has been added by the author):

> "If the Sequence is a burst write and is disconnected either by the initiator *(by issuing a Disconnect At Next ADB)* or target *(by issuing a Disconnect At Next ADB, or a Single Data Phase Disconnect)*, the Sequence has more than one transaction. After a disconnection, the initiator must resume the sequence *(using the same Sequence ID)* by initiating another burst write transaction using the same command and adjusting the starting address and

byte count for the data already sent. The initiator must deliver the full byte count of the Sequence no matter how many times the Sequence is disconnected and regardless of whether continuations after a disconnection are terminated with Retry."

...Or Unless First Data Phase of Memory Write Receives Retry

The spec says the following regarding Retry and memory writes:

"If the Sequence is a burst write and the target signals Retry on the first Data Phase of the Sequence, the Sequence ends immediately. The requester is not obligated to repeat a Sequence terminated with Retry on the first Data Phase (unless it is required by the application, e.g., a PCI-X bridge forwarding a memory write Sequence). However, if the requester repeats the burst write, it is considered a new Sequence and is permitted to use the same or a different command and attributes (byte count, Tag, etc.). The requester is permitted to reuse a Tag as soon as the memory write Sequence completes on the requester's bus, independent of whether there are one or more PCI-X bridges between the requester and completer, and if so, when those bridges forward the Sequence to the completer."

Memory Writes Are Posted

General

Targets handle Memory Write and Memory Write Block transactions by posting the write data in a posted-write buffer and writing the data to memory at a later time when it flushes its buffers.

Can Be Initiated Before All Write Data Is Ready

A Requester can initiate a Memory Write or a Memory Write Block transaction when it has some of the write data (but not all of it) buffered up and ready to write. During the transaction, as it approaches the block boundary where it will have a buffer dry condition, it issues a Disconnect At Next ADB to the target. When it has more of the write accumulated and ready to write, it would then rearbitrate for the bus and pick up where it left off.

Split Transactions

What Problem Do Split Transactions Solve?

Upon receipt of a transaction request (other than a Memory Write, Memory Write Block, Split Completion, or Special Cycle), the target (either the Completer or an intervening bridge) may determine that it would take in excess of 16 clocks from the assertion of FRAME# before it is ready to start transferring data. In this case, the target memorizes the request and issues a Split Response to the initiator. The completer performs the read or write and then initiates one or more Split Completion transactions to return the previously requested read data or the write completion notice to the Requester.

In PCI, this same problem is handled by treating the request as a Delayed Read or a Delayed Write request. But, as described in "PCI Delayed Transactions Are Inefficient" on page 15, Delayed Transactions are very inefficient.

Split Completion Uses Sequence ID as the Address

When it receives the Subsequent Split Completion transaction, the Requester (acting as the target of the Split Completion transaction) receives the Sequence ID (Requester's Bus Number, Device Number, Function Number, and Tag) that it issued in the original request and decodes it. The Requester compares this to its Requester ID and, if it's a match, claims the transaction by asserting DEVSEL#. The Requester compares the Tag received with the Requester ID to the suspended transactions currently resident in its Split Transaction Queue. Detecting a match, it picks up the thread of that transaction.

- If it was a read request, the Requester accepts the read data delivered by the Completer (or an error message if the Completer encountered an internal problem when attempting the read; see "Read Completion Indication" on page 323).
- If it was a write request, the Requester accepts the write completion message (see "Write Completion Indication" on page 322) delivered in the single Data Phase of the Split Completion transaction (or an error message if the Completer encountered an internal problem when attempting the write).

Requester and Completer May Reside on the Same Bus

Example

Consider Figure 9-2 on page 121. In this example, the Requester and Completer reside on the same bus. When the Requester issues a request to the Completer, the Completer may either treat it as an Immediate transaction or, if it would take longer than 16 clocks from the assertion of FRAME# to start transferring data, the Completer may split it.

1. If it chooses to split the transaction, the Completer memorizes the request (and the data if it's an IO or Configuration Write transaction) and issues a Split Response to the Requester.
2. Upon receipt of the Split Response, the Requester must commit sufficient buffer space to receive all of the data that will ultimately be returned in the Split Completion transaction(s). This buffer commitment requirement is explained in "On Split Response, Requester Must Commit Buffer Space" on page 125.
3. In addition, the Requester moves the transaction into its Split Transaction Queue and suspends it.
4. After issuing the Split Response, the Completer now assembles the requested read data in a buffer, or performs the write to its internal location(s).
5. The Completer then arbitrates for bus ownership and initiates a Split Completion transaction.
6. Because of the buffer commitment rule stated in step 2, the Requester is not permitted to respond to the Split Completion with a Retry or a Disconnect At Next ADB. Retry would mean that it reserved no buffer space, while issuance of a Disconnect At Next ADB would indicate it had some buffer space available, but not enough to hold the full, requested byte count.
7. Acting as the target of the Split Completion transaction, the Requester decodes its Requester ID and asserts DEVSEL# to claim the transaction. It uses the Tag supplied in the Split Completion address to identify the suspended transaction whose thread is being resumed.

Split Completion May Contain a Message

If the request was an IO or Configuration Write, the Completer delivers a Split Completion Message (SCM) in the Split Completion's one and only Data Phase. The message indicates good or bad completion. In the case of a Memory Read

Block (or a Memory Read Dword) that is split, a subsequent Split Completion transaction may contain a SCM indicating that a problem was encountered during the read within the Completer. For more information, refer to "Read Completion Indication" on page 323.

Memory Read May Result in Multiple Split Completion Transactions

Completer Has All Data Buffered Up: One Split Completion. If the request was a Memory Read Block, the Completer starts delivering the requested read data in the Split Completion's Data Phase(s). If the Completer has all of the data buffered up and ready to deliver, it delivers the full byte count in this Split Completion transaction. In this case, the Split Sequence actually consisted of two transactions:

- The initial request issued by the Requester, and
- The subsequent Split Completion returning all of the requested data or a Split Completion Message (see "Read Completion Indication" on page 323).

Some Data Buffered Up: Multiple Split Completions. If the Completer had some but not all of the requested data buffered up and ready to deliver, it issues a Disconnect At Next ADB as it approaches a buffer dry condition. In this case, the Split Sequence consisted of three or more transactions:

- The initial request issued by the Requester, and
- The series of two or more Split Completion transactions returning all of the requested data or a Split Completion Message (see "Read Completion Indication" on page 323).

Figure 9-2: Example With Requester and Completer on Same Bus

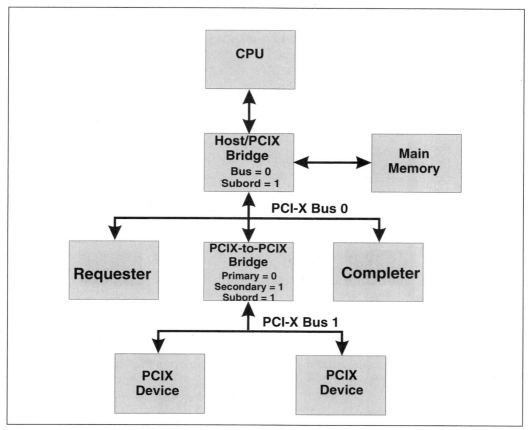

Requester and Completer May Reside on Different Buses

Example

Refer to Figure 9-3 on page 124. In this example, the Requester and Completer reside on different buses. In this scenario, an example request proceeds as follows:

1. Assuming that the transaction is not a Memory Write or a Memory Write Block (because they are posted rather than split), the bridge will split the transaction. However, if the bridge's primary interface cannot currently memorize any additional transactions that must be split (because its Split Transaction Queue is full), it issues a Retry to the Requester.
2. Assuming the bridge accepts the split request, it memorizes the request (including the data if it's an IO or Configuration Write transaction) and issues a Split Response to the Requester.
3. Upon receipt of the Split Response, the Requester must commit sufficient buffer space to receive all of the data that will ultimately be returned in the Split Completion transaction(s). This buffer commitment requirement is explained in "On Split Response, Requester Must Commit Buffer Space" on page 125.
4. In addition, the Requester moves the transaction into its Split Transaction Queue and suspends it.
5. After issuing the Split Response, the bridge now reissues the Requester's original transaction on its secondary interface using the Sequence ID issued by the Requester.
6. The Completer may issue a Split Response, or may start transferring data immediately (see the next two sections).

Case One: Completer Issues a Split Response. The following numbered list describes this case:

1. After issuing the Split Response, the Completer now assembles the requested read data in a buffer, or performs the write to its internal location(s).
2. The Completer then arbitrates for bus ownership and initiates a Split Completion transaction.
3. Acting as the target of the Split Completion transaction, the bridge decodes the Bus Number portion of the Requester ID issued in the Split Completion transaction's Address Phase. Since the target bus is its primary bus, it asserts DEVSEL# to claim the transaction.
4. The bridge may or may not have sufficient buffer space reserved to accept all of the read data. In the latter case, it will issue a Retry if it currently has no buffer space available, or a Disconnect At Next ADB as it approaches a buffer full condition. Otherwise, it accepts all of the data.
5. The bridge then passes the Split Completion transaction to its primary bus and the Requester accepts the data.

Case Two: Completer Transfers Data Immediately. Assuming that the transaction is a Memory Read Block, the Completer may be able to start supplying the data very rapidly. In this case, it asserts TRDY# and starts transferring the requested data to the bridge. There are several possibilities:

- The bridge may have sufficient buffer space to accept all of the data and the Completer may send all of the data immediately.
- The bridge may have sufficient buffer space to accept all of the data, but the Completer may have to issue a Disconnect At Next ADB before all of the data has been transferred. In this case, the bridge would have to rearbitrate for the bus and would reinitiate the transaction to read the remaining data.
- The bridge may not have sufficient buffer space to accept all of the data. In this case, the bridge would issue a Retry or a Disconnect At Next ADB to the Completer. In this case, when the bridge has sufficient buffer space for at least some of the remaining data, the bridge would rearbitrate for the bus and would reinitiate the transaction to read the remaining data.

Once the bridge has part of or all of the requested read data, or has completed the IO or Configuration Write, it will then initiate a series of one or more Split Completion transactions on its primary bus to return the results to the Requester.

In this scenario, the bridge was not given a Split Completion transaction by the Completer, but it must nevertheless issue a Split Completion transaction to the Requester. It must therefore form its own Split Completion transaction. This issue is covered in "Bridge Creation of a Split Completion" on page 548.

Figure 9-3: Example With Requester and Completer on Different Buses

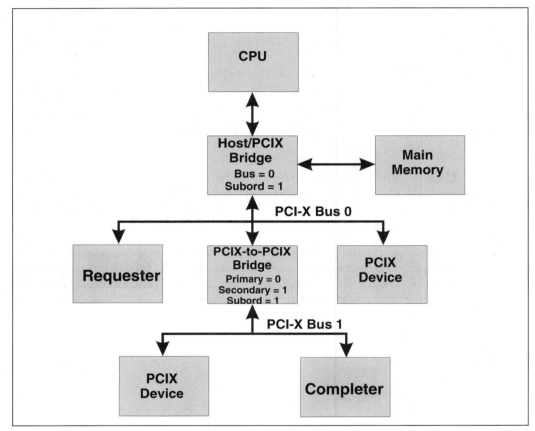

Requester Buffer Space Management

Allocate Buffer to Hold All of the Data, Then Arbitrate

Before initiating a Memory Read Block transaction, the Requester must allocate a buffer large enough to hold all of the requested data. This is necessary to properly handle a Split Response (see next section).

On Split Response, Requester Must Commit Buffer Space

As stated earlier (see step 2 in "Example" on page 119), it is a rule that upon receipt of a Split Response from a target, the Requester must commit a buffer large enough to all of the data requested in the transaction. This buffer must be held in reserve until the Split Completion returns the previously requested read data at a later time.

The necessity for the buffer commitment stems from the fact that the Requester is not permitted to Retry or to issue a Disconnect At Next ADB in response to a Split Completion. In other words, it must be prepared to accept at full speed the full requested byte count in a single Split Completion transaction.

On Immediate Response, Requester Can Release Buffer Space

If the Requester's transaction receives some data immediately (i.e., an Immediate transaction), it can deallocate any unused buffer space if the target does not return all of the requested read data (i.e., the target may issue a Disconnect At Next ADB). If the Requester still desires the remaining read data (alternatively, it may have been prefetching data at that point), it can issue a new transaction request with the adjusted start byte address and byte transfer count.

Bridge Can Retry or Disconnect Split Completion

A PCIX-to-PCIX bridge can issue a Retry or a Disconnect At Next ADB in response to a Split Completion transaction:

- It will issue a **Retry** in response to a Split Completion if its buffers are currently full. This could happen if the bridge has been configured to pass more requests through than it has buffer space for the resulting return data.
- It can issue a **Disconnect At Next ADB** if has some buffer space available, but not enough to hold all of the return data supplied in a Split Completion.

Requesters Must Implement a Split Request Timeout

Although it doesn't say it anywhere in the spec, the designer of a Requester must implement a timer that starts ticking when a request is issued and is cancelled if and when the request completes. The Requester might issue a request, receive a Split Response, but not receive the Split Completion data to fulfill the request within a reasonable amount of time. The spec doesn't say any of this and therefore doesn't suggest a timeout value. The designer should choose a value that he or she considers to be an excessive amount of time. If the timer times out, the Requester should set an error bit in a device-specific status register and generate an interrupt request to invoke its driver which will then check its status.

Part 2:
Transaction Protocol

The Previous Part

Part 1 introduced basic concepts and terminology and consists of the following chapters:

- Chapter 1: PCI Needed Improvement
- Chapter 2: PCI-X Improves on PCI
- Chapter 3: Lowest Common Denominator Defines Mode
- Chapter 4: Device Types and Bus Initialization
- Chapter 5: PCI-X Is a Registered Bus
- Chapter 6: Intro to Commands
- Chapter 7: Intro to Transaction Phases
- Chapter 8: Intro to Transaction Termination
- Chapter 9: Intro to Split and Immediate Transactions

This Part

Part 2 provides a detailed description of the PCI-X bus protocol and consists of the following chapters:

- Chapter 10: Bus Arbitration
- Chapter 11: Detailed Command Description
- Chapter 12: Latency Rules
- Chapter 13: The Address, Attribute and Response Phases
- Chapter 14: Dword Transactions
- Chapter 15: Burst Transactions
- Chapter 16: Transaction Terminations
- Chapter 17: Split Completion Messages
- Chapter 18: 64-Bit Transactions
- Chapter 19: Parity Generation and Checking

The Next Part

Part 3 covers device configuration and consists of the following chapters:

- Chapter 20: Configuration Transactions
- Chapter 21: Non-Bridge Configuration Registers
- Chapter 22: Bridge Configuration Registers

10 Bus Arbitration

The Previous Chapter

In PCI-X, Split Transactions take the place of PCI Delayed transactions. The previous chapter introduced the concepts and terminology associated with PCI-X Split Transactions. In addition, it defined PCI-X Immediate transactions.

This Chapter

This chapter provides a detailed description of bus arbitration in the PCI-X bus environment. It includes:

- a detailed, step-by-step description of an example arbitration among a number of initiators,
- the initiator design rules,
- the arbiter design rules,
- a discussion of bus parking, and
- a detailed description of preemption and the initiator's Latency Timer.

The Next Chapter

The next chapter provided a detailed description of the Dword commands, the Burst commands, and the Dual-Address Cycle (DAC) command.

Stepping Not Permitted

Address and Data Stepping are not permitted on a bus operating in PCI-X mode, so this behavior does not need to be accounted for by the arbiter.

Request and Grant Signals Are Registered

Refer to Figure 10-1 on page 130. The arbiter clocks all of the REQ# signals into its input register on the rising-edge of the clock and submits the registered versions of the REQ# signals to its internal arbitration logic during that clock cycle. The GNT# outputs of its arbitration logic are clocked out of its output register on the next rising-edge of the clock.

The spec refers to the arbiter's registered version of a REQ# signal as s1_REQ# and to its internal version of a GNT# signal as s1_GNT#.

Figure 10-1: The Arbiter

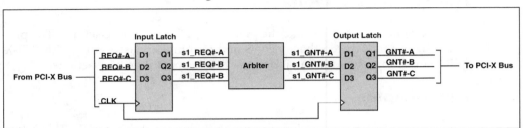

Example Arbitration

Refer to Figure 10-2 on page 131 during the following discussion. In this scenario, there are three initiators competing for bus ownership. The example scenario has the following characteristics:

- Initiator A has the lowest priority, B has mid-level priority, and C has the highest priority.
- At some point earlier in time, A had requested bus ownership, had received its grant and had initiated a bus transaction.
- When A started its transaction, it kept its REQ#-A line asserted because it has a second transaction that it wishes to perform after it completes the first one.

Figure 10-2: Arbitration Example

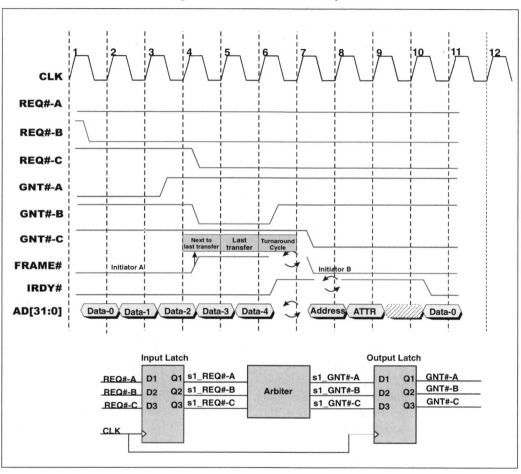

CLOCK 1. At some earlier point in time, initiator A had requested bus owner-ship (REQ#-A asserted), the arbiter had granted it ownership (GNT#-A asserted), and initiator A had started a transaction (FRAME# and IRDY# asserted).

During clock cycle one:

- Initiator B asserts REQ#-B to request bus ownership.

CL CK 2.

ON the rising-edge of clock two:

- The arbiter registers REQ#-B and submits s1_REQ#-B to its internal arbitration logic during clock two.

DURING clock cycle two:

- The arbiter detects s1_REQ#-B and determines that initiator B is to be the next owner of the bus (because it has a higher priority than initiator A). As a result, the arbiter deasserts s1_GNT#-A during clock two.

CL CK 3.

ON the rising-edge of clock three:

- The arbiter clocks the s1_GNT# signals through its output register onto the external bus GNT# signals. This causes GNT#-A to be deasserted in clock three.

DURING clock cycle three:

- The arbiter asserts its s1_GNT#-B output to indicate that initiator B will be the next bus owner (after A has completed its transaction).

CL CK 4.

ON the rising-edge of clock four:

- The arbiter clocks the s1_GNT# outputs through to the external bus grant signals, causing the external GNT#-B signal to be asserted.
- Initiator A latches the state of GNT#-A (deasserted) and presents s1_GNT#-A to its internal logic (not shown) during clock four. This informs A that it has been preempted and must surrender bus ownership.
- Initiator A deasserts FRAME#, thereby indicating that it will, at the latest, stop driving the bus two clocks later (during clock six). In this example, it is deasserting FRAME# at the exact moment that it registers GNT#-A in the deasserted state. It should be stressed that there is no connection between the loss of its GNT#-A and the fact that it's wrapping up its transaction (i.e., it's a coincidence!). It is finishing up the transaction because it has transferred all of the data or because it is disconnecting at an ADB.
- Initiator C decides that it needs to use the bus and asserts REQ#-C.

CL CK 5.

ON the rising-edge of clock five:

- GNT#-B is registered by initiator B, and its s1_GNT# signal is submitted to its internal logic (not shown) during clock five.
- Initiator B also registers the state (deasserted) of FRAME#, and its s1_FRAME# signal is submitted to its internal logic (not shown).
- The arbiter registers the state of REQ#-C and submits s1_REQ#-C for arbitration during clock five. The arbitration takes place during clock five and the result (s1_GNT#-B deasserted) is available to clock out of

the arbiter's output register on the rising-edge of clock six.

CL CK 6.

ON the rising-edge of clock six:

- Initiator B's internal logic samples s1_GNT# asserted and s1_FRAME# deasserted.
  - GNT#-B is deasserted.
  - s1_GNT# asserted indicates that B is to be the next bus owner.
  - s1_FRAME# deasserted indicates that, at the latest, the current bus owner (A) is backing its output drivers from the bus during clock six.
  - As a result of seeing s1_REQ#-C asserted during clock five, the arbiter deasserted s1_GNT#-B during clock five. This is reflected on the external GNT#-B signal when the inputs of the arbiter's output register are clocked through the output register on the rising-edge of clock six. This causes GNT#-B to be deasserted.

DURING clock cycle six:

- Initiator B may therefore internally initiate its transaction in clock six. It internally initiates the transaction by:
  - asserting its s1_FRAME#signal,
  - driving the address onto its internal s1_AD bus, and
  - the driving the command onto its internal s1_C/BE bus.
- The arbiter asserts s1_GNT#-C to its output register.

CL CK 7.

ON the rising-edge of clock seven:

- Initiator B starts its transaction by clocking out the address, command, and by asserting FRAME#.
- The arbiter's output register clocks out the s1_GNT# signals and drives them onto the external GNT# signals. This causes GNT#-C to be asserted. Initiator C cannot start its transaction, however, until initiator B finishes up its transaction (not illustrated).

Device Design Rules

The design rules applying to the design of an initiator are covered in the sections that follow.

No Fast Back-to-Back

When operating in PCI-X mode, PCI Fast Back-to-Back transactions are not permitted.

REQ# Can Be Asserted or Deasserted at Any Time

In PCI, the initiator is required to deassert its REQ# for two clocks after a transaction in progress has been disconnected by the target (by the assertion of STOP#). This requirement does not exist when a device is operating in PCI-X mode. The initiator is permitted to assert and deassert REQ# on any clock. The PCI-X arbiter tracks the transaction in progress and would therefore know if the initiator has received Disconnect At Next ADB from its target, or if the initiator itself is in the process of ending a transaction.

Issuing REQ# and Then Changing Your Mind

An initiator is permitted to deassert REQ# without initiating a transaction after GNT# is asserted. In other words, an initiator could arbitrate for bus ownership in order to perform a transaction and then discover that its need to perform the transaction has been eliminated.

After REQ# Is Asserted, Assert FRAME# or Deassert REQ#

If the initiator does assert REQ#, it must either assert FRAME# (to start the transaction) or deassert REQ# (if the need to perform the transaction has been eliminated) within six clocks after the arbiter asserts GNT# and the bus is Idle. The six clock delay allows the initiator time to pre-drive the address bus before asserting FRAME# in a configuration transaction. A detailed description of the configuration transaction can be found in Chapter 20, entitled "Configuration Transactions," on page 425.

Initiator Can Start Transaction Two Clocks After GNT# Is Asserted

Refer to Figure 10-3 on page 136. Due to the registered nature of the bus, an initiator cannot start a transaction until two clocks after the clock in which the arbiter asserted its GNT#:

CLOCK N-2.

ON the rising-edge of clock N-2:
- The arbiter asserts GNT# to the initiator.

CLOCK N-1.

ON the rising-edge of clock N-1:
- The initiator registers the state of its GNT# signal.

DURING clock cycle N-1:
- The initiator's internal logic determines that its registered version of its GNT# is asserted. As a result, it drives its internal version of the FRAME# signal asserted before the rising-edge of clock n.

CLOCK N.

ON the rising-edge of clock N:
- The initiator clocks out an asserted level onto the bus FRAME# signal.

GNT# Removal in Clock Prior to FRAME# Too Late to Stop Initiation

Refer to Figure 10-3 on page 136. If the arbiter removes an initiator's GNT# (see Clock N-1) during the clock cycle when its internal logic detects that it has received its GNT#, the initiator can still start a transaction on the next rising-edge of the clock (Clock N). This is because it's clocking the deasserted state of its GNT# signal into its input register on the same clock edge (the rising-edge of clock N) on which it's starting the transaction. By the time it determines that it's lost its GNT#, it's already in the Address Phase of its transaction (Clock N). Its transaction has been preempted, however, so it must relinquish bus ownership on the next block boundary after it exhausts its Master Latency Timer value (typically set to the default of 64d).

Single Idle Clock Between Transactions

By observing the previous transaction, the initiator can start a transaction immediately following the previous transaction's Idle clock. Refer to Figure 10-3 on page 136.

CLOCK N-3. When an initiator is ending a transaction due to byte count satisfaction or because it is issuing a Disconnect At Next ADB, it deasserts FRAME# in the clock during which it transfers the next-to-last data item (see clock N-3). It keeps IRDY# asserted.

CL CK N-2.

ON the rising-edge of clock N-2:

- Tracking bus activity, the next initiator registers the state of FRAME# and IRDY# on the rising-edge of clock N-2.

DURING clock cycle N-2:

- The current initiator keeps IRDY# asserted for one more clock (see clock N-2) while it transfers the final data item.
- The next initiator detects the deasserted state of its registered copy of FRAME# and the asserted state of its registered copy of IRDY#. This informs it that the current initiator is in the final clock of its transfer and that the next clock (see clock N-1) is the current transaction's backoff clock. The next initiator may therefore start its transaction on the rising-edge of clock n if its GNT# was registered asserted on the rising-edge of clock N-1.

CL CK N-1.

ON the rising-edge of clock N-1:

- The next initiator registers the state of its GNT#.

DURING clock cycle N-1:

- The initiator and target back their respective output drivers off of the bus.
- The next initiator detects the asserted state of the registered copy of its GNT#.

CL CK N. The new initiator can start a transaction on the rising-edge of clock N.

Figure 10-3: One Idle Clock Between Transactions

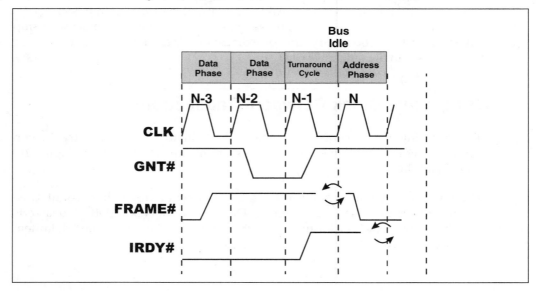

Multiple Idle Clocks Between Transactions

Refer to Figure 10-4 on page 137. An initiator awaiting bus acquisition may initiate a transaction in clock N if both of the following are true:

- It registers a bus Idle condition (FRAME# and IRDY# both deasserted) on the rising-edge of clock N-2; and
- it registers its GNT# asserted on the rising-edge of clock N-1.

In this case, the bus has been Idle for at least two clock cycles (clocks N-2 and N-1) prior to the clock in which it starts its transaction (clock N). Note that clock N-3 in the figure may:

- be an Idle clock, or
- (as pictured) an initiator may have just transferred its final data item on the rising-edge of clock N-3 and is returning IRDY# to the deasserted state and is backing its output driver off of the FRAME# signal line during clock N-3.

Figure 10-4: Two or More Idle Clocks Between Transactions

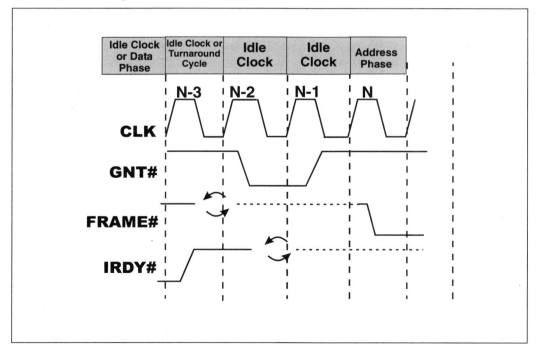

Back-to-Back Transactions by Same Initiator

If an initiator needs to perform a series of transactions, and its GNT# is still asserted on the last clock of its first transaction (that is, one clock before the Idle clock and two clocks before the start of the next transaction), the initiator is permitted to start the next transaction with a single Idle clock between the two transactions.

Device Containing Multiple Initiators

Some devices include multiple sources of initiator activity. Examples of these include the following:

- A multi-function device.
- A single-function device with multiple sources of initiator traffic, like a UART or LAN controller with separate receiver and transmitter logic.
- A device that, when addressed as a target, responds with a Split Response (which means that it will initiate a Split Completion later in time) and also initiates its own requests.

Obviously, these separate initiators reside within the same device (i.e., package) and must therefore share a single REQ# and GNT# signal pair. The device must incorporate an internal arbiter to determine which of the internal initiators uses the bus when next GNT# is asserted. This internal arbitration algorithm is outside the scope of the PCI-X spec, but it is recommended that it be fair to each of the internal initiators. If the device initiates Split Completion transactions, each initiator must have fair access to the bus (relative to transactions requested by other initiators within the same device).

Arbiter Design Rules

No GNT# Asserted and REQ# Detected

If no GNT# signals are currently asserted and the arbiter has a REQ# from one or more initiators, the arbiter may assert GNT# to the next bus owner on any clock.

Must Allow Opportunity to Start Configuration Transaction

As described later in Chapter 20, entitled "Configuration Transactions," on page 425, configuration transactions are initiated in a manner different from other transaction types. In all transaction other than configuration transactions, upon bus acquisition the initiator immediately drives out the address and command and asserts FRAME# to indicate that it has started a transaction.

Refer to Figure 10-5 on page 140. When starting a configuration transaction, however, upon bus acquisition (rising-edge of clock two) the initiator drives out the address and possibly the configuration read or write command but does not assert FRAME# until the fifth clock of the transaction (see clock six). As described later in Chapter 20, entitled "Configuration Transactions," on page 425, this gives the IDSEL values on AD[31:16] time to propagate through the series resistors on the system board and settle at the correct value on the IDSEL pin of each device.

If the current initiator is in the process of starting a configuration transaction, the bus will appear to remain Idle (FRAME# and IRDY# deasserted) until the rising-edge of the sixth clock of the possible transaction (in the figure, the rising-edge of clock seven). If this appears to be the case, the arbiter must be designed so as to keep the initiator's GNT# asserted for five clocks (clocks zero through four in the figure; GNT# could be removed in clock five) while the bus is Idle to ensure that the initiator has the opportunity to start a configuration transaction.

Figure 10-5: Example Configuration Read Transaction

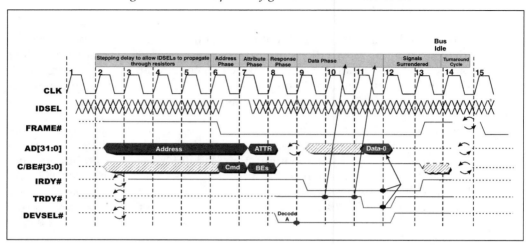

When Bus Not Idle, GNT# Can Be Deasserted Sooner

When an initiator starts a transaction other than a configuration access, it asserts FRAME# in the same clock where it drives out the address and command. In this case, the arbiter can deassert GNT# sooner than five clocks (see previous section) in order to preempt the current initiator and pass ownership to a higher priority device before the bus is in the Idle state.

If Transaction Not Started, Arbiter May Ignore Master

If a device does not assert FRAME# (i.e., start a transaction) or deassert REQ# (because it no longer needs to perform a transaction) after GNT# has been asserted for six consecutive clocks while the bus is Idle, the arbiter will be designed so as to assume that the device is broken, deassert its GNT#, and never service a request from that initiator again.

So, be forewarned in case you're thinking of designing a device that arbitrates for bus ownership just to get the bus parked on itself in case it may need the bus in the future.

Removing GNT# From One Initiator and Giving It to Another

If the arbiter deasserts one initiator's GNT#, it must not assert another initiator's GNT# until the next clock.

Parking Recommendation

If only one device is requesting bus ownership, the spec recommends that the arbiter park ownership on that device (i.e., keep GNT# asserted to that device). See the next section.

Bus Parking

Floating Bus Causes Power Drain

During periods of time when the bus is not in use, the AD and C/BE buses and the parity signal(s) are not being driven by any device. Immediately after the previous bus owner completed a transaction, the bus signals have been pre-charged to certain logic levels by the initiator and the target of the last transaction. After several clocks, however, they will begin to lose their charge and will float. When they have floated down around the switching points at all of the CMOS input receivers that are attached to the bus (each and every device has input receivers attached to these signals), all of these input transistors will begin rapidly switching on and off and will draw a large amount of current. This is a violation of the power conservation portion of the 2.2 PCI spec (as well as the PCI-X spec).

Bus Parking Prevents Bus Float

The arbiter must prevent this from happening. To do so, it implements one of the following policies:

- During bus Idle time, the arbiter (which typically resides within the bus's Source Bridge) issues an output enable to the bridge's bus output drivers. A stable pattern is driven onto the AD and C/BE buses and the parity signal(s) during bus Idle time.

- Alternatively, the arbiter can give responsibility for driving the bus to a device. To do so, it asserts GNT# to an initiator even though the master has not asserted its REQ# signal. If GNT# is asserted and the bus is Idle for four consecutive clocks, the device must actively drive the bus (AD, C/BE#, PAR, and, if it's a 64-bit device, PAR64) on the sixth clock. The device must stop driving the bus two clocks after GNT# is deasserted.

Rules Associated with Bus Parking

The bus parking rules are as follows:

- When a device that is not asserting its REQ# detects its GNT# asserted and a bus Idle condition (FRAME# and IRDY# deasserted) for four clock cycles, the device must enable its bus output drivers no later than the sixth clock.
- The device must stop driving the bus two clocks after its GNT# is deasserted.
- If the device intends to initiate a transaction and the bus is currently parked on it, it does not asserts its REQ# signal (because it already has bus ownership). It just asserts FRAME# and starts the transaction (see clock five in Figure 10-6 on page 143).
- If however, the device intends to start a series of two or more transactions, it must assert its REQ# when it starts the first transaction to inform the arbiter that, if possible, it would like the arbiter to keep its GNT# asserted so it can retain bus ownership to perform its second transaction.
- The parked initiator can start a transaction anytime within two clocks after it sees its GNT# asserted (this is shown in clock five of the example in Figure 10-6 on page 143).
- The arbiter cannot assert GNT# to another initiator until one clock after it deasserts GNT# to the parked initiator (see clocks four and five in Figure 10-6 on page 143). There is only one turn-around clock when bus ownership is moved from a parked initiator to one that is starting a transaction.
- Target devices that never initiate Split Completions do not implement a REQ#/GNT# signal pair.
- If only one device is requesting bus ownership, the spec recommends that the arbiter park ownership on that device (i.e., keep GNT# asserted to that device).

Figure 10-6: Bus Parking Example

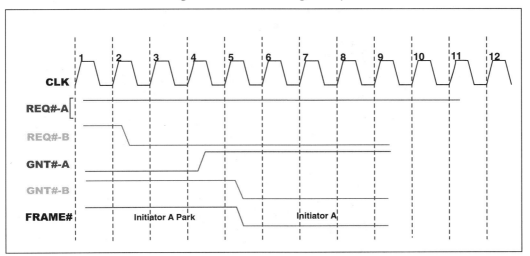

How the Initiator Deals With Preemption

The Basics

Preemption occurs when the arbiter removes the GNT# from the current bus owner while it is performing a transaction. As in PCI, the value in the initiator's Master Latency Timer (MLT or LT) configuration register defines the initiator's timeslice whenever it initiates a new transaction. The timeslice value defines the period of time that the initiator is guaranteed bus ownership even if it loses its GNT#. As in PCI, the initiator starts decrementing its LT on each rising-edge of the clock after it asserts FRAME# to start the transaction.

- As long as it has not yet exhausted its assigned timeslice, it does not have to honor a preemption (i.e., the removal of its GNT#) if one should occur.
- If it is preempted during its timeslice, it must honor the preemption as soon as possible after it exhausts its timeslice.
- If it exhausts its timeslice but still has its GNT# (i.e., it hasn't been preempted), it can continue the transaction either until it's done or it loses its GNT#. During this period (i.e., after it has exhausted its timeslice), it's living on borrowed time.

- If it's exhausted its timeslice and then loses its GNT#, it must honor the pre-emption as soon as possible.

After Timeslice Exhaustion and Preemption, How Soon Must It Yield?

In the previous section, it says that the initiator must yield "as soon as possible." The spec defines this as follows:

"In most cases, this means the initiator disconnects on the next ADB. However, if the Latency Timer expires during a burst transaction less than four Data Phases from the ADB, the initiator does not have enough time to deassert FRAME# for this ADB. In such cases, the initiator continues past this ADB and disconnects on to the next one."

The problem wherein the initiator issues a Disconnect At Next ADB very close to a block boundary is discussed in detail in "Initiator Issues Disconnect at Next ADB" on page 289.

What Is the Recommended LT Value?

When a function is operating in PCI-X mode, the default value loaded into its LT on the removal of RST# is 64d. The configuration software is discouraged from changing the LT from its default value (64d) in PCI-X mode without a good understanding of the needs of each device in the system and the effects such a change has on all devices.

How Much Data Can Be Transferred During Default Timeslice?

The best case transaction performance scenario when performing 32-bit transfers assumes the following:

- The start byte address is aligned on a block boundary (i.e., an address divisible by 128d).
- The target claims the transaction as quickly as possible.
- The target asserts TRDY# at the earliest opportunity to indicate its readiness to start transferring the first data block.

A block consists of 128 bytes (32 dwords). Assuming 32-bit transfers, it therefore takes 32 clock cycles to transfer one block.

Assuming that the initiator loses its GNT# during its timeslice, the timeslice expires 64d clocks into the transaction. Subtracting three clock cycles (64 - 3 = 61) to account for the Address Phase, the Attribute Phase, and the best-case, single-clock Response Phase, 61d dwords are transferred before the timeslice expires. However, after preemption and upon expiration of its timeslice, the initiator must yield the bus on the next block boundary. 61d dwords have already been transferred; a total of 244 bytes of data. The next block boundary would be three dwords later for a total of 256 bytes transferred. As the initiator approaches that block boundary, it issues a Disconnect At Next ADB to the target. They end the transaction upon completion of the second block transfer.

If the example assumed 64-bit transfers, a total of four blocks could have been transferred for a total of 512 bytes.

11 Detailed Command Description

The Previous Chapter

The previous chapter provided a detailed description of bus arbitration in the PCI-X bus environment. It included:

- a detailed, step-by-step description of an example arbitration among a number of initiators,
- the initiator design rules,
- the arbiter design rules,
- a discussion of bus parking, and
- a detailed description of preemption and the initiator's Latency Timer.

This Chapter

This chapter provides a detailed description of the Dword commands, the Burst commands, and the Dual-Address Cycle (DAC) command.

The Next Chapter

The next chapter provides a detailed description of how quickly the initiator and the target must be capable of transferring data. This includes the target's rules of behavior during both startup time and run-time, as well as a description of the Maximum Completion Time limit imposed upon non-bridge devices.

Dword Commands

General

As mentioned in "Dword Commands" on page 92, the dword commands are used to transfer a single dword or a subset thereof. The dword commands are:

- IO Read and Write Commands
- Memory Read Dword Command
- Configuration Read and Write Commands
- Interrupt Acknowledge Command
- Special Cycle Command

The sections that follow describe each of these commands.

Command Encoding

Table 11-1 on page 148 defines the encoding of the PCI-X dword commands. The command is always issued on C/BE#[3:0] during the transaction's Address Phase.

Table 11-1: PCI-X Dword Command Encoding

C/BE[3:0]#	PCI-X Command
0000	Interrupt Acknowledge
0001	Special Cycle
0010	IO Read
0011	IO Write
0110	Memory Read Dword
1010	Configuration Read
1011	Configuration Write

Illegal to Assert REQ64# in Dword Transactions

Because Dword transactions by definition only transfer one dword or a subset thereof, it is illegal for the initiator to assert REQ64# in the transaction's Address Phase. This would indicate that it wished to transfer a full qword in the Data Phase.

IO Read and Write Commands

Basic Description

The IO Read and IO Write commands are used to access a device's control/status/data registers when they are mapped into IO space rather than memory space. Hypothetically, in PCI the IO Read and Write commands can be used to perform burst IO reads or writes. In reality, however, they have only been implemented to transfer a single IO dword or a subset thereof. The PCI-X spec is therefore just recognizing reality in only permitting single Data Phase IO transactions.

The settings on C/BE#[3:0] identify which locations in the IO dword are to be read or written. For a detailed description of the IO Read and Write transactions, refer to "IO Read and Memory Read Dword" on page 216 and "IO Write" on page 224.

Start Address and Byte Enable Format

Start Address Is Byte-Aligned. The initiator must issue a byte-aligned start address on AD[31:0] in the Address Phase of the transaction. If any Byte Enables are asserted in the Attribute Phase, the start byte address issued in the Address Phase must be the address associated with the least-significant Byte Enable asserted. If no Byte Enables are asserted, the start byte address may be that of any of the four locations in the IO dword.

Byte Enable Usage. Any combination of Byte Enables (including none) is permitted in the Attribute Phase. There is one constraint, however. If any Byte Enables are asserted, it is illegal to assert any Byte Enables associated with IO addresses numerically lower than the IO start byte address issued in the Address Phase. Table 11-2 on page 150 lists some example start byte address/Byte Enable combinations.

IO Transaction With No Byte Enables Asserted. It might not seem to make any sense that the spec permits an IO transaction with no Byte Enables asserted. This indicates that the initiator doesn't really want to read or write any bytes. An example implementation that this would make sense for would be an IO address associated with a hardware device's trigger port. The initiator addresses the IO port address for a read or a write, but doesn't care what it reads (if it's an IO read), or, if it's a write, the IO port doesn't expect to receive any write data. The simple act of addressing that IO port for a read or a write triggers the IO device to take some action (e.g., it might be a BIOS flash update trigger port).

Table 11-2: Some Example Start Address/Byte Enable Combinations in IO Read, IO Write, and Memory Read Dword Transactions

Start Byte Address Issued in Address Phase (hex)	BE#[3:0] in Attribute Phase	Comment
00000100h	0000b	Valid combination. Initiator is addressing all four locations in the IO dword consisting of locations 00000100h through 00000103h.
00000101h	0001b	Valid combination. Initiator is addressing the last three locations (00000101h through 00000103) in the IO dword consisting of locations 00000100h through 00000103h.
00000101h	0000b	Invalid combination. Initiator is addressing IO address 00000101h in the Address Phase, but has asserted BE#[0] in the Attribute Phase (which corresponds to IO address 00000100h). It means the initiator lied in the Address Phase when it said it was starting at IO address 00000101h.
00000102h	0011b	Valid combination. Initiator is addressing the last two locations in the IO dword consisting of locations 00000100h through 00000103h.
00000103h	0111b	Valid combination. Initiator is addressing only the last location in the IO dword consisting of locations 00000100h through 00000103h.
00000100h	0110b	Valid combination. Initiator is addressing the first and last locations in the IO dword consisting of locations 00000100h through 00000103h.
00000102h	1111b	Valid combination. Initiator is addressing location 0000102h in the Address Phase, but has no Byte Enables asserted in the Attribute Phase.

Chapter 11: Detailed Command Description

Target Response to an IO Access

General. The device that acts as the target (i.e., it asserts DEVSEL# to claim the transaction) of the IO Read or Write transaction could be a simple, non-bridge IO target (in other words, it is the Completer and resides on the same bus as the Requester). Alternately, the device acting as the target could be a PCI-X bridge claiming the transaction. The next two sections discuss both of these possible cases.

Completer Handling of an IO Access. The Completer can handle the transaction in one of two ways:

- If it can perform the read or write within 16 clocks from the assertion of FRAME#, the Completer can complete the transaction immediately by asserting TRDY# and providing the read data (if it's an IO Read) or accepting the write data (if it's an IO Write).
- If the Completer cannot complete the access within 16 clocks from the assertion of FRAME#, it will memorize the transaction (including the write data) and issue a Split Response to the initiator within 8 clocks from the assertion of FRAME#. When it has successfully performed the internal read or write (or has incurred an internal error), the Completer arbitrates for the bus and performs a Split Completion transaction to deliver the read data, the write completion message (see "Write Completion Indication" on page 322), or an error message to the Requester.

When Bridge Acts as Target of IO Access. There are two possible cases wherein a bridge acts as the target of an IO access:

- the IO access targets an internal location within the bridge. In other words, the bridge is the addressed target (i.e., the Completer).
- the IO Access targets a Completer on the other side of the bridge. In this case, the bridge must split the transaction. It memorizes the transaction (including the write data if it's an IO write) and issues a Split Response to the initiator. It then performs the IO Read or Write on the destination side of the bridge. When the bridge has successfully performed the read or write on the destination side of the bridge (or has incurred an error in the attempted transaction), the bridge arbitrates for the originating bus and performs a Split Completion transaction to deliver the read data, the write completion message, or an error message to the originator of the IO transaction (see Chapter 17, entitled "Split Completion Messages," on page 313).

Memory Read Dword Command

The Memory Read Dword command is used to read a single dword or a subset thereof from memory-mapped IO ports (i.e., a device's control/status/data registers mapped into memory space rather than memory space).

The settings on C/BE#[3:0] identify which locations in the memory dword are to be read. For a detailed description of the Memory Read Dword transaction, refer to "IO Read and Memory Read Dword" on page 216.

Start Address and Byte Enable Format

Start Address Is Byte-Aligned. The start address format issued in the Memory Read Dword transaction is the same as that issued in an IO transaction. See "Start Address Is Byte-Aligned" on page 152 for a detailed description.

Byte Enable Usage. The Byte Enable usage in the Memory Read Dword transaction is the same as for an IO transaction. See "Byte Enable Usage" on page 149 for a detailed description.

Transaction With No Byte Enables Asserted. A Memory Read Dword transaction may be issued with no Byte Enables asserted (as is the case for an IO transaction). See "Transaction With No Byte Enables Asserted" on page 152 for a detailed description.

Target Response to a Memory Read Dword Access

General. The device that acts as the target (i.e., it asserts DEVSEL# to claim the transaction) of the Memory Read Dword transaction could be a simple, non-bridge IO target (in other words, it is the Completer and resides on the same bus as the Requester). Alternately, the device acting as the target could be a PCI-X bridge claiming the transaction. The next two sections discuss both of these possible cases.

Completer Handling of a Memory Read Dword Access. The Completer can handle the transaction in one of two ways:

- If it can perform the read within 16 clocks from the assertion of FRAME#, the Completer can complete the transaction immediately by asserting TRDY# and providing the read data.

- If the Completer cannot complete the access within 16 clocks from the assertion of FRAME#, it will memorize the transaction and issue a Split Response to the initiator within 8 clocks from the assertion of FRAME#. When it has successfully performed the internal read (or has incurred an internal error), the Completer arbitrates for the bus and performs a Split Completion transaction to deliver the read data or an error message (see "Read Completion Indication" on page 323) to the Requester.

Bridge Acts as Target of Memory Read Dword Access. There are two possible cases wherein a bridge acts as the target of a Memory Read Dword access:

- Access targets an internal location within the bridge. In other words, the bridge is the addressed target (i.e., the Completer).
- Access targets a Completer on the other side of the bridge. In this case, the bridge must split the transaction. It memorizes the transaction and issues a Split Response to the initiator. It then performs the Memory Read Dword access on the destination side of the bridge. When the bridge has successfully performed the read on the destination side of the bridge (or has incurred an error in the attempted transaction), the bridge arbitrates for the originating bus and performs a Split Completion transaction to deliver the read data or an error message (see "Read Completion Indication" on page 323) to the originator of the Memory Read Dword transaction.

Configuration Read and Write Commands

The Configuration Read and Write commands are used to access a function's configuration registers. Hypothetically, in PCI the Configuration Read and Write commands can be used to perform burst Configuration reads or writes. In reality, however, they have only been implemented to transfer a single Configuration dword or a subset thereof. The PCI-X spec is therefore just recognizing reality in only permitting single Data Phase Configuration transactions.

The settings on C/BE#[3:0] identify which locations in the Configuration dword are to be read or written.

For a detailed description of the configuration transactions, refer to Chapter 20, entitled "Configuration Transactions," on page 425.

Interrupt Acknowledge Command

General

The following sections provide background on the purpose of the Interrupt Acknowledge command. For a detailed description of the Interrupt Acknowledge transaction, refer to "Interrupt Acknowledge Command" on page 234.

Background

In an Intel x86-based system, the processor is usually the device that services interrupt requests received from subsystems that require servicing. In a PC-compatible system, the subsystem requiring service issues a request by asserting one of the system interrupt request signals, IRQ0 through IRQ15. When the IRQ is detected by the interrupt controller within the South Bridge (see Figure 11-1 on page 156), it asserts INTR to the host processor. Assuming that the host processor is enabled to recognize interrupt requests (the Interrupt Flag bit in the EFLAGS register is set to one), the processor responds by requesting the interrupt vector from the interrupt controller. This is accomplished by the processor performing the following sequence:

1. **The processor generates an Interrupt Acknowledge bus cycle**. *Please note that a P6 family processor (the Pentium Pro and later processors) does not generate this first Interrupt Acknowledge bus cycle.* No address is output by the processor because the address of the target device, the interrupt controller, is implicit in the bus cycle type. The purpose of this bus cycle is to **command the interrupt controller to prioritize** its **currently pending requests** and select the request to be processed. The processor doesn't expect any data to be returned by the interrupt controller during this bus cycle.

2. **The processor generates a second Interrupt Acknowledge bus cycle** to **request the interrupt vector** from the interrupt controller. If this is a P6 family processor, this is the only Interrupt Acknowledge transaction it generates. BE0# is asserted by the processor, indicating that an 8-bit vector is expected to be returned on the lower data path, D[7:0]. To state this more precisely, the processor requests that the interrupt controller return the index into the interrupt table in memory. This tells the processor which table entry to read. The table entry contains the start address of the device-specific interrupt service routine in memory. In response to the second Interrupt Acknowledge bus cycle, the interrupt controller must drive the interrupt table index, or vector, associated with the highest-priority request currently pending back to the processor over the lower data path, D[7:0].

Chapter 11: Detailed Command Description

The processor reads the vector from the bus and uses it to determine the start address of the interrupt service routine that it must execute.

Host/PCIX Bridge Handling of Interrupt Acknowledge

The following description assumes that the processor belongs to the P6 processor family and therefore only generates one Interrupt Acknowledge transaction in response to the assertion of INTR.

When the Host/PCIX bridge detects the start of an Interrupt Acknowledge on the host side, the bridge acquires ownership of the PCI-X bus and initiates a PCI-X Interrupt Acknowledge transaction. When the PCI-X target that contains the interrupt controller (the South Bridge) detects the Interrupt Acknowledge transaction, it asserts DEVSEL# to claim the transaction. It then internally generates two, back-to-back interrupt acknowledge pulses to the 8259A interrupt controller, thereby emulating the double Interrupt Acknowledge generated by a pre-P6 Intel x86 processor. In response, the interrupt controller drives the interrupt vector onto the lower data path (AD[7:0]) and asserts TRDY# to indicate the presence of the vector to the initiator (the Host/PCIX bridge). When the Host/PCIX bridge samples TRDY# and IRDY# asserted, it reads the vector from the lower data path and terminates the PCI-X Interrupt Acknowledge transaction. During this period, the bridge was either inserting Wait States into the processor's Interrupt Acknowledge transaction, or could have handled it as a Deferred Transaction (refer to MindShare's *Pentium Pro and Pentium II System Architecture* book, published by Addison-Wesley). It then drives the 8-bit interrupt vector onto the processor's lower data path and the processor reads the vector from the bus. The processor then uses it to index into the memory-based interrupt table to get the start address of the interrupt service routine to execute.

Figure 11-1: Example System Block Diagram

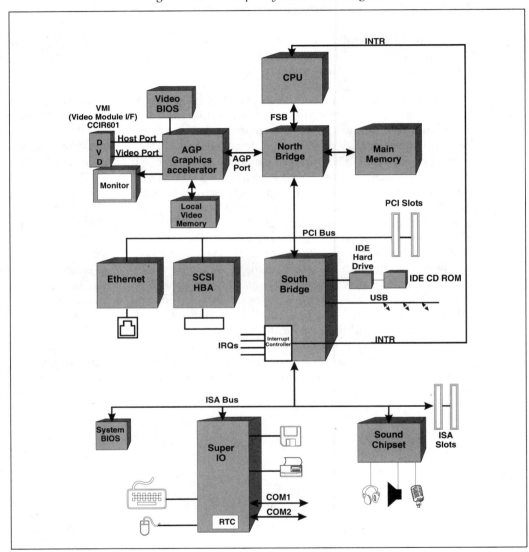

Chapter 11: Detailed Command Description

System Using APIC Bus to Deliver Interrupts To Processors

Refer to Figure 11-2 on page 158. In an Intel-based system with multiple processors, interrupt requests from hardware devices are typically delivered to the array of processors over the APIC bus rather than the INTR signal line. The interrupt request is delivered by the IO APIC module to the processors in the form of a message packet that identifies the target processor as well as the interrupt vector. There is therefore no need for the processor to generate any Interrupt Acknowledge transactions on its Front Side Bus (i.e., the host processor bus). In this case, no Interrupt Acknowledge transactions will ever be generated on the PCI-X bus by the Host/PCIX Bridge (or anyone else, for that matter).

Figure 11-2: Multi-Processor System Using APIC Bus to Deliver Request to Array of CPUs

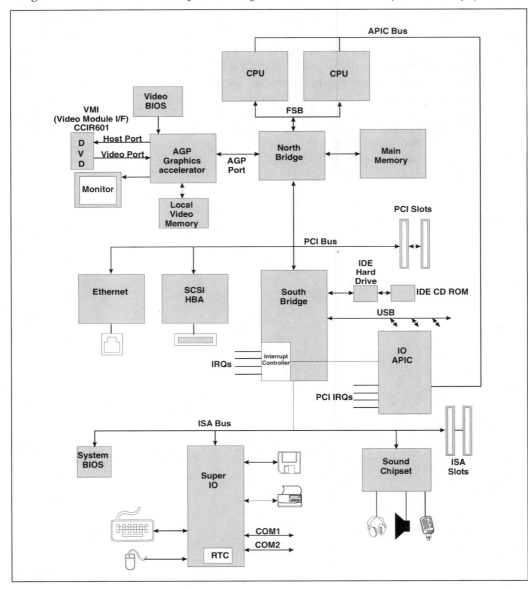

Non-Intel System Implementation

As an example, in a PowerPC PReP-compliant platform, the programmer performs a one to four byte memory read from memory location BFFFFFF0h. When the Host/PCIX bridge detects this read, it acquires ownership of the PCI-X bus and initiates the PCI-X Interrupt Acknowledge transaction. When the interrupt controller supplies the requested vector to the Host/PCIX bridge, the bridge in turn supplies it to the processor and asserts TA# (Transfer Acknowledge) to indicate its presence. The processor reads the vector and places it into the GPR (General Purpose Register) indicated by the load instruction being executed. The programmer then uses the vector as an index into the interrupt table.

In a system based on a processor other than an x86, the interrupt vector requested by the processor may be four bytes rather one byte wide. If this were the case, the Host/PCIX bridge would assert all four byte enables to request a 32-bit vector.

Finally, a non-Intel processor may implement an interrupt mechanism that never requires the performance of a PCI-X Interrupt Acknowledge transaction.

Special Cycle Command

General

The following section provides an introduction to the Special Cycle command. A detailed description can be found in "Special Cycle Command" on page 235.

Basic Description

The Special Cycle command is issued by an initiator to broadcast a message to one or more targets residing on a target PCI-X bus. Each target on the PCI-X bus must examine the message to determine whether the message applies to it (a target may be designed not to recognize any messages or to recognize only specific messages; most targets don't pay any attention to messages delivered via the Special Cycle transaction). Via the Special Cycles bit in its configuration Command register (see Figure 11-3 on page 161), a target's ability to monitor Special Cycle messages can be enabled or disabled. As an example of message passing using the Special Cycle transaction, Intel x86 processors use the Special Cycle to indicate when they are going into a Halt or Shutdown condition.

Address Phase

During the Address Phase, a valid address is not driven onto the AD bus (because Intel x86 processors do not supply a valid address when they initiate a Special Cycle transaction). The AD bus must be driven with a stable pattern, however, so that the parity of the AD bus, the PAR signal, and the command bus content can be checked for correctness. In the Address Phase, the initiator uses C/BE#[3:0] to indicate that this is a Special Cycle transaction.

Attribute Phase

The PCI-X spec states:

> "Such devices are permitted also to utilize the PCI-X attribute fields to further define the transaction."

The information presented in the Attribute Phase of a Special Cycle transaction consists solely of the Requester ID, the transaction Tag, and the Byte Enables (all of which are asserted). The author interprets the spec statement as follows: a target could be designed to only pay attention to messages broadcast by a specific Requester and/or with a specific Byte Enable combination.

Data Phase

During the Data Phase, the initiator broadcasts the message type on the AD bus. Although the PCI Special Cycle command hypothetically can consist of more than one Data Phase, the reality is that there are no multiple Data Phase messages defined in the 2.2 PCI spec. The PCI-X version recognizes this reality by defining the Special Cycle command as a dword command.

In PCI-X Special Cycle Transaction, No Wait States Permitted

If necessary, a PCI initiator may insert Wait States into the transaction by deasserting IRDY#, but this is not true in PCI-X. The initiator must immediately drive out the message and assert IRDY#.

No Target Is Permitted to Respond

No target is permitted to assert DEVSEL# when it recognizes a message. Since multiple targets can recognize the message type, there would be contention on the DEVSEL# line if they all tried to claim the transaction by asserting DEVSEL#. Since all Special Cycle transactions on the PCI-X bus are intended to pass messages only to PCI and PCI-X targets, a subtractive decode bridge (i.e., the ISA or EISA bus bridge if one is present) must not pass the transaction onto the ISA or EISA bus if it doesn't see any PCI or PCI-X target claim the transaction by asserting DEVSEL#.

Ending the Transaction

Since no target is permitted to respond to the Special Cycle transaction (DEVSEL# is not asserted), another means must be used to end the transaction. The initiator performs a Master Abort to end the transaction (in other words, return the bus to the Idle state in a graceful fashion). Master Abort is explained in "Initiator Termination Due to Connection Timeout" on page 290. It must be noted that when the initiator terminates the Special Cycle transaction with a Master Abort (because DEVSEL# was not asserted by a target), it must not set the Received Master Abort bit in its configuration Status register (see Figure 11-4 on page 162). That bit should only be set in a transaction wherein DEVSEL# is expected but not received.

During system design, each PCI-X device that is capable of recognizing or broadcasting message types must be hardwired with the message types it recognizes or broadcasts. Upon recognition of any of its assigned message types, a PCI-X target should take the application-specific action defined by the message type received.

Figure 11-3: PCI Configuration Command Register

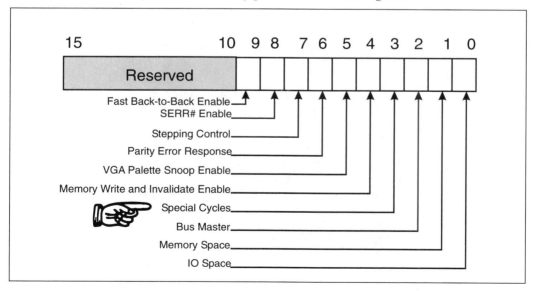

Figure 11-4: PCI Configuration Status Register

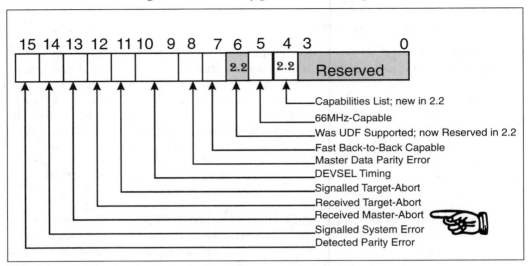

The Message Types

The messages permitted in the PCI-X environment are the same as those defined in the PCI 2.2 spec. Table 11-3 on page 162 lists the currently defined message codes.

Table 11-3: Message Types Defined in the PCI 2.2 Specification

Message Code (on AD[15:0])	Message Type
0000h	**Shutdown**. Processor is going into a Shutdown condition due to a severe, unrecoverable software problem.
0001h	**Halt**. The processor has fetched and is executing a Halt instruction. In response, the processor issues the Halt message using the Special Cycle transaction to indicate to all external devices that it is going to cease fetching and executing instructions.
0002h	**x86-specific message**. AD[31:16] contains the Intel device-specific message. None are currently defined.
0003h-FFFFh	**Reserved**.

Chapter 11: Detailed Command Description

Devices That May Initiate a Special Cycle Transaction

The main reason that the Special Cycle transaction was included in the PCI and PCI-X specs is that Intel x86 processors broadcast messages when a processor internal event occurs that may be of interest to logic external to the processor. When the Host/PCIX Bridge detects a processor-initiated Special Cycle transaction on the processor's Front Side Bus (FSB), it determines if the message is one that needs to appear on PCI-X bus zero. If so, the Host/PCIX Bridge performs the PCI-X Special Cycle transaction to broadcast the message on PCI-X bus zero.

The spec does not preclude generation of Special Cycle transactions by initiators other than the Host/PCIX Bridge. However, the message broadcast by an initiator other than the Host/PCIX Bridge would not be the Halt or the Shutdown message as these are solely the province of the Host/PCIX Bridge acting as the processor's surrogate on the PCI-X bus. An exception is a PCIX-to-PCIX bridge. If requested to do so by an initiator, the bridge will broadcast a message on either its primary or secondary bus. This subject is covered in "Generation of Special Cycle Under Software Control" on page 450.

Software-Initiated Special Cycle Transactions

The PCI 2.2 spec permits an optional Host/PCIX Bridge design that supports generation of a Special Cycle transaction under software control. This optional mechanism is described in "Generation of Special Cycle Under Software Control" on page 450.

Burst Commands

All Burst-Oriented Commands Are Memory Transfers

The PCI-X burst-oriented commands are used to perform memory transfers of between 1 and 4096 bytes of information. The spec writers constrained the maximum byte transfer count of each transfer request to 4KB in the interest of a fair sharing of bus bandwidth and target resources among multiple masters.

Burst Command Encoding

Table 11-4 on page 164 provides a list of the burst commands. The command is always issued on C/BE#[3:0] in the transaction's Address Phase. If the transaction is an attempt to perform 64-bit data transfers with a memory device that resides above the 4GB boundary, in the first of the two Address Phases:

- The command placed on C/BE#[3:0] is the Dual-Address Cycle (DAC) command.
- The actual memory command (e.g., Memory Read Block) is placed on C/BE#[7:4].
- The lower 32-bits of the 64-bit memory address are placed on AD[31:0].
- The upper 32-bits of the 64-bit memory address are placed on AD[63:32].

In the second Address Phase:

- The command placed on C/BE#[3:0] is the actual memory command.
- The actual memory command is duplicated on C/BE#[7:4].
- The upper 32-bits of the 64-bit memory address are placed on AD[31:0].
- The upper 32-bits of the 64-bit memory address are duplicated on AD[63:32].

A detailed explanation of 64-bit memory addressing and the DAC command can be found in "Addressing Memory Above 4GB Boundary" on page 372.

Table 11-4: PCI-X Burst Commands

C/BE[3:0]# or C/BE[7:4]# (binary)	PCI-X Command	Byte Enable Usage
0111	Memory Write	Byte Enables define bytes to be transferred within target dword. Any combination of Byte Enables is valid.
1000	Alias to Memory Read Block	Byte Enables are reserved during Data Phases and must be driven deasserted (high) by initiator.
1001	Alias to Memory Write Block	
1100	Split Completion	
1110	Memory Read Block	
1111	Memory Write Block	

Chapter 11: Detailed Command Description

Start Address Is Byte Aligned

PCI Memory Addressing

In a PCI memory transaction, the start address is dword- or qword-aligned and has the following format:

- AD[31:2] identifies the dword-aligned start dword address. Alternatively, when starting a 64-bit transfer, AD[31:3] identifies the qword-aligned start qword address. In this case, AD[2] must be zero to make it an address divisible by eight.
- The target latches the start dword or qword address into its address counter when the transaction begins and AD[1:0] tells the PCI memory target what to do with its address counter as the transaction proceeds from Data Phase to Data Phase. There are two possibilities:
  - AD[1:0] = 00b indicates Linear addressing. The target increments its address counter by four (to point to the next dword start address) if performing 32-bit transfers, or by eight if performing 64-bit transfers (to point to the next qword start address).
  - AD[1:0] = 10b indicates Cache Line Wrap addressing. This would only be used by a Host/PCIX Bridge if the processor were permitted to cache from PCI memory targets. Prior to the 2.2 PCI spec, the PCI spec permitted the system designer to permit caching from memory on the PCI bus. However, this results in more system design complexity and slower performance, so no PCI designs ever supported processor caching from any memory other than main memory. The reality, therefore, is that this addressing sequence has never been used. The 2.2 PCI spec does not permit caching from PCI memory.

PCI-X Memory Addressing

In PCI-X memory-oriented transactions, the start address is always byte-aligned and is delivered on AD[31:0]. The PCI-X memory target latches the start address into its address counter:

- A 32-bit memory target latches the start dword address on AD[31:2] into its address counter. AD[1:0] identify the exact start byte address within the dword.
- A 64-bit memory target latches the start qword address on AD[31:3] into its address counter. AD[2:0] identify the exact start byte address within the qword.

Linear Addressing Is Implied

Notice that, unlike PCI memory addressing, no addressing sequence information is delivered on AD[1:0]. In essence, the spec writers have eliminated Cache Line Wrap addressing and all memory addressing is Linear by implication. As the transaction proceeds from Data Phase to Data Phase:

- A 32-bit memory target increments its address counter by four to point to the start address of the next dword. In each Data Phase of a Memory Write transaction (see "Memory Write Command" on page 174), the Byte Enables issued by the initiator identify which locations within the currently addressed dword are to be written. If the transaction is a Memory Read Block (see "Memory Read Block Command" on page 167) or Memory Write Block (see "Memory Write Block Command" on page 169), the Byte Enables are reserved and driven high and all bytes are to be transferred. The only exceptions are:
  - bytes in the first dword prior to the start byte address are not transferred.
  - bytes in the final dword after the end address are not transferred.
- A 64-bit memory target increments its address counter by eight to point to the start address of the next qword. In each Data Phase of a Memory Write transaction, the Byte Enables issued by the initiator identify which locations within the currently addressed qword are to be written. If the transaction is a Memory Read Block or Memory Write Block, the Byte Enables are reserved and driven high and all bytes are to be transferred. The only exceptions are:
  - bytes in the first qword prior to the start byte address are not transferred.
  - bytes in the final qword after the end address are not transferred.

Transfer Length

In PCI, Transfer Length Is Unknown

In PCI memory transactions, the initiator does not in any way indicate how much data it intends to transfer. The only case where the target would know how much data is to be transferred is if the initiator asserts IRDY# and deasserts FRAME# in the first Data Phase. This indicates to the target that the initiator is ready to transfer the first data item and that it's the only one.

Chapter 11: Detailed Command Description

In PCI-X, Byte Transfer Count Defines End Address

In every burst memory transaction, the PCI-X initiator indicates a precise byte transfer count in the Attribute Phase of the transaction.

Memory Read Block Command

Basic Description

The Memory Read Block command is an all-inclusive read starting at the start byte address (issued in the Address Phase) and encompassing all locations up to and including the end address identified by the byte transfer count issued by the initiator (in the Attribute Phase). Since the command type defines this as an all-inclusive read, the Byte Enables are not needed and are reserved and driven high in all Data Phases of the transaction.

The end address equals the start byte address + the byte transfer count - 1. The addressed memory target will not return the contents of any locations before the start byte address within the start dword (or qword if performing 64-bit transfers). Likewise, it also will not return the contents of any locations after the end byte address within the end dword (or qword if performing 64-bit transfers).

Can Be Purely Speculative

The PCI-X spec states that upon receipt of a Retry response from the target, the initiator can choose to not retry the transaction. This is quite different than PCI where a transaction that receives a Retry must be repeated until at least the first data item is successful transferred.

This essentially means that, while a purely speculative access is not permitted in PCI, it is in PCI-X. Assume that bus ownership is currently parked on a PCI-X initiator even though it did not ask for the bus. Since it already owns the bus, the initiator might start a Memory Read Block transaction to prefetch data that it may need in the future. If it receives a Retry from the target and the arbiter removes its GNT# due to assertion of REQ# by one or more other initiators, the initiator could choose not to repeat the transaction.

Target Response to Memory Read Block Access

The target of a Memory Read Block transaction can respond in any of the following ways:

1. The Completer could complete it as an Immediate transaction **by transferring all of the requested data** in this transaction.

2. The Completer could complete it as an Immediate transaction **by transferring some of the requested data now**, but due to an approaching, temporary buffer dry condition, the Completer issues a **Disconnect At Next ADB** to the initiator. In this case, the Requester may or may not choose to rearbitrate for the bus to resume the transaction at the point of disconnection.
   - If it was speculatively prefetching when it was disconnected, it almost certainly will not resume the transaction.
   - If it needs to complete the read, it will resume the transaction. As an example, if the SCSI Host Bus Adapter was reading a block of data from memory to write to a hard drive, it most assuredly will resume the transaction.

3. The Completer could complete it as an Immediate transaction by transferring the first data item and simultaneously issuing a **Single Data Phase Disconnect** to the initiator (e.g., because the Completer doesn't support bursting). In this case, the Requester may or may not choose to rearbitrate for the bus to resume the transaction at the point of disconnection.
   - If it was speculatively prefetching when it was disconnected, it almost certainly will not resume the transaction.
   - If it needs to complete the read, it will resume the transaction.

4. The Completer or a bridge between the Requester and Completer could issue a **Retry** to the initiator. In this case, the Requester may or may not choose to rearbitrate for the bus to resume the transaction at the point of disconnection.
   - If it was speculatively prefetching, it almost certainly will not resume the transaction.
   - If it needs to complete the read, it will resume the transaction.

5. The Completer could complete it as an Immediate transaction by issuing a **Target Abort** to the initiator in the first or a subsequent Data Phase. This is a fatal error and the initiator will not resume the transaction.
   - The initiator will set the Received Target Abort bit in its configuration Status register and will generate an interrupt to invoke its interrupt handler to check its status.
   - The target will set the Signaled Target Abort bit in its configuration Status register.

6. The Completer or a bridge between the Requester and Completer could memorize the transaction and issue a **Split Response** to the initiator.
   - The initiator moves the transaction to its Split Transaction Queue and suspends it until it receives a Split Completion from the Completer at a later time.

- The target performs the read (internally or, if it's a bridge, on the destination bus) and then performs a Split Completion transaction to return the requested read data or, possibly, a Split Completion error message (see "Read Completion Indication" on page 323) to the Requester.

Must Commit Buffer Space Before Initiating

Before initiating the Memory Read Block transaction, the Requester must reserve enough buffer space to all of the requested read data. If the Completer responds with a Split Response, the Requester must suspend the transaction and must hold the buffer space in reserve while awaiting the subsequent Split Completion transaction generated by the Completer to return the requested read data (or an error). For more information, refer to:

- "On Split Response, Requester Must Commit Buffer Space" on page 125.
- "On Immediate Response, Requester Can Release Buffer Space" on page 125.

Alias To Memory Read Block Command

This command is really a place-holder for a possible future command. Currently, no bus masters are permitted to issue this command. If a target is addressed using this command, it must treat it as if it's a Memory Read Block command.

As an example, this could be used in the future to indicate a double-data rate transfer request wherein a block of data might be transferred using both of the clock edges to double throughput.

Memory Write Block Command

Basic Description

The Memory Write Block command is an all-inclusive write starting at the start byte address and encompassing all locations up to and including the end address identified by the byte transfer count issued by the initiator. Since the command type defines this as an all-inclusive write, the Byte Enables are not needed and are reserved and driven high in all Data Phases of the transaction.

The end byte address equals the start byte address + the byte transfer count - 1. The addressed memory target will not update (i.e., write into) the contents of any locations before the start byte address within the start dword (or qword if performing 64-bit transfers). Likewise, it also will not update (i.e., write into) the contents of any locations after the end byte address within the end dword (or qword if performing 64-bit transfers).

If Disconnected, Must Resume With Same Sequence ID

The following text is a direct quote from the spec (note that the author has added the italicized text):

> "If the Sequence is a burst write and is disconnected either by the initiator *(by issuing a Disconnect At Next ADB)* or target *(by issuing a Disconnect At Next ADB, or a Single Data Phase Disconnect)*, the Sequence has more than one transaction. After a disconnection, the initiator must resume the sequence *(using the same Sequence ID)* by initiating another burst write transaction using the same command and adjusting the starting address and byte count for the data already sent. The initiator must deliver the full byte count of the Sequence no matter how many times the Sequence is disconnected and regardless of whether continuations after a disconnection are terminated with Retry. If the Sequence is a burst write and the target signals Target Abort or no target responds (Master Abort), the Sequence ends when the transaction terminates."

It should be noted that this text only addresses the issue of a memory write that has successfully written some of the data and is then disconnected. It does not address the issue of a burst memory write that receives a Retry upon the initial issuance of the write request (see the next section).

If Requester Cannot Complete Memory Write

A Requester may initiate a burst memory write Sequence intending to transfer a block of data, but an internal problem may prevent it from supplying all of the promised data to the Completer. In this case, the Requester must keep its promise to supply all of the data. The spec says:

> "The value of the data used by the requester in such situations is beyond the scope of this specification. If the requester uses the Memory Write command, the requester has the option of deasserting byte enables for bytes that it supplied after the error occurred. After such an error condition, the device must use other means beyond the scope of this specification to notify its device driver that the problem occurred and that not all of the data is valid."

Technically, a Write Can Be Purely Speculative, But...

The spec says the following regarding Retry and memory writes:

> "If the Sequence is a burst write and the target signals Retry on the first Data Phase of the Sequence, the Sequence ends immediately. The requester is not obligated to repeat a Sequence terminated with Retry on the first Data Phase (unless it is required by the application, e.g., a PCI-X bridge forwarding a memory write Sequence). However, if the requester repeats the burst write, it is considered a new Sequence and is permitted to use the same or a different command and attributes (byte count, Tag, etc.). The requester is permitted to reuse a Tag as soon as the memory write Sequence completes on the requester's bus, independent of whether there are one or more PCI-X bridges between the requester and completer, and if so, when those bridges forward the Sequence to the completer."

A purely speculative burst memory read transaction is permitted and could very well occur (see "Can Be Purely Speculative" on page 167). Although the spec text (see previous paragraph) permits a speculative burst memory write transaction, the author is of the opinion that would be a very rare occurrence. Not retrying a write (either a memory, IO, or configuration write) that receives a Retry seems to be a rather bizarre and dangerous concept: the idea that you were going to update a memory location, IO port, or configuration register, received a Retry and decided not to do it after all is very atypical.

Target Never Permitted to Split a Memory Write

The target is never permitted to handle a Memory Write Block or a Memory Write transaction as a Split Transaction. The possible valid responses are listed in the next section.

Target Response to Memory Write Block Transaction

The target of a Memory Write Block transaction can respond in any of the following ways:

1. The target could complete it as an Immediate transaction **by accepting all of the requested data** in this transaction.
2. The target could complete as an Immediate transaction by issuing a **Target Abort**. This can occur in any Data Phase, is a fatal error, and the initiator will not resume the transaction. If the transaction is not a Split Completion:

- The initiator will set the Received Target Abort bit in its configuration Status register and will generate an interrupt to invoke its interrupt handler to check its status.
- The target will set the Signaled Target Abort bit in its configuration Status register.

If the transaction is a Split Completion and it receives a Target Abort, it is handled differently. For more information, refer to "Completer Receives Target Abort on Split Completion" on page 606.

3. The target could complete it as an Immediate transaction by transferring the first data item and simultaneously issuing a **Single Data Phase Disconnect** to the initiator (e.g., because the target doesn't support bursting). In this case, the Requester must rearbitrate for the bus to resume the transaction at the point of disconnection (for more information, refer to "If Disconnected, Must Resume With Same Sequence ID" on page 170). As stated earlier, it must use the same Sequence ID and must update the byte transfer count and the start byte address.

4. **Retry**. If the target has a temporary posted memory write buffer full condition, it will issue a Retry to the Requester. For additional information, refer to "Maximum Completion Time" on page 193.

5. **Disconnect at Next ADB**. The target may start accepting the write data into its posted memory write buffer, but, as it approaches a buffer full condition, it issues a Disconnect At Next ADB to the Requester. The Requester must resume the write at the point of disconnection (for more information, refer to "If Disconnected, Must Resume With Same Sequence ID" on page 170). As stated earlier, it must use the same Sequence ID and must update the byte transfer count and the start byte address.

Doesn't Need All of the Write Data Ready Before Initiating

A Requester can initiate a Memory Write or a Memory Write Block transaction when it has some of the write data (but not all of it) buffered up and ready to write. During the transaction, as it approaches the block boundary where it will have a buffer dry condition, it issues a Disconnect At Next ADB to the target. When it has more of the write data accumulated and ready to write, it would then rearbitrate for the bus and pick up where it left off (and it must do so; see "If Disconnected, Must Resume With Same Sequence ID" on page 170).

Emulating the PCI Memory Write and Invalidate Command

As described in MindShare's *PCI System Architecture* book, a Requester can achieve better performance when performing a burst write to main memory if its uses the PCI Memory Write and Invalidate command. Although this command does not exist in the PCI-X protocol, a PCI-X Requester may emulate it using either the Memory Write or the Memory Write Block PCI-X command (Memory Write Block would be the more likely candidate for this). In order to do this, the following criteria must be met:

1. The Requester's device driver must ensure that it assigns a memory buffer in main memory for its Requester's use wherein the start address is aligned on a cache line boundary (i.e., it is divisible by the processor's cache line size).

2. To ensure good performance, the driver should also ensure that the transfer size to be performed by the Requester is a multiple of the cache line size. This would permit the Requester to perform one transaction to write all of the data. If the transfer size causes the end address to be a memory address other than the end address of a cache line, the Requester would be forced to perform two transactions: the first one to write all lines from the start address through the end of the last full line to be written, and a second transaction to write the fragment of the last line.

3. The Requester function must implement the PCI Cache Line Size configuration register.

4. The Requester's device driver must instruct the Requester as to whether or not to set the NS (No Snoop) attribute bit in the Attribute Phase of the transaction. The spec does not define how the driver would tell the Requester whether or not the processor(s) need to snoop its accesses to memory. The Requester function's PCI-X Command register does not contain a bit to control this aspect of the Requester's functionality, so the designer must implement a control bit in a device-specific register within the Requester.

   • If the driver knows that the processor(s) are not caching from the Requester's buffer in main memory, it would tell the Requester to set the NS bit whenever it accesses its buffer in memory. The Host/PCIX bridge does not generate snoop transactions on the processor(s) bus when the Requester is attempting to access its buffer in main memory with the No Snoop attribute bit set to one.

   • If the driver knows that the processor(s) are caching from the Requester's buffer in main memory, it would tell the Requester to clear the NS bit whenever it accesses its buffer in memory. The Host/PCIX bridge would then generate snoop transactions on the processor(s) bus when the Requester is attempting to access its buffer in main memory.

When the Host/PCIX bridge sees that an initiator is performing a PCI-X Memory Write or Memory Write Block transaction that meets the above criteria, the PCI-X initiator is essentially promising to write all of the memory lines included in the byte transfer count specified in the transaction's Attribute Phase. In response, the Host/PCIX bridge will send a series of one or more snoop transactions back to the processors, but will not wait for the snoop result before permitting the initiator to write the data to memory. The type of snoop transaction used is processor bus-specific, but its net effect will be to kill the processor's copy of the line(s) being written by the PCI-X initiator (even if the processor has a modified copy of the line). Although the processor may have a modified copy of a line and it was the freshest copy of the line until this instant in time, the full cache line of data to be written by the PCI-X initiator is by definition now the freshest copy and should therefore be written to memory.

Alias To Memory Write Block Command

This command is really a place-holder for a possible future command. Currently, no bus masters are permitted to issue this command. If a target is addressed using this command, it must treat it as if it's a Memory Write Block command.

As an example, this could be used in the future to indicate a double-data rate transfer request wherein a block of data might be transferred using both of the clock edges to double throughput.

Memory Write Command

Basic Description

A master uses the Memory Write command if it wishes to write bytes into some but not all locations within the range defined by the start byte address and the byte transfer count. The Byte Enables issued by the initiator in each Data Phase identify the locations to be written to within the current dword (or qword if performing 64-bit transfers). Any combination of Byte Enables is valid in each Data Phase. It should be noted that this command could also be used to write all (rather than some) bytes within the defined range.

It's interesting to note that when using this command, the byte transfer count issued by the initiator (in the Attribute Phase) is not really a byte transfer count. Rather, it defines the end address of the range within which the initiator wishes to write some (but not necessarily all) bytes, and the Byte Enables issued in each Data Phase define the actual bytes to be written.

This is an excellent command for an initiator to use for the following purposes:

- When writing to some but not necessarily all memory-mapped IO ports within a memory address range.

- When updating random locations within a memory buffer (such as a video frame buffer). As an example, an Intel P6 processor accumulates writes to the video frame buffer in its Write Combining Buffers and then performs a series of memory write transactions on its Front Side Bus (FSB) to write them to memory. If the video frame buffer is implemented within a PCI-X function, the Host/PCIX Bridge accumulates these writes in its outbound posted memory write buffer. It then arbitrates for ownership of the PCI-X bus and, if only some bytes are to be written within the range, initiates a PCI-X Memory Write command to dump its buffer to the video frame buffer.
- If a PCIX-to-PCIX bridge has accumulated memory writes in its posted memory write buffer and the dwords to be written were posted in ascending address order, the bridge can use the Memory Write command to dump its buffer.

Can Be Purely Speculative

Refer to "Technically, a Write Can Be Purely Speculative, But..." on page 171.

Target Never Permitted to Split a Memory Write

The target is never permitted to handle a Memory Write Block or a Memory Write transaction as a Split Transaction. The possible valid responses are listed in the next section.

Target Response to Memory Write Transaction

The target of a Memory Write transaction can respond in any of the ways listed in "Target Response to Memory Write Block Transaction" on page 171.

Doesn't Need All of the Write Data Ready Before Initiating

A Requester can initiate a Memory Write or a Memory Write Block transaction when it has some of the write data (but not all of it) buffered up and ready to write. During the transaction, as it approaches the block boundary where it will have a buffer dry condition, it issues a Disconnect At Next ADB to the target. When it has more of the write accumulated and ready to write, it would then rearbitrate for the bus and pick up where it left off (and it must do so; see "If Disconnected, Must Resume With Same Sequence ID" on page 170).

Split Completion Command

Basic Description

The target uses this transaction type to return one of the following to the Requester:

- the previously requested read data (either a single dword when fulfilling an IO Read or a Configuration Read; or a block of read data when fulfilling a Memory Read Block), or
- a Split Completion Message (SCM; see Chapter 17, entitled "Split Completion Messages," on page 313) indicating the success/failure indication of a previously issued write, or an error on a previously requested read.

More information on the Split Completion command can be found in "Split Completion Transaction" on page 274, and in Chapter 17, entitled "Split Completion Messages," on page 313.

At Minimum, Completer Must Handle One Split Transaction

A target that never splits transactions has no need for the Split Transaction capability. If a target responds to any requests by issuing a Split Response, however, it must have the ability to deal with a minimum of one Split Transaction at a time. The spec recommends that, for performance reasons, a target that splits transactions should implement a Split Transaction Queue capable of dealing with a number of outstanding split requests simultaneously.

Can Be Initiated Even If Bus Master Bit Is Off

If a target has issued a Split Response to at least one transaction request, it will be capable of arbitrating for bus ownership and initiating the Split Completion transaction even if software has not set the Bus Master bit in the function's configuration Command register (see Figure 11-5 on page 177).

Figure 11-5: Configuration Command Register

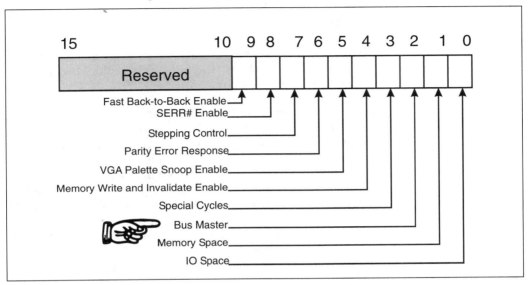

Split Transactions Never Associated With Memory Writes

As explained in "Commands That Will Not Receive a Split Response" on page 110, memory writes are always posted and are never split.

One or More Split Completions to Fulfill One Request

The Completer will fulfill the Requester's transfer request with a series of one or more Split Completion transactions that will return the requested read data (assuming that it was a Memory Read Block request) in strict address order.

Separate Requests May Be Fulfilled out of Order

Assume that one Requester issues a series of three requests (think of them as request 1, request 2, and request 3) to the same Completer and the Completer issues a Split Response to each of them. The Completer can issue the Split Completions for the three requests in any order (e.g., 1-2-3, 3-1-2, 3-2-1, etc.). The Requester must be able to deal with this behavior. The Completer, however, will always return the memory read data associated with a specific request in strict order.

If, to ensure proper operation, a Requester requires that two requests be completed in order, then the request that must complete second must not be issued until the first request completes.

The Address Phase

In the Address Phase of the Split Completion Transaction, the Completer supplies the following information (pictured in "Split Completion Transaction's Address Phase Information Format" on page 178):

- C/BE#[3:0] contains the **Split Completion command** code.
- **Requester ID**. This is decoded by any bridges in the path back to the Requester to determine if the transaction needs to be passed through to the other side of the bridge. It is decoded by the Requester to determine if it is the target of the Split Completion transaction. It will assert DEVSEL# if it is.
- Requester's transaction **Tag**. The Requester uses the Tag to identify which of its currently suspended transactions the Completer is picking up the thread of.
- **Relaxed Ordering attribute bit**. Explained in "Relaxed Ordering Effect on Transaction Ordering" on page 569.
- **Lower Address field**. Explained in "Disconnecting First Split Completion Is Problematic" on page 184.

Figure 11-6: Split Completion Transaction's Address Phase Information Format

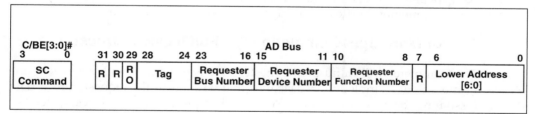

The Attribute Phase

In the Attribute Phase of the Split Completion transaction, the Completer supplies the following information (pictured in "Split Completion Transaction's Attribute Phase Information Format" on page 180):

- **Completer ID**. Identifies the Completer (by its Bus, Device, and Function number) that initiated the transaction. This information is only of interest to a tool (such as the Agilent Technologies PCI-X Bus Exerciser) so it can identify the initiator of the Split Completion transaction.

- **Remaining Byte Count**. This 12-bit field (actually presented as two fields) identifies how many bytes remain to be returned. In the initial Split Completion transaction, this will indicate the full byte count requested by the Requester (also refer to the explanation of the BCM bit below). In subsequent Split Completions (assuming that the requested read data is returned in a series of Split Completions), this field indicates the number of bytes of the requested read data that remain to be transferred.

- **Byte Count Modified (BCM) bit**. The start byte address issued by the Requester in a Memory Read Block request may have been very close to a block boundary (i.e., within three Data Phases of the boundary). When the Completer subsequently initiates the first Split Completion transaction, it may only have the data fragment at the end of that block ready to deliver at this time. It would therefore need to disconnect the transaction on that imminent block boundary. If the Completer were to start the Split Completion and attempt to issue a Disconnect At Next ADB to the target, this is not enough prior warning and the target will not disconnect the transaction until the subsequent block boundary. The only way to force the target to end the transaction on the imminent block boundary is to artificially adjust the byte transfer count (see Figure 11-7 on page 180) to end the transfer on the imminent block boundary. In addition, the Completer must set the BCM bit to indicate that this is the case. The only device that will pay attention to the BCM bit is a tool that is monitoring bus activity. Setting this bit tells the tool that the actual overall transfer length is greater than this adjusted byte transfer count and that one or more additional Split Completion transactions will subsequently be performed to finish the transfer.

  BCM Special Case Scenario: Assume that the Completer responds to a burst memory read issued by a PCIX-to-PCIX bridge with immediate read data and then disconnects on an ADB. The bridge can initiate a Split Completion on the Sequence's originating bus to return the first part of the read data to the Requester. In this case, the bridge uses its own ID as the Completer ID when creating the Split Completion transaction. When the bridge resumes the memory read on the Completer's bus, it will use the same Sequence ID (because it's part of the same Requester memory read request). Assume that when the bridge resumes the memory read, the Completer issues a Split Response to the bridge. In this case, when the Completer subsequently initiates the Split Completion transaction it is not permitted to set the BCM bit and modify the byte count because this is actually not the beginning of the Sequence. To preclude this possibility, the Completer must not set the BCM bit and modify the byte count when the starting address of the Sequence is aligned to an ADB and the Completer is designed to use immediate completion in the range before the ADB.

- **Split Completion Message (SCM) bit**. The Completer will set the SCM bit when the Split Completion transaction's one and only Data Phase contains a completion message (see Chapter 17, entitled "Split Completion Messages," on page 313). Also see next bullet item.
- **Split Completion Error (SCE) bit**. If both the SCM and SCE bits are set, the Split Completion transaction's one and only Data Phase contains a completion error message. Also refer to Chapter 17, entitled "Split Completion Messages," on page 313.

Figure 11-7: Split Completion Transaction's Attribute Phase Information Format

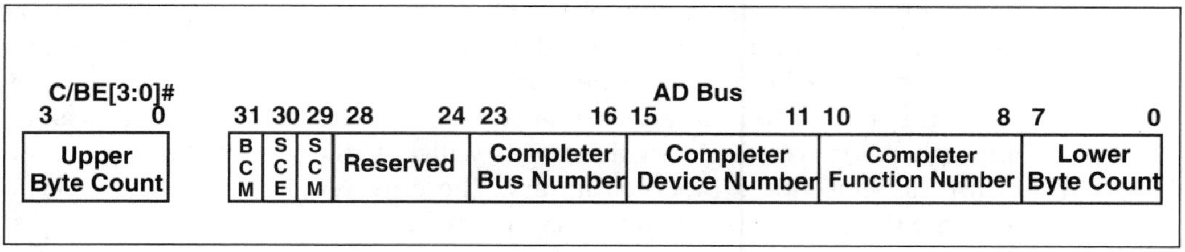

Claiming a Split Completion Transaction

The Requester and Completer may or may not reside on the same bus. The following two sections discuss these two cases.

Requester and Completer Are on the Same Bus. If the Requester and Completer reside on the same bus, the Requester acts as the target of the Split Completion and will have to claim the transaction. The spec permits implementation of either of two decode strategies:

METHOD 1. The Requester decodes the Requester ID and Tag delivered in the transaction's Address Phase. If it matches its own Requester ID and one of its outstanding Tags, it asserts DEVSEL# to claim the transaction. It then uses the Tag to determine which of its previously suspended requests it is picking up the thread of.

METHOD 2. The Requester could decode just the Requester ID (not the Tag) and assert DEVSEL# if it matches its own Requester ID. Subsequently, it looks at the Tag to determine which of its previously suspended requests it is picking up the thread of. If the Tag does not match any of its currently outstanding requests, it accepts all of the Split Completion data and then discards it. The Requester must also set the Unexpected Split Completion bit in its PCI-X Status register (see "Unexpected Split Completion (this is also not a good thing!)" on page 480).

Requester and Completer Are on Different Buses. If they are not on the same bus, the Split Completion will have to traverse one or more bridges to get back to the Requester that originated the transfer request. In this case, a bridge will have to act as the target of the transaction and must decide whether to claim it and pass it through to the bus on the opposite side of the bridge. There are a number of cases:

- If the Split Completion originated on the bridge's primary side, it compares the Requester Bus Number (delivered in the Address Phase) to its Secondary Bus Number Register. If it does not match it, and also does not fall within the range of buses defined by the bridge's Secondary and Subordinate Bus Number register values, the bridge will not assert DEVSEL# to claim the transaction and will not pass it through to its secondary bus.
- If the Split Completion originated on the bridge's primary side, it compares the Requester Bus Number (delivered in the Address Phase) to its Secondary Bus Number Register. If it matches, it asserts DEVSEL# and will pass the transaction through to its secondary bus.
- If the Split Completion originated on the bridge's primary side, it compares the Requester Bus Number (delivered in the Address Phase) to its Secondary Bus Number Register. If it does not match it, but it falls within the range of buses defined by the bridge's Secondary and Subordinate Bus Number register values, the bridge asserts DEVSEL# and will pass the transaction through to its secondary bus (because it needs to be delivered to a bus subordinate to the bridge's secondary bus).
- If the Split Completion originated on the bridge's secondary side, it compares the Requester Bus Number (delivered in the Address Phase) to its Primary Bus Number Register. If it matches, it asserts DEVSEL# and will pass the transaction through to its primary bus.
- If the Split Completion originated on the bridge's secondary side, and the target bus is neither the bridge's primary bus nor is it in the range of buses defined by the bridge's Secondary and Subordinate Bus registers, the bridge will claim the transaction and will pass it through to the primary bus (because it needs to be delivered to a bus that is not beneath this bridge).
- If the Split Completion originated on the bridge's secondary side, and the target bus is not the bridge's primary bus, but it is within the range of buses defined by the bridge's Secondary and Subordinate Bus Number registers, the bridge will not claim it and pass it through to its primary side (because the target bus is one which is subordinate to the bridge's secondary bus).

Master Abort or Target Abort on a Split Completion. If the Requester doesn't claim the transaction (see the previous two sections), the initiator of the Split Completion transaction will experience a Master Abort (it cannot deliver the Split Completion). Alternatively, the Requester may claim the transaction but may issue a Target Abort in the first or any other Data Phase of the Split Completion.

If the Split Request is a write or if it addresses a location that has no read side effects (i.e., Prefetchable memory), the Completer must discard the Split Completion and take no further action.

If the Split Request is a read and the location has read side effects (i.e., it is Non-Prefetchable memory), the Completer must discard the Split Completion, set the Split Completion Discarded bit in its PCI-X Status Register, and assert SERR# (if enabled by the SERR# enable bit in its configuration Command register). In neither case does the Completer set the Received Master Abort or Received Target Abort bits in its configuration Status register, since the completer is not the original initiator of the request.

Treatment of Byte Enables

In a Split Completion transaction, the Byte Enables are reserved and driven high for all Data Phases of the transaction. They are not required because the Requester that issued the Memory Read Block transaction request knows the start and end byte addresses of the range being read and it is an all-inclusive read within that range.

Requester Must Accept the Split Completion Data

As stated earlier, the Requester is not permitted to respond to a Split Completion with a Retry or a Disconnect At Next ADB.

The Requester may have issued the Memory Read Block request to fetch data that it might have a use for in the future, and it might subsequently decide that it doesn't need the data. Nonetheless, it must accept all of the read data when it is returned and can then discard it.

When Bridge Is Target of Completion, Can Retry or Disconnect

A bridge residing between the Completer and Requester will have to act as the target of the Split Completion(s) so that it can then pass it to the bus that the Requester resides on. Unlike the Requester that a originated a request, the bridge doesn't have to reserve buffer space for all of the read data that will be returned by the subsequent Split Completion(s). For this reason, if it needs to, the bridge is permitted to respond to a Split Completion with either a Retry or a Disconnect At Next ADB. Refer to "Bridge Can Retry or Disconnect Split Completion" on page 125.

Initiator of Split Completion Can Disconnect

The initiator of a Split Completion transaction (either the Completer or a bridge on the path back to the Requester) doesn't have to have all of the requested read data buffered up and ready to go when it starts a Split Completion transaction. In this case, the Completer or bridge would issue a Disconnect At Next ADB as it approached the block boundary where it will run out of data (before satisfying the full byte count requested).

After Disconnect, Pick Up Where You Left Off

If a Disconnect At Next ADB is issued by either party (the Completer or a bridge that is acting as the target of the Split Completion) during a Split Completion transaction, the initiator of the Split Completion transaction will rearbitrate for bus ownership and issue another Split Completion until the full requested byte count has been returned.

Split Completion Messages

If the SCM bit in the Completer Attributes (see Figure 11-7 on page 180) is set, the transaction includes a message. A Split Completion transaction that contains a message is always a single Data Phase transaction. The message consists of a 32-bit value delivered in the Data Phase (see Figure 11-8 on page 184). The message indicates one the following:

- Successful completion of an IO Write or a Configuration Write.
- For a Memory Read Block request, that there is no message and the transaction will return the requested data.
- An error was incurred on an attempt to deliver write data for an IO or Configuration Write request.
- An error was incurred during a memory read operation.

In the Address Phase (see Figure 11-6 on page 178) of a Split Completion transaction that contains a message, the Lower Address field is set to zero. In the Attribute Phase (see Figure 11-7 on page 180), the Byte Count field is set to four.

Receipt of a Split Completion Message terminates a Sequence regardless of how many bytes remain to be sent. If the request was a Memory Read Block and an error was incurred at some point during the read:

- The Remaining Byte Count field in the Split Completion Message (see Figure 11-8 on page 184) indicates the number of bytes that were not sent for this request.
- The Remaining Lower Address field (see Figure 11-8 on page 184) indicates the lower seven bits of the starting address of the remainder of the Sequence. Upon receipt of a read error message, a bridge will release any remaining buffer space that was reserved to hold the read data that will not be returned due to the error condition.

Additional information on Split Completion Messages can be found in Chapter 17, entitled "Split Completion Messages," on page 313.

Figure 11-8: Split Completion Message Format

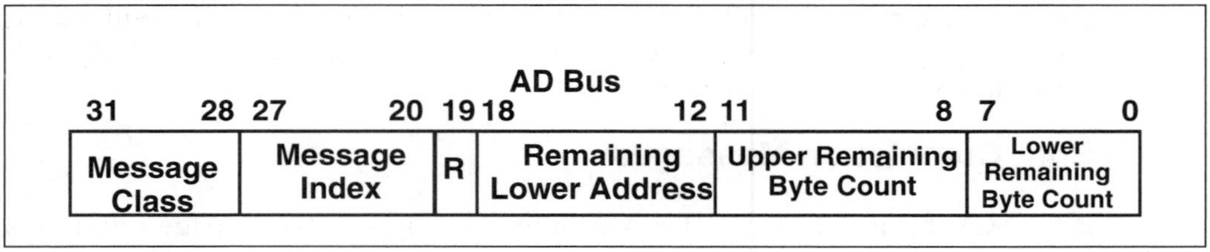

To Disconnect First Split Completion at Imminent ADB

See the explanation of the BCM bit in "The Attribute Phase" on page 178.

Disconnecting First Split Completion Is Problematic

The Problem. Refer to Figure 11-9 on page 186.

1. Assume that the Requester on bus one issues a Memory Read Block to the Completer on bus zero.
2. Since the request must cross the bridge, the bridge splits the request.
3. The bridge then reinitiates the Memory Read Block transaction on bus zero.
4. The Completer on bus zero issues a Split Response to the bridge.

5. After accumulating some or all of the requested read data, the Completer initiates a Split Completion transaction on bus zero to return the data to the Requester. The bridge accepts some or all of the read data into its internal buffer.
6. The bridge then reinitiates the Split Completion transaction on bus one.
7. Assume that the bridge decides to issue a Disconnect At Next ADB during its performance of the Split Completion transaction on bus one.

Now, here's the problem. How does the bridge know where the block boundary is relative to the start point of its transfer? The address that it issued in the Address Phase of the Split Completion is the address that was provided to it by the Completer and that address is not a memory address. Rather, it is the Requester ID and Tag.

The Solution. Refer to the illustration of the Split Completion transaction's Address Phase information in Figure 11-6 on page 178. When the Completer initiated the first Split Completion transaction, it provided the bridge with the lower 7-bits of the byte-aligned memory start address that was provided by the Requester in its Memory Read Block request. This information is provided in the 7-bit Lower Address field of the Address Phase information.

In step seven of the previous section's example, when the bridge issues the Disconnect At Next ADB, it uses the value in the Lower Address field to figure out where the Split Completion transfer of read data was initiated relative to the next block start address. It then knows exactly where to disconnect the transaction.

If there are any subsequent Split Completions issued by the Completer for the same request, the Lower Address field will always contain zero in them because the remaining Split Completions of the Sequence are always resuming at a block boundary (i.e., offset zero within the next block of data to be transferred).

Figure 11-9: Example System Block Diagram

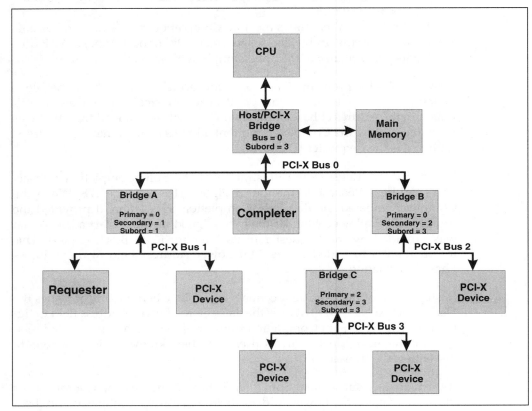

Bridge Buffer Space Problem Due to Corrupted Split Completion

There a number of ways in which a Split Completion transaction's information could become corrupted and the corruption may not cause a parity error (i.e., it's a multi-bit failure, but still resulting in an even number of one bits on the AD bus, the C/BE# bus, and the parity bit). The transaction would therefore appear to be a good transaction. This can cause a bridge's internal buffer management to become inaccurate. Some examples are:

- A corrupted Requester Bus Number (see Figure 11-6 on page 178) may cause the bridge not to claim the transaction. The initiator of the Split Completion will experience a Master Abort (see "Master Abort or Target Abort on a Split Completion" on page 182) and will not re-attempt the transaction. The Split Completion data will therefore never arrive at the Requester and the Requester would experience a timeout (see "Requesters Must Implement a Split Request Timeout" on page 125). The bridge still has buffer space reserved to receive that Split Completion's read data, however, and that buffer space will not be released. The bridge may therefore end up issuing a Retry or Disconnect At Next ADB to one or more subsequent Split Completions due to insufficient buffer space.
- The **Byte Count** field (see Figure 11-7 on page 180) is **corrupted**. In this case, the bridge may use the Byte Count value to select how much buffer space to release after the transfer is completed.

Dual-Address Cycle (DAC) Command

The Dual-Address Cycle (DAC) command may only be used when issuing a start memory address located above the 4GB address boundary. For a detailed description of the DAC, refer to "Addressing Memory Above 4GB Boundary" on page 372.

12 *Latency Rules*

The Previous Chapter

The previous chapter provided a detailed description of the Dword commands, the Burst commands, and the Dual-Address Cycle (DAC) command.

This Chapter

This chapter provides a detailed description of how quickly the initiator and target must be capable of transferring data. This includes the target's rules of behavior during both startup time and run-time, as well as a description of the Maximum Completion Time limit imposed upon non-bridge target devices.

The Next Chapter

The previous chapter provided a detailed description of the Address, Attribute, and Response Phases of memory burst transactions, Dword transactions, Configuration transactions, and Split Completion transactions.

Initiator Latency Rules

Don't Start Transfer If You're Not Ready

When starting a transaction, the initiator of a transaction must (at a minimum) immediately have the data to be transferred within the first block ready to transfer. This is necessary because the initiator of a PCI-X transaction is not permitted to delay (by keeping IRDY# deasserted) the transfer of the data in the first block.

Refer to Figure 12-1 on page 190. It is a rule that the initiator must assert IRDY# in the fourth clock cycle of the transaction (the fifth clock cycle if it uses the Dual-Address Cycle command, as it adds a second Address Phase).

- If it's a Memory Read Block transaction, the initiator's assertion of IRDY# indicates that it's immediately ready to start receiving the data within the first block at full speed. In other words, at a minimum, it has reserved sufficient buffer space to hold the data between the start byte address and the current block boundary.
- If it's a Memory Write Block or Memory Write transaction, the initiators assertion of IRDY# indicates that it's immediately ready to start transferring the data within the first block at full speed. In other words, at a minimum, it has buffered up the data between the start byte address and the current block boundary.

No Initiator Wait States Permitted...Ever

Once the transfer of a data block begins (IRDY# and TRDY# both asserted), neither party is permitted to temporarily deassert its respective ready signal to delay the transfer of a data item within a block. In other words, once you assert IRDY# to start the transmission of a block, you must keep it asserted during the entire period while the remainder of that block is transferred.

Figure 12-1: Example Memory Read Block Transaction

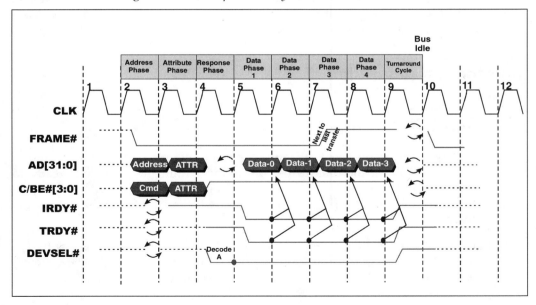

Behavior When Preempted

For a detailed discussion of preemption, refer to "How the Initiator Deals With Preemption" on page 143.

Target Latency Rules

Target Response Time During Initialization Period

What's Going on During Initialization Time?

During initialization time, the startup configuration software is accessing the configuration registers within each function to determine the presence of a function as well as its resource requirements. Immediately after RST# is removed from a PCI or a PCI-X function, it may not be prepared to service configuration accesses on a timely basis. As an example, a function's configuration registers might not contain valid default values immediately after RST# is removed. Perhaps the function must start backloading this information into its configuration registers from a serial EEPROM. In this case, it could be a substantial amount of time after RST# removal before the function can provide read data from or accept write data into its configuration registers. For this reason, functions do not have to obey the 16 clock first Data Phase completion rule during initialization time.

Definition of Initialization Period in PCI

As defined in the PCI 2.2 spec, initialization time (Trhfa) begins when RST# is deasserted and completes 2^{25} PCI clocks later (32 mega-cycles). This parameter is referred to in the spec as Trhfa (Time from Reset High-to-First-Access). At a bus speed of 33MHz, this equates to 1.0066 seconds, while it equates to 0.5033 seconds at a bus speed of 66MHz. Run-time follows initialization time. If a target is accessed during initialization time, it is allowed to do any of the following:

- Ignore the request (except if it is a boot device). A boot device is one that must respond as a target in order to allow the processor to access the boot ROM. In a typical PC design, this would be the PCI-to-ISA bridge. Devices in the processor's path to the boot ROM should be prepared to be the target of a transaction immediately after Trhff expires (five clock cycles after RST# is deasserted).

- Claim the access and hold in Wait States until it can complete the request, not to exceed the end of initialization time.
- Claim the access and terminate with Retry.

Definition of Initialization Period in PCI-X

In PCI-X, Trhfa is 2^{26} clocks (64 mega-cycles) in duration rather than 2^{25} as it is in PCI. This is because the PCI-X clock speed can be substantially faster than (up to 133MHz) the PCI clock speed, and if this parameter remained the same as the PCI Trhfa spec, initialization time would be reduced to 0.25 seconds (at a clock speed of 133MHz).

During initialization time, a PCI-X target has the same options available as a PCI target does (see previous section).

Initialization Period and Hot-Plug

See "Early Configuration Access to Newly-Installed Device" on page 80.

Target Can Ignore 16-Clock Rule During ROM Shadowing

The PCI-X spec also states that during system setup, a PCI-X target is permitted to ignore the 16-clock rule when software is performing the memory reads to copy (i.e., shadow) the function's device ROM code into main memory (because the ROM typically has a very slow access time).

Target Response Time Limit During Run-Time

Response Time Limit When No Data Transferred

A target can terminate a transaction with no data transferred. The following target terminations result in no data being transferred:

- Retry.
- Split Response.
- Target Abort.

If a target is going to issue one these responses to the initiator, it must do so within eight clocks from the assertion of FRAME#. In other words, issue it quickly to free up the bus for someone else to use.

Response Time Limit When Data Transferred

If the target intends to transfer any data at all in the transaction, it must assert TRDY# within 16 clocks from the assertion of FRAME#. This would include the following target terminations:

- Single Data Phase Disconnect.
- Disconnect At Next ADB.

Host/PCIX Bridge Must Obey 16-Clock Rule

In PCI. A Host/PCI bridge that is snooping is optionally permitted to exceed the 16-clock limit, but may never exceed 32 clocks. Assume that a PCI master is accessing main memory. The Host/PCI bridge can start inserting Wait States in the first Data Phase while it sends the memory address back to the processors to be snooped in their caches. In the event of a snoop hit on a modified line, the processor with the modified line will transfer the line to the bridge. If the bridge knows that this process can be accomplished within 32 PCI clocks from the start of the PCI master's transaction, then it is legal for it to hold the PCI bus in Wait States while the snoop and possibly the memory update take place.

In PCI-X. The Host/PCIX bridge must obey the 16-clock rule just like any other PCI-X target.

Subsequent Data Phase Target Latency Rule

Like the initiator (see "No Initiator Wait States Permitted...Ever" on page 190), once the target asserts TRDY# to indicate its readiness to start the transfer of the first data block, it must keep TRDY# asserted for the remainder of the transmission of the block.

Maximum Completion Time

In PCI

When data is written to a memory target, the target can handle it in one of three ways:

METHOD 1. The target can immediately accept the data and write it into memory. How fast this can be accomplished is dependent on the write latency of the memory being written to (but it must be able to accomplish the write within 16 clocks).

METHOD 2. The target can immediately accept the data into a posted memory write buffer.

METHOD 3. If the target has a temporary condition (e.g., a temporarily full posed memory write buffer) that prevents it from accepting the data within 16 clocks, it can issue a Retry to the master. The key word here is temporary. The target is not allowed to issue Retries indefinitely to the master attempting the write. The Maximum Completion Limit on memory writes applies to this case.

After a target terminates a memory write transaction with a Retry, it must complete at least one Data Phase of a memory write within:

- 334 clocks from the first Retry termination for systems running at 33MHz or slower.
- 668 clocks from the first Retry termination for systems running at 66MHz.

This 10 microsecond (at both 33 MHz and 66 MHz) time limit is called the Maximum Completion Time. If a target is presented with multiple memory writes, the Maximum Completion Time is measured from the time the first memory write transaction is terminated with Retry until the time the first Data Phase of any memory write to the target completes with something other than Retry.

When a termination other than a Retry occurs, the time limit starts over again with the next Retry on a memory write. The actual time that the Data Phase completes also depends upon when the master repeats the transaction. Targets must be designed to meet the Maximum Completion Time requirements assuming the master will repeat the memory write transaction precisely at the limit of the Maximum Completion Time.

PCI devices are not required to honor this time limit during Trhfa (i.e., for 2^{25} clock cycles after RST# is deasserted). For more information, refer to "Target Response Time During Initialization Period" on page 191.

Note that bridges do not have to adhere to the Maximum Completion Time (because it's problematic how long it will take a bridge to flush its posted-memory write buffers to the other bus so it can start accepting more write data).

How PCI-X Is Different

In PCI-X, the Maximum Completion Time limit is two microseconds rather than ten. Unlike PCI, it applies to IO Write as well as Memory Write and Memory Write Block transactions. As in PCI, bridges do not have to obey the Maximum Completion Time limit (because it's problematic how long it will take a bridge to flush its posted-memory write buffers to the other bus so it can start accepting more write data).

How Can You Prevent Violation of This Time Limit?

A function's device driver is the software entity that stimulates its Requester to perform memory writes and IO writes to the function's memory or IO registers. When the driver detects that the function is temporarily unable to handle additional write data, it must cease performing writes to the function's memory or IO registers until the function indicates that it's prepared to accept additional write data. Before writing to the device, the driver would check a status bit in a device-specific status register to determine if the device is prepared to accept additional write data.

13 *The Address, Attribute and Response Phases*

The Previous Chapter

The previous chapter provided a detailed description of how quickly the initiator and target must be capable of transferring data. This included the target's rules of behavior during both startup time and run-time, as well as a description of the Maximum Completion Time limit imposed upon non-bridge devices.

This Chapter

This chapter provides a detailed description of the Address, Attribute, and Response Phases of memory burst transactions, Dword transactions, Configuration transactions, and Split Completion transactions.

The Next Chapter

The next chapter provides detailed examples of the Dword transaction types:

- IO Read and Write transactions.
- The Memory Read Dword transaction.
- The Interrupt Acknowledge transaction.
- The Special Cycle transaction.

Although the Configuration Read and Write transactions are Dword transactions, a detailed discussion of them is deferred until Chapter 20, entitled "Configuration Transactions," on page 425.

All Transactions Begin With Address and Attribute Phases

Refer to Figure 13-1 on page 198. Each transaction begins with the Address Phase (clock two), immediately followed by the Attribute Phase (clock three).

During the Address Phase, the initiator outputs:

- The start address on the AD bus (the address type is defined as a memory, IO, or configuration address by the command type).
- The command (i.e., transaction) type on the C/BE# bus. The format of the start address is defined by the command type.

During the Attribute Phase, the initiator delivers additional information about the transaction. This information is delivered on AD[31:0] and C/BE#[3:0]. The format of the Attribute information is defined by the command type.

Subsequent sections in this chapter define the Address/Attribute format for each type of command.

Figure 13-1: Example PCI-X Transaction

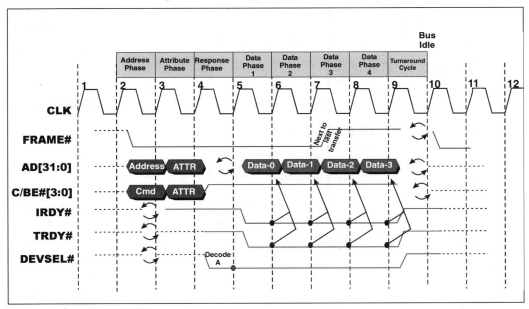

Chapter 13: The Address, Attribute and Response Phases

Memory Transaction May Have Two Address Phases

Refer to Figure 13-2 on page 199. When an initiator issues a start memory address that is above the 4GB address boundary, it uses the Dual-Address Cycle command in the first Address Phase (clock two) to inform the targets that this is the first of two Address Phases. The initiator delivers a 64-bit memory start address in two packets over AD[31:0], and it delivers the actual memory command (e.g., Memory Read Block) on C/BE#[3:0] during the second Address Phase (clock three). The Attribute Phase (clock four) immediately follows the second Address Phase.

A detailed description of 64-bit memory addressing can be found in "Addressing Memory Above 4GB Boundary" on page 372.

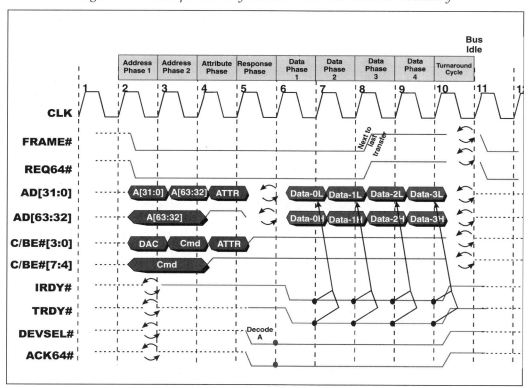

Figure 13-2: Example Memory Access Above 4GB Address Boundary

Attributes Always Delivered on Lower Half of Bus

Refer to Figure 13-1 on page 198. The Attributes are always delivered over AD[31:0] and C/BE#[3:0]. During the Attribute Phase of memory transactions initiated by a 64-bit initiator (see clock four in Figure 13-2 on page 199), AD[63:32] and C/BE#[7:4] are always reserved and driven high.

Address/Attribute Format Depends on Command Type

As mentioned earlier, the format of the Address/Attribute information is defined by the command type. The sections that follow define the formats for the various command types.

Memory Burst Format

Description

The memory burst-oriented commands are:

- Memory Read Block
- Memory Write Block
- Memory Write
- Alias To Memory Read Block
- Alias To Memory Write Block

Figure 13-3 on page 201 illustrates the information output during the Address Phase of any of these transaction types. The initiator issues the start byte address on AD[31:0] and the memory command type on C/BE#[3:0]. When initiating a transaction with a start memory address above the 4GB address boundary, there are two Address Phases in the transaction. A detailed description of this can be found in "Addressing Memory Above 4GB Boundary" on page 372.

Figure 13-4 on page 201 illustrates the information output during the transaction's Attribute Phase:

Chapter 13: The Address, Attribute and Response Phases

- **Requester ID**. Consists of the Requester's Bus Number, Device Number, and Function Number supplied from its PCI-X Status register (see Figure 21-9 on page 462).
- **Transaction Tag**. The Requester's transaction number.
- **Byte Transfer Count**. This 12-bit field indicates the transfer size in bytes.
  - 000h = 4096 bytes
  - 001h-FFFh = 1 through 4096 bytes.
- **No Snoop (NS) attribute bit**. See "No Snoop Attribute Bit" on page 201.
- **Relaxed Ordering (RO) attribute bit**. See "Relaxed Ordering Effect on Transaction Ordering" on page 569.

Figure 13-3: Memory Transaction Address Phase Format

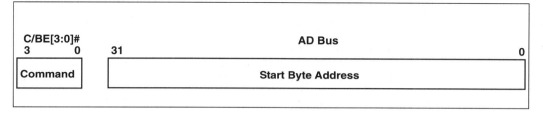

Figure 13-4: Memory Burst Transaction Attribute Phase Format

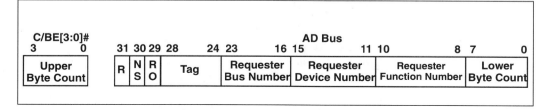

No Snoop Attribute Bit

Background

Bridge Knows AGP's Area of Memory Is Non-Cacheable. Refer to Figure 13-5 on page 204. The Host/PCIX bridge typically contains the main memory controller. It is also the communication path between the AGP graphics adapter and main memory. The AGP 2.0 spec dictates that the region of main memory allocated to the AGP graphics adapter must be designated as non-cacheable memory. This means that the processors do not cache copies of memory lines from this region. There is therefore no reason for the Host/PCIX bridge to generate snoop transactions on the processor bus whenever the AGP adapter accesses its designated area of memory.

Memory Used by PCI Masters May or May Not Be Cached. Other than the region of main memory assigned to the AGP adapter, the Host/PCIX bridge does not know what areas of main memory are cached by the processor(s). This means that it must generate a snoop transaction on the processor bus whenever a PCI master attempts to access main memory.

Snoops Slow Down PCI Accesses to Main Memory. When a PCI adapter starts an access to main memory, the Host/PCIX bridge acts as the target of the PCI transaction. Because the master may be addressing a stale line in system memory, the Host/PCIX bridge cannot allow the PCI master to start transferring data with memory until the results of the snoop have been presented to the Host/PCIX bridge by the processor(s). While awaiting the snoop result, the Host/PCIX bridge may insert Wait States into the first Data Phase or may issue a Retry to the PCI master. This delay in the transfer of the first data item certainly impacts the performance of the PCI master.

Snoop Traffic on Processor Bus Can Hurt Processor(s). Each time that the Host/PCIX bridge generates a snoop transaction on the processor bus, the processor bus is a little less available to the processor(s). If PCI bus masters access main memory frequently, this can have an adverse effect on the performance of the processor(s).

Main Memory Less Available to Processors. In addition, during periods of time when PCI masters are generating a lot of traffic to main memory, the memory bus is less available for the processors to use.

PCI-X Driver Can Make Requester's Buffer Uncacheable

When a Requester's device driver makes a memory allocation call to the OS to reserve a region of main memory for the use of its Requester, it may request that the OS make that memory range uncacheable. If this is the case, the device driver then sets a bit in one of the Requester's device-specific registers to indicate that the Requester can set the No Snoop (NS) attribute bit whenever it performs a memory transaction to access its assigned buffer.

Only Host/PCIX Bridge Pays Attention to NS Bit

If the memory transaction has to traverse one or more PCIX-to-PCIX bridges to get to the Requester's buffer in main memory, the bridges will pass along the NS bit unmodified and will pay no attention to it. The only device that will pay attention to the NS bit is the Host/PCIX bridge because it typically contains the main memory controller. If the NS bit is set to one, the Host/PCIX bridge will not delay the initiator's access to memory while it sends a snoop transaction back to the processor(s). It will let the initiator have immediate access to main memory.

As discussed earlier (see "Snoops Slow Down PCI Accesses to Main Memory" on page 202), this yields better performance for the PCI-X initiator and also diminishes snoop traffic on the processor bus (see "Snoop Traffic on Processor Bus Can Hurt Processor(s)" on page 202).

When NS Is Set and CPU Has a Lock in Force

Many processors cannot snoop their caches while performing a locked transaction series. During this period of time, the Host/PCIX bridge will not permit PCI-X masters to access main memory unless the NS attribute bit is set in the transaction's Attribute Phase (indicating that snooping is not necessary). Otherwise, the Host/PCIX bridge issues a Retry to the PCI-X initiator.

NS Must Be 0 in Some Transactions

The No Snoop (NS) attribute bit must be cleared to zero (or doesn't exist) in the following transactions:

- Special Cycle.
- A Memory Write or Memory Write Block (or Alias To Memory Write Block) being performed to generate an interrupt via the MSI (Message-Signaled Interrupt) mechanism.
- IO Read or Write.
- Configuration Read or Write.
- Split Completion.
- Interrupt Acknowledge.

Note that the NS and RO attribute bits can be set in a Memory Read Dword transaction.

Figure 13-5: Typical System Block Diagram

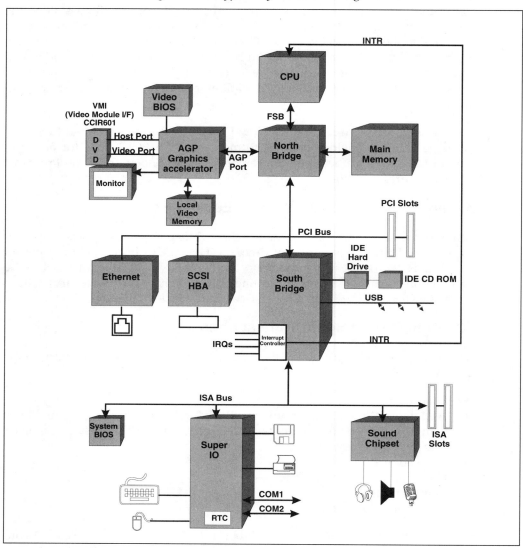

Chapter 13: The Address, Attribute and Response Phases

Dword Command (other than Config) Format

Memory Read Dword and IO Format

Figure 13-6 on page 205 illustrates the format of the memory or IO address issued in the Address Phase of an IO Read, IO Write, or Memory Read Dword transaction. As shown, the start address is always byte-aligned.

Figure 13-7 on page 206 illustrates the format of the Attribute Phase information:

- **Requester ID**. Consists of the Requester's Bus Number, Device Number, and Function Number supplied from its PCI-X Status register (see Figure 21-9 on page 462).
- **Transaction Tag**. The Requester's transaction number.
- **Byte Enables**. See "Byte Enable Usage" on page 149, "IO Transaction With No Byte Enables Asserted" on page 149, "Byte Enable Usage" on page 152, and "Transaction With No Byte Enables Asserted" on page 152.
- **No Snoop (NS) attribute bit**. This bit must be zero for an IO Read or Write, while it may be set for a Memory Dword transaction. See "No Snoop Attribute Bit" on page 201.
- **Relaxed Ordering (RO) attribute bit**. This bit must be zero for an IO Read or Write, while it may be set for a Memory Dword transaction. See "Relaxed Ordering Effect on Transaction Ordering" on page 569.

Figure 13-6: Memory Read Dword Transaction Address Phase Format

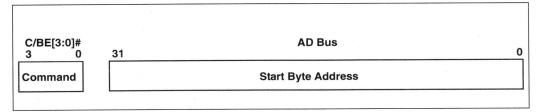

Figure 13-7: Memory Read Dword or IO Transaction Attribute Phase Format

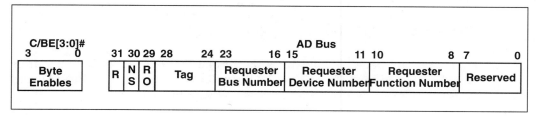

Special Cycle and Interrupt Acknowledge Format

In the Address Phase of a Special Cycle or Interrupt Acknowledge transaction, the initiator does not present a valid address. It must, however, present a stable pattern on AD[31:0] to ensure proper parity on the Address Phase information.

The Attribute Phase format for these two transactions is the same as that shown in Figure 13-7 with the following exceptions:

- The NS bit must be zero.
- The RO bit must be zero.

Configuration Command Format

Two Types of Configuration Transactions

When instructed to do so, a bridge must perform a configuration access on its secondary bus. If the target device resides on its secondary bus, the bridge performs a Type 0 configuration access. If the target device resides on a bus subordinate to the bridge's secondary bus, the bridge must perform a Type 1 configuration access on the secondary bus. The following two sections introduce these two variations on the configuration access.

For a detailed description of the configuration transactions, refer to Chapter 20, entitled "Configuration Transactions," on page 425.

Type 0 Configuration Access

If the target bus is the bridge's secondary bus, the bridge must initiate a PCI-X configuration transaction and in some way indicate to the devices on the secondary bus that one of them is the target of this configuration transaction. This is accomplished by setting AD[1:0] to 00b during the Address Phase of the configuration transaction. This identifies the transaction as a Type 0 configuration transaction targeting one of the devices on this bus. This bit pattern tells the community of devices on the PCI-X bus that the Source Bridge has already performed the bus number comparison and verified that the request targets a device on its secondary bus. A detailed description of the Type 0 configuration transaction can be found in "Type 0 Configuration Transactions" on page 435.

Type 1 Configuration Access

If, on the other hand, the target bus is a bus that is subordinate to the bridge's secondary bus, the bridge still must initiate the configuration transaction on its secondary bus, but must indicate in some manner that none of the devices on this bus is the target of the transaction. Rather, only PCIX-to-PCIX bridges residing on the secondary bus should pay attention to the transaction because it targets a device on a bus further out in the hierarchy beyond a PCIX-to-PCIX bridge that is attached to the secondary bus. This is accomplished by setting AD[1:0] to 01b during the Address Phase of the configuration transaction. This pattern instructs all functions other than PCIX-to-PCIX bridges that the transaction is not for any of them and is referred to as a Type 1 configuration transaction. A detailed description of the Type 1 configuration access can be found in "Type 1 Configuration Transactions" on page 447.

Type 0 Configuration Access Format

Figure 13-8 on page 208 illustrates the information supplied by the Source Bridge in the Address Phase of the Type 0 configuration access.

Figure 13-9 on page 208 illustrates the information supplied by the Source Bridge in the Attribute Phase of a Type 0 configuration access.

A detailed explanation of the Type 0 configuration access can be found in "Type 0 Configuration Transactions" on page 435.

Figure 13-8: Type 0 Configuration Transaction Address Phase Format

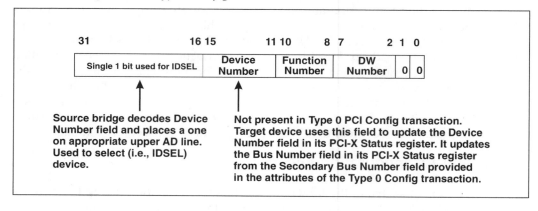

Figure 13-9: Configuration Transaction Attribute Phase Format

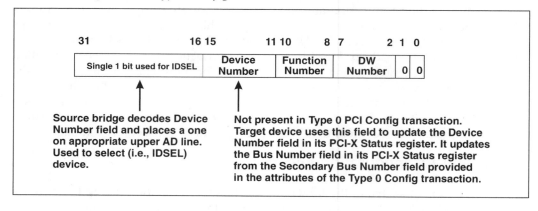

Type 1 Configuration Access Format

Figure 13-10 on page 209 illustrates the information supplied by the Source Bridge in the Address Phase of the Type 1 configuration access.

Figure 13-9 on page 208 illustrates the information supplied by the Source Bridge in the Attribute Phase of a Type 1 configuration access.

A detailed explanation of the Type 1 configuration access can be found in "Type 1 Configuration Transactions" on page 447.

Chapter 13: The Address, Attribute and Response Phases

Figure 13-10: Type 1 Configuration Transaction Address Phase Format

Figure 13-10: Type 1 Configuration Transaction Address Phase Format

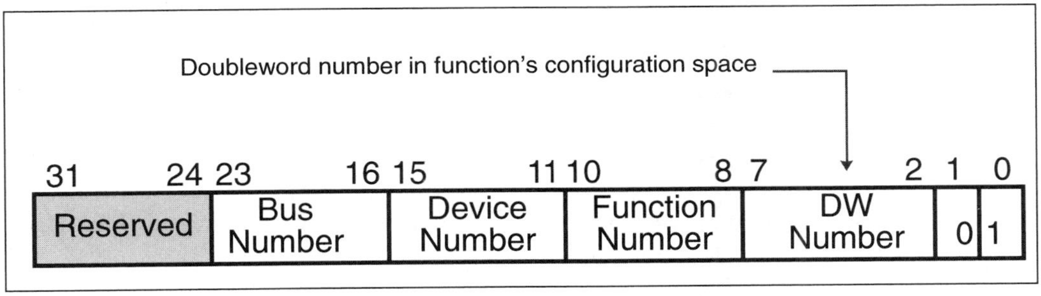

Split Completion Command Format

Figure 13-11 on page 210 illustrates the information supplied by the initiator in the Address Phase of the Split Completion transaction. The following information is supplied:

- **Requester ID**. The Completer addresses the Requester using the Requester ID and the Requester's transaction Tag supplied in the original request (for more information, refer to "Claiming a Split Completion Transaction" on page 180).
- Requester's transaction **Tag**. See previous bullet.
- Requester's **Lower Address field**. See "Disconnecting First Split Completion Is Problematic" on page 184.
- **Relaxed Ordering (RO) bit**. See "Relaxed Ordering Effect on Transaction Ordering" on page 569.
- **Split Completion command**.

Figure 13-12 on page 210 illustrates the information supplied by the initiator in the Attribute Phase of the Split Completion transaction. The following information is supplied:

- Completer ID.
- Byte Count.
- Byte Count Modified (BCM) bit.
- Split Completion Error (SCE) bit.
- Split Completion Message (SCM) bit.

For a description of each of these fields, refer to "The Attribute Phase" on page 178.

Figure 13-11: Split Completion Transaction Address Phase Format

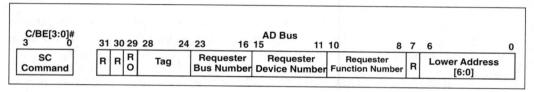

Figure 13-12: Split Completion Transaction Attribute Phase Format

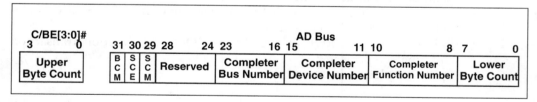

The Response Phase: Connecting With the Target

Unlike the Address, Attribute, and Data Phases, no information is transferred during the Response Phase. The initiator is awaiting the assertion of DEVSEL# by the target to indicate that a connection has been established. As in the PCI environment, the initiator will test the state of the DEVSEL# signal up to four times. If it is deasserted all four times, the initiator will Master Abort the transaction (refer to "Initiator Termination Due to Connection Timeout" on page 290 for a detailed description of the Master Abort termination).

Chapter 13: The Address, Attribute and Response Phases

Refer to Figure 13-13 on page 214 during the following discussion.

CLOCK 1. The transaction has not yet begun.

CLOCK 2.

DURING clock cycle two:

- Clock two is the Address Phase. The initiator drives out the address and command and asserts FRAME#.

CLOCK 3.

ON the rising-edge of clock three:

- This is the end of the Address Phase. All of the targets on the bus clock the address, command, and the state of the FRAME# signal into their respective input registers.

DURING clock cycle three:

- Within each target the registered address and command are submitted to each function's decoders (i.e., its Base Address Registers, or BARs). If the target function has a fast decoder and it is the target addressed by the transaction, it asserts its internal version of DEVSEL# before the rising-edge of clock four. If it is not being addressed or its decoder is a little slow, its internal version of DEVSEL# will be not be asserted.

CLOCK 4.

ON the rising-edge of clock four:

- If the currently addressed target has a fast decoder, it clocks an asserted level (low) onto the external DEVSEL# signal on the rising-edge of clock four. Assertion of DEVSEL# during this clock cycle is referred to as Decode Speed A.

CLOCK 5.

ON the rising-edge of clock five:

- The initiator and the ISA bridge (if one is present) clock the state of the DEVSEL# signal into their respective input registers for the first time on the rising-edge of clock five.

DURING clock cycle five:

- The initiator checks the state of its registered copy of DEVSEL#. If asserted, a connection has been established with the target and the initiator will not check the state of DEVSEL# again. In this case, the Response Phase is only one clock in duration. This defines the rising-edge of clock six as the first point at which the initiator will register the state of the target's TRDY# signal to see if it's ready to start the transmission of the first data block. If DEVSEL# is not asserted, the initiator will register the state of DEVSEL# again on the rising-edge of clock six.
- The ISA bridge checks the state of its registered copy of DEVSEL#. If it sees it asserted, it ignores the rest of the transaction (because it's obviously for a PCI-X target). If DEVSEL# is not asserted, the ISA bridge will register the state of DEVSEL# again on the rising-edge of clock six.

- Assertion of DEVSEL# during this clock cycle is referred to as Decode Speed B.

CLOCK 6.

ON the rising-edge of clock six:

- The initiator and the ISA bridge (if one is present) clock the state of the DEVSEL# signal into their respective input registers for the second time on the rising-edge of clock six.

DURING clock cycle six:

- The initiator checks the state of its registered copy of DEVSEL#. If asserted, a connection has been established with the target and the initiator will not check the state of DEVSEL# again. In this case, the Response Phase is two clocks in duration. This defines the rising-edge of clock seven as the first point at which the initiator will register the state of the target's TRDY# signal to see if it's ready to start the transmission of the first data block. If DEVSEL# is not asserted, the initiator will register the state of DEVSEL# for the final time on the rising-edge of clock seven.
- The ISA bridge is also checking the state of its registered copy of DEVSEL#. If it sees it asserted, it ignores the rest of the transaction (because it's obviously for a PCI-X target). If DEVSEL# is not asserted, the ISA bridge will register the state of DEVSEL# for the final time on the rising-edge of clock seven.
- Assertion of DEVSEL# during this clock cycle is referred to as Decode Speed C.

CLOCK 7.

ON the rising-edge of clock seven:

- The initiator and the ISA bridge (if one is present) clock the state of the DEVSEL# signal into their respective input registers.

DURING clock cycle seven:

- The initiator checks the state of its registered copy of DEVSEL#. If asserted, a connection has been established with the target and the initiator will not check the state of DEVSEL# again. In this case, the Response Phase is three clocks in duration. This defines the rising-edge of clock eight as the first point at which the initiator will register the state of the target's TRDY# signal to see if it's ready to start the transmission of the first data block. If DEVSEL# is not asserted, the initiator will register the state of DEVSEL# for the final time on the rising-edge of clock nine.
- The ISA bridge is also checking the state of its registered copy of DEVSEL# (for the final time). If it sees it asserted, it ignores the rest of the transaction (because it's obviously for a PCI-X target). If DEVSEL# is not asserted, and if the memory or IO address is one which could be

for an ISA device, the ISA bridge will assert DEVSEL# on the rising-edge of clock eight. If the address is not one that could be for an ISA device, the ISA bridge will not claim the transaction and the transaction will end in a Master Abort.

CLOCK 8.

ON the rising-edge of clock eight:

- If the ISA bridge is claiming the transaction, it asserts DEVSEL#.

CLOCK 9.

ON the rising-edge of clock nine:

- The initiator clocks the state of the DEVSEL# signal into its input register for the final time on the rising-edge of clock nine.

DURING clock cycle nine:

- The initiator checks the state of its registered copy of DEVSEL#. If asserted, a connection has been established with the target. In this case, the Response Phase is six clocks in duration. This defines the rising-edge of clock ten as the first point at which the initiator will register the state of the target's TRDY# signal to see if it's ready to start the transmission of the first data block. If DEVSEL# is not asserted, the initiator will timeout and experience a Master Abort. In that case, the initiator will return the bus to the Idle state starting on the rising-edge of clock ten.

CLOCK 10.

ON the rising-edge of clock 10:

- The initiator clocks a deasserted level onto FRAME# and IRDY# to return the bus to the Idle state.

If transaction is not a Split Completion or a Special Cycle transaction, the initiator also sets the Received Master Abort bit in its configuration Status register and generates an interrupt. This invokes its driver, which checks its status to see what happened.

If the transaction is a Split Completion, the initiator discards the completion data. For more information, refer to "Completer Handling of Master Abort on a Split Completion" on page 610.

Figure 13-13: DEVSEL# Sampling

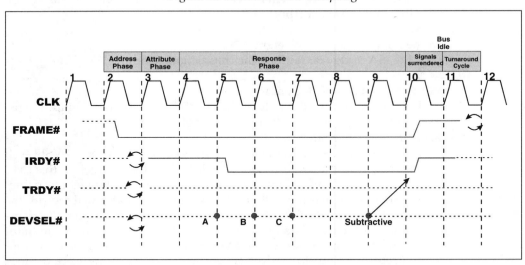

14 *Dword Transactions*

The Previous Chapter

The previous chapter provided a detailed description of the Address, Attribute, and Response Phases of memory burst transactions, Dword transactions, Configuration transactions, and Split Completion transactions.

This Chapter

This chapter provides detailed examples of the Dword transaction types:

- IO Read and Write transactions.
- The Memory Read Dword transaction.
- The Interrupt Acknowledge transaction.
- The Special Cycle transaction.

Although the Configuration Read and Write transactions are Dword transactions, a detailed discussion of them is deferred until Chapter 20, entitled "Configuration Transactions," on page 425.

The Next Chapter

The next chapter provides detailed examples of the Burst transaction types:

- Memory Read Block.
- Memory Write Block.
- Memory Write.
- Split Completion.Alias To Memory Read and Write Block commands.

General

All timing diagrams in this chapter assume that the initiator already arbitrated for and has now achieved bus ownership (i.e., its GNT# is asserted and it detects bus Idle [FRAME# and IRDY# both high]).

General Format of Timing Diagram Descriptions

The sections that follow provide a detailed description of various transaction scenarios. Each transaction is described clock-by-clock, with the events during each clock divided into two categories:

- **ON** the rising-edge of clock n.
- **DURING** clock n.

Please keep in mind that some events could actually be correctly placed in either of these event categories.

IO Read and Memory Read Dword

Background on the IO Read command may be found in "IO Read and Write Commands" on page 149. Background on the Memory Read Dword command may be found in "Memory Read Dword Command" on page 152.

Figure 14-1 on page 220 and Figure 14-2 on page 224 are two examples of either Memory Read Dword or IO Read transactions. The two sections that follow provide a detailed description of each transaction example.

Example One

CLOCK 1. The transaction has not yet begun. The initiator detected its GNT# asserted (not shown) on the rising-edge of clock one, informing it that it will be the next bus owner. The initiator has been tracking bus activity, so it also knows that the bus will be Idle on the rising-edge of clock two (for more information, refer to Chapter 10, entitled "Bus Arbitration," on page 129).

CLOCK 2.
ON the rising-edge of clock two:
- The initiator starts the IO Read or Memory Read Dword transaction by:
  - driving out the byte-specific IO or memory address onto AD[31:0].
  - driving out the IO Read or Memory Read Dword command onto C/BE#[3:0].
  - asserting FRAME#.

CLOCK 3.
ON the rising-edge of clock three:
- All targets on the bus clock the address, command, and the state of the FRAME# signal into their input registers.
- The initiator drives out the attributes (see Figure 13-7 on page 206) onto AD[31:0] and the Byte Enables onto C/BE#[3:0]. The Byte Enables identify the bytes to be read from the IO or memory dword.

DURING clock cycle three:
- All targets begin the decode of the registered copy of the address and command. In this example, the currently addressed target asserts its internal version of the DEVSEL# signal prior to the rising-edge of clock four.

CLOCK 4.
ON the rising-edge of clock four:
- The initiator backs its output drivers off of AD[31:0] (in preparation for the target's delivery of the data over the AD bus).
- The currently addressed target clocks an asserted level onto DEVSEL#. This is the Decode A time slot.

DURING clock four:
- The initiator places the Byte Enables in the Reserved and Driven High state for the remainder of the transaction.

CLOCK 5.
ON the rising-edge of clock five:
- The initiator asserts IRDY#, indicating that it has buffer space available to hold the requested data.
- The rising-edge of clock five is the first point at which the initiator clocks the state of DEVSEL# into its input register. In this case, it detects an asserted level on its registered copy of DEVSEL# during clock cycle five. This tells the initiator it has established a connection with the addressed target, and it defines the first point at which the initiator will register the read data and the state of TRDY# as the rising-edge of clock six.

- The earliest time slot in which the target can assert TRDY# is the clock immediately following its assertion of DEVSEL#. In this case, the target does not assert TRDY# on the rising-edge of clock five, thereby indicating that it is not yet supplying the requested read data on the AD bus.
- On any form of a read, it is a rule that the target must take ownership of the AD bus in the clock immediately following its assertion of DEVSEL#. In this case, the target is not yet ready to drive the requested read data onto the AD bus, so it drives a dummy data pattern to keep the bus from floating until it does have the data ready to deliver.

CLOCK 6.

ON the rising-edge of clock six:

- The initiator clocks the content of the AD bus and the state of the TRDY# signal into its input register on the rising-edge of clock 6. In this case, the deasserted state of its registered copy of TRDY# tells the initiator that the requested data was not yet present on the AD bus, so the initiator discards the registered data during clock cycle six.

DURING clock six:

- The deasserted state of its registered copy of TRDY# causes the initiator to insert a Wait State in clock cycle six.

CLOCK 7.

ON the rising-edge of clock seven:

- The initiator once again clocks the content of the AD bus and the state of the TRDY# signal into its input register. In this case, the deasserted state of its registered copy of TRDY# tells the initiator that the requested data was not yet present on the AD bus, so the initiator discards the registered data during clock cycle seven.

DURING clock seven:

- The deasserted state of its registered copy of TRDY# causes the initiator to insert a second Wait State in clock cycle seven.

CLOCK 8.

ON the rising-edge of clock eight:

- The initiator once again clocks the content of the AD bus and the state of the TRDY# signal into its input register on the rising-edge of clock eight. In this case, the asserted state of its registered copy of TRDY# tells the initiator that the requested data was present on the AD bus, so the initiator places the registered read data into its read buffer during clock cycle eight.

DURING clock eight:
- Knowing that the initiator read the data on the rising-edge of clock eight, the target:
  - Deasserts TRDY#. Since it's a sustained tri-state signal, the deassertion protocol is to drive it high for one clock cycle and then back off the output driver from the signal line.
  - Deasserts DEVSEL# (also a sustained tri-state signal line).
  - Backs off its output drivers from the AD bus.

CLOCK 9.

ON the rising-edge of clock nine:
- Because it received the requested read data on the rising-edge of clock eight, on the rising-edge of clock nine the initiator ends the transaction. It:
  - Deasserts FRAME#. Since it's a sustained tri-state signal, the deassertion protocol is to drive it high for one clock cycle and then back off the output driver from the signal line.
  - Deasserts IRDY# (also a sustained tri-state signal line).
  - Regarding the Byte Enables, in clock cycle nine it may continue to drive them high, drive some other pattern, or back off its output drivers.

CLOCK 10.

ON the rising-edge of clock 10:
- The bus returns to the Idle state (FRAME# and IRDY# both high).

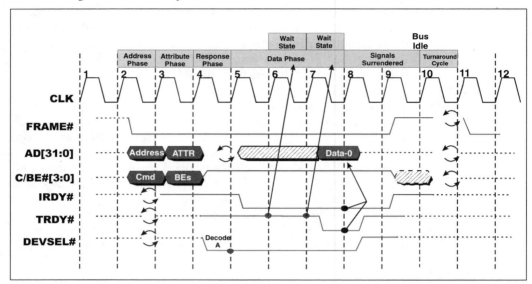

Figure 14-1: Memory Read Dword or IO Read, Decode A, Two Wait States

Example Two

CLOCK 1. The transaction has not yet begun. The initiator detected its GNT# asserted (not shown) on the rising-edge of clock one, informing it that it will be the next bus owner. The initiator has been tracking bus activity, so it also knows that the bus will be Idle on the rising-edge of clock two (for more information, refer to Chapter 10, entitled "Bus Arbitration," on page 129).

CLOCK 2.

ON the rising-edge of clock two:
- The initiator starts the IO Read or Memory Read Dword transaction by:
  - driving out the byte-specific IO or memory address onto AD[31:0].
  - driving out the IO Read or Memory Read Dword command onto C/BE#[3:0].
  - asserting FRAME#.

CLOCK 3.

ON the rising-edge of clock three:
- All targets on the bus clock the address, command, and the state of the FRAME# signal into their input registers.

- The initiator drives out the attributes (see Figure 13-7 on page 206) onto AD[31:0] and the Byte Enables onto C/BE#[3:0]. The Byte Enables identify the bytes to be read from the IO or memory dword.

DURING clock cycle three:

- All targets begin the decode of the registered copy of the address and command. In this example, the currently addressed target asserts its internal version of the DEVSEL# signal prior to the rising-edge of clock four.

CLOCK 4.

ON the rising-edge of clock four:

- The currently addressed target clocks an asserted level onto DEVSEL#. This is the Decode A time slot.

DURING clock four:

- The initiator backs its output drivers off of AD[31:0] (in preparation for the target's delivery of the data over the AD bus).
- The initiator places the Byte Enables in the Reserved and Driven High state for the remainder of the transaction.

CLOCK 5.

ON the rising-edge of clock five:

- The initiator asserts IRDY#, indicating that it has buffer space available to hold the requested data.
- The rising-edge of clock five is the first point at which the initiator clocks the state of DEVSEL# into its input register. In this case, it detects a deasserted level on its registered copy of DEVSEL# during clock cycle five. This tells the initiator that it has not yet established a connection with the addressed target.

CLOCK 6.

ON the rising-edge of clock six:

- The rising-edge of clock six is the second point at which the initiator clocks the state of DEVSEL# into its input register. In this case, it still does not detect an asserted level on its registered copy of DEVSEL# during clock cycle six. This tells the initiator that it still not established a connection with the addressed target.

CLOCK 7.

ON the rising-edge of clock seven:

- The rising-edge of clock seven is the third point at which the initiator clocks the state of DEVSEL# into its input register. In this case, it detects an asserted level on its registered copy of DEVSEL# during clock cycle seven. This tells the initiator that it has established a connection with the addressed target, and it defines the first point at which the initiator will register the read data and the state of TRDY# as the rising-edge of clock eight.

- The earliest time slot in which the target can assert TRDY# is the clock immediately following its assertion of DEVSEL#. In this case, the target does not assert TRDY# on the rising-edge of clock seven, thereby indicating that it is not yet supplying the requested read data on the AD bus.

DURING clock seven:

- On any form of a read, it is a rule that the target must take ownership of the AD bus in the clock immediately following its assertion of DEVSEL#. In this case, the target is not yet ready to drive the requested read data onto the AD bus, so it drives a dummy data pattern to keep the bus from floating until it does have the data ready to deliver.
- It should be noted that when a target uses a decode speed other than A, it optionally can take ownership of the AD bus in the same clock wherein it asserts DEVSEL# (clock six in the figure).

CLOCK 8.

ON the rising-edge of clock eight:

- The initiator clocks the content of the AD bus and the state of the TRDY# signal into its input register. In this case, the deasserted state of its registered copy of TRDY# tells the initiator that the requested data was not yet present on the AD bus, so the initiator discards the registered data during clock cycle eight.

DURING clock eight:

- The deasserted state of its registered copy of TRDY# causes the initiator to insert a Wait State in clock cycle eight.

CLOCK 9.

ON the rising-edge of clock nine:

- The initiator once again clocks the content of the AD bus and the state of the TRDY# signal into its input register. In this case, the deasserted state of its registered copy of TRDY# tells the initiator that the requested data was not yet present on the AD bus, so the initiator discards the registered data during clock cycle nine.

DURING clock nine:

- The deasserted state of its registered copy of TRDY# causes the initiator to insert a second Wait State in clock cycle nine.

CLOCK 10.

ON the rising-edge of clock 10:

- The initiator once again clocks the content of the AD bus and the state of the TRDY# signal into its input register. In this case, the asserted state of its registered copy of TRDY# tells the initiator that the requested data was present on the AD bus, so the initiator places the registered read data into its read buffer during clock cycle 10.

DURING clock 10:

- Knowing that the initiator read the data on the rising-edge of clock 10, the target:
  - Deasserts TRDY#. Since it's a sustained tri-state signal, the deassertion protocol is to drive it high for one clock cycle and then back off the output driver from the signal line.
  - Deasserts DEVSEL# (also a sustained tri-state signal line).
  - Backs off its output drivers from the AD bus.

CLOCK 11.

ON the rising-edge of clock 11:

- Because it received the requested read data on the rising-edge of clock 10, the initiator ends the transaction on the rising-edge of clock 11. It:
  - Deasserts FRAME#. Since it's a sustained tri-state signal, the deassertion protocol is to drive it high for one clock cycle and then back off the output driver from the signal line.
  - Deasserts IRDY# (another sustained tri-state signal line).
  - Regarding the Byte Enables, in clock cycle 11 it may continue to drive them high, drive some other pattern, or back off its output drivers.

CLOCK 12. The bus returns to the Idle state (FRAME# and IRDY# both high) on the rising-edge of clock 12.

Figure 14-2: Memory Read Dword or IO Read, Decode C, Two Wait States

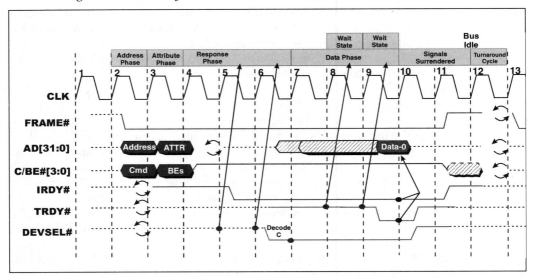

IO Write

Background on the IO Write command may be found in "IO Read and Write Commands" on page 149.

Example One

CLOCK 1. The transaction has not yet begun. The initiator detected its GNT# asserted (not shown) on the rising-edge of clock one, informing it that it will be the next bus owner. The initiator has been tracking bus activity, so it also knows that the bus will be Idle on the rising-edge of clock two (for more information, refer to Chapter 10, entitled "Bus Arbitration," on page 129).

CLOCK 2.

ON the rising-edge of clock two:

- The initiator starts the IO Write transaction on the rising-edge of clock two by:
  - driving out the byte-specific IO address onto AD[31:0].
  - driving out the IO Write command onto C/BE#[3:0].
  - asserting FRAME#.

CLOCK 3.

ON the rising-edge of clock three:

- All targets on the bus clock the address, command, and the state of the FRAME# signal into their input registers.
- The initiator drives out the attributes (see Figure 13-7 on page 206) onto AD[31:0] and the Byte Enables onto C/BE#[3:0]. The Byte Enables identify the bytes to be written to the IO dword.

DURING clock cycle three:

- All targets begin the decode of the registered copy of the address and command. In this example, the currently addressed target asserts its internal version of the DEVSEL# signal prior to the rising-edge of clock four.

CLOCK 4.

ON the rising-edge of clock four:

- The currently addressed target clocks an asserted level onto DEVSEL#. This is the Decode A time slot.

DURING clock four:

- The initiator has the option of doing one of the following:
  - It can back its output drivers off of AD[31:0].
  - It can drive the attributes for an extra clock cycle before supplying the write data.
  - It can start driving the write data a clock early.
  - It can drive a dummy stable pattern.
- The initiator places the Byte Enables in the Reserved and Driven High state for the remainder of the transaction.

CLOCK 5.

ON the rising-edge of clock five:

- The initiator asserts IRDY#, indicating that it is driving the write data onto the AD bus.
- The rising-edge of clock five is the first point at which the initiator clocks the state of DEVSEL# into its input register. In this case, it detects an asserted level on its registered copy of DEVSEL# during clock cycle five. This tells the initiator that it has established a connection with the addressed target, and it defines the first point at which the initiator will register the state of TRDY# as the rising-edge of clock six.
- The earliest time slot in which the target can assert TRDY# is the clock immediately following its assertion of DEVSEL#. In this case, the target does assert TRDY# on the rising-edge of clock five, thereby indicating that it will register the write data from the AD bus on the rising-edge of clock six.

CLOCK 6.

ON the rising-edge of clock six:

- The target clocks the write data on the AD bus into its input register. It does not need to check the state of IRDY# to validate the presence of the data because it's a rule that the initiator must assert IRDY# and start driving the write data in clock five.
- The initiator clocks the state of the TRDY# signal into its input register on the rising-edge of clock six and examines its registered copy of TRDY# during clock six. In this case, it detects that it's asserted, indicating that the target accepted the write data on the rising-edge of clock six. The initiator can therefore surrender the bus during clock seven.

DURING clock six:

- The initiator continues to drive the write data until it has verified acceptance by the target.
- The target deasserts TRDY#. Since it's a sustained tri-state signal, the deassertion protocol is to drive it high for one clock cycle and then back off the output driver from the signal line.
- The target deasserts DEVSEL# (also a sustained tri-state signal line).

CLOCK 7.

ON the rising-edge of clock seven:

- Because the target accepted the write data on the rising-edge of clock six, on the rising-edge of clock seven the initiator ends the transaction. It:
    - Deasserts FRAME#. Since it's a sustained tri-state signal, the deassertion protocol is to drive it high for one clock cycle and then back off the output driver from the signal line.
    - Deasserts IRDY# (also a sustained tri-state signal line).

DURING clock seven:

- Regarding the Byte Enables, in clock cycle seven the initiator may continue to drive them high, drive some other pattern, or back off its output drivers.
- Regarding the AD bus, the initiator can continue to drive the write data during clock seven, may drive a dummy data pattern, or may back its output drivers off of the AD bus.

CLOCK 8.

ON the rising-edge of clock eight:

- The bus returns to the Idle state (FRAME# and IRDY# both high) on the rising-edge of clock eight.
- If the initiator has not yet backed its output drivers off the AD bus and the Byte Enables, it does so on the rising-edge of clock eight.

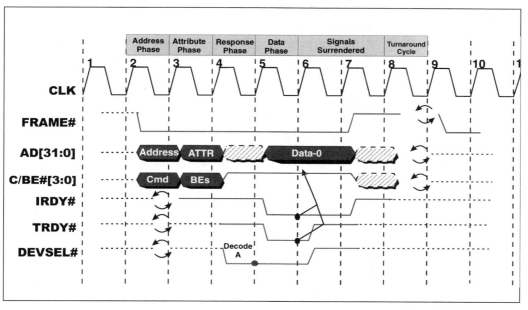

Figure 14-3: IO Write, Decode A, No Wait States

Example Two

CLOCK 1. The transaction has not yet begun. The initiator detected its GNT# asserted (not shown) on the rising-edge of clock one, informing it that it will be the next bus owner. The initiator has been tracking bus activity, so it also knows that the bus will be Idle on the rising-edge of clock two (for more information, refer to Chapter 10, entitled "Bus Arbitration," on page 129).

CLOCK 2.

ON the rising-edge of clock two:

- The initiator starts the IO Write transaction by:
    - driving out the byte-specific IO address onto AD[31:0].
    - driving out the IO Write command onto C/BE#[3:0].
    - asserting FRAME#.

CLOCK 3.

ON the rising-edge of clock three:

- All targets on the bus clock the address, command, and the state of the FRAME# signal into their input registers.

- The initiator drives out the attributes (see Figure 13-7 on page 206) onto AD[31:0] and the Byte Enables onto C/BE#[3:0]. The Byte Enables identify the bytes to be written to the IO dword.

DURING clock cycle three:

- All targets begin the decode of the registered copy of the address and command. In this example, the currently addressed target asserts its internal version of the DEVSEL# signal prior to the rising-edge of clock four.

CLOCK 4.

ON the rising-edge of clock four:

- The currently addressed target clocks an asserted level onto DEVSEL#. This is the Decode A time slot.

DURING clock cycle four:

- The initiator has the option of doing one of the following:
  - It can back its output drivers off of AD[31:0].
  - It can drive the attributes for an extra clock cycle before supplying the write data.
  - It can start driving the write data a clock early.
  - It can drive a dummy stable pattern.
- The initiator places the Byte Enables in the Reserved and Driven High state for the remainder of the transaction.

CLOCK 5.

ON the rising-edge of clock five:

- The initiator asserts IRDY#, indicating that it is driving the write data onto the AD bus.
- The rising-edge of clock five is the first point at which the initiator clocks the state of DEVSEL# into its input register. In this case, it detects an asserted level on its registered copy of DEVSEL# during clock cycle five. This tells the initiator that it has established a connection with the addressed target, and it defines the first point at which the initiator will register the state of TRDY# as the rising-edge of clock six.
- The earliest time slot in which the target can assert TRDY# is the clock immediately following its assertion of DEVSEL#. In this case, the target does not assert TRDY# on the rising-edge of clock five, thereby indicating that it will not register the write data from the AD bus on the rising-edge of clock six.

CLOCK 6.

ON the rising-edge of clock six:

- The target once again does not assert TRDY#, thereby indicating that it will not register the write data from the AD bus on the rising-edge of clock seven.

DURING clock cycle six:

- The initiator continues to drive the write data because it has not yet been accepted.

CLOCK 7.

ON the rising-edge of clock seven:

- The target finally asserts TRDY#, thereby indicating that it will register the write data from the AD bus on the rising-edge of clock eight.

DURING clock cycle seven:

- The initiator continues to drive the write data because it has not yet been accepted.

CLOCK 8.

ON the rising-edge of clock eight:

- The target clocks the write data on the AD bus into its input register. It does not need to check the state of IRDY# to validate the presence of the data because it's a rule that the initiator must assert IRDY# and start driving the write data in clock five.
- The initiator clocks the state of the TRDY# signal into its input register and examines its registered copy of TRDY# during clock eight. In this case, it detects that it's asserted, indicating that the target accepted the write data on the rising-edge of clock eight. The initiator can therefore surrender the bus during clock nine.

DURING clock cycle eight:

- The target deasserts TRDY#. Since it's a sustained tri-state signal, the deassertion protocol is to drive it high for one clock cycle and then back off the output driver from the signal line.
- The target deasserts DEVSEL# (also a sustained tri-state signal line).

CLOCK 9.

ON the rising-edge of clock nine:

- Because the target accepted the write data on the rising-edge of clock eight, the initiator ends the transaction on the rising-edge of clock nine. It:
  - Deasserts FRAME#. Since it's a sustained tri-state signal, the deassertion protocol is to drive it high for one clock cycle and then back off the output driver from the signal line.
  - Deasserts IRDY# (also a sustained tri-state signal line).

DURING clock cycle nine:

- Regarding the Byte Enables, in clock cycle nine the initiator may continue to drive them high, drive some other pattern, or back off its output drivers.
- Regarding the AD bus, the initiator can continue to drive the write data during clock nine, may drive a dummy data pattern, or may back its output drivers off of the AD bus.

CLOCK 10.

ON the rising-edge of clock 10:

- The bus returns to the Idle state (FRAME# and IRDY# both high) on the rising-edge of clock 10.
- If the initiator has not yet backed its output drivers off the AD bus and the Byte Enables, it does so on the rising-edge of clock 10.

Figure 14-4: IO Write, Decode A, Two Wait States

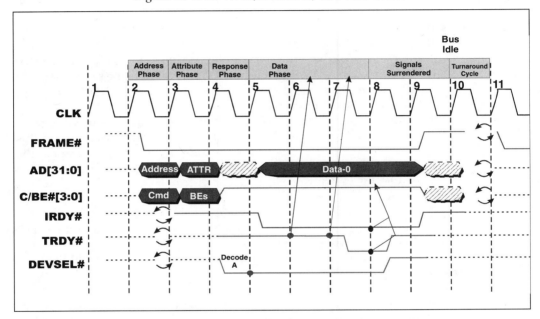

Example Three

CLOCK 1. The transaction has not yet begun. The initiator detected its GNT# asserted (not shown) on the rising-edge of clock one, informing it that it will be the next bus owner. The initiator has been tracking bus activity, so it also knows that the bus will be Idle on the rising-edge of clock two (for more information, refer to Chapter 10, entitled "Bus Arbitration," on page 129).

CLOCK 2.

ON the rising-edge of clock two:

- The initiator starts the IO Write transaction by:
  - driving out the byte-specific IO address onto AD[31:0].
  - driving out the IO Write command onto C/BE#[3:0].
  - asserting FRAME#.

CLOCK 3.

ON the rising-edge of clock three:

- All targets on the bus clock the address, command, and the state of the FRAME# signal into their input registers.
- The initiator drives out the attributes (see Figure 13-7 on page 206) onto AD[31:0] and the Byte Enables onto C/BE#[3:0]. The Byte Enables identify the bytes to be written to the IO dword.

DURING clock cycle three:

- All targets begin the decode of the registered copy of the address and command. In this example, the currently addressed target asserts its internal version of the DEVSEL# signal prior to the rising-edge of clock four.

CLOCK 4.

ON the rising-edge of clock four:

- The currently addressed target clocks an asserted level onto DEVSEL#. This is the Decode A time slot.

DURING clock cycle four:

- The initiator has the option of doing one of the following:
  - It can back its output drivers off of AD[31:0].
  - It can drive the attributes for an extra clock cycle before supplying the write data.
  - It can start driving the write data a clock early.
  - It can drive a dummy stable pattern.
- The initiator places the Byte Enables in the Reserved and Driven High state for the remainder of the transaction.

CLOCK 5.

ON the rising-edge of clock five:

- The initiator asserts IRDY#, indicating that it is driving the write data onto the AD bus.
- The rising-edge of clock five is the first point at which the initiator clocks the state of DEVSEL# into its input register. In this case, it detects a deasserted level on its registered copy of DEVSEL# during clock cycle five. This tells the initiator that it has not yet established a connection with the addressed target.

CLOCK 6.

ON the rising-edge of clock six:

- The rising-edge of clock six is the second point at which the initiator clocks the state of DEVSEL# into its input register. In this case, it once again detects a deasserted level on its registered copy of DEVSEL# during clock cycle six. This tells the initiator that it has not yet established a connection with the addressed target.

DURING clock cycle six:

- The initiator continues to drive the write data until it is accepted by the target.

CLOCK 7.

ON the rising-edge of clock seven:

- The rising-edge of clock seven is the third point at which the initiator clocks the state of DEVSEL# into its input register. In this case, it detects an asserted level on its registered copy of DEVSEL# during clock cycle seven. This tells the initiator that it has established a connection with the addressed target, and it establishes the rising-edge of clock eight as the first time the initiator will register the state of TRDY# to see if the target has accepted the write data.

DURING clock cycle seven:

- The initiator continues to drive the write data until it is accepted by the target.

CLOCK 8.

ON the rising-edge of clock eight:

- The target once again does not assert TRDY#, thereby indicating that it will not register the write data from the AD bus on the rising-edge of clock nine.

DURING clock cycle eight:

- The initiator continues to drive the write data because it has not yet been accepted.

CLOCK 9.

ON the rising-edge of clock nine:

- The target finally asserts TRDY# on the rising-edge of clock nine, thereby indicating that it will register the write data from the AD bus on the rising-edge of clock 10.

DURING clock cycle nine:

- The initiator continues to drive the write data because it has not yet been accepted.

Clock 10.

On the rising-edge of clock 10:

- The target clocks the write data on the AD bus into its input register on the rising-edge of clock 10. It does not need to check the state of IRDY# to validate the presence of the data because it's a rule that the initiator must assert IRDY# and start driving the write data in clock five.
- The target deasserts TRDY#. Since it's a sustained tri-state signal, the deassertion protocol is to drive it high for one clock cycle and then back off the output driver from the signal line.
- The target deasserts DEVSEL# (also a sustained tri-state signal line).
- The initiator clocks the state of the TRDY# signal into its input register on the rising-edge of clock 10 and examines its registered copy of TRDY# during clock 10. In this case, it detects that it's asserted, indicating that the target accepted the write data on the rising-edge of clock 10. The initiator can therefore surrender the bus during clock 11.

Clock 11.

On the rising-edge of clock 11:

- Because the target accepted the write data on the rising-edge of clock 10, on the rising-edge of clock 11 the initiator ends the transaction. It:
  - Deasserts FRAME#. Since it's a sustained tri-state signal, the deassertion protocol is to drive it high for one clock cycle and then back off the output driver from the signal line.
  - Deasserts IRDY# (also a sustained tri-state signal line).

During clock cycle 11:

- Regarding the Byte Enables, in clock cycle 11 the initiator may continue to drive them high, drive some other pattern, or back off its output drivers.
- Regarding the AD bus, the initiator can continue to drive the write data during clock 11, may drive a dummy data pattern, or may back its output drivers off of the AD bus.

Clock 12.

On the rising-edge of clock 12:

- The bus returns to the Idle state (FRAME# and IRDY# both high).
- If the initiator has not yet backed its output drivers off the AD bus and the Byte Enables, it does so on the rising-edge of clock 12.

Figure 14-5: IO Write, Decode C, Two Wait States

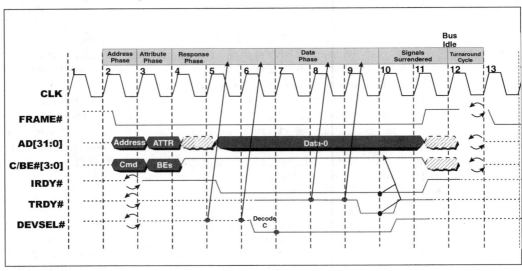

Configuration Read and Write Transactions

A complete description of the PCI-X Configuration Read and Write transactions can be found in Chapter 20, entitled "Configuration Transactions," on page 425.

Interrupt Acknowledge Command

Background on the Interrupt Acknowledge command can be found in "Interrupt Acknowledge Command" on page 154. Figure 14-6 on page 235 is an example Interrupt Acknowledge transaction. Essentially, it is a read performed by the Host/PCIX bridge to obtain the interrupt vector from the interrupt controller. The vector is then passed back to the processor. Assuming it is an x86 processor, C/BE#[0] is asserted in the Attribute Phase to indicate that the Host/PCIX bridge is requesting the one-byte vector to be delivered on Data Path 0 (AD[7:0]) in the Data Phase.

Other than the following differences, this transaction is identical to the IO Read or Memory Read dword example described in Figure 14-1 on page 220:

- The address driven in the Address Phase is just a stable pattern to ensure good Address Phase parity.
- The command issued on C/BE#[3:0] in the Address Phase is the Interrupt Acknowledge command.

Figure 14-6: Interrupt Acknowledge, Decode A, Two Wait States

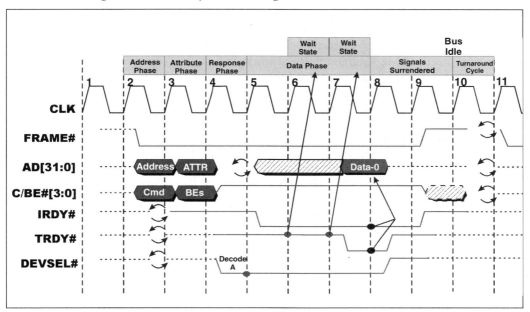

Special Cycle Command

Background on the Special Cycle command may be found in "Special Cycle Command" on page 159. Refer to Figure 14-7 on page 238.

CLOCK 1. The transaction has not yet begun. The initiator detected its GNT# asserted (not shown) on the rising-edge of clock one, informing it that it will be the next bus owner. The initiator has been tracking bus activity, so it also knows that the bus will be Idle on the rising-edge of clock two (for more information, refer to Chapter 10, entitled "Bus Arbitration," on page 129).

CLOCK 2.

ON the rising-edge of clock two:

- The initiator starts the Special Cycle transaction by:
  - driving a stable pattern onto AD[31:0] to ensure good Address Phase parity.
  - driving out the Special Cycle command onto C/BE#[3:0].
  - asserting FRAME#.

CLOCK 3.

ON the rising-edge of clock three:

- All targets on the bus clock the address, command, and the state of the FRAME# signal into their input registers.
- The initiator drives out the attributes (see Figure 13-7 on page 206 and "Special Cycle and Interrupt Acknowledge Format" on page 206) onto AD[31:0] and the Byte Enables onto C/BE#[3:0]. The Byte Enables identify the data lanes that contain the message.

DURING clock cycle three:

- All targets begin the decode of the registered copy of the address and command. Since this is a Special Cycle transaction, no target will respond to the transaction (i.e., it is illegal for any device to assert DEVSEL#).
- Targets that are not designed to recognize any form of message delivered via the Special Cycle transaction will ignore the remainder of the transaction.
- The initiator does not sample DEVSEL# at all in this transaction.

CLOCK 4.

DURING clock cycle four:

- The initiator has the option of doing one of the following:
  - It can back its output drivers off of AD[31:0].
  - It can drive the attributes for an extra clock cycle before supplying the message data.
  - It can start driving the message data a clock early.
  - It can drive a dummy stable pattern.
- The initiator places the Byte Enables in the Reserved and Driven High state for the remainder of the transaction.

CLOCK 5. The initiator asserts IRDY# on the rising-edge of clock five, indicating that it is driving the message data onto the AD bus.

CLOCK 6. Any targets designed to recognize one or more message types will register the message data on the rising-edge of clock six.

CLOCKS 7 THROUGH 9. The initiator keeps driving the message data and also keeps FRAME# and IRDY# asserted for four additional clocks. The asserted state of FRAME# and IRDY# keeps the bus from returning to the Idle state until the rising-edge of clock 11. This gives any targets that are processing the message four clocks of guaranteed processing time to interpret and handle the message without having to worry about a new transaction beginning that may target one of them.

CLOCK 10.

ON the rising-edge of clock 10:

- The initiator ends the transaction. It:
    - Deasserts FRAME#. Since it's a sustained tri-state signal, the deassertion protocol is to drive it high for one clock cycle and then back off the output driver from the signal line.
    - Deasserts IRDY# (also a sustained tri-state signal line).

DURING clock cycle 10:

- Regarding the Byte Enables, in clock cycle 10 the initiator may continue to drive them high, drive some other pattern, or back off its output drivers.
- Regarding the AD bus, the initiator can continue to drive the message data during clock 10, may drive a dummy data pattern, or may back its output drivers off the AD bus.

CLOCK 11.

ON the rising-edge of clock 11:

- The bus returns to the Idle state (FRAME# and IRDY# both high).
- If the initiator has not yet backed its output drivers off the AD bus and the Byte Enables, it does so on the rising-edge of clock 11.

Figure 14-7: Special Cycle Transaction

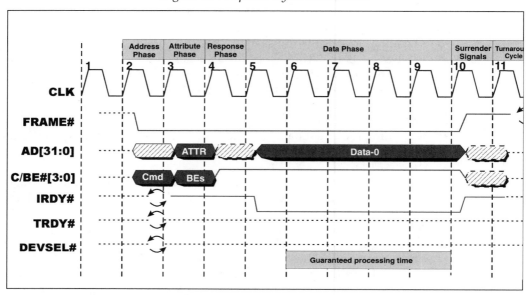

15 *Burst Transactions*

The Previous Chapter

The previous chapter provided detailed examples of the Dword transaction types:

- IO Read and Write transactions.
- The Memory Read Dword transaction.
- The Interrupt Acknowledge transaction.
- The Special Cycle transaction.

Although the Configuration Read and Write transactions are Dword transactions, a detailed discussion of them is deferred until Chapter 20, entitled "Configuration Transactions," on page 425.

This Chapter

This chapter provides detailed examples of the Burst transaction types:

- Memory Read Block.
- Memory Write Block.
- Memory Write.
- Split Completion.
- Alias To Memory Read and Write Block commands.

The Next Chapter

The next chapter provides a detailed description of both initiator and target terminations of a transaction. It includes clock-by-clock descriptions of example timing diagrams.

Introduction

With the exception of the final timing diagram in this chapter (Figure 15-23 on page 276), all of the examples consist of four Data Phases and represent one of the two possible scenarios defined in the next two sections. In both of these cases, the end of the transaction is identical and appears as illustrated in each timing diagram in this chapter. For example, refer to Figure 15-5 on page 249:

- In clock eight, the initiator deasserts FRAME to inform the target that the next-to-last data item (dword or qword) is being transferred in this clock.
- In clock nine, the last data item is transferred.
- The initiator and target surrender the bus in clock 10.

Short Transfer Within a Block

An initiator issues a memory start byte address and a byte transfer count wherein all of the data to be transferred falls within one block. As each data item is transferred, the initiator and target decrement the specified byte transfer count and recognize the approaching transaction end.

Long Transfer, But Disconnect on First Block Boundary

Consider the following set of assumptions:

- An initiator issues a memory start byte address that is four (or more) Data Phases from a block boundary.
- The byte transfer count identifies an end byte address somewhere beyond the imminent block boundary.
- However, the initiator issues a Disconnect At Next ADB to the target as it approaches the imminent block boundary to force a disconnect before all of the data has been transferred.

General Format of Timing Diagram Descriptions

The sections that follow provide a detailed description of various transaction scenarios. Each transaction is described clock-by-clock, with the events during each clock divided into two categories:

- **On** the rising-edge of clock N.
- **During** clock N.

Please keep in mind that some events could actually be correctly placed in either of these event categories.

Memory Read Block Transaction

The Memory Read Block transaction is an all-inclusive read starting at the byte-specific memory start address through the end byte address as defined by the byte transfer count. Additional detail about the Memory Read Block transaction can be found in "Memory Burst Format" on page 200 and in "Memory Read Block Command" on page 167.

Memory Read Block: Detailed Example

Refer to Figure 15-5 on page 249.

Clock 1. The transaction has not yet begun. The initiator detected its GNT# asserted (not shown) on the rising-edge of clock one, informing it that it will be the next bus owner. The initiator has been tracking bus activity, so it also knows that the bus will be Idle on the rising-edge of clock two (for more information, refer to Chapter 10, entitled "Bus Arbitration," on page 129).

Clock 2.
On the rising-edge of clock two:
- The initiator starts the Memory Read Block transaction by:
  - driving out the byte-specific memory start address onto AD[31:0]. In this example, the start byte address could be any address within the first block.
  - driving out the Memory Read Block command onto C/BE#[3:0].
  - asserting FRAME#.

Clock 3.
On the rising-edge of clock three:
- All targets on the bus clock the address, command, and the state of the FRAME# signal into their input registers.
- The initiator drives out the attributes (see Figure 13-4 on page 201) onto AD[31:0] and C/BE#[3:0]. Among other things, the attributes contain the byte transfer count. In this example, there are two possibilities:
  - The start byte address issued in the Address Phase could be any byte within the first block and the byte transfer count encompasses four Data Phases but does not cross the next block boundary.

- The start byte address issued in the Address Phase is one of the locations in the fourth dword from the end of the block and the byte transfer count identifies an end address that is beyond the imminent block boundary.

DURING clock cycle three:

- All targets begin the decode of the registered copy of the address and command. In this example, the currently addressed target asserts its internal version of the DEVSEL# signal prior to the rising-edge of clock four.

CLOCK 4.

ON the rising-edge of clock four:

- The currently addressed target clocks an asserted level onto DEVSEL#. This is the Decode A time slot.

DURING clock cycle four:

- The initiator backs its output drivers off AD[31:0] (in preparation for the target's delivery of the data over the AD bus).
- The initiator places the Byte Enables in the Reserved and Driven High state for the remainder of the transaction.

CLOCK 5.

ON the rising-edge of clock five:

- The initiator asserts IRDY#, indicating that it has buffer space available to hold at least the first block (or a subset thereof) of the requested data.
- The rising-edge of clock five is the first point at which the initiator clocks the state of DEVSEL# into its input register. In this case, it detects an asserted level on its registered copy of DEVSEL# during clock cycle five. This tells the initiator that it has established a connection with the addressed target. This defines the first point at which the initiator will register the state of TRDY# and the content of the AD bus as the rising-edge of clock six.
- The target drives the first read data item and asserts TRDY#.

CLOCK 6.

ON the rising-edge of clock six:

- The initiator clocks the first read data item and the state of TRDY# into its input register.
- The target drives out the second data item.

DURING clock cycle six:

- The initiator determines that its internal copy of the TRDY# signal is asserted, indicating that good data was registered on the rising-edge of clock six. The initiator places this data item into its read buffer.

- Internally, both the initiator and the target adjust the byte count remaining and increment their current address pointers to point to the start address of the next dword.

CLOCK 7.

ON the rising-edge of clock seven:

- The initiator clocks the second read data item and the state of TRDY# into its input register.
- The target drives out the third data item.
- The initiator deasserts FRAME# for one of two reasons:
  - This transaction of four (or more) Data Phases is a small transfer, wholly contained within a block (i.e., it does not cross a block boundary). In this clock, both parties realize (by checking the byte count remaining) that the next-to-last data item is being transferred.
  - The start byte address issued in the Address Phase was a location in the fourth dword from the upcoming block boundary. Although the transfer count specified in the Attribute Phase indicates that the transfer would cross at least the upcoming block boundary, in this example the initiator must force the target to Disconnect At Next ADB. As an example, the initiator of the Memory Read Block may be a PCIX-to-PCIX bridge and it may not have enough buffer space reserved to go beyond the upcoming block boundary. In this case, the initiator deasserts FRAME# to inform the target that it's disconnecting the transaction on the upcoming block boundary.

DURING clock cycle seven:

- The initiator determines that its internal copy of the TRDY# signal is asserted, indicating that good data was registered on the rising-edge of clock seven. The initiator places the second data item into its read buffer.
- Internally, both the initiator and the target adjust the byte count remaining.

CLOCK 8.

ON the rising-edge of clock eight:

- The initiator clocks the third read data item and the state of TRDY# into its input register.
- The target clocks the state of the FRAME# signal into its input register and determines that it has been deasserted by the initiator. This informs the target that the data item to be transferred on the rising-edge of clock nine is the final one to be transferred (even if it doesn't exhaust the transfer count).
- The target drives out the fourth data item. This is either the final data item of the current block, or it is the last data item to be transferred within the block (as defined by the byte transfer count).

DURING clock cycle eight:

- The initiator determines that its internal copy of the TRDY# signal is asserted, indicating that good data was registered on the rising-edge of clock eight. The initiator places the third data item into its read buffer.
- Internally, both the initiator and the target adjust the byte count remaining.

CLOCK 9.

ON the rising-edge of clock nine:

- The initiator clocks the fourth and final read data item and the state of TRDY# into its input register.
- Both parties release the bus. The initiator deasserts IRDY# and ceases to drive the Byte Enables, and the target deasserts TRDY# and DEVSEL# and ceases to drive the final data item.

DURING clock cycle nine:

- The initiator determines that its internal copy of the TRDY# signal is asserted, indicating that good data was registered on the rising-edge of clock nine. The initiator places the fourth and final data item into its read buffer.
- Internally, both the initiator and the target adjust the byte count remaining. There are two possibilities:
  - One possibility is that the byte count has been exhausted and the transaction is therefore completed.
  - The second possibility is that, although the byte transfer count is not exhausted, the initiator deasserted FRAME# in clock seven to inform the target that the initiator needed to disconnect on this block boundary. The last data item of the current block was just read on the rising-edge of clock nine, so the transaction is completed.

Figure 15-1: Memory Read Block, Decode A, No Wait States

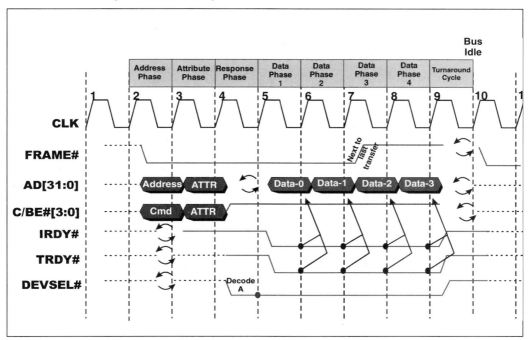

Memory Read Block: Variation One

Figure 15-2 on page 246 differs from Figure 15-1 on page 245 in the following ways:

- The target doesn't assert DEVSEL# until the decode B time slot, but then quickly asserts TRDY# in the next clock.
- On read, a target with decode speed B, C, or Subtractive is permitted to take ownership of the AD bus in the same clock that it asserts DEVSEL# (clock five in the figure).

Figure 15-2: Memory Read Block, Decode B, No Wait States

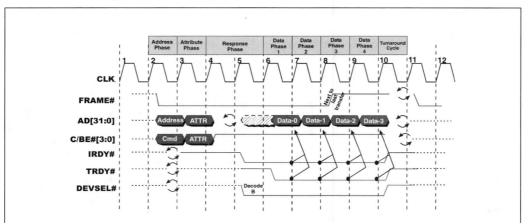

Memory Read Block: Variation Two

Figure 15-3 on page 247 differs from Figure 15-1 on page 245 in the following ways:

- The target asserts DEVSEL# in the decode C time slot and then quickly asserts TRDY# in the next clock.
- On read, a target with decode speed B, C, or Subtractive is permitted to take ownership of the AD bus in the same clock that it asserts DEVSEL# (clock six in the figure).

Figure 15-3: Memory Read Block, Decode C, No Wait States

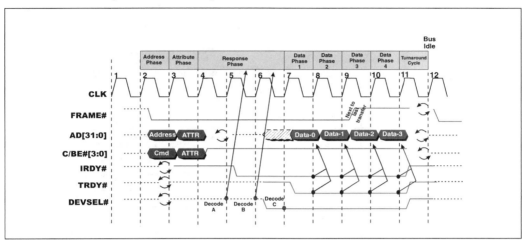

Memory Read Block: Variation Three

Figure 15-4 on page 248 differs from Figure 15-1 on page 245 in the following ways:

- The transaction is claimed by the ISA bridge (i.e., the Subtractive decode agent) in clock eight.
- The target then quickly asserts TRDY# in the next clock.
- On read, a target with decode speed B, C, or Subtractive is permitted to take ownership of the AD bus in the same clock that it asserts DEVSEL# (clock eight in the figure).

Figure 15-4: Memory Read Block, Subtractive Decode, No Wait States

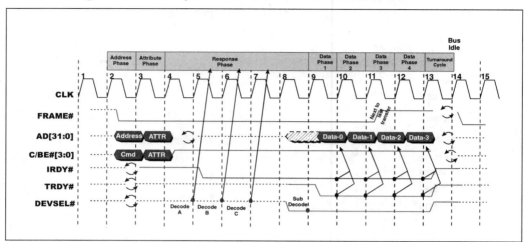

Memory Read Block: Variation Four

Figure 15-5 on page 249 differs from Figure 15-1 on page 245 in the following ways:

- The target quickly asserts DEVSEL# in the decode A time slot.
- Rather than asserting TRDY# at the earliest opportunity (clock five), it delays its assertion until clock six.
- Optionally, the target can take ownership of the AD bus one clock after it asserted DEVSEL# and drive a dummy data pattern until it drives the real data (in clock six in the figure).

Figure 15-5: Memory Read Block, Decode A, One Wait State

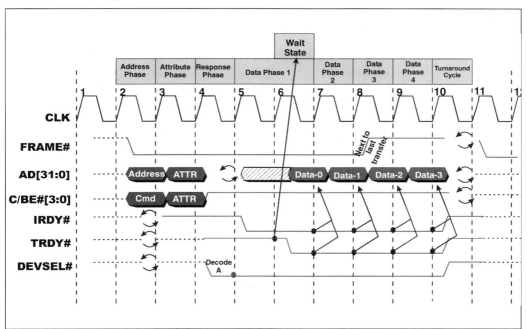

Memory Read Block: Variation Five

Figure 15-6 on page 250 differs from Figure 15-1 on page 245 in the following ways:

- The target quickly asserts DEVSEL# in the decode A time slot.
- Rather than asserting TRDY# at the earliest opportunity (clock five), it delays its assertion until clock seven.
- The target must take ownership of the AD bus one clock after it asserted DEVSEL# and drive a dummy data pattern until it drives the real data (in clock seven in the figure).

Figure 15-6: Memory Read Block, Decode A, Two Wait States

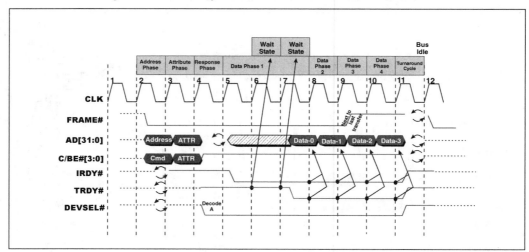

Memory Read Block: Variation Six

Figure 15-7 on page 251 differs from Figure 15-1 on page 245 in the following ways:

- The target asserts DEVSEL# in the decode C time slot.
- Rather than asserting TRDY# at the earliest opportunity (clock seven), it delays its assertion until clock nine.
- The target must take ownership of the AD bus one clock after it asserted DEVSEL# and drive a dummy data pattern until it drives the real data (in clock nine in the figure).
- Optionally, it could take ownership of the AD bus in the same clock in which it asserted DEVSEL# (clock six).

Figure 15-7: Memory Read Block, Decode C, Two Wait States

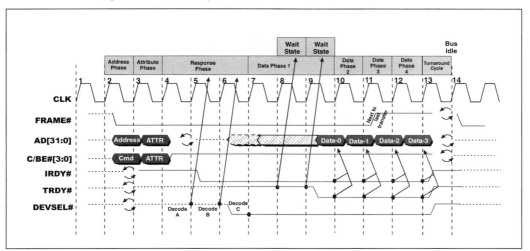

Memory Read Block: Variation Seven

Figure 15-8 on page 252 differs from Figure 15-1 on page 245 in the following ways:

- The target quickly asserts DEVSEL# in the decode A time slot.
- Rather than asserting TRDY# at the earliest opportunity (clock five), it delays its assertion until clock eight.
- The target must take ownership of the AD bus one clock after it asserted DEVSEL# and drive a dummy data pattern until it drives the real data (in clock eight in the figure).

Figure 15-8: Memory Read Block, Decode A, Three Wait States

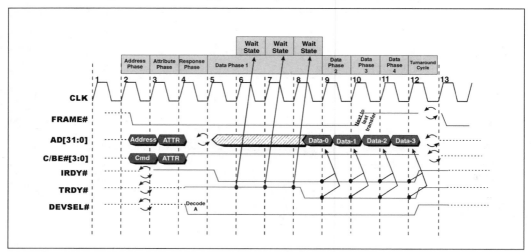

Memory Read Block: Variation Eight

Figure 15-9 on page 253 differs from Figure 15-1 on page 245 in the following ways:

- The target quickly asserts DEVSEL# in the decode A time slot.
- Rather than asserting TRDY# at the earliest opportunity (clock five), it delays its assertion until clock nine.
- The target must take ownership of the AD bus one clock after it asserted DEVSEL# and drive a dummy data pattern until it drives the real data (in clock nine in the figure).

Figure 15-9: Memory Read Block, Decode A, Four Wait States

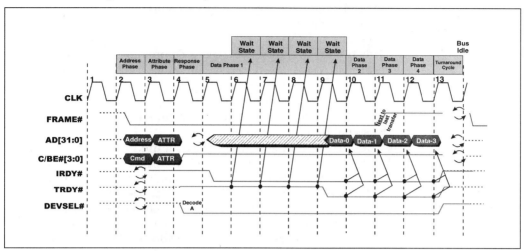

Memory Write Block Transaction

The Memory Write Block transaction is an all-inclusive write to memory starting at the byte-specific memory start address through the end byte address as defined by the byte transfer count. Additional detail about the Memory Write Block transaction can be found in "Memory Burst Format" on page 200 and in "Memory Write Block Command" on page 169.

Memory Write Block: Detailed Example

Refer to Figure 15-10 on page 257.

CLOCK 1. The transaction has not yet begun. The initiator detected its GNT# asserted (not shown) on the rising-edge of clock one, informing it that it will be the next bus owner. The initiator has been tracking bus activity, so it also knows that the bus will be Idle on the rising-edge of clock two (for more information, refer to Chapter 10, entitled "Bus Arbitration," on page 129).

CLOCK 2.

ON the rising-edge of clock two:
- The initiator starts the Memory Write Block transaction by:
  - driving out the byte-specific memory start address onto AD[31:0]. In this example, the start byte address could be any address within the first block.
  - driving out the Memory Write Block command onto C/BE#[3:0].
  - asserting FRAME#.

CLOCK 3.

ON the rising-edge of clock three:
- All targets on the bus clock the address, command, and the state of the FRAME# signal into their input registers.
- The initiator drives out the attributes (see Figure 13-4 on page 201) onto AD[31:0] and C/BE#[3:0]. Among other things, the attributes contain the byte transfer count. In this example, there are two possibilities:
  - The start byte address issued in the Address Phase could be any byte within the first block and the byte transfer count encompasses four Data Phases but does not cross the next block boundary.
  - The start byte address issued in the Address Phase is one of the locations in the fourth dword from the end of the block and the byte transfer count identifies an end address that is beyond the imminent block boundary.

DURING clock cycle three:
- All targets begin the decode of the registered copy of the address and command. In this example, the currently addressed target asserts its internal version of the DEVSEL# signal prior to the rising-edge of clock four.

CLOCK 4.

ON the rising-edge of clock four:
- The currently addressed target clocks an asserted level onto DEVSEL#. This is the Decode A time slot.

DURING clock cycle four:
- The initiator has the option of doing one of the following:
  - It can back its output drivers off AD[31:0].
  - It can drive the attributes for an extra clock cycle before supplying the first write data item.
  - It can start driving the first write data item a clock early.
  - It can drive a dummy stable pattern.
- The initiator places the Byte Enables in the Reserved and Driven High state for the remainder of the transaction.

CLOCK 5.

ON the rising-edge of clock five:
- The initiator asserts IRDY#, indicating that it is driving the first write data item onto the AD bus.
- The rising-edge of clock five is the first point at which the initiator clocks the state of DEVSEL# into its input register. In this case, it detects an asserted level on its registered copy of DEVSEL# during clock cycle five. This tells the initiator that it has established a connection with the addressed target and it defines the first point at which the initiator will register the state of TRDY# as the rising-edge of clock six.
- The earliest time slot in which the target can assert TRDY# is the clock immediately following its assertion of DEVSEL#. In this case, the target does assert TRDY# on the rising-edge of clock five, thereby indicating that it will register the first write data item from the AD bus on the rising-edge of clock six.

CLOCK 6.

ON the rising-edge of clock six:
- The target clocks the write data from the AD bus into its input register. It does not need to check the state of IRDY# to validate the presence of the data because it's a rule that the initiator must assert IRDY# and start driving the first write data item in clock five.
- The initiator starts driving the second write data item on the rising-edge of clock six.

DURING clock cycle six:
- The target places the first write data item into its buffer.
- The initiator determines that its registered copy of TRDY# is asserted, indicating that the target has begun to accept the data to be written within the first block.
- Internally, both the initiator and the target adjust the byte count remaining.

CLOCK 7.

ON the rising-edge of clock seven:
- The target clocks the second write data item into its input register.
- The initiator drives out the third data item.
- The initiator deasserts FRAME# for one of two reasons:
  - This transaction of four (or more) Data Phases is a small transfer, wholly contained within a block (i.e., it does not cross a block boundary). In this clock, both parties realize (by checking the byte count remaining) that the next-to-last data item is being transferred.
  - The start byte address issued in the Address Phase was a location in the fourth dword from the upcoming block boundary. Although the transfer count specified in the Attribute Phase indicates that the

transfer would cross at least the upcoming block boundary, in this example the initiator must force the target to Disconnect At Next ADB. As an example, the initiator of the Memory Write Block may only have the data to be written within the first block buffered and ready to write. In this case, the initiator deasserts FRAME# to inform the target that it's disconnecting the transaction on the upcoming block boundary.

DURING clock cycle seven:

- The target places the second write data item into its buffer.
- Internally, both the initiator and the target adjust the byte count remaining.

CLOCK 8.

ON the rising-edge of clock eight:

- The target clocks the third write data item into its input register.
- The target clocks the state of the FRAME# signal into its input register and determines that it has been deasserted by the initiator. This informs the target that the data item to be transferred on the rising-edge of clock nine is the final one to be transferred (even if it doesn't exhaust the transfer count).
- The target drives out the fourth write data item. This is either the final data item of the current block, or it is the last data item to be transferred within the block (as defined by the byte transfer count).

DURING clock cycle eight:

- The initiator places the third write data item into its buffer.
- Internally, both the initiator and the target adjust the byte count remaining.

CLOCK 9.

ON the rising-edge of clock nine:

- The target clocks the fourth and final write data item into its input register.

DURING clock cycle nine:

- The initiator places the fourth and final data item into its internal buffer.
- Internally, both the initiator and the target adjust the byte count remaining. There are two possibilities:
  - One possibility is that the byte count has been exhausted and the transaction is therefore completed.
  - The second possibility is that, although the byte transfer count is not exhausted, the initiator deasserted FRAME# in the previous clock to inform the target that the initiator needs to disconnect on this block boundary. The last data item of the current block was written on the rising-edge of clock nine, so the transaction is completed.

CLOCK 10.

ON the rising-edge of clock 10:

- Both parties release the bus. The initiator deasserts IRDY# and ceases to drive the final data item and the Byte Enables, and the target deasserts TRDY# and DEVSEL#.

Figure 15-10: Memory Write Block, Decode A, No Wait States

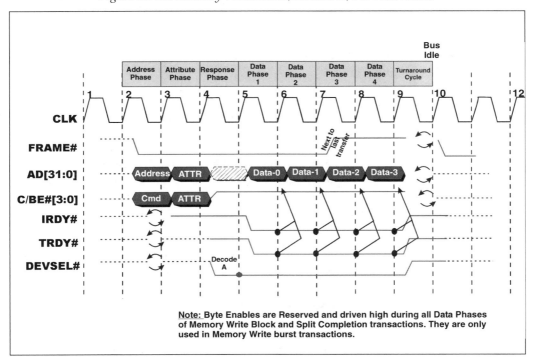

Note: Byte Enables are Reserved and driven high during all Data Phases of Memory Write Block and Split Completion transactions. They are only used in Memory Write burst transactions.

On Burst Writes, Insert Wait States in Pairs

Figure 15-11 on page 260 differs from Figure 15-10 on page 257 in the following ways:

- The target uses decode speed B.
- The target inserts Wait States to delay acceptance of first data block. For a detailed explanation, refer to the next section.

Refer to Figure 15-11 on page 260; the target is delaying its assertion of TRDY# because it is not immediately ready to start accepting the first block of write data. The following is a detailed explanation of the behavior of both parties under these circumstances. The explanation starts with clock cycle five.

CLOCK 5.

ON the rising-edge of clock five:

- The initiator asserts IRDY# and begins driving the first write data item. It must continue to drive the first data item until the earliest clock edge where TRDY# may be registered in the asserted state (i.e., one clock cycle after DEVSEL# is registered in the asserted state). In this example, this would be until the rising-edge of clock seven.
- The target asserts DEVSEL# in the decode speed B time slot (i.e., in clock five).

CLOCK 6.

ON the rising-edge of clock six:

- The initiator clocks the state of DEVSEL# into its input register.

DURING clock cycle six:

- The asserted state of the initiator's registered copy of DEVSEL# defines the rising-edge of clock seven as the first point to register the state of TRDY# to see if the target has started accepting the first block of write data yet.
- The initiator continues to drive the first write data item.

CLOCK 7.

ON the rising-edge of clock seven:

- The initiator starts driving the second data item (in the hope that the target started accepting write data on this edge) and simultaneously registers the state of TRDY# to determine if the target has started to accept the first block of write data on this clock edge.

DURING clock cycle seven:

- In this example, the initiator discovers that its registered copy of TRDY# is deasserted, indicating that the target did not accept the first data item on the rising-edge of clock seven.
- It is a rule that if the target refused acceptance of the first data item in the previous clock, it must not assert TRDY# in the current clock to indicate that it is accepting the second data item. This would result in out-of-order delivery of write data and that is not allowed. In other words, on a burst memory write (i.e., Memory Write Block or Memory Write transaction), the target must always insert Wait States in pairs.

CLOCK 8.

ON the rising-edge of clock eight:
- The target has TRDY# deasserted, indicating its refusal of the second data item.

DURING clock cycle eight:
- Because the target refused the delivery of the first and second data items, the initiator must once again drive out the first and second data items during clocks eight and nine.
- The target now asserts TRDY# to indicate that is ready to start accepting the first block of write data.

CLOCK 9.

ON the rising-edge of clock nine:
- The target clocks the first data item into its input register.
- The initiator starts driving out the second data item again.
- The initiator registers the state of TRDY#. Its asserted state indicates that the target has accepted the first write data item of the block and will accept all subsequent data items to be written into the first block at full-speed.

CLOCK 10. Starting with the rising-edge of clock 10, the target starts accepting the remaining data items to be written into the first block at full-speed.

The spec refers to this repeating of the first and second data items until the target starts accepting the first data block as data toggling.

Figure 15-11: Memory Write Block, Decode B, One Wait State Pair

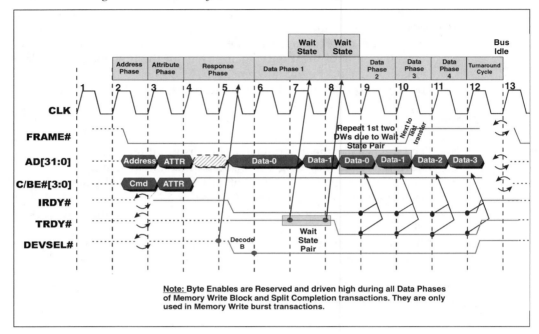

Note: **Byte Enables are Reserved and driven high during all Data Phases of Memory Write Block and Split Completion transactions. They are only used in Memory Write burst transactions.**

Memory Write Transaction

The Memory Write transaction writes data into the area defined by the byte-specific memory start address through the end byte address defined by the byte transfer count. In this transaction, the byte transfer count is not necessarily a byte transfer count. Rather, it defines the end address of the area within which the initiator intends to write some but possibly not all locations. In each Data Phase, the Byte Enables define the locations to be written within the current dword or qword. Additional detail about the Memory Write transaction can be found in "Memory Burst Format" on page 200 and in "Memory Write Command" on page 174.

Memory Write: Detailed Example

Refer to Figure 15-12 on page 265.

CLOCK 1.

DURING clock cycle one:

- The transaction has not yet begun. The initiator detected its GNT# asserted (not shown) on the rising-edge of clock one, informing it that it will be the next bus owner. The initiator has been tracking bus activity, so it also knows that the bus will be Idle on the rising-edge of clock two (for more information, refer to Chapter 10, entitled "Bus Arbitration," on page 129).

CLOCK 2.

ON the rising-edge of clock two:

- The initiator starts the Memory Write transaction by:
  - driving out the byte-specific memory start address onto AD[31:0]. In this example, the start byte address could be any address within the first block.
  - driving out the Memory Write command onto C/BE#[3:0].
  - asserting FRAME#.

CLOCK 3.

ON the rising-edge of clock three:

- All targets on the bus clock the address, command, and the state of the FRAME# signal into their input registers.
- The initiator drives out the attributes (see Figure 13-4 on page 201) onto AD[31:0] and C/BE#[3:0]. Among other things, the attributes contain the byte transfer count. In this example, there are two possibilities:
  - The start byte address issued in the Address Phase could be any byte within the first block and the byte transfer count encompasses four Data Phases but does not cross the next block boundary.
  - The start byte address issued in the Address Phase is one of the locations in the fourth dword from the end of the block and the byte transfer count identifies an end address that is beyond the imminent block boundary.

DURING clock cycle three:

- All targets begin the decode of the registered copy of the address and command. In this example, the currently addressed target asserts its internal version of the DEVSEL# signal prior to the rising-edge of clock four.

CLOCK 4.

ON the rising-edge of clock four:

- The currently addressed target clocks an asserted level onto DEVSEL#. This is the Decode A time slot.

DURING clock cycle four:

- The initiator has the option of doing one of the following:
    - It can back its output drivers off AD[31:0].
    - It can drive the attributes for an extra clock cycle before supplying the first write data item.
    - It can start driving the first write data item a clock early.
    - It can drive a dummy stable pattern.
    - It can place the Byte Enables in the Reserved and Driven High state for one clock cycle.

CLOCK 5.

ON the rising-edge of clock five:

- The initiator asserts IRDY#, indicating that it is driving the first write data item and its associated Byte Enables.
- The rising-edge of clock five is the first point at which the initiator clocks the state of DEVSEL# into its input register. In this case, it detects an asserted level on its registered copy of DEVSEL# during clock cycle five. This tells the initiator that it has established a connection with the addressed target and it defines the first point at which the initiator will register the state of TRDY# as the rising-edge of clock six.
- The earliest time slot in which the target can assert TRDY# is the clock immediately following its assertion of DEVSEL#. In this case, the target does assert TRDY# on the rising-edge of clock five, thereby indicating that it will register the first write data item from the AD bus on the rising-edge of clock six.

CLOCK 6.

ON the rising-edge of clock six:

- The target clocks the write data from the AD bus and the Byte Enables into its input register. It does not need to check the state of IRDY# to validate the presence of the data because it's a rule that the initiator must assert IRDY# and start driving the first write data item in clock five.
- The initiator starts driving the second write data item and its associated Byte Enables.

DURING clock cycle six:

- The target places the first write data item and its Byte Enables into its buffer.
- The initiator determines its copy of TRDY# is asserted, indicating that target has begun to accept the data to be written within the first block.

- Internally, both the initiator and the target adjust the byte count remaining.

Clock 7.

On the rising-edge of clock seven:

- The target clocks the second write data item and its Byte Enables into its input register.
- The initiator drives out the third data item and its associated Byte Enables.
- The initiator deasserts FRAME# for one of two reasons:
  - This transaction of four (or more) Data Phases is a small transfer, wholly contained within a block (i.e., it does not cross a block boundary). In this clock, both parties realize (by checking the byte count remaining) that the next-to-last data item is being transferred.
  - The start byte address issued in the Address Phase was a location in the fourth dword from the upcoming block boundary. Although the transfer count specified in the Attribute Phase indicates that the transfer would cross at least the upcoming block boundary, in this example the initiator must force the target to Disconnect At Next ADB. As an example, the initiator of the Memory Write may only have the data to be written within the first block buffered and ready to write. In this case, the initiator deasserts FRAME# to inform the target that it's disconnecting the transaction on the upcoming block boundary.

During clock cycle seven:

- The target places the second write data item and its Byte Enables into its buffer.
- Internally, both the initiator and the target adjust the byte count remaining.

Clock 8.

On the rising-edge of clock eight:

- The target clocks the third write data item and its Byte Enables into its input register.
- The target clocks the state of the FRAME# signal into its input register and determines that it has been deasserted by the initiator. This informs the target that the data item to be transferred on the rising-edge of clock nine is the final one to be transferred (even if it doesn't exhaust the transfer count).
- The initiator drives out the fourth write data item and its associated Byte Enables. This is either the final data item of the current block, or it is the last data item to be transferred within the block (as defined by the byte transfer count).

DURING clock cycle eight:
- The target places the third write data item and its Byte Enables into its buffer.
- Internally, both the initiator and the target adjust the byte count remaining.

CLOCK 9.

ON the rising-edge of clock nine:
- The target clocks the fourth and final data item into its input register.
- Both parties release the bus. The initiator deasserts IRDY# and ceases to drive the final data item and the Byte Enables, and the target deasserts TRDY# and DEVSEL#.

DURING clock cycle nine:
- The initiator places the fourth and final data item and its Byte Enables into its internal buffer.
- Internally, both the initiator and the target adjust the byte count remaining. There are two possibilities:
  - One possibility is that the byte count has been exhausted and the transaction is therefore completed.
  - The second possibility is that, although the byte transfer count is not exhausted, the initiator deasserted FRAME# in clock seven to inform the target that the initiator needs to disconnect on this block boundary. The last data item of the current block was just written on the rising-edge of clock nine, so the transaction is completed.

Figure 15-12: Memory Write, Decode A, No Wait States

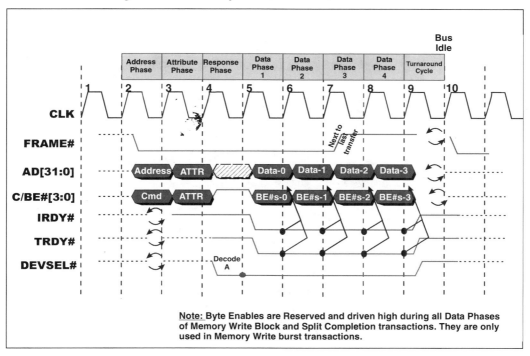

Note: Byte Enables are Reserved and driven high during all Data Phases of Memory Write Block and Split Completion transactions. They are only used in Memory Write burst transactions.

Memory Write: Variation One

With the following exceptions, the Memory Write transaction illustrated in Figure 15-13 on page 266 is the same as the Memory Write Block transaction pictured in Figure 15-11 on page 260:

- The target has decode speed A rather than B.
- The Byte Enables are not Reserved and Driven high. Rather, the Byte Enable setting in each Data Phase defines which locations within the current dword or qword are to be written.

Figure 15-13: Memory Write, Decode A, One Wait State Pair

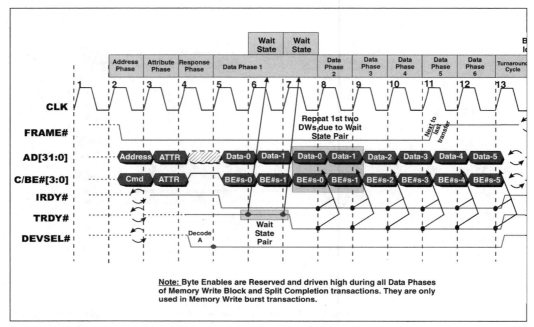

Note: Byte Enables are Reserved and driven high during all Data Phases of Memory Write Block and Split Completion transactions. They are only used in Memory Write burst transactions.

Memory Write: Variation Two

With the following exception, the Memory Write transaction illustrated in Figure 15-14 on page 267 is the same as the Memory Write transaction pictured in Figure 15-13 on page 266:

- The target inserts two Wait State pairs rather than one, forcing the initiator to repeat the transmission of the first two data items and their respective Byte Enables two times. The target then starts accepting the data to be written into the first block on the rising-edge of clock 10.

Figure 15-14: Memory Write, Decode A, Two Wait State Pairs

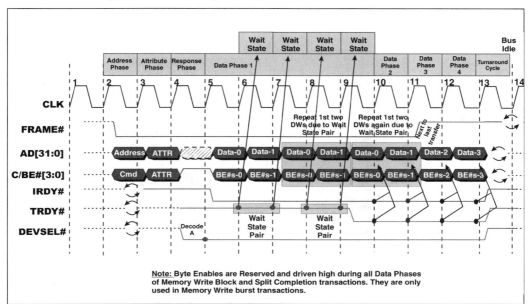

Memory Write: Variation Three

With the following exceptions, the Memory Write transaction illustrated in Figure 15-15 on page 268 is the same as the Memory Write transaction pictured in Figure 15-12 on page 265:

- The target has decode speed B rather than A.
- The initiator must continue to drive the first data item until the clock edge on which it samples TRDY# for the first time (rising-edge of clock seven in the example). The initiator then registers the state of TRDY# and, in the hope that the target did take the first data item, the initiator starts driving the second data item on the same clock edge.

Figure 15-15: Memory Write, Decode B, No Wait States

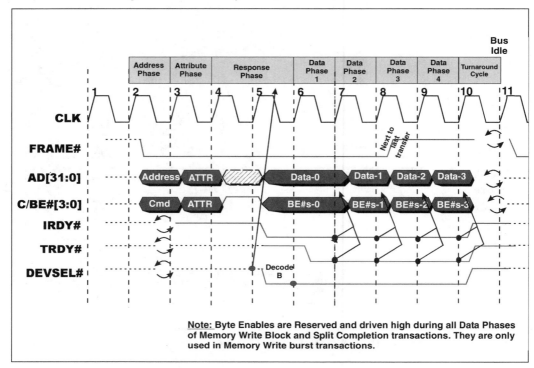

Note: Byte Enables are Reserved and driven high during all Data Phases of Memory Write Block and Split Completion transactions. They are only used in Memory Write burst transactions.

Memory Write: Variation Four

With the following exceptions, the Memory Write transaction illustrated in Figure 15-16 on page 269 is the same as the Memory Write transaction pictured in Figure 15-15 on page 268:

- The target inserts one Wait State pair to indicate that it's not yet ready to start accepting the data to be written within the first block. This forces the initiator to repeat the transmission of the first two data items one time. The target then starts accepting the data to be written into the first block on the rising-edge of clock 9.

Figure 15-16: Memory Write, Decode B, One Wait State Pair

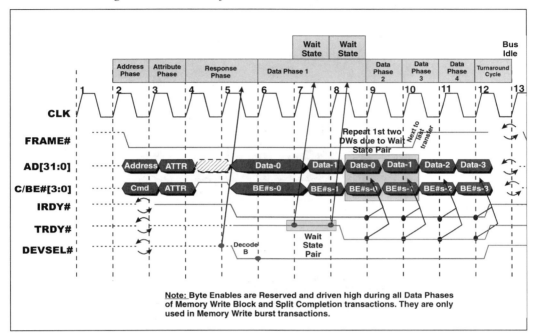

Memory Write: Variation Five

With the following exceptions, the Memory Write transaction illustrated in Figure 15-17 on page 270 is the same as the Memory Write transaction pictured in Figure 15-16 on page 269:

- The target inserts two Wait State pairs to indicate that it's not yet ready to start accepting the data to be written within the first block. This forces the initiator to repeat the transmission of the first two data items and their respective Byte Enables two times. The target then starts accepting the data to be written into the first block on the rising-edge of clock 11.

Figure 15-17: Memory Write, Decode B, Two Wait State Pairs

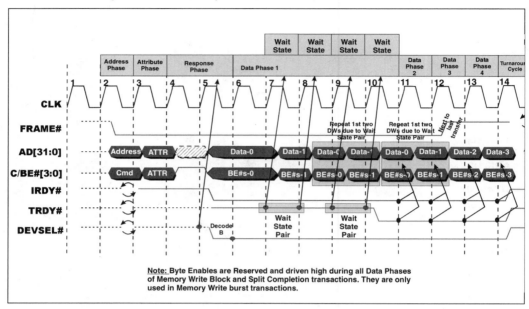

Note: Byte Enables are Reserved and driven high during all Data Phases of Memory Write Block and Split Completion transactions. They are only used in Memory Write burst transactions.

Memory Write: Variation Six

In Figure 15-18 on page 271:

- The target has decode speed C and inserts no Wait States prior to its acceptance of the data to be written within the first block. The initiator must continue to drive the first data item until the clock edge on which it samples TRDY# for the first time (rising-edge of clock eight in the example).
- The initiator then registers the state of TRDY# and, in the hope that the target did take the first data item, the initiator starts driving the second data item on the same clock edge.

Figure 15-18: Memory Write, Decode C, No Wait States

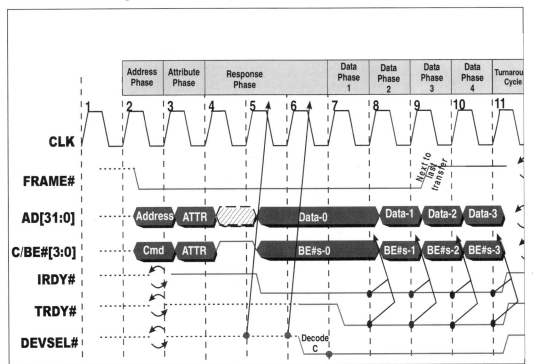

Memory Write: Variation Seven

In the previous example (Figure 15-18 on page 271), the target had decode speed C and did not insert any Wait States prior to its acceptance of the data to be written within the first block. In Figure 15-19 on page 272, the target once again has decode speed C, but it inserts one Wait State pair prior to its acceptance of the data to be written within the first block.

Figure 15-19: Memory Write, Decode C, One Wait State Pair

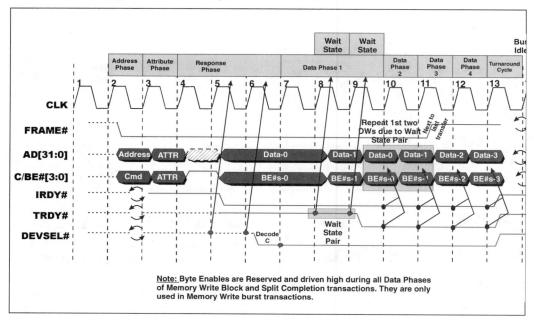

Note: Byte Enables are Reserved and driven high during all Data Phases of Memory Write Block and Split Completion transactions. They are only used in Memory Write burst transactions.

Memory Write: Variation Eight

While the target in Figure 15-19 on page 272 inserted one Wait State pair prior to its acceptance of the data to be written within the first block, the target in Figure 15-20 on page 273 inserts two Wait State pairs.

Figure 15-20: Memory Write, Decode C, Two Wait State Pairs

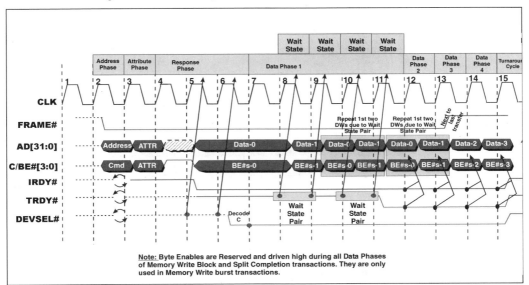

Memory Write: Variation Nine

In the final example, Figure 15-21 on page 274, the ISA bridge claims the transaction (i.e., it asserts DEVSEL#) using subtractive decode speed. Notice that the initiator must continue to drive the first data item until the clock edge on which it samples TRDY# for the first time (rising-edge of clock 10 in the example).

Figure 15-21: Memory Write, Subtractive Decode, No Wait States

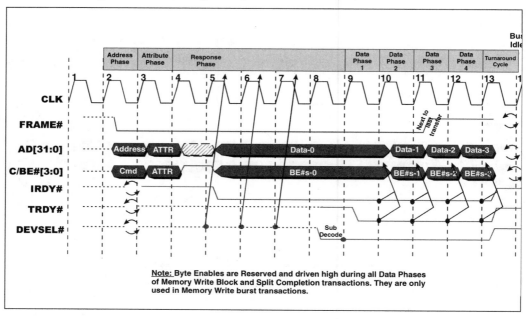

Note: Byte Enables are Reserved and driven high during all Data Phases of Memory Write Block and Split Completion transactions. They are only used in Memory Write burst transactions.

Split Completion Transaction

The Split Completion transaction is initiated by the Completer to return one of the following:

- block of memory read data requested by a Memory Read Block transaction issued by the Requester.
- a Split Completion Message signaling the successful delivery of IO or Configuration write data.
- an error Split Completion Message signaling an error while attempting delivery of IO or Configuration write data.
- an error Split Completion Message signaling an error while fetching a block of memory data requested by a Memory Read Block transaction.

Additional detail about the Split Completion transaction can be found in "Split Completion Command Format" on page 209 and in "Split Completion Command" on page 176.

Split Completion Returning Block of Read Data

Figure 15-22 on page 275 illustrates a Split Completion transaction returning data requested by a previously issued Memory Read Block transaction. The PCI-X spec takes the point of view that there is a lot of similarity between a Split Completion transaction returning requested read data and a Memory Write Block transaction (see Figure 15-11 on page 260). In both situations, the initiator of the transaction drives the following information onto the AD bus:

- the address during the Address Phase.
- the attributes during the Attribute Phase.
- the data during the Data Phases.

Just as in a write burst, Wait State pairs are inserted by the target (in this case, the target of the Split Completion) when the target is not yet ready to start accepting the first block of data.

Figure 15-22: Split Completion Returning Previously-Requested Read Data, Decode B, One Wait State Pair

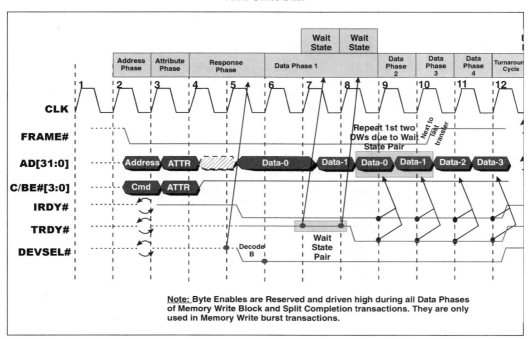

Returning a Split Completion Error Message

Figure 15-23 on page 276 illustrates a Split Completion transaction returning a message rather than previously requested memory read data. As mentioned earlier, the Completer sends a message under the following circumstances:

- a Split Completion Message to signal the successful delivery of IO or Configuration write data.
- an error Split Completion Message to signal an error while attempting delivery of IO or Configuration write data.
- an error Split Completion Message to signal an error while fetching a block of memory data requested by a Memory Read Block transaction.

A Split Completion transaction that is returning a message always consists of a single Data Phase. The message consists of a 32-bit data structure. The SCM bit will be set in the Attribute Phase (see "Split Completion Command Format" on page 209) to indicate that the transaction is delivering a message rather than previously requested read data. A detailed description of the various messages can be found in Chapter 17, entitled "Split Completion Messages," on page 313.

Figure 15-23: Split Completion Returning a Split Completion Message

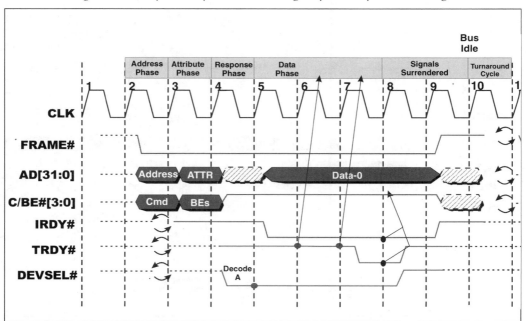

Alias To Memory Block Commands

Although the Alias to Memory Read Block and Alias to Memory Write Block commands are burst commands, no initiator is currently permitted to issue these commands and all targets are to treat them as if they are the Memory Read Block and Memory Write Block commands. These commands may be implemented in a later version of the PCI-X spec.

16 *Transaction Terminations*

The Previous Chapter

The previous chapter provided detailed examples of the Burst transaction types:

- Memory Read Block.
- Memory Write Block.
- Memory Write.
- Split Completion.
- Alias To Memory Block commands.

This Chapter

This chapter provides a detailed description of both initiator and target terminations of a transaction. It includes clock-by-clock descriptions of example timing diagrams.

The Next Chapter

The next chapter describes the purpose of the Split Completion Message, its format, the messages associated with writes and reads, and device-specific error handling.

General Format of Timing Diagram Descriptions

The sections that follow provide a detailed description of various transaction scenarios. Each transaction is described clock-by-clock, with the events during each clock divided into two categories:

- **ON** the rising-edge of clock N.
- **DURING** clock N.

Please keep in mind that some events could actually be correctly placed in either of these event categories.

Termination by the Initiator

General

The initiator of a transaction may terminate a transaction for any of the following reasons:

- Byte count satisfaction.
- The initiator issues a Disconnect At Next ADB.
- The initiator fails to connect with a target.

These terminations are covered in the next three sections. It should also be noted that the initiator may terminate a transaction because the target has instructed it to do so. These target-initiated terminations are covered in "Termination By the Target" on page 290.

Byte Count Satisfaction

Introduction

The protocol used by the initiator when ending a transaction due to byte count satisfaction is defined by the number of Data Phases in the transaction. There are two possibilities:

- Ending a transaction consisting of four or more Data Phases.
- Ending a transaction consisting of less than four Data Phases.

The next two sections describe the methodology used by the initiator in each of these two cases.

Chapter 16: Transaction Terminations

Ending Transaction of Four or More Data Phases

With the exception of Figure 15-23 on page 276, every example transaction in Chapter 15, entitled "Burst Transactions" consisted or four Data Phases and therefore illustrated how the initiator ends a transaction of four (or more) Data Phases due to byte count satisfaction.

Refer to Figure 16-1 on page 281. In short, both the initiator and the target are decrementing the byte transfer count in each Data Phase. In the Data Phase where the next-to-last data item (as defined by the remaining byte transfer count) is transferred, the initiator deasserts FRAME#. The final data item is then transferred in the next Data Phase. Both parties then release the bus. For a more detailed description of this example, refer to "Memory Read Block: Detailed Example" on page 241.

Figure 16-1: Ending Transaction of Four (or More) Data Phases

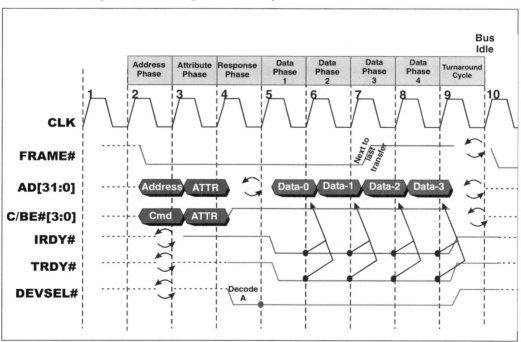

Ending Transaction of Less Than Four Data Phases

Introduction. The protocol used when ending a transaction of less than four Data Phases is defined in the following three sections.

Three-Data-Phase Transaction. Refer to Figure 16-2 on page 284.

CLOCK 1. The transaction has not yet begun. The initiator detected its GNT# asserted (not shown) on the rising-edge of clock one, informing it that it will be the next bus owner. The initiator has been tracking bus activity, so it also knows that the bus will be Idle on the rising-edge of clock two (for more information, refer to Chapter 10, entitled "Bus Arbitration," on page 129).

CLOCK 2.

ON the rising-edge of clock two:
- The initiator starts the burst memory transaction by:
  - driving out the byte-specific memory start address onto AD[31:0]. In this example, the start byte address could be any address within the block.
  - driving out the burst memory command onto C/BE#[3:0].
  - asserting FRAME#.

CLOCK 3.

ON the rising-edge of clock three:
- All targets on the bus clock the address, command, and the state of the FRAME# signal into their input registers.
- The initiator drives out the attributes (see Figure 13-4 on page 201) onto AD[31:0] and C/BE#[3:0]. Among other things, the attributes contains the byte transfer count. In this example, the start byte address issued in the Address Phase could be any byte within the block and the byte transfer count encompasses three Data Phases within the same block.

DURING clock cycle three:
- All targets begin the decode of the registered copy of the address and command during clock cycle three. In this example, the currently addressed target asserts its internal version of the DEVSEL# signal prior to the rising-edge of clock four.

CLOCK 4. The currently addressed target clocks an asserted level onto DEVSEL# on the rising-edge of clock 4. This is the Decode A time slot.

CLOCK 5.

ON the rising-edge of clock five:
- The initiator asserts IRDY#, indicating that it is ready to start transferring data. If it's a burst write transaction, the initiator drives out the first data item onto the AD bus.

- The rising-edge of clock five is the first point at which the initiator clocks the state of DEVSEL# into its input register. In this case, it detects an asserted level on its registered copy of DEVSEL# during clock cycle five. This tells the initiator that it has established a connection with the addressed target. This defines the first point at which the initiator will register the state of TRDY# as the rising-edge of clock six.
- The target asserts TRDY# to indicate that it's ready to transfer the first data item. If it's a burst read, the target drives out the first data item.

CLOCK 6.

ON the rising-edge of clock six:

- The initiator registers the state of TRDY#. The asserted state of TRDY# indicates that the target has started the transfer (i.e., it is not inserting Wait States to delay the transfer of the data).
- The device sourcing the data (the initiator if it's a write or a Split Completion; the target if it's a read) drives out the second data item. This is the next-to-last data item.

DURING clock cycle six:

- Both parties decrement the remaining byte transfer count. Realizing that the next-to-last data item will be transferred on the rising-edge of clock seven, the initiator prepares to deassert FRAME# on the rising-edge of clock seven. Note that the initiator could not turn off FRAME# if TRDY# had been registered in the deasserted state on the rising-edge of clock six.

CLOCK 7.

ON the rising-edge of clock seven:

- The device sourcing the data (the initiator if it's a write or a Split Completion; the target if it's a read) drives out the last data item.
- The initiator deasserts FRAME#.

DURING clock cycle seven:

- Both parties decrement the remaining byte transfer count. Realizing that the last data item will be transferred on the rising-edge of clock eight, the initiator prepares to deassert IRDY#, and the target prepares to deassert TRDY# and DEVSEL# on the rising-edge of clock eight.

CLOCK 8.

ON the rising-edge of clock eight:

- The final data item is transferred.
- The initiator deasserts IRDY# to return the bus to the Idle state.
- The target deasserts TRDY# and DEVSEL#.

Figure 16-2: Ending Transaction of Three Data Phases

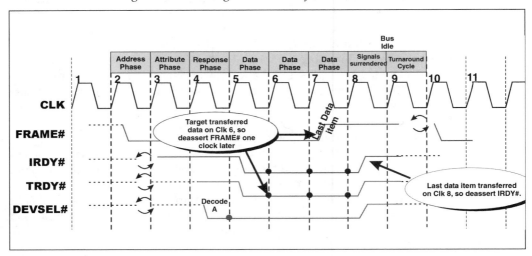

Two-Data-Phase Transaction. Refer to Figure 16-3 on page 286.

Clock 1.

During clock cycle one:

- The transaction has not yet begun. The initiator detected its GNT# asserted (not shown) on the rising-edge of clock one, informing it that it will be the next bus owner. The initiator has been tracking bus activity, so it also knows that the bus will be Idle on the rising-edge of clock two (for more information, refer to Chapter 10, entitled "Bus Arbitration," on page 129).

Clock 2.

On the rising-edge of clock two:

- The initiator starts the burst memory transaction by:
  - driving out the byte-specific memory start address onto AD[31:0]. In this example, the start byte address could be any address within the block.
  - driving out the burst memory command onto C/BE#[3:0].
  - asserting FRAME#.

Clock 3.

On the rising-edge of clock three:

- All targets on the bus clock the address, command, and the state of the FRAME# signal into their input registers.

- The initiator drives out the attributes (see Figure 13-4 on page 201) onto AD[31:0] and C/BE#[3:0]. Among other things, the attributes contains the byte transfer count. In this example, the start byte address issued in the Address Phase could be any byte within the block and the byte transfer count encompasses two Data Phases within the same block.

DURING clock cycle three:

- All targets begin the decode of the registered copy of the address and command during clock cycle three. In this example, the currently addressed target asserts its internal version of the DEVSEL# signal prior to the rising-edge of clock four.

CLOCK 4.

ON the rising-edge of clock four:

- The currently addressed target clocks an asserted level onto DEVSEL#. This is the Decode A time slot.

CLOCK 5.

ON the rising-edge of clock five:

- The initiator asserts IRDY#, indicating that it is ready to start transferring data. If it's a burst write transaction, the initiator drives out the first data item onto the AD bus. This is the next-to-last data item.
- The rising-edge of clock five is the first point at which the initiator clocks the state of DEVSEL# into its input register. In this case, it detects an asserted level on its registered copy of DEVSEL# during clock cycle five. This tells the initiator that it has established a connection with the addressed target. This defines the first point at which the initiator will register the state of TRDY# as the rising-edge of clock six.
- The target asserts TRDY# to indicate that it's ready to transfer the first data item. If it's a burst read, the target drives out the first data item. This is the next-to-last data item.

CLOCK 6.

ON the rising-edge of clock six:

- The initiator registers the state of TRDY#. The asserted state of TRDY# indicates that the target has started the transfer (i.e., it is not inserting Wait States to delay the transfer of the data).
- The device sourcing the data (the initiator if it's a write or a Split Completion; the target if it's a read) drives out the last data item.

DURING clock cycle six:

- Both parties decrement the remaining byte transfer count. Realizing that the last data item will be transferred on the rising-edge of clock seven, the initiator prepares to deassert FRAME# and IRDY#, and the target prepares to deassert TRDY# and DEVSEL# on the rising-edge of clock seven. Note that the initiator could not turn off FRAME# and IRDY# if TRDY# had been registered in the deasserted state on the rising-edge of clock six.

CLOCK 7.

ON the rising-edge of clock seven:
- The final data item is transferred.
- The initiator deasserts IRDY# and FRAME# to return the bus to the Idle state.
- The target deasserts TRDY# and DEVSEL#.

Figure 16-3: Ending Transaction of Two Data Phases

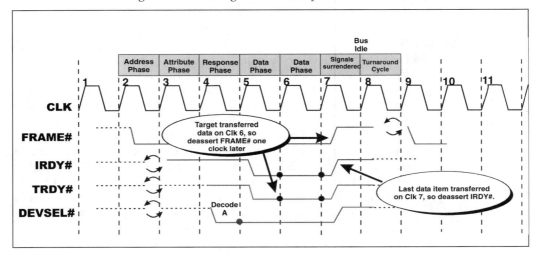

One-Data-Phase Transaction. Refer to Figure 16-4 on page 288.

CLOCK 1.

DURING clock cycle one:
- The transaction has not yet begun. The initiator detected its GNT# asserted (not shown) on the rising-edge of clock one, informing it that it will be the next bus owner. It has been tracking bus activity and also knows the bus will be Idle on the rising-edge of clock two (for more information, refer to Chapter 10, entitled "Bus Arbitration," on page 129).

CLOCK 2.

ON the rising-edge of clock two:
- The initiator starts the burst memory transaction by:

- driving out the byte-specific memory start address onto AD[31:0]. In this example, the start byte address could be any address within the block.
- driving out the burst memory command onto C/BE#[3:0].
- asserting FRAME#.

CLOCK 3.

ON the rising-edge of clock three:
- All targets on the bus clock the address, command, and the state of the FRAME# signal into their input registers.
- The initiator drives out the attributes (see Figure 13-4 on page 201) onto AD[31:0] and C/BE#[3:0]. Among other things, the attributes contain the byte transfer count. In this example, the start byte address issued in the Address Phase could be any byte within the block and the byte transfer count encompasses one Data Phase.

DURING clock cycle three:
- All targets begin the decode of the registered copy of the address and command during clock cycle three. In this example, the currently addressed target asserts its internal version of the DEVSEL# signal prior to the rising-edge of clock four.

CLOCK 4.

ON the rising-edge of clock four:
- The currently addressed target clocks an asserted level onto DEVSEL#. This is the Decode A time slot.

CLOCK 5.

ON the rising-edge of clock five:
- The initiator asserts IRDY#, indicating that it is ready to start transferring data. If it's a burst write transaction, the initiator drives out the first (and only) data item onto the AD bus.
- The rising-edge of clock five is the first point at which the initiator clocks the state of DEVSEL# into its input register. In this case, it detects an asserted level on its registered copy of DEVSEL# during clock cycle five. This tells the initiator that it has established a connection with the addressed target. This defines the first point at which the initiator will register the state of TRDY# as the rising-edge of clock six.
- The target asserts TRDY# to indicate that it's ready to transfer the first (and only) data item. If it's a burst read, the target drives out the data item.

CLOCK 6.

ON the rising-edge of clock six:
- The initiator registers the state of TRDY#. The asserted state of TRDY# indicates that the target has transferred the one and only

data item (i.e., it is not inserting Wait States to delay the transfer of the data item).

- The target deasserts TRDY# and DEVSEL#.

DURING clock cycle six:

- Realizing that the last (and only) data item was transferred on the rising-edge of clock six, the initiator prepares to deassert FRAME# and IRDY# to return the bus to the Idle state in clock seven. Note that the initiator could not turn off FRAME# and IRDY# on the rising-edge of clock seven if TRDY# had been registered in the deasserted state on the rising-edge of clock six.

Figure 16-4: Ending Transaction of One Data Phase

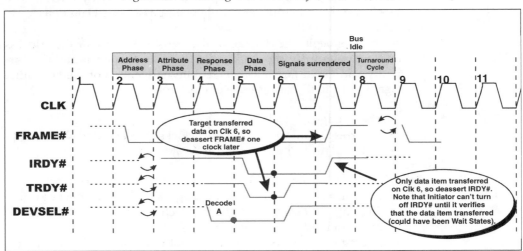

Chapter 16: Transaction Terminations

Initiator Issues Disconnect at Next ADB

The initiator of a transaction may need to disconnect a transaction on an upcoming block boundary. As examples:

- It may be a Memory Write or a Memory Write Block transaction and the Requester does not have all of the data buffered and ready to write. It will therefore have to issue a Disconnect At Next ADB to the target as it approaches the block boundary where it will run out of data.
- It may be a Memory Read Block transaction issued by a PCIX-to-PCIX bridge and the bridge has not allocated sufficient buffer space to hold all of the read data. If the target responds immediately with data, the bridge will therefore have to issue a Disconnect At Next ADB to the target as it approaches the block boundary where it will run out of buffer space.
- The Completer may start a Split Completion transaction to return previously requested read data and it may not actually have all of the data buffered up and ready to deliver. The Completer will therefore have to issue a Disconnect At Next ADB to the target as it approaches the block boundary where it will run out of data.

There are two basic scenarios:

SCENARIO 1. The initiator is performing a transaction with four or more Data Phases and wishes to disconnect on an upcoming block boundary. With the exception of Figure 15-23 on page 276, all of the transactions in Chapter 15, entitled "Burst Transactions" illustrate this scenario. A detailed description can be found in "Memory Read Block: Detailed Example" on page 241.

SCENARIO 2. The initiator is performing a transaction with a start address very close to the next block boundary (less than four Data Phases from the block boundary) and it wishes to disconnect on the imminent block boundary. In this case, the only way that the initiator can force the target to end the transaction on the imminent block boundary is to trick it. This is accomplished by adjusting the byte transfer count issued in the Attribute Phase to make the target end the transaction in three, two, or one Data Phases. "Ending Transaction of Less Than Four Data Phases" on page 282 describes the protocol.

Initiator Termination Due to Connection Timeout

This subject is covered in "The Response Phase: Connecting With the Target" on page 210.

Termination By the Target

Target Abort

Target Abort Is Always Fatal

Reception of a Target Abort always forces the initiator to terminate the transaction and the transaction will not be repeated.

Some Reasons Target Issues Target Abort

Broken Target. If a target is broken and unable to transfer data, it may indicate this by issuing a Target Abort to the master.

IO Addressing Error. The byte enable combination is not one supported by the target (in other words, it doesn't "own" all of the addressed locations within the current dword). For more information, refer to "IO Read and Write Commands" on page 149.

Address Phase Parity Error. If a target appears to be addressed in a transaction but there is a Address Phase parity error, the target may end the transaction by issuing a Target Abort to the master (in addition to asserting SERR#).

Initiator's and Target's Response to Target Abort

In response to a Target Abort, the initiator and target take the following actions:

- The initiator sets the **Received Target Abort bit** in its Status register.
- The target sets the **Signaled Target Abort bit** in its Status register.
- The initiator generates an **interrupt** to alert its related device driver to check its status.
- The initiator generates **SERR#** (assuming the initiator's SERR# Enable bit is set to one in its PCI configuration Command register).

Chapter 16: Transaction Terminations

Example Target Abort Issued in First Data Phase

Refer to Figure 16-5 on page 293.

CLOCK 1.

DURING clock cycle one:

- The transaction has not yet begun. The initiator detected its GNT# asserted (not shown) on the rising-edge of clock one, informing it that it will be the next bus owner. The initiator has been tracking bus activity, so it also knows that the bus will be Idle on the rising-edge of clock two (for more information, refer to Chapter 10, entitled "Bus Arbitration," on page 129).

CLOCK 2.

ON the rising-edge of clock two:

- The initiator starts the transaction:
    - driving out the byte-specific memory start address onto AD[31:0]. In this example, the start byte address could be any address within the block.
    - driving out the command onto C/BE#[3:0].
    - asserting FRAME#.

CLOCK 3.

ON the rising-edge of clock three:

- All targets on the bus clock the address, command, and the state of the FRAME# signal into their input registers.
- The initiator drives out the attributes (see Figure 13-4 on page 201) onto AD[31:0] and C/BE#[3:0]. Among other things, the attributes contain the byte transfer count.

DURING clock cycle three:

- All targets begin the decode of the registered copy of the address and command. In this example, the currently addressed target asserts its internal version of the DEVSEL# signal prior to the rising-edge of clock four.

CLOCK 4.

ON the rising-edge of clock four:

- The currently addressed target clocks an asserted level onto DEVSEL#. This is the Decode A time slot.

CLOCK 5.

ON the rising-edge of clock five:

- The initiator asserts IRDY# indicating that it is ready to start transferring data.
- The rising-edge of clock five is the first point at which the initiator clocks the state of DEVSEL# into its input register. In this case, it detects an asserted level on its registered copy of DEVSEL# during clock cycle

five. This tells the initiator that it has established a connection with the addressed target. This defines the first point at which the initiator will register the state of TRDY# as the rising-edge of clock six.

- In this example, the target asserts STOP# and deasserts DEVSEL# on the rising-edge of clock five. It does not assert TRDY# because it's not ready to transfer the data. This transition from DEVSEL# asserted in the previous clock to a deassertion of DEVSEL# and assertion of STOP# in the next clock signals a Target Abort to the initiator.

CLOCK 6.

ON the rising-edge of clock six:

- The initiator clocks the state of TRDY#, STOP# and DEVSEL# into its input register.
- The target deasserts STOP# after a one-clock assertion.

DURING clock cycle six:

- Upon detecting the Target Abort indication during clock six:
    - the initiator sets the Received Target Abort bit in its Status register.
    - the target sets the Signaled Target Abort bit in its Status register.
    - the initiator prepares to release the bus on the rising-edge of clock seven.

CLOCK 7. As a result of detecting the Target Abort in clock seven, the initiator deasserts IRDY# and FRAME# to return the bus to the Idle state.

Note that the target has up to eight clocks from the assertion of FRAME# to issue the Target Abort in the first Data Phase. The reason that the limit is set at eight clocks is because the target might perform a subtractive decode, asserting DEVSEL# in the seventh clock of the transaction and issuing the Target Abort in the eighth clock of the transaction. If the target takes several clocks to determine that it wishes to issue a Target Abort, it keeps DEVSEL# asserted until it has decided, and then deasserts DEVSEL# and asserts STOP# for one clock cycle.

Figure 16-5: Target Abort in First Data Phase

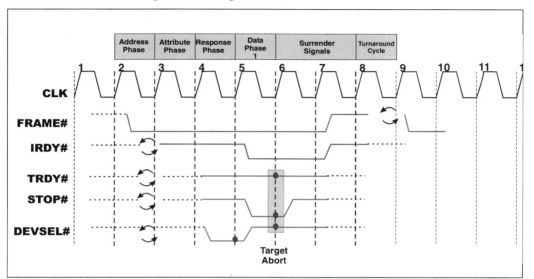

Example Target Abort Issued in Subsequent Data Phase

Refer to Figure 16-6 on page 294. This example illustrates the case where a transaction has been in progress for a while and then the target issues a Target Abort in a subsequent Data Phase. In this example, the first and second data items transfer successfully, but the target issues a Target Abort in the third Data Phase (clock cycle seven). This forces the initiator to terminate the transaction one clock later (in clock nine).

Figure 16-6: Target Abort in Subsequent Data Phase

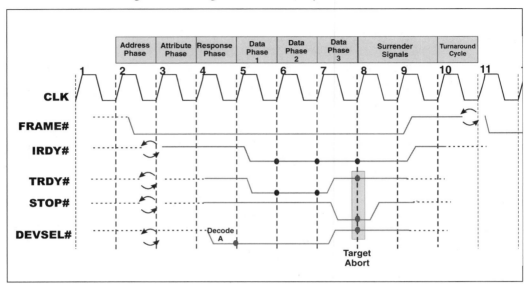

Target Issues a Retry

For a discussion of why a target might issue a Retry to the initiator, refer to "Reasons for Issuing a Retry" on page 107. For a discussion of how the initiator responds to a Retry, refer to "Initiator's Response to a Retry" on page 108.

Refer to Figure 16-7 on page 296.

CLOCK 1.

DURING clock cycle one:
- The transaction has not yet begun. The initiator detected its GNT# asserted (not shown) on the rising-edge of clock one, informing it that it will be the next bus owner. The initiator has been tracking bus activity, so it also knows that the bus will be Idle on the rising-edge of clock two (for more information, refer to Chapter 10, entitled "Bus Arbitration," on page 129).

CLOCK 2.

ON the rising-edge of clock two:
- The initiator starts the transaction by:
  - driving out the byte-specific memory start address onto AD[31:0]. In this example, the start byte address could be any address within the block.
  - driving out the command onto C/BE#[3:0].
  - asserting FRAME#.

CLOCK 3.

ON the rising-edge of clock three:
- All targets on the bus clock the address, command, and the state of the FRAME# signal into their input registers.
- The initiator drives the attributes (see Figure 13-4 on page 201) onto AD[31:0] and C/BE#[3:0]. Among other things, the attributes contain the byte transfer count.

DURING clock cycle three:
- All targets begin the decode of the registered copy of the address and command. In this example, the currently addressed target asserts its internal version of the DEVSEL# signal prior to the rising-edge of clock four.

CLOCK 4.

ON the rising-edge of clock four:
- The currently addressed target clocks an asserted level onto DEVSEL#. This is the Decode A time slot.

CLOCK 5.

ON the rising-edge of clock five:
- The initiator asserts IRDY#, indicating that it is ready to start transferring data.
- The rising-edge of clock five is the first point at which the initiator clocks the state of DEVSEL# into its input register. In this case, it detects an asserted level on its registered copy of DEVSEL# during clock cycle five. This tells the initiator that it has established a connection with the addressed target. This defines the first point at which the initiator will register the state of TRDY# as the rising-edge of clock six.
- In this example, the target asserts STOP# while leaving DEVSEL# asserted. It does not assert TRDY# because it's not ready to transfer the data. This transition from DEVSEL# asserted in the previous clock to a continued assertion of DEVSEL# and the assertion of STOP# without TRDY# asserted in the next clock signals a Retry to the initiator.

CLOCK 6.

ON the rising-edge of clock six:

- The initiator clocks the state of TRDY#, STOP# and DEVSEL# into its input register.
- The target deasserts STOP# and DEVSEL#.

DURING clock cycle six:

- Upon detecting the registered Retry indication during clock six, the initiator prepares to release the bus on the rising-edge of clock seven.

CLOCK 7. As a result of detecting the Retry in clock six, the initiator deasserts IRDY# and FRAME# to return the bus to the Idle state.

Note that the target has up to eight clocks from the assertion of FRAME# to issue the Retry in the first Data Phase. The reason that the limit is set at eight clocks is because the target might perform a subtractive decode, asserting DEVSEL# in the seventh clock of the transaction and issuing the Retry in the eighth clock of the transaction. If the target takes several clocks to determine that it wishes to issue a Retry, it keeps DEVSEL# asserted until it has decided, and then asserts STOP# for one clock cycle after which it deasserts both STOP# and DEVSEL#.

Figure 16-7: Target Issues a Retry

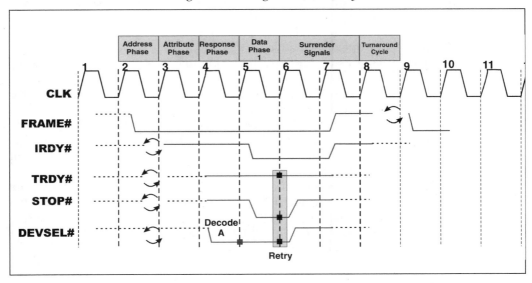

Target Issues Single Data Phase Disconnect

General

A classic example wherein a target would issue a Single Data Phase Disconnect is the case where an initiator attempts a burst with a target that doesn't support bursting. In other words, the target doesn't implement an address counter to latch the start address into and increment as the transaction moves from Data Phase to Data Phase.

Refer to Figure 16-8 on page 299.

CLOCK 1.
> **DURING** clock cycle one:
> - The transaction has not yet begun. The initiator detected its GNT# asserted (not shown) on the rising-edge of clock one, informing it that it will be the next bus owner. The initiator has been tracking bus activity, so it also knows that the bus will be Idle on the rising-edge of clock two (for more information, refer to Chapter 10, entitled "Bus Arbitration," on page 129).

CLOCK 2.
> **ON** the rising-edge of clock two:
> - The initiator starts the transaction by:
>   - driving out the byte-specific memory start address onto AD[31:0]. In this example, the start byte address could be any address within the block.
>   - driving out the command onto C/BE#[3:0].
>   - asserting FRAME#.

CLOCK 3.
> **ON** the rising-edge of clock three:
> - All targets on the bus clock the address, command, and the state of the FRAME# signal into their input registers.
> - The initiator drives the attributes (see Figure 13-4 on page 201) onto AD[31:0] and C/BE#[3:0]. Among other things, the attributes contain the byte transfer count.
>
> **DURING** clock cycle three:
> - All targets begin the decode of the registered copy of the address and command. In this example, the currently addressed target asserts its internal version of the DEVSEL# signal prior to the rising-edge of clock four.

CLOCK 4.

ON the rising-edge of clock four:
- The currently addressed target clocks an asserted level onto DEVSEL#. This is the Decode A time slot.

CLOCK 5.

ON the rising-edge of clock five:
- The initiator asserts IRDY#, indicating that it is ready to start transferring data.
- The rising-edge of clock five is the first point at which the initiator clocks the state of DEVSEL# into its input register. In this case, it detects an asserted level on its registered copy of DEVSEL# during clock cycle five. This tells the initiator that it has established a connection with the addressed target, defining the first point at which the initiator will register the state of TRDY# as the rising-edge of clock six.
- In this example, the target asserts STOP# and TRDY# and deasserts DEVSEL# on the rising-edge of clock five. It asserts TRDY# because it's ready to transfer the first data item. It asserts STOP# to prevent the initiator from proceeding beyond the first data transfer. This transition from DEVSEL# asserted in the previous clock to a deassertion of DEVSEL# and assertion of STOP# and TRDY# in the next clock signals a Single Data Phase Disconnect to the initiator.

CLOCK 6.

ON the rising-edge of clock six:
- The initiator clocks the state of TRDY#, STOP# and DEVSEL# into its input register.
- The first data item is registered by the receiving device (initiator if a read; target if a write).

DURING clock cycle six:
- Upon detecting the registered Single Data Phase Disconnect indication during clock six, the initiator prepares to release the bus on the rising-edge of clock seven.
- The target deasserts STOP# and TRDY# after a one-clock assertion.

CLOCK 7. As a result of detecting the Single Data Phase Disconnect in clock six, the initiator deasserts IRDY# and FRAME# to return the bus to the Idle state.

Note that the target has up to 16 clocks from the assertion of FRAME# to issue the Single Data Phase Disconnect in the first Data Phase. If the target takes several clocks to determine that it wishes to issue a Single Data Phase Disconnect, it keeps DEVSEL# asserted until it has decided, and then deasserts DEVSEL# and asserts STOP# and TRDY# for one clock cycle.

Special Case Scenario

The PCI SIG issued an update to the spec too late for its inclusion in this edition of the book (the author offers his apologies, but did not have sufficient time to analyze the change and incorporate it). It deals with the usage of Single Data Phase Disconnect in response to memory write burst transactions. The reader is urged to read clarifications C35 and C46 in the spec "AF" version Errata and Clarifications document dated 6/26/00.

Figure 16-8: Target Issues Single Data Phase Disconnect

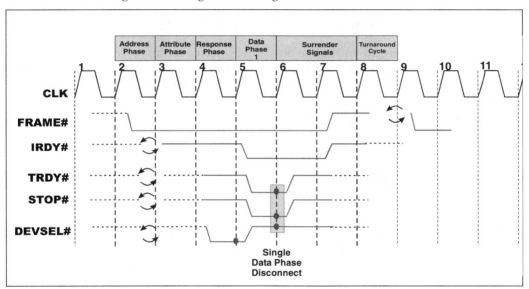

Target Issues Disconnect At Next ADB

During a transaction, the target may need to force the initiator to disconnect the transaction at the next block boundary. "Disconnect At Next ADB" on page 109 provides background on why this might be necessary.

There are three possible scenarios:

- The target issues a disconnect four or more Data Phases from the next block boundary.
- The target issues a disconnect too close to an imminent block boundary.

- The target must disconnect a transaction that starts very close to a block boundary.

The following sections provide a detailed description of the protocol in these three cases.

To issue a Disconnect At Next ADB to the initiator, the target asserts STOP#. Once STOP# is asserted, it must stay asserted until the transaction ends. If the target incurs a severe problem in a Data Phase after the issuance of STOP# but before the upcoming block boundary, it must change the indication from a disconnect (STOP# asserted) to a Target Abort (keep STOP# asserted, but deassert TRDY# and DEVSEL#).

Disconnect Issued Four or More Data Phases From ADB

Refer to Figure 16-9 on page 301. During Data Phase N (clock 17), the target asserts STOP# to tell the initiator to disconnect at the upcoming ADB. In this example, STOP# is asserted in the fourth Data Phase before the next block boundary. This is sufficient warning to the initiator and so it will honor the disconnect on the upcoming block boundary.

CLOCK 17.
ON the rising-edge of clock 17:
- The target asserts STOP# because it wishes the initiator to disconnect the transaction on the upcoming ADB. The target must keep STOP# asserted until the transfer ends.

CLOCK 18.
ON the rising-edge of clock 18:
- The fourth data item from the ADB is transferred.
- The initiator registers the state of STOP# on the rising-edge of clock 18. Its asserted state instructs the initiator to disconnect at the upcoming ADB. As a result, the initiator prepares to deassert FRAME# on the rising-edge of clock 19.

CLOCK 19.
ON the rising-edge of clock 19:
- The third data item from the ADB is transferred.
- As a result of seeing STOP# asserted on the previous rising-edge of the clock, the initiator drives FRAME# to the deasserted state.

CLOCK 20.
ON the rising-edge of clock 20:
- The next-to-last data item from the ADB is transferred.
- The target registers FRAME# deasserted, verifying that the initiator will honor the disconnect upon completion of this block transfer.

CLOCK 21.

ON the rising-edge of clock 21:

- The last data item of the current block is transferred.
- The initiator deasserts IRDY# to return the bus to the Idle state.
- The target deasserts TRDY#, STOP#, and DEVSEL#.

Figure 16-9: Target Disconnects Transaction of Four or More Data Phases

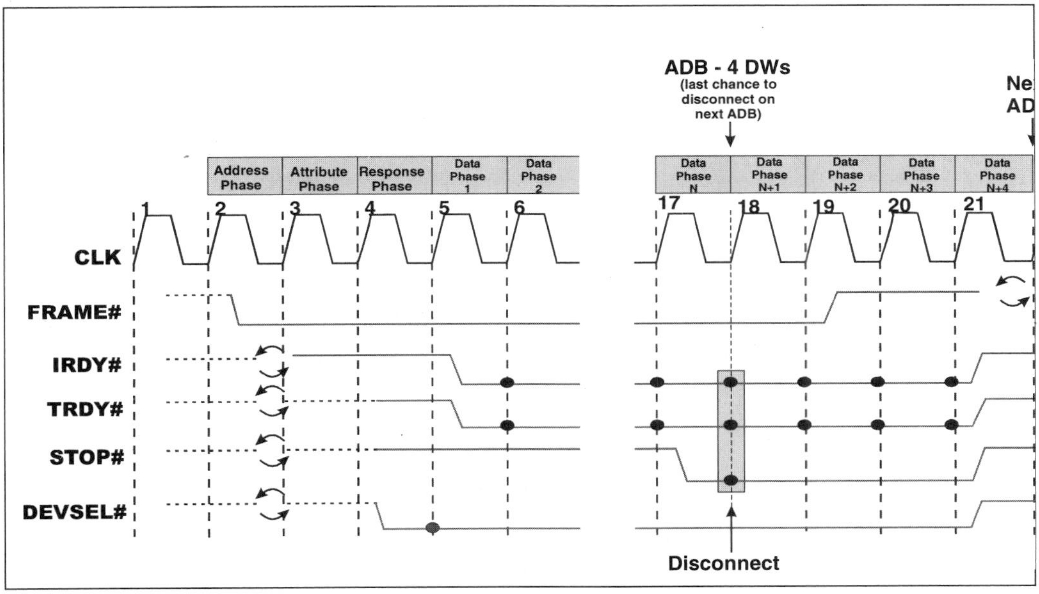

Target Issues Disconnect Too Close to Block Boundary

Refer to Figure 16-10 on page 302. In the figure, the last data item of the first block transfers on the rising-edge of clock nine, and first data item of the next block is transferred on the rising-edge of clock 10. If the target were to issue STOP# in clock six, seven, or eight, this is too close to the block N boundary to force the initiator to end the transaction on the transfer of the final data item of the first block (on the rising-edge of clock nine). The initiator will not honor the disconnect request until the next block boundary (the rising-edge of clock 26 in the figure).

If the target were to assert STOP# starting in any clock in the range from 10 through 21, the disconnect will be honored upon the completion of block N.

Figure 16-10: If Target Issues Disconnect Too Late, Transaction Disconnects at Next ADB

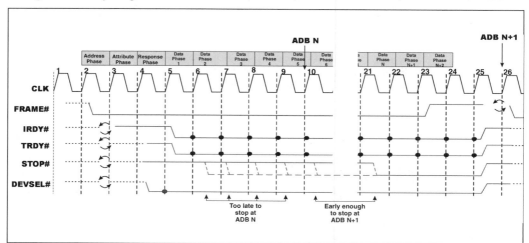

To Disconnect When Start Address Very Close to ADB

Consider a scenario where all of the following are true:

- The start byte address issued by the initiator is close to the end of the current block (i.e., three, two, or one Data Phases from the start of the next block).
- The byte transfer count issued by the initiator identifies an end address beyond the upcoming block boundary.
- The target wishes to force a disconnect upon completing the transfer of the current block.

In this case, the target must assert STOP# in the very first Data Phase of the transaction. The next three sections describe the actions taken by the initiator and target when the start byte address is three, two, or one Data Phases from the upcoming block boundary and the target issues a disconnect request in the very first Data Phase.

Start Address Three Data Phases From Block Boundary. Refer   to Figure 16-11 on page 304.

Clock 2.

During clock cycle two:

- The start byte address issued by the initiator is three Data Phases from the next block boundary.

Clock 3.

During clock cycle three:

- The byte transfer count issued by the initiator identifies an end address beyond the upcoming block boundary.

Clock 4.

On the rising-edge of clock four:

- The target asserts DEVSEL# to claim the transaction.
- The initiator asserts IRDY# to indicate that is ready to start transferring data.
- The initiator drives out the third-to-last data item of the current block.

Clock 5.

On the rising-edge of clock five:

- When the target is ready to start transferring the remainder of the first block, it asserts TRDY#.
- The target also asserts STOP# to force the initiator to terminate the transaction on the imminent block boundary.

Clock 6.

On the rising-edge of clock six:

- The target accepts the first write data item.

During clock six:

- Both parties decrement the remaining byte transfer count.
- The initiator drives out the next-to-last data item of the first block.
- The initiator registers STOP# asserted. As a result, it prepares to deassert FRAME# on the next rising-edge of the clock.

Clock 7.

On the rising-edge of clock seven:

- The initiator drives out the last data item of the current block.
- Because the initiator detected STOP# asserted in the previous clock, it deasserts FRAME#.
- The target accepts the next-to-last data item of the current block.

During clock seven:

- Both parties decrement the remaining byte transfer count.

CLOCK 8.

ON the rising-edge of clock eight:
- The target accepts the final data item of the current block.
- The target deasserts STOP#, TRDY#, and DEVSEL#.
- The initiator stops driving the final data item of the current block and deasserts IRDY# to return the bus to the Idle state.

Although the remaining byte transfer count has not been exhausted, the transaction ends.

Figure 16-11: Target Disconnects Transaction That Starts Three Data Phases From ADB

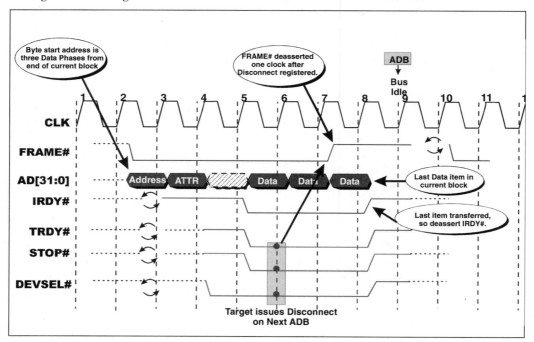

Start Address Two Data Phases From Block Boundary. Refer to Figure 16-12 on page 306.

CLOCK 2.

DURING clock cycle two:
- The start byte address issued by the initiator is two Data Phases from the next block boundary.

CLOCK 3.

DURING clock cycle three:

- The byte transfer count issued by the initiator identifies an end address beyond the upcoming block boundary.

CLOCK 4.

ON the rising-edge of clock four:

- The target asserts DEVSEL# to claim the transaction.
- The initiator asserts IRDY# to indicate that is ready to start transferring data. It drives out the next-to-last data item of the current block.

CLOCK 5.

ON the rising-edge of clock five:

- Because the target is ready to start transferring the remainder of the first block, it asserts TRDY#.
- In this example, the target also asserts STOP# to force the initiator to terminate the transaction on the imminent block boundary.

CLOCK 6.

ON the rising-edge of clock six:

- The target accepts the first write data item.
- The initiator registers STOP# asserted. As a result, it prepares to deassert FRAME# and IRDY# on the next rising-edge of the clock.

DURING clock six:

- Both parties decrement the remaining byte transfer count.
- The initiator drives out the last data item of the first block.

CLOCK 7.

ON the rising-edge of clock seven:

- The target accepts the final data item of the current block.
- The target deasserts STOP#, TRDY#, and DEVSEL#.
- The initiator stops driving the final data item of the current block and deasserts FRAME# and IRDY# to return the bus to the Idle state.

Although the remaining byte transfer count has not been exhausted, the transaction ends.

Figure 16-12: Target Disconnects Transaction That Starts Two Data Phases From ADB

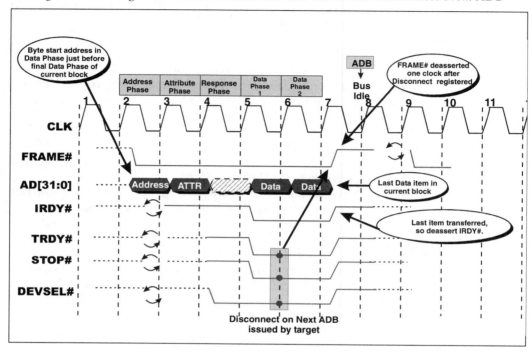

Start Address One Data Phase From Block Boundary. Refer to Figure 16-13 on page 308.

CLOCK 2.
DURING clock cycle two:
- The start byte address issued by the initiator is within the last dword (or qword) of the current block.

CLOCK 3.
DURING clock cycle three:
- The byte transfer count issued by the initiator identifies an end address beyond the upcoming block boundary.

CLOCK 4.
ON the rising-edge of clock four:
- The target asserts DEVSEL# to claim the transaction.
- The initiator asserts IRDY# to indicate that is ready to start transferring data and drives out the last data item of the current block.

CLOCK 5.

ON the rising-edge of clock five:

- When the target is ready to start transferring the end of the first block, it asserts TRDY#. In this example, it also asserts STOP# to force the initiator to terminate the transaction on the imminent block boundary.

CLOCK 6.

ON the rising-edge of clock six:

- The target accepts the write data item.
- The initiator registers STOP# asserted. As a result, it prepares to deassert FRAME# and IRDY# on the next rising-edge of the clock.

DURING clock six:

- Both parties decrement the remaining byte transfer count.
- The initiator drives out the first data item of the next block. Note that this data item will not be accepted by the target.
- The target deasserts STOP#, TRDY#, and DEVSEL# (because the transaction is over).

CLOCK 7.

ON the rising-edge of clock seven:

- The target does not accept the first data item of the next block.
- The initiator stops driving the first data item of the next block and deasserts FRAME# and IRDY# to return the bus to the Idle state.

Although the remaining byte transfer count has not been exhausted, the transaction ends.

Figure 16-13: Target Disconnects Transaction That Starts One Data Phase From ADB

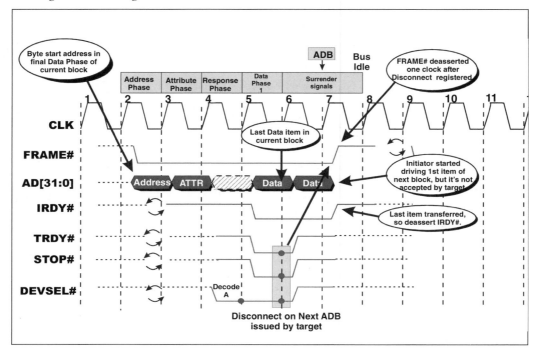

Target Issues a Split Response

For background on Split Transactions, refer to "Split Transactions" on page 118.

Split Response for a Read

Figure 16-14 on page 310 illustrates a read request that receives a Split Response from the target.

CLOCK 3.

ON the rising-edge of clock three:
- The target registers and memorizes the address and command.

CLOCK 4.

ON the rising-edge of clock four:

- The target registers and memorizes the attributes.
- The target asserts DEVSEL#.
- The initiator backs its output drivers off the AD bus in preparation for the target's delivery of read data.

CLOCK 5.

ON the rising-edge of clock five:

- The initiator registers the state of DEVSEL#. Its asserted state verifies that a connection has been made with the target.
- The initiator asserts IRDY# to indicate its readiness to receive the requested read data.

DURING clock cycle five:

- The target drives data of all Fs and asserts TRDY# and deasserts DEVSEL#. It does not assert STOP#. This signaling pattern on TRDY#, DEVSEL# and STOP# indicates a Split Response to the initiator.

CLOCK 6.

ON the rising-edge of clock six:

- The initiator registers the state of TRDY# (asserted), STOP# (deasserted), DEVSEL# (deasserted), and the data from the AD bus.
- The initiator prepares to deassert FRAME# and IRDY# on the next rising-edge of the clock.

DURING clock cycle six:

- The initiator recognizes that it has received a Split Response from the target, thereby indicating that the requested read data will be returned by the target at a later time in a Split Completion transaction.
- The target deasserts TRDY# and stops driving the data pattern.

CLOCK 7.

DURING clock cycle seven:

- The initiator deasserts FRAME# and IRDY#.

Note that if the target is going to deliver a Split Response, it must do so within eight clocks from the assertion of FRAME#. The reason that the limit is set at eight clocks is because the target might perform a subtractive decode, asserting DEVSEL# in the seventh clock of the transaction and issuing the Split Response in the eighth clock of the transaction.

Also note that it is a rule that the target must supply a data pattern of all Fs in the Data Phase. Although this pattern has no meaning currently, future versions of the spec may assign meaning to non-F patterns.

PCI-X System Architecture

Figure 16-14: Target Issues a Split Response to a Memory Read Block, Memory Read Dword, or IO Read

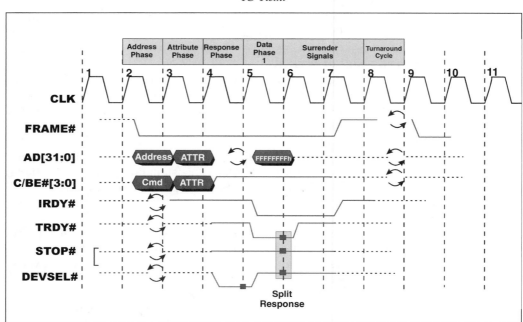

Split Response for an IO or Configuration Write

Figure 16-15 on page 312 illustrates an IO Write request that receives a Split Response from the target. It should be noted that a Configuration Write could also receive a Split Response. It would look the same as Figure 16-15 on page 312 for clocks three through the end of the transaction. The Address Phase would look different, however. A complete description of Configuration transactions can be found in Chapter 20, entitled "Configuration Transactions," on page 425.

CLOCK 3.
    ON the rising-edge of clock three:
      • The target registers and memorizes the address and command.

CLOCK 4.
    ON the rising-edge of clock four:
      • The target registers and memorizes the attributes.
      • The target asserts DEVSEL#.

CLOCK 5.

ON the rising-edge of clock five:
- The initiator registers the state of DEVSEL#. Its asserted state verifies that a connection has been made with the target.
- The initiator asserts IRDY# to indicate that it's driving the write data.

CLOCK 6.

ON the rising-edge of clock six:
- The initiator registers the state of TRDY# (asserted), STOP# (deasserted), DEVSEL# (deasserted).
- The target registers and memorizes the write data to be delivered.

DURING clock cycle six:
- The initiator recognizes that it has received a Split Response from the target. As a result, it recognizes that the target will initiate a Split Completion transaction at a later time with a Split Completion Message to indicate success or failure in delivering the write data.
- The initiator prepares to deassert FRAME# and IRDY# on the next rising-edge of the clock.
- The target deasserts TRDY#.

CLOCK 7.

ON the rising-edge of clock seven:
- The initiator deasserts FRAME# and IRDY# and stops driving the data.

Note that if the target is going to deliver a Split Response, it must do so within eight clocks from the assertion of FRAME#.

Figure 16-15: Target Issues a Split Response to an IO Write

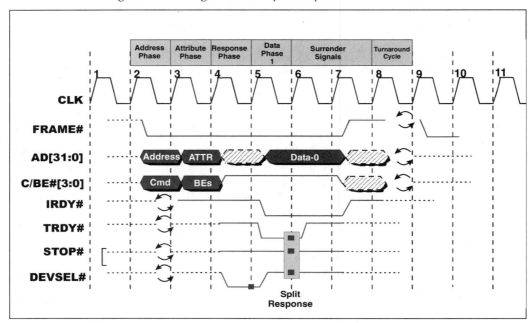

17 *Split Completion Messages*

The Previous Chapter

The previous chapter provided a detailed description of both initiator and target terminations of a transaction. It included clock-by-clock descriptions of example timing diagrams.

This Chapter

This chapter describes the purpose of the Split Completion Message, its format, the messages associated with writes and reads, and device-specific error handling.

The Next Chapter

The next chapter provides a detailed discussion of 64-bit data transfers, 64-bit memory addressing, and additional issues associated with 64-bit devices and 64-bit memory addressing.

Purpose of Split Completion Messages

A device sends a Split Completion Message (SCM) back to a Requester if a problem is encountered while attempting to perform the Split Transaction request. The following types of transactions may be split:

- Memory Read Block
- Alias to Memory Read Block
- Memory Read Dword
- Interrupt Acknowledge
- IO Read
- IO Write

- Configuration Read
- Configuration Write

Remember that Memory Write and Memory Write Block transactions are never split; they are posted in the target's posted-memory write buffer.

After issuing a Split Response to a request, the target is required to deliver one or more Split Completion transactions at a later time to fulfill the request or report an error. Table 17-1 on page 314 defines the possible results that may be delivered back to the Requester for a transaction that has been split.

Table 17-1: After Splitting Transaction, Target Must Deliver Some Form of Completion

Split Request Type	Target is required to deliver:
Memory Read Block (or Alias To Memory Read Block) IO Read Configuration Read Memory Read Dword	• Requested read data, or • A message indicating an error occurred when the Completer attempted to read the requested data from its internal locations. Note that while the Completer may read and supply the requested read data to the Requester without a problem, the data may become corrupted somewhere in its flight path back to the Requester. In this case, the Requester will check the parity of the returning data and determine that it is bad.
Interrupt Acknowledge	• The interrupt vector, or • A message indicating an error occurred when the Completer attempted to read the vector from the Interrupt Controller. Note that while the Completer may read and supply the interrupt vector to the Requester without a problem, the vector may become corrupted somewhere in its flight path back to the Requester. In this case, the Requester will check the parity of the returning vector and determine that it is bad.
IO Write	• A message indicating successful delivery of the write data, or • A message indicating that the write data was corrupted in flight.

Chapter 17: Split Completion Messages

Table 17-1: After Splitting Transaction, Target Must Deliver
Some Form of Completion (Continued)

Split Request Type	Target is required to deliver:
Configuration Write	• A message indicating successful delivery of the write data, or • A message indicating that the write data was corrupted in flight.

SCM Always Terminates a Sequence

Receipt of an SCM associated with a request completes the request. The SCM may have been preceded by one or more Split Completion transactions returning previously requested memory read data.

Upon Receipt of Error Message, Set Status Bit

Upon receipt of a Split Completion Message with the Split Completion Error (SCE) bit set to one in the Attribute Phase (see Figure 17-3 on page 317), the Requester must set the Received Split Completion Error Message bit in its PCI-X status register (see Figure 17-1 on page 315).

Figure 17-1: PCI-X Status Register

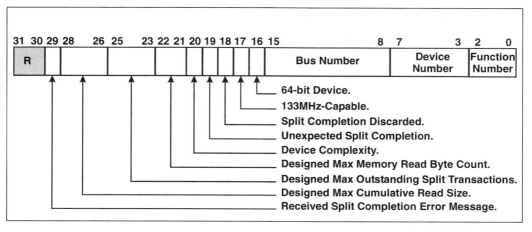

Message Format

A Split Completion transaction that contains a Split Completion Message (SCM) always consists of a single Data Phase during which the initiator of the Split Completion supplies the SCM to the Requester.

Address Phase Format

The information delivered in the Address Phase is pictured in Figure 17-2 on page 316 and has the following characteristics:

- **Requester ID and Transaction Tag.** Decoded by the Requester to identify which of its previous Split Transactions the Split Completion Message is associated with.
- **Lower Address field**. Always cleared to zero.
- **Relaxed Ordering bit**. Always cleared to zero.

Figure 17-2: Split Completion Address Format

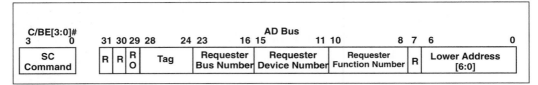

Attribute Phase Format

The information delivered in the Attribute Phase is pictured in Figure 17-3 on page 317 and has the following characteristics:

- **Completer ID**. Identifies the originator of the Split Completion transaction for the benefit of a diagnostic tool that may be monitoring transaction flow.
- **Upper and Lower Byte Count fields**. Always set to a byte count of four (because a message always consists of a single dword value).
- **Byte Count Modified (BCM) bit**. Always cleared to zero.
- **Split Completion Message (SCM) and Split Completion Error (SCE) bits**. The SCM bit is always set to one in a Split Completion transaction that contains a message. Refer to Table 17-2 on page 317.

Figure 17-3: Split Completion Attribute Format

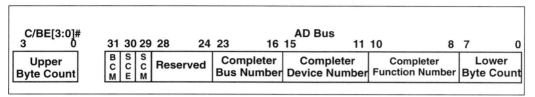

Table 17-2: Encoding of SCM and SCE Bits in Attribute Phase

SCM	SCE	Meaning
0	0	The transaction does not contain a message. This would be the bit setting for a Split Completion transaction returning previously requested read data without error.
0	1	Reserved.
1	0	Error-free completion of a split IO or Configuration Write transaction. A message is included in the Data Phase (but the only message currently defined indicates good completion of the write). Refer to "Good Completion of Split IO or Configuration Write" on page 322.
1	1	Error completion of a read or write. A message is included in the Data Phase. Refer to: <ul><li>"Bad Completion of a Split IO or Configuration Write" on page 323.</li><li>"Bad Completion of a Split Burst Memory Read" on page 324.</li><li>"Byte Count Out-of-Range" in Table 17-6 on page 321.</li><li>"Target Abort" in Table 17-5 on page 319.</li><li>"Master Abort" in Table 17-5 on page 319.</li></ul>

Data Phase Message Format

The format of a message is pictured in Figure 17-4 on page 318 and consists of the following elements:

- **Message Class**. Identifies the basic category of the message. The currently defined Message Classes are listed in Table 17-3 on page 318. They are:
  - **Write Completion Class**. Indicates good completion of an IO or Configuration Write.
  - **PCI-X Bridge Error Class**. Indicates a bridge encountered a problem when attempting the transaction on the destination bus.
  - **Completer Error Class**. Indicates that the Completer encountered a problem with the transaction.
- **Message Index**. Identifies a specific message within the indicated Message Class (refer to Table 17-4 through Table 17-6).
- **Remaining Byte Count**. This value only has meaning if the request was a burst memory read (refer to "Bad Completion of a Split Burst Memory Read" on page 324). If the request was any form of a dword transaction, this field is always set to four.
- **Remaining Lower Address field**. This value only has meaning if the request was a burst memory read (refer to "Bad Completion of a Split Burst Memory Read" on page 324); otherwise, it's value is zero.

Table 17-4 through Table 17-6 provide a detailed description of each Message Class and its currently assigned Message Index values. The remaining sections in this chapter provide a detailed description of each of the Split Completion message scenarios.

Figure 17-4: Split Completion Message Format

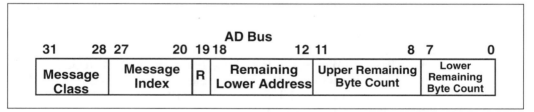

Table 17-3: Currently Defined Message Classes

Message Class	Description
0h	**Write Completion Class** (see Table 17-4 on page 319).
1h	**PCI-X Bridge Error Class.** An error was encountered on the other side of a bridge. See Table 17-5 on page 319.

Table 17-3: Currently Defined Message Classes (Continued)

Message Class	Description
2h	**Completer Error Class**. An error was encountered within the Completer. See Table 17-6 on page 321.
3h-Fh	Reserved for future assignment.

Table 17-4: Message Class 0h: Write Completion Message Class Index Values

Message Index Value	Description
00h	Normal completion of an IO or Configuration Write.
01h-FFh	Reserved for future assignment.

Table 17-5: Message Class 1h: PCI-X Bridge Error Class Index Values

Message Index Value	Description
00h	A **Master Abort** occurred when the transaction was attempted on the destination bus. In other words, no target asserted DEVSEL# to claim the transaction. • The bridge generates an SCM back to the Requester with a Class/Index of 1h/00h. Since the bridge did not connect with the Completer, it must create the Split Completion transaction itself. This subject is covered in detail in "Bridge Creation of a Split Completion" on page 548. • The bridge sets the Received Master Abort bit in the status register associated with the destination bus (Status register if the Master Abort occurred on the bridge's primary side; Secondary Status register if it occurred on its secondary side).

Table 17-5: Message Class 1h: PCI-X Bridge Error Class Index Values (Continued)

Message Index Value	Description
01h	A **Target Abort** occurred when the transaction was attempted on the destination bus. Although a connection was established with the target (i.e., DEVSEL# was asserted), the target issued a Target Abort to the bridge in one of the Data Phases of the transaction. • The bridge generates an SCM back to the Requester with a Class/Index of 1h/01h. Since the bridge received a Split Completion from the Completer, it must create the Split Completion transaction itself. This subject is covered in detail in "Bridge Creation of a Split Completion" on page 548. • The bridge sets the Received Target Abort bit in the status register associated with the destination bus (Status register if the Target Abort occurred on the bridge's primary side; Secondary Status register if it occurred on its secondary side). • The target that issued the Target Abort sets the Signaled Target Abort bit in its Status register.
02h	**Write Data Parity Error.** When the bridge attempted an IO or Configuration Write on the destination bus, the target asserted PERR# to indicate receipt of a corrupted write data item. • The bridge generates an SCM back to the Requester with a Class/Index of 1h/02h. • The target that asserted PERR# sets the Detected Parity Error bit in its Status register. • The bridge sets the Master Data Parity Error bit in the status register associated with the destination bus (Status register if the parity error occurred on the bridge's primary side; Secondary Status register if it occurred on its secondary side).
03h-FFh	Reserved for future assignment.

Note: for a detailed discussion of bridge error handling scenarios, refer to "Error Handling" on page 549.

Table 17-6: Message Class 2h: Completer Error Message Class Index Values

Message Index Value	Description
00h	**Byte Count Out-of-Range**. This message can only occur for a burst memory read wherein the end address (as specified by the byte count) exceeds the end address of the Completer addressed in the Address Phase. • Prior to initiating the Split Completion containing this SCM, the Completer must return all data between the start address and the Completer's end address in one or more Split Completion transactions. • When the Requester receives this message, it generates an interrupt request to invoke the interrupt handler within its device driver. The driver then checks a device-specific status register to determine the nature of the problem. • The spec takes the point of view that a Requester attempting to perform a burst read beyond a target's address boundary is a rare case. The device driver may or may not implement an error handler for this condition. If it doesn't, the error is fatal. The driver may have a handler, however, that will issue another read request to its Requester, causing it to initiate another burst memory read starting at the next address.
01h	**Split Write Data Parity Error**. On an IO or Configuration Write, the Completer may signal a Split Response, but also detect corrupted write data. In this case, the Completer asserts PERR# to the initiator of the write and sends it this SCM message. The initiator of the write sets the Master Data Parity Error bit in its Status register. If the initiator of the write is a bridge, it sets the Master Data Parity Error bit in the status register associated with the destination bus (Status register if the parity error occurred on the bridge's primary side; Secondary Status register if it occurred on its secondary side).
02h-7Fh	Reserved for future assignment.

Table 17-6: Message Class 2h: Completer Error Message Class Index Values (Continued)

Message Index Value	Description
8Xh	**Device-Specific Error**. If the Completer detects an error other than Byte Count Out-of-Range or a Split Write Data Parity Error, it sends a device-specific error message back to the Requester. The message value is 8Xh, where "Xh" represents one of 16 possible device-specific error codes. Naturally, only device-specific software (such as the device's driver) would know how to interpret these error codes. Also refer to "Device-Specific Error Handling" on page 325.
90h-FFh	Reserved for future assignment.

Write Completion Indication

Good Completion of Split IO or Configuration Write

On a successful completion of an IO or Configuration Write, an SCM with a Message Class of 00h (Write Completion Message Class) and a Message Index value of 00h (Good Completion) will be issued by either the Completer or by an intervening bridge:

1. It is issued by the Completer under either of the following circumstances:
   a) The Completer is located on the same bus as the Requester, it has split the transaction, and it has successfully delivered the write data to internal IO or Configuration location(s).
   b) The Completer is located on the other side of a PCIX-to-PCIX bridge and it responded to the bridge's initiation of the IO or Configuration Write with a Split Response. The Completer successfully delivers the write data to internal IO or Configuration location(s), and subsequently initiates a Split Completion transaction with an SCM indicating good completion.
2. If the Completer accepts the write data immediately when the bridge initiates the IO or Configuration Write, the bridge then initiates a Split Completion transaction with an SCM indicating good completion.

Bad Completion of a Split IO or Configuration Write

Earlier in time, the Requester issued an IO or Configuration Write and received a Split Response from the Completer (if the Completer resides on the same bus as the Requester) or from a bridge that resides between the Requester and the Completer. If the data is written successfully, a Split Completion Message is issued with Message Class 0h and a Message Index value of 00h (see Table 17-4 on page 319). The error scenarios are:

1. Message Class 1h (PCI-X Bridge Error Class) and:
   a) Message Index Value 00h: a Master Abort occurred when the bridge attempted the write on the destination bus. Refer to Table 17-5 on page 319 for a detailed description.
   b) Message Index Value 01h: a Target Abort occurred when the bridge attempted the write on the destination bus. Refer to Table 17-5 on page 319 for a detailed description.
   c) Message Index Value 02h: a Write Data Parity Error occurred when the bridge attempted the write on the destination bus. Refer to Table 17-5 on page 319 for a detailed description.
2. Message Class 2h (Completer Error Message Class) and:
   a) Message Index Value 01h: a Split Write Data Parity Error. Refer to Table 17-6 on page 321 for more information.
   b) Message Index Value 8Xh: a Device-Specific Error. Refer to Table 17-6 on page 321 for more information.

Read Completion Indication

Good Completion of a Split Dword Read

Good completion of a split IO Read, Configuration Read, or Memory Read Dword transaction is indicated by a Split Completion transaction with a single Data Phase returning the requested read data. Neither the SCM nor the SCE bit is set to one in the Split Completion's Attribute Phase.

Good Completion of a Split Burst Memory Read

Good completion of a split burst memory read is indicated by the Completer's return of all of the requested read data in a series of one or more Split Completion transactions. Neither the SCM nor the SCE bit is set to one in the Attribute Phase of each of the Split Completion transactions.

Bad Completion of a Split Dword Read

Bad completion of a split IO Read, Configuration Read, or Memory Read Dword transaction is indicated by a single Split Completion transaction containing an error message. The possible error messages are:

- **Device-Specific Error**. See Table 17-6 on page 321.
- **Master Abort Error**. See Table 17-5 on page 319.
- **Target Abort Error**. See Table 17-5 on page 319.

Bad Completion of a Split Burst Memory Read

General

Bad completion of a split burst memory read transaction is indicated by a single Split Completion transaction containing an error message. The possible scenarios are:

- **Device-Specific Error**. See Message Index Value 8Xh in Table 17-6 on page 321. This message could be sent in the first (and only) Split Completion transaction, or may be preceded by one or more Split Completions returning good read data (assuming that the Completer can read some but not all of the data without error).
- **Master Abort Error**. See Message Index Value 00h in Table 17-5 on page 319. By definition, this message would be contained within the one and only Split Completion transaction.
- **Target Abort Error**. See Message Index Value 01h in Table 17-5 on page 319. This message could be sent in the first (and only) Split Completion transaction, or may be preceded by one or more Split Completions returning good read data (assuming that the Completer can read some but not all of the data without error).
- **Byte Count Out-of-Range Error**. For a detailed explanation, refer to the description of Message Index Value 00h in Table 17-6 on page 321. Also see "Handling Completer Byte Count Out-of-Range Error" on page 627.

Remaining Byte Count and Remaining Lower Address Fields

Refer to Figure 17-4 on page 318. Upon receipt of a Split Completion Message associated with a burst memory read request, a bridge uses the **Remaining Byte Count** and the **Remaining Lower Address** fields provided in the message to release buffer space previously reserved to receive the Split Completion read data (all of the read data will not be returned due to an error). These two fields have the following meaning in a Split Completion Message associated with a burst memory read request:

- **Remaining Byte Count**. This value indicates the number of bytes of read data that have not already been sent in the previous Split Completions associated with this burst memory read request.
- **Remaining Lower Address field**. This value represents the least-significant seven bits of the address of the first byte of read data that has not already been sent in the previous Split Completions associated with this burst memory read request.

Device-Specific Error Handling

Refer to Table 17-6 on page 321. One way to report the receipt of a device-specific error is for the Requester to store the lower nibble (four bits) of the Message Index Value in a device-specific location and cause an interrupt to the processor. The device driver servicing the interrupt would read the location to determine the nature of the problem.

The designer may choose to reserve one nibble value (such as 0h) to indicate that no error condition exists. In this case, software would clear the register after the occurrence of each error, so it could tell the difference between new errors and errors it had already recorded.

Alternatively, all 16 possible values could be assigned to different errors and an additional device-specific bit assigned to indicate that the register contains a new error condition.

18 64-Bit Transactions

The Previous Chapter

The previous chapter described the purpose of the Split Completion Message, its format, the messages associated with writes and reads, and device-specific error handling.

This Chapter

This chapter provides a detailed discussion of 64-bit data transfers, 64-bit memory addressing, and additional issues associated with 64-bit devices and 64-bit memory addressing.

The Next Chapter

The next chapter provides a detailed discussion of parity generation, parity checking, Address and Attribute Phase parity, and Data Phase parity.

General Format of Timing Diagram Descriptions

The sections that follow provide a detailed description of various transaction scenarios. Each transaction is described clock-by-clock, with the events during each clock divided into two categories:

- **ON** the rising-edge of clock N.
- **DURING** clock N.

Please keep in mind that some events could actually be correctly placed in either of these event categories.

64-Bit Data Transfers and 64-Bit Addressing: Separate Capabilities

The PCI and PCI-X specifications provide a mechanism that permits a 64-bit initiator to perform 64-bit data transfers with a 64-bit target. At the beginning of a transaction, the 64-bit PCI-X initiator automatically senses if the responding target is a 64-bit or a 32-bit device. If it's a 64-bit device, up to eight bytes (a qword) may be transferred during each Data Phase. Throughput of 1.06GB/second can be achieved at a bus speed of 133MHz (8 bytes/transfer x 133.33 million transfers/second). If the responding target is a 32-bit device, the initiator automatically senses this and steers all data to or from the target over the lower four data paths (AD[31:0]).

The specifications also define 64-bit memory addressing capability. This capability is only used to address memory targets that reside above the 4GB address boundary. While this capability is optional in the PCI environment, PCI-X requires that all initiators (both 32- and 64-bit initiators) that address memory must be capable of using 64-bit memory addressing. Furthermore, in PCI-X all memory BARs (Base Address Registers; i.e. memory decoders) must be implemented as 64-bit BARs rather than 32-bit BARs. In PCI, they may be either 32- or 64-bits wide.

It is important to note that 64-bit addressing and 64-bit data transfer capability are two features, separate and distinct from each other.

- An initiator that performs any memory transactions is required to support 64-bit memory addressing, while one that never addresses memory (or memory-mapped IO locations) will not support it.
- A target that contains memory (or memory-mapped IO locations) must support 64-bit memory addressing, while one that contains no memory (or memory-mapped IO locations) will not support it.
- An initiator may or may not support the ability to perform 64-bit data transfers.
- A target may or may not support the ability to perform 64-bit data transfers.

64-Bit Extension Signals

In order to support the 64-bit data transfer capability, the PCI and PCI-X buses implement an additional thirty-nine pins:

- **REQ64#** is asserted by a 64-bit initiator to indicate that it would like to perform 64-bit data transfers. REQ64# has the same timing and duration as the FRAME# signal. The REQ64# signal line must be **supplied with a pullup** resistor on the system board. REQ64# cannot be permitted to float when a 32-bit initiator is performing a transaction.
- **ACK64#** is asserted by a target in response to REQ64# assertion by the initiator (if the target supports 64-bit data transfers). ACK64# has the same timing and duration as DEVSEL# (but ACK64# must not be asserted unless REQ64# is asserted by the initiator). Like REQ64#, the ACK64# signal line must also be **supplied with a pullup** resistor on the system board. ACK64# cannot be permitted to float when a 32-bit device is the target of a transaction.
- **AD[63:32]** comprise the upper four address/data paths. The system board designer **must provide pullup resistors** on these signal lines so they will not float during bus Idle time or during transactions that are only using the lower half of the bus.
- **C/BE#[7:4]** comprise the upper four command/byte enable signals. The system board designer **must provide pullup resistors** on these signal lines so they will not float during bus Idle time or during transactions that are only using the lower half of the bus.
- **PAR64** is the parity bit that provides even parity for the upper four AD paths and the upper four C/BE signal lines. The system board designer **must provide a pullup resistor** on this signal line so it will not float during bus Idle time or during transactions that are only using the lower half of the bus.

The following sections provide a detailed discussion of 64-bit data transfer and addressing capability.

REQ64# and ACK64# Have Same Timing as FRAME# and DEVSEL#

Just as in 64-bit PCI, the initiator always asserts REQ64# and FRAME# together when it starts a 64-bit transaction and deasserts them simultaneously.

Likewise, the target of a 64-bit transaction always asserts and deasserts ACK64# along with DEVSEL# (assuming that it's a 64-bit target and that the initiator asserted REQ64#). Refer to Figure 18-7 on page 346. This is also true in the case where a 64-bit initiator connects with a 64-bit target and the target issues a Single Data Phase Disconnect in the first Data Phase (see Figure 16-8 on page 299). The target must deassert ACK64# in the same clock that it deasserts DEVSEL#.

In Attribute Phase, Upper Bus Reserved and Driven High

During the Attribute Phase, the upper half of the bus (AD[63:32] and C/BE#[7:4]) is treated as follows:

- If the initiator is a 64-bit initiator, the upper half of the bus is reserved and must be driven high.
- If the initiator is a 32-bit initiator, the required pullup resistors on the system board maintain these signals in the logic high state.

Block Length Remains the Same

Irrespective of whether the current transaction is a 64- or 32-bit transfer, the block length (i.e., the ADQ length) is always 128 bytes. Obviously then, a block can be transferred in half the number of Data Phases when performing 64-bit transfers.

Bursts Cannot Cross 2^{64} Boundary

Memory burst transactions are forbidden to cross the 2^{64} address boundary.

REQ64# Not Permitted in Dword Transactions

General

Since the nature of a dword transaction is that it transfers a dword or a subset thereof, it is illegal for an initiator to assert REQ64# when it initiates any of the dword transactions. This includes the Memory Read Dword transaction.

When a 64-bit capable initiator starts a dword transaction, it does not use the upper half of the bus. The required pullups on the system board maintain the upper half of the bus in the logic high state during periods when it is not in use.

...Unless It's a Split Completion

The Completer can initiate a Split Completion as a 64-bit transfer if the Split Request was a dword transaction. In the Data Phase, the Completer drives the dword of read data or the Split Completion Message onto AD[31:0]. The Lower Address field in the Split Completion address is cleared to zero (see Figure 13-11 on page 210).

MSI Write Always Writes a Single 32-Bit Data Value

The PCI 2.2 spec stipulates that the memory write that is performed to write the MSI (Message Signaled Interrupt) data value always consists of a single, 32-bit data value:

- The 16-bit message value is driven onto the lower two data paths, AD[15:0].
- The upper two data paths, AD[31:16], must be driven to zero.
- C/BE#[3:0] are asserted.

For additional information regarding MSI generation in the PCI-X environment, refer to "MSI Feature Optional in PCI Environment" on page 22. For a complete description of the MSI capability, refer to the chapter on interrupts in Mind-Share's *PCI System Architecture* book (Fourth Edition or later; published by Addison-Wesley).

Bridge Must Support DAC on Both Interfaces

Refer to Figure 18-1 on page 332. The 1.1 PCI-to-PCI Bridge Architecture spec states that a PCI-to-PCI bridge must support upstream movement of a memory transaction that uses the DAC command (for a detailed description of the DAC command and 64-bit memory addressing, refer to "Addressing Memory Above 4GB Boundary" on page 372). In the figure, this would be a memory transaction initiated on bus one that targets a memory address above the 4GB address boundary in main memory. In other words, the bridge must recognize the DAC command when it latches the transaction from bus one, and must be capable of re-issuing the transaction on bus zero. However, a PCI-to-PCI bridge does not have to support downstream movement of a memory transaction (from bus zero to bus one).

PCI-X System Architecture

The PCI-X spec, on the other hand, dictates that a PCI-X bridge must support both upstream and downstream movement of the DAC command. It must be capable (on both of its interfaces) of acting as the target of a memory transaction using the DAC command and furthermore must be capable (on both of its interfaces) of re-issuing a memory transaction that uses the DAC command.

Figure 18-1: Example System

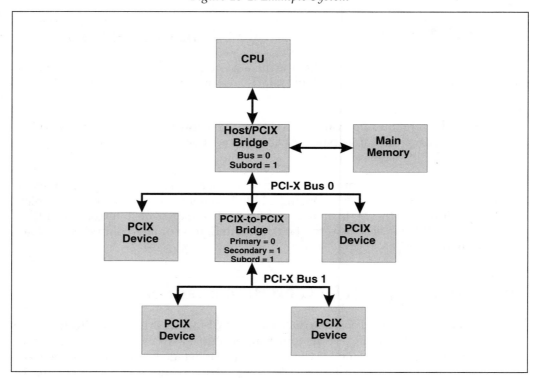

Width of Function's Connection to Bus

General

Software can determine the width of a PCI-X function's connection to the AD bus by reading a status bit in the function's PCI-X Status register (see bit 16 in Figure 18-2 on page 333). The PCI-X Status register is implemented as a configuration register. A complete description of the configuration registers in non-bridge PCI-X functions can be found in Chapter 21, entitled "Non-Bridge Configuration Registers," on page 453, while a description of the configuration registers in PCI-X bridge function can be found in Chapter 22, entitled "Bridge Configuration Registers," on page 487.

The state of this status bit indicates the width of the function's connection to the AD bus. The configuration software uses this bit to determine if a card is installed in the appropriate type of slot. As an example, a function with a 64-bit interface to the AD bus may have been installed in a 32-bit add-in connector, thereby limiting it to 32-bit data transfers and radically reducing its performance level.

It is assumed that the platform-specific configuration software knows which device positions on each embedded bus are populated by connectors and also knows the width of each connector.

The PCI-X spec says that this status bit has no meaning for a function that is embedded on the system board. This is because it would obviously be fruitless for the configuration software to prompt the end user to move the card to a connector of the appropriate width (unless, of course, the software expects the end-user to use power tools).

If software determines that one or more functions within a multi-function card installed in a 32-bit add-in connector have a 64-bit connection to the bus while other functions within the same card do not, the spec suggests that software prompt the end user to move the card to a 64-bit connector.

Figure 18-2: PCI-X Status Register

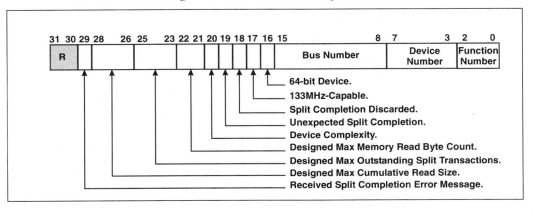

Add-In Card With a Bridge

If the software determines that an add-in card incorporates a PCIX-to-PCIX bridge, it is possible that the bus on the secondary side of the bridge might implement add-in connectors. However, the configuration software may or may not be able to determine this:

- If the bridge implements the Slot Numbering New Capability register set, software can use this register set to determine the presence and the number of add-in connectors that are on the bridge's secondary bus. Unfortunately, although these registers will indicate the number of connectors, there is no way to determine the width of each connector.
- If the bridge does not implement this register set, then software cannot determine the presence or absence of add-in connectors on the bridge's secondary bus.

For a complete description of the Slot Numbering register set, refer to Mind-Share's *PCI System Architecture* book (Fourth Edition or later; published by Addison-Wesley).

Determining the Width of a Bridge's Interfaces

A PCIX-to-PCIX bridge may implement either 32- or 64-bit interfaces. Software can determine the width of a bridge's primary and secondary interfaces by checking a status bit in the bridge's PCI-X Secondary Status register (bit 0 in Figure 18-3 on page 334) and PCI-X Bridge Status register (bit 16 in Figure 18-4 on page 335).

Figure 18-3: PCI-X Secondary Status Register

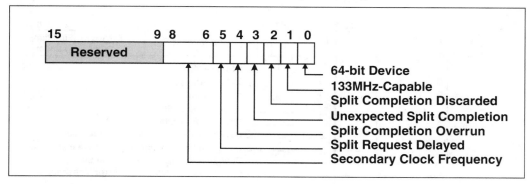

Figure 18-4: PCI-X Bridge Status Register

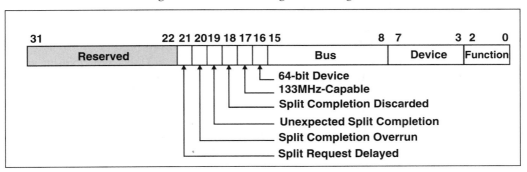

64-Bit Cards in 32-Bit Add-In Connectors

A 64-bit card installed in a 32-bit expansion slot automatically only uses the lower half of the bus to perform transfers. This is true because the system board designer connects the REQ64# output pin and the ACK64# input pin on the 32-bit connector to individual pullups on the system board and to nothing else.

When a 64-bit initiator is installed in a 32-bit card slot and it initiates a transaction, its assertion of REQ64# is not visible to any of the targets. In addition, its ACK64# input is always sampled deasserted (because it's pulled up on the system board). This forces the initiator to use only the lower part of the bus during the transfer. Furthermore, if the target addressed in the transaction is a 64-bit target, it samples REQ64# deasserted (because it's pulled up on the system board), forcing it to only utilize the lower half of the bus during the transaction and to disable its ACK64# output.

The 64-bit extension signal lines on the card itself cannot be permitted to float when they are not in use. The CMOS input receivers attached to the upper half of the bus on the card would oscillate and draw excessive current, thus violating the "green" aspect of the specification. When the card is installed in a 32-bit slot, it cannot use the upper half of the bus. The manner in which the card detects the type of slot (REQ64# sampled deasserted at startup time) and ensures that the CMOS input receivers attached to the upper half of the bus on the card do not oscillate is described in the next section.

Pullups Prevent 64-Bit Extension From Floating When Not in Use

If the 64-bit extension signals (AD[63:32], C/BE#[7:4] and PAR64) are permitted to float when not in use, the CMOS input buffers on the card will oscillate and draw excessive current. In order to prevent the extension from floating when not in use, the system board designer is required to include pullup resistors on the extension signals to keep them from floating. Because these pullups are guaranteed to keep the extension from floating when not in use, 64-bit devices that are embedded on the system board and 64-bit cards installed in 64-bit PCI add-in connectors don't need to take any special action to keep the extension from floating when they are not using it.

The 64-bit extension is not in use under the following circumstances:

- The PCI bus is Idle.
- A 32-bit initiator is performing a transaction with a 32-bit target.
- A 32-bit initiator is performing a transaction with a 64-bit target. Upon detecting REQ64# deasserted at the start of the transaction, the target will not use the upper half of the bus.
- A 64-bit initiator addresses a target to perform 32-bit data transfers (REQ64# deasserted) and the target resides below the 4GB address boundary (the upper half of the bus is not used during the Address Phase and is also not used in the Data Phases). Whether the target is a 32-bit or a 64-bit target, the upper half of the bus isn't used during the Data Phases (because REQ64# is deasserted).
- A 64-bit initiator attempts a 64-bit data transfer (REQ64# asserted) with a 32-bit memory target that resides below the 4GB boundary. In this case, the initiator only uses the lower half of the bus during the Address Phase (because it's only generating a 32-bit address). When it discovers that the currently addressed target is a 32-bit target (ACK64# not asserted when DEVSEL# asserted), the initiator ceases to use the upper half of the bus during the Data Phases.

Problem: A 64-Bit Card in a 32-Bit PCI Connector

Refer to Figure 18-5 on page 337. Installation of a 64-bit card in a 32-bit card connector is permitted. The main (32-bit) portion of the connector contains all of the 32-bit PCI-X signals, while an extension to the connector contains the 64-bit extension signals (with the exception of REQ64# and ACK64# which are located on the 32-bit portion of the connector).

When a 64-bit device is installed in a 32-bit PCI-X expansion slot, the system board pullups on AD[63:32], C/BE#[7:4] and PAR64 are not available to the add-in card. This means that the add-in card's input buffers that are connected to the extension signal pins will float, oscillate, and draw excessive current.

The PCI specification states that the add-in card designer must *not* solve this problem by supplying pullup resistors on the extension lines on the add-in card. Using this approach would cause problems when the card is installed in a 64-bit expansion slot. There would then be two sets of pullup resistors on these signal lines (the ones on the card plus the ones on the system board). If all designers solved the problem in this manner, a machine with multiple 64-bit cards inserted in 64-bit card connectors would have multiple pullups on the extension signals, resulting in pullup current overload.

The specification provides a method for a 64-bit card to determine at startup time whether it's installed in a 32- or 64-bit connector. If the card detects that it is plugged into a 64-bit connector, the pullups on the system board will keep the input receivers on the card from floating when the extension is not in use. On the other hand, if a 64-bit card detects that it is installed in a 32-bit card connector, the logic on the card must keep the input receivers from switching. The specification states that an approach similar to one of the following should be used:

- Biasing the input buffer to turn it off.
- Actively driving the outputs continually (since they aren't connected to anything).

Figure 18-5: 64- and 32-Bit Connectors

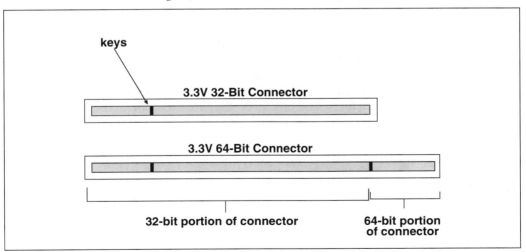

How 64-Bit Card Determines Type of Slot Its Installed In

Refer to Figure 18-6 on page 339. When the system is powered up, the reset signal is automatically asserted. During this period of time, the logic on the system board must assert the REQ64# signal as well as RST#. REQ64# has a single pullup resistor on it and is connected to the REQ64# pin on all 64-bit devices integrated onto the system board and on all 64-bit expansion slots. The specification states that the REQ64# signal line on each 32-bit expansion slot (REQ64# and ACK64# are located on the 32-bit portion of the connector), however, must each have its own independent pullup resistor.

During reset time, the system board reset logic initially asserts the bus RST# signal while the POWERGOOD signal from the power supply is deasserted. During the assertion of RST#, the system board logic asserts REQ64# (REQ64# must be held asserted for a minimum of 10 clock cycles prior to the deassertion of RST#; this is the setup time) and keeps it asserted until after it removes the RST# signal (for a minimum of 0ns and a maximum of 50ns; this is the hold time). When POWERGOOD is asserted by the power supply logic, the system board reset logic deasserts the bus RST# signal. On the trailing-edge of RST# assertion, all 64-bit devices are required to sample the state of the REQ64# signal.

All 64-bit devices that are embedded on the system board or that are installed in 64-bit expansion slots sample REQ64# asserted on the trailing-edge of RST#. This informs them that they are connected to the extension pullups on the system board and need take no special action to keep the extension from floating when not using it.

All 64-bit devices that are installed in 32-bit card slots, however, detect REQ64# deasserted on the trailing-edge of RST#. This informs them that they are not connected to the system board-resident pullups on the extension signals. The card logic must therefore take responsibility for the state of its own on-card 64-bit extension signal lines. The card must therefore use one of the methods cited in the previous section to prevent excessive current draw by the card's input receivers.

Figure 18-6: REQ64# Signal Routing

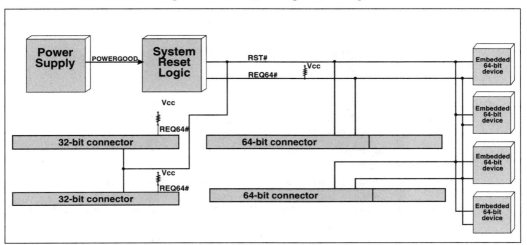

64-Bit Data Transfer Capability

The agreement to perform 64-bit transfers is established by a handshake between the initiator and the target. When the initiator supports 64-bit transfers and wishes to perform 64-bit transfers, it asserts REQ64# along with FRAME# during the Address Phase. If the currently addressed target supports 64-bit data transfers, it replies with ACK64#. Because they are both pulled high, the quiescent state of REQ64# and ACK64# is deasserted. If either the initiator or the target, or both, do not support 64-bit data transfers, 32-bit data transfers are used instead.

During 64-bit transfers, all transfer timing during Data Phases is identical to that used during 32-bit data transfers. One to eight bytes (or no bytes) may be transferred between the initiator and the target during each Data Phase. As in 32-bit transfers, the usage of the Byte Enables during a transaction's Data Phase(s) is defined by the type of transaction:

- The Byte Enables are Reserved and Driven High in all Data Phases of Memory Read Block, Alias To Memory Read Block, Memory Write Block, Alias To Memory Write Block, and Split Completion transactions.
- The Byte Enables can vary from Data Phase to Data Phase during a Memory Write transaction. Any combination of Byte Enables is valid, including none asserted (the initiator may wish to "skip" a qword). The initiator is not per-

mitted to assert any Byte Enables associated with locations prior to the start byte address. Likewise, it is not permitted to assert any Byte Enables associated with locations after the end address (which is defined by the byte transfer count).

- The Byte Enables are delivered during the Attribute Phase in all Dword transactions and they are Reserved and Driven High during the transaction's Data Phase.

64-Bit Transfers: Only Burst Memory Operations

As in PCI, only memory commands may utilize 64-bit data transfer capability. The PCI specification provides the following arguments for not implementing support for 64-bit data transfers for the other types of commands:

- During the special cycle transaction, no target responds with DEVSEL#. ACK64#, therefore, is also not asserted.
- Configuration transactions do not require the level of throughput achievable with 64-bit data transfers and therefore do not justify the added complexity and cost necessary to support 64-bit data transfer capability. The author has heard arguments from some designers (of large mainframes and supercomputers) that devices that require large streams of configuration information would benefit from 64-bit configuration support.
- As with configuration transactions, IO transactions do not require a high level of throughput and therefore do not justify the added complexity and cost necessary to support 64-bit data transfer capability.
- By definition, the Interrupt Acknowledge command only performs a single Data Phase consisting of a one, two, three or four byte transfer.

Start Address Byte-Aligned

In PCI, the start memory address issued by the initiator of a 64-bit transfer has the following characteristics:

- The start address it issues is qword-aligned (e.g., address 00000100h, 00000108h, 00000110h, etc.).
- This means that AD[2] must be set to zero.
- AD[1:0] convey the addressing sequence to the target (for more information see the chapter *Memory and IO Addressing* in MindShare's *PCI System Architecture, Fourth Edition* book).

In PCI-X, the start memory address is byte-aligned, rather than qword-aligned, and identifies a start byte address within the qword identified by the address information supplied on AD[31:3] during the Address Phase. Unlike PCI memory addressing, there is only one form of memory addressing, and that is linear addressing. Cache Line Wrap addressing has been eliminated in PCI-X.

64-Bit Target's Interpretation of Address

Assuming that the target supports 64-bit data transfers (it asserts ACK64#), the target latches the start qword address presented on AD[31:3] into its address counter (if it supports burst mode). The target increments the address in its address counter by eight at the completion of each Data Phase to point to the next sequential qword. If the transaction is a Memory Write, the target samples the Byte Enables during each Data Phase to determine which of the eight bytes within the currently addressed qword is to be written (and therefore which of the eight data paths are to be used).

32-Bit Target's Interpretation of Address

If the target that responds to the transaction is a 32-bit target (ACK64# not asserted), the target latches the start dword address presented on AD[31:2] into its address counter (if it supports burst mode). The target increments the address in its address counter by four at the completion of each Data Phase to point to the next sequential dword. If the transaction is a Memory Write, the target samples the four lower Byte Enables, C/BE#[3:0], during each Data Phase to determine which of the four bytes within the currently addressed dword is to be written and which of the four data paths (on the AD[31:0] portion of the bus) are to be used.

64-Bit Memory Read Block With 64-Bit Target

Refer to Figure 18-7 on page 346.

CLOCK 1.

DURING clock cycle one:

- The transaction has not yet begun. The initiator detected its GNT# asserted (not shown) on the rising-edge of clock one, informing it that it will be the next bus owner. The initiator has been tracking bus activity, so it also knows that the bus will be Idle on the rising-edge of clock two (for more information, refer to Chapter 10, entitled "Bus Arbitration," on page 129).

- The required pullup resistors (located on the system board) on the upper half of the bus keep the upper half of the bus from floating during periods of time when they aren't in use.

CLOCK 2.

ON the rising-edge of clock two:

- The initiator starts the Memory Read Block transaction by:
  - driving the byte-specific memory start address onto AD[31:0]. In this example, the start byte address could be any address within the first block.
  - driving the Memory Read Block command onto C/BE#[3:0].
  - asserting FRAME#.
  - asserting REQ64# to indicate that it wishes to perform 64-bit data transfers. REQ64# will remain asserted until FRAME# is deasserted.

DURING clock cycle two:

- The upper half of the bus is not in use in the Address Phase. The initiator has the option of not driving these signals (letting the system board pullups keep them high)or may drive any desired pattern onto them.

CLOCK 3.

ON the rising-edge of clock three:

- All targets on the bus clock the address, command, and the state of the FRAME# signal into their input registers.
- The initiator drives out the attributes (see Figure 13-4 on page 201) onto AD[31:0] and C/BE#[3:0]. Among other things, the attributes contain the byte transfer count. In this example, there are two possibilities:
  - The start byte address issued in the Address Phase could be any byte within the first block and the byte transfer count encompasses four Data Phases but does not cross the next block boundary.
  - The start byte address issued in the Address Phase is one of the locations in the sixth qword from the end of block and the byte transfer count identifies an end address that is beyond the imminent block boundary.

DURING clock cycle three:

- All targets begin the decode of the registered copy of the address and command. In this example, the currently addressed target asserts its internal version of the DEVSEL# and ACK64# signals prior to the rising-edge of clock four.
- The upper half of the bus is Reserved and Driven High during the Attribute Phase. C/BE#[7:4] are Reserved and Driven High for the remainder of the transaction.

CLOCK 4.

ON the rising-edge of clock four:

- The currently addressed target clocks an asserted level onto DEVSEL#. This is the decode A time slot.

DURING clock cycle four:

- The initiator backs its output drivers off AD[63:0] (in preparation for the target's delivery of the data over the AD bus).
- The initiator places the Byte Enables in the Reserved and Driven High state for the remainder of the transaction.

CLOCK 5.

ON the rising-edge of clock five:

- The initiator asserts IRDY#, indicating that it has buffer space available to hold at least the first block (or a subset thereof) of the requested data.
- The rising-edge of clock five is the first point at which the initiator clocks the state of DEVSEL# and ACK64# into its input register. In this case, it detects an asserted level on its registered copies of DEVSEL# and ACK64# during clock cycle five. This tells the initiator that it has established a connection with the addressed target and that it supports 64-bit data transfers. The asserted state of DEVSEL# defines the first point at which the initiator will register the state of TRDY# and the content of the AD bus as the rising-edge of clock six.
- The target drives the first read data item and asserts TRDY#.

CLOCK 6.

ON the rising-edge of clock six:

- The initiator clocks the first read data item (up to eight bytes of data) and the state of TRDY# into its input register.
- The target drives out the second qword.

DURING clock six:

- The initiator determines that its internal copy of the TRDY# signal is asserted, indicating that good data was registered on the rising-edge of clock six. The initiator places the first data item into its read buffer.
- Internally, both the initiator and the target adjust the byte count remaining and increment the current address pointer to point to the start address of the next qword.

CLOCK 7.

ON the rising-edge of clock seven:

- The initiator clocks the second qword and the state of TRDY# into its input register.
- The target drives out the third qword.

DURING clock seven:

- The initiator determines that its internal copy of the TRDY# signal is asserted, indicating that good data was registered on the rising-edge of clock seven. The initiator places the second qword into its read buffer.
- Internally, both the initiator and the target adjust the byte count remaining and increment the current address pointer to point to the start address of the third qword.

CLOCK 8.

ON the rising-edge of clock eight:

- The initiator clocks the third qword and the state of TRDY# into its input register.
- The initiator drives out the fourth qword.

DURING clock eight:

- The initiator determines that its internal copy of the TRDY# signal is asserted, indicating that good data was registered on the rising-edge of clock eight. The initiator places the third qword into its read buffer.
- Internally, both the initiator and the target adjust the byte count remaining and increment the current address pointer to point to the start address of the next qword.

CLOCK 9.

ON the rising-edge of clock nine:

- The initiator clocks the fourth qword and the state of TRDY# into its input register.
- The target drives out the fifth qword.
- The initiator deasserts FRAME# (and REQ64#) for one of two reasons:
  - This transaction of four or more Data Phases (six, in this case) is a small transfer, wholly contained within a block (i.e., it does not cross a block boundary). In this clock, both parties realize (by checking the byte count remaining) that the next-to-last data item is being transferred.
  - The start byte address issued in the Address Phase was a location in the sixth qword from the upcoming block boundary. Although the transfer count specified in the Attribute Phase indicates that the transfer would cross at least the upcoming block boundary, in this example the initiator must force the target to Disconnect At Next ADB. As an example, the initiator of the Memory Read Block may be a PCIX-to-PCIX bridge and it may not have enough buffer space reserved to go beyond the upcoming block boundary. In this case, the initiator deasserts FRAME# to inform the target that it's disconnecting the transaction on the upcoming block boundary.

Chapter 18: 64-Bit Transactions

DURING clock nine:

- The initiator determines that its internal copy of the TRDY# signal is asserted, indicating that good data was registered on the rising-edge of clock nine. The initiator places the fourth qword into its read buffer.
- Internally, both the initiator and the target adjust the byte count remaining and increment the current address pointer to point to the start address of the next qword.

CLOCK 10.

ON the rising-edge of clock 10:

- The initiator clocks the fifth qword and the state of TRDY# into its input register.
- The target clocks the state of the FRAME# signal into its input register on the rising-edge of clock 10 and determines that it has been deasserted by the initiator. This informs the target that the data item to be transferred on the rising-edge of clock 11 is the final one to be transferred (even if it doesn't exhaust the transfer count).
- The target drives out the sixth qword on the rising-edge of clock 10. This is either the final data item of the current block, or it is the last data item to be transferred within the block (as defined by the byte transfer count).

DURING clock 10:

- The initiator determines that its internal copy of the TRDY# signal is asserted, indicating that good data was registered on the rising-edge of clock 10. The initiator places the fifth qword into its read buffer.
- Internally, both the initiator and the target adjust the byte count remaining and increment the current address pointer to point to the start address of the next qword.

CLOCK 11.

ON the rising-edge of clock 11:

- The initiator clocks the sixth and final qword and the state of TRDY# into its input register.
- Both parties release the bus. The initiator deasserts IRDY# and ceases to drive the Byte Enables, and the target deasserts TRDY#, DEVSEL# and ACK64# and ceases to drive the final data item.

DURING clock 11:

- The initiator determines that its internal copy of the TRDY# signal is asserted, indicating that good data was registered on the rising-edge of clock 11. The initiator places the sixth and final qword into its read buffer.
- Internally, both the initiator and the target adjust the byte count remaining and increment the current address pointer to point to the start address of the next qword. There are two possible results:
  - One possibility is that the byte count has been exhausted and the transaction is therefore completed.
  - The second possibility is that, although the byte transfer count is not exhausted, the initiator deasserted FRAME# in the previous clock to inform the target that the initiator needs to disconnect on this block boundary. The last qword of the current block was just read on the rising-edge of clock 11, so the transaction is completed.

Figure 18-7: 64-Bit Memory Read Block (or Alias To Memory Read Block) From 64-Bit Target

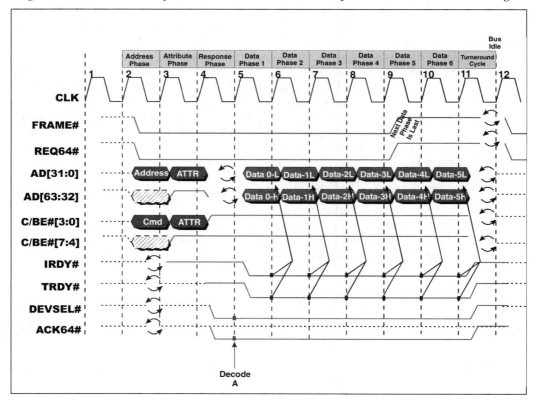

64-Bit Write Block or Split Completion With 64-Bit Target

Refer to Figure 18-8 on page 352. This is an example of one of the following:

- Memory Write Block transaction between a 64-bit initiator and a 64-bit target.
- 64-bit Completer performing a Split Completion transaction to return a block of previously requested read data to the Requester that issued the earlier Memory Read Block (or Alias to Memory Read Block) request. The target that responds to the Split Completion (either the Requester or a Bridge) is a 64-bit target.

CLOCK 1.

DURING clock cycle one:
- The transaction has not yet begun. The initiator detected its GNT# asserted (not shown) on the rising-edge of clock one, informing it that it will be the next bus owner. The initiator has been tracking bus activity, so it also knows that the bus will be Idle on the rising-edge of clock two (for more information, refer to Chapter 10, entitled "Bus Arbitration," on page 129).
- The required pullup resistors (located on the system board) on the upper half of the bus keep the upper half of the bus from floating during periods of time when they aren't in use.

CLOCK 2.

ON the rising-edge of clock two:
- The initiator starts the Memory Write Block transaction by:
    - driving out the byte-specific memory start address onto AD[31:0]. In this example, the start byte address could be any address within the first block.
    - driving out the Memory Write Block command onto C/BE#[3:0].
    - asserting FRAME#.
    - asserting REQ64# to indicate that it wishes to perform 64-bit data transfers. REQ64# is deasserted when FRAME# is deasserted.

DURING clock cycle two:
- The upper half of the bus is not in use in the Address Phase. The initiator has the option of not driving these signals (and letting the system board pullups keep them high), or may drive any desired pattern onto them.

CLOCK 3.

ON the rising-edge of clock three:

- All targets on the bus clock the address, command, and the state of the FRAME# signal into their input registers.
- The initiator drives out the attributes (see Figure 13-4 on page 201) onto AD[31:0] and C/BE#[3:0]. Among other things, the attributes contain the byte transfer count. In this example, there are two possibilities:
  - The start byte address issued in the Address Phase could be any byte within the first block and the byte transfer count encompasses four Data Phases but does not cross the next block boundary.
  - The start byte address issued in the Address Phase is one of the locations in the fourth dword from the end of the block and the byte transfer count identifies an end address that is beyond the imminent block boundary.

DURING clock cycle three:

- All targets begin the decode of the registered copy of the address and command. In this example, the currently addressed target asserts its internal version of the DEVSEL# and ACK64# signals prior to the rising-edge of clock four.
- The upper half of the bus is Reserved and Driven High during the Attribute Phase. C/BE#[7:4] are Reserved and Driven High for the remainder of the transaction.

CLOCK 4.

ON the rising-edge of clock four:

- The currently addressed target clocks an asserted level onto DEVSEL# and ACK64#. This is the decode A time slot.

DURING clock cycle four:

- The initiator has the option of doing one of the following:
  - It can back its output drivers off AD[63:0].
  - It can back its output drivers off AD[63:32] and drive the attributes onto AD[31:0] for an extra clock cycle before supplying the first write data item.
  - It can start driving the first write data item onto AD[31:0] a clock early and back its output drivers off AD[63:32].
  - It can drive a dummy stable pattern onto AD[63:0].
- The initiator places the Byte Enables in the Reserved and Driven High state for the remainder of the transaction.

CLOCK 5.

ON the rising-edge of the clock:

- The initiator asserts IRDY#, indicating that it is driving the first write data item onto the AD bus.

- The rising-edge of clock five is the first point at which the initiator clocks the state of DEVSEL# and ACK64# into its input register. In this case, it detects an asserted level on its registered copies of DEVSEL# and ACK64# during clock cycle five. This tells the initiator that it has established a connection with the addressed target and that the target is capable of 64-bit data transfers. It defines the first point at which the initiator will register the state of TRDY# as the rising-edge of clock six.
- The earliest time slot in which the target can assert TRDY# is the clock immediately following its assertion of DEVSEL#. In this case, the target does assert TRDY# on the rising-edge of clock five, thereby indicating that it will register the first write data item from the AD bus on the rising-edge of clock six.

CLOCK 6.

ON the rising-edge of clock six:
- The target clocks the write data from the AD bus into its input register. It does not need to check the state of IRDY# to validate the presence of the data because it's a rule that the initiator must assert IRDY# and start driving the first write data item in clock five.
- The initiator starts driving the second write data item.

DURING clock cycle six:
- The target places the first write data item into its buffer.
- The initiator determines that its registered copy of TRDY# is asserted, indicating that the target has begun to accept the data to be written within the first block.
- Internally, both the initiator and the target adjust the byte count remaining and increment the current address pointer to point to the start address of the next qword.

CLOCK 7.

ON the rising-edge of clock seven:
- The target clocks the write data from the AD bus into its input register.
- The initiator starts driving the next write data item.

DURING clock cycle seven:
- The target places the registered write data item into its buffer.
- Internally, both the initiator and the target adjust the byte count remaining and increment the current address pointer to point to the start address of the next qword.

CLOCK 8.

ON the rising-edge of clock eight:
- The target clocks the write data from the AD bus into its input register.
- The initiator starts driving the next write data item.

DURING clock cycle eight:
- The target places the registered write data item into its buffer.
- Internally, both the initiator and the target adjust the byte count remaining and increment the current address pointer to point to the start address of the next qword.

CLOCK 9.

ON the rising-edge of clock nine:
- The target clocks the next write data item into its input register.
- The initiator drives out the next-to-last data item.
- The initiator deasserts FRAME# and REQ64# for one of two reasons:
  - This transaction of four or more Data Phases (six, in this case) is a small transfer, wholly contained within a block (i.e., it does not cross a block boundary). In this clock, both parties realize (by checking the byte count remaining) that the next-to-last data item is being transferred.
  - The start byte address issued in the Address Phase was a location in the sixth qword from the upcoming block boundary. Although the transfer count specified in the Attribute Phase indicates that the transfer would cross at least the upcoming block boundary, in this example the initiator must force the target to Disconnect At Next ADB. As an example, the initiator of the Memory Write Block may only have the data to be written within the first block buffered and ready to write. In this case, the initiator deasserts FRAME# and REQ64# to inform the target that it's disconnecting the transaction on the upcoming block boundary.

DURING clock nine:
- The target places the registered write data item into its buffer.
- Internally, both the initiator and the target adjust the byte count remaining and increment the current address pointer to point to the start address of the next qword.

CLOCK 10.

ON the rising-edge of clock 10:
- The target clocks the next-to-last write data item into its input register.
- The target clocks the state of the FRAME# signal into its input register on the rising-edge of clock 10 and determines that it has been deasserted by the initiator. This informs the target that the data item to be transferred on the rising-edge of clock 11 is the final one to be transferred (even if it doesn't exhaust the transfer count).
- The target drives out the last write data item on the rising-edge of clock 10. This is either the final data item of the current block, or it is the last data item to be transferred within the block (as defined by the byte transfer count).

DURING clock 10:

- The initiator places the registered write data item into its buffer.
- Internally, both the initiator and the target adjust the byte count remaining and increment the current address pointer to point to the start address of the next qword.

CLOCK 11.

ON the rising-edge of clock 11:

- The target clocks the final write data item into its input register.
- Both parties release the bus. The initiator deasserts IRDY# and ceases to drive the final data item and the Byte Enables, and the target deasserts TRDY#, DEVSEL#, and ACK64#.

DURING clock 11:

- The initiator places the registered data item into its internal buffer.
- Internally, both the initiator and the target adjust the byte count remaining. This has one of two possible results:
    - One possibility is that the byte count has been exhausted and the transaction is therefore completed.
    - The second possibility is that, although the byte transfer count is not exhausted, the initiator deasserted FRAME# in the previous clock to inform the target that the initiator needs to disconnect on this block boundary. The last data item of the current block was just written on the rising-edge of clock 11, so the transaction is completed.

Figure 18-8: 64-Bit Memory Write Block, Alias To Memory Write Block, or Split Completion with 64-Bit Target

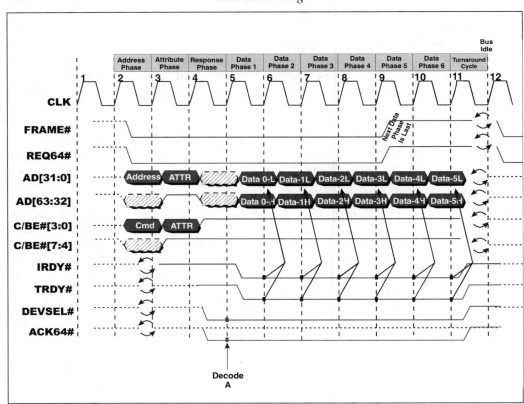

64-Bit Memory Write With 64-Bit Target

Figure 18-9 on page 353 illustrates a 64-bit initiator performing a Memory Write transaction with a 64-bit target. The only difference between the Memory Write and the Memory Write Block (see Figure 18-8 on page 352) is that the Memory Write transaction is not an all-inclusive write. The initiator is permitted to assert any combination of Byte Enables in each Data Phase. The only exceptions are the first and last Data Phases.

- In the first Data Phase, the initiator is not permitted to asserted any Byte Enables associated with locations before the start byte address issued in the Address Phase.
- In the last Data Phase, the initiator is not permitted to asserted any Byte Enables associated with locations after the end address defined by the byte transfer count issued in the Attribute Phase.

Figure 18-9: 64-bit Memory Write With 64-bit Target

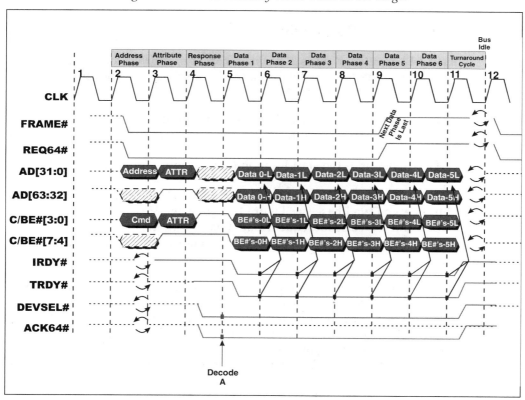

Start Address Alignment Defines Data Path Usage

Introduction

While it is correct to say that the PCI-X data bus is 64-bits wide (in a 64-bit implementation), it is more correct to say that it consists of eight data paths, designated as data paths 0 through 7. Refer to Table 18-2 on page 358. The eight data paths are aligned with the eight locations within the currently addressed qword.

64-Bit to 64-Bit Connection

When a 64-bit initiator starts a 64-bit transaction, it drives out a byte-specific start address in the Address Phase. Assuming that the initiator connects with a 64-bit target (the target asserts ACK64#), the following are true:

- AD[31:3] identifies the qword that contains the start byte address.
- The 64-bit target latches this qword-aligned start address into its address counter.
- AD[2:0] identifies the start location (one of eight locations) within the first qword.
- Data can be transferred a qword at a time using the full-width of the data bus in each Data Phase (see Figure 18-10 on page 358).
- Upon entry to each subsequent Data Phase, both the initiator and the target increment their respective address counters by eight to point to the next qword.

Assuming that the 64-bit initiator connects with a 64-bit target (see Figure 18-10 on page 358), the contents of locations 0 through 3 within the start qword are always read or written over data paths 0 through 3 (the lower half of the bus), while the contents of locations 4 through 7 within the start qword are always read or written over data paths 4 through 7 (the upper half of the bus). Since a 64-bit target is attached to both halves of the bus, this does not present a problem.

64-Bit to 32-Bit Connection

See Figure 18-11 on page 359. Assuming that the 64-bit initiator connects with a 32-bit target (the target does not assert ACK64#), the following are true:

- The initiator starts out believing that it can use the full-width of the bus.
- From the perspective of the 32-bit target, AD[31:2] identifies the dword that contains the start byte address.

- The 32-bit target latches this dword-aligned start address into its address counter.
- AD[1:0] identifies the start location (one of four locations) within the first dword.
- Data can be transferred a dword at a time using the lower half of the data bus in each Data Phase (see Figure 18-11 on page 359).
- Upon entry to each subsequent Data Phase, both the initiator and the target increment their respective address counters by four to point to the next dword.

Although the initiator starts out attempting to use the full-width of the bus, upon detecting that it has connected with a 32-bit target, it must stream all dwords, both upper and lower, over the lower half of the bus.

If the start address issued by the 64-bit initiator is any location within the first dword of the first qword (i.e., AD[2] is 0), data will be transferred (read or written) over at least some of the data paths that comprise the lower half of the bus (the data path associated with the start byte address and, perhaps, the paths associated with higher addressed locations within the same dword).

On the other hand, the start address could be a location within the second dword of the first qword (i.e., AD[2] is 1). These locations are normally associated with the upper half of the bus (and the 32-bit target is not attached to this part of the bus). The possible 64-bit to 32-bit connection scenarios are described in Table 18-1 on page 356.

Table 18-1: 64-Bit to 32-Bit Connection Scenarios

Read or Write?	Dword that start address is located in	Description
Read	Lower	The initiator initially thinks it will receive the lower and upper dwords simultaneously (over both halves of the bus) in the first Data Phase. However, when the initiator detects ACK64# deasserted, it realizes that the 32-bit target will only supply the lower dword over the lower part of the bus in the first Data Phase. In the second Data Phase, it will then receive the upper dword over the lower part of the bus. All subsequent dwords are streamed over the lower part of the bus. Both the initiator and target increment their respective address counters by four as they proceed from Data Phase to Data Phase.
	Upper	The initiator initially thinks it will receive the upper dword over the upper half of the bus in the first Data Phase. However, when the initiator detects ACK64# deasserted, it realizes that it will receive the upper dword (and all subsequent dwords) over the lower part of the bus. Both the initiator and target increment their respective address counters by four as they proceed from Data Phase to Data Phase.

Table 18-1: 64-Bit to 32-Bit Connection Scenarios (Continued)

Read or Write?	Dword that start address is located in	Description
Write	Lower	The initiator starts out driving the first qword of write data onto the full-width of the data bus. However, when the initiator detects ACK64# deasserted, it realizes that, in the first Data Phase, the target will only accept the dword it is presenting on the lower part of the bus. The dword it has been driving onto the upper half of the bus cannot be seen by the 32-bit target. In the second Data Phase, the initiator must therefore copy the dword that it was driving onto the upper half of the bus to the lower half (to make it visible to the target). All subsequent dwords will be streamed over the lower half of the bus. Both the initiator and target increment their respective address counters by four as they proceed from Data Phase to Data Phase.
	Upper	In this case, the initiator does not intend to write anything into the first dword of the first qword, but it does intend to write data into the upper dword of the first qword. The initiator starts out driving the data to be written into the upper dword onto the upper half of the bus.

If it connects with a 32-bit target, however, the target can only receive write data over the lower half of the bus. To efficiently handle this possibility, the initiator duplicates the data destined for the upper dword on both halves of the bus. When the initiator detects ACK64# deasserted, it realizes that, in the first Data Phase, the target accepted the dword it is presenting on the lower part of the bus into the upper dword of the first qword. All subsequent dwords will be streamed over the lower half of the bus. Both the initiator and target increment their respective address counters by four as they proceed from Data Phase to Data Phase. |

Table 18-2: Start Address/Data Path Alignment

Start Byte Address in Qword	is associated with data path	Dword it's located in
0	0, AD[7:0]	The first dword of the qword, often referred to as the even or lower dword.
1	1, AD[15:8]	
2	2, AD[23:16]	If the start byte address is any location within the first dword, AD[2] of the start address is 0.
3	3, AD[31:24]	
4	4, AD[39:32]	The second dword of the qword, often referred to as the odd or upper dword.
5	5, AD[47:40]	
6	6, AD[55:48]	If the start byte address is any location within the second dword, AD[2] of the start address is 1.
7	7, AD[63:56]	

Figure 18-10: 64-Bit to 64-Bit Connection

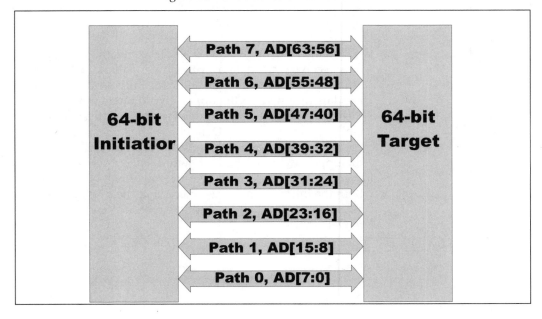

Figure 18-11: 64-Bit to 32-Bit Connection

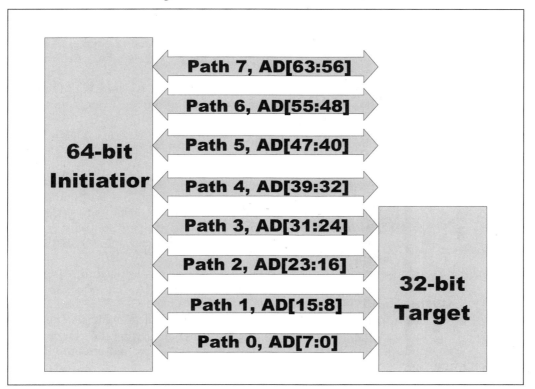

64-Bit Memory Reads From 32-Bit Targets

Starting on Even Dword

Refer to Figure 18-12 on page 365. The initiator initially thinks it will receive the lower and upper dwords simultaneously (over both halves of the bus) in the first Data Phase (in clock five). However, when the initiator detects ACK64# deasserted, it realizes that the 32-bit target will only supply the lower dword over the lower part of the bus in the first Data Phase. In the second Data Phase, it will then receive the upper dword (of the first qword) over the lower part of the bus. All subsequent dwords are streamed over the lower part of the bus. Both the initiator and target increment their respective address counters by four as they proceed from Data Phase to Data Phase.

PCI-X System Architecture

CLOCK 1.

DURING clock cycle one:

- The transaction has not yet begun. The initiator detected its GNT# asserted (not shown) on the rising-edge of clock one, informing it that it will be the next bus owner. The initiator has been tracking bus activity, so it also knows that the bus will be Idle on the rising-edge of clock two (for more information, refer to Chapter 10, entitled "Bus Arbitration," on page 129).
- The required pullup resistors (located on the system board) on the upper half of the bus keep the upper half of the bus from floating during periods of time when they aren't in use.

CLOCK 2.

ON the rising-edge of clock two:

- The initiator starts the Memory Read Block transaction by:
  - driving out the byte-specific memory start address onto AD[31:0]. In this example, the start byte address is a location within the lower dword of the first qword (e.g., location 00000100h, 00000101h, 00000102h, or 00000103h).
  - driving out the Memory Read Block command onto C/BE#[3:0].
  - asserting FRAME#.
  - asserting REQ64# to indicate that it wishes to perform 64-bit data transfers. REQ64# remains asserted until FRAME# is deasserted.

DURING clock cycle two:

- The upper half of the bus is not in use in the Address Phase. The initiator has the option of not driving these signals (letting the system board pullups keep them high) or may drive any desired pattern onto them.

CLOCK 3.

ON the rising-edge of clock three:

- All targets on the bus clock the address, command, and the state of the FRAME# and REQ64# signals into their input registers.
- The initiator drives out the attributes (see Figure 13-4 on page 201) onto AD[31:0] and C/BE#[3:0]. Among other things, the attributes contain the byte transfer count. In this example, there are two possibilities:
  - The start byte address issued in the Address Phase could be any byte within the first block and the byte transfer count encompasses four Data Phases but does not cross the next block boundary. As stated in the description of clock two, the start byte address is a location within the lower dword of the first qword.
  - The start byte address issued in the Address Phase is one of the locations in the sixth dword from the end of block and the byte transfer count identifies an end address that is beyond the imminent block boundary.

DURING clock cycle three:

- All targets begin the decode of the registered copy of the address and command. In this example, the currently addressed target asserts its internal version of DEVSEL# prior to the rising-edge of clock four, but does not assert ACK64#.
- The upper half of the bus is Reserved and Driven High during the Attribute Phase. C/BE#[7:4] are Reserved and Driven High until clock six.

CLOCK 4.

ON the rising-edge of clock four:

- The currently addressed target clocks an asserted level onto DEVSEL#. This is the decode A time slot.

DURING clock cycle four:

- The initiator backs its output drivers off AD[63:0] (in preparation for the target's delivery of the data over the AD bus).
- The initiator keeps the Byte Enables in the Reserved and Driven High state.

CLOCK 5.

ON the rising-edge of clock five:

- The initiator asserts IRDY#, indicating that it has buffer space available to hold at least the first block (or a subset thereof) of the requested data.
- The rising-edge of clock five is the first point at which the initiator clocks the state of DEVSEL# and ACK64# into its input register. In this case, it detects an asserted level on its registered copy of DEVSEL# and a deasserted level on ACK64# during clock cycle five. This tells the initiator that it has established a connection with the addressed target and that it does not support 64-bit data transfers. The asserted state of DEVSEL# defines the first point at which the initiator will register the state of TRDY# and the content of the AD bus as the rising-edge of clock six. The deasserted state of ACK64# means that a connection has been established with a 32-bit target. It will only source the requested data a dword at a time over the lower half of the bus.
- The target drives the first read data item (i.e., the lower dword of the first qword) onto the lower half of the bus and asserts TRDY#.

CLOCK 6.

ON the rising-edge of clock six:

- The initiator clocks the first read data item (the lower dword of the first qword) and the state of TRDY# into its input register.
- The target drives out the upper dword of the first qword.
- The deasserted state of ACK64# on the rising-edge of clock five indicated to the initiator that the upper half of the bus will not be used for the remainder of this transaction. As a result, the initiator has the option

of either driving the upper Byte Enables to an unspecified value for the remainder of the transaction, or may cease driving them. In the latter case, the required system board pullups will maintain the upper Byte Enables in the high state for the remainder of the transaction.

DURING clock six:

- The initiator determines that its internal copy of the TRDY# signal is asserted, indicating that good data was registered on the rising-edge of clock six. The initiator places this data item into its read buffer.
- Internally, both the initiator and the target adjust the byte count remaining and increment the current address pointer (by four, not by eight) to point to the start address of the next dword.
- Since the 32-bit target cannot source data over the upper half of the bus, the required system board pullups will maintain the upper half of the bus in the high state for the remainder of the transaction.

CLOCK 7.

ON the rising-edge of clock seven:

- The initiator clocks the second dword and the state of TRDY# into its input register.
- The target drives out the third dword.

DURING clock seven:

- The initiator determines that its internal copy of the TRDY# signal is asserted, indicating that good data was registered on the rising-edge of clock seven. The initiator places this dword into its read buffer.
- Internally, both the initiator and the target adjust the byte count remaining and increment the current address pointer to point to the start address of the next dword.

CLOCK 8.

ON the rising-edge of clock eight:

- The initiator clocks the third dword and the state of TRDY# into its input register.
- The target drives out the fourth dword.

DURING clock eight:

- The initiator determines that its internal copy of the TRDY# signal is asserted, indicating that good data was registered on the rising-edge of clock eight. The initiator places this dword into its read buffer.
- Internally, both the initiator and the target adjust the byte count remaining and increment the current address pointer to point to the start address of the next dword.

CLOCK 9.

ON the rising-edge of clock nine:

- The initiator clocks the fourth dword and the state of TRDY# into its input register.
- The target drives out the fifth dword.
- The initiator deasserts FRAME# (and REQ64#) for one of two reasons:
    - This transaction of four or more Data Phases (six, in this case) is a small transfer, wholly contained within a block (i.e., it does not cross a block boundary). In this clock, both parties realize (by checking the byte count remaining) that the next-to-last data item is being transferred.
    - The start byte address issued in the Address Phase was a location in the sixth dword from the upcoming block boundary. Although the transfer count specified in the Attribute Phase indicates that the transfer would cross at least the upcoming block boundary, in this example the initiator must force the target to Disconnect At Next ADB. As an example, the initiator of the Memory Read Block may be a PCIX-to-PCIX bridge and it may not have enough buffer space reserved to go beyond the upcoming block boundary. In this case, the initiator deasserts FRAME# to inform the target that it's disconnecting the transaction on the upcoming block boundary.

DURING clock nine:

- The initiator determines that its internal copy of the TRDY# signal is asserted, indicating that good data was registered on the rising-edge of clock nine. The initiator places this dword into its read buffer.
- Internally, both the initiator and the target adjust the byte count remaining and increment the current address pointer to point to the start address of the next dword.

CLOCK 10.

ON the rising-edge of clock 10:

- The initiator clocks the fifth dword and the state of TRDY# into its input register.
- The target clocks the state of the FRAME# signal into its input register and determines that it has been deasserted by the initiator. This informs the target that the dword to be transferred on the rising-edge of clock 11 is the final one to be transferred (even if it doesn't exhaust the transfer count).
- The target drives out the sixth dword. This is either the final dword of the current block, or it is the last dword to be transferred within the block (as defined by the byte transfer count).

DURING clock 10:
- The initiator determines that its internal copy of the TRDY# signal is asserted, indicating that good data was registered on the rising-edge of clock 10. The initiator places the fifth dword into its read buffer.
- Internally, both the initiator and the target adjust the byte count remaining and increment the current address pointer to point to the start address of the next dword.

CLOCK 11.

ON the rising-edge of clock 11:
- The initiator clocks the sixth and final dword and the state of TRDY# into its input register.
- Both parties release the bus. The initiator deasserts IRDY# and ceases to drive the Byte Enables, and the target deasserts TRDY#, DEVSEL# and ACK64# and ceases to drive the final data item.

DURING clock 11:
- The initiator determines that its internal copy of the TRDY# signal is asserted, indicating that good data was registered on the rising-edge of clock 11. The initiator places the sixth and final dword into its read buffer.
- Internally, both the initiator and the target adjust the byte count remaining and increment the current address pointer to point to the start address of the next dword. There are two possible results:
  - One possibility is that the byte count has been exhausted and the transaction is therefore completed.
  - The second possibility is that, although the byte transfer count is not exhausted, the initiator deasserted FRAME# in the previous clock to inform the target that the initiator needs to disconnect on this block boundary. The last dword of the current block was just read on the rising-edge of clock 11, so the transaction is completed.

Figure 18-12: 64-Bit Memory Read Block or Alias To Memory Read Block From 32-Bit Target Starting on Even Dword

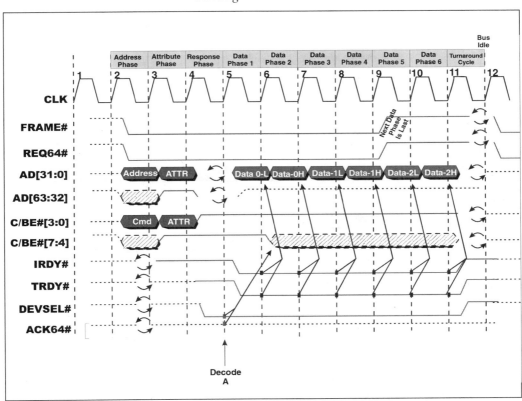

Starting on Odd Dword

Refer to Figure 18-13 on page 366. This is the same as the previous example with the following exception: the start byte address issued by the 64-bit initiator is a location within the upper dword of the first qword. The initiator initially thinks it will receive the upper dword over the upper half of the bus in the first Data Phase (clock five). However, when the initiator detects ACK64# deasserted, it realizes that it will receive the upper dword (and all subsequent dwords) over the lower part of the bus. Both the initiator and target increment their respective address counters by four as they proceed from Data Phase to Data Phase.

Figure 18-13: 64-Bit Memory Read Block or Alias To Memory Read Block From 32-Bit Target Starting on Odd Dword

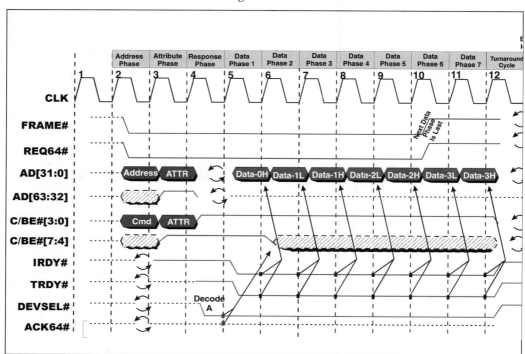

64-bit Memory Writes to 32-Bit Targets

Starting on Even Dword

Refer to Figure 18-14 on page 367. The initiator starts (on the rising-edge of clock five) driving the first qword of write data and its associated Byte Enables onto the full-width of the bus. However, when it detects ACK64# deasserted (on the rising-edge of clock six), it realizes that, in the first Data Phase (clock cycle five) the target will only accept the dword presented on the lower part of the bus. The dword it's driving on the upper half of the bus cannot be seen by the 32-bit target. In the second Data Phase (clock cycle six), the initiator must therefore copy the dword (and its associated Byte Enables) it was driving on the upper half of the bus to the lower half (to make it visible to the target). All subsequent dwords are streamed over the lower half of the bus. Both the initiator and target increment their respective address counters by four as they proceed from Data Phase to Data Phase.

After discovering (on the rising-edge of clock five) it has connected with a 32-bit target, the initiator no longer drives valid information onto the upper half of the bus (starting in clock six). It can either turn off its upper bus output drivers and let the pullups keep those signals from floating, or can drive an unspecified pattern on the upper bus signals for the remainder of the transaction.

Figure 18-14: 64-Bit Memory Write to 32-Bit Target Starting on Even Dword

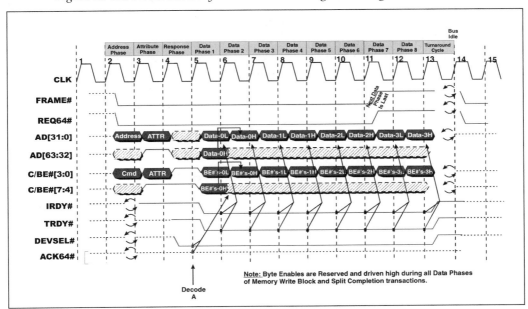

Starting on Odd Dword

Example One. Refer to Figure 18-15 on page 368. In this case, the initiator does not intend to write anything into the first dword of the first qword, but it does intend to write data into the upper dword of the first qword. The initiator starts out driving the data to be written into the upper dword onto the upper half of the bus.

If it connects with a 32-bit target, however, the target can only receive write data over the lower half of the bus. To efficiently handle this possibility, the initiator duplicates the data and Byte Enables destined for the upper dword on both halves of the bus (see clock five). When the initiator detects ACK64# deasserted (in clock five), it realizes that, in the first Data Phase, the target accepted the dword presented on the lower part of the bus into the upper dword of the first qword. All subsequent dwords are streamed over the lower half of the bus. Both the initiator and target increment their respective address counters by four as they proceed from Data Phase to Data Phase.

Figure 18-15: 64-Bit Memory Write to 32-Bit Target Starting on Odd Dword

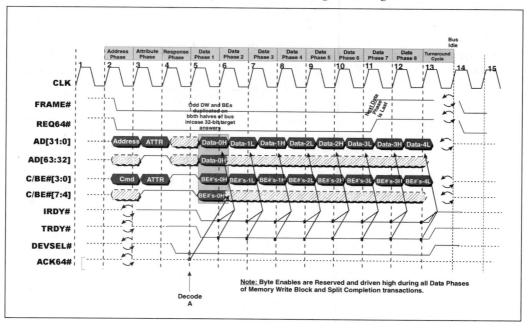

Example Two. Refer to Figure 18-16 on page 369. The only difference between this figure and Figure 18-15 on page 368 is that the target once again claims the transaction using decode speed A, but it keeps TRDY# deasserted for two clock cycles (clocks five and six) because it is not yet ready to start accepting the write data. As described in "On Burst Writes, Insert Wait States in Pairs" on page 257, if the target keeps TRDY# deasserted to temporarily refuse acceptance of the first write data item, it must also keep it deasserted in the next clock to refuse acceptance of the second one as well. The initiator is then forced to repeat the transmission of the first and second data items until the target asserts TRDY# (on the rising-edge of clock seven) to indicate that it has begun accepting the data to be written within the first block.

Figure 18-16: 64-Bit Memory Write to 32-Bit Target Starting on Odd Dword With Decode A and 2 Wait States

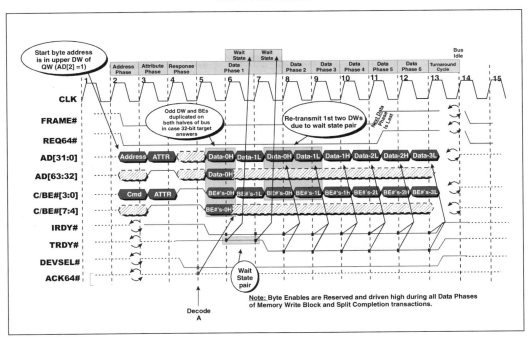

Example Three. While the target in Figure 18-16 on page 369 only inserted one Wait State pair before it started accepting the data to be written within the first block, the target in Figure 18-17 on page 370 inserts two Wait State pairs before it starts accepting the data. The initiator is therefore forced to repeat the transmission of the first two dwords two times before the target starts accepting the data.

Figure 18-17: 64-Bit Memory Write to 32-Bit Target Starting on Odd Dword With Decode A and 4 Wait States

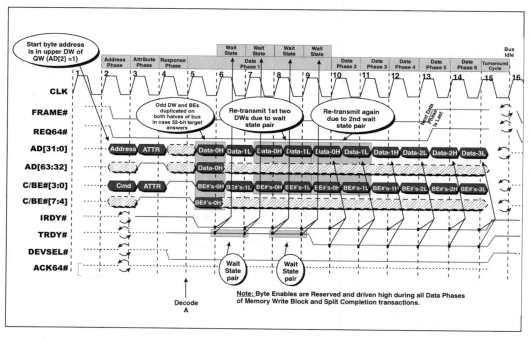

Example Four. Refer to Figure 18-18 on page 371. In this example, the target has decode speed B and inserts no Wait States before it begins accepting the data to be written within the first block. The initiator must keep driving the upper dword to be written into the first qword until the first point at which it registers the state of TRDY# (in this example, the rising-edge of clock seven).

Figure 18-18: 64-Bit Memory Write to 32-Bit Target Starting on Odd Dword With Decode B and No Wait States

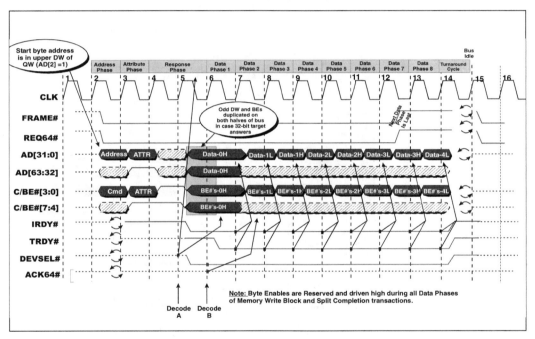

Note: Byte Enables are Reserved and driven high during all Data Phases of Memory Write Block and Split Completion transactions.

Example Five. Refer to Figure 18-19 on page 372. In this example, the target has decode speed C and inserts one pair of Wait States before it begins accepting the data to be written within the first block. The initiator must keep driving the upper dword to be written into the first qword until the first point at which it registers the state of TRDY# (in this example, the rising-edge of clock eight).

Figure 18-19: 64-Bit Memory Write to 32-Bit Target Starting on Odd Dword With Decode C and 2 Wait States

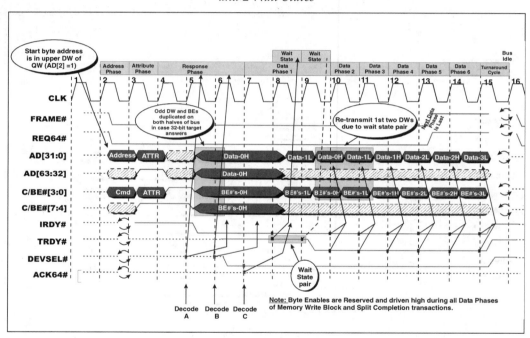

Addressing Memory Above 4GB Boundary

Introduction

Initiators are only permitted to use 64-bit addressing when communicating with memory that resides above the 4GB address boundary. Standard 32-bit addressing (generated using the normal memory commands and a single

Address Phase) must be used if the start address resides below this boundary (i.e., the upper 32 bits of the address are all zero).

Introduction to the DAC Command

Using the basic command set, the address bus, AD[31:0], permits the initiator to address memory devices that reside within the first 4GB of address space (using a single Address Phase); any command that uses a single Address Phase is referred to as a Single Address Command (SAC).

The specification also provides support for addressing memory devices that reside above the 4GB boundary. The Dual Address Cycle command, or DAC, is used by an initiator to inform the community of targets that it is broadcasting a 64-bit memory address in two, back-to-back Address Phases. 64-bit addressing capability is not restricted to 64-bit initiators. Initiators fall into two categories:

- Those that are capable of generating only 32-bit addresses on AD[31:0] using a single Address Phase.
- Those that are capable of generating 32- and 64-bit addresses.

The sections that follow discuss the methods used by both 32-bit and 64-bit initiators in presenting a 64-bit address to the community of targets. Targets fall into two categories:

- Those that recognize the 64-bit addressing protocol (i.e., they have memory that resides above the 4GB address boundary).
- Those that only recognize the 32-bit addressing protocol (i.e., they do not have any memory that resides above the 4GB address boundary).

DAC Support Mandatory for All Initiators

In PCI, an initiator that performs memory transactions may or may not implement 64-bit memory addressing capability. In PCI-X, however, it is mandatory that all initiators that perform memory transactions must implement this capability. The reason for this is as follows.

When an initiator accesses memory, the region of memory it accesses is assigned to it by its device driver. The device driver, in turn, is assigned this memory buffer region by the OS memory allocation routine. In order to give the memory allocation routine maximum flexibility when assigning memory buffers to drivers, all initiators must be capable of addressing memory that resides below or above the 4GB address boundary.

Memory Targets Must Support Wide BARs and DAC

Every memory target implements a programmable memory decoder, or Base Address Register (BAR). The configuration software probes each BAR to discover whether it's a memory or IO BAR and how much address space it needs assigned to it. The configuration software then assigns a base address to the decoder.

In PCI, a memory BAR may be implemented as either a 32- or 64-bit register (see Figure 18-20 on page 374 and Figure 18-21 on page 375). If it were implemented as a 32-bit BAR, then the configuration software is restricted to assigning memory address ranges that reside below the 4GB address boundary. In PCI-X, however, all memory BARs must be implemented as 64-bit BAR registers, thereby giving the configuration software maximum flexibility in assigning memory ranges to PCI-X functions. This also implies that all PCI-X memory targets must recognize the DAC command.

Figure 18-20: PCI 32-Bit Memory BAR

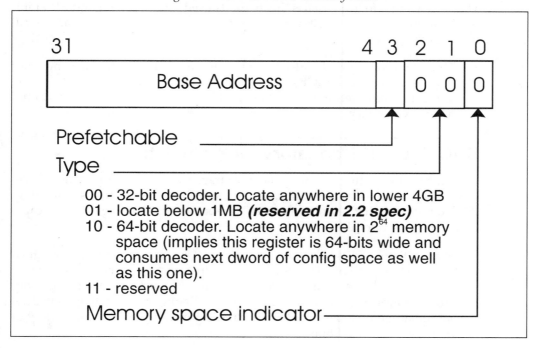

Figure 18-21: PCI-X (or PCI) 64-Bit Memory BAR

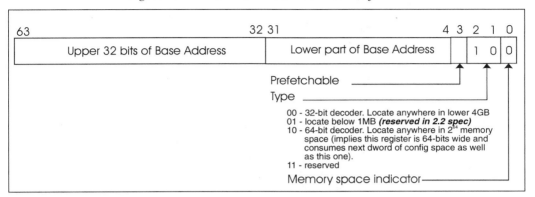

Use of DAC Command Changes DEVSEL# and Master Abort Timing

Refer to Figure 18-22 on page 376. The insertion of an extra Address Phase pushes out the decode time slots (A, B, C, and Subtractive) by one clock. In addition, in the event that DEVSEL# is not asserted by any target, Master Abort occurs one clock later than it normally would.

Example 32-Bit Transaction Using DAC Command

Figure 18-22 on page 376 illustrates a 32-bit initiator performing a block memory read from a memory target that resides above the 4GB address boundary.

CLOCK 1.
   DURING clock cycle one:
   - The transaction has not yet begun. The initiator detected its GNT# asserted (not shown) on the rising-edge of clock one, informing it that it will be the next bus owner. The initiator has been tracking bus activity, so it also knows that the bus will be Idle on the rising-edge of clock two (for more information, refer to Chapter 10, entitled "Bus Arbitration," on page 129).

CLOCK 2.
   ON the rising-edge of clock two:
   - The initiator starts the Memory Read Block transaction by:
     - driving out the lower 32-bits of the 64-bit, byte-specific memory start address onto AD[31:0].

- driving out the DAC command onto C/BE#[3:0]. This indicates that this is the first of two, back-to-back Address Phases. The lower 32 bits of the 64-bit memory address is delivered over AD[31:0] in the first Address Phase (clock two), while the actual memory command (Memory Read Block) and the upper 32 bits of the 64-bit memory address in the second Address Phase (clock three).
- asserting FRAME#.

CLOCK 3.

DURING clock cycle three:

- The memory command (Memory Read Block or Alias To Memory Read Block) and the upper 32 bits of the 64-bit memory address are delivered over AD[31:0] in the second Address Phase.

CLOCK 4. This is the Attribute Phase. From this point forward, this is a perfectly normal, 32-bit burst read transaction.

Figure 18-22: 32-Bit Memory Read Block or Alias To Memory Read Block From Memory Above 4GB Boundary

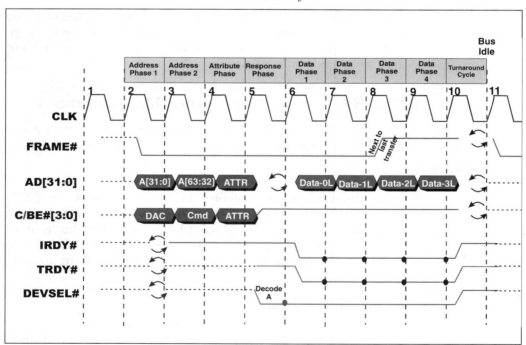

Example 64-Bit Transaction Using DAC Command

In Figure 18-23 on page 378, a 64-bit initiator is using the DAC command to address memory above the 4GB address boundary. In addition, it wishes to perform 64-bit data transfers (it asserts REQ64# when it asserts FRAME#).

CLOCK 2.
ON the rising-edge of clock two:
- The initiator starts the transaction by asserting FRAME# and REQ64#, and driving the Dual Address Cycle command onto C/BE#[3:0].
- The initiator also drives the lower 32 bits of the address onto AD[31:0], the upper 32 bits of the address onto AD[63:32], and the memory read command (Memory Read Block or Alias To Memory Read Block) onto C/BE#[7:4]. It continues to drive the upper part of the address onto AD[63:32] and the memory read command onto C/BE#[7:4] for the duration of both Address Phases (clocks two and three).
- REQ64# is asserted, indicating that the initiator is using the entire 64-bit bus for address output (during the first Address Phase) and that the initiator wishes to perform 64-bit data transfers (if the addressed target is a 64-bit device).

CLOCK 3.
ON the rising-edge of clock three:
- The community of 32-bit targets latch the DAC (Dual Address Cycle) command from C/BE#[3:0] and the lower 32 bits of the address from AD[31:0].
- The community of 64-bit memory targets that reside above the 4GB boundary latch the entire 64-bit address from AD[63:0] and the memory read command from C/BE#[7:4].

DURING clock three:
- All 32-bit targets other than memory targets residing above the 4GB address boundary quit listening to the transaction. All 64-bit memory targets residing below the 4GB boundary also quit listening.
- The initiator starts the second Address Phase by driving the upper part of the address onto AD[31:0] (in case the currently addressed target is not a 64-bit device) and the memory read command onto C/BE#[3:0].
- 64-bit memory targets that reside above the 4GB address boundary have received the entire 64-bit address and the command and begin the decode.

CLOCK 4. This is the Attribute Phase. From this point forward, this is a perfectly normal, 64-bit burst read transaction.

Figure 18-23: 64-bit Memory Read Block or Alias To Memory Read Block From Memory Above 4GB Boundary With 64-Bit Target

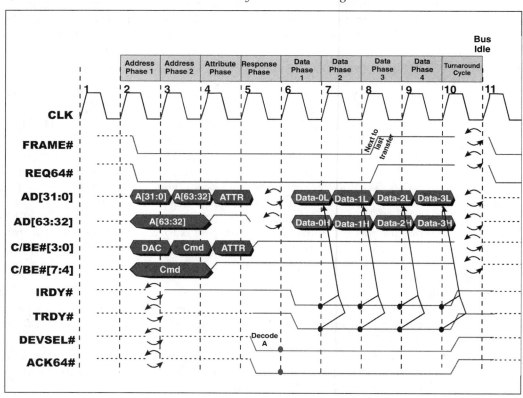

DEVSEL# Must Not Be Asserted Too Soon

Refer to Figure 15-1 on page 245. A transaction that accesses a memory device residing below the 4GB address boundary only has a single Address Phase. The target registers the 32-bit address and the command at the end of the Address Phase and begins the decode during the Attribute Phase. If the memory target has a decode speed A decoder, it can assert DEVSEL# at the end of the Attribute Phase.

Refer to Figure 18-23 on page 378. A 64-bit memory target residing above the 4GB address boundary can latch the entire 64-bit memory address and the command (from C/BE#[7:4]) on the rising-edge of clock three and begin the decode. Assuming it has a fast decoder, theoretically it could assert DEVSEL# on the rising-edge of clock four.

This is not permitted. It is not permitted to assert DEVSEL# until the rising-edge of clock five at the earliest. The only advantage that a 64-bit memory target has is that it could have a relatively slow decoder and still appear to use decode speed A.

Add-In Card Trace Length

Table 18-3 on page 380 defines the minimum and maximum trace lengths that may be implemented on an add-in card.

Due to the reflected-wave nature of the bus, the lengths of the 32- and 64-bit interface signals are critical. The system board designer has closely budgeted those trace lengths on the system board and depends on the add-in card designer to adhere to the spec.

The length of the CLK trace (CLK is not a reflected-wave signal) on the card is very critical. Every aspect of the bus protocol is synchronized to the rising-edge of the CLK signal and it is critical that every device on the bus detect the clock's rising-edge simultaneously (or as close as possible). The maximum allowable device-to-device clock skew is:

- 2ns in 33MHz PCI.
- 1ns in 66MHz PCI.
- 0.5ns in PCI-X.

In order to ensure that this parameter is met, the system board designer matches the lengths of the separate clock traces to each other and depends on the clock trace length on the add-in card on being *exactly* the length specified in the spec (see the table; essentially, the trace length must be 2.5 inches plus or minus 0.1 inch).

The reader will notice that the 64-bit extension signal traces are permitted to be longer than the 32-bit signal traces. Refer to Figure 18-24 on page 381. The PCI spec recommends that, in order to minimize trace lengths, the pinouts on a PCI package (or, in this case, a PCI-X package) be laid out (i.e., wrapped around one end of the component) in the same order as the pinouts on the add-in connector. If the device implements the 64-bit extension signals, those signals should continue wrapping around the component in the same order as the 64-bit extension signals on the connector. The reader can see in the figure that this would necessitate longer on-card traces for the 64-bit signals. That's why the PCI spec (see Table 18-3 on page 380) has a higher max value for the 64-bit signals.

However, it's interesting to note that while the max length for the 64-bit signals in PCI is 2.0 inches, it is spec'd at 2.75 inches in the PCI-X spec. This was done because the authors of the PCI-X spec knew that many PCI designers have found it almost impossible to comply with the max value of 2.0 inches. In addition, while PCI doesn't spec a minimum trace length for the 64-bit signals, PCI-X specifies a minimum trace length of 1.75 inches to make the system board designer's estimation of the trace lengths on add-in cards easier.

Although the PCI spec does not specify a minimum or maximum trace length for the RST# trace, the PCI-X spec does (see the table). This is to ensure that REQ64# (see "How 64-Bit Card Determines Type of Slot Its Installed In" on page 338) and the Initialization Pattern (see "Init Pattern Setup and Hold Time" on page 67) are stable for the appropriate time after the rising-edge of RST#.

Table 18-3: Add-In Card Trace Lengths (all values in inches)

Parameter	PCI-X		PCI	
	Min	Max	Min	Max
CLK length	2.4	2.6	2.4	2.6
32-bit interface signal length	0.75	1.5	-	1.5
64-bit interface extension signal length	1.75	2.75	-	2.0
RST# length	0.75	3.0	-	-

Figure 18-24: Suggested Component Layout

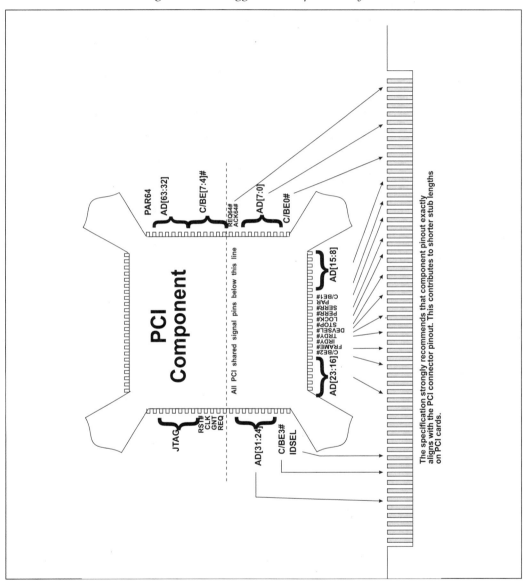

Parity Generation and Checking

Refer to Chapter 19, entitled "Parity Generation and Checking," on page 383.

19 *Parity Generation and Checking*

The Previous Chapter

The previous chapter provided a detailed discussion of 64-bit data transfers, 64-bit memory addressing, and additional issues associated with 64-bit devices and 64-bit memory addressing.

This Chapter

This chapter provides a detailed discussion of parity generation, parity checking, Address and Attribute Phase parity, and Data Phase parity.

The Next Chapter

The next chapter provides a detailed description of Type 0 and Type 1 Configuration transactions, Special Cycle Requests, and the arbiter's treatment of configuration transactions.

General Discussion of Parity Generation

Parity Generation Is Mandatory

The agent driving the AD bus in any phase (other than the Response Phase) is required to provide correct parity for the information driven on the AD and the C/BE buses in that phase.

In Data Phases of Writes and Split Completions

Initiator Must Generate Correct Data Phase Parity

During a write or a Split Completion transaction, the initiator is required to generate the correct parity for the data and Byte Enables it provides in each Data Phase (including all clocks of the first Data Phase when the target is inserting Wait States in the first data transfer; see next section).

Toggle Data and Parity When Target Inserts Wait State Pairs

When a target inserts Wait States in the initial Data Phase of a burst write, it must always insert Wait States in pairs (see "On Burst Writes, Insert Wait States in Pairs" on page 257). This forces the initiator to toggle between the first and second data item until the target begins to accept the write or Split Completion data. In this case, the initiator must toggle between the parity for the first and second data items as well.

In Reads, the Target Sources Data and Parity

First Data Phase Data and Parity Can Be Delayed

In the first Data Phase of a read transaction, the target may insert Wait States to delay the delivery of the first data item as well as its parity bit. When the target finally drives the first data item and asserts TRDY# to indicate its presence, it must then drive the correct parity one clock later.

Subsequent Data Phase Data and Parity Never Delayed

Each subsequent Data Phase of a read burst transaction is a single clock in duration. The target provides the next data item, followed immediately by its associated parity bit in the next clock.

General Discussion of Parity Checking

Checking Required in Address and Attribute Phases

All devices on the bus are required to check the parity of the Address and Attribute Phases of each transaction.

Parity Checking Is Generally Required In Data Phases

The device receiving the data in each Data Phase is generally required to check the Data Phase parity. As in PCI, some exceptions are acceptable. As an example, the designer of a video frame buffer might decide not to check the integrity of data being written into the buffer. If any data corruption should occur, the only thing affected would be the visual image presented to the end-user.

Target Data Parity Checking During Write or Split Completion

The target of a write or Split Completion transaction must not check data parity while it is inserting Wait States in the first Data Phase. Once it asserts TRDY# to indicate its readiness to start accepting the write or Split Completion data, it then begins checking parity.

Initiator Parity Checking During Reads

Parity Not Checked During First Data Phase Wait States

Since the target has not yet presented the first data item, the initiator may not check its parity.

Parity Checked One Clock After Each Subsequent Data Phase

The device receiving data in each Data Phase checks the associated parity bit on the clock rising-edge that immediately follows the edge on which the data is received.

In Any Phase, Agent Driving AD Bus Supplies Parity

As in PCI, the agent that owns and is driving the AD bus is responsible for providing the parity bit. This means:

- In the Address Phase, the initiator drives the address onto the AD bus and the command onto the C/BE bus. The initiator is therefore responsible for providing the parity that covers the address and command.
- In the Attribute Phase, the initiator drives the attributes onto the AD bus and the C/BE bus. The initiator is therefore responsible for providing the parity that covers these attributes.
- In the Response Phase, parity is neither presented nor checked for correctness.
- In the Data Phase, the agent sourcing the data is responsible for providing proper parity for the data it is presenting as well as the Byte Enable setting.
  - In any form of a read transaction (including Interrupt Acknowledge), the agent sourcing the read data is the target. It is therefore also responsible for presenting the parity that covers the read data it is presenting as well as the Byte Enables received from the initiator.
  - In any form of a write transaction (including Special Cycle), the agent sourcing the write data is the initiator. It is therefore also responsible for presenting the parity that covers the write data and the Byte Enables it is driving to the target.

As in PCI, Even Parity Is Used

Just as in PCI, the agent that supplies the parity must set the parity bit either high or low to force an even number of one bits in the 37-bit pattern consisting of AD[31:0], C/BE#[3:0], and PAR.

During 64-bit transfers, the agent driving the upper half of the bus must set the parity bit for the upper half of the bus either high or low to force an even number of one bits in the 37-bit pattern consisting of AD[63:32], C/BE#[7:4], and PAR64.

No Parity in Response Phase

Since no data is transferred during the Response Phase, no device checks for parity errors on the AD and C/BE# buses in the clock following the Attribute Phase.

Chapter 19: Parity Generation and Checking

Address Phase Parity

Address Phase Parity Checking Required

All devices on the bus must check the parity associated with the information driven during the Address Phase (i.e., the address and the command).

When DAC Is Used, Check Both Packets

When an initiator uses the DAC command, it is indicating that it is issuing two address/command packets. All devices must perform a parity check on both address/command packets. For more information on the DAC command, refer to "Addressing Memory Above 4GB Boundary" on page 372.

On Error, SERR# Required

When a function detects a parity error on an Address Phase, the function is required to set the Detected Parity Error bit in its Status register. In addition, if the SERR# Enable bit is set to one in the function's Command register, the function is also required to assert SERR#. In that case, the function will also set the Signaled System Error bit to one in its Status register (in addition to setting the Detected Parity Error bit).

Error Detected Before Transaction Claimed

A target that uses a decode speed other than A may detect an Address Phase parity error prior to finishing its decode and asserting DEVSEL#. As already stated, the target will set the Detected Parity Error and Signaled System Error bits in its Status register and will assert SERR#. Regarding how the target (assuming that it appears to be addressed by the transaction) terminates the transaction, it has two options:

OPTION 1. The target may choose not to claim the transaction and just let it end in a Master Abort. The initiator terminates the transaction without establishing a connection and sets the Received Master Abort bit in its Status register. In addition, the initiator generates an interrupt to invoke its driver to check its status.

OPTION 2. See the next section.

Error Detected After Transaction Claimed

If a target with a decode speed other than A detects an Address Phase parity error after it has decoded the transaction and asserted DEVSEL#, as already stated the target will set the Detected Parity Error and Signaled System Error bits in its Status register and will assert SERR#. It may terminate the transaction in one of two ways:

- It may issue a Target Abort to the initiator. In this case, the target sets the Signaled Target Abort bit in its Status register and the initiator sets the Received Target Abort bit in its Status register. Upon receipt of the Target Abort, the initiator generates an interrupt to invoke its driver to check its status.
- It may allow the transaction to proceed to completion normally.

Parity Error in Split Completion Address Phase

As with any Address Phase parity error, any function that detects the error will set the Detected Parity Error and Signaled System Error bits in its Status register and will assert SERR#.

The spec permits the same options for the target's treatment of the Split Completion Address Phase as for any other transaction type, so the target that appears to be selected by the Sequence ID may choose to not claim the transaction, or may claim it and then issue a Target Abort to the initiator (the Completer or a bridge residing in the path between the Completer and the Requester). The parity error means that the Sequence ID (Requester ID plus the transaction Tag) has been corrupted in flight. If no target claims the transaction, the initiator experiences a Master Abort. For more information on the actions taken by the initiator in this case, refer to "Completer Handling of Master Abort on a Split Completion" on page 610. If the target issues a Target Abort in response to the Split Completion transaction, the actions taken by the initiator are defined in "Completer Receives Target Abort on Split Completion" on page 606.

Attribute Phase Parity

Means Sequence ID and/or Byte Count Corrupted

If a function detects an Attribute Phase parity error, it means that the Sequence ID and/or the byte transfer count have been corrupted. Because this is quite serious, as is the case in the Address Phase, all devices are required to check the parity of the information delivered in the Attribute Phase. Any function that detects an Attribute Phase parity error is required to set the Detected Parity Error bit in its Status register and, if enabled to do so, it must also assert SERR# and set the Signaled System Error status bit.

When Attributes Corrupted and Split Response Issued

If the target of a transaction issues a Split Response and also detects an Attribute Phase parity error, the target must:

- Discard the transaction.
- Assert SERR# and set the Signaled System Error bit to one in its Status register (if enabled to do so by a one in the SERR# Enable bit in the target's Command register).
- Set the Detected Parity Error bit to one in its Status register.

Data Phase Parity

Parity Always Covers Full Width of Data Bus

As in PCI, in the Data Phase of the transaction the agent driving the data must always drive the full width of the data bus (i.e., the AD bus):

- In a 32-bit transaction, the agent driving data onto AD[31:0] must always drive a stable 32-bit pattern onto the data bus, even if it's not reading or writing all bytes within the currently addressed dword. This is necessary because the PAR bit always covers AD[31:0] and C/BE#[3:0].
- In a 64-bit transaction, the agent driving data onto AD[63:0] must always drive a stable 64-bit pattern onto the data bus, even if it's not reading or

writing all bytes within the currently addressed qword. This is necessary because the PAR64 bit always covers AD[63:32] and C/BE#[7:4].

Parity Driven One Clock After Information Presented

As in PCI, the parity bit (or bits, when performing a 64-bit transfer) is always driven one clock after the owner of the AD bus drives information (address, attributes, or data) onto the AD bus. The parity bit is therefore guaranteed to be presented one clock after:

- FRAME# is asserted and the address and command are driven.
- the attributes are driven.
- (in a read transaction) TRDY# is asserted in a Data Phase.
- (in a write transaction) IRDY# is asserted in a Data Phase.

Similar to PCI, But Different (due to registered bus)

Due to the registered nature of the PCI-X bus (see Chapter 5, entitled "PCI-X Is a Registered Bus," on page 83), in the event of a Data Phase parity error PERR# is asserted one clock later than it would be in PCI. This is covered in more detail in this chapter.

Parity-Related Initiator Responsibilities

Initiator May Be a Requester, a Bridge, or a Completer

The initiator of a transaction may be the Requester that originates the request, a PCIX-to-PCIX bridge residing between the Requester and the targeted Completer, or the Completer initiating a Split Completion transaction. In any case, the initiator of a transaction has certain responsibilities regarding parity generation and/or checking. The following sections define the initiator's responsibilities during writes, Split Completions, and reads.

Requester's Parity-Related Responsibilities During a Write

During the Data Phase(s) of a write transaction, the Requester has the following parity-related responsibilities:

Drive Data, Byte Enables and the Parity. One clock after entering a Data Phase the Requester must drive the parity bit related to the data and Byte Enables it drove in the previous clock cycle. Refer to Figure 19-1 on page 405. As an example, the first Data Phase begins on the rising-edge of clock five (the fourth clock cycle of the transaction) when the Requester asserts IRDY# and drives the first data item and its related Byte Enables. The Requester must drive the parity bit associated with this data item and its Byte Enables on the rising-edge of clock six.

Requester Checks PERR#. Four clocks after a Data Phase begins (the rising-edge of clock nine in Figure 19-1 on page 405), the Requester must clock the state of the PERR# signal into its input register and examine it to determine if the related data item and/or its related Byte Enables were received correctly by the target.

Requester Actions When PERR# Asserted by Target. The actions taken by the Requester upon detecting PERR# asserted during a write are defined by the current state of the Parity Error Response bit in its Command register:

CASE 1. If the Parity Error Response bit = 1 in its Command register, the Requester sets the Master Data Parity Error bit in its Status register. Additional action taken by the Requester depends on the current state of the Data Parity Error Recovery Enable bit in its PCI-X Command register (for more information, refer to "Requester's Data Parity Error Recovery Enable Bit" on page 613):
- **Data Parity Error Recovery Enable bit = 0**: the Requester will assert SERR# (if the SERR# Enable bit is set to one in its Command register; if the SERR# Enable bit is cleared to zero, the Requester takes no further action).
- **Data Parity Error Recovery Enable bit = 1**: the Requester will generate an interrupt to invoke the interrupt handler within its driver.

CASE 2. If the Parity Error Response bit = 0 in its Command register, the Requester takes no action.

Requester's Actions on PERR# and Split Response. This subject is covered in "Data Error Received With Split Response on Dword Write" on page 618.

Bridge's Parity-Related Responsibilities During a Write

During the Data Phase(s) of a write transaction, the bridge has the following parity-related responsibilities:

Drive Data, Byte Enables and the Parity. One clock after entering a Data Phase, the bridge must drive the parity bit related to the data and Byte Enables it drove in the previous clock cycle. As an example, in Figure 19-1 on page 405, the first Data Phase begins on the rising-edge of clock five when the bridge asserts IRDY# and drives the first data item and its related Byte Enables. The bridge must drive the parity bit associated with this data item and its Byte Enables on the rising-edge of clock six.

Bridge Checks PERR#. Four clocks after a Data Phase begins (the rising-edge of clock nine in Figure 19-1 on page 405), the bridge must clock the state of the PERR# signal into its input register and examine it to determine if the related data item and/or its related Byte Enables were received correctly by the target.

Bridge Actions When PERR# Asserted by Target. The actions taken by the bridge upon detecting PERR# asserted during a write are defined by:

- whether it was performing a Split or a Posted write.
- the current state of the Parity Error Response bit in either its Command register (if it's performing the write on its primary side), or its Bridge Control register (if it's performing the write on its secondary side).

There are four basic scenarios:

SCENARIO 1. The bridge is performing a Split IO or Configuration Write received from an initiator on the other side of the bridge using write data that was received without error on the originating bus. It then performs the requested write on the destination bus and detects PERR# asserted by the target. Assuming that the Parity Error Response bit in the control register associated with the destination bus (Command register for the primary bus; Bridge Control register for the secondary side) is set to one, the bridge sets the Master Data Parity Error bit in the status register associated with the destination bus (Status register for the primary side; Secondary Status register for the secondary side). There are two possible cases:
- The target treated the write as an immediate transaction (asserts TRDY#, or signals a Single Data Phase Disconnect or a Disconnect at Next ADB). In this case, the bridge will initiate a Split Completion transaction on the originating bus to deliver a Split Completion error message back to the Requester. In the Split Completion error message, the bridge indicates the Bridge Error Class (1h) and the Index value 02h (Write Data Parity Error).

- In addition to asserting PERR#, the target signaled Split Response to the bridge. In this case, the agent that acted as the target of the write (and asserted PERR#) has committed to initiate a Split Completion transaction at a later time and will return a Split Completion error message as a result of delivering the corrupted data to the Completer.

SCENARIO 2. The bridge is performing a Split IO or Configuration Write received from an initiator on the other side of the bridge and is using write data that was corrupted when it was received from the initiator on the originating bus. When it then performs the requested write on the destination bus, it must be a faithful messenger and drive the bad parity to the target. Obviously, it then detects PERR# asserted by the target upon receipt of the bad parity. In this case, the actions taken by the bridge are identical to those listed for Scenario 1.

SCENARIO 3. The bridge is performing a posted memory write for an initiator on the other side of the bridge, and the write data was received without error on the originating bus. It then performs the requested memory write on the destination bus and detects PERR# asserted by the target. In this case, assuming that the Parity Error Response and SERR# Enable bits are set to one in the control register for the bridge's destination bus (Command register for the primary interface; Bridge Control register for the secondary interface), the bridge asserts SERR# and sets the Signaled System Error and Master Data Parity Error bits in the status register associated with the destination bus (the Status register for an error on its primary side; the Secondary Status register for an error on its secondary side).

SCENARIO 4. The bridge is performing a posted memory write for an initiator on the other side of the bridge using write data that was corrupted when it was received from the initiator on the originating bus. Acting as the target of the write on the originating side, it asserts PERR# to the initiator on the originating bus and sets the Detected Parity Error bit in the status register associated with that side of the bridge (Status register if it's the primary side; Secondary Status register if it's the secondary side). The bridge then must perform the posted memory write on the destination bus using the bad parity. When the target on the destination bus receives the bad parity and asserts PERR# back to the bridge, the bridge sets the Master Data Parity bit in the status register associated with the destination bus (Status register if it's the primary side; Secondary Status register if it's the secondary side). The bridge takes no further action.

Initiator's Parity-Related Responsibilities During a Split Completion

Who Initiates Split Completion Transactions? A Split Completion transaction is initiated in any of the following three scenarios:

- The Completer that issued a Split Response earlier in time now initiates a Split Completion transaction.
- A bridge in the path between the Completer and Requester is passing along the Split Completion originated by the Completer.
- A bridge passes a transaction to the destination bus on which the Completer resides, and the Completer treats it as an Immediate transaction. In this case, the bridge must originate a Split Completion transaction to return to the Requester.

Initiator Drives Data, Byte Enables and Parity. One clock after entering a Data Phase the initiator must drive the parity bit related to the data and Byte Enables it drove in the previous clock cycle. As an example, in Figure 19-1 on page 405, the first Data Phase begins on the rising-edge of clock five when the initiator asserts IRDY# and drives the first data item and its related Byte Enables. The initiator must drive the parity bit associated with this data item and its Byte Enables on the rising-edge of clock six.

Initiator Does Not Monitor PERR#. During a Split Completion transaction, the initiator (either a bridge or the Completer) supplies either previously requested read data or an SCM back to the Requester. The initiator supplies both the data (or SCM) and its parity to the device acting as the target of the transaction (either the Requester or a bridge in the path between the Completer and the Requester). The target device checks the parity and, if the parity is incorrect, is responsible for handling the reporting of the error to software (because, if it's the Requester, it originated the read or write request at an earlier point in time). A detailed discussion of this topic can be found in "Target's Responsibilities During a Split Completion" on page 399.

The spec does not describe whether or not the initiator of a Split Completion transaction must monitor PERR# during the transaction's Data Phases. It is the author's opinion that it does not. The device acting as the target of the Split Completion is either the Requester that originated the request or a bridge in the path back to the Requester. It is therefore the target's rather than the initiator's responsibility to handle the error (see "Target's Responsibilities During a Split Completion" on page 399).

Chapter 19: Parity Generation and Checking

Initiator's Parity-Related Responsibilities During a Read

General. During a read transaction, the initiator (either the Requester or a bridge) receives either the read data and its related parity or a Split Response from the target. The initiator is therefore responsible for checking the parity for correctness and reporting the error in the event of a parity error. Read transactions include:

- Memory Read Dword
- IO Read
- Configuration Read
- Interrupt Acknowledge
- Memory Read Block
- Alias to Memory Read Block

First Read Data Item and Parity Can Be Delayed by Target. In the initial Data Phase of a read transaction, the presentation of the first data item (and its parity bit) can be delayed by the target. The delay is the result of either or both of the following:

- The target may implement a less-than optimal decoder and may not assert DEVSEL# until the B, C, or the Subtractive decode time slot (for more information on decode, refer to "The Response Phase: Connecting With the Target" on page 210).
- The target has up to 16 clocks from the assertion of FRAME# to present the first data item and assert TRDY#.

The target does not provide the parity bit associated with the first data item until one clock after it presents the first data item and asserts TRDY#.

Subsequent Data Phases of a Read. Each subsequent Data Phase of a read transaction is one clock in duration, during which the target must keep TRDY# asserted as it delivers the next data item to the initiator. The parity bit associated with that data item and its aassociated Byte Enables is delivered by the target in the following clock and is checked by the initiator (see next section).

Parity Checking by Initiator During a Read. The initiator of the read latches the data item on the rising-edge of one clock and the parity bit for that data item on the next rising-edge of the clock. The initiator then checks the correctness of the parity. If the parity is incorrect, the initiator sets the Detected Parity Error bit in its Status register. If the Parity Error Response bit in its Command register is set to one, the initiator also asserts PERR# (or

SERR#; see "Requester's Parity-Related Responsibilities During a Read" on page 396) and sets the Master Data Parity Error bit in its Status register. Any further actions taken by the initiator depend on whether the initiator performing the read is the Requester or a bridge residing between the Requester and the Completer (see "Requester's Parity-Related Responsibilities During a Read" on page 396 and "Bridge's Parity-Related Responsibilities During a Read" on page 397). If the Parity Error Response bit is cleared to zero, the initiator takes no further action beyond setting the Detected Parity Error bit in its Status register.

Split Response Dummy Data Corrupted. This subject is covered in "Data Error Received With Split Response on Read" on page 616.

The next two sections focus on the parity-related responsibilities of a Requester that initiates a read and a bridge that initiates a read, respectively.

Requester's Parity-Related Responsibilities During a Read

A Requester that initiates a read may detect a Data Phase parity error on a read in any of three different scenarios:

SCENARIO 1. The target may supply the data immediately (i.e., it does not split the transaction) and the parity on one or more data items is incorrect.

SCENARIO 2. The target may issue a Split Response to the Requester and the parity on the dummy data pattern (all ones) may be incorrect. This subject is covered in "Data Error Received With Split Response on Read" on page 616.

SCENARIO 3. The target may issue a Split Response to the Requester and initiate a Split Completion transaction at a later time to return the previously requested read data. One or more of the read data items may have bad parity. This subject is covered in "Initiator's Parity-Related Responsibilities During a Split Completion" on page 394.

In Scenario 1, as stated earlier in "Parity Checking by Initiator During a Read" on page 395, the Requester sets the Detected Parity Error bit in its Status register. If the Parity Error Response bit in its Command register is set to one, the initiator asserts either PERR# or SERR# (based on the state of the Data Parity Error Recovery Enable bit in the PCI-X Command register; see "Requester's Data Parity Error Recovery Enable Bit" on page 613) and sets the Master Data Parity Error bit in its Status register. The next two sections discuss whether PERR# or SERR# is asserted.

Read Error and Data Parity Error Recovery Enable Bit = 1. If   the Data Parity Error Recovery Enable bit in its PCI-X Command register is set to one, it asserts PERR# and generates an interrupt to invoke the interrupt handler within its device driver. The interrupt handler checks the status, determines that there was a Data Phase parity error and attempts recovery in a device-specific manner (i.e., outside the scope of the spec). For more information on the Data Parity Error Recovery Enable bit, refer to "Requester's Data Parity Error Recovery Enable Bit" on page 613.

Read Error and Data Parity Error Recovery Enable Bit = 0. If   the Data Parity Error Recovery Enable bit in its PCI-X Command register is cleared to zero, the Requester asserts SERR# rather than PERR# (assuming that the SERR# Enable bit in its Command register is set to one). For additional information, refer to "Requester's Data Parity Error Recovery Enable Bit" on page 613.

Bridge's Parity-Related Responsibilities During a Read

General. A bridge that initiates a read may detect a Data Phase parity error on a read in any of three different scenarios:

SCENARIO 1. The target may supply the data immediately (i.e., it does not split the transaction) and the parity on one or more data items is incorrect. See "Bridge Handling of Parity Error in Immediate Read" on page 397.

SCENARIO 2. The target may issue a Split Response to the bridge and the parity on the dummy data pattern (all ones) may be incorrect. This subject is covered in "Data Error Received With Split Response on Read" on page 616.

SCENARIO 3. The target may issue a Split Response to the bridge and initiate a Split Completion transaction at a later time to return the previously requested read data. One or more of the read data items may have bad parity. This subject is covered in "Initiator's Parity-Related Responsibilities During a Split Completion" on page 394.

Bridge Handling of Parity Error in Immediate Read. When   the bridge detects a Data Phase parity error on immediate read data, it sets the Detected Parity Error bit in the appropriate status register (Status register if the read was performed on its primary bus; Secondary Status register if performed on its secondary bus). If the Parity Error Response bit is set to one in the control register for that bus (Command register if the read was performed on its primary side; Bridge Control register if performed on its secondary side), the bridge asserts PERR# and sets the Master Data Parity

Error bit in the appropriate status register (Status register if the read was performed on its primary bus; Secondary Status register if performed on its secondary bus).

When the bridge performs the Split Completion transaction to return the requested read data to the Requester, the bridge acts as a faithful messenger and drives bad parity. The bridge continues to fetch read data until the byte count is satisfied or the target on the destination bus ends the Sequence in some other way.

Parity-Related Target Responsibilities

Target May Be a Completer, a Requester, or a Bridge

The device responding as the target of a transaction may be any of the following:

- The transaction is being performed on the bus that the Completer resides on and the Completer is acting as the target of the transaction.
- The transaction may be a Split Completion transaction and the device acting as the target is the Requester that issued the initial request.
- The transaction may be a Split Completion transaction and the device acting as the target is a bridge in the path back to the Requester.
- A transaction may be one other than a Split Completion and the device acting as the target of the transaction is a bridge on the path out to the Completer.

In any case, the target of a transaction has certain responsibilities regarding parity generation and/or checking. The following sections define the target's responsibilities during writes, Split Completions, and reads.

Target's Responsibilities During a Write

During a write transaction, the device acting as the target of the write receives the data and the Byte Enables from the initiator and checks the information for correctness. If it's incorrect, the target takes the actions defined in the following two sections.

Note that the target does not check parity while it is inserting Wait States in the initial Data Phase.

When Completer Acts as the Target of the Write. If the target of a write is the Completer, it takes the following actions:

- Sets the Detected Parity Error bit in its Status register.
- If the Parity Error Response bit in its Command register is set to one, the Completer asserts PERR# back to the initiator.
- If the Completer also issues a Split Response to the initiator, it takes the actions described in "Data Error Received With Split Response on Dword Write" on page 618.

When a Bridge Acts as the Target of the Write. If the target of the write is a bridge residing between the Requester and the Completer, the bridge takes the following actions:

- It sets the Detected Parity Error bit in its appropriate status register (Status register if its primary interface is the target of the write; Secondary Status register if its secondary interface is the target of the write).
- If the Parity Error Response bit in the control register (Command register if the bridge's primary interface is the target of the write; Bridge Control register if the secondary interface is the target) is set to one, the bridge asserts PERR# back to the initiator.
- If the bridge also issues a Split Response to the initiator, it takes the actions described in "Data Error Received With Split Response on Dword Write" on page 618.
- If the transaction is a memory write, it is posted in the bridge. When the bridge forwards the memory write to the destination side of the bridge, it is a faithful messenger and delivers the bad parity to the Completer.

Target's Responsibilities During a Split Completion

The device acting as the target of a Split Completion transaction can either be the Requester that originated the request or a bridge in the path between the Completer and the Requester. The following two sections define the actions of a Requester or a bridge when it is acting as the target of a Split Completion transaction.

Note that the target does not check parity while it is inserting Wait States in the initial Data Phase.

When Requester Acts as the Target of a Split Completion. The Requester may detect bad parity when it is receiving previously requested read data or an SCM in the Data Phase(s) of a Split Completion transaction.

For a description of the Requester actions in this case, refer to "Requester/ Completer Handling of Data Error During Split Completion" on page 620.

When a Bridge Acts as the Target of a Split Completion. The bridge forwards SCMs without decoding the message, regardless of whether they indicate normal completion or that some other device detected an error. When a bridge is acting as the target of a Split Completion transaction that is headed back toward the Requester, it takes the following actions in the event of a Data Phase parity error:

SCENARIO 1. If the Split Completion does not contain an SCM (i.e., the SCM bit is cleared to zero in the attributes):
- Assuming that the Parity Error Response bit is set to one in the control register for that interface of the bridge (Command register if it's the primary interface; Bridge Control register if it's the secondary interface), the bridge asserts PERR#.
- The bridge sets the Detected Parity Error bit in the status register for that interface of the bridge (Status register if it's the primary interface; Secondary Status register if it's the secondary interface).
- When the bridge initiates the Split Completion transaction on the destination side of the bridge, it is a faithful messenger and drives bad parity back toward the Requester.

SCENARIO 2. If the Split Completion contains an SCM (i.e., the SCM bit is set to one in the attributes) and the bridge has detected bad parity on the SCM, the bridge:
- Asserts SERR# on its primary side (if the SERR# Enable bit is set to one in its Command register).
- Sets the Signaled System Error bit to one in its Status register.
- Discards the transaction.

Target's Responsibilities During a Read

During a read transaction, in each Data Phase it is the target's responsibility to provide proper parity based on the data it is driving onto the AD bus and the Byte Enables it is receiving from the initiator. The target device generates parity information and supplies it to the initiator of the read. It does not check parity and report parity errors. The device acting as the target of a read transaction may be the Completer or a bridge in the path between the Requester and the Completer.

Data Parity Generation/Checking in PCI-X

General Format of Timing Diagram Descriptions

The sections that follow provide a detailed description of parity generation and checking in various transaction scenarios. Each transaction is described clock-by-clock, with the events during each clock divided into two categories:

- On the rising-edge of clock N.
- During clock N.

Please keep in mind that some events could actually be correctly placed in either of these event categories, so the author has chosen to place it in one or the other.

Parity in Memory Write Block (or Alias) or Split Completion

Figure 19-1 on page 405 illustrates either a Memory Write Block or a Split Completion transaction that is returning a block of read data previously requested using a Memory Read Block (or Alias to Memory Read Block) transaction. In both cases, the Byte Enables are reserved and driven high during each Data Phase of the transaction. The following is a detailed description of the illustrated transaction.

CLOCK 1. The transaction has not yet begun.
CLOCK 2. The initiator issues the address and command and asserts FRAME#.
CLOCK 3.
    ON the rising-edge of clock three:
- All agents on the bus register the address and command.
- The initiator drives the parity bit associated with the address and command. The number of one bits in the address and command plus the parity bit must be an even number of one bits.
- The initiator drives the attributes onto AD[31:0] and the Byte Enable bus.

    DURING clock cycle three:
- All targets begin the decode to determine which of them is the target.
- All bus agents compute the expected Address Phase parity based on the registered content of AD[31:0] and C/BE#[3:0].

CLOCK 4.
    ON the rising-edge of clock four:
- All bus agents register the Address Phase parity bit.
- All bus agents register the attributes.

DURING clock cycle four:

- All bus agents compare the registered Address Phase parity to the computed parity. If they are the same, there was no corruption of Address Phase information (as far as a simple-minded single-bit parity algorithm can detect) and no error action is taken. Any agent that detects a difference will drive SERR# asserted (if enabled to do so via the SERR# Enable bit in its Command register) on the rising-edge of clock five. It also sets the Signaled System Error and Detected Parity Error bits in its Status register.
- The initiator must drive the Byte Enable signals to the high state during the Response Phase.
- All bus agents compute the expected Attribute Phase parity.
- The initiator's treatment of AD[31:0] during the Response Phase (clock four) can be anything it desires (drive some value or turn off its output drivers). The initiator must drive the Byte Enables high.
- The targeted function asserts DEVSEL# (this is the decode A time slot).

CLOCK 5.

ON the rising-edge of clock five:

- All bus agents register the Attribute Phase parity bit.
- The initiator drives the first data item onto AD[31:0] and asserts IRDY# to indicate that it has begun to source data within the first block.
- In this example, the target asserts TRDY# on the rising-edge of clock five, thereby indicating its readiness to begin accepting the data within the first block.

DURING clock cycle five:

- The initiator is required to drive the Byte Enables high throughout all of the transaction's Data Phases.
- All bus agents compare the actual Attribute Phase parity to the computed parity. If they are the same, there was no corruption of Attribute Phase information (once again, as far as a simple-minded single-bit parity algorithm can detect) and no error action is taken. Any agent that detects a difference will drive SERR# asserted (if enabled to do so via the SERR# Enable bit in its Command register) on the rising-edge of clock six. It also sets the Signaled System Error and Detected Parity Error bits in its Status register.

CLOCK 6.

ON the rising-edge of clock six:

- The initiator drives out the second data item and maintains the Byte Enables in the high state.
- The target clocks the first data item and the Byte Enables (all high) into its input register.

- The initiator drives the parity bit associated with the first data item and Byte Enables.

DURING clock cycle six:

- The target computes the expected parity based on the registered copy of the first data item and its Byte Enables.

CLOCK 7.

ON the rising-edge of clock seven:

- The target clocks the first Data Phase's parity bit into its input register.
- The initiator drives out the third data item and maintains the Byte Enables in the high state.
- The target clocks the second data item and the Byte Enables (all high) into its input register.
- The initiator drives the parity bit associated with the second data item and Byte Enables.
- The initiator deasserts FRAME# to indicate one of the following:
  - During this clock, the initiator is driving the next-to-last data item in the current block and it has deasserted FRAME# to inform the target that it wishes to disconnect the transaction on the block boundary.
  - As dictated by the byte transfer count issued in the Attribute Phase, this is the next-to-last Data Phase of the transaction.

DURING clock cycle seven:

- The target compares the expected parity to the actual. If it's the same, it assumes that no data/Byte Enable corruption occurred in the first Data Phase. If it's different, a parity error has been detected.
- The target computes the expected parity based on the registered copy of the second data item and its Byte Enables.

CLOCK 8.

ON the rising-edge of clock eight:

- The target registers the FRAME# signal.
- The target registers the third data item and Byte Enables.
- The target registers the parity bit associated with the second data item.
- If the target detected a parity error on the first data item during clock seven, it asserts PERR# for one clock (assuming that the Parity Error Response bit is set in its Command register) starting on the rising-edge of clock eight and sets the Detected Parity Error bit in its Status register. If not, it leaves PERR# high.
- The initiator drives out the final data item.
- The initiator drives out the parity bit associated with the third data item.

DURING clock cycle eight:

- The target examines the registered copy of FRAME# and determines that the data item being transferred in clock eight is the final data item.
- The target computes the parity expected for the second data item.

CLOCK 9.

ON the rising-edge of clock nine:

- The target registers the final data item and Byte Enables.
- The target registers the parity bit associated with the third data item.
- If the transaction is a Memory Write Block (or Alias) rather than a Split Completion transaction, the initiator registers the state of the PERR# signal to see if the target detected a parity error on receipt of the first data item. If PERR# is asserted, the initiator sets the Master Data Parity Error bit in its Status register.
- The initiator drives the parity bit associated with the final data item.
- If the target detected a parity error on the second data item during clock eight, it asserts PERR# for one clock (assuming that the Parity Error Response bit is set in its Command register) starting on the rising-edge of clock nine and also sets the Detected Parity Error bit in its Status register. If not, it leaves PERR# high.

DURING clock cycle nine:

- The target computes the expected parity for the final data item.
- The target also compares the computed and actual parity bits for the third data item.
- The initiator backs off its output drivers from FRAME#, AD[31:0], and the Byte Enables.
- The target drives TRDY# and DEVSEL# back to the deasserted state.
- The initiator drives IRDY# back to the deasserted state.

CLOCK 10.

ON the rising-edge of clock 10:

- If the transaction is a Memory Write Block (or Alias) rather than a Split Completion transaction, the initiator registers the state of the PERR# signal to see if the target detected a parity error on receipt of the second data item. If PERR# is asserted, the initiator sets the Master Data Parity Error bit in its Status register.
- If the target detected a parity error for the third data item and Byte Enables, it asserts PERR# (assuming that the Parity Error Response bit is set in its Command register) and also sets the Detected Parity Error bit in its Status register. If not, it leaves PERR# high.
- In the example, the same or a different initiator starts a new transaction.

DURING clock cycle 10:

- The initiator of the previous transaction backs its output driver off of the PAR signal line.

CLOCK 11.

ON the rising-edge of clock 11:

- If the transaction is a Memory Write Block (or Alias) rather than a Split Completion transaction, the initiator registers the state of the PERR# signal to see if the target detected a parity error on receipt of the third data item. If PERR# is asserted, the initiator sets the Master Data Parity Error bit in its Status register.
- If the target detected a parity error for the fourth data item and Byte Enables, it asserts PERR# (assuming that the Parity Error Response bit is set in its Command register) starting on the rising-edge of clock 11 and also sets the Detected Parity Error bit in its Status register. If not, it leaves PERR# high.
- The initiator of the next transaction drives out the attributes for the transaction.
- The initiator of the next transaction drives out the parity bit for that transaction's Address Phase.

Figure 19-1: Parity in Memory Write Block or Split Completion Transaction

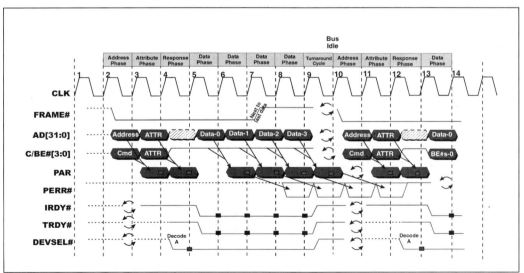

Parity in a Memory Write Transaction

Figure 19-2 on page 406 illustrates a Memory Write transaction. Unlike the Memory Write Block and Split Completion transactions (see Figure 19-1 on page 405), the Byte Enables can change from Data Phase to Data Phase.

Figure 19-2: Parity in Memory Write Transaction

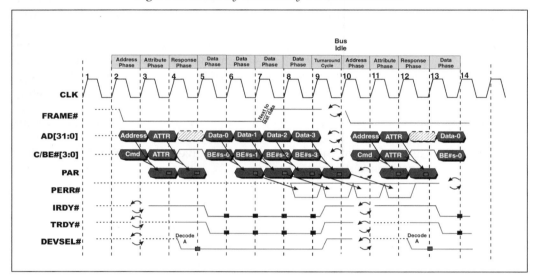

Parity in Memory Read Block (or Alias) Transaction

Figure 19-3 on page 411 illustrates parity in a Memory Read Block (or Alias to Memory Read Block) transaction. The following is a detailed description of this figure.

CLOCK 1. The transaction has not yet begun.

CLOCK 2. The initiator issues the address and command and asserts FRAME#.

CLOCK 3.

ON the rising-edge of clock three:

- All agents on the bus register the address and command.
- The initiator drives the parity bit associated with the address and command. The number of one bits in the address and command plus the parity bit must be an even number of one bits.
- The initiator drives the attributes onto AD[31:0] and the Byte Enable bus.

DURING clock cycle three:
- All agents on the bus begin the decode to determine which of them is the target.
- All bus agents compute the expected Address Phase parity based on the registered content of AD[31:0] and C/BE#[3:0].

CLOCK 4.

ON the rising-edge of clock four:
- All bus agents register the Address Phase parity bit.
- All bus agents register the attributes.
- The targeted function asserts DEVSEL# on the rising-edge of clock four (the decode A time slot).

DURING clock cycle four:
- All bus agents compare the registered Address Phase parity to the computed parity. If they are the same, there was no corruption of Address Phase information (as far as a simple-minded single-bit parity algorithm can detect) and no error action is taken. If they are different, any agent that detects a difference will drive SERR# asserted (if enabled to do so via the SERR# Enable bit in its Command register) on the rising-edge of clock five. It also sets the Detected Parity Error and Signaled System Error bits to one in its Status register.
- The initiator must drive the Byte Enable signals to the high state during the Response Phase.
- All bus agents compute the expected Attribute Phase parity.
- During the Response Phase (clock four), the initiator must back its output drivers off of the AD bus in preparation for the target returning read data.

CLOCK 5.

ON the rising-edge of clock five:
- All bus agents register the Attribute Phase parity bit on the rising-edge of clock five.
- The target registers the Byte Enables to be used in generating the parity for the first Data Phase.
- The target drives the first data item onto AD[31:0] and asserts TRDY# to indicate that it has begun to source data within the first block.
- The initiator asserts IRDY#, thereby indicating its readiness to begin accepting the data within the first block.

DURING clock cycle five:
- The initiator is required to drive the Byte Enables high throughout all of the transaction's Data Phases (because a Memory Read Block is an all-inclusive read).

- All bus agents compare the actual Attribute Phase parity to the computed parity. If they are the same, there was no corruption of Attribute Phase information (once again, as far as a simple-minded single-bit parity algorithm can detect) and no error action is taken. If they are different, any agent that detects a difference will drive SERR# asserted (if enabled to do so via the SERR# Enable bit in its Command register) on the rising-edge of clock six. It also sets the Detected Parity Error and Signaled System Error bits to one in its Status register.
- The initiator backs its output driver off of the PAR signal in preparation for the target starting to source the parity for the read data it presents.

CLOCK 6.

ON the rising-edge of clock six:
- The target drives out the second data item.
- The target drives out the parity bit for the first Data Phase. It was computed using the Byte Enables registered on the rising-edge of clock five and the data driven during clock five.
- The target registers the Byte Enables to be used in generating the parity for the second Data Phase.
- The initiator clocks the first read data item into its input register.

DURING clock cycle six:
- The initiator computes the first Data Phase expected parity based on the registered copy of the first read data item and the state of the Byte Enables on the rising-edge of clock five.

CLOCK 7.

ON the rising-edge of clock seven:
- The initiator clocks the first Data Phase's parity bit into its input register.
- The target drives out the third data item while the initiator maintains the Byte Enables in the high state.
- The initiator clocks the second read data item into its input register.
- The target drives the parity bit associated with the second data item and the state of the Byte Enables at the time of clock six's rising-edge.

DURING clock cycle seven:
- The initiator compares the expected parity to the actual. If it's the same, it assumes that no data/Byte Enable corruption occurred in the first Data Phase. If it's different, a parity error has been detected.
- The initiator computes the second Data Phase expected parity based on the registered copy of the second data item and the state of the Byte Enables at the time of clock six's rising-edge.

- The initiator deasserts FRAME# to indicate one of the following:
  - During this clock, the target is driving the next-to-last data item in the current block and the initiator has deasserted FRAME# to inform the target that it wishes to disconnect the transaction on the block boundary.
  - As dictated by the byte transfer count issued in the Attribute Phase, this is the next-to-last Data Phase of the transaction.

CLOCK 8.

ON the rising-edge of clock eight:
- The target registers the FRAME# signal.
- The initiator registers the third read data item.
- The initiator registers the parity bit associated with the second data item.
- If the initiator detected a parity error on the first data item during clock seven, it asserts PERR# for one clock (assuming that the Parity Error Response bit is set in its Command register) starting on the rising-edge of clock eight and also sets the Detected Parity Error and Master Data Parity Error bits to one in its Status register. If not, it leaves PERR# high.
- The target drives out the final data item.
- The target drives out the parity bit associated with the third read data item.

DURING clock cycle eight:
- The initiator compares the expected parity to the actual. If it's the same, it assumes that no data/Byte Enable corruption occurred in the second Data Phase. If it's different, a parity error has been detected.
- The target examines the registered copy of FRAME# and determines that the data item being transferred in clock eight is the final data item.
- The initiator computes the parity expected for the third data item.

CLOCK 9.

ON the rising-edge of clock nine:
- The initiator registers the final read data item.
- The initiator registers the parity bit associated with the third data item and the Byte Enables that were registered on the rising-edge of clock eight.
- The target drives the parity bit associated with the final read data item.
- If the initiator detected a parity error on the second read data item during clock eight, it asserts PERR# for one clock (assuming that the Parity Error Response bit is set in its Command register) starting on the rising-edge of clock nine and also sets the Detected Parity Error and Master Data Parity Error bits to one in its Status register. If not, it leaves PERR# high.

DURING clock cycle nine:
- The initiator computes the expected parity for the final read data item.
- The initiator compares the computed and actual parity bits for the third read data item. If they are different, a parity error was detected and the initiator sets the Detected Parity Error and Master Data Parity Error bits to one in its Status register.
- The initiator backs off its output drivers from FRAME# and the Byte Enables, while the target backs off its output drivers from AD[31:0].
- The target drives TRDY# and DEVSEL# back to the deasserted state.
- The initiator drives IRDY# back to the deasserted state.

CLOCK 10.

ON the rising-edge of clock 10:
- If the initiator detected a parity error for the third read data item and the state of the Byte Enables on the rising-edge of clock nine, it asserts PERR# (assuming that the Parity Error Response bit is set in its Command register) and sets the Detected Parity Error and Master Data Parity Error bits to one in its Status register. If not, it leaves PERR# high.
- In the example, the same or a different initiator starts a new transaction.
- The target of the previous transaction backs its output driver off the PAR signal line.
- The initiator registers the parity bit for the final data item.

DURING clock cycle 10:
- The initiator compares the computed and actual parity bits for the final read data item. If they are different, a parity error was detected and the initiator sets the Detected Parity Error and Master Data Parity Error bits to one in its Status register.
- The initiator backs off its output drivers from IRDY# and the PAR signal, while the target backs off its output drivers from TRDY# and DEVSEL#.

CLOCK 11.

ON the rising-edge of clock 11:
- If the initiator detected a parity error for the fourth read data item and the state of the Byte Enables that was registered on the rising-edge of clock 10, it asserts PERR# (assuming that the Parity Error Response bit is set in its Command register) starting on the rising-edge of clock eleven and sets the Detected Parity Error and Master Data Parity Error bits to one in its Status register. If not, it leaves PERR# high.
- The initiator of the next transaction drives out the attributes for the transaction.
- The initiator of the next transaction drives out the parity bit for that transaction's Address Phase.

Chapter 19: Parity Generation and Checking

Figure 19-3: Parity in Memory Read Block (or Alias) Transaction

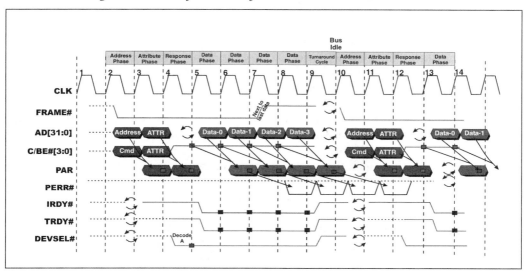

Parity in Memory Read Dword or IO Read Transaction

Figure 19-4 on page 414 and Figure 19-5 on page 415 illustrate parity in Memory Read Dword and IO Read transactions.

The following is a detailed description of Figure 19-4 on page 414.

CLOCK 1. The transaction has not yet begun.
CLOCK 2. The initiator issues the address and command and asserts FRAME#.
CLOCK 3.
    ON the rising-edge of clock three:
- All agents on the bus register the address and command.
- The initiator drives the parity bit associated with the address and command. The number of one bits in the address and command plus the parity bit must be an even number of one bits.
- The initiator drives the attributes onto AD[31:0] and also issues the Byte Enables to identify the bytes to be read within the target dword.

    DURING clock cycle three:
- All agents on the bus begin the decode to determine which of them is the target.
- All bus agents compute the expected Address Phase parity based on the registered content of AD[31:0] and C/BE#[3:0].

CLOCK 4.

ON the rising-edge of clock four:

- All bus agents register the Address Phase parity bit.
- All bus agents register the attributes.
- The targeted function asserts DEVSEL# on the rising-edge of clock four (the decode A time slot).

DURING clock cycle four:

- All bus agents compare the registered Address Phase parity to the computed parity. If they are the same, there was no corruption of Address Phase information (as far as a simple-minded single-bit parity algorithm can detect) and no error action is taken. If they are different, any agent that detects a difference will drive SERR# asserted (if enabled to do so via the SERR# Enable bit in its Command register) on the rising-edge of clock five and sets the Detected Parity Error and Signaled System Error bits to one in its Status register.
- The initiator must drive the Byte Enable signals to the high state during the Response Phase.
- All bus agents compute the expected Attribute Phase parity.
- During the Response Phase (clock four), the initiator must back its output drivers off of the AD bus in preparation for the target returning read data.

CLOCK 5.

ON the rising-edge of clock five:

- All bus agents register the Attribute Phase parity bit on the rising-edge of clock five.
- The target registers the Byte Enables to be used in generating the parity for the first Data Phase.
- The target drives the first data item onto AD[31:0] and asserts TRDY# to indicate that it is sourcing the data requested within the target dword.
- The initiator asserts IRDY#, thereby indicating its readiness to accept the requested data.
- The initiator registers the state of DEVSEL# to determine if the target has claimed the transaction.

DURING clock cycle five:

- The initiator is required to drive the Byte Enables high until it has received the requested data.
- All bus agents compare the actual Attribute Phase parity to the computed parity. If they are the same, there was no corruption of Attribute Phase information (once again, as far as a simple-minded single-bit parity algorithm can detect) and no error action is taken. If they are different, any agent that detects a difference will drive SERR# asserted (if enabled to do so via the SERR# Enable bit in its Command register) on

the rising-edge of clock six and sets the Detected Parity Error and Signaled System Error bits to one in its Status register.
- The initiator backs its output driver off of the PAR signal in preparation for the target starting to source the parity for the read data it presents.
- The initiator checks the state of its registered state of DEVSEL# and determines that the target has claimed the transaction.

CLOCK 6.

ON the rising-edge of clock six:
- The target drives out the parity bit for the Data Phase. It was computed using the Byte Enables registered on the rising-edge of clock five and the data driven during clock five.
- The initiator clocks the read data item into its input register.
- The initiator registers the state of TRDY#.

DURING clock cycle six:
- The target backs its output drivers off of the AD bus.
- The asserted state of the registered copy of TRDY# informs the initiator that it has received the requested read data.
- The target deasserts TRDY# and DEVSEL# (because the data was delivered to the initiator on the rising-edge of clock six).
- The initiator computes the expected Data Phase parity based on the registered copy of the read data item and the state of the Byte Enables on the rising-edge of clock five.

CLOCK 7.

ON the rising-edge of clock seven:
- Because the requested read data was received on the rising-edge of clock six, the initiator deasserts FRAME# and IRDY#.
- The initiator registers the parity bit associated with the read data it received on the rising-edge of clock six.

DURING clock cycle seven:
- The initiator can either back its output drivers off of the Byte Enables or may drive any pattern it wishes.
- The target backs its output driver off the PAR signal.
- The target backs its output drivers off TRDY# and DEVSEL#.
- The initiator compares the actual and computed parity to determine if any corruption occurred.

CLOCK 8.

ON the rising-edge of clock eight:
- The initiator backs its output drivers off FRAME# and IRDY#.
- If the initiator did not already do so during clock seven, it backs its output drivers off the Byte Enables.
- If the initiator had a miscompare on the computed versus the actual parity in clock seven, it asserts PERR# on the rising-edge of clock eight

(assuming that the Parity Error Response bit in its Command register is set to one) and sets the Detected Parity Error and Master Data Parity Error bits to one in its Status register.

Figure 19-4: Parity on Memory Read Dword or IO Read (Decode A and No Wait States)

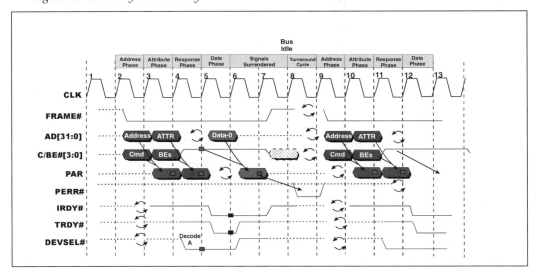

Figure 19-5 on page 415 is the same as Figure 19-4 on page 414 except that the target is slightly slower at decoding the address and command and claiming the transaction (it uses decode speed B, than A). As a result, it does not assert DEVSEL# until the rising-edge of clock five and then asserts TRDY# on the rising-edge of clock six when it presents the data to the initiator. It must then present the parity one clock later.

Figure 19-5: Parity on Memory Read Dword or IO Read (Decode B and No Wait States)

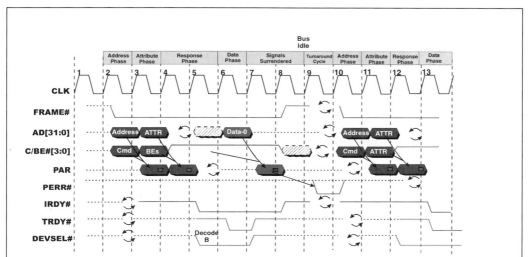

Parity in Configuration Read

Figure 19-6 on page 416 illustrates a Configuration Read transaction. Although the initiator starts driving the address in clock two, it does not assert FRAME# and actually start the transaction until four clocks later (on the rising-edge of clock six). This is referred to as address pre-drive and is described in detail in "Type 0 Configuration Transactions" on page 435. Once the transaction starts in clock six, it proceeds identically to a Memory Read Dword or an IO Read transaction.

Figure 19-6: Parity in Configuration Read

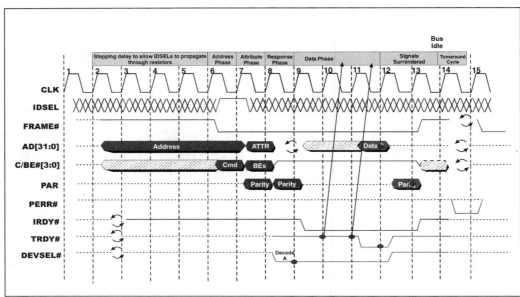

Parity in IO Write Transaction

Figure 19-7 on page 420 illustrates an IO Write transaction.

CLOCK 1. The transaction has not yet begun.

CLOCK 2. The initiator issues the address and command and asserts FRAME#.

CLOCK 3.

ON the rising-edge of clock three:

- All agents on the bus register the address and command.
- The initiator drives the parity bit associated with the address and command. The number of one bits in the address and command plus the parity bit must be an even number of one bits.
- The initiator drives the attributes onto AD[31:0] and also issues the Byte Enables to identify the bytes to be written within the target dword.

DURING clock cycle three:

- All agents on the bus begin the decode to determine which of them is the target.
- All bus agents compute the expected Address Phase parity based on the registered content of AD[31:0] and C/BE#[3:0].

CLOCK 4.

ON the rising-edge of clock four:
- All bus agents register the Address Phase parity bit.
- All bus agents register the attributes.
- The targeted function asserts DEVSEL# on the rising-edge of clock four (the decode A time slot).

DURING clock cycle four:
- All bus agents compare the registered Address Phase parity to the computed parity. If they are the same, there was no corruption of Address Phase information (as far as a simple-minded single-bit parity algorithm can detect) and no error action is taken. If they are different, any agent that detects a difference will drive SERR# asserted (if enabled to do so via the SERR# Enable bit in its Command register) on the rising-edge of clock five and sets the Detected Parity Error and Signaled System Error bits to one in its Status register.
- The initiator must drive the Byte Enable signals to the high state during the Response Phase.
- All bus agents compute the expected Attribute Phase parity.
- The initiator can either back its output drivers off of the AD bus or may drive an undefined pattern.

CLOCK 5.

ON the rising-edge of clock five:
- All bus agents register the Attribute Phase parity bit.
- The initiator drives the write data onto AD[31:0] and asserts IRDY# to indicate that it is sourcing the data to be written into the target dword.
- The initiator registers the state of DEVSEL# to determine if the target has claimed the transaction.

DURING clock cycle five:
- The initiator is required to drive the Byte Enables high until one clock after the target has accepted the write data (clock eight in the example).
- All bus agents compare the actual Attribute Phase parity to the computed parity. If they are the same, there was no corruption of Attribute Phase information (once again, as far as a simple-minded single-bit parity algorithm can detect) and no error action is taken. If they are different, any agent that detects a difference will drive SERR# asserted (if enabled to do so via the SERR# Enable bit in its Command register) on the rising-edge of clock six and sets the Detected Parity Error and Signaled System Error bits to one in its Status register.
- The initiator checks the state of its registered copy of DEVSEL# and determines that the target has claimed the transaction.

CLOCK 6.

ON the rising-edge of clock six:

- The initiator drives the parity bit onto the PAR signal (generated using the write data and Byte Enables driven during clock five). It must continue to drive the parity bit until one clock after the target has accepted the write data.
- The initiator registers the state of TRDY# to determine if the target accepted the write data.

DURING clock cycle six:

- The initiator checks the state of its registered copy of TRDY# and determines that the target did not accept the write data on the rising-edge of clock six. This results in a Wait State in clock seven during which the initiator must continue to drive the write data.

CLOCK 7.

ON the rising-edge of clock seven:

- The initiator once again registers the state of TRDY# to determine if the target accepted the write data on the rising-edge of clock seven.
- The target asserts TRDY# to indicate that it will accept the write data.

DURING clock cycle seven:

- The initiator must continue to drive the write data until the target accepts it.
- The initiator must continue to drive the parity until the target accepts it.

CLOCK 8.

ON the rising-edge of clock eight:

- The initiator once again registers the state of TRDY# to determine if the target accepted the write data.
- The target accepts the write data into its input register.
- The target deasserts TRDY# and DEVSEL# (because it just accepted the write data).

DURING clock cycle eight:

- The initiator must continue to drive the write data until it has verified that the target has accepted it.
- The initiator must continue to drive the parity until it verifies that the target accepted it.
- The initiator examines the state of its registered copy of TRDY# and determines that the target has accepted the write data.
- The target computes the expected parity.

CLOCK 9.

ON the rising-edge of clock nine:

- The initiator deasserts IRDY# and FRAME# (because the target accepted the write data on the rising-edge of the previous clock).
- The target registers the parity bit.

DURING clock cycle nine:

- The target backs its output drivers off TRDY# and DEVSEL#.
- The initiator may either continue to drive an undefined pattern on to AD[31:0] and the Byte Enables, or may turn off those output drivers.
- The initiator must continue to drive the parity bit until the target accepts it.
- The target compares the actual versus the computed parity to determine if any corruption occurred.

CLOCK 10.

ON the rising-edge of clock 10:

- The initiator backs its output drivers off IRDY# and FRAME#.
- The initiator backs its output driver off the PAR signal line.
- If it hadn't already done so one clock earlier, the initiator backs its output drivers off of AD[31:0] and the Byte Enables.
- If the target had a miscompare on the computed versus the actual parity in clock nine, it asserts PERR# on the rising-edge of clock 10 (assuming that the Parity Error Response bit in its Command register is set to one). The target also sets the Detected Parity Error bit to one in its Status register.

Figure 19-7: Parity in IO Write Transaction

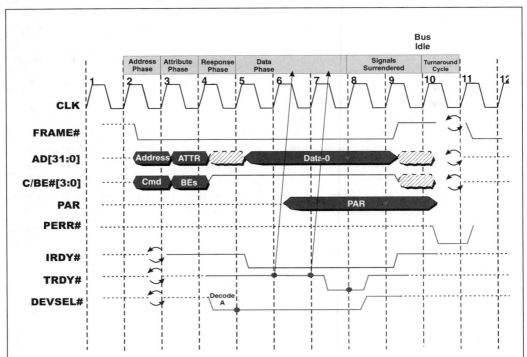

Parity in Configuration Write

Figure 19-8 on page 421 illustrates a Configuration Write transaction. Although the initiator starts driving the address in clock two, it does not assert FRAME# and actually start the transaction until four clocks later (on the rising-edge of clock six). This is referred to as address pre-drive and is described in detail in "Type 0 Configuration Transactions" on page 435. Once the transaction starts in clock six, it proceeds identically to an IO Write transaction.

Figure 19-8: Parity in Configuration Write

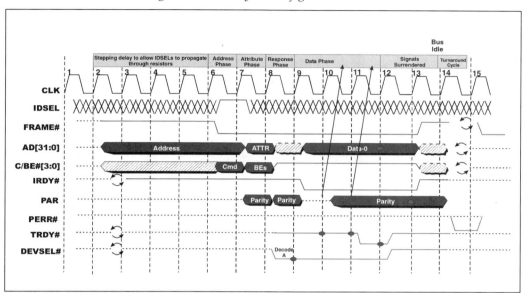

Part 3:
Device Configuration

The Previous Part

Part 2 provided a detailed description of the PCI-X bus protocol and consists of the following chapters:

- Chapter 10: Bus Arbitration
- Chapter 11: Detailed Command Description
- Chapter 12: Latency Rules
- Chapter 13: The Address, Attribute and Response Phases
- Chapter 14: Dword Transactions
- Chapter 15: Burst Transactions
- Chapter 16: Transaction Terminations
- Chapter 17: Split Completion Messages
- Chapter 18: 64-Bit Transactions
- Chapter 19: Parity Generation and Checking

This Part

Part 3 covers device configuration and consists of the following chapters:

- Chapter 20: Configuration Transactions
- Chapter 21: Non-Bridge Configuration Registers
- Chapter 22: Bridge Configuration Registers

The Next Part

Part 4 addresses issues to related to the PCI-X load-tuning mechanisms that the programmer may use to control the manner in which Requesters and bridges use the buses in the system. This part consists only of Chapter 23: Load Tuning Mechanisms.

20 *Configuration Transactions*

The Previous Chapter

The previous chapter provided a detailed discussion of parity generation, parity checking, Address and Attribute Phase parity, and Data Phase parity.

This Chapter

This chapter provides a detailed description of Type 0 and Type 1 Configuration transactions, Special Cycle Requests, and the arbiter's treatment of configuration transactions.

The Next Chapter

The next chapter describes the detection of a PCI-X bridge, the determination of a function's capabilities, how a function's PCI configuration registers are affected by mode selection, and the implementation and usage of the function's PCI-X capability register set.

Configuration Software Mechanism Same as PCI

The method software uses to stimulate the Host/PCIX bridge to generate a PCI-X configuration transaction is identical to that used in the PCI environment. For a detailed description of this mechanism, refer to the chapter entitled *Configuration Transactions* in the MindShare book entitled *PCI System Architecture, Fourth Edition* (published by Addison-Wesley).

Configuration Transactions Can Only Flow Downstream

With one exception (refer to the next section), PCIX-to-PCIX bridges will only pass configuration transactions downstream (i.e., away from the processor and main memory). The theory is that configuration registers are only accessed by the software executing on the processor. This means that, in order for a tool (such as the Agilent Technology PCI-X Bus Exerciser) to access configuration registers within functions on buses other than the one it resides on, the tool must be located on a bus upstream from the targeted function.

Special Cycle Request Can Flow Upstream or Downstream

Any Requester is permitted to issue a specially-formatted configuration write transaction that is really a request for a bridge to pass a Special Cycle Request from one bus to another. Bridges are designed to pass this type of request in either direction. For more information on the Special Cycle Request, refer to "Generation of Special Cycle Under Software Control" on page 450.

Type 0: Access Registers in Function on This Bus

Device Selection

The Type 0 Configuration transaction is used to access the configuration registers within a PCI-X function residing on the bus that the transaction is being performed on. It is being performed either by the source bridge for this bus or by a PCI-X bus exerciser tool (such as the Agilent Technologies PCI-X bus exerciser). Prior to initiating the transaction, the source bridge decodes the target device number specified by the programmer (see the Host/PCIX bridge to bus four in Figure 20-2 on page 428). The source bridge is always device 0 on the bus. Table 20-1 on page 427 illustrates the decoder's routing of its IDSEL outputs onto the upper address lines during the Address Phase of the Type 0 Configuration transaction. Figure 20-1 on page 427 illustrates the format of the address generated by the source bridge during the transaction's Address Phase. Figure 20-3 on page 429 illustrates the connection of the upper AD lines to each device. Just as in PCI, the system board designer must ensure that the coupling resistor is located in close proximity to the physical device.

Figure 20-1: Type 0 Configuration Address Format

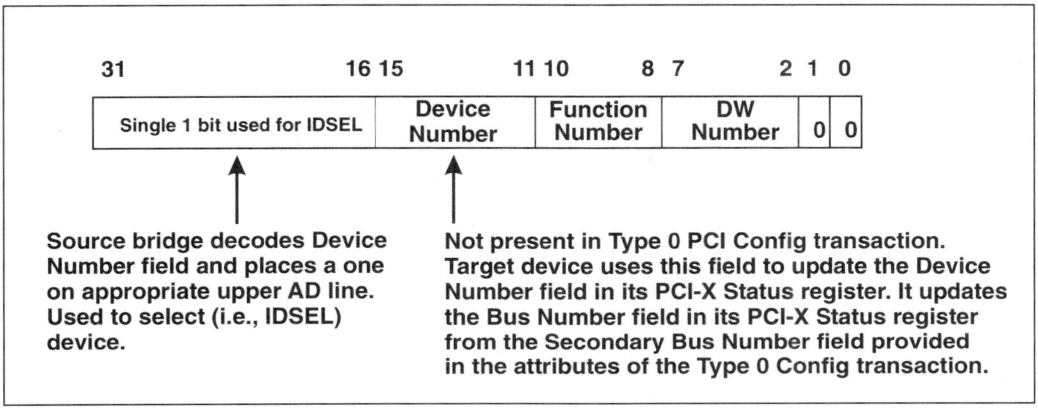

31	16 15	11 10	8 7	2 1 0
Single 1 bit used for IDSEL	Device Number	Function Number	DW Number	0 0

Source bridge decodes Device Number field and places a one on appropriate upper AD line. Used to select (i.e., IDSEL) device.

Not present in Type 0 PCI Config transaction. Target device uses this field to update the Device Number field in its PCI-X Status register. It updates the Bus Number field in its PCI-X Status register from the Secondary Bus Number field provided in the attributes of the Type 0 Config transaction.

Table 20-1: Routing of IDSELs to Upper AD Lines

IDSEL for Device Number:	Is always routed to the Device over AD Line:
0	AD[16]. Note that Device 0 is always the source bridge for the bus.
1	AD[17]
2	AD[18]
3	AD[19]
4	AD[20]
5	AD[21]
6	AD[22]
7	AD[23]
8	AD[24]
9	AD[25]
10	AD[26]

Table 20-1: Routing of IDSELs to Upper AD Lines (Continued)

IDSEL for Device Number:	Is always routed to the Device over AD Line:
11	AD[27]
12	AD[28]
13	AD[29]
14	AD[30]
15	AD[31]

Figure 20-2: Each Source Bridge Incorporates a Device-to-IDSEL Decoder

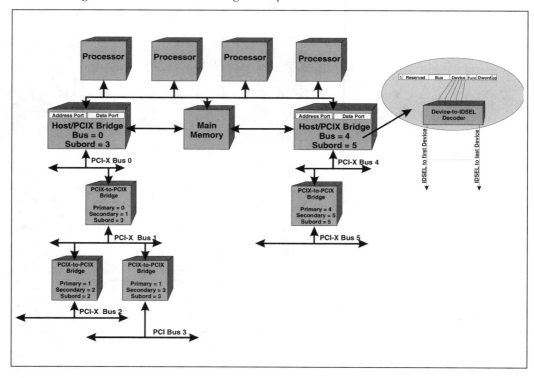

Figure 20-3: Resistive Coupling of Upper AD Lines to IDSEL Pins at Each Physical Device

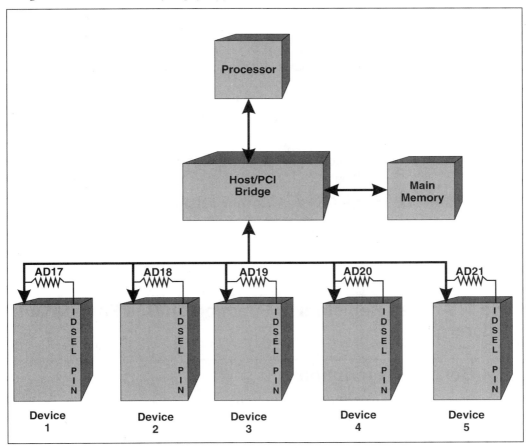

Bus/Device Auto-Updated by Each Type 0 Config Write

General

Whenever a Requester initiates a transaction request, it must provide its Requester ID in the Attribute Phase of the transaction. Likewise, whenever a Completer initiates a Split Completion transaction, it must provide its Completer ID in the transaction's Attribute Phase. The Requester or Completer obtains this information from its PCI-X Status register, which is automatically updated each time that a Type 0 Configuration Write is performed to any of the function's configuration registers. For more information on this topic, refer to "Bus, Device and Function Number Fields" on page 477.

Host/PCIX Bridge Device Number Assignment

Since the source bridge is always Device 0 on its secondary bus, the Host/PCIX bridge must automatically assign the value 00h to the Device Number field in its PCI-X Status register (see Figure 21-5 on page 457) on power-up.

Type 1: Access Registers in Function on Bus Farther Out in Hierarchy

General Description

When a bridge initiates a Type 1 Configuration access, it is ignored by non-bridge functions on the bus. Only PCIX-to-PCIX bridges pay attention to the Type 1 access. Furthermore, the source bridge that is performing the Type 1 access does not internally decode the target device number specified by the programmer. Rather, it generates an address with the format illustrated in Figure 20-4 on page 431. The 01b on AD[1:0] differentiates this from a Type 0 Configuration access. The IDSELs have no meaning in the Type 1 access (because the initiator is not attempting to access a device on this bus).

All PCI-X bridges that latch the Type 1 access compare the target bus number specified in the address to their Secondary Bus Number and Subordinate Bus Number configuration registers. If the target bus matches the value in a bridge's Secondary Bus Number register (see Figure 20-5 on page 432), the bridge claims the transaction (i.e., it asserts DEVSEL#), passes the transaction on to its secondary bus and converts it into a Type 0 access (because the Configuration access has arrived at the destination bus).

If the target bus does not match the value in a bridge's Secondary Bus Number register but is greater than that value and equal to or less than the value in the bridge's Subordinate Bus Number register, the bridge claims the transaction (i.e., it asserts DEVSEL#) and passes the transaction on to its secondary bus as a Type 1 access (because the Configuration access needs to be cascaded out to a bus beyond the bridge's secondary bus through another bridge).

Figure 20-4: Address Used in Type 1 Configuration Access

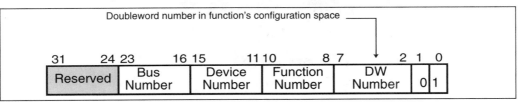

Figure 20-5: Bridge Configuration Header Registers

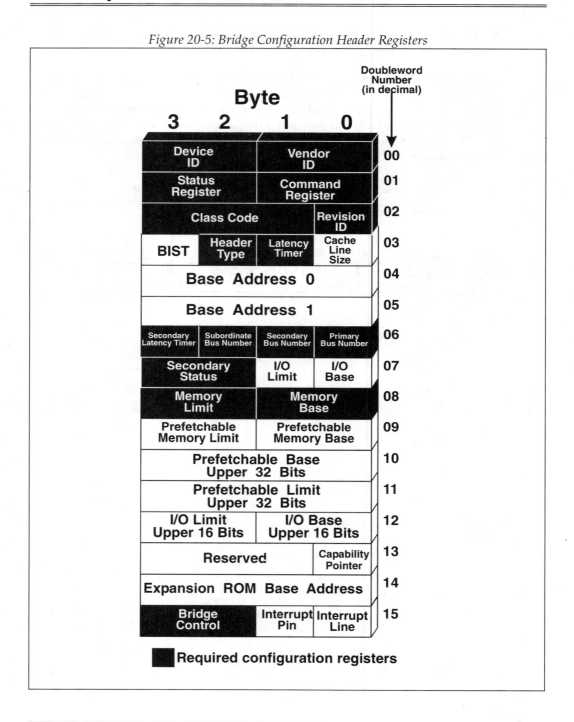

Some Example Scenarios

Refer to Figure 20-6 on page 435.

Example One

Assume that the configuration software executing on the processor instructs the Host/PCIX bridge to perform a Configuration access with a PCI-X function that resides on PCI-X bus 0. In this case, the bridge has a match on its Bus Number register (0), so it initiates a Type 0 Configuration on bus 0 and the IDSELs select a target device on that bus. The function decoder within the device determines that the targeted function is implemented within the device, so it asserts DEVSEL# and claims the transaction.

Example Two

Assume that the configuration software executing on the processor instructs the Host/PCIX bridge to perform a Configuration access with a PCI-X function that resides on PCI-X bus 1. In this case, the Host/PCIX bridge does not have a match on its Bus Number register (0), but the target bus is greater than its Bus Number register value but less than or equal to the value in its Subordinate Bus Number register (3). This means that the target bus is beyond the bridge farther out in the hierarchy than bus 0. As a result, the bridge initiates a Type 1 Configuration access on bus 0 and outputs the address specified in Figure 20-4 on page 431. The transaction is latched by all devices on bus 0. Because it is a Type 1 Configuration access, however, all non-bridge functions ignore the transaction. PCIX-to-PCIX bridges compare the specified target bus number (1) to the values in their Secondary and Subordinate Bus Number registers. In this case, the specified target bus number is equal to the value in bridge A's Secondary Bus Number register (1), so the bridge claims the transaction (i.e., it asserts DEVSEL#) and passes it through to bus 1. It also converts it from a Type 1 to a Type 0 access and selects a device on bus 1. The function decoder within the device determines that the targeted function is implemented within the device, so it asserts DEVSEL# and claims the transaction.

Example Three

Assume that the configuration software executing on the processor instructs the Host/PCIX bridge to perform a Configuration access with a PCI-X function that resides on PCI-X bus 3. In this case, the Host/PCIX bridge does not have a match on its Bus Number register (0), but the target bus is greater than its Bus Number register value and less than or equal to the value in its Subordinate Bus

Number register (3). This means that the target bus is beyond the bridge farther out in the hierarchy than bus 0. As a result, the bridge initiates a Type 1 Configuration access on bus 0 and outputs the address specified in Figure 20-4 on page 431. The transaction is latched by all devices on bus 0. Because it is a Type 1 Configuration access, however, all non-bridge functions ignore the transaction. PCIX-to-PCIX bridges compare the specified target bus number to the values in their Secondary and Subordinate Bus Number registers.

In this case, bridge B does not have a match on its Secondary Bus Number register, but the target bus is greater than its Secondary Bus Number register value (2) and less than or equal to the value in its Subordinate Bus Number register (3). This means that the target bus is beyond the bridge farther out in the hierarchy than bus 2. As a result, the bridge claims the transaction and passes through unaltered as a Type 1 Configuration access.

The transaction is then latched by bridge C and the specified target bus number is equal to the value in bridge C's Secondary Bus Number register (3), so the bridge claims the transaction (i.e., it asserts DEVSEL#) and passes it through to bus 3. It also converts it from a Type 1 to a Type 0 access and selects a device on bus 3. The function decoder within the device determines that the targeted function is implemented within the device, so it asserts DEVSEL# and claims the transaction.

Example Four

In this example, an exerciser tool on bus 2 initiates a Type 1 Configuration access targeting a function on bus 3. The transaction is latched by all devices on bus 2 and is ignored by all non-bridge devices. The transaction is latched by bridge C and the specified target bus number (3) is equal to the value in bridge C's Secondary Bus Number register (3), so the bridge claims the transaction (i.e., it asserts DEVSEL#) and passes it through to bus 3. It also converts it from a Type 1 to a Type 0 access and selects a device on bus 3. The function decoder within the device determines that the targeted function is implemented within the device, so it asserts DEVSEL# and claims the transaction.

Figure 20-6: Example System

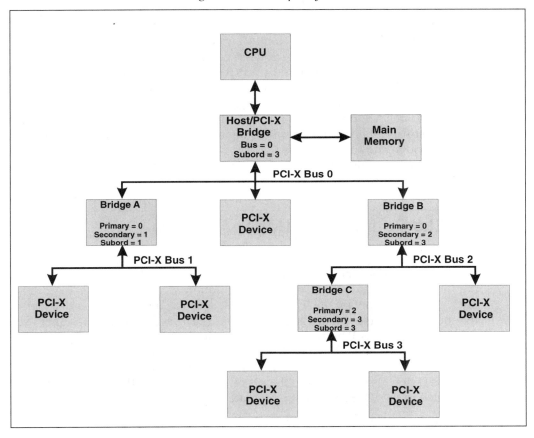

Type 0 Configuration Transactions

Action Taken on Master Abort

The actions taken by the source bridge when a configuration access results in a Master Abort are the same as those taken in a PCI bus environment under the same circumstances. There are two possible scenarios:

1. The transaction was **initiated by** a **Host/PCIX bridge**. In this case, the bridge sets the Received Master Abort bit to one in its Secondary Status register. In addition,
   - If the transaction is a Type 0 Configuration Read, the bridge returns all ones to the processor as the read data.
   - If the transaction is a Type 0 Configuration Write, the bridge tells the processor that the transaction has completed.
2. The transaction was **initiated by** a **PCIX-to-PCIX bridge**. The actions taken by the bridge are determined by the state of the Master Abort Mode bit in its Bridge Control register (see Figure 20-5 on page 432).
   - **Master Abort Mode bit = 0**. If the transaction is a read, the transaction returns all ones. If the transaction is a write, the data is accepted by the bridge and then discarded.
   - **Master Abort Mode bit = 1**. The bridge signals a Target Abort to the Requester.

IDSELs Routed Over Upper AD Lines

This is the method used in all PCIX-to-PCIX bridge designs and in most host/PCIX bridge and system board designs. Refer to Figure 20-3 on page 429. During the Address Phase of a Type 0 Configuration access, the upper 16 address lines, AD[31:16], contain the IDSELs generated by the device number decoder in the source bridge (see Figure 20-1 on page 427). The system board designer uses these signal lines as IDSEL signals to the various physical devices (up to 16 of them). Internally, the bridge decodes the target device number specified by the programmer (see the bridge to bus four in Figure 20-2 on page 428) to select which AD line to set to one. On the system board, each of these address lines is connected to the IDSEL input of a separate device (see Figure 20-7 on page 437).

This approach places an additional load on each AD line, however, and it's a rule that each PCI-X device is only permitted to place one electrical load on each PCI-X bus signal. This effect is mitigated by resistively coupling (using a 2K Ohm series resistor) the device's IDSEL pin to the appropriate AD pin at the embedded device or at the connector on the system board (see Figure 20-3 on page 429).

Although this approach supports the implementation of up to 16 devices on a PCI-X bus (from a configuration standpoint), realistically the bus will not work correctly with too many electrical loads present.

Figure 20-7: Direct-Connect of Upper AD Lines to IDSEL Pins

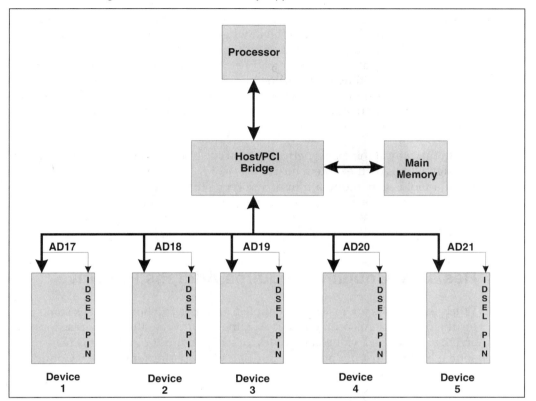

IDSEL Output Pins/Traces Allowed on Host/PCIX Bridge

Description

Although PCIX-to-PCIX bridge designers are required to resistively couple the upper AD lines to the IDSEL pin at each device, the Host/PCIX bridge designer has the option of implementing actual IDSEL output pins on the bridge. These pins would then be connected to traces which connect each bridge output pin to a separate device's IDSEL input pin. Most Host/PCIX bridge designs probably will not implement IDSEL output pins because it is a pin- and trace-intensive solution.

Type 0 Access by a Tool

If a Host/PCIX bridge implements IDSEL output pins (as described in the previous section), this presents a problem when a PCI-X bus exerciser tool (such as the Agilent Technologies PCI-X bus exerciser) installed on PCI-X bus 0 initiates a Type 0 Configuration access to read or write configuration registers within a PCI-X function residing on the same bus. Since the tool is not connected to the bridge's IDSEL output pins, whenever the tool initiates any transaction, the bridge must route the upper 16 bits (AD[31:16]) of the tool's address information onto its IDSEL output pins.

- In this way, if the tool is performing a Type 0 access, it can control the IDSEL signal lines on the system board.
- If a tool is generating a transaction type other than a Type 0 Configuration access, the upper address bus information is still presented to all bus devices over the upper AD lines, but devices ignore their IDSEL pins in all transactions other than a Type 0 Configuration transactions.

Resistive Coupling Requires Address Pre-Drive

When the IDSELs are resistively-coupled to upper AD lines, it takes some time for the ones or zeros on the upper AD lines to traverse the series resistors and arrive at the correct value at each device's IDSEL input pin. For this reason, the source bridge must use address pre-drive when performing Type 0 Configuration transactions.

Refer to Figure 20-8 on page 443. The source bridge initiates the Type 0 Configuration transaction by driving the address (see Figure 20-1 on page 427) onto the AD bus with AD[1:0] set to 00b to indicate that this is a Type 0 Configuration transaction. It also outputs its internal device decoder's IDSEL outputs onto the upper AD lines (AD[31:16]). The Configuration Read or Write command may be simultaneously driven onto C/BE#[3:0]. If the bridge designer chooses not to output the command when it begins pre-driving the address, the bridge must drive something (anything) onto C/BE#[3:0] to keep the command bus from floating during the address pre-drive period.

Chapter 20: Configuration Transactions

The source bridge doesn't assert FRAME# yet, however. It delays the assertion of FRAME# for four clock cycles to let the bits on the upper AD lines propagate through the series resistors to the IDSEL pins at the devices and settle to the correct state and then asserts FRAME#. If the bridge hadn't already done so, it also drives the command (Configuration Read or Write) onto C/BE#[3:0] when it asserts FRAME#. No devices will pay any attention to the transaction until FRAME# is asserted.

Bridge With IDSEL Pins Also Requires Address Pre-Drive

When a tool (rather than the Host/PCIX bridge) is performing a Type 0 access, the four clock address pre-drive period permits time for a Host/PCIX bridge with IDSEL output pins to route the upper AD bus IDSEL information supplied by the tool onto the bridge's IDSEL output pins. This permits the tool to select a device as the target of the Type 0 Configuration access.

Type 0 Configuration Read

Refer to Figure 20-8 on page 443.

CLOCK 1. The transaction has not yet begun.
CLOCK 2.
>   **ON** the rising-edge of clock two:
>   - The initiator begins driving the address onto the AD bus and will drive it for a total of five clock cycles. The address has the format illustrated in Figure 20-1 on page 427. It will assert FRAME# on the rising-edge of the fifth clock cycle (clock six in the example). As described in "IDSELs Routed Over Upper AD Lines" on page 436, in addition to the device number, function number, and dword address, the initiator is also driving the IDSELs (i.e., the device selects) onto AD[31:16].
>   - Optionally, the initiator begins driving the command onto the C/BE# bus. At the latest, it will begin driving the command on the rising-edge of clock six.

CLOCK 3.
>   **DURING** clock cycle three:
>   - The initiator continues to pre-drive the address onto the AD bus (and perhaps the command onto the C/BE# bus).

CLOCK 4.

DURING clock cycle four:

- The initiator continues to pre-drive the address onto the AD bus (and perhaps the command onto the C/BE# bus).

CLOCK 5.

DURING clock cycle five:

- The initiator continues to pre-drive the address onto the AD bus (and perhaps the command onto the C/BE# bus).

CLOCK 6.

ON the rising-edge of clock six:

- The initiator continues to drive the address.
- If it didn't start driving the command in clock two, the initiator now drives the command onto the C/BE# bus.
- The initiator asserts FRAME#, thereby indicating that it has started the transaction.

DURING clock cycle six:

- By this time, the IDSEL values should have traversed the series resistors on the system board and settled at the correct values on the IDSEL pins of all devices.

CLOCK 7.

ON the rising-edge of clock seven:

- All agents on the bus register the address and command and the state of their respective IDSEL signals.
- The initiator drives the attributes onto AD[31:0] and also issues the Byte Enables to identify the bytes to be read within the target dword.

DURING clock cycle seven:

- All agents on the bus begin the decode to determine which of them is the target. The command is a Configuration Read, so the decoder checks the following:
  - AD[1:0] = 00b, indicating that this is a Type 0 Configuration Read targeting one of the devices on this bus.
  - Each device therefore tests the state of the registered copy of its IDSEL pin to determine if it is the targeted device.
  - The targeted device decodes the function number delivered in the Address Phase. If the targeted function exists within the device, it will assert DEVSEL# in the A, B, or C decode timeslot.
  - In this example, a function with decode speed A asserts its internal DEVSEL# signal during clock seven.

CLOCK 8.

ON the rising-edge of clock eight:

- All bus agents register the attributes, including the Byte Enables.
- The targeted function asserts DEVSEL# on the rising-edge of clock eight (the decode A time slot).

DURING clock cycle eight:

- The initiator must drive the Byte Enable signals to the high state during the Response Phase.
- During the Response Phase (clock eight), the initiator must back its output drivers off of the AD bus in preparation for the target returning read data.

CLOCK 9.

ON the rising-edge of clock nine:

- In this example, the targeted function is not yet ready to supply the data, so it does not assert TRDY# in clock nine.
- The targeted function must take ownership of the data bus in clock nine (the clock after it asserted DEVSEL#) to keep the bus from floating until it is ready to present the requested read data.
- The initiator asserts IRDY#, thereby indicating its readiness to accept the requested data.
- The initiator registers the state of DEVSEL# to determine if the target has claimed the transaction.

DURING clock cycle nine:

- The initiator is required to drive the Byte Enables high until it has received the requested data.
- The initiator checks the state of its registered copy of DEVSEL# and determines that the target has claimed the transaction. This defines the rising-edge of clock 10 as the first time that the state of TRDY# will be checked by the initiator.

CLOCK 10.

ON the rising-edge of clock 10:

- The initiator clocks the read data and the state of TRDY# into its input register.
- The targeted function is not yet ready to deliver the requested read data, so it does not assert TRDY# and continues to drive the data bus to keep it from floating.

DURING clock cycle 10:

- The initiator checks the state of its registered copy of TRDY#. Its deasserted state indicates that the target did not deliver valid read data on the rising-edge of clock 10, so the initiator discards the read data.

CLOCK 11.

ON the rising-edge of clock 11:

- The initiator clocks the read data and the state of TRDY# into its input register.
- The targeted function is now ready to deliver the requested read data, so it asserts TRDY# and drives the requested read data onto the data bus.

DURING clock cycle 11:

- The initiator checks the state of its registered copy of TRDY#. Its deasserted state indicates that the target did not deliver valid read data on the rising-edge of clock 11, so the initiator dicards the read data.

CLOCK 12.

ON the rising-edge of clock 12:

- The initiator clocks the read data and the state of TRDY# into its input register.
- The targeted function deasserts TRDY# and DEVSEL#.

DURING clock cycle 12:

- The initiator checks the state of its registered copy of TRDY#. Its asserted state indicates that the target did deliver valid read data on the rising-edge of clock 12, so the initiator keeps the read data.
- The initiator prepares to deassert FRAME# and IRDY# on the rising-edge of clock 13.
- The targeted function ceases to drive the read data onto the data bus.

CLOCK 13.

ON the rising-edge of clock 13:

- The initiator deasserts FRAME# and IRDY#.

DURING clock cycle 13:

- The initiator may either continue to drive the Byte Enables to the deasserted state or may back its output drivers off the bus.

CLOCK 14.

ON the rising-edge of clock 14:

- The initiator backs its output drivers off the FRAME# and IRDY# signals.
- If the initiator had continued driving the Byte Enables during the previous clock, it turns off its output drivers.

Figure 20-8: Type 0 Configuration Read

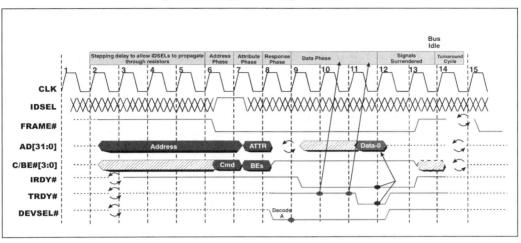

Type 0 Configuration Write

Refer to Figure 20-9 on page 447.

CLOCK 1. The transaction has not yet begun.
CLOCK 2.
> **ON** the rising-edge of clock two:
> - The initiator begins driving the address onto the AD bus and will drive it for a total of five clock cycles. It will assert FRAME# on the rising-edge of the fifth clock cycle (clock six in the example). The address has the format illustrated in Figure 20-1 on page 427. As described in "IDSELs Routed Over Upper AD Lines" on page 436, in addition to the device number, function number, and dword address, the initiator is also driving the IDSELs (i.e., the device selects) onto AD[31:16].
> - Optionally, the initiator begins driving the command onto the C/BE# bus. At the latest, it will begin driving the command on the rising-edge of clock six.

CLOCK 3.
> **DURING** clock cycle three:
> - The initiator continues to pre-drive the address onto the AD bus (and perhaps the command onto the C/BE# bus).

CLOCK 4.

DURING clock cycle four:

- The initiator continues to pre-drive the address onto the AD bus (and perhaps the command onto the C/BE# bus).

CLOCK 5.

DURING clock cycle five:

- The initiator continues to pre-drive the address onto the AD bus (and perhaps the command onto the C/BE# bus).

CLOCK 6.

ON the rising-edge of clock six:

- The initiator continues to drive the address.
- If it didn't start driving the command in clock two, the initiator now drives the command onto the C/BE# bus.
- The initiator asserts FRAME#, thereby indicating that it has started the transaction.

DURING clock cycle six:

- By this time, the IDSEL values should have traversed the series resistors on the system board and settled at the correct values on the IDSEL pins of all devices.

CLOCK 7.

ON the rising-edge of clock seven:

- All agents on the bus register the address and command and the state of their respective IDSEL signals.
- The initiator drives the attributes onto AD[31:0] and also issues the Byte Enables to identify the bytes to be read within the target dword.

DURING clock cycle seven:

- All agents on the bus begin the decode to determine which of them is the target. The command is a Configuration Read, so the decoder checks the following:
  - AD[1:0] = 00b, indicating that this is a Type 0 Configuration Write targeting one of the devices on this bus.
  - Each device therefore tests the state of the registered copy of its IDSEL pin to determine if it is the targeted device.
  - The targeted device decodes the function number delivered in the Address Phase. If the targeted function exists within the device, it will assert DEVSEL# in the A, B, or C decode timeslot.
- In this case, a function with decode speed A asserts its internal DEVSEL# signal during clock seven.

CLOCK 8.

ON the rising-edge of clock eight:

- The currently addressed target clocks an asserted level onto DEVSEL#. This is the Decode A time slot.

DURING clock cycle eight (the Response Phase):
- The initiator has the option of doing one of the following:
  - It can back its output drivers off of AD[31:0].
  - It can drive the attributes for an extra clock cycle before supplying the write data.
  - It can start driving the write data a clock early.
  - It can drive a dummy stable pattern.
- The initiator places the Byte Enables in the Reserved and Driven High state for the remainder of the transaction.

CLOCK 9.

ON the rising-edge of clock nine:
- The initiator asserts IRDY#, indicating that it is driving the write data onto the AD bus.
- The rising-edge of clock nine is the first point at which the initiator clocks the state of DEVSEL# into its input register. In this case, it detects an asserted level on its registered copy of DEVSEL# during clock cycle nine. This tells the initiator that it has established a connection with the addressed target and it defines the first point at which the initiator will register the state of TRDY# as the rising-edge of clock 10.
- The earliest time slot in which the target can assert TRDY# is the clock immediately following its assertion of DEVSEL#. In this case, the target does not assert TRDY# on the rising-edge of clock nine, thereby indicating that it will not accept the write data from the AD bus on the rising-edge of clock 10.

CLOCK 10.

ON the rising-edge of clock 10:
- The target once again does not assert TRDY#, thereby indicating that it will not accept the write data from the AD bus on the rising-edge of clock 11.

DURING clock cycle 10:
- The initiator continues to drive the write data because it has not yet been accepted.

CLOCK 11.

ON the rising-edge of clock 11:
- The target finally asserts TRDY#, thereby indicating that it will register the write data from the AD bus on the rising-edge of clock 12.

DURING clock cycle 11:
- The initiator continues to drive the write data because it has not yet been accepted.

CLOCK 12.

ON the rising-edge of clock 12:

- The target accepts the write data on the AD bus. It does not need to check the state of IRDY# to validate the presence of the data because it's a rule that the initiator must assert IRDY# and start driving the write data in clock nine.
- The initiator clocks the state of the TRDY# signal into its input register and examines its registered copy of TRDY# during clock 12. In this case, it detects that it's asserted, indicating that the target accepted the write data on the rising-edge of clock 12. The initiator can therefore surrender the bus during clock 13.

DURING clock cycle 12:

- The target deasserts TRDY#. Since it's a sustained tri-state signal, the deassertion protocol is to drive it high for one clock cycle and then back off the output driver from the signal line.
- The target deasserts DEVSEL# (also a sustained tri-state signal line).

CLOCK 13.

ON the rising-edge of clock 13:

- Because the target accepted the write data on the rising-edge of clock 12, the initiator ends the transaction on the rising-edge of clock 13. It:
    - Deasserts FRAME#. Since it's a sustained tri-state signal, the deassertion protocol is to drive it high for one clock cycle and then back off the output driver from the signal line.
    - Deasserts IRDY# (also a sustained tri-state signal line).

DURING clock cycle 13:

- Regarding the Byte Enables, in clock cycle 13 the initiator may continue to drive them high, drive some other pattern, or back off its output drivers.
- Regarding the AD bus, the initiator can continue to drive the write data during clock 13, may drive a dummy data pattern, or may back its output drivers off the AD bus.

CLOCK 14.

ON the rising-edge of clock 14:

- The bus returns to the Idle state (FRAME# and IRDY# both high) on the rising-edge of clock 14.
- If the initiator has not yet backed its output drivers off the AD bus and the Byte Enables in the previous clock cycle, it does so on the rising-edge of clock 14.

Figure 20-9: Type 0 Configuration Write

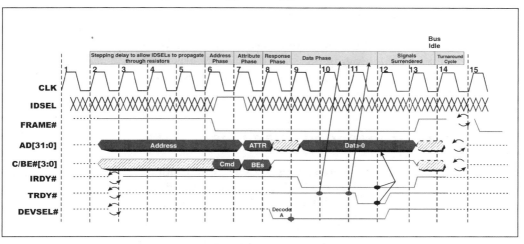

Type 1 Configuration Transactions

Although Not Necessary, Address Pre-Drive Used

Devices only pay attention to the state of their IDSEL pins during a Type 0 Configuration access. IDSEL has no meaning during any other type of transaction, including a Type 1 Configuration access.

In order to keep the protocol used during configuration transactions consistent and simple, however, address pre-drive is also used during the Type 1 access.

Type 1 Configuration Access Address Format

Refer to Figure 20-4 on page 431. The address issued during the Address Phase of a Type 1 access consists of:

- AD[23:16] identifies the target **bus** upon which the Type 0 Configuration access must be performed.
- AD[15:11] identifies the target **device** on the target bus.
- AD[10:8] identifies the target **function** within the target device.
- AD[7:2] identifies the target **dword** within the target function's configuration space.

Target Bus's Source Bridge Converts Type 1 to Type 0 Access

When the Type 1 Configuration access arrives at the bridge to the target bus specified by the programmer, that bridge converts the Type 1 access to a Type 0 access and selects the specified target device on that bus (by asserting its IDSEL).

Type 1 Transaction Examples

The only differences between the Type 1 Configuration Read and Write transactions illustrated in Figure 20-10 on page 448 and Figure 20-11 on page 449 and the Type 0 transactions illustrated in Figure 20-8 on page 443 and Figure 20-9 on page 447 are:

- The source bridge performing the Type 1 transaction does not supply IDSELs over upper AD lines (because this transaction is not accessing a device on the bus that the Type 1 access is being performed on).
- The address format is that illustrated in Figure 20-4 on page 431 rather than that illustrated in Figure 20-1 on page 427.

Figure 20-10: Type 1 Configuration Read

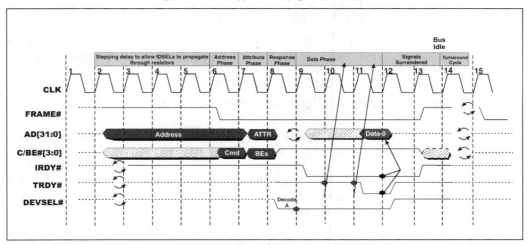

Figure 20-11: Type 1 Configuration Write

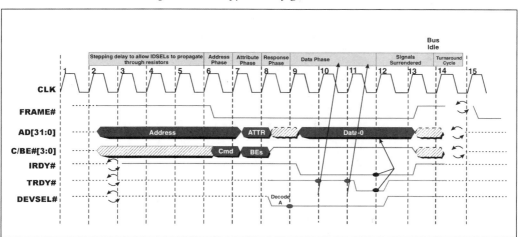

Arbiter's Treatment of Configuration Access

When the bus is not Idle (i.e., a transaction is currently in progress), the arbiter can keep GNT# asserted to the current initiator for a period of less than five clocks. In other words, it can remove GNT# from the device in order to grant bus ownership to another device.

The arbiter must ensure that a device has a fair opportunity to initiate configuration transactions. Refer to Figure 20-12 on page 450. In order for a device to successfully initiate a configuration transaction, GNT# must remain asserted to the device for five clocks while the bus is Idle for the device to initiate a configuration transaction.

Just as in any other transaction type, the arbiter must assert GNT# to a device in clock N-2 for the device to start a configuration transaction on the rising-edge of clock N. In Figure 20-12 on page 450, the device registers its GNT# in the asserted state on the rising-edge of clock N-1 and the bus is Idle. As a result, the device initiates a configuration access on the rising-edge of clock N. It drives out the address (and perhaps the command as well) but delays the assertion of FRAME# for four clocks to pre-drive the address (and IDSELs).

If the arbiter deasserts GNT# to the device during clock N, N+1, or N+2, the device must surrender the bus without starting the transaction. It must back its output drivers off the bus and not assert FRAME#.

Figure 20-12: Preemption During Start of Configuration Access

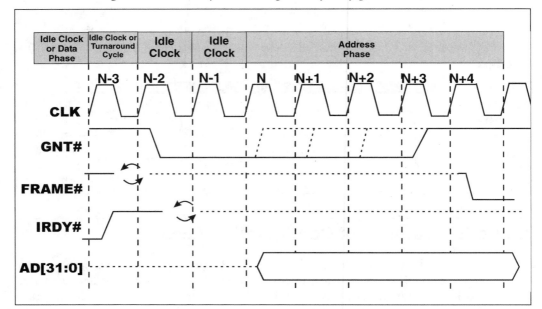

Generation of Special Cycle Under Software Control

General

Host/PCIX bridges are not required to provide a means that allows software to cause the initiation of a Special Cycle transaction on a target PCI-X bus. If this capability is provided by the bridge, however, this section describes how it must be implemented.

To prime the Host/PCIX bridge to generate a PCI-X Special Cycle transaction, the host processor must write a 32-bit value with the following content to the Configuration Address Port at IO address 0CF8h:

- Bus Number = the target PCI Bus that the Special Cycle transaction is to be performed on.
- Device Number = all ones (31d, or 1Fh).
- Function Number = all ones (7d).
- Dword Number = all zeros.

After this has been accomplished, the next write to the Configuration Data Port at IO port 0CFCh supplies the Host/PCIX bridge with the data that represents the message. The bridge then takes the following actions:

- If the target bus is bus zero, the Host/PCIX bridge initiates a Special Cycle transaction on bus zero and, in the transaction's Data Phase, drives out the programmer-supplied data as the message.
- If the value in the Host/PCIX bridge's Secondary Bus Number register does not match the specified target bus number but the target bus number is within the range of buses subordinate to the bridge's bus, the bridge passes the transaction through as a Type 1 Configuration Write (so that it can be submitted to PCIX-to-PCIX bridges farther out in the hierarchy) and, in the transaction's Data Phase, drives out the programmer-supplied data as the message.

If the Host/PCIX bridge has been primed to generate a PCI-X Special Cycle transaction (by writing the appropriate data to the Configuration Address Port) and an IO read is performed from the Configuration Data Port, the result is undefined. The bridge may pass it through as a Type 0 Configuration Read (which will result in a Master Abort with all ones returned as data).

PCIX-to-PCIX Bridges Pass Special Cycle Request to Target Bus

When a PCIX-to-PCIX bridges receives a Type 1 Configuration Write on either side of the bridge with the Device Number, Function Number, and Dword Number fields in the address set to all ones, all ones, and all zeros respectively, the bridge treats this as a Special Cycle Request. If the target bus is the bus directly on the other side of the bridge, the bridge translates the Special Cycle Request into a Special Cycle transaction on the target bus and delivers the Type 1's write data as the message in the transaction's Data Phase. If the target bus isn't the one directly on the other side of the bridge, but is a bus that lies beyond the bus on the other side of the bridge, the bridge passes it through as a Type 1 transaction (i.e., without translating it).

Special Cycle by Device Other Than Host/PCIX Bridge

Any Requester is permitted to initiate either a Special Cycle or a Special Cycle Request transaction in order to transmit a message to the devices that reside on the targeted bus.

21 *Non-Bridge Configuration Registers*

The Previous Chapter

The previous chapter provided a detailed description of Type 0 and Type 1 Configuration transactions, Special Cycle Requests, and the arbiter's treatment of configuration transactions.

This Chapter

This chapter describes the detection of a PCI-X bridge, the determination of a function's capabilities, how a function's PCI configuration registers are affected by mode selection, and the implementation and usage of the function's PCI-X capability register set.

The Next Chapter

The next chapter describes the bridge's configuration registers. It identifies the PCI registers that are unaffected by the mode, those that are affected (and how), and describes the bridge's PCI-X capability register set.

Detecting a PCI-X Capable Bridge

Detecting Presence of PCI-X Capable Bridge/Bus

The presence of a PCI-X capable bridge indicates that the bus on its secondary side is a PCI-X bus. This being the case, the configuration programmer then checks the capabilities of each function present on that bus to ensure the highest possible performance on that bus. Remember that the PCI-X bus is essentially a lowest common denominator bus: the presence of a less-capable device causes the bridge to force all devices on the bus to operate using a protocol and frequency that ensures proper operation of the less-capable device.

A PCI-X capable bridge is detected by checking for the presence of the PCI-X Capability register set.

1. Refer to Figure 21-1 on page 454. The programmer checks the state of the Capabilities List bit in the bridge function's PCI Status register. A one indicates that the function implements one or more New Capability configuration registers sets, while a zero indicates that none are implemented (including the PCI-X Capability register set). A zero would therefore indicate that the function resides within a PCI device rather than a PCI-X capable device, while a one indicates that the function may or may not reside within a PCI-X capable device (see the next step).

2. A one in the Capabilities List bit indicates that the Capabilities Pointer register is implemented (see dword 13, byte 0 in Figure 21-2 on page 455). The dword-aligned value in this register is used by the programmer to select and read the indicated dword within the bridge function's configuration space.

3. New Capability register sets have the general format indicated in Figure 21-3 on page 456. The first byte indicates which New Capability register set this is, while the second byte either contains a dword-aligned pointer to position of the next New Capability register set, or zero if the function has no additional New Capabilities. As indicated in Table 21-1 on page 456, Capability ID 07h indicates that this is the bridge function's PCI-X Capability register set. Its format is illustrated in Figure 21-4 on page 457.

Figure 21-1: PCI Status Register

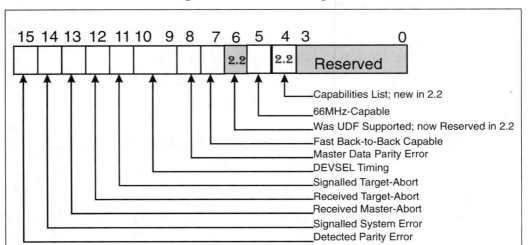

Chapter 21: Non-Bridge Configuration Registers

Figure 21-2: Configuration Header Type 1 Register Set Template

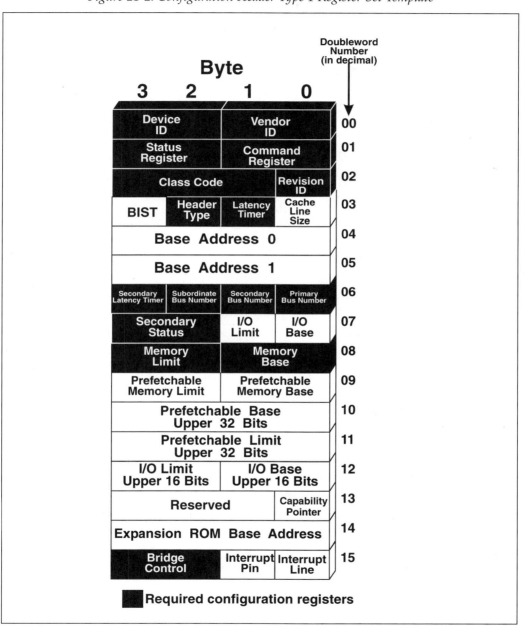

Figure 21-3: General Format of New Capability Registers Sets

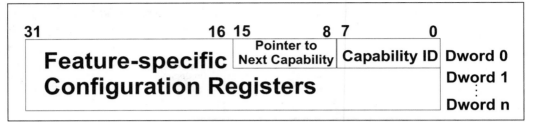

Table 21-1: Currently Assigned Capability IDs

ID	Description
00h	Reserved.
01h	**PCI Power Management Interface**. Refer to the Power Management chapter in MindShare's book entitled *PCI System Architecture, Fourth Edition* (published by Addison-Wesley).
02h	**AGP**. Refer to the MindShare book entitled *AGP System Architecture, Second Edition* (published by Addison-Wesley).
03h	**VPD**. Refer to the description in MindShare's book entitled *PCI System Architecture, Fourth Edition* (published by Addison-Wesley).
04h	**Slot Identification**. This capability identifies a bridge that provides external expansion capabilities (i.e., an expansion chassis containing add-in card slots). Full documentation of this feature can be found in the revision 1.1 *PCI-to-PCI Bridge Architecture Specification*. For a detailed description, refer to the topics entitled *Introduction To Chassis/Slot Numbering Registers* and *Chassis and Slot Number Assignment* in MindShare's book entitled *PCI System Architecture, Fourth Edition* (published by Addison-Wesley).
05h	**Message Signaled Interrupts**. Refer to the topic entitled *Message Signaled Interrupts (MSI)* in MindShare's book entitled *PCI System Architecture, Fourth Edition* (published by Addison-Wesley).
06h	**CompactPCI Hot Swap**. Refer to the topic entitled *CompactPCI and PMC* in MindShare's book entitled *PCI System Architecture, Fourth Edition* (published by Addison-Wesley).
7d	Reserved in 2.2 PCI spec, but ID 07h was subsequently assigned to PCI-X devices.
8-255d	Reserved in 2.2 PCI.

Figure 21-4: PCI-X Bridge Capability Register Set Format

31 16	15 Next 8	7 0	
PCI-X Secondary (I/F) Status Register	Next Capability	Capability ID = 7	Dword 0
PCI-X Bridge (Primary I/F) Status Register			Dword 1
Upstream Split Transaction Control Register			Dword 2
Downstream Split Transaction Control Register			Dword 3

Detecting Width of Bridge's Interfaces

Refer to Figure 21-5 on page 457 and Figure 21-6 on page 458. Software may determine the width of the bridge's connection to the buses by checking the state of the 64-Bit Device status bit. The programmer may then check the width of each device's connection to the bridge's secondary bus to ensure that devices of the appropriate width are installed in the connectors on that bus. For more information, refer to "Detecting Width of PCI-X Functions" on page 461.

Figure 21-5: Bridge's PCI-X Status Register

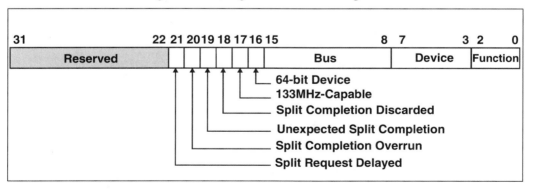

Figure 21-6: Bridge's PCI-X Secondary Status Register

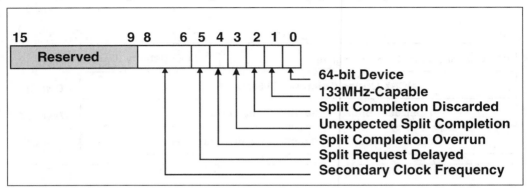

Detecting Frequency Support of Bridge's Interfaces

Frequency Support of Bridge's Primary Interface

A card with a PCIX-to-PCIX bridge may be installed in a connector on a bus. As with any other function, software may determine the maximum bus frequency supported on the bridge's primary interface by checking the state of the 133MHz-Capable bit in the bridge's PCI-X Status register (see Figure 21-5 on page 457). In the event that the bus on the bridge's primary side is a 133MHz-Capable bus (as indicated by the 133MHz-Capable bit of that bus's Source Bridge PCI-X Secondary Status register), the programmer may wish to suggest the removal of the card if the bridge on the card only supports 66MHz PCI-X operation on its primary interface.

Frequency Support on Bridge's Secondary Interface

The 133MHz-Capable bit in the PCI-X Secondary Status register (see Figure 21-6 on page 458) indicates whether the bridge's secondary bus is capable of running in 66MHz or 133MHz PCI-X mode. The programmer may then check the frequency and mode supported by each device on the secondary bus to ensure that devices with the appropriate capabilities are installed in connectors on the secondary bus. For more information, refer to "Detecting Frequency Support of PCI-X Functions" on page 462.

Checking Current Frequency/Protocol of Secondary Bus

During a power-up session, the programmer may check the protocol and clock frequency currently in use on the bridge's secondary bus by reading the Secondary Clock Frequency field from the bridge's PCI-X Secondary Status register. This is very useful in a Hot-Plug PCI-X environment in determining the appropriateness of attaching a newly installed card to the bus before actually doing so.

Detecting Capabilities of Functions on Bus

Format of Non-Bridge Function's PCI-X Capability Registers

Figure 21-7 on page 460 illustrates the configuration header registers for a non-bridge function. Assuming that the Capabilities List bit (bit 4) is set in the Status register, then the Capabilities Pointer register points to the beginning of the linked-list of New Capability configuration registers sets. Figure 21-8 on page 461 illustrates the layout of a non-bridge function's PCI-X Capability register set.

Figure 21-7: Non-Bridge Function's Configuration Header Registers

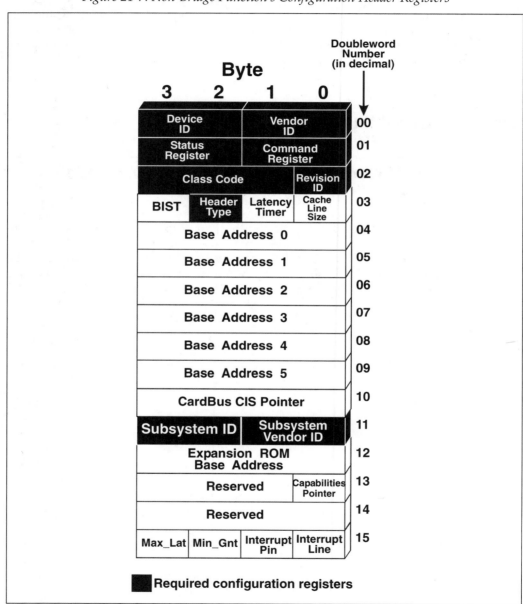

Chapter 21: Non-Bridge Configuration Registers

Figure 21-8: Format of Non-Bridge Function's PCI-X Capability Registers

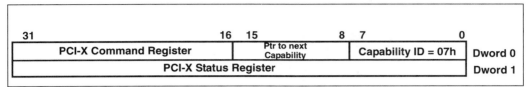

Detecting PCI Functions

A PCI function residing on a PCI-X bus may be found by checking each function on the bus to determine if it implements the PCI-X Capability register set. If it doesn't, then the function resides within a device that is only capable of the PCI bus protocol. When such a device is discovered on a PCI-X bus, the programmer should urge the end-user to remove the card, advising the user of the performance implications if the card is left in the system.

Detecting Width of PCI-X Functions

As indicated in an earlier section (see "Detecting Width of Bridge's Interfaces" on page 457) software may determine the width of the bus connected to a bridge's secondary interface by checking the state of the 64-Bit Device status bit in the bridge's PCI-X Secondary Status register.

Figure 21-9 on page 462 illustrates the PCI-X Status register for a non-bridge function, while Figure 21-5 on page 457 illustrates a PCIX-to-PCIX bridge's PCI-X Status register format. A card installed in a connector on the bus may contain only a non-bridge device (containing one or more functions) or a device that incorporates a bridge function (and, possibly, additional functions). The programmer checks the 64-Bit Device status bit in each function's status register (PCI-X Status register in a non-bridge function, or the PCI-X Bridge Status register in a bridge function) to determine the width of the function's connection to the AD bus pins on the connector. If it is a single-function device, software prompts the end-user to remove the card if it's ill-suited to the connector width. If it's a multi-function device, some of the functions may have a 32-bit interface while others have a 64-bit interface. In this case, software should recommend that the card be installed in a 64-bit card connector.

Figure 21-9: Non-Bridge Function's PCI-X Status Register

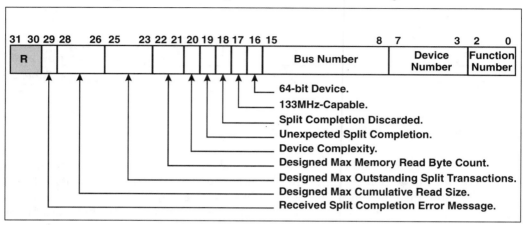

Detecting Frequency Support of PCI-X Functions

To determine the bus frequency supported by a PCI-X capable device, the programmer checks the state of each function's 133MHz-Capable bit. In both non-bridge and bridge functions, this bit resides in the function's PCI-X Status register (see Figure 21-9 on page 462 and Figure 21-5 on page 457). The programmer checks the 133MHz-Capable bit in the appropriate register to determine the width of the device's connection to the AD bus pins on the connector and prompts the end-user to remove the card if it's ill-suited to the Source Bridge's secondary bus frequency capability.

Most PCI Configuration Registers Remain Unchanged

Refer to Figure 21-7 on page 460. In a PCI-X capable function, the following PCI Configuration header registers have the same purpose and usage as in the PCI environment (in both the PCI-X and PCI protocol modes):

- Device ID register.
- Vendor ID register.
- Revision ID register.
- Class Code register.
- BIST register.

- Header Type register.
- CardBus CIS Pointer register.
- Subsystem Vendor ID register.
- Subsystem ID register.
- Expansion ROM Base Address register.
- Capabilities Pointer register.
- Max_Lat register.
- Min_Gnt register.
- Interrupt Pin register.
- Interrupt Line register.

Some PCI Config Registers Affected by Protocol Mode

Some Register Default Values Affected

As described in Chapter 4, entitled "Device Types and Bus Initialization," on page 55, each PCI-X capable device receives an initialization pattern from the Source Bridge on the rising-edge of RST#. This pattern instructs the device as to the protocol and bus clock frequency that will be used during this power-on session. Each function within each device must set the default values within a subset of its PCI configuration registers based on the protocol selected. The affected PCI configuration registers are:

- **Status register**. When the function is initialized in PCI-X mode, the Fast Back-to-Back Capable status bit is always zero (because Fast Back-to-Back transactions are not permitted when using the PCI-X protocol). Also see "Status Register Bits Affected by Protocol Mode" on page 469.
- **Latency Timer** register. When the function is initialized in PCI-X mode, the Latency Timer is initialized to a value of 64d. For more information, refer to "What Is the Recommended LT Value?" on page 144 and "How Much Data Can Be Transferred During Default Timeslice?" on page 144.

Implementation of Some Registers Affected

- **Memory Base Address registers**. See "Memory Base Address Registers" on page 464.
- **IO Base Address registers**. See "IO Base Address Registers" on page 467.
- **Cache Line Size Configuration register**. See "Cache Line Size Configuration Register" on page 470.

Usage of Some Registers Affected

The usage of the following registers is affected by the protocol mode selected:

- **Command register**. See "Command Register Bits Affected by Protocol Mode" on page 467.
- **Status register**. See "Status Register Bits Affected by Protocol Mode" on page 469.
- **Latency Timer register**. See "Latency Timer Default Affected by Protocol Mode" on page 469.

A detailed description of the changes in the usage of each of these registers can be found in the sections that follow. A detailed description of all of the PCI configuration registers can be found in the *Configuration Registers* chapter of the MindShare book *PCI System Architecture, Fourth Edition* (published by Addison-Wesley).

Base Address Registers (BARs)

Memory Base Address Registers

PCI and Memory BARs. Refer to Figure 21-10 on page 466 and Figure 21-11 on page 466. In the PCI environment, the designer has the option of implementing memory BARs as either 32- or 64-bit decoders.

Must Be Implemented as 64-bit Decoders. Refer to Figure 21-7 on page 460. In order to give the configuration software maximum flexibility in assigning memory addresses ranges to programmable memory decoders, all memory BARs must be implemented as 64-bit decoders (and must appear so whether the function is in either PCI-X or PCI mode). This gives the configuration software the flexibility to assign a decoder a memory range below or above the 4GB address boundary.

Definition of Prefetchable Memory. As defined in the PCI specification and in MindShare's book *PCI System Architecture, Fourth Edition*, Prefetchable memory is well behaved from both a read and write perspective. With one small exception, the definition of Prefetchable memory remains the same in the PCI-X spec. While a PCI Prefetchable memory target is required to return all bytes in each Data Phase, this is not true of PCI-X Prefetchable memory.

There are currently two types of PCI-X memory read commands:

- **Memory Read Dword**. This command is used to read from memory-mapped IO registers and the target device only supplies the bytes for which the respective Byte Enables are asserted in the transaction's Attribute Phase. Memory-mapped IO devices are typically not well-behaved, Prefetchable memory.
- **Memory Read Block**. This command is used to read an all-inclusive block of information from the target memory. The start byte address is issued in the Address Phase and identifies the start byte address of the least-significant location to be read, while the byte count is issued in the Attribute Phase and identifies the end byte address of the last location to be read. The Byte Enables are Reserved and Driven High during all Data Phases of the transaction. The target memory only supplies the contents of the locations within the specified range and does not supply any bytes from locations prior to the start byte address in the start dword or qword or after the end byte address in the end dword or qword (even if the target is Prefetchable memory). However, it would not be a violation for the target to supply these unrequested bytes if those memory locations are well behaved from a read perspective (i.e., reading from a location does not alter the contents of that location or alter the state of the device in any other way).

Minimum Memory Range. While the PCI spec recommends that a memory BAR be designed to request a minimum memory address range of 4KB (to save on address decode logic), the PCI-X spec dictates that the minimum size of the requested range must be 128 bytes. The decoder should be designed to only ask for a range that is "no larger than the smallest integral power of two that is larger than the range actually used by the device."

In other words, the designer must only ask for a memory space assignment that meets the memory's needs and no more. In a machine that supports Hot-Plug PCI-X, after the machine is already up and running and space has already been assigned to various other memory decoders throughout the system, it can be problematic for the Hot-Plug configuration software to find an unassigned memory range to assign to a function's decoders.

Diminishes Overall Number of BARs. If any of a function's BARs are memory decoders, each of them consumes two dwords of the area in the function's configuration space that is set aside for the implementation of BAR registers. This would, of course, diminish the overall number of BAR registers that could be implemented for the function.

Figure 21-10: 32-Bit Memory BAR

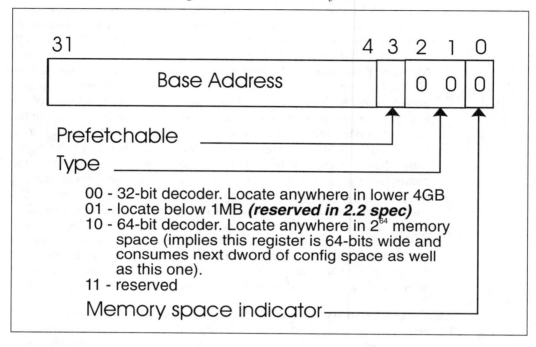

Figure 21-11: 64-Bit Memory BAR

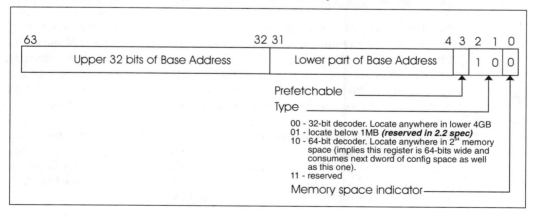

IO Base Address Registers

To give the configuration software maximum flexibility, each IO BAR must have a matching Memory BAR. In this way, the configuration software could assign both an IO and a memory range to the function's device-specific register set (which is what an IO BAR is typically used for).

Command Register Bits Affected by Protocol Mode

Introduction

Refer to Figure 21-12 on page 467. The following Command register bits have their traditional role if the function is in PCI mode, but their roles are altered when the function is in PCI-X mode:

- Fast Back-to-Back Enable Bit
- Stepping Control Bit
- Memory Write and Invalidate Bit
- Bus Master Enable Bit

The sections that follow describe how PCI-X mode alters the role of each of these bits.

Figure 21-12: PCI Command Register

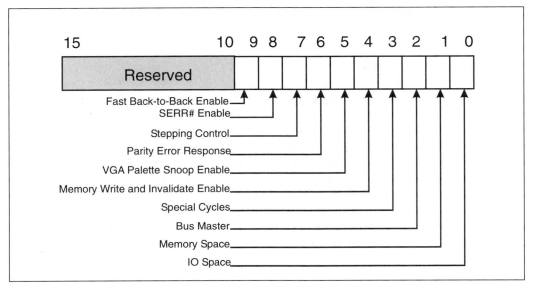

Fast Back-to-Back Enable Bit

Unlike PCI, there is no such thing as fast back-to-back transactions in the PCI-X bus protocol. Therefore, when a function is initialized in PCI-X mode, the function ignores the state of the Fast Back-to-Back bit in its Command register (and it therefore doesn't matter what value it is initialized to). For a complete description of PCI fast back-to-back transactions, refer to MindShare's book entitled *PCI System Architecture, Fourth Edition* (published by Addison-Wesley).

Stepping Control Bit

Unlike PCI, there is no such thing as address or data stepping in the PCI-X bus protocol. Therefore, when a function is initialized in PCI-X mode, the function ignores the state of the Stepping Control bit in its Command register. For a complete description of PCI address and data stepping, refer to MindShare's book entitled *PCI System Architecture, Fourth Edition* (published by Addison-Wesley).

Memory Write and Invalidate Bit

Unlike PCI, there is no such thing as the Memory Write and Invalidate transaction in the PCI-X bus protocol. Therefore, when a function is initialized in PCI-X mode, the function ignores the state of the Memory Write and Invalidate bit in its Command register. For a complete description of PCI Memory Write and Invalidate transaction, refer to MindShare's book entitled *PCI System Architecture, Fourth Edition* (published by Addison-Wesley). For information about emulation of the PCI Memory Write and Invalidate command by a PCI-X Requester, refer to "Emulating the PCI Memory Write and Invalidate Command" on page 172.

Bus Master Bit

Earlier sections of the book detailed Split Transaction capability. A target that issues a Split Response in response to a transaction request has committed to initiate a series of one or more Split Completion transactions at a later time in order to deliver the requested read data or to acknowledge completion of a write (either IO or Configuration). The PCI-X spec states that a target device that has made this commitment must initiate the corresponding Split Completion(s) irrespective of the setting of the Bus Master bit in the function's Command register. In other words, if software had neglected to set this bit to one, the function would nonetheless arbitrate for bus ownership and then initiate the Split Completion transaction(s).

Status Register Bits Affected by Protocol Mode

Refer to Figure 21-13 on page 469. When a PCI-X capable function is initialized in PCI mode, the usage and interpretation of the **Master Data Parity Error** and the **Detected Parity Error** bits adhere to the PCI spec. When the function is initialized in PCI-X mode, however, these bits are used and interpreted identically to PCI except in one case. That case is described in "Requester/Completer Handling of Data Error During Split Completion" on page 620.

Figure 21-13: PCI Status Register

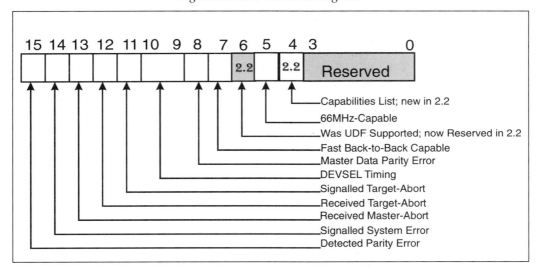

Latency Timer Default Affected by Protocol Mode

When a PCI-X capable function is initialized in PCI mode, the default value loaded in the function's Latency Timer register (see Figure 21-7 on page 460) is 00h (as dictated by the PCI spec). The configuration software must then consult each bus master-capable device's Min_Gnt register to determine the guaranteed timeslice desired by each bus master and then assign values to each of the bus masters' Latency Timer registers.

When the function is initialized in PCI-X mode, however, a default value of 64d is loaded into its Latency Timer register. For a detailed discussion of this register's role in PCI-X mode, refer to "How the Initiator Deals With Preemption" on page 143.

Cache Line Size Configuration Register

In the PCI environment, a PCI bus master-capable device uses its Cache Line Size configuration register (see Figure 21-7 on page 460) in order to make intelligent use of the PCI Memory Read, Memory Read Line, Memory Read Multiple, and Memory Write and Invalidate commands (refer to MindShare's book entitled *PCI System Architecture, Fourth Edition* for a detailed description of these commands).

These commands do not exist in the PCI-X protocol, however, so the usefulness of this register is function-specific. A situation wherein the implementation of this register is quite useful is described in "Emulating the PCI Memory Write and Invalidate Command" on page 172.

Capabilities Pointer Register

In both modes, a PCI-X capable function has the Capabilities List bit set in its Status register (see Figure 21-13 on page 469) and the dword pointer value is present in its Capabilities Pointer register (see Figure 21-7 on page 460). This is true because the function does implement at least one New Capability register set: the PCI-X Capability register set.

Function's PCI-X Capability Register Set

Register Set Format

Figure 21-14 on page 471 illustrates the PCI-X Capability register set as implemented in a non-bridge function. The sections that follow provide a detailed description of these registers.

Figure 21-14: PCI-X Capability Register Set (as implemented in a non-bridge function)

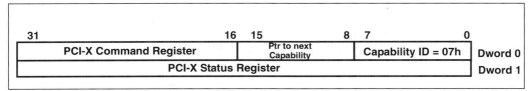

Background on Load Tuning

A well-designed, high-end OS will schedule a load-tuning task to run on a periodic basis to check on the smooth flow of traffic throughout the platform. If any problems are detected, the task determines what action(s) may be taken to increase the platform efficiency. Two possible scenarios are described in the following two sections.

Adjusting Requester's Split Transaction Queue Size

Problem. A Requester is dominating Split Transaction Queues in one or more Completers or bridges. A specific Requester is initiating too many transactions that receive Split Responses from one or more Completers or PCIX-to-PCIX bridges. The Completers or bridges are then forced to issue Retries to other Requesters due to full Split Transaction Queues.

Solution. By checking a bit-field in a Requester's PCI-X Status register, the load-tuning software can determine the maximum number of Split Transactions that it can handle. The load-tuning software may then limit the Requester to a lower maximum number of Split Transactions by changing the content of a bit-field in the Requester's PCI-X Command register. Refer to "Max Outstanding Split Transaction Field" on page 473 and "Designed Max Outstanding Split Transactions" on page 484.

Adjusting Requester's Memory Read Transaction Size

Problem. A Requester is dominating the Split Completion read data buffers in one or more bridges. A specific Requester is initiating Memory Read Block transactions, each with a large byte count, that receive Split Responses from one or more Completers or PCIX-to-PCIX bridges. The targeted Completers or bridges are forced to commit a large percentage of their internal buffers to service memory read requests from this specific Requester. This is causing one or both of the following problems:

- The targeted Completers or bridges are forced (due to insufficient buffer space to hold the requested Split Completion read data) to delay the performance of requests issued by other Requesters.
- Although the targeted bridges accept Split Requests issued by other Requesters, they are forced (due to insufficient buffer space to hold the resulting Split Completion read data) to issue Retries or Disconnects in response to the Split Completion transactions returning read data for other Requesters. In other words, the Requester issuing the large memory read requests tends to dominate the usage of the bridge's internal buffers that are used to hold requested Split Completion read data.

Solution. By checking a bit-field in a Requester's PCI-X Status register, the load-tuning software can determine the maximum size memory read transaction that the Requester is capable of issuing. The load-tuning software may then limit the Requester to a lower maximum memory read transaction size by changing the content of a bit-field in the Requester's PCI-X Command register. Refer to "Max Memory Read Byte Count Field" on page 474 and "Designed Max Memory Read Byte Count" on page 484.

PCI-X Command Register

Figure 21-15 on page 472 illustrates the PCI-X Command register as implemented in a non-bridge PCI-X function. The sections that follow provide a detailed description of each bit field.

Figure 21-15: PCI-X Command Register (as implemented in a non-bridge function)

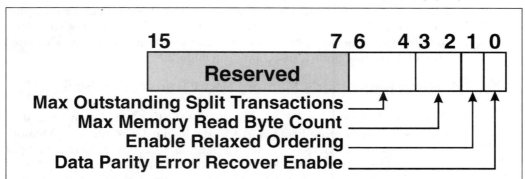

Chapter 21: Non-Bridge Configuration Registers

Max Outstanding Split Transaction Field

- 3-bit, Read/Write field.
- Default state after RST# (see Table 21-2 on page 473).

For background, refer to "Adjusting Requester's Split Transaction Queue Size" on page 471.

Refer to Figure 21-15 on page 472 and Table 21-2 on page 473. This 3-bit read/write bit field is used by the system load-tuning software to control the maximum number of Split Transactions the Requester is permitted to have outstanding at a given moment in time. A corresponding 3-bit, hard-wired, read-only bit field (Designed Max Outstanding Split Transactions) in the Requester's PCI-X Status register (see Figure 21-16 on page 477) indicates the size of the Requester's Split Transaction Queue.

The default value in this field after RST# assertion equals the maximum number of Split Transactions the device is designed to have outstanding when the Maximum Memory Read Byte Count field (see "Max Memory Read Byte Count Field" on page 474) is set to 0 (512 bytes).

Table 21-2: Max Outstanding Split Transactions Field in Requester's PCI-X Command Register

Binary Value	Max Number of Split Transaction Requester Supports
000	1
001	2
010	3
011	4
100	8
101	12
110	16
111	32
The default value in this field after RST# assertion equals the maximum number of Split Transactions the device is designed to have outstanding when the Maximum Memory Read Byte Count field (see "Max Memory Read Byte Count Field" on page 474) is set to 0 (512 bytes).	

Max Memory Read Byte Count Field

- 2-bit, Read/Write field.
- Default state after RST# = 00b (512 bytes).

For background, refer to "Adjusting Requester's Memory Read Transaction Size" on page 471.

Refer to Figure 21-15 on page 472 and Table 21-3 on page 474. This 2-bit read/write bit field is used by the system load-tuning software to control the maximum size memory read transaction that the Requester is permitted to initiate. A corresponding 2-bit, hard-wired, read-only bit field (Designed Max Memory Read Byte Count) in the Requester's PCI-X Status register (see Figure 21-16 on page 477) indicates the maximum size memory read transaction that the Requester can issue.

Table 21-3: Max Memory Read Byte Count Field in Requester's PCI-X Command Register

Binary Value	Max Size Memory Read Requester Can Issue
00	512 (default value)
01	1024
10	2048
11	4096

Enable Relaxed Ordering

- Typically a Read/Write bit, but may be hardwired to zero if the Requester never sets the Relaxed Ordering (RO) bit in the Attribute Phase of its transactions.
- Default after RST# = 1 (Relaxed Ordering Enabled), unless this bit is hardwired to zero (see previous bullet item).

Refer to Figure 21-15 on page 472.

RO Command Bit Enables/Disables Use of RO Attribute Bit. The Requester is never permitted to set the RO attribute bit to one when performing memory accesses if the RO bit in its PCI-X Command register is cleared to zero. The remainder of this discussion assumes that the RO Command bit is set to one. When this bit is set to one (its default state), the Requester is permitted to set the Relaxed Ordering (RO) bit in the Attribute

Phase of transactions it initiates to access the memory buffer assigned for its use by its device driver.

General Description. A Requester is permitted to set the RO attribute bit in a memory transaction only if its programming model and device driver guarantee that its memory write or read transactions are not required to remain in strict order. In general, a Requester can set the RO attribute bit when performing a memory access to a data buffer (commonly referred to as the Payload buffer), while the Requester must clear the RO attribute bit to zero when performing a memory access to access control, status, or flag locations.

Usage in Memory Read. A Requester can set the RO attribute bit to one in a memory read transaction if its memory usage model does not require Split Read Completions for this transaction to stay in order with respect to posted memory writes moving in the same direction (as the Split Read Completion data). If the target (a Completer or an intervening bridge) does pay attention to the RO attribute bit (optional whether it does or doesn't) when it receives a transaction, and the RO bit is set for a read transaction, the target is permitted to allow read-completion transactions for this Sequence to pass posted memory write transactions moving in the same direction. If the RO bit is not set or if the target (completer or bridge) does not implement the bit, the target keeps all read-completion transactions in strict order relative to memory write transactions moving in the same direction.

Usage in Memory Write. A requester can set the RO bit to one in a memory write transaction to main memory if its memory usage model does not require this main memory write be performed in order with respect to other memory writes when the memory writes arrive at main memory. PCI-X bridges ignore the state of the RO bit for memory write transactions traversing the bridge and always forward them in the order in which they were received (i.e., PCIX-to-PCIX bridges always use strong write-ordering). In other words, on a memory write the only target device that pays attention to the state of the RO attribute bit is the Host/PCIX bridge (when the memory write arrives at the Host/PCI bridge). If this bit is set, the Host/PCIX bridge has permission to write this data to main memory in whatever order will yield the best performance. The Host/PCIX bridge (acting as the target) is permitted to allow this memory write transaction to pass previously posted memory write transactions moving towards main memory. The Host/PCIX bridge is also permitted to allow bytes within the transaction to be written to main memory in any order. The bytes must be written to the correct main memory locations, but, to achieve the best performance, the Host/PCIX bridge can write the bytes to those locations in any order.

After Disconnect, Be Consistent. If a memory transaction is disconnected, the Requester must not change the value of this attribute bit in any subsequent transaction in the same Sequence.

Restrictions on Use. This attribute is used only for memory transactions that are not Message Signaled Interrupts (i.e., MSI; a memory write being performed to deliver an MSI must have the RO attribute bit cleared to zero). The Requester must not set this attribute bit if the transaction is an MSI, IO, Configuration, Split Completion, or a Special Cycle transaction.

For Additional Information. For additional discussion of Relaxed Ordering, refer to "Relaxed Ordering Effect on Transaction Ordering" on page 569.

Data Parity Error Recover Enable

- Read/Write bit.
- Default after RST# = 0 (Data Phase Parity Error Recovery Disabled).

A Requester's device driver sets this bit in the Requester's PCI-X Command register if the driver implements a Data Phase parity error recovery routine. When set to one, this bit enables the Requester to set the Master Data Parity Error bit in its PCI Status register and generate an interrupt in the event of a Data Phase parity error. This causes the Requester's device driver to be invoked. The driver then checks the Requester's status, discovers that the Master Data Parity Error bit is set to one, and executes the Data Phase parity error recovery routine.

If this bit is 0 and the device is in PCI-X mode, the Requester asserts SERR# (if enabled via the SERR# Enable bit in its PCI Command register) whenever the Master Data Parity Error bit is set (as the result of a Data Phase Parity Error).

For a detailed description of this bit, refer to "Requester's Data Parity Error Recovery Enable Bit" on page 613.

PCI-X Status Register

Figure 21-16 on page 477 illustrates a non-bridge function's PCI-X Status register. The sections that follow provide a description of each bit field within the register.

Chapter 21: Non-Bridge Configuration Registers

Figure 21-16: PCI-X Status Register (as implemented in a non-bridge function)

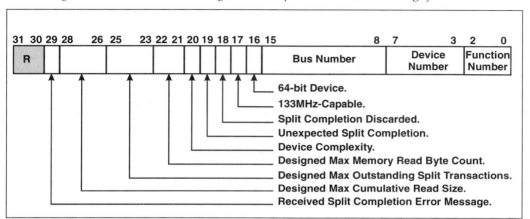

Bus, Device and Function Number Fields

- Read-only fields.
- State after RST#:
    - Function Number = the function number within the device.
    - Device Number = 1Fh
    - Bus Number = FFh.

Why They Are Necessary. Whenever a Requester initiates a transaction request it must provide its Requester ID in the Attribute Phase of the transaction (see Figure 13-4 on page 201, Figure 13-7 on page 206, Figure 13-9 on page 208, and Figure 13-12 on page 210). Likewise, whenever a Completer initiates a Split Completion transaction, it must provide its Completer ID in the transaction's Attribute Phase (see Figure 13-12 on page 210). The Requester or Completer obtains this information from its PCI-X Status register. The sections that follow describe how this information is placed in this register.

Function Number Is Hardwired. The function "knows" which function it is within the package and this value is hardwired into the Function Number field of the PCI-X Status register.

Bus/Device Auto-Updated by Type 0 Configuration Write. Each time that a Type 0 Configuration Write transaction selects this function, the function automatically updates the Bus Number and Device Number fields in its PCI-X Status register (irrespective of which of the function's Configuration registers are actually targeted by the Configuration Write). The function receives the Device Number information from AD[15:11] in the transaction's Address Phase (see Figure 21-17 on page 478) and receives the Bus Number from AD[7:0] in the transaction's Attribute Phase (see Figure 21-18 on page 478).

Note for PCI-X Tool Designer. When a PCI-X bus exerciser initiates a Type 0 Configuration Write transaction targeting a function within another device residing on the same bus as the tool, the tool must provide its Bus Number from its PCI-X Status register in the transaction's Attribute Phase.

Figure 21-17: Type 0 Configuration Address Phase Information

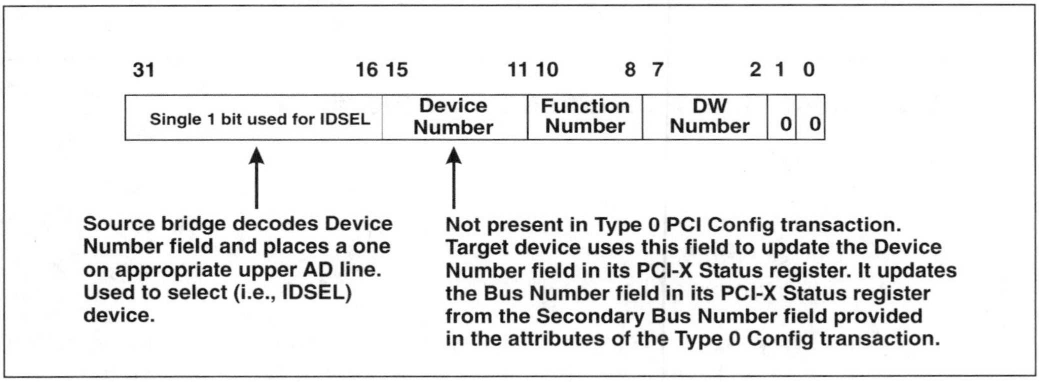

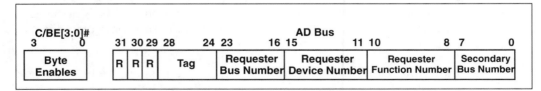

Figure 21-18: Type 0 Configuration Attribute Phase Information

Chapter 21: Non-Bridge Configuration Registers

64-Bit Device Status Bit

- Read-Only bit.

This bit indicates the width of the device's connection to the AD bus:

- 0 = 32 bits.
- 1 = 64 bits.

If the function is part of a device that is installed on an add-in card and connects directly to the PCI connector (not through a bridge), this bit is set if and only if all of the following are true:

1. The function implements a 64-bit AD interface.
2. The device that contains the function also implements a 64-bit AD interface.
3. The add-in card implements a 64-bit PCI connector. This requirement is independent of the width of the slot in which the card is installed.

If the device is subordinate to a bridge on an add-in card, or if the device is embedded on the system board (rather than on an add-in card), this bit is permitted to have any value.

For more information, refer to "Detecting Width of PCI-X Functions" on page 461.

133MHz-Capable Status Bit

- Read-Only bit.

This bit indicates the maximum bus clock frequency supported by the device:

- 0 = 66MHz.
- 1 = 133MHz.

This bit is used by software to assist the user in identifying the best slot for an add-in card. It is also used in some hot-plug systems to determine whether an add-in card would function properly if the bus were changed to PCI-X 133MHz mode.

- All functions within a multi-function device must have the same value for this bit.
- If the device is installed on an add-in card and connects directly to the card's PCI connector, this bit indicates whether the device is capable of 133MHz PCI-X operation. The connection of the card's PCIXCAP pin must accurately reflect the state of this bit.

- If the device is subordinate to a bridge on an add-in card, or if the device is embedded on the system board (rather than on an add-in card), this bit is permitted to have any value.

For more information, refer to "Detecting Frequency Support of PCI-X Functions" on page 462.

Split Completion Discarded (this is not a good thing!)

- Read/Write bit.
- Write a 1 to a 1 to clear it to 0.
- Default state after RST# = 0.

This bit is set if the device discards a Split Completion because the Requester would not accept it (i.e., the Split Completion ended in a Target Abort or a Master Abort). For more detail, see:

- "Master Abort or Target Abort on a Split Completion" on page 182.
- "Discard of Completion for IO, Config, or Prefetchable Memory Read" on page 608.
- "Discard of Completion of IO, Config, or Prefetchable Memory Read" on page 611.
- "Bridge Split Completion Ends in Master Abort" on page 633.
- "Bridge Split Completion Ends in Target Abort" on page 641.

Once set to one, this bit remains set until software writes a one to this bit.

- 0 = no Split Completion has been discarded.
- 1 = a Split Completion has been discarded.

Unexpected Split Completion (this is also not a good thing!)

When set to one, this bit indicates that a Requester received an unexpected Split Completion. Although the Requester ID supplied in the Address Phase of the Split Completion transaction matched this Requester's ID, the transaction Tag did not match any of its previously issued transaction requests that had received Split Responses. For a detailed discussion of this topic, refer to "Requester Handling of Unexpected Split Completion" on page 626.

Chapter 21: Non-Bridge Configuration Registers

Device Complexity

- Read-Only bit.

    General. The Device Complexity bit indicates whether this function is a simple device or a bridge device.

    - 0 = simple device
    - 1 = bridge device

    The spec dictates a set of rules governing transaction ordering by simple devices as well as a set of rules governing under what circumstances a simple device is permitted to reject a transaction (i.e., issue a Retry or a Disconnect).

    What Use Is This Bit? This is one of those unavoidable times when the author must admit complete ignorance. After thinking about how this bit might prove useful to software and, finally, having asked the spec writers this question, the answer still is, "I don't know."

    Definition of a Simple Device. Refer to Figure 21-19 on page 483. A simple device is one that does not implement internal posting of memory write transactions that must be initiated by the device on the PCI-X interface. Assume that the local CPU in the figure starts execution of a memory write instruction that causes it to initiate a memory write going outbound towards a memory target on the PCI-X bus. The CPU cannot complete its internally generated memory write transaction until the transaction has been initiated on the PCI-X bus and a target has accepted the write data. Only then can the local CPU move on and begin execution of its next instruction.

    Rules Governing Behavior of a Simple Device. The following rules govern the behavior of a simple PCI-X device (they are numbered for ease of reference):

    1. As in conventional PCI, simple PCI-X devices are never allowed to make the acceptance of a transaction when acting as the target (with the exception of Split Completions) contingent upon the prior completion of another transaction acting as an initiator.
    2. A simple PCI-X device is never allowed to make the completion of a Sequence for which it is the Completer contingent upon another device completing a Sequence for which the simple device is the Requester. That is, a simple PCI-X device that has terminated a transaction with

Split Response is required to request the bus to initiate the Split Completion for that Sequence independent of other Sequences that the simple device initiates.

3. Refer to Figure 21-19 on page 483. A simple PCI-X device is permitted to terminate an inbound PCI-X-initiated memory write to its local memory with Retry only for temporary conditions that are guaranteed to resolve over time (such as a temporarily full inbound posted memory write buffer). After terminating such a memory write transaction with Retry, a PCI-X device must start accepting inbound memory write data within:
    *   267 clocks on buses initialized to 133MHz mode,
    *   200 clocks on buses initialized to 100MHz mode,
    *   and 133 clocks on buses initialized to 66MHz PCI-X mode.

    This corresponds to **2 microseconds** in systems running at the maximum frequency of each mode. This is referred to as the **Maximum Completion Time Limit**. This same limit is 10 microseconds in the PCI environment. This requirement applies to all devices in their normal mode of operation and to their respective device drivers. This requirement does not apply to diagnostic modes or device-specific cases that are not intended for normal use in a system with other PCI-X devices. In its normal mode of operation, the device driver must not initiate a memory write to the device unless the device is able to accept it within the 2 microsecond time limit. In other words, before writing data into the device's local memory, its driver should first check a device-specific status bit to determine if it's ready to start accepting new data (i.e., its inbound posted memory write buffer is no longer full). It should be noted that in PCI-X (unlike in PCI) the 2 microsecond limit also applies to inbound IO writes to the simple device. In addition, if the Simple device responds to an IO Write with a Split Response, it must request the bus to initiate the corresponding Split Completion within the Maximum Completion Time Limit.

4. To provide backward compatibility with PCI-to-PCI bridges designed prior to the PCI 2.1 spec and the revision 1.1 PCI-to-PCI Bridge Architecture Specification, all PCI-X devices are required to accept inbound memory write transactions even when they may have one or more previously issued transactions that received Split Responses and are awaiting Split Completions. This is analogous to the requirement in the PCI 2.2 spec for PCI devices to accept (i.e., not Retry) memory write transactions even while awaiting completion of a Delayed Transaction.

5. A simple PCI-X device that has already accepted a transaction request and issued a Split Response to its initiator is permitted to issue a Retry in response to another transaction that must be Split (because its Split Transaction Queue is currently full). Once it has performed the corresponding Split Completion transaction, it can then accept and Split the next transaction request that it had retried earlier.

6. A simple PCI-X device is required to accept all Split Completion transactions that correspond to Split Requests that it had previously issued. In other words, it must have reserved sufficient internal buffer space to hold all of the requested Split Completion data.

7. A Simple device that implements a Split Transaction Queue that can hold more than one Split Request can initiate the Split Completions for different Sequences in any order, but Split Completions for the same Sequence must be initiated in address order.

Figure 21-19: Simple Device

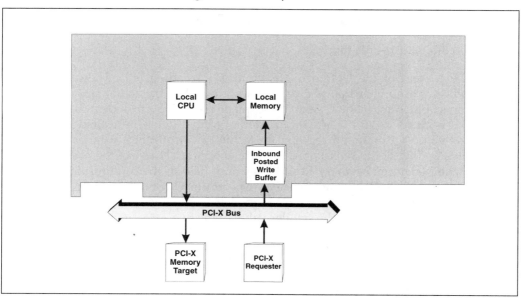

Designed Max Memory Read Byte Count

- 2-bit, Read-only field.

The Designed Maximum Memory Read Byte Count field in the non-bridge function's PCI-X Status register (see Figure 21-7 on page 460 and Table 21-3 on page 474) indicates a number that is greater than or equal to the maximum byte count the function is designed to use when initiating a Sequence using the Memory Read Block or Alias To Memory Read Block command. The content of this field indicates the smallest value that correctly indicates the function's maximum byte count capability. If the configuration software sets the Maximum Memory Read Byte Count field in the PCI-X Command register (see Figure 21-15 on page 472) to a value less than this field, the function uses the smaller value of the two.

For additional information, refer to "Max Memory Read Byte Count Field" on page 474 and to "Background on Load Tuning" on page 471.

Designed Max Outstanding Split Transactions

- 3-bit, Read-only field.

The content of the Designed Maximum Outstanding Split Transactions field indicates a number that is greater than or equal to the actual size of the function's Split Transaction Queue. If the queue size it reports depends on the value that is currently in the Maximum Memory Read Byte Count field in the function's PCI-X Command register, the value read from the Designed Maximum Outstanding Split Transactions field must accurately reflect the present setting of the Maximum Memory Read Byte Count field. If the configuration software sets the PCI-X Command register's Maximum Outstanding Split Transaction field to a value lower than the Designed Maximum Memory Read Byte Count field, the function uses the smaller value of the two.

For additional information, refer to "Max Outstanding Split Transaction Field" on page 473 and to "Background on Load Tuning" on page 471.

Designed Max Cumulative Read Size

- 3-bit read-only field.

The hardwired read-only value in the Designed Maximum Cumulative Read Size field (see Figure 21-9 on page 462 and Table 21-4 on page 485) indicates a number that is greater than or equal to the maximum cumulative size of all burst memory read transactions that the function is designed to have outstanding at one time. The value in this field must report the smallest value that correctly indicates the function's capability. If the value depends on the current value in the Maximum Memory Read Byte Count field in the PCI-X Command register, then the number must accurately reflect the present setting of the Maximum Memory Read Byte Count field. Remember, an ADQ is a 128-byte block.

Table 21-4: Designed Maximum Cumulative Read Size Field

Value (binary)	Number of ADQs	Size in Bytes
000	8	1KB
001	16	2KB
010	32	4KB
011	64	8KB
100	128	16KB
101	256	32KB
110	512	64KB
111	1024	128KB

22 *Bridge Configuration Registers*

The Previous Chapter

The previous chapter described the detection of a PCI-X bridge, the determination of a function's capabilities, how a function's PCI configuration registers are affected by mode selection, and the implementation and usage of the function's PCI-X capability register set.

This Chapter

This chapter describes the bridge's configuration registers. It identifies the PCI registers that are unaffected by the mode, those that are affected (and how), and describes the bridge's PCI-X capability register set.

The Next Chapter

The next chapter identifies the load tuning mechanisms available for both non-bridge and bridge functions. These mechanisms permit system software to alter the manner in which devices use the bus, thereby allowing software to smooth the flow of data throughout the system.

Discovering a PCIX-to-PCIX Bridge

This topic is covered in "Detecting a PCI-X Capable Bridge" on page 453.

Many Bridge PCI Configuration Registers Unchanged

Refer to Figure 22-1 on page 489. The implementation and usage of the following bridge PCI Configuration registers does not change no matter what mode (PCI or PCI-X) the bridge's two interfaces are in:

- Vendor ID register and Device ID register.
- Revision ID register.
- Class Code register.
- BIST register.
- Header Type register.
- Primary Bus Number register.
- Subordinate Bus Number register.
- IO Limit and IO Base registers.
- Memory Base and Memory Limit registers.
- IO Base and IO Limit Extension registers.
- Expansion ROM Base Address register.
- Interrupt Pin and Interrupt Line registers.

Some Bridge PCI Configuration Registers Affected by Mode

Refer to Figure 22-1 on page 489. If either interface of the bridge is in PCI-X mode, the following bridge PCI Configuration registers are affected:

- Command register.
- Status register.
- Capability Pointer register.
- Secondary Status register.
- Cache Line Size register.
- Latency Timer and Secondary Latency Timer registers.
- Base Address registers.
- Secondary Bus Number register.
- Prefetchable Memory Base and Prefetchable Memory Limit registers.
- Prefetchable Memory Base and Limit Extension registers.
- Bridge Control register.

The sections that follow provide a description of how each of these registers are affected if either interface of the bridge is in PCI-X mode.

Figure 22-1: PCIX-to-PCIX Bridge Configuration Header Registers

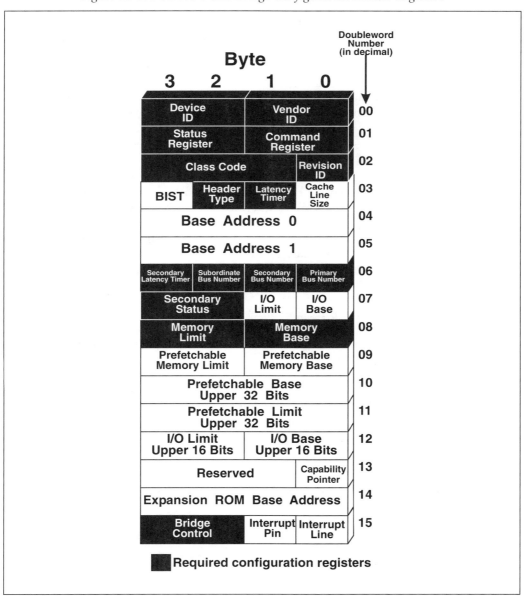

Command Register Affected

The bridge's Command register controls its operational characteristics on its primary interface. If the bridge's primary interface has been initialized to PCI-X mode (by the Source Bridge for the primary bus), the functionality of some of the Command register bits are altered. A complete description of the changes can be found in "Command Register Bits Affected by Protocol Mode" on page 467. If the primary interface has been initialized in PCI mode, however, the Command register bits operate exactly as defined by the PCI spec.

Status Register Affected

The bridge's Status register reflects the status of its operation on its primary interface. If the bridge's primary interface has been initialized to PCI-X mode (by the Source Bridge for the primary bus), the functionality of some of the Status register bits are altered. A complete description of the changes can be found in "Status Register Bits Affected by Protocol Mode" on page 469. If the primary interface has been initialized in PCI mode, however, the Status register bits operate exactly as defined by the PCI spec.

It should be noted that the Capabilities List bit (bit 4) is set to one in both modes (because the bridge implements at least one new capability, PCI-X). This also means that, in both modes, the Capabilities Pointer register contains the pointer to the first New Capability register set.

Capability Pointer Register Affected

See the previous section.

Secondary Status Register Affected

General

When the bridge's secondary interface is initialized in PCI-X mode, the following bits are affected:

• Fast Back-to-Back Capable bit.
• Master Data Parity Error bit.

- Detected Parity Error bit.
- DEVSEL# Timing bit field.

The sections that follow describe how these bits operate differently if the bridge's secondary interface is in PCI-X mode.

Fast Back-to-Back Capable Bit Affected

In PCI-X mode, the Fast Back-to-Back Capable bit is ignored (because there is no such thing as Fast Back-to-Back transactions on a bus operating in PCI-X mode). It can be initialized to any value.

Master Data Parity Error/Detected Parity Error Bits Affected

In a read transaction in the PCI environment, the Master Data Parity Error and Detected Parity Error bits are normally only set in the Status register of the initiator of the transaction when it receives a corrupted read data item. While this is generally true in PCI-X mode, there is one exception:

- In a Split Completion transaction returning previously requested read data, the device acting as the target is the Requester that originated the read request or a bridge on the path from the Completer back to the Requester.

When the bridge's secondary interface is acting as the target of a Split Completion transaction returning previously requested read data, it checks the parity of each read data item being returned to it by the initiator of the transaction. In the event of a read parity error, the bridge sets the Detected Parity Error and Master Data Parity Error bits in its Secondary Status register.

DEVSEL# Timing Bit Field

This bit field always indicates PCI DEVSEL# timing (i.e., Fast, Medium, or Slow assertion of DEVSEL#) no matter which mode the bridge's secondary interface is operating in. This indicates how quickly the bridge's secondary interface asserts DEVSEL# when it is acting as the target of a transaction initiated by an initiator on the bridge's secondary bus.

Cache Line Size Register Affected

A bridge interface (primary and/or secondary) operating in PCI-X mode ignores the Cache Line Size configuration register, while an interface operating in PCI mode uses it as defined by the PCI spec:

- to intelligently deal with Memory Read Line and Memory Read Multiple (line) commands issued by PCI masters on the bus that either targets memory within the bridge itself or must traverse the bridge to the bus on the opposite side.
- to correctly handle a Memory Write-and Invalidate command issued by a PCI master on the interface that either targets memory within the bridge itself or that must traverse the bridge to the bus on the opposite side.

Both Latency Timer Registers Affected

When either of the bridge's interfaces is operating in PCI-X mode, the respective Latency Timer register is loaded with a default value of 64d after RST#. Otherwise that interface's register is loaded with 0d after RST#. For background on this, refer to "How the Initiator Deals With Preemption" on page 143.

Base Address Registers (BARs) Affected

Refer to Figure 22-1 on page 489. Both the revision 1.1 PCI Bridge Architecture and PCI-X specs permit the implementation of one or two BAR registers. These would be the programmable address decoders for the bridge's internal, bridge-specific register set and/or internal memory (if it implements a bridge-specific internal memory buffer). The PCI-X spec says that if the bridge's primary interface is in PCI-X mode and if either of the Base Address Registers (BARs) is implemented as a memory BAR, then it must be implemented as a 64-bit rather than 32-bit memory decoder. Obviously, in this case this would restrict the designer to one memory BAR that would consume both BAR register positions in the bridge's configuration space (dwords 4 and 5).

The PCI-X spec also states that if either of the BAR registers is an IO BAR, then the designer must implement a corresponding 64-bit memory BAR. It's pretty obvious that this would not be possible because the memory BAR would consume both of the configuration dwords that are reserved for the implementation of BAR registers.

On a final note, the PCI-X spec states:

"If the primary interface is in PCI-X mode and the Base Address registers (other than the Expansion ROM Base Address register) request memory resources, the BARs must support 64-bit addressing as described in PCI 2.2."

In a sense, this makes it sound like the spec is saying that the memory BAR must be 64 bits wide if the primary interface is in PCI-X mode, but that it would be acceptable for the register to appear as a 32-bit memory BAR if the primary interface is in PCI mode. I believe that the spec writers really intended that the memory BARs in a PCI-X capable function must always be 64-bits wide, thus giving the configuration software the flexibility of assigning a memory address to the BAR that is either below or above the 4GB address boundary in either operational mode.

Secondary Bus Number Register Affected

In PCI Mode, No Change

When the bridge's secondary bus is operating in PCI mode, the Secondary Bus Number register is only used so the bridge can determine whether or not a Type 1 Configuration transaction received on its primary interface must be claimed and passed through to the bridge's secondary bus. This is identical to normal PCI operation.

In PCI-X Mode, Secondary Requesters May Have Pending Split Accesses

Assume that the bridge's secondary bus is operating in PCI-X mode and that the machine has already booted the OS and is up and running. At a given moment in time, one or more of the Requesters that reside on the bridge's secondary bus may have outstanding Split Transactions that are awaiting the receipt of Split Completions. When each of the Requesters issued these transaction requests earlier in time, each supplied the targeted Completers (any of which may reside on the other side of the bridge) with their respective Requester IDs (consisting of its Bus Number, Device Number and Function Number). The resulting Split Completion transactions use the Requester ID to address the Requester that originated the request. If software should change the bridge's Secondary Bus Number register before each of these outstanding Split Completions arrives back at the bridge, the bridge will not claim the Split Completions and pass them to the bridge's secondary bus (because the number of that bus has been changed). The net result is that the Split Completions will not arrive back at the Requesters. On the primary side of the bridge, the Split Completions will end in a Master Abort, while on the secondary side the Requesters will time out and generate interrupts to report fatal errors (an unfulfilled Split Request) to their respective drivers.

Hot-Plug Event May Cause Bus Renumbering

The only event that, if not handled correctly, might cause the scenario described in the previous section would be the installation or removal of a card (in a Hot-Plug PCI-X bus environment) that contains a PCI-to-PCI bridge or a PCIX-to-PCIX bridge (for background, refer to "Hot-Plug PCI-X Bus Initialization" on page 71; specifically, the sections on "Hot-Install of Card With PCIX-to-PCIX Bridge on It" on page 75 and "Hot-Install of Card With PCI-to-PCI Bridge on It" on page 77). This would necessitate a change of the bridge's Secondary Bus Number register and this must be done in the correct manner.

If software must change the number of a bus that has been operating in PCI-X mode for awhile, the following actions must be taken:

1. The Hot-Plug software must issue a request to the OS to quiesce all Requesters on the bridge's secondary bus.
2. The OS then issues a Quiesce Request to each of the drivers associated with the Requesters that reside on the bridge's secondary bus.
3. Each driver will cease issuing any new requests to its respective Requester and will wait until all outstanding requests have been completed (thereby ensuring that all outstanding Split Transactions have received their corresponding Split Completions). The driver then reports back to the OS that the Quiesce operation has been successfully completed.
4. When the OS has received confirmation of quiescence from all of the affected drivers, it informs the Hot-Plug software.
5. The Hot-Plug software then changes the bridge's Secondary Bus Number register.
6. Finally, the Hot-Plug software issues at least one Type 0 Configuration Write transaction to any Configuration register within each function residing on the secondary bus to re-prime the Device Number and Bus Number fields in each of their PCI-X Status registers. For more information on why the Type 0 Writes are required, refer to "Bus, Device and Function Number Fields" on page 477.

For more information on Hot-Plug, refer to the chapter entitled *Hot-Plug PCI* in MindShare's book *PCI System Architecture, Fourth Edition* (published by Addison-Wesley).

RST# Causes Functions to Forget Bus/Device Numbers

RST# can be asserted to the devices on a bridge's secondary bus under two circumstances:

- The bridge has detected RST# asserted to it by the Source Bridge on its primary side.
- The programmer has written a one into the Secondary Bus Reset bit in the bridge's Bridge Control register.

In either case, the assertion of RST# to the secondary bus functions causes them to "forget" the Bus and Device Numbers in their respective PCI-X Status registers. The programmer must then issue (after ensuring that RST# has been deasserted on the secondary side) at least one Type 0 Configuration Write transaction to any Configuration register within each function residing on the secondary bus to re-prime the Device Number and Bus Number fields in each of their PCI-X Status registers. For more information on why the Type 0 Writes are required, refer to "Bus, Device and Function Number Fields" on page 477.

Prefetchable Base/Limit Registers Affected

The PCI-X spec states:

"If the primary interface is in PCI-X mode, the Prefetchable Memory Base and Limit registers and Prefetchable Base and Limit Upper 32 Bits registers are required."

This is intended to give the configuration software the flexibility of assigning a Prefetchable memory base and end address range that is either below or above the 4GB address boundary. All of the Prefetchable memory devices that exist on the bridge's secondary side are assigned sub-ranges within this overall range.

As stated earlier in "Base Address Registers (BARs) Affected" on page 492, this makes it sound like the spec is saying that the Prefetchable memory base and end address register pair must each be 48 bits wide if the primary interface is in PCI-X mode, but that it would be acceptable for the register pair to appear as two 16-bit registers if the primary interface is in PCI mode. I believe that the spec writers really intended that this register pair in a PCI-X capable function must always be 48 bits wide, regardless of the current operational mode.

Prefetchable Base/Limit Extension Registers Affected

See the previous section.

Bridge Control Register Affected

Refer to Figure 22-2 on page 497. When the bridge's secondary interface is initialized in PCI-X mode, the following bits are affected (if the secondary interface is in PCI mode, then these bits have the same effect as in PCI):

- **Fast Back-to-Back Enable bit**. This bit is ignored by the bridge if the secondary interface is in PCI-X mode (because there is no such thing as Fast Back-to-Back transactions on a bus operating in PCI-X mode). It can be initialized to any value.
- **Primary Discard Timer bit**. This bit is ignored by the bridge if the primary interface is in PCI-X mode. An interface that is operating in PCI-X mode is connected to a bus that uses the PCI-X rather than the PCI bus protocol. There are no such thing as Delayed transactions on a PCI-X bus (they are replaced by Split Transactions), so there can be no such thing as a discard of an orphan Delayed Completion.

  For a detailed discussion of PCI Delayed transaction, refer to the chapter entitled *Master and Target Latency*, specifically the section entitled *Delayed Transactions* in MindShare's book entitled *PCI System Architecture, Fourth Edition* (published by Addison-Wesley).
- **Secondary Discard Timer bit**. This bit is ignored by the bridge if the secondary interface is in PCI-X mode. See the previous bullet item.
- **Discard Timer Status bit**. This bit is never set for an interface that is in PCI-X mode (because that interface will never discard an orphan Delayed transaction).
- **Discard Timer SERR# Enable bit**. This bit is ignored by the bridge if both of the bridge's interfaces are in PCI-X mode (once again, because neither interface will ever discard an orphan Delayed transaction).

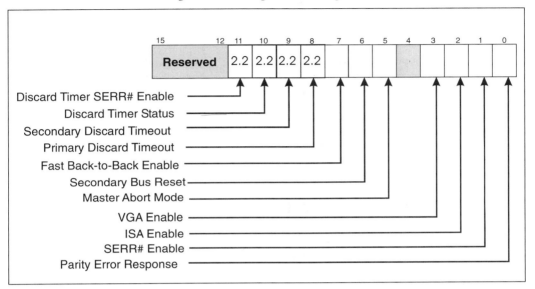

Figure 22-2: Bridge Control Register

Bridge's PCI-X Capability Register Set

PCI-X Capability Register Set Format

Refer to Figure 22-3 on page 498. The Capability ID for the PCI-X capability register set is 07h. The sections that follow provide a detailed description of this register set.

Figure 22-3: PCIX-to-PCI Bridge's PCI-X Capability Register Set

31 16	15 Next Capability 8	7 Capability ID = 7 0	
PCI-X Secondary (I/F) Status Register	Next Capability	Capability ID = 7	Dword 0
PCI-X Bridge (Primary I/F) Status Register			Dword 1
Upstream Split Transaction Control Register			Dword 2
Downstream Split Transaction Control Register			Dword 3

PCI-X Secondary Status Register

Figure 22-4 on page 498 illustrates the PCI-X Secondary Status register in a PCIX-to-PCIX bridge. The sections that follow provide a detailed description of each bit field.

Figure 22-4: Bridge's Secondary Status Register

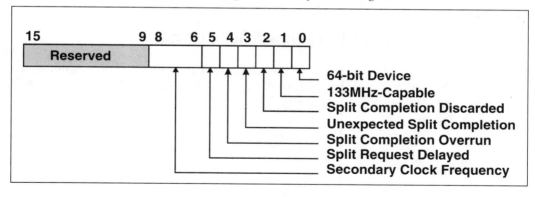

64-Bit Device Status Bit

- Read-only bit.

The state of this bit indicates the width of the bridge's secondary bus:

- 0 = 32 bits.
- 1 = 64 bits.

The configuration software uses this information and the state of the 64-bit Device bit in the PCI-X Status register of each secondary bus function to determine the appropriateness of cards installed in connectors on the secondary bus.

133MHz Capable Status Bit

- Read-only bit.

The state of this bit indicates the maximum speed capability of the bridge's secondary interface:

- 0 = 66MHz.
- 1 = 133MHz.

The configuration software uses this information and the state of the 133MHz Capable bit in the PCI-X Status register of each secondary bus function to determine the appropriateness of cards installed in connectors on the secondary bus.

Split Completion Discarded Bit

- Default after RST# = 0.
- Write a 1 to a 1 to clear it to 0.

Essentially, when this bit is set to one it means that the secondary bridge interface has an **orphan Split Completion** transaction on its hands. It is set to one when the secondary interface of the bridge initiates a Split Completion transaction (to return transaction results to a Requester) and the Requester either does not claim the transaction (i.e., it doesn't assert DEVSEL#) and the bridge experiences a **Master Abort**, **or** the transaction is claimed but the target then issues a **Target Abort** to the bridge.

Unexpected Split Completion Bit

- Default after RST# = 0.
- Write a 1 to a 1 to clear it to 0.

PCI Master Addresses PCI-X Target on Secondary. Assume that bridge's primary bus is in PCI mode and its secondary bus is in PCI-X mode. A PCI master initiates a transaction (other than a memory write; a memory write would be posted in the bridge) targeting a PCI-X device. Naturally, the PCI master does not supply the bridge with a Requester ID or a transaction tag. On the primary interface, the bridge treats it as a Delayed transaction and then initiates the equivalent PCI-X transaction on the secondary bus. As a Sequence ID, the secondary interface uses:

- Its secondary bus number.
- A device number of 00h.
- A function number of 00h.
- The bridge creates a unique transaction Tag for the transaction.

Assume that the target of the transaction provides a Split Response to the bridge, so the bridge suspends the transaction and will expect a Split Completion transaction at a later time. The target device then initiates the corresponding Split Completion transaction to return the results of the request. This discussion continues in the next section.

Problem: Bridge's Requester ID, but Bad Tag. When set to one, the Unexpected Split Completion bit indicates that the bridge's secondary interface received an unexpected Split Completion. Although the Requester ID supplied to the secondary interface in the Address Phase of the Split Completion transaction matched the secondary interface's Requester's ID (Bus = bridge's secondary bus number, Device = 00, Function = 0), the transaction Tag did not match any of its previously issued transaction requests that had received Split Responses.

Error Handling. A detailed discussion of this topic can be found in "Requester Handling of Unexpected Split Completion" on page 626. As described in that section, the bridge could handle the error in one of the following ways:

- Accept all of the Split Completion data, discard it, and then generate an interrupt to invoke the bridge's driver.
- Ignore the transaction (i.e., do not assert DEVSEL#), thereby causing the initiator of the Split Completion to experience a Master Abort (for more information, refer to "Completer Handling of Master Abort on a Split Completion" on page 610).

- The spec doesn't supply this as an error reporting option, but perhaps the bridge might accept all of the data, discard it, and then assert SERR#.

Bridge Secondary Interface Efficiency Status Bits

Background on Efficiency Status Bits. The Split Completion Overrun and Split Request Delayed status bits indicate (to the load tuning software) how well the bridge is doing in managing the buffer space (associated with its secondary interface) that it uses to hold Split Completion data being returned to its secondary interface by Completers that reside on its secondary side.

- If the load tuning software checks these two bits and both are zero, this indicates that this bridge interface is doing just fine.
- If either or both bits are set to one, however, it means that, since the last time the load tuning software checked, the bridge's secondary interface has had to delay the forwarding of some transaction headed towards the secondary interface (i.e., delay the forwarding of one or more queued Split requests), or has had to Retry or Disconnect one or more Split Completions coming inbound towards the secondary interface due to insufficient buffer space.

In response, the load tuning software will clear the status bits and adjust how the bridge's secondary interface makes use of its internal buffer space. The software will then check back periodically to see if the adjustment has helped and make additional adjustments if necessary. Additional information can be found in Chapter 23, entitled "Load Tuning Mechanisms," on page 515. Both of these bits have the following characteristics:

- Default after RST# = 0.
- Write a 1 to a 1 to clear it to 0.

Split Completion Overrun Bit. When this bit is set to one, it indicates that, due to a temporary lack of Split Completion buffer space, the bridge's secondary interface was forced to issue a Retry or to a issue a Disconnect in response to one or more Split Completion transactions since the last time the load tuning software looked at this bit.

When the bridge re-initiates a split memory read burst transaction, the Completer may supply the requested read data immediately. In this case, if the bridge stores the immediate read data in the same buffer area as Split Completion data, the bridge may disconnect the transaction because the buffers became full. The bridge may set the Split Completion Overrun status bit in this case.

Split Request Delayed Bit. When this bit is set to one, it indicates that, due to insufficient buffer space to hold the Split Completion data that would result from passing transaction requests from its primary to its secondary side, the bridge's secondary interface logic was forced to delay the forwarding of (i.e., not arbitrated for ownership of the bus to forward) inbound requests received on the bridge's primary interface that would need to be passed to the bridge's secondary interface.

Secondary Clock Frequency Bit Field

- 3-bit, read-only field.

Refer to Table 22-1 on page 502. This information field allows the programmer to determine the clock frequency and bus protocol currently in use on the bridge's secondary bus. This information is very useful in a Hot-Plug PCI-X environment, permitting software to determine the suitability of a new card before attaching it to the already-operational secondary bus.

Table 22-1: Secondary Clock Frequency Bit Field Encoding

Bit Field Value (binary)	Mode	Frequency (MHz)
000	PCI	Determined by state of M66EN signal from all cards.
001	PCI-X	66
010	PCI-X	100
011	PCI-X	133
100		
101	Reserved	
110		
111		

PCI-X Bridge (Primary Interface) Status Register

Figure 22-5 on page 503 illustrates the PCI-X Bridge (Primary Interface) Status register in a PCIX-to-PCIX bridge. The sections that follow provide a detailed description of each bit field.

Figure 22-5: PCI-X Bridge (Primary Interface) Status Register

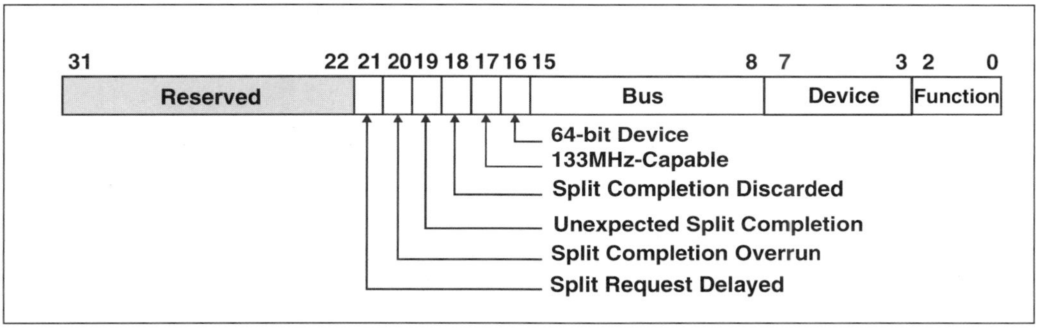

64-Bit Device Status Bit

- Read-only bit.

The state of this bit indicates the width of the bridge's primary interface:

- 0 = 32 bits.
- 1 = 64 bits.

This is **not** necessarily the width of the bus on the bridge's primary side. That would be indicated by the state of the 64-bit Device status bit in the PCI-X Secondary Status register in the Source Bridge for the primary bus.

The configuration software uses this information to determine the appropriateness of this card for installation in a connector on the primary bus.

133MHz Capable Status Bit

- Read-only bit.

The state of this bit indicates the maximum speed capability of the bridge's primary interface:

- 0 = 66MHz.
- 1 = 133MHz.

This is **not** necessarily the speed of the bus on the bridge's primary side. That would be indicated by the state of the 133MHz Capable status bit in the PCI-X Secondary Status register in the Source Bridge for the primary bus.

The configuration software uses this information to determine the appropriateness of this card for installation in a connector on the primary bus.

Split Completion Discarded Bit

- Default after RST# = 0.
- Write a 1 to a 1 to clear it to 0.

Essentially, when this bit is set to one it means that the primary bridge interface has an **orphan Split Completion** transaction on its hands. It is set to one when the primary interface of the bridge initiates a Split Completion transaction (to return transaction results to a Requester) and the Requester either does not claim the transaction (i.e., it doesn't assert DEVSEL#) and the bridge experiences a **Master Abort, or** the transaction is claimed but the target then issues a **Target Abort** to the bridge.

Unexpected Split Completion Bit

- Default after RST# = 0.
- Write a 1 to a 1 to clear it to 0.

PCI Master Addresses PCI-X Target on Primary. Assume that bridge's secondary bus is in PCI mode and its primary bus is in PCI-X mode. A PCI master initiates a transaction (other than a memory write; a memory write would be posted in the bridge) targeting a PCI-X device. Naturally, the PCI master does not supply the bridge with a Requester ID or a transaction tag. On the secondary interface, the bridge treats it as a Delayed transaction and then initiates the equivalent PCI-X transaction on the primary bus. As a Sequence ID, the primary interface uses:

- The bridge's primary bus number.
- The bridge's device number on the primary bus.
- The bridge's function number.
- A unique transaction Tag for the transaction.

Assume that the target of the transaction provides a Split Response to the bridge, so the bridge suspends the transaction and will expect a Split Completion transaction at a later time. The target device then initiates the corresponding Split Completion transaction to return the results of the request. This discussion continues in the next section.

Problem: Bridge's Requester ID, but Bad Tag. When set to one, the Unexpected Split Completion bit indicates that the bridge's primary interface received an unexpected Split Completion. Although the Requester ID supplied to the primary interface in the Address Phase of the Split Completion transaction matched the primary interface's Requester's ID (Bus = bridge's primary bus number and the bridge's Device and Function number), the transaction Tag did not match any of its previously issued transaction requests that had received Split Responses.

Error Handling. A detailed discussion of this topic can be found in "Requester Handling of Unexpected Split Completion" on page 626. As described in that section, the bridge could handle the error in one of the following ways:

- Accept all of the Split Completion data, discard it, and then generate an interrupt to invoke the bridge's driver.
- Ignore the transaction (i.e., do not assert DEVSEL#), thereby causing the initiator of the Split Completion to experience a Master Abort (for more information, refer to "Completer Handling of Master Abort on a Split Completion" on page 610).
- The spec doesn't supply this as an error reporting option, but perhaps the bridge might accept all of the data, discard it, and then assert SERR#.

Bridge Primary Interface Efficiency Status Bits

Background on Efficiency Bits. Refer to "Background on Efficiency Status Bits" on page 501.

Split Completion Overrun Bit. When this bit is set to one, it indicates that, due to a temporary lack of Split Completion buffer space, the bridge's primary interface was forced to issue a Retry or to a issue a Disconnect in response to one or more Split Completion transactions since the last time the load tuning software looked at this bit.

When the bridge re-initiates a split memory read burst transaction, the Completer may supply the requested read data immediately. In this case, if the bridge stores the immediate read data in the same buffer area as Split Completion data, the bridge may disconnect the transaction because the buffers became full. The bridge may set the Split Completion Overrun status bit in this case.

Split Request Delayed Bit. When this bit is set to one, it indicates that, due to insufficient buffer space to hold the Split Completion data that would result from passing transaction requests from its secondary to its primary side, the bridge's primary interface logic was forced to delay the forwarding of (i.e., not arbitrated for ownership of the bus to forward) inbound requests received on the bridge's secondary interface that would need to be passed to the bridge's primary interface.

Bus/Device/Function Number Fields

- Read-only bits fields.

The bridge is just another function residing on the bus connected to its primary side. These read-only fields contain the bridge's Bus Number, Device Number and Function Number as an entity on the primary bus. For a detailed discussion on how these fields obtain the values in them, refer to "Bus, Device and Function Number Fields" on page 477.

Split Transaction Control Registers

Basic Register Format

Refer to Figure 22-3 on page 498. The Bridge's PCI-X Capability register set contains two Split Transaction Control registers, each consisting of the following register pair (see Figure 22-6 on page 506):

- Split Transaction Capacity register.
- Split Transaction Commitment Limit register.

Figure 22-6: PCIX-to-PCIX Bridge's Split Transaction Control Register Format

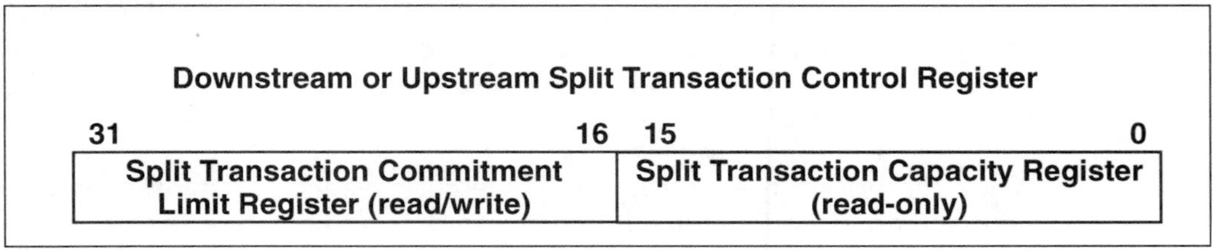

Downstream or Upstream Split Transaction Control Register	
31 16	15 0
Split Transaction Commitment Limit Register (read/write)	Split Transaction Capacity Register (read-only)

The Bridge's Split Completion Data Buffers

Refer to Figure 22-7 on page 510. As discussed in "Background on Efficiency Status Bits" on page 501, in order to achieve more efficient use of the bridge's internal buffers, the programmer can adjust how the bridge makes use of those buffers. The illustrated bridge data buffers are used in the following manner:

- **The Upstream Data Buffer holds Split Completion read data returned from Completers on the primary (upstream) side of the bridge for Requesters on the secondary side of the bridge.** Earlier in time, one or more Requesters on the bridge's secondary bus had issued memory read requests targeting Completers on the primary side of the bridge. The bridge's secondary interface memorized those requests and issued Split Responses to the Requesters. The bridge then re-initiates the requests on the bridge's primary bus and receives Split Responses either from the targeted Completers or from bridges in the paths to the targeted Completers. At later points in time, Split Completion transactions are initiated to return the previously requested memory read data to the Requesters. The bridge's primary interface receives the Split Completion memory read data into its Upstream Data Buffer and then initiates Split Completion transactions on the bridge's secondary side to return the requested read data to the Requesters.
- **The Downstream Data Buffer holds Split Completion read data returned from Completers on the secondary (downstream) side of the bridge for Requesters on the primary side of the bridge.** Earlier in time, one or more Requesters on the bridge's primary bus had issued memory read requests targeting Completers on the secondary side of the bridge. The bridge's primary interface memorized those requests and issued Split Responses to the Requesters. The bridge then re-initiates the requests on the bridge's secondary side and receives Split Responses either from the targeted Completers or from bridges in the paths to the targeted Completers. At later points in time, Split Completion transactions are initiated to return the previously requested memory read data to the Requesters. The bridge's secondary interface receives the Split Completion memory read data into the Downstream Data Buffer and then initiates Split Completion transactions on the bridge's primary side to return the requested read data to the Requesters.

Controlling Bridge's Use of Its Split Completion Data Buffers

Capacity Value Indicates Size of Respective Data Buffer. The Capacity register contains a 16-bit, hardwired, read-only value.

A bridge may be designed to store the Split Completion data being returned for memory reads in a buffer separate from that used to store the Split Completion data associated with Split Transactions other than memory reads. In such a bridge, the 16-bit Capacity register value indicates the size of buffer (in ADQs; i.e., 128 byte blocks) in which the bridge stores Split Completion memory read data. If the bridge is designed to store all Split Completion data (for memory reads as well as other transaction types) in a single buffer, the Capacity register value indicates the size of the buffer.

Limit Value Controls Bridge's Perception of Buffer Size. The Limit register is a 16-bit, read/write register. Immediately after reset it contains the same value as that found in its associated Capacity register (in other words, its actual buffer size).

The programmer has four choices, the last of which is not viable:

- Leave **Limit = Capacity**. This places the bridge in Allocation mode (see "Allocation Mode" on page 508).
- Set **Limit** to a value **greater than** the **Capacity** value but less than FFFFh. This places the bridge in Virtual Buffer Space mode (see "Virtual Buffer Space Mode" on page 509).
- Set **Limit** value = **FFFFh**. This places the bridge in Flood mode (see "Flood Mode" on page 509).
- If the **Limit** is set to a value **less than** that of the **Capacity** register value, the results are indeterminate.

The following three sections define the effects of each of the three viable settings on the bridge's operation.

Allocation Mode. When a bridge's interface is programmed to operate in Allocation mode (Limit = Capacity), it must follow the following rules:

- When the bridge has queued up a Split memory read to pass to the opposite side of the bridge, it is permitted to request ownership of the bus (i.e., assert REQ#) on the opposite side only if the bridge has sufficient buffer space to reserve for the purpose of accepting all of the requested data when it is returned to the bridge in a subsequent series of one or more Split Completions. In other words, the bridge must be capable of accepting all of the resulting Split Completion read data without issuing a Retry or a Disconnect At Next ADB to the initiator of the Split Completion(s).
- If the bridge does not have sufficient buffer space to reserve for this purpose, it is not permitted to request ownership of the bus on the other

side until it has serviced a sufficient number of previously forwarded Split memory reads and has freed up sufficient buffer space to hold all of the read data for this request.

- If the bridge stores Split Completion data for all transactions in a common buffer, it is also not permitted to forward Split Transactions other than memory reads until it has sufficient buffer space to accept the resulting Split Completion data.

The Split Completion Overrun bit will never get set when the interface is in Allocation mode (because the bridge cannot forward a transaction to the destination bus unless it has reserved sufficient buffer space to hold all of the data).

Virtual Buffer Space Mode. When a bridge's interface is programmed to operate in Virtual Buffer Space mode (the programmer has set its Limit to a value greater than its actual buffer capacity), it acts as if it has a Split Completion data buffer (a virtual buffer) larger than its actual buffer. Before arbitrating for ownership of the opposite bus for the purpose of forwarding the Split request, it first checks if it has sufficient buffer space in its Virtual data buffer to hold the returning Split Completion data. If it does, it forwards the transaction, otherwise it delays forwarding it until it does have a sufficient amount of Virtual buffer space to reserve to hold the resulting Split Completion data.

However, the reality is that by tricking the bridge into thinking its buffer is bigger than it actually is, the bridge may be forced to issue Retries or Disconnect At Next ADBs when Split Completions start returning data to the bridge.

Flood Mode. When a bridge's interface is programmed to operate in Flood mode (the programmer has set its Limit to a FFFFh), it acts as if it has a Split Completion data buffer of infinite size. It does not check for buffer availability before forwarding a request. This heightens the possibility that the bridge may be forced to issue Retries or Disconnect At Next ADBs when Split Completions start returning data to the bridge.

Regaining Control After Operating in Flood Mode. As pointed out in the previous section ("Flood Mode" on page 509), while the Limit register value is set to FFFFh the bridge is not required to keep track of the size of Split requests that it has forwarded across the bridge. However, at some point the programmer may wish to regain control and force the bridge to once more check its available buffer space (real or virtual) before forwarding additional transactions across the bridge. This is a problem because, at that point, the bridge has no idea how much of its buffer space will be used up to hold the Split Completion data associated with transactions it forwarded without checking for available buffer space (while it was in Flood mode). The spec defines the following mechanism for the bridge to regain an accurate view of buffer space availability so it can once again intelligently evaluate whether to forward or delay a Split request.

"To synchronize the bridge's commitment counters, the bridge must set its commitment count to zero and immediately begin incrementing it when new Split Requests are forwarded across the bridge and decrementing it when Split Completions are forwarded to their requesters across the bridge. However, if a Split Completion would decrement the commitment count below zero, the commitment count must be set to zero. If at some point all outstanding Split Transactions finish, the bridge's commitment count is also zero. From that point on, the commitment limit is accurate."

Figure 22-7: Upstream/Downstream Buffering Illustration

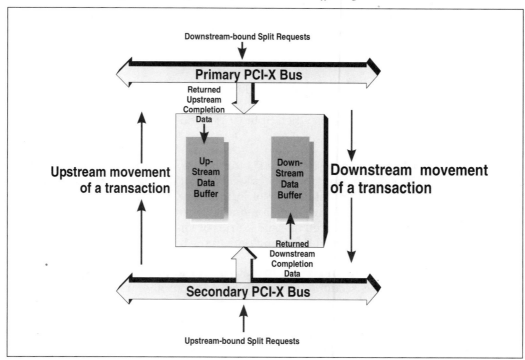

For More Information on Load Tuning...

For more information on the usage of the bridge's Limit/Capacity registers and its efficiency bits, refer to Chapter 23, entitled "Load Tuning Mechanisms," on page 515.

Optional Bridge Registers

Unlike a simple PCI-X function, a bridge does not implement the PCI-X Status and Command registers found in a simple function. This means that the bridge does not include the following tuning fields in the PCI-X Command register:

- Maximum Memory Read Byte Count register.
- Maximum Outstanding Split Transactions register.

A special-purpose bridge may have the ability to initiate transactions on its own. In this case, if the load-tuning software had access to the bits fields indicated above, it could exercise some control over how the bridge utilized the bus when it acts as the originator (i.e., the Requester) of transfer requests. The spec recommends that this be accomplished by implementing a second function within the device that contains the bridge function (which is typically function zero within the device). The second function would implement the PCI-X capability register set for a simple device, but these registers would allow the load-tuning software additional control over the bridge's operational characteristics.

Inclusion of the PCI-X Command register in a bridge also permits control of the bridge's usage of:

- Data Phase parity error recovery.
- The Relaxed Ordering capability.

Part 4:
Load Tuning

The Previous Part

Part 3 covered device configuration and consists of the following chapters:

- Chapter 20: Configuration Transactions
- Chapter 21: Non-Bridge Configuration Registers
- Chapter 22: Bridge Configuration Registers

This Part

Part 4 addresses issues to related to the PCI-X load tuning mechanisms that the programmer may use to control the manner in which Requesters and bridges use the buses in the system. This part consists only of Chapter 23: Load Tuning Mechanisms.

The Next Part

Part 5 covers the operation of PCIX-to-PCIX bridges as well as some operational aspects of Host/PCIX bridges. It consists of the following chapters:

- Chapter 24: PCIX-to-PCIX Bridges
- Chapter 25: Locked Transaction Series

23 *Load Tuning Mechanisms*

The Previous Chapter

The previous chapter described the bridge's configuration registers. It identified the PCI registers that are unaffected by the mode, those that are affected (and how), and described the bridge's PCI-X capability register set.

This Chapter

This chapter identifies the load tuning mechanisms available for both non-bridge and bridge functions. These mechanisms permit system software to alter the manner in which devices use the bus, thereby allowing software to smooth the flow of data throughout the system.

The Next Chapter

This chapter covers the following bridge-related topics:

- Support for the DAC command.
- Posting of memory writes.
- Split Transaction handling.
- Claiming Split Completions.
- Translating PCI transactions to PCI-X transactions.
- Translating PCI-X transactions to PCI transactions.
- Error handling.
- Buffer size.

Introduction to Load Tuning

In a well-designed, high-end platform, the OS would schedule a utility to run on a periodic basis, the purpose of which is to analyze how well data is flowing throughout the platform. Based on its assessment of the situation, the utility will, if necessary, tune the operational characteristics of the system's Requesters, Completers, and bridges to make better use of the buses and of the buffers within bridges in order to achieve a smooth flow of data between Requesters and Completers with minimum delay incurred.

This chapter describes the mechanisms available at both the device/function- and bridge-levels that may be adjusted to achieve this goal.

Non-Bridge Function Tuning

Information Fields

In a non-bridge function, the programmer has the following read-only register fields available to discover the operational limits of the function:

- The **Designed Max Memory Read Byte Count field** in the function's PCI-X Status register (see Figure 23-1 on page 517).
- The **Designed Max Cumulative Read Size field** in the function's PCI-X Status register (see Figure 23-1 on page 517). For more information, refer to "Designed Max Memory Read Byte Count" on page 484.
- The **Designed Max Outstanding Split Transactions field** in the function's PCI-X Status register (see Figure 23-1 on page 517).

Adjustable Fields/Registers

The programmer has the following mechanisms available to adjust the manner in which the function utilizes the bus:

- The **Max Memory Read Byte Count field** in the PCI-X Command register (see Figure 23-2 on page 517). For more information, refer to "Max Memory Read Byte Count Field" on page 474 and "Adjusting Requester's Memory Read Transaction Size" on page 471. By adjusting this value, software can adjust the maximum size memory read transaction that the Requester is permitted to initiate. This field is useful in adjusting the amount of a bridge's internal, Split Completion buffer space that this Requester utilizes.
- The **Max Outstanding Split Transactions field** in the PCI-X Command register (see Figure 23-2 on page 517). For more information, refer to "Adjusting Requester's Split Transaction Queue Size" on page 471. This field is used to adjust how many outstanding Split Transactions the Requester is

capable of handling. Software may choose to decrease the size of the Requester's queue because it has a tendency to dominate the Split Transaction Queues of one or more Completers or bridges.

- The **Latency Timer** register in the function's configuration header region (see Figure 23-3 on page 518). By adjusting the timeslice assigned to a Requester or Completer, the software can increase the amount of bus time available to a function (so it can transfer large amounts of data more quickly), or it may decrease the amount of bus time available to a function in order to increase the amount of bus time available to other Requesters or Completers. For more information on the Latency Timer, refer to "How the Initiator Deals With Preemption" on page 143.

Figure 23-1: PCI-X Status Register in Non-Bridge Function

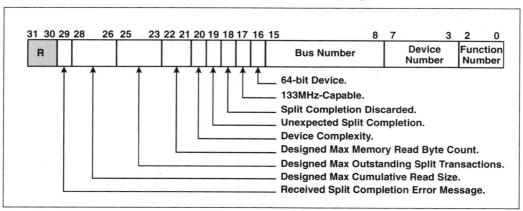

Figure 23-2: PCI-X Command Register in Non-Bridge Function

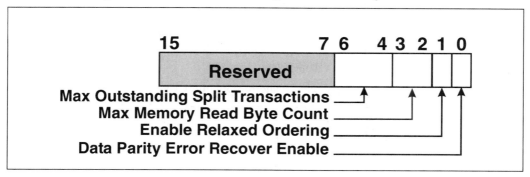

Figure 23-3: Latency Timer Register In Non-Bridge Function

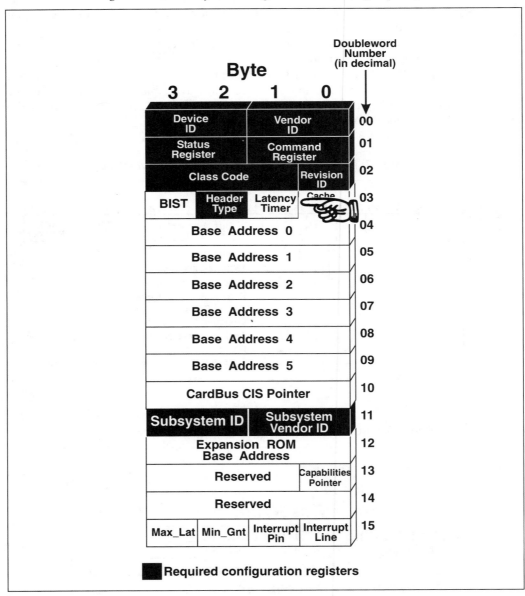

Bridge Tuning

Adjusting Usage of Split Completion Buffers

Introduction

For background on the bridge's efficiency status bits, refer to "Bridge Secondary Interface Efficiency Status Bits" on page 501 and "Bridge Primary Interface Efficiency Status Bits" on page 505. For an introduction to the mechanism used to adjust how the bridge utilizes its internal Split Completion buffers, refer to "Split Transaction Control Registers" on page 506.

Interpreting the Efficiency Bits

On a dynamic, on going basis the load-tuning utility software performs the following sequence of steps. Table 23-1 on page 521 provides a more detailed description of the interpretation of the efficiency bits and the actions taken if one or both bits should become set.

1. The default setting after reset is Limit = Capacity.
2. Wait an appropriate time interval before checking the state of the efficiency bits associated with each of the bridge's interfaces. The interval depends upon the rate at which traffic patterns in the system change.
3. Check the Split Request Delayed bit and the Split Completion Overrun bit and adjust the Split Transaction Commitment Limit register as follows:
   - If neither bit is set, the Limit value is good.
   - If the Split Request Delayed bit is set and the Split Completion Overrun bit is not set, the Limit is too low. Increase the Limit.
   - If the Split Request Delayed bit is not set and the Split Completion Overrun bit is set, the Limit is too high. Decrease the Limit.
   - If both bits are set, the Limit is too high. Decrease the Limit.
4. Loop back to step 2.

Additional Spec Comments

The spec also contains the following comments regarding the efficiency bits and the Capacity and Limit fields (in some cases, the author has edited and/or annotated the spec text):

1. Regarding the algorithm: "In a system where traffic patterns change over time, an algorithm such as the one described in "Interpreting the Efficiency Bits" on page 519 tracks those changes and adjusts the Limit appropriately. More sophisticated algorithms that adapt to historical traffic patterns, or use varying change increments for the register, or varying delay-time intervals are also possible."

2. "If a bridge whose primary bus is connected directly to the Host/PCIX bridge has a Capacity of at least 4KB, and the Host/PCIX bridge has a typical read latency of 3 microseconds or less, setting the upstream Limit = Capacity generally allows requests to be forwarded upstream (towards main memory) as quickly as necessary without any risk of terminating a Split Completion with Retry."

3. "The read latency for downstream transactions and for transactions that cross multiple PCI-X bridges is generally harder to predict. One method for identifying the optimum setting for the Limit in these cases is to adjust it based on the behavior of previous traffic as indicated by the Split Request Delayed and Split Completion Overrun status bits. The general guideline for setting the Limit is that if the Split Request Delayed bit is set, the Limit is potentially too low. If the Split Completion Overrun bit is set, the Limit is too high. The optimum setting of the Limit is one less than the smallest setting for which the Split Completion Overrun bit sets. If bus traffic is heavy on the Requester side, or if the Requester-side bus width or frequency is less than the Completer side, the Split Request Delayed bit may set even though the Limit is set optimally."

Table 23-1: Interpretation of Efficiency Bits and Recommended Actions

Split Request Delayed Bit	Split Completion Overrun Bit	What This Means	What You Should Do
0	0	1. The respective bridge interface (primary or secondary) has not had to delay the forwarding of any Split Transactions to the opposite interface due to unavailable buffer space. 2. The respective bridge interface has not had to Retry or Disconnect any Split Completions coming inbound to its Split Completion Data Buffer.	Nothing. Everything's great!

Table 23-1: Interpretation of Efficiency Bits and Recommended Actions (Continued)

Split Request Delayed Bit	Split Completion Overrun Bit	What This Means	What You Should Do
0	1	1. The respective bridge interface (primary or secondary) has not had to delay the forwarding of any Split Transactions to the opposite interface due to unavailable buffer space. 2. The respective bridge interface has had to Retry or Disconnect one or more Split Completions coming inbound to its Split Completion Data Buffer due to insufficient buffer space.	**The interface is, to some degree, too aggressive in forwarding transactions. The Limit field is set too high, so decrease it and clear the bit.** The respective bridge interface has not had to delay the forwarding of any Split Transactions, indicating that the Limit is set high enough so that the bridge always has sufficient buffer space to allow the forwarding of Split Transactions. However, the reality is that the bridge has had to reject (i.e., Retry or Disconnect) one or more returning Split Completions due to insufficient buffer space. This means that the interface has forwarded more transactions than, in reality, it had buffer space reserved for.

Table 23-1: Interpretation of Efficiency Bits and Recommended Actions (Continued)

Split Request Delayed Bit	Split Completion Overrun Bit	What This Means	What You Should Do
1	0	1. The respective bridge interface (primary or secondary) has had to delay the forwarding of one or more Split Transactions to the opposite interface due to unavailable buffer space. 2. The respective bridge interface has not had to Retry or Disconnect any Split Completions coming inbound to its Split Completion Data Buffer.	**Either the buffer size (i.e., the Limit) is set too low, or it may be alright. The limit should be increased and the bit cleared.** The respective bridge interface has had to delay the forwarding of one or more Split Transactions, indicating that the interface did not think that there was sufficient buffer space to allow the forwarding of some Split Transactions. However, the reality is that the bridge did not · have to reject (i.e., Retry or Disconnect) any returning Split Completions due to insufficient buffer space.

Table 23-1: Interpretation of Efficiency Bits and Recommended Actions (Continued)

Split Request Delayed Bit	Split Completion Overrun Bit	What This Means	What You Should Do
1	1	1. The respective bridge interface (primary or secondary) has had to delay the forwarding of one or more Split Transactions to the opposite interface due to unavailable buffer space. 2. The respective bridge interface has had to Retry or Disconnect one or more Split Completions coming inbound to its Split Completion Data Buffer due to insufficient buffer space.	**The Limit field is set too high, so decrease it and clear the bits.** The respective bridge interface has had to delay the forwarding of one or more Split Transactions, indicating that the interface did not think that there was sufficient buffer space to allow the forwarding of some Split Transactions. In addition, the bridge had to reject (i.e., Retry or Disconnect) one or more returning Split Completions due to insufficient buffer space.

Adjusting Bridge's Timeslice Values

Bridge Is Surrogate for Initiators on Both Sides of Bridge

Refer to Figure 23-4 on page 526. The PCIX-to-PCIX bridge resides in between bus 0 and bus 1. When an initiator on bus 0 starts a transaction targeting a Completer on the bus 1 side of the bridge, the bridge must re-initiate the transaction on bus 1. Likewise, when an initiator on bus 1 starts a transaction targeting a Completer on the bus 0 side of the bridge, the bridge must re-initiate the transaction on bus 0. In other words, sometimes the bridge must act as the surrogate initiator for a device in the community of initiators that reside on its primary bus, and sometimes it must act as the surrogate initiator for a device in the community of initiators that reside on its primary bus.

Software Must Assign Bridge Two Timeslices

Refer to Figure 23-5 on page 527. A PCIX-to-PCIX bridge implements two Latency Timer registers:

- One (the Latency Timer register) that defines its timeslice when performing a transaction on its primary side for an initiator that resides on its secondary side.
- Another (the Secondary Latency Timer register) that defines its timeslice when performing a transaction on its secondary side for an initiator that resides on its primary side.

At startup time, the configuration software must assign the bridge two timeslice values using these two registers. The value programmed in each of these registers defines the guaranteed number of PCI-X clock cycles that the bridge will own the respective bus (primary or secondary) whenever it has initiated a transaction for an initiator on that bus. For background on the function of the Latency Timer, refer to "How the Initiator Deals With Preemption" on page 143. In the case of a bridge, the software must assign a timeslice that it considers an appropriate value to each of the two registers when the bridge is re-initiating a transaction for any of the initiators residing on the opposite bus.

Load-Tuning Software Can Choose Timeslice Other Than 64d

As discussed in "What Is the Recommended LT Value?" on page 144, the PCI-X spec recommends a timeslice value of 64d (the default value) for each PCI-X initiator, so this would typically be the value assigned to the two bridge Latency Timer registers as well. However, changing the value assigned in either or both of the bridge's Latency Timer registers to something other than 64d is an option that the load-tuning software has available to change the manner in which the bridge utilizes either or both buses.

Figure 23-4: Example System

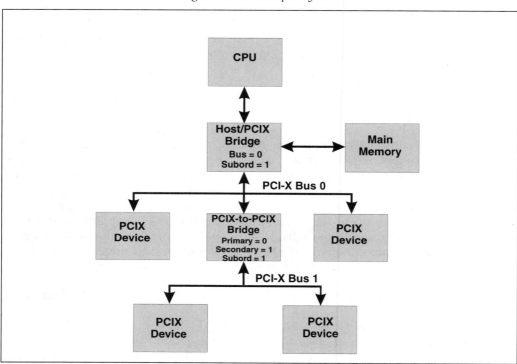

Figure 23-5: PCIX-to-PCIX Bridge's Configuration Header Registers

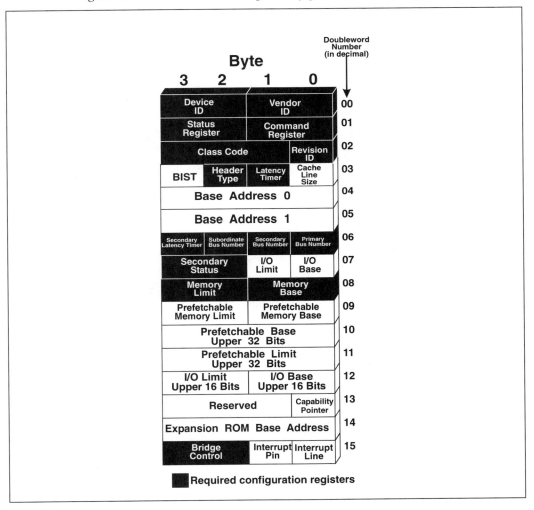

Part 5:
PCI-X Bridges

Previous Part

Part 4 addressed issues related to the PCI-X load tuning mechanisms that the programmer may use to control the manner in which Requesters and bridges use the buses in the system. This part consists only of Chapter 23: Load Tuning Mechanisms.

This Part

Part 5 covers the operation of PCIX-to-PCIX bridges as well as some operational aspects of Host/PCIX bridges. It consists of the following chapters:

- Chapter 24: PCIX-to-PCIX Bridges
- Chapter 25: Locked Transaction Series

The Next Part

Part 6 covers error detection and handling and consists of Chapter 26: Error Detection and Handling.

24 PCIX-to-PCIX Bridges

The Previous Chapter

The previous chapter identified the load tuning mechanisms available for both non-bridge and bridge functions. These mechanisms permit system software to alter the manner in which devices use the bus, thereby allowing software to smooth the flow of data throughout the system.

This Chapter

This chapter covers the following bridge-related topics:

- Support for the DAC command.
- Posting of memory writes.
- Split Transaction handling.
- Claiming Split Completions.
- Translating PCI transactions to PCI-X transactions.
- Translating PCI-X transactions to PCI transactions.
- Error handling.
- Buffer size.

The Next Chapter

The next chapter describes the locking mechanism that permits the processor, through the Host/PCIX bridge, to perform a series of transactions to a Completer with the guarantee that no PCI-X Requester upstream of the Completer will be able to access the Completer. In addition, no Requester other than the Host/PCIX bridge (in other words, the processor) will be able to access main memory.

Performs Same Function as a PCI-to-PCI Bridge

As is the case in a PCI-to-PCI bridge, a PCIX-to-PCIX bridge is a traffic director between two buses. It acts as the surrogate initiator for the two communities of initiators that reside on its primary and secondary sides. Unless this chapter states differently, its operation is identical to that of a PCI-to-PCI bridge. The bridge contains a set of PCI configuration registers as well as a set of PCI-X Capability registers. Chapter 22, entitled "Bridge Configuration Registers," on page 487, provided a detailed description of the bridge's configuration registers. This included a description of:

- How the bridge's PCI configuration registers operate when one or both interfaces are in PCI-X mode (see "Some Bridge PCI Configuration Registers Affected by Mode" on page 488).
- How the bridge's PCI-X Capability registers are implemented and how they operate (see "Bridge's PCI-X Capability Register Set" on page 497.)

This chapter focuses on the differences between PCIX and PCI bridges. If an operational characteristic of the bridge is not covered in this chapter, that means that it is the same as that of a PCI-to-PCI bridge. A complete description of the PCI-to-PCI bridge can be found in the chapter entitled *The PCI-to-PCI Bridge* in the MindShare book entitled *PCI System Architecture, Fourth Edition* (published by Addison-Wesley).

Support for DAC Command

Downstream Movement of DAC Optional for PCI Bridge

Refer to Figure 24-1 on page 533. In a PCI system, it would not be uncommon for a Requester on a subordinate bus to initiate a memory access with main memory at an address above the 4GB address boundary. For this reason, PCI-to-PCI bridges are required to support upstream movement of a transaction using the DAC command. Whether or not the bridge supports downstream movement of the DAC command is optional, however (wherein a Requester on a bridge's primary side is addressing a memory target on the bridge's secondary side at an address above the 4GB address boundary).

PCI-X Bridge Must Support Downstream DAC Movement

Earlier sections of the book (see "Base Address Registers (BARs)" on page 464) highlighted the fact that memory decoders (i.e., Base Address registers) in PCI-X functions must be implemented as 64-bit registers. This gives the configuration software the flexibility of assigning them memory address ranges either below or above the 4GB address boundary.

The configuration software may assign memory addresses above the 4GB address boundary to PCI-X functions that reside on the secondary side of a PCIX-to-PCIX bridge. This being the case, it is mandatory that the bridge must support downstream movement of the DAC command through the bridge. This means that the bridge must implement the extension registers for the Prefetchable Memory Base and Limit registers (see "Prefetchable Base/Limit Extension Registers Affected" on page 495).

Figure 24-1: Example System

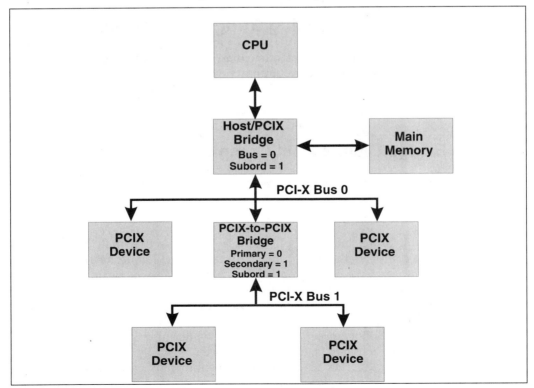

Bus Width

The bridge's primary and secondary bus interfaces may be implemented as either 32- or 64-bit interfaces.

Memory Writes Crossing Bridge Are Always Posted

Just as in a PCI bridge, a PCIX bridge always deals with transactions using the Memory Write, Memory Write Block, and Alias To Memory Write Block that must traverse the bridge by immediately accepting the write data into its posted memory write buffer. From the perspective of the initiator, the data has already been written to the target memory. At a later time, the bridge will arbitrate for ownership of the opposite bus and perform the memory writes and will ensure that it uses the same Sequence IDs that were given to it by the Requesters that originated the memory write transactions.

Other Transactions Crossing Bridge Are Always Split

In a PCI bridge, all transactions other than memory writes that must traverse the bridge are treated as Delayed transactions. When a PCIX bridge interface is operating in PCI-X mode, however, these transactions are treated as Split Transactions.

How the Bridge Claims Split Completions

When one of the bridge's interfaces latches a Split Completion transaction, it uses its internal bus number registers to decide whether or not to claim the Split Completion and pass it to the opposite bridge interface:

- When the bridge latches a Split Completion transaction on its primary interface, it compares the Bus Number portion of the Requester ID (see Figure 24-2 on page 535) to its Secondary Bus Number and Subordinate Bus Number register values. If the target bus number falls within the range of buses defined by the bridge's Secondary Bus Number and Subordinate Bus Number registers, the bridge claims the transaction (i.e., it asserts DEVSEL#). It accepts the Split completion data and, at a later time, passes the Split Completion transaction to its opposite interface.
- When the bridge latches a Split Completion transaction on its secondary

interface, it compares the Bus Number portion of the Requester ID to its Primary Bus Number register. If it matches it, the bridge claims the transaction (i.e., it asserts DEVSEL#). If it doesn't match the bridge's Primary Bus Number register and it's outside the range of buses defined by the bridge's Secondary Bus Number and Subordinate Bus Number registers, the bridge claims the transaction (because the target bus is not on the downstream side of the bridge). The bridge accepts the Split completion data and, at a later time, passes the Split Completion transaction to its opposite interface.

Figure 24-2: Split Completion Address Phase Information Format

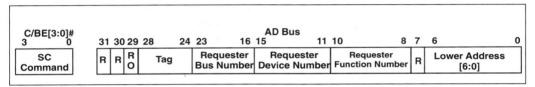

When Bridge Can Use Retry or Disconnect At Next ADB

When Bridge Can Issue a Retry

A bridge interface that is operating in PCI-X mode is permitted to issue a Retry in response to a transaction under the following circumstances:

- The transaction is a memory write and the bridge's posted memory write buffer is temporarily full.
- The transaction needs to be Split and this bridge interface's Split Transaction Queue is currently full.
- The bridge has been locked and an attempt is made to cross the bridge by an initiator other than the one that locked the bridge. For more information, refer to Chapter 25, entitled "Locked Transaction Series," on page 579.
- A corrupted Split Completion (i.e., a Split Completion whose size or address did not match its Split Request or a corrupt Requester Bus Number field in the Split Completion address caused it to cross the wrong bridge) crossed the bridge some time since the last rising-edge of RST#. For more information, refer to "Corrupted Split Completion" on page 562.

When Bridge Can Issue a Disconnect At Next ADB

When acting as the target of a transaction, a bridge interface that is operating in PCI-X mode is permitted to issue a Disconnect At Next ADB in response to a transaction under the following circumstances:

- During a memory write transaction, the interface's Posted Memory Write Buffer is approaching a buffer full condition.
- During a Split Completion transaction, the interface's Split Completion Data Buffer is approaching a buffer full condition.
- A corrupted Split Completion (i.e., a Split Completion whose size or address did not match its Split Request or a corrupt Requester Bus Number field in the Split Completion address caused it to cross the wrong bridge) crossed the bridge some time since the last rising edge of RST#. For more information, refer to "Corrupted Split Completion" on page 562.

Interfaces Can Be in Different Modes/Speeds

As discussed in "Bridge Must Support Interfaces in Different Modes" on page 70, the bridge's two interfaces must support operation in either PCI-X or PCI mode.

Translating PCI to PCI-X

General

In Figure 24-3 on page 537, the primary interface of the PCI-X bridge is operating in PCI mode, while its secondary bus is in PCI-X mode. In this example, a PCI bus master initiates a transaction targeting a Completer on the PCI-X side of the bridge. The bridge latches the transaction request on its primary interface and must translate it into the appropriate PCI-X transaction. The sections that follow provide a detailed description of this process.

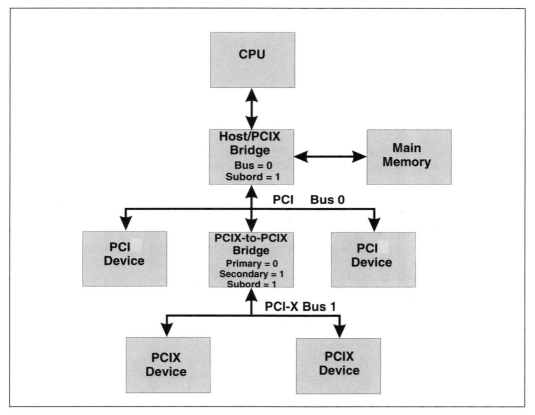

Figure 24-3: PCI-X Bridge With Interfaces in Different Modes

Writes Are Posted

A PCI Memory Write or Memory Write and Invalidate transaction will be posted in the bridge, so the PCI Memory Write transaction can complete immediately.

All Others Treated as PCI Delayed Transaction

Any other type of PCI transaction that must traverse the bridge from primary to secondary is treated as a PCI Delayed transaction by the bridge's primary interface. In other words, it memorizes the request and issues Retry to the PCI bus master. The PCI master must then repeat the transaction on a regular basis until it receives completion from the bridge's primary interface.

On PCI Side, Bridge Follows PCI Ordering Rules

On the PCI side of the bridge, the bridge follows the PCI ordering and dead-lock-avoidance rules. All of the bypass cases required to avoid deadlock are the same for PCI and PCI-X, so the translation introduces no additional rules to avoid deadlocks. The Relaxed Order (RO) attribute is never set for transactions the bridge translates from conventional PCI (see "Creating the Attributes" on page 541), so the special case for Split Transactions in PCI-X bridges that applies only when this bit is set does not apply to these transactions (for more information, refer to "Relaxed Ordering Effect on Transaction Ordering" on page 569). All of the ordering rules that apply when the transaction is re-initiated on the PCI-X side of the bridge are the same as (or are more conservative than) the PCI rules.

Translating the Transaction Type

Table 24-1 on page 539 describes the rules regarding the translation of the PCI command into the appropriate PCI-X command.

Table 24-1: PCI-to-PCIX Command Translation

PCI Command	Translates to PCI-X Command	Description
IO Read or IO Write	IO Read or IO Write	Hypothetically, a PCI master could initiate a burst IO transaction. In reality, the author is not aware of, nor has the author ever met anyone who is aware of, a device that actually implements this capability. However, if the PCI master did initiate a burst IO transaction, the bridge's interface would issue a PCI Disconnect to the master in the first Data Phase and would translate it to a PCI-X IO transaction, which, by definition, only has a single Data Phase.
Configuration Read or Configuration Write	Configuration Read or Configuration Write	Hypothetically, a PCI master could initiate a burst Configuration transaction. In reality, the author is not aware of, nor has the author ever met anyone who is aware of, a device that actually implements this capability. However, if the PCI master did initiate a burst Configuration transaction, the bridge's interface would issue a PCI Disconnect to the master in the first Data Phase and would translate it to a PCI-X Configuration transaction, which, by definition, only has a single Data Phase.

Table 24-1: PCI-to-PCIX Command Translation (Continued)

PCI Command	Translates to PCI-X Command	Description
Memory Read	Memory Read Dword	If the bridge's primary interface detects that the PCI master's transaction only has one Data Phase (it deasserts FRAME# when it asserts IRDY#) and it is performing a 32-bit transfer (REQ64# is not asserted), then the bridge translates it into a PCI-X Memory Read Dword command.
	Memory Read Block	If the PCI transaction has more than a single Data Phase, the length of the transfer is not known. In this case, the bridge uses the same prefetch algorithms used by conventional PCI bridges. Such prefetch algorithms are beyond the scope of the PCI-X spec. The byte count is controlled by the bridge's prefetch algorithm.
Memory Read Line	Memory Read Block	If the PCI master has initiated a multiple Data Phase Memory Read Line transaction, the length of the transfer is not known. In this case, the bridge uses the same prefetch algorithms used by conventional PCI bridges. Such prefetch algorithms are beyond the scope of the PCI-X spec. The byte count is controlled by the bridge's prefetch algorithm.
Memory Read Multiple (Line)	Memory Read Block	If the PCI master has initiated a multiple Data Phase Memory Read Multiple (Line) transaction, the length of the transfer is not known. In this case, the bridge uses the same prefetch algorithms used by conventional PCI bridges. Such prefetch algorithms are beyond the scope of the PCI-X spec. The byte count is controlled by the bridge's prefetch algorithm.

Table 24-1: PCI-to-PCIX Command Translation (Continued)

PCI Command	Translates to PCI-X Command	Description
Memory Write (posted in bridge)	Memory Write	If the bridge's Posted Write Buffer entries for this transaction indicate that not all bytes are to be written within the specified range, then the bridge will translate it into the PCI-X Memory Write command.
	Memory Write Block	If the bridge's Posted Write Buffer entries for this transaction indicate that all bytes are to be written within the specified range, then the bridge will translate it into the PCI-X Memory Write Block command.
Memory Write and Invalidate	Memory Write Block	Since the PCI Memory Write and Invalidate command is an all-inclusive write within the specified line (or lines), it translates into the PCI-X Memory Write Block command.

Creating the Attributes

There is no Attribute Phase in a PCI transaction. That being the case, the PCI master did not supply the bridge with any of the following when it initiated its transaction:

- No Snoop (NS) attribute bit.
- Relaxed Ordering (RO) attribute bit.
- Requester ID (Bus Number, Device Number, Function Number).
- Transaction Tag.
- Byte transfer count.

The sections that follow describe how the bridge creates the transaction attributes.

Attribute Bits

When the bridge translates the PCI transaction into a PCI-X transaction, it must clear to zero both the Relaxed Ordering (RO) and the No Snoop (NS) attribute bits in the Attribute Phase.

Requester ID

In the Attribute Phase, the bridge sets the Requester ID fields as follows:

- Requester Bus Number is set equal to the contents of the bridge's Primary Bus Number register.
- Requester Device Number is cleared to zero.
- Requester Function Number is cleared to zero.

Transaction Tag

The transaction Tag number that the bridge assigns to the transaction can be assigned in any manner that will ensure a unique transaction number (relative to other PCI-X transactions that the bridge initiates). For example, the bridge could use the entry number that the PCI Delayed transaction occupies in the primary interface's Delayed Transaction Queue.

Byte Transfer Count

The Byte Transfer Count field is set according to the rules set forth in Table 24-2 on page 542.

Table 24-2: PCI-to-PCIX Byte Count Translation

PCI Command	Description
IO Read or IO Write	Converts to dword PCI-X transaction, and they do not have a Byte Transfer Count.
Configuration Read or Configuration Write	Converts to dword PCI-X transaction, and they do not have a Byte Transfer Count.
Memory Read	If it converts into a Memory Read Dword transaction, there is no Byte Transfer Count.
	If it converts into a Memory Read Block transaction, the bridge uses its design-specific prefetch algorithm to generate the Byte Transfer Count. See Table 24-1 on page 539.
Memory Read Line	The bridge uses its design-specific prefetch algorithm to generate the Byte Transfer Count. See Table 24-1 on page 539.

Table 24-2: PCI-to-PCIX Byte Count Translation (Continued)

PCI Command	Description
Memory Read Multiple (Line)	The bridge uses its design-specific prefetch algorithm to generate the Byte Transfer Count. See Table 24-1 on page 539.
Memory Write (posted in bridge)	The Byte Transfer Count is generated based on the difference between the start byte address and the end byte address to be written to.
Memory Write and Invalidate	The Byte Transfer Count is generated based on the difference between the start byte address and the end byte address to be written to. The Byte Transfer Count will be a multiple of the cache line size.

Target May Treat as Immediate or as Split Transaction

When the bridge initiates the PCI-X transaction on its secondary bus, the target (the Completer or a bridge in the path to the Completer) may treat the transaction as either an Immediate or a Split Transaction:

- If the target treats it as an Immediate transaction, then the bridge creates a Delayed Completion to give to the PCI master the next time it repeats the transaction.
- If the target treats it as a Split Transaction, then the bridge does not yet have the Delayed Completion to give to the PCI master. The bridge's secondary interface moves the transaction to its Split Transaction Queue to await the subsequent Split Completion(s) associated with the request (see "Bridge Creation of a Split Completion" on page 548).

Translating PCI-X to PCI

General

In Figure 24-3 on page 537, the primary interface of the PCI-X bridge is operating in PCI mode, while its secondary bus is in PCI-X mode. In this example, a PCI-X Requester initiates a transaction addressing a target on the PCI side of the bridge. The bridge latches the transaction request on its secondary interface and must translate it into the appropriate PCI transaction. The sections that follow provide a detailed description of this process.

Writes Are Posted

A PCI-X Memory Write, Memory Write Block, or Alias To Memory Write Block transaction will be posted in the bridge, allowing the PCI-X Memory Write transaction to complete immediately.

All Others Treated as Split Transactions

Any other type of PCI-X transaction that must traverse the bridge from secondary to primary is treated as a PCI-X Split Transaction by the bridge's secondary interface. In other words, it memorizes the request and issues a Split Response to the PCI-X Requester. The PCI-X Requester then moves the transaction to its Split Transaction Queue and awaits the subsequent Split Completion(s).

Translating the Transaction Type

Table 24-3 on page 544 describes the rules regarding the translation of the PCI-X command into the appropriate PCI command.

Table 24-3: PCIX-to-PCI Command Translation

PCI-X Command	Translates to PCI Command	Description
IO Read or IO Write	IO Read or IO Write	The PCI-X IO Read or Write transaction translates into the equivalent PCI single Data Phase transaction.
Configuration Read or Configuration Write	Configuration Read or Configuration Write	The Configuration Read or Write transaction translates into a single Data Phase PCI Configuration Read or Write transaction.

Table 24-3: PCIX-to-PCI Command Translation (Continued)

PCI-X Command	Translates to PCI Command	Description
Memory Read Dword	Memory Read	The Memory Read Dword transaction translates into a single Data Phase PCI Memory Read transaction.
Memory Read Block	Memory Read	If the start byte address and the byte transfer count indicate a single dword or a subset thereof is being transferred, then the PCI-X Memory Read Block transaction translates into a single Data Phase PCI Memory Read transaction.
	Memory Read Line	If the PCI-X Memory Read Block transaction reads more than one dword but does not cross a cache line boundary, then the bridge translates it into a PCI Memory Read Line transaction. The bridge uses its Cache Line Size configuration register to make this determination.
	Memory Read Multiple (Line)	If the PCI-X Memory Read Block transaction reads more than one dword and crosses a cache line boundary, then the bridge translates it into a PCI Memory Read Multiple (Line) transaction. The bridge uses its Cache Line Size configuration register to make this determination.

Table 24-3: PCIX-to-PCI Command Translation (Continued)

PCI-X Command	Translates to PCI Command	Description
Memory Write	Memory Write	The PCI-X transaction is posted in the bridge. If not all bytes in the specified address range are to be written (i.e., there are holes) or if the transaction does not start on a cache line boundary or doesn't end at the end of a cache line, then the bridge translates it into a Memory Write transaction. The bridge uses its Cache Line Size configuration register to make this determination.
	Memory Write and Invalidate	The PCI-X transaction is posted in the bridge. If all bytes in the specified address range are to be written (i.e., no holes) and the transaction starts on a cache line boundary and ends at the end of a cache line, then the bridge translates it into either a PCI Memory Write and Invalidate or a Memory Write transaction (although Memory Write and Invalidate is preferred). The bridge uses its Cache Line Size configuration register to make this determination.

Table 24-3: PCIX-to-PCI Command Translation (Continued)

PCI-X Command	Translates to PCI Command	Description
Memory Write Block	Memory Write	The PCI-X transaction is posted in the bridge. If the transaction does not start on a cache line boundary or doesn't end at the end of a cache line, then the bridge translates it into a Memory Write transaction. The bridge uses its Cache Line Size configuration register to make this determination.
	Memory Write and Invalidate	The PCI-X transaction is posted in the bridge. If the transaction starts on a cache line boundary and ends at the end of a cache line, then the bridge translates it into either a PCI Memory Write and Invalidate or a Memory Write transaction (although Memory Write and Invalidate is preferred). The bridge uses its Cache Line Size configuration register to make this determination.

PCI Target May Treat as Immediate or Delayed Transaction

When the bridge initiates the PCI transaction on its primary bus, the PCI target may respond immediately (i.e., transfer data) or may issue a Retry to the bridge:

- If the target responds by transferring data, and assuming that it's not a memory write, then the bridge must create a Split Completion transaction on the secondary bus to give the completion to the PCI-X Requester (refer to "Bridge Creation of a Split Completion" on page 548).
- If the target issues a Retry to the bridge, the target may be treating it as a PCI Delayed transaction. The bridge must Retry the transaction on the PCI bus on a regular basis until the target responds with something other than Retry. When the target stops issuing Retry and transfers the data, the bridge must create a Split Completion transaction on the secondary bus to give the completion to the PCI-X Requester (refer to "Bridge Creation of a Split Completion" on page 548).

Bridge Creation of a Split Completion

When the bridge has transferred the data (or incurred an error) with the PCI target, and assuming that the transaction was not a memory write (which are posted rather than Split), the bridge must create a Split Completion transaction to return the results to the PCI-X Requester on the secondary bus. It creates it in the following manner:

- The Split Completion address (see Figure 24-4 on page 548) uses the Sequence ID supplied by the Requester in the original transaction.
- In the Attribute Phase (see Figure 24-5 on page 548) of the Split Completion transaction, the Completer ID is formulated as follows:
  - If the PCI transaction was performed by the bridge on its primary interface, then the bridge supplies the Completer Bus Number from its Primary Bus Number register.
  - If the PCI transaction was performed by the bridge on its secondary interface, then the bridge supplies the Completer Bus Number from its Secondary Bus Number register.
- The Completer Device Number and Completer Function Number fields are cleared to zero.

Figure 24-4: Split Completion Address Format

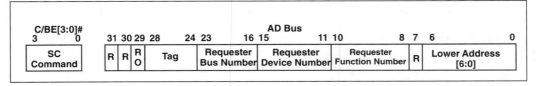

Figure 24-5: Split Completion Attribute Format

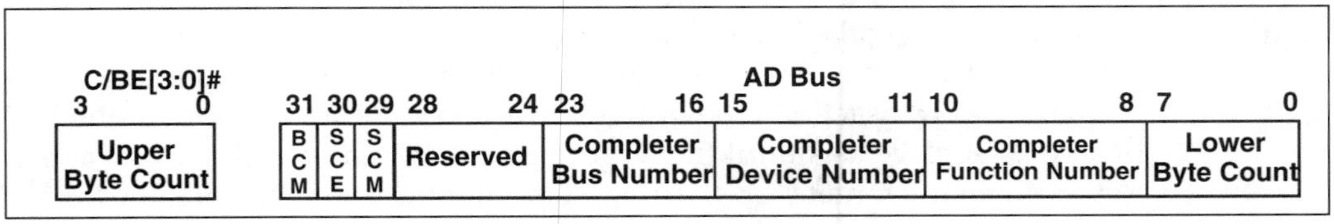

Effect of Relaxed Ordering Attribute Bit

If the PCI-X Requester had set the Relaxed Ordering (RO) attribute bit in the original request, the bridge will honor it. For a detailed description, refer to "Relaxed Ordering Effect on Transaction Ordering" on page 569.

Error Handling

Bridge Error Class SCMs

When a bridge encounters a problem while attempting a Split Transaction on the destination side of the bridge, it sends a Split Completion Error Message back to the Requester in a Split Completion transaction. A description of the Bridge Error Class messages can be found in Table 17-5 on page 319.

Error Handling Defined by Mode of Originating Interface

How an error associated with a specific transaction is handled depends on whether the bridge interface that originated the transaction is operating in PCI-X or PCI mode:

- For a memory write or a transaction that is Split, the originating bridge interface is the one that receives the write or the Split Request, while the destination interface is the one that re-initiates the transaction.
- For a Split Completion, the originating interface is the one that receives the Split Completion from another entity, while the destination interface is the one that re-initiates it to pass it back toward the Requester that originated the request earlier in time.

The next two sections define error handling when the originating interface is in PCI-X mode and PCI mode, respectively.

Error Handling When the Originating Bus Is in PCI-X Mode

This section assumes that a PCI-X Requester originated a transaction that must traverse a bridge. Alternatively, a PCI-X Completer has initiated a Split Completion transaction that must traverse the bridge. In either case, the bridge may experience an error condition while attempting to handle the transaction. The sections that follow define the actions taken by the bridge in the event of various types of error conditions, regardless of the mode (PCI or PCI-X) that the bridge's opposite interface is operating in.

Scenario 1: Data Parity Error in Immediate Read on Destination Bus

Refer to Figure 24-6 on page 551. Any read (step 1) initiated on a PCI-X bus that must traverse a bridge must be handled as a Split Request. The bridge's originating bus interface issues a Split Response to the initiator (step 2). The bridge's destination bus interface then re-initiates the transaction on the destination bus. This scenario assumes that the target on the destination bus responds immediately with read data (step 3) and that one or more of the data items have bad parity. The bridge responds in the following manner:

- The bridge's destination bus interface asserts PERR# (step 4a) on the destination side of the bridge (assuming that the Parity Error Response bit is set to one in the control register for the destination interface: Command register if it's the primary interface; Bridge Control register if it's the secondary interface).
- The bridge's destination bus interface sets the Master Data Parity Error and Detected Parity Error bits in the status register (step 4b) associated with the destination interface (Status register if it's the primary interface; Secondary Status register if it's the secondary interface).
- The bridge's destination interface continues to accept all of the requested read data from the target until the byte count is exhausted or until the target terminates the Sequence in some other way (e.g., by issuing a Target Abort).
- The bridge's originating interface initiates one or more Split Completion transactions and returns all of the requested read data along with any bad parity (step 5) to the PCI-X initiator that originated the read request.

Figure 24-6: Scenario 1: PCI-X Originated Read Results in Immediate Read Parity Error

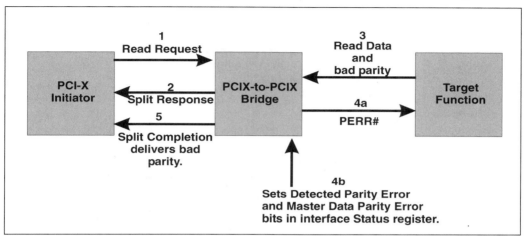

Scenario 2: Data Parity Error on Split Write

General. In this scenario, the PCI-X initiator initiates an IO or Configuration Write that must traverse the bridge. The write data is corrupted either on the originating bus or on the destination bus. There are four possible scenarios, discussed in the next four sections, Scenario 2a through Scenario 2d.

Scenario 2a. Refer to Figure 24-7 on page 552. In this scenario, the bridge's interface that acts as the target of the write is designed to delay the acceptance of the write and the issuance of the Split Response until it has first verified the correctness of the write data. If it detects bad parity on the write data, rather than accepting the write and issuing the Split Response, the bridge takes the following actions:

- The bridge asserts PERR# (assuming that the Parity Error Response bit is set to one in the control register associated with this bridge interface: Bridge Control register if it's the secondary interface; Command register if it's the primary interface).
- The bridge sets the Detected Parity Error bit to one in the status register associated with this interface (Status register if it's the primary interface; Secondary Status register if it's the secondary interface).
- The bridge's originating interface also asserts TRDY# to the initiator.
- It discards the write and does not forward it.

Figure 24-7: Scenario 2a: PCI-X Originated IO or Configuration Write Receives Parity Error and TRDY# on Originating Bus

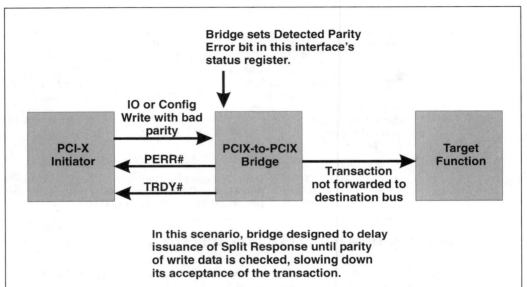

Scenario 2b. Refer to Figure 24-8 on page 553. In this scenario, the bridge's interface that acts as the target of the write is designed to issue the Split Response and accept the write before it has checked the parity of the write data. If the bridge detects bad data parity after the issuance of the Split Response, it has committed to deliver the write on the destination bus and subsequently return a Split Completion transaction indicating the results of the write on the destination bus. Upon detecting the parity error on the originating bus, the bridge takes the following actions:

- The bridge asserts PERR# to the PCI-X initiator (assuming that the Parity Error Response bit is set to one in the control register associated with this bridge interface: Bridge Control register if it's the secondary interface; Command register if it's the primary interface).
- The bridge sets the Detected Parity Error bit to one in the status register associated with this interface (Status register if it's the primary interface; Secondary Status register if it's the secondary interface).
- The bridge forwards the transaction to the destination bus with the bad parity.

Figure 24-8: Scenario 2b: PCI-X Originated IO or Configuration Write Receives Parity Error and Split Response on Originating Bus

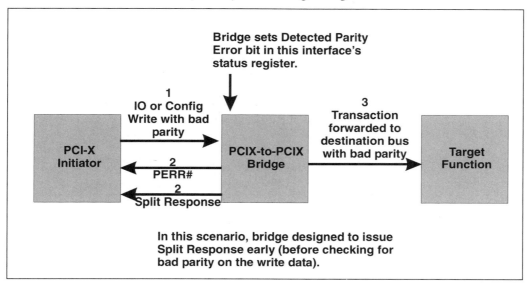

Scenario 2c. Refer to Figure 24-9 on page 554. In this scenario, the bridge's interface that acts as the target of the write is designed to issue the Split Response and accept the write before it has checked the parity of the write data. In this example, there may or may not be a parity error on the originating PCI-X bus. If the bridge detects bad data parity after the issuance of the Split Response, it has committed to deliver the write on the destination bus and subsequently return a Split Completion transaction indicating the results of the write on the destination bus. The bridge takes the following actions:

- If there was a parity error on the originating bus, the bridge asserts PERR# to the PCI-X initiator (assuming that the Parity Error Response bit is set to one in the control register associated with this bridge interface: Bridge Control register if it's the secondary interface; Command register if it's the primary interface).
- If there was a parity error on the originating bus, the bridge sets the Detected Parity Error bit to one in the status register associated with this interface (Status register if it's the primary interface; Secondary Status register if it's the secondary interface).

- The bridge forwards the transaction to the destination bus (with the bad parity, if it was bad on the originating bus).
- This scenario assumes that the target on the destination bus accepts the write data immediately (i.e., it asserts TRDY#, issues a Single Data Phase Disconnect, or issues a Disconnect At Next ADB).
- This scenario also assumes that the target also asserts PERR# (because it detected bad parity on the write data).
- When the bridge detects PERR# asserted by the target, it sets the Master Data Parity Error status bit and then initiates a Split Completion transaction on the originating bus. The Split Completion transaction contains a Bridge Class error message indicating that a Data Phase write parity error was detected on the destination bus.

Figure 24-9: Scenario 2c: PCI-X Originated IO or Configuration Write Receives Parity Error and Immediate Completion on Destination Bus

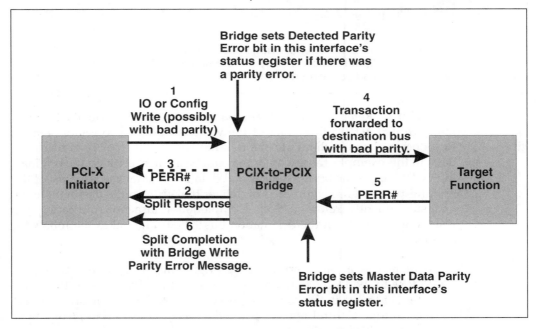

Scenario 2d. Refer to Figure 24-10 on page 555. This scenario assumes that the target on the destination bus accepts the write with a Split Response. It also assumes that there was no write data parity error detected on either bus. In this case, the target has committed to perform a subsequent Split Completion transaction to indicate the success or failure of the write. When

the bride's destination interface receives the subsequent Split Completion Message, it will pass it back to the initiator on the originating bus.

Figure 24-10: Scenario 2d: PCI-X Originated IO or Configuration Write Receives Split Response on Destination Bus

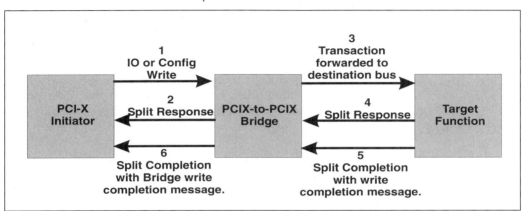

Scenario 3: Data Parity Error on Split Completion

Originating Bus Parity Error on Split Completion Read Data. If the bridge detects a data parity error on the originating bus for Split Completion read data:

- The bridge asserts PERR# on the originating bus (assuming that the Parity Error Response bit is set to one in the control register associated with the originating interface: Command register if it's the primary interface; Bridge Control register if it's the secondary interface).
- Acting as the target of the Split Completion, it sets the Detected Parity Error bit in the status register associated with the originating interface (Status register if it's the primary interface; Secondary Status register if it's the secondary interface).
- The bridge then supplies the bad parity when it forwards the Split Completion to the destination bus. The bridge takes no other action on that data parity error.

Originating Bus Parity Error on SCM. If the bridge detects a data parity error on the originating bus for a Split Completion Message (SCM):

- It asserts SERR# (assuming that the SERR# Enable bit is set to one in the control register associated with the originating interface: Command register if it's the primary interface; Bridge Control register if it's the secondary interface).

- The bridge sets the Signaled System Error bit in the status register associated with the originating interface (Status register if it's the primary interface; Secondary Status register if it's the secondary interface).
- The bridge discards the transaction.

Destination Bus Parity Error on Data or SCM. If the bridge detects PERR# asserted (by the target of the Split Completion) on the destination bus when it forwards a Split Completion, the spec states that the bridge:

> "sets the appropriate error status bits as described in Section 5.4.1 for that interface. The bridge takes no other action on that data parity error."

In section 5.4.1, the spec states:

> "The Master Data Parity Error (bit 8) in the Status register in a PCI-X device is set in... the target (requester or PCI-X bridge) if the target of a Split Completion calculates a data parity error in either read data or a Split Completion Message."

Since in this scenario the bridge is the initiator of the Split Completion, not the target, it would therefore not set any bits in the status register associated with the destination bus. Rather, the device acting as the target of the Split Completion would set the Master Data Parity Error and Detected Parity Error bits in its Status register.

Bridge Forwards SCMs Quietly (without getting involved). The bridge forwards Split Completion Messages without decoding the message. The bridge forwards Split Completion Messages the same way regardless of whether they indicate normal completion or an error message.

Scenario 4: Data Parity Error on Posted Memory Write

There two possible cases:

1. The bridge detects bad parity on one or more memory write data items that it receives on the originating bus.
    - The bridge asserts PERR# to the initiator of the memory write (assuming that the Parity Error Response bit is set to one in the control register associated with the originating interface: Command register if it's the primary interface; Bridge Control register if it's the secondary interface).

- The bridge sets the Detected Parity Error bit in the status register associated with the originating interface (Status register if it's the primary interface; Secondary Status register if it's the secondary interface).
- The bridge then forwards the posted write transaction to the destination interface and drives bad parity. The bridge takes no other action on that data parity error.

2. The bridge receives the memory write data into its Posted Memory Write Buffer without error, but then detects PERR# asserted by the target when it performs the memory write on the destination interface. In this case:

- The bridge sets the Master Data Parity Error bit (assuming that the Parity Error Response bit is set to one in the control register associated with the destination interface: Command register if it's the primary interface; Bridge Control register if it's the secondary interface) in the status register associated with the destination interface (Status register if it's the primary interface; Secondary Status register if it's the secondary interface).
- The bridge asserts SERR# (if enabled) as well as setting the Signaled System Error bit in its status register.

Scenario 5: Master Abort on Destination Bus

General. The actions taken by a PCI-X bridge that experiences a Master Abort when forwarding a transaction depends on both of the following:

- The state of the Master Abort Mode bit in the Bridge Control register.
- The type of transaction.

The PCI-X bridge's reaction to a Master Abort on the destination bus differs from a PCI-to-PCI bridge. While a PCI-to-PCI bridge would signal Target Abort to the origination master when it retries its transaction, a PCI-X bridges sends a Split Completion Message back to the Requester (the bridge reacts the same way for both locked and un-locked transactions). The sections that follow detail the PCI-X bridge's responses to the a Master Abort under each of the following conditions:

- Master Abort when forwarding a Split Transaction.
- Master Abort on a posted memory write transaction.
- Master Abort when forwarding a Split Completion transaction.

Master Abort When Forwarding Split Request. If a bridge experiences a Master Abort on the destination bus when forwarding a Split Transaction request, the bridge takes the following actions (and the state of the Master Abort Mode bit in the Bridge Control register has no effect).

The bridge sets the Received Master Abort status bit in the status register associated with its destination interface (the Status register if it's the primary interface; the Secondary Status register if it's the secondary interface) and creates a Split Completion Message (SCM) to send back to the Requester in a Split Completion transaction. The Split Completion transaction's address and attributes are created as follows:

- It creates the Split Completion address from the original request the same way a Completer would: it uses the Requester ID and Tag that were given to it by the Requester.
- For the Completer Attributes, the bridge creates the Completer ID for the bus on which the Master Abort occurred:
  - If the Master Abort occurred on the primary interface, the bridge supplies the bus number, device number, and function number of the Completer ID from its PCI-X Bridge Status register.
  - If the Master Abort occurred on the secondary interface, the bridge supplies the bus number from its Secondary Bus Number register and sets the Device Number and Function Number fields of the Completer ID to zero.

The SCM uses the PCI-X Bridge Error class code and Master Abort error message index as described in "Data Phase Message Format" on page 317. If the transaction that ended in a Master Abort is a dword transaction, the error SCM replaces the normal Split Completion for this transaction (i.e., the dword of read data or the SCM that indicates good completion of a Split write).

Master Abort on Posted Memory Write. The actions taken by a PCI-X bridge that experiences a Master Abort when attempting to perform a posted memory write on the destination bus are the same as those taken by a PCI bridge. The bridge sets the Received Master Abort bit in the status register associated with its destination interface (the Status register if it's the primary interface; the Secondary Status register if it's the secondary interface). If the burst memory transaction that is sourcing the data is still in progress on the originating bus, the bridge disconnects the transaction as soon as possible (at the next ADB, or if it's too close to that ADB, then at the one after that) and discards the entire transaction.

- If the Master Abort Mode bit in the Bridge Control register is cleared to zero, the bridge takes no further action on the error.
- If the Master Abort Mode bit is set to one, the bridge asserts SERR# on its primary interface (if the SERR# Enable bit is set to one in its Command register) and sets the Signaled System Error bit in its status register.

Master Abort on Split Completion. A bridge may experience a Master Abort while attempting to pass along a Split Completion transaction from the Completer back to the Requester. The Master Abort Mode bit has no effect and the bridge takes the following actions:

- If the Master Abort occurs on the primary bus, the bridge sets the Received Master Abort bit in its Status register as well as the Split Completion Discarded bit in its PCI-X Bridge Status register.
- If the Master Abort occurs on the secondary bus, the bridge sets the Received Master Abort status bit in its Secondary Status register and the Split Completion Discarded bit in its PCI-X Secondary Status register.

In both cases, the bridge discards the Split Completion and takes no further action.

Scenario 6: Target Abort on Destination Bus

Bridge Signals Target Abort. A PCI-X bridge signals a Target Abort if it asserts DEVSEL# to claim a transaction but internal error conditions prevent the bridge from signaling any other termination. The bridge sets the Signaled Target Abort bit in the status register associated with its destination interface (the Status register if it's the primary interface; the Secondary Status register if it's the secondary interface).

Bridge Receives A Target Abort on Split Transaction. If the bridge receives a Target Abort on the destination bus for a transaction that it has Split and is forwarding, the bridge takes the following actions:

- It sets the Received Target Abort status bit in the status register associated with its destination interface (the Status register if it's the primary interface; the Secondary Status register if it's the secondary interface).
- The bridge performs a Split Completion transaction to report the error back to the Requester. The Split Completion address and attributes are created as described in "Master Abort When Forwarding Split Request" on page 557. The Split Completion Message uses the PCI-X Bridge Error class code and Target Abort error message index (see "Data Phase Message Format" on page 317).
  - If the transaction was a dword transaction, the error Split Completion Message replaces the normal completion message for this transaction.
  - If the transaction was a burst, the bridge may send the error Split Completion Message in the first or any subsequent Split Completion transaction associated with this Sequence.

Bridge Receives Target Abort on Memory Write. In this case, the bridge takes the following actions:

- The bridge sets the Received Target Abort status bit to one (in the Status register if the abort occurred on its primary side; Secondary Status register if the abort occurred on its secondary side).
- If the memory write transaction is still in progress on the originating side of the bridge, the bridge must issue a Disconnect At Next ADB to the initiator as soon as possible.
- The bridge discards all of the memory write data in its posted memory write buffer that is associated with this transaction.
- The bridge asserts SERR# on its primary side and sets the Signaled System Error bit in its Status register (assuming that the SERR# Enable bit is set to one in its Command register).

Bridge Receives Target Abort on Split Completion. The bridge takes the following actions:

- If the Target Abort occurred on its primary side, the bridge sets the Received Target Abort bit in its Status register and the Split Completion Discarded bit in its PCI-X Bridge Status register.
- If the Target Abort occurred on its secondary side, the bridge sets the Received Target Abort bit in its Secondary Status register and the Split Completion Discarded bit in its PCI-X Secondary Status register.
- The bridge discards the Split Completion data.
- The bridge asserts SERR# and sets the Signaled System Error bit in its Status register on its primary side (assuming that the SERR# Enable bit is set to one in its Command register).

Error Handling When Originating Bus in PCI Mode

Background

When one interface of a PCI-X bridge is operating in PCI mode and it receives a transaction (other than a memory write: they are posted) that must cross the bridge onto a PCI-X bus, the bridge's originating interface handles it as a PCI Delayed transaction and issues a Retry to the PCI master. The PCI master is then obliged to retry the transaction on a periodic basis until it receives a response other than a Retry. The bridge translates the transaction into its equivalent PCI-X transaction (see "Translating PCI to PCI-X" on page 536) and initiates it on its PCI-X side.

Bridge Handles Errors Same as PCI Bridge Unless SCM Error

When the originating bus is in PCI mode, the bridge handles all errors in the same manner as a PCI-to-PCI bridge unless the error occurs on a PCI-X bus and the error is reported to the bridge in the form of a Split Completion Message.

SCM Error on a Split Read

When a PCI-X bridge forwards a read transaction from the PCI side of a bridge to its PCI-X side, the bridge's PCI-X interface may first receive a Split Response from the target and then subsequently receive a Split Completion Message. There are two possible scenarios:

SCENARIO 1. The bridge returns read data of all ones to the PCI master if all of the following are true:
- The SCM indicates a Master Abort condition (i.e., PCI-X Bridge class and Master Abort error index),
- the Master Abort Mode bit in the Bridge Control register is cleared to zero (it's still configuration time), and
- the read transaction is not a locked transaction.

During initialization time (i.e., system configuration is still in progress), the bridge will return all ones for a Configuration Read that ends in a Master Abort. In this way, receipt of all ones when a function's Vendor ID register is read informs the configuration software that the targeted function does not exist.

SCENARIO 2. In all other cases, when a Split read receives a Split Completion Message, the bridge terminates the transaction on the PCI side (when the PCI master retries it) with Target Abort (and sets the Signaled Target Abort bit to one in the status register associated with its originating interface: Status register if it's the primary interface; Secondary Status register if it's the secondary interface).

SCM on Split Write

If the PCI-X bridge forwards a write transaction (i.e., an IO or Configuration Write) from its PCI side to its PCI-X side, receives a Split Response, and then subsequently receives a Split Completion Message, the bridge completes the transaction normally on the PCI side (i.e., it asserts TRDY# when the PCI master retries the transaction) in the following two cases:

- When the transaction receives an SCM indicating normal Completion (i.e., Write Completion class and Normal Completion index).

- When the transaction receives an SCM indicating Master Abort (i.e., PCI-X Bridge class and Master Abort error index), and the Master Abort Mode bit in the Bridge Control register is cleared to zero (indicating that it's still configuration time), and the write transaction is not locked.

If the SCM indicates that a write data parity error occurred (i.e., PCI-X Bridge class and Write Data Parity Error index), the bridge, acting as the target of the PCI transaction, takes the following actions the next time that the PCI master retries the transaction:

- The bridge asserts PERR# to the PCI master.
- The bridge sets the Detected Parity Error bit in the status register associated with its PCI interface (the Status register if it's the primary interface; the Secondary Status register if it's the secondary interface).

In any other case where a Split write completes with an SCM, the bridge signals a Target Abort to the PCI master the next time that it retries the transaction.

Corrupted Split Completion

Refer to "Bridge Buffer Space Problem Due to Corrupted Split Completion" on page 186.

Buffer Size

Posted Memory Write Buffer Size

A PCI-X bridge must implement at least two 128-byte ADQs (blocks) of buffer space to hold posted memory write data. The bridge's posted write buffer is considered full when less than two blocks of buffer are currently available.

This is the minimum buffer size for the following reason (the following text is from the spec):

"If a memory write Sequence addresses a completer on the other side of a PCI-X bridge, a bridge with less than two ADQs of buffer space for memory write transactions must not signal Disconnect at Next ADB if such a disconnection would cause the bridge to hold a portion of the memory write Sequence that is too small (*less than four Data Phases*) to forward correctly on the destination bus. The problem occurs if the byte count of the Sequence indicates the Sequence extends beyond the next ADB, but the portion of the Sequence that the bridge holds would require less than four data phases on the destination bus. If the bridge attempted to forward such a portion of a memory write Sequence, and the target on the destination bus (completer or bridge) signaled Data Transfer (indicating its ability to accept data beyond the ADB), the bridge would be unable to disconnect the transaction at the ADB. The byte count of the Sequence would indicate to the target that the transaction should continue, but the write data would not be available in the bridge.

Although that PCI-X bridge would be allowed to signal Disconnect at Next ADB for transactions other than the problem case described above, the logic required to select precisely this case is complex. The problem case is a function of the starting address, the width of the destination bus, and the width of the completer. The recommended simpler alternative is to provide a minimum of two ADQs of buffer space for memory write transactions. In such an implementation, the bridge would signal Retry to memory write transactions if the buffer space available in the bridge for memory write data was less than two ADQs. With a minimum of two ADQs of buffer space, a bridge would not signal Disconnect at Next ADB until it reached the end of the second ADQ, thereby eliminating the risk of holding too little of the write data."

Bridge designers, however, are encouraged to implement much larger buffers to enable the posting of multiple and/or longer burst memory write transactions.

Split Completion Data Buffer Size

A PCI-X bridge must implement at least one 128-byte ADQ of buffer space to hold Split Completion data. This is the minimum buffer size because, when acting as the target of a Split Completion transaction, the bridge can only disconnect on block boundaries. It must therefore be prepared to accept a full block of Split Completion data at full-speed. Bridge designers, however, are encouraged to implement much larger buffers to enable the storing of multiple and/or longer Split Completions.

Buffer Space for Memory Read Data

General

Before initiating a burst memory read transaction, a PCI-X bridge must have at least two ADQs (i.e., blocks) of buffer space available. This is necessary in case the addressed Completer starts supplying the read data immediately (i.e., it doesn't issue a Split Response to the bridge).

The Problem

If a bridge forwards a long burst memory read transaction and the Completer responds immediately with data, the bridge must be able to accept the data at least to the first ADB. If the start memory address is less than four Data Phases from an ADB, the bridge (acting as the initiator of the transaction) is not able to disconnect on the imminent ADB and must proceed to the next one. For this reason, the bridge must have two blocks of buffer space available, one to hold the data between the starting address and the first block boundary and the other to hold the data between the first and second block boundaries.

When Limit = Capacity, This Is Not a Problem

If the value currently in the Limit field of the bridge's Split Transaction Control register is set equal to the value in the Split Transaction Capacity field, the bridge will only pass a Split request across if it has sufficient buffer space available to hold the resulting Split Completion read data. In this case, the bridge will always have two blocks of buffer space available when it initiates a memory read.

When a Request Is Bigger Than the Bridge Buffer

If a Split memory read request must be forwarded by a bridge and the byte transfer count in the memory read is larger than that indicated in the respective Capacity field, the bridge must wait to forward that memory read until it has no other Split Transactions to be forwarded in that direction. If the bridge allows other Split Requests to pass the large one, it must forward the large request eventually (in other words, be fair to the big guy).

Application Bridge

While a device may not actually be a PCIX-to-PCIX bridge (i.e., it does not have a Class/SubClass of 06h/04h, and it implements the Header Type 0 configura-

---

tion register template rather than the Header Type 1 template), its design may include features that require it to follow the same design rules as Simple devices (see "Device Complexity" on page 481), as well as a number of the design rules applicable to PCIX-to-PCIX bridges.

Refer to Figure 24-12 on page 567. A device that implements internal posting of memory write transactions that the device must initiate on the PCI-X interface is considered a bridge. In the illustration, when the intelligent microcontroller on the card initiates a memory write transaction on its internal bus that targets a memory device outside the device on the PCI-X bus, the memory write is posted in the card's outbound posted memory write buffer. The on-card microcontroller considers the write completed even though it has not yet been performed on the PCI-X bus. The card also implements an inbound posted memory write buffer. This makes the device very similar to a PCIX-to-PCIX bridge in that both implement posted memory write buffers going in both directions and, like the bridge, the card may both initiate and act as the target of Split Transactions.

The PCI-X spec refers to such devices as application bridges. The programmer may identify an application bridge by checking the state of the Device Complexity bit in the function's PCI-X Status register (see Figure 24-11 on page 566). A Host/PCIX bridge would be an example of an application bridge.

An application bridge must meet at least the following bridge requirements (additional PCI-X bridge requirements may be necessary, depending upon the complexity of the application bridge):

1. The bridge transaction ordering and deadlock avoidance rules (see "Bridge Acceptance Rules" on page 567).
2. The bridge transaction acceptance rules (see "Bridge Acceptance Rules" on page 567).
3. Unless the system design guarantees that no locked accesses ever address a Completer on the other side of the bridge, the bridge must adhere to the locking rules (see Chapter 25, entitled "Locked Transaction Series," on page 579).

PCI-X bridges and application bridges do not have to meet the following PCI-X requirements for Simple device design for transactions that cross from one interface to another:

- A Simple device design (see "Device Complexity" on page 481) has a great deal of control over its internal environment. It is therefore bound by the 2 microsecond Maximum Completion Time limit (see "Maximum Completion Time" on page 193) in dumping its inbound posted memory write buffer to its internal memory. Since it is more problematic for a bridge design to accurately predict how long it will take to dump its posted write buffer to the other side of the bridge, the Maximum Completion Time limit does not apply to bridges.

- A bridge terminates Split Completions with Retry or Disconnect at Next ADB when it is required by the transaction ordering rules or if its Split Completion data buffer space is currently full of previously received Split Completion data.

Figure 24-11: PCI-X Status Register

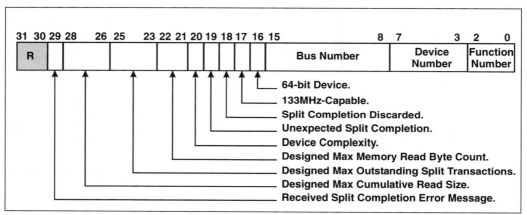

Figure 24-12: A Complex Device

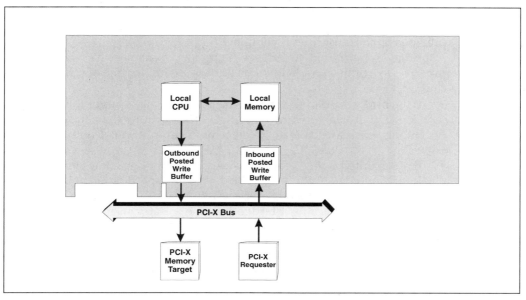

Bridge Acceptance Rules

The bridge acceptance rules define the circumstances under which a bridge (either a PCI-X bridge or an application bridge) is permitted to issue a Retry or a Disconnect At Next ADB in response to a transaction.

1. A bridge must never make the acceptance (posting) of a memory write transaction as a target contingent on the prior completion of a non-locked transaction that the bridge initiates on the same bus.
2. A bridge is permitted to terminate with Retry or Disconnect At Next ADB a memory write transaction that crosses the bridge only if the bridge's posted memory write buffer is full of previously posted memory write transactions moving in the same direction.
3. Bridges are not subject to the Maximum Completion Time limit that simple devices have for accepting memory write transactions. However, to provide backward compatibility with PCI-to-PCI bridges designed prior to the revision 2.1 PCI spec, all PCI-X bridges are required to accept memory write transactions regardless of how many previous Split Transactions the bridge

has enqueued. This is analogous to the requirement in the PCI 2.2 spec for a PCI bridge to accept memory writes even while it has one or more Delayed Transactions outstanding as a master.

4. A bridge that has a temporarily full Split Transaction Queue will issue a Retry to another transaction that must be Split on that interface until the previous Split Transaction is complete.

5. A bridge is permitted to issue a Retry or Disconnect at Next ADB in response to a Split Completion if its buffers are full for one of following reasons:

   - If the bridge's Limit register has been set to a value larger than its actual Capacity, it can forward more Split Transactions than it actually has buffer space available to receive the resulting Split Completion read data.
   - If a corrupted Split Completion crossed the bridge some time since the last rising-edge of RST# (see "Bridge Buffer Space Problem Due to Corrupted Split Completion" on page 186).

6. The PCI 2.2 spec permits a bridge to issue a Retry in response to a read transaction when the ordering rules require the bridge to initiate a previously posted memory write transaction. This case is not allowed for a PCI-X bridge operating in PCI-X mode. In most cases, a PCI-X bridge issues a Split Response to any read that must cross the bridge. The ordering rules require the bridge to initiate any previously posted memory writes before initiating the Split Completion returning the read data. If the bridge's Split Request Queue is currently full, the bridge must respond to any reads that must traverse the bridge with Retry until completion of a previously latched Split request permits the bridge to memorize the next read and issue a Split Response to its initiator. During the period of time that one or more reads are being rejected (i.e., Retries are issued), the transaction ordering rules require the bridge to continue to initiate posted memory writes.

Ordering and Passing Rules

The rules presented in this section apply both to PCI-X bridges and to application bridges. They exist for two reasons:

- They ensure that transactions complete in such an order as to guarantee proper operation of system software.
- They ensure that PCI devices designed to comply with the 2.2 PCI spec and with the PCI-X spec will not cause deadlocks when interacting with older PCI devices designed prior to the PCI 2.1 spec (in other words, prior to the introduction of PCI Delayed transactions).

Same Rules as PCI Except...

PCI-X bridges adhere to all of the same rules as PCI bridges built to the 2.2 PCI spec. In addition, two features that affect transaction ordering and passing rules that are not present in PCI are:

- The Relaxed Ordering attribute bit.
- Split Transactions.

For a detailed description of the PCI 2.2 ordering and deadlock-avoidance rules, refer to the chapter entitled *Transaction Ordering and Deadlock Avoidance* in the MindShare book entitled *PCI System Architecture, Fourth Edition* (published by Addison-Wesley).

Relaxed Ordering Effect on Transaction Ordering

Relaxed Ordering Effects on Memory Reads. Refer to Figure 24-14 on page 570. This scenario makes the following assumptions:

- A bridge detects that the Relaxed Ordering attribute bit is set for a memory read transaction that must cross the bridge.
- The bridge issues a Split Response to the initiator of the read and then passes the memory read to the destination side of the bridge.
- Before the Completer returns the Split Completion read data for that transaction, one or more unrelated memory writes are posted in the bridge going toward the bus that had earlier originated the memory read.
- The Completer returns the previously requested read data in a series of one or more Split Completions.
- Because the Relaxed Ordering bit is set in the Address Phase of the Split Completion transaction (see Figure 24-13 on page 570), the bridge is permitted to pass the Split Completion memory read data back to its Requester (even though the unrelated posted memory writes moving in the same direction were received by the bridge interface before the Split Completion memory read data arrived). This rule is documented in Table 24-4 on page 573.

The fact that the Requester's driver has permitted this means that it is guaranteeing that the memory write data is unrelated to the memory read data and there is therefore no requirement that the affected memory locations be updated before the memory read data is delivered to the Requester.

Figure 24-13: Split Completion Transaction Address Phase Format

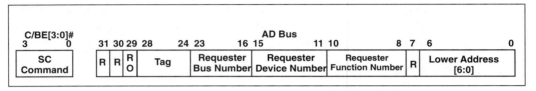

Figure 24-14: Relaxed Ordering Effect on Memory Reads

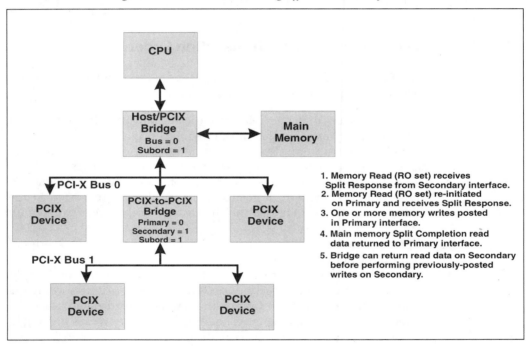

Relaxed Ordering Effects on Memory Writes. PCI-X bridges and application bridges pay no attention to the Relaxed Ordering attribute bit in a memory write transaction (other than to pass it along faithfully when it passes the posted memory write to the destination bus). They always perform all posted memory writes on the destination bus in precisely the same order that they were received on the originating bus.

The only device that does pay attention to the Relaxed Ordering (RO) attribute bit in a memory write transaction is the Host/PCIX bridge. If the RO bit is set to one in the Attribute Phase of a memory write, the Host/PCIX bridge is permitted to (but doesn't have to) write the data associated with this memory write to main memory before data associated with main memory writes that were received by the bridge prior to this one. This rule is documented in Table 24-4 on page 573. In addition, the bytes within the affected memory write transaction are permitted to be written to the targeted main memory locations in any order (but of course they must be written to the correct main memory locations). This out-of-order writing to main memory gives the Host/PCIX bridge the ability to perform main memory updates in whatever order will yield the best possible performance. As an example, it could perform writes to rows of main memory that are currently open first.

Split Transaction Effects on Transaction Ordering

General. The second PCI-X feature that does not exist in PCI and affects the ordering rules is Split Transactions. Split Transaction ordering and deadlock-avoidance rules are almost identical to the rules for Delayed Transactions in PCI. As with Delayed transactions, the order of transactions is established when they complete (i.e., a transaction is considered not to have taken place until it completes: a PCI Delayed transaction is not considered to have taken place until it receives a termination other than a Retry; a PCI-X Split Transaction is not considered to have taken place until it receives a Split Completion).

Split Completions have the same ordering requirements as PCI Delayed Completions, except in the two cases described in the next two sections.

Same Sequence Split Completions Must Remain in Order. Split Read Completions with the same Sequence ID must stay in address order (see Table 24-4 on page 573). The Completer must supply the Split Read Completions in strict address order, and any intervening bridges must preserve this order, thus guaranteeing that the Requester always receives the data in its expected order. Split Read Completions associated with different Sequence IDs have no relationship to each other and can be delivered out of order with reference to each other (see Table 24-4 on page 573). If an initiator requires two Split Transactions to complete in order, the initiator must not issue the second request until the first Split Transaction completes.

Relaxed Ordering Can Affect Split Completion Delivery. As described in "Relaxed Ordering Effects on Memory Reads" on page 569, the second case in which Split Read Completion ordering rules are different from Delayed Read Completion rules is if the Relaxed Ordering bit is set.

The Rules

Table 24-4 on page 573 lists the ordering rules for all Split Transactions and memory write transactions crossing a bridge in the same direction. Each entry in the first column (e.g., PMW) represents a previously latched transaction that must cross the bridge, while each entry in the second column (e.g., SRR) represents a transaction that was just latched and also has to cross the bridge going in the same direction. The following is the key to the transaction types:

- **PMW**. Posted Memory Write transaction.
- **SRR**. Split Read Request.
- **SRC**. Split Read Completion.
- **SWR**. Split Write Request.
- **SWC**. Split Write Completion.

Table 24-4: The Bridge Ordering and Passing Rules

1st	2nd	Description
PMW	PMW	The 2nd PMW cannot be performed before the 1st. When the RO bit is cleared in a memory write, both PCI-X and Host/PCIX bridges must perform all posted memory writes to memory in the same order that they are received.
		When the RO bit is set to one in a memory write, the Host/PCIX bridge is permitted to perform the write to memory before previously posted writes to main memory. In addition, the bytes within the write can be written to memory in any order. PCI-X bridges pay no attention to the RO bit and always perform PMWs in the order received.
	SRR	The bridge is not permitted to perform the SRR before the PMW. If it did and the PMW was to the same location(s) as the read, the read would return stale data.
	SWR	The bridge is not permitted to perform the SWR before the PMW. A SWR that has just been latched may not be performed on the destination bus before a previously latched PMW is performed on the destination bus. Since the SWR's write was initiated *after* the PMW data was written to the bridge, it must be written to the target on the destination bus *after* the previously latched PMW data. This ensures strong write ordering. In the Producer/Consumer example (in MindShare's *PCI System Architecture* book), the SWR could be the Producer's write to set the Flag that indicates the data is all in the Data buffer. It wouldn't do to have the Flag get set *before* all of the data has actually arrived in the Data buffer.
	SRC	RO= 0. Unless the Relaxed Ordering attribute bit is set in the SRC, the bridge is not permitted to perform the SRC before the PMW.
		RO = 1. If the Relaxed Ordering attribute bit is set in SRC, the bridge may (if it wishes) perform the SRC on the destination bus before it performs a previously posted memory write transaction.
	SWC	The bridge has the option of performing these two transactions in either order. One is a memory write traveling toward the destination bus, while the other is a SWC returning the results of a write performed on the opposite bus to a Requester on the destination side of the bridge.

Table 24-4: The Bridge Ordering and Passing Rules (Continued)

1st	2nd	Description
SRR	PMW	The bridge must perform the just-latched PMW before it performs the previously latched SRR. This rule exists to avoid a possible deadlock scenario. A deadlock can occur when bridges that support Delayed Transactions (i.e., designed to the PCI 2.1 or 2.2 spec) are transferring data with bridges that do not support Delayed Transactions (i.e., bridges designed to a pre-2.1 version of the PCI spec). For a complete description of this scenario, refer to the discussion of Rule 5 on page 663 of the MindShare book *PCI System Architecture, Fourth Edition* (published by Addison-Wesley).
	SRR	A bridge can reorder Split Requests. As an example, a bridge might delay one SRR due to insufficient buffer space to hold the resulting read data, while it can pass the other SRR to the destination bus because it is requesting less data for which there is sufficient bridge buffer space.
	SWR	A bridge can reorder Split Requests. As an example, a bridge might delay the SRR due to insufficient buffer space to hold the resulting read data, while it can pass the SWR to the destination bus because it only requires one dword of buffer space to hold the resulting SCM.
	SRC	The bridge must perform the SRC before the SRR to avoid a deadlock that can occur between two bridges. A detailed description can be found in the description of Rule 6 on page 666 of the MindShare book *PCI System Architecture, Fourth Edition* (published by Addison-Wesley).
	SWC	The bridge must perform the SWC before the SRR to avoid a deadlock that can occur between two bridges. A detailed description can be found in the description of Rule 6 on page 666 of the MindShare book *PCI System Architecture, Fourth Edition* (published by Addison-Wesley).

Table 24-4: The Bridge Ordering and Passing Rules (Continued)

1st	2nd	Description
SWR	PMW	The bridge must perform the just-latched PMW before it performs the previously latched SWR. This rule exists to avoid a possible deadlock scenario. A deadlock can occur when bridges that support Delayed Transactions (i.e., designed to the PCI 2.1 or 2.2 spec) are transferring data with bridges that do not support Delayed Transactions (i.e., bridges designed to a pre-2.1 version of the PCI spec). For a complete description of this scenario, refer to the discussion of Rule 5 on page 663 of the MindShare book *PCI System Architecture, Fourth Edition* (published by Addison-Wesley).
	SRR	A bridge can reorder Split Requests.
	SWR	A bridge can reorder Split Requests.
	SRC	The bridge must perform the SRC before the SWR to avoid a deadlock that can occur between two bridges. A detailed description can be found in the description of Rule 6 on page 666 of the MindShare book *PCI System Architecture, Fourth Edition* (published by Addison-Wesley).
	SWC	The bridge must perform the SWC before the SWR to avoid a deadlock that can occur between two bridges. A detailed description can be found in the description of Rule 6 on page 666 of the MindShare book *PCI System Architecture, Fourth Edition* (published by Addison-Wesley).

Table 24-4: The Bridge Ordering and Passing Rules (Continued)

1st	2nd	Description
SRC	PMW	The bridge must perform the PMW on the destination bus before the SRC. This is necessary to avoid possible deadlocks between the PCI-X bridge and old PCI bridges that were designed prior to the inception of PCI Delayed Transaction. A complete description can be found in the description of Rule 7 on page 667 of the MindShare book *PCI System Architecture, Fourth Edition.*
	SRR	The bridge can perform the two transactions in either order on the destination bus. In most PCI-X bridges, Split Requests are managed in separate buffers from Split Completions, so Split Requests naturally pass Split Completions. However, no deadlocks occur if Split Completions block Split Requests.
	SWR	The bridge can perform the two transactions in either order on the destination bus. In most PCI-X bridges, Split Requests are managed in separate buffers from Split Completions, so Split Requests naturally pass Split Completions. However, no deadlocks occur if Split Completions block Split Requests.
	SRC	If the two SRCs are associated with separate Sequences, the bridge can perform the two transactions in either order on the destination bus.
		SRCs with the same Sequence ID must remain in address order.
	SWC	The bridge can perform the two transactions in either order on the destination bus. An SWC is permitted to be blocked by or to pass an SRC.

Table 24-4: The Bridge Ordering and Passing Rules (Continued)

1st	2nd	Description
SWC	PMW	The bridge must perform the PMW on the destination bus before the SWC. This is necessary to avoid possible deadlocks between the PCI-X bridge and old PCI bridges that were designed prior to the inception of the PCI Delayed Transaction. A complete description can be found in the description of Rule 7 on page 667 of the MindShare book *PCI System Architecture, Fourth Edition.*
	SRR	The bridge can perform the two transactions in either order on the destination bus. An SRR is permitted to be blocked by or to pass an SWC.
	SWR	The bridge can perform the two transactions in either order on the destination bus. A Split Request is permitted to be blocked by or to pass a Split Completion. In most PCI-X bridges, Split Requests are managed in separate buffers from Split Completions, so Split Requests can pass Split Completions. However, no deadlocks occur if Split Completions block Split Requests.
	SRC	The bridge can perform the two transactions in either order on the destination bus. SRCs are permitted to be blocked by or to pass SWCs.
	SWC	The bridge can perform the two transactions in either order on the destination bus. SWCs are permitted to be blocked by or to pass SRCs and SWCs.

Decomposing Split Transactions (sounds morbid!)

When a bridge receives a Split Read Request to be forwarded to the destination bus, it would typically forward it identically (same Sequence ID, same byte transfer count, etc.). However, the bridge designer may choose to forward it as a series of smaller requests. The spec takes the point of view that although this is permissible, it increases the complexity of the bridge design and results in decreased performance (because the bridge must arbitrate for bus ownership to perform each of the smaller transactions).

If the bridge issues a Split Response to a transaction received on the originating bus, it may (as described above) choose to forward it to the destination bus as a series of smaller requests. In this case, the bridge must generate unique Sequence IDs for each of the smaller requests. In order to guarantee that the Sequence IDs are unique, the bridge uses its own Requester ID for the destination bus:

- If the destination bus is the one on the primary side of the bridge, the Requester ID is supplied from the Bus/Device/Function fields in the bridge's PCI-X Bridge Status register (see Figure 22-5 on page 503).
- If the destination bus is the one on the secondary side of the bridge, the Requester ID consists of the bus number from the bridge's Secondary Bus Number register, the device number is 00h (because the bridge is always device 0 on its secondary bus), and the function number is 0.

When the Split Completions resulting from these requests return on the destination bus, the bridge must convert them back to the original Sequence ID and must return the data in address order.

25 *Locked Transaction Series*

The Previous Chapter

The previous chapter covered the following bridge-related topics:

- Support for the DAC command.
- Posting of memory writes.
- Split Transaction handling.
- Claiming Split Completions.
- Translating PCI transactions to PCI-X transactions.
- Translating PCI-X transactions to PCI transactions.
- Error handling.
- Buffer size.

This Chapter

This chapter describes the locking mechanism that permits the processor, through the Host/PCIX bridge, to perform a series of transactions to a Completer with the guarantee that no PCI-X Requester upstream of the Completer will be able to access the Completer. In addition, no Requester other than the Host/PCIX bridge (in other words, the processor) will be able to access main memory.

The Next Chapter

The next chapter provides a detailed description of error handling both for non-bridge and bridge functions.

Definition of Downstream and Upstream

Refer to Figure 25-1 on page 586. As defined earlier in the book, a transaction is moving downstream if it is moving away from the processor(s) and main memory, while a transaction is moving upstream if it is moving towards the processor(s) and main memory.

Basics

Refer to Figure 25-1 on page 586. The locking mechanism was included in the PCI and PCI-X specs to support an operational characteristic of Intel x86 processors. In some circumstances, the Intel processor instructs the Host/PCIX bridge to perform a locked transaction series (the first of which is always a memory read) that targets a Completer on a PCI-X bus. This means that the processor needs to perform a series of two (or more) transactions in the PCI-X realm (i.e., the Completer resides on a bus beyond the Host/PCIX bridge). The Host/PCIX bridge is the only device that is allowed to originate a locked transaction series.

The completion of the first transaction of the locked transaction series (a memory read) locks all of the bridges in the path between the processor and the Completer. The bridges will remain locked until the locked transaction series completes or until a fatal error is detected (Master Abort, Target Abort, or the receipt of a Split Completion Message that contains an error). While the bridges remain locked, they have the following operational characteristics (including the Host/PCIX bridge):

- The bridges' secondary interfaces have the following operational characteristics:
    - It keeps LOCK# asserted (to keep the target it addressed earlier in the locked state) either until the locked transaction series completes, or a fatal error occurs in a subsequent transaction of the series (Target Abort, Master Abort, or it receives a Split Completion Error Message).
    - It will not accept any transactions moving upstream towards main memory (with the exception of Split Completion transactions).
- The primary interface of any PCIX-to-PCIX bridges in the path to the Completer have the following operational characteristics:
    - It will not accept (i.e., will issue a Retry in response to) any transactions moving downstream from any initiator other than the one that locked it (see the exception stated in the next item).
    - It will accept any Split Completion transactions that are moving downstream and will pass them to its secondary bus.
    - It will remain in the full-lock state until FRAME# and LOCK# are both sampled deasserted on the same rising-edge of the clock on its primary interface.

After the first memory read has been completed and the lock on all bridges along the path to the Completer has been established, the following conditions are in force:

- No PCI-X Requesters on any PCI-X bus can access main memory. They will receive a Retry from the Host/PCIX bridge.
- The Host/PCI-X bridge will accept Split Completion transactions moving towards the processor.
- No Requesters (other than the Host/PCIX bridge) residing on intervening buses along the path can access any device that resides on the Completer's bus.
- The Completer itself is not locked.
- The Completer can be accessed by Requesters that reside on its bus or on any bus downstream of its bus.
- Requesters on each bus can perform unlocked transactions with Completers that reside on the same bus as them.
- PCIX-to-PCIX bridges along the path will accept Split Completion transactions moving in both directions through the bridge.

Only Host/PCIX Bridge Originates Downstream Locked Series

The Host/PCIX bridge is the only device that is permitted to originate a locked transaction series moving in the downstream direction (i.e., away from the processor and main memory). No other device (including PCIX-to-PCIX bridges) ever originates a locked transaction series that addresses a target that resides downstream of the Host/PCIX bridge.

The Host/PCIX bridge only initiates a locked transaction series when instructed to do so by the processor and only passes it to the PCI-X bus when the processor is targeting a memory device that resides beyond the Host/PCIX bridge (in the PCI-X or PCI bus environment).

PCI-X Bridges Only Pass Locked Series Downstream

A PCI-X bridge will pass a locked transaction series from its primary to its secondary side, but never in the opposite direction. This permits the processor, through the auspices of the Host/PCIX bridge, to perform a locked transaction series with any Completer in the system. It does not, however, permit devices on subordinate PCI-X buses to originate locked transaction series targeting main memory (which would require PCI-X bridge support for upstream movement of locked transactions through the bridge):

- If a PCI-X bridge latches a transaction on its secondary side with LOCK# asserted, it ignores LOCK# (i.e., it does not lock itself) and passes the transaction to its primary side without asserting LOCK# on the primary side.
- If a PCI-X bridge latches a transaction on its primary side with LOCK# asserted, it honors the LOCK# (i.e., it does lock itself) and passes the transaction to its secondary side with LOCK# asserted on the secondary side.

Only EISA Bridge Originates Upstream Locked Traffic

Refer to Figure 25-1 on page 586. The only device that is permitted to originate a locked transaction series moving upstream towards main memory is the PCIX-to-EISA bridge. However, the EISA bridge is not permitted to utilize the PCI-X LOCK# signal to lock the PCI-X bus. Rather, it must utilize sideband signaling to establish a lock on the PCI-X bus. In addition, since PCIX-to-PCIX bridges will not pass a locked transaction series from secondary to primary side with the lock intact, the EISA bridge must reside on PCI-X bus 0 in order to establish a lock on main memory.

As an example, the EISA bridge could assert a sideband signal to the PCI-X bus arbiter in the Host/PCIX bridge to request exclusive ownership of PCI-X bus 0. The Host/PCIX bridge then asserts a return signal to the EISA bridge indicating that the PCIX/EISA bridge will retain ownership of PCI-X bus 0 until it removes the request. The EISA bridge can then perform its locked transaction series with main memory without fear that another master on bus 0 will gain bus ownership. When it has completed its locked transaction series, the EISA bridge releases the arbiter lock by deasserting the signal it had asserted to the arbiter.

In versions of the PCI spec prior to 2.2, the target memory was recommended to lock a 16 byte block of memory (aligned on an address divisible by 16), but could lock its entire memory address space. This still applies for an upstream locked access to main memory by the EISA bridge. For downstream locked accesses, the locked resources are the PCIX-to-PCIX bridges in the path to the Completer (and the Completer could be the EISA bridge).

Application Bridge May or May Not Support Locking

If the system software and the platform hardware design guarantee that a locked transaction series will never cross an application bridge, the bridge would not have to support downstream movement of a locked transaction series through the bridge. If this guarantee does not exist, the bridge must support locking.

EISA Bridge Supports LOCK# As Input, Not as Output

The EISA bridge supports LOCK# as an input because the processor may instruct the Host/PCIX bridge to perform a locked transaction series targeting a memory location on the EISA bus. The EISA bridge does not, however, implement LOCK# as an output pin on its PCI-X interface because (as described in "Only EISA Bridge Originates Upstream Locked Traffic" on page 582) it is not permitted to use the PCI-X locking mechanism.

Non-Bridge Devices Ignore LOCK#

Only the following devices implement the PCI-X LOCK# signal:

- The Host/PCIX bridge implements it as an output so it can originate locked transactions series on the PCI-X bus on behalf of the processor.
- A PCIX-to-PCIX bridge implements LOCK# as an input on its primary interface (because it acts as the target of locked transactions initiated either by the Host/PCIX bridge or by the secondary interface of a PCIX-to-PCIX bridge that resides between the Host/PCIX bridge and this bridge).
- A PCIX-to-PCIX bridge implements LOCK# as an output on its secondary interface (so it can pass locked transactions received on its primary side to its secondary side).

Devices other than bridges do not implement the LOCK# signal either as an output or as an input. When a non-bridge device (such as the Completer in Figure 25-1 on page 586) is targeted and instructed to lock itself, it permits the access but does not lock itself against accesses from initiators other than the initiator that locked it.

Sequence of Events

Refer to Figure 25-1 on page 586. As mentioned earlier in this chapter, the locking mechanism was included in the PCI and PCI-X specs to support an operational characteristic of Intel x86 processors. In some circumstances, the Intel processor instructs the Host/PCIX bridge to perform a locked transaction series (the first of which is always a memory read) that targets a Completer on a PCI-X bus. This means that the processor needs to perform a series of two (or more) transactions in the PCI-X realm (i.e., the Completer resides on a bus beyond the Host/PCIX bridge). This following list details the steps involved in performing a locked transaction series with the Completer illustrated in Figure 25-1 on page 586:

1. The processor initiates a locked transaction series on its Front Side Bus. The first transaction in this series is a memory read.
2. The Host/PCIX bridge initiates the memory read on PCI-X bus 0 and asserts LOCK# to the target.
3. The PCIX-to-PCIX bridge's primary interface is the target of the transaction. It treats the memory read as an SRR (Split Read Request) and issues a Split Response to the initiating bridge's (in this case, the Host/PCIX bridge's) secondary interface.
4. Upon issuing the Split Response, the target bridge's primary interface enters the **target-lock state**. While in the target-locked state, the target bridge's primary interface has the following operating characteristics:
   - It will not accept (i.e., will issue a Retry in response to) any transactions moving downstream from any initiator other than the one that locked it.
   - It will accept any Split Completion transactions that are moving downstream and will pass them to its secondary bus.
5. Upon receiving the Split Response, the initiating bridge's (i.e., the Host/PCIX bridge's) secondary interface enters the **initiator-lock state**. While in the initiator-locked state, the initiating bridge's secondary interface has the following operating characteristics:
   - Upon receipt of the Split Response, it terminates the memory read transaction.
   - It continues to assert LOCK# on its secondary bus to keep the target bridge's primary interface locked.
   - Its secondary interface continues to accept transactions moving upstream to main memory.
   - It can issue unlocked transactions that are not part of its locked transaction series (but it must keep LOCK# asserted throughout them to keep the previously locked target locked). As an example, it can initiate Split Completion transactions returning main memory read data that had been requested in earlier transactions.

     However, the initiating bridge must not depend upon such transactions completing until after the locked transaction series completes (because one or more of these unlocked transactions could address a Completer on the other side of a locked downstream bridge and be terminated with Retry by the bridge until the locked transaction series completes and the bridge is unlocked).
6. The target bridge's secondary interface initiates the memory read on PCI-X bus 1 and asserts LOCK# to instruct the target (the Completer in this case) to lock itself.

7. The Completer issues a Split Response to the PCIX-to-PCIX bridge's secondary interface. This causes the bridge's secondary interface to enter the initiator-lock state.

8. The Completer subsequently initiates a Split Completion transaction to return either the requested read data or a Split Completion Error Message to the PCIX-to-PCIX bridge's secondary interface.

9. When the PCIX-to-PCIX bridge's secondary interface accepts the first Data Phase's data item, its initiator-lock is transformed into a **full-lock**. While in full-lock, the PCIX-to-PCIX bridge's secondary interface has the following operational characteristics:

    - It keeps LOCK# asserted either until the locked transaction series completes, or a fatal error occurs in a subsequent transaction of the series (Target Abort, Master Abort, or it receives a Split Completion Error Message).
    - It will not accept any transactions moving upstream towards main memory (with the exception of Split Completion transactions).

10. The Completer does not lock itself because it is not a bridge.

11. The PCIX-to-PCIX bridge's primary interface initiates the Split Completion transaction to return the read data to the Host/PCIX bridge. Note that the Host/PCIX bridge's secondary interface is still keeping LOCK# asserted to the PCIX-to-PCIX bridge's primary interface while the PCIX-to-PCIX bridge's primary interface performs the Split Completion transaction.

12. When the Host/PCIX bridge's secondary interface has accepted the first data item of the Split Completion, the Host/PCIX bridge's secondary interface transitions from the initiator-lock to the full-lock state. While it remains in the full-lock state, the Host/PCIX bridge's primary interface has the following operational characteristics:

    - It keeps LOCK# asserted either until the locked transaction series completes, or a fatal error occurs in a subsequent transaction of the series (Target Abort, Master Abort, or it receives a Split Completion Error Message).
    - It will not accept any transactions moving upstream towards main memory (with the exception of Split Completion transactions).

13. In addition, the PCIX-to-PCIX bridge's primary interface transitions from the target-lock to the full-lock state. While it remains in the full-lock state, the PCIX-to-PCIX bridge's primary interface has the following operational characteristics:

    - It will not accept (i.e., will issue a Retry in response to) any transactions moving downstream from any initiator other than the one that locked it.
    - It will accept any Split Completion transactions that are moving downstream and will pass them to its secondary bus.

- It will remain in the full-lock state until FRAME# and LOCK# are both sampled deasserted on the same rising-edge of the clock on its primary interface.

Split Completion Error Message Terminates Lock

If an initiating bridge's interface receives a Split Completion transaction that contains an error message (or if it receives a Target Abort or Master Abort), this terminates the locked transaction series. The bridge's secondary interface deasserts LOCK# and exits the locked state. Upon detecting LOCK# and FRAME# deasserted, the PCIX-to-PCIX bridge's primary interface exits the locked state as well.

Figure 25-1: Example System

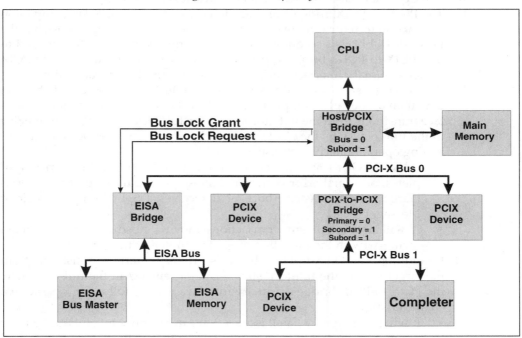

Chapter 25: Locked Transaction Series

Upstream Bridge (Initiating Bridge) Rules

The following rules govern the behavior of a bridge that originates (this would be the Host/PCIX bridge) or passes a locked transaction series downstream to its secondary interface:

1. All Sequences that are part of a locked transaction series must address the same Completer.
2. The first transaction of a locked transaction series must be a read transaction.
3. LOCK# must be deasserted in the Address Phase, then asserted in the clock following the Address Phase (in a DAC transaction, in the clock after the first Address Phase), and, to maintain the lock, must remain asserted until the final transaction in the series completes.
4. LOCK# must be released (i.e., deasserted) if the initial transaction of the locked transaction series is terminated with Retry (the lock was not established).
5. LOCK# must be deasserted whenever a locked Sequence is terminated by Target Abort or Master Abort.
6. To prevent the Host/PCIX bridge from monopolizing the bus, LOCK# must be deasserted between consecutive locked transaction series.
7. To release LOCK#, the initiator must deassert LOCK# for a minimum of one clock while the bus is in the Idle state.

Downstream Bridge (Target Bridge) Rules

The following rules govern the behavior of the primary bridge interface when the primary interface acts as the target of a locked transaction series:

1. A bridge acting as a target of a transaction locks its primary interface when LOCK# is deasserted during the first (or only) Address Phase and is then asserted during the following clock.
2. Once in a locked state, a bridge's primary interface remains locked until both FRAME# and LOCK# are sampled deasserted on the primary bus, regardless of how transactions are terminated on the primary bus.
3. The bridge is not allowed to accept any new requests from the primary bus while it is in a locked state except from the initiator of the locked transaction series. The bridge must accept Split Completions from any initiator while in a locked state.

Arbitration

In case it will have a need to use the locking mechanism, a bridge's secondary interface registers the state of LOCK# and FRAME# on every rising-edge of the clock. If it has a need to perform a locked transaction series, it takes the following actions:

1. If the bridge's copy of LOCK# that it registered from its secondary interface is asserted, this indicates that some other bridge is currently performing a locked transaction series. The bridge will not assert REQ# to request bus ownership to perform its series. Instead, it will keep registering and checking the state of its secondary bus LOCK# and FRAME# signals until it sees both deasserted.
2. Once it has determined that FRAME# and LOCK# are deasserted, the bridge asserts its REQ# signal to arbitrate for bus ownership.
3. While waiting for its GNT#, the bridge's secondary interface continues to monitor the state of LOCK#. If it sees it asserted, this means that some other bridge was granted bus ownership and has started a locked transaction series.
4. When the bridge's secondary interface has acquired bus ownership and LOCK# is still deasserted, it may initiate the first transaction of its locked transaction series.

Starting Locked Transaction Series

Retry/Target Abort/Master Abort Cancels Lock

First Access of Series Receives Retry

General. If the first access (a memory read) of a locked transaction series receives a Retry response from the target, the bridge that initiated the memory read must deassert the LOCK# signal. The initiator has been rejected by the target. The bridge must therefore periodically repeat the memory read until it receives some response other than a Retry from the target.

If Target Is a PCI-to-PCI Bridge. If the device acting as the target of the memory read is a PCI-to-PCI bridge, it issues a Retry to the initiator and enqueues the memory read as a DRR (Delayed Read Request). The target bridge's primary interface is considered locked at that point (even though the bridge that initiated the memory read has not yet received the requested memory read data).

If the Target Is a PCIX-to-PCIX Bridge. If the device acting as the target of the memory read is a PCIX-to-PCIX bridge, it issues a Split Response to the initiator and enqueues the memory read as an SRR (Split Read Request). The target bridge's primary interface is considered locked at that point (even though the bridge that initiated the memory read has not yet received the requested memory read data).

First Access of Series Receives Target or Master Abort

If the first access (a memory read) of a locked transaction series receives a Target Abort response from the target, or if no target responds to the transaction (i.e., the initiator experiences a Master Abort), the bridge that initiated the memory read must deassert the LOCK# signal. As with any Target Abort or Master abort, this is a fatal error and the initiator will not repeat the memory read. Rather, it will register the error and generate an interrupt to invoke its driver to come check its status.

First Transaction Has Immediate Completion

Figure 25-2 on page 592 illustrates a bridge initiating the first transaction of the locked series. As stated in the rules, this must be a memory read transaction. In this example, the Completer responds immediately with the data, indicating that the Completer resides on the secondary bus of the bridge performing the access.

If the device responding as the target had been the primary interface of a bridge on the path to the Completer, it would have issued a Split Response to the initiator and handled the transaction as a Split Read Request (SRR). This is described in the next section.

CLOCK 2.
ON the rising-edge of clock two:
- The initiator (the secondary interface of the Host/PCIX bridge or a PCIX-to-PCIX bridge) starts the memory read transaction.
- As stated in the rules, the initiator must keep LOCK# deasserted during the Address Phase.

CLOCK 3.

ON the rising-edge of clock three:

- The initiator asserts LOCK# on the rising-edge of the clock that immediately follows the Address Phase.
- If the device acting as the target were the primary interface of a bridge in the path to the Completer, the target registers the state of LOCK#. In this case, the device acting as the target is the Completer rather than a bridge, so it ignores the state of LOCK#.
- The target registers the address and command.

DURING clock cycle three:

- If the device acting as the target were the primary interface of a bridge in the path to the Completer (in this case, it is not; the Completer is acting as the target), the target examines the state of its registered copy of LOCK# and establishes that it is deasserted. This is the first prerequisite for establishing a lock.
- The target decodes the address and command and asserts its internal DEVSEL# signal.

CLOCK 4.

ON the rising-edge of clock four:

- If the device acting as the target were the primary interface of a bridge in the path to the Completer, the target registers the state of LOCK#. In this case, the device acting as the target is the Completer rather than a bridge, so it ignores the state of LOCK#.
- The target clocks out its internal, asserted DEVSEL# onto the external DEVSEL# signal.

DURING clock cycle four:

- The initiator backs its output drivers off the AD and C/BE buses in preparation for the target returning the requested read data.
- The target determines that its registered copy of LOCK# is asserted:
  - If the device acting as the target is the Completer, it ignores LOCK# and does not prepare to lock itself.
  - If the device acting as the target is the primary interface of a bridge in the path to the Completer, it prepares to lock itself.

CLOCK 5.

ON the rising-edge of clock five:

- The initiator registers the state of DEVSEL#.
- The target asserts TRDY# and drives out the requested read data. Note that if the device acting as the target were the primary interface of a bridge in the path to the Completer, it would signal Split Response rather than Data Transfer.
- The initiator asserts IRDY# indicating that it's ready to accept the read data item.

DURING clock cycle five:

- The initiator examines its registered copy of DEVSEL# and determines that it has established a connection with the target. This defines the rising-edge of clock six as the first point at which the initiator will register the state of TRDY# to see if the target has presented the read data.

CLOCK 6.

ON the rising-edge of clock six:

- The initiator registers the data and the state of TRDY#.
- The target deasserts TRDY# and DEVSEL# and ceases to drive the data.

DURING clock cycle six:

- The initiator examines the state of its registered copy of TRDY#. Its asserted state indicates that the initiator received the requested read data on the rising-edge of clock five. The lock has been established on the initiating bridge's secondary interface at this point.
- The initiator deasserts its internal IRDY# and FRAME# signals.

CLOCK 7.

ON the rising-edge of clock seven:

- The initiator clocks its internal, deasserted IRDY# and FRAME# signals onto the external IRDY# and FRAME# signals. This returns the bus to the Idle state.
- Although the initiator is backing off the bus, it continues to assert LOCK#, thereby instructing the target to stay locked. Since the device acting as the target is the Completer, it ignores LOCK# and does not lock itself.

Figure 25-2: First Transaction (a read) Experiences Immediate Completion

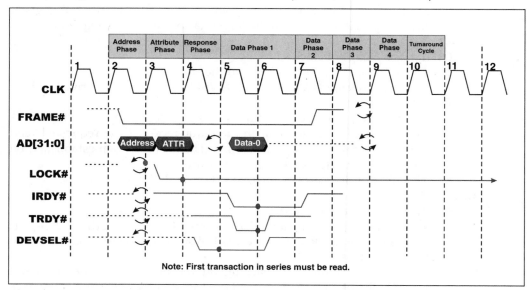

Note: First transaction in series must be read.

First Transaction Receives Split Response

If the device acting as the target of the first transaction (a memory read) is the primary interface of a bridge in the path to the Completer, it treats the read as an SRR and responds with a Split Response. This is illustrated in Figure 25-3 on page 595 and is described below.

It should be noted that if the device acting as the target were the Completer, it also could issue a Split Response to the read, but, unlike the bridge, it will not lock itself.

CLOCK 2.
ON the rising-edge of clock two:
- The initiator (the secondary interface of the Host/PCIX bridge or a PCIX-to-PCIX bridge) starts the memory read transaction.
- As stated in the rules, the initiator must keep LOCK# deasserted during the Address Phase.

Clock 3.

On the rising-edge of clock three:

- The initiator asserts LOCK# on the rising-edge of the clock that immediately follows the Address Phase.
- Since the device acting as the target is the primary interface of a bridge in the path to the Completer, the target registers the state of LOCK#. If the device acting as the target was the Completer rather than a bridge, it ignores the state of LOCK#.
- The target registers the address and command.

During clock cycle three:

- Since the device acting as the target is the primary interface of a bridge in the path to the Completer, the target examines the state of its registered copy of LOCK# and establishes that it is deasserted. This is the first prerequisite for establishing a lock.
- The target decodes the address and command and asserts its internal DEVSEL# signal.

Clock 4.

On the rising-edge of clock four:

- Since the device acting as the target is the primary interface of a bridge in the path to the Completer, the target registers the state of LOCK#.
- The target clocks out its internal, asserted DEVSEL# onto the external DEVSEL# signal.

During clock cycle four:

- The initiator backs its output drivers off of the AD and C/BE buses in preparation for the target returning the requested read data.
- The target determines that its registered copy of LOCK# is asserted (the second prerequisite when establishing a lock on a target bridge's interface):
  - If the device acting as the target were the Completer, it ignores LOCK# and does not prepare to lock itself.
  - Since the device acting as the target is the primary interface of a bridge in the path to the Completer, it prepares to lock itself.

Clock 5.

On the rising-edge of clock five:

- The initiator registers the state of DEVSEL#.
- Since the device acting as the target is the primary interface of a bridge in the path to the Completer, it signals Split Response rather than Data Transfer. The bridge's primary interface asserts TRDY#, deasserts DEVSEL#, and drives out a data pattern of all Fs (a requirement when issuing a Split Response to a read transaction).
- The initiator asserts IRDY# indicating that it's ready to accept the read data item.

Clock 6.

ON the rising-edge of clock six:

- The initiator registers the data, as well as the state of TRDY# and DEVSEL#.
- Having already issued the Split Response to the initiator, the target deasserts TRDY# and backs its output drivers off the AD bus.

DURING clock cycle six:

- The initiator determines that it has received a Split Response from the target. It moves the memory read transaction into its Split Transaction Queue. The lock has been established on:
  - The initiating bridge's secondary interface is in the initiator-lock state.
  - The target bridge's primary interface is in the target-lock state.
- The initiator deasserts its internal IRDY# and FRAME# signals, in preparation for returning the bus to the Idle state, but it keeps its internal LOCK# signal asserted (to maintain the lock on the target).

Clock 7.

ON the rising-edge of clock seven:

- The initiator clocks out a deasserted state onto the external IRDY# and FRAME# signals, returning the bus to the Idle state.
- The initiator keeps LOCK# asserted, however, to maintain the lock on the target.

Figure 25-3: First Transaction (a read) Receives Split Response

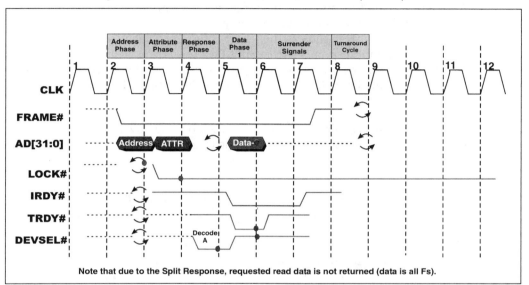

Note that due to the Split Response, requested read data is not returned (data is all Fs).

Continuing Locked Transaction Series

Once the initial locked read has arrived at the Completer, the bridges that reside between the Host/PCIX bridge and the Completer are locked. This means:

- The primary interfaces of the locked bridges will not accept (i.e., will respond with Retry) any transactions (other than Split Completions) initiated by a device other than the one that locked them. If the initiator of a subsequent transaction does not demonstrate its control of the LOCK# signal by deasserting it in the Address Phase and then reasserting it in the clock immediately following the Address Phase (see the LOCK# signal in clocks two and three of Figure 25-4 on page 596 and in Figure 25-5 on page 597), the locked target will respond with a Retry.
- The secondary interfaces of the locked bridges will not accept any transactions that are attempting to move upstream towards main memory (other than Split Completions). Retry will be issued to any transactions that are initiated by devices residing on the bridge's secondary bus.

When the initiating bridge performs a subsequent access in the locked transaction series, there are three possible cases:

- The device that responds as the target is the Completer (see Figure 25-4 on page 596) and it responds immediately.
- The device that responds as the target is the Completer (see Figure 25-5 on page 597) and it responds with a Split Response.
- The device that responds as the target is the primary interface of a bridge in the path to the Completer. It will respond with a Split Response (see Figure 25-5 on page 597).

In Figure 25-4 on page 596 and in Figure 25-5 on page 597, the initiator keeps LOCK# asserted to maintain the lock on the target.

Figure 25-4: Completer Responds Immediately to Subsequent Read Access

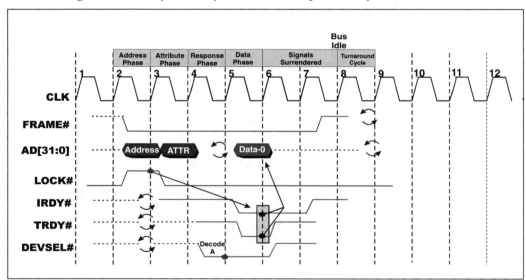

Figure 25-5: Bridge Responds to Subsequent Read Access From Completer

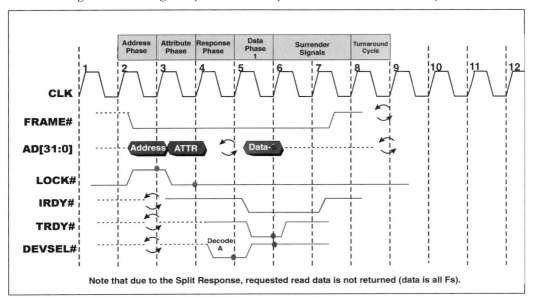

Note that due to the Split Response, requested read data is not returned (data is all Fs).

Attempted Access to Bridge by Device Other Than Owner

In Figure 25-6 on page 598, a device other than the bridge that owns the LOCK# signal issues a transaction request to a target bridge's primary interface which is currently locked. The target bridge's primary interface does not see LOCK# deasserted on the rising-edge of the clock at the end of the transaction's Address Phase (i.e., on the rising-edge of clock three). If the initiator were the one that had established the lock earlier, it would have demonstrated its control of the LOCK# signal by deasserting it in the Address Phase and then reasserting it in the following clock. Upon sensing this attempted access by someone other than its owner, the bridge's primary interface issues a Retry to the initiator on the rising-edge of clock five.

Figure 25-6: Attempted Access by Device Other Than Owner

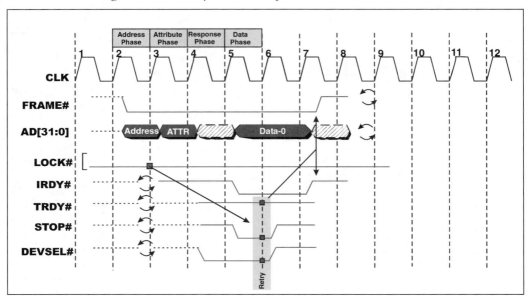

Last Transaction in Locked Series

If Last Transaction Receives Immediate Completion

Assume that a bridge's secondary interface initiates the final transaction of the locked transaction series and that the Completer resides on that bus and responds immediately (i.e., it does not Split the transaction).

As in any transaction after the first one of the series, the initiator (to identify itself to the target) deasserts LOCK# during the Address Phase and then re-asserts it in the clock that immediately follows the Address Phase. The initiator then keeps LOCK# asserted until the data has been transferred. Although the initiating bridge can deassert LOCK# in any clock after the transaction has completed, the spec recommends that the initiating bridge deassert LOCK# when it deasserts IRDY# following the completion of the transaction's last Data Phase (in other words, surrender LOCK# quickly). Waiting longer to deassert LOCK# will keep the target locked unnecessarily and another transaction that addresses the same target would unnecessarily receive a Retry.

Chapter 25: Locked Transaction Series

If Last Transaction Receives Split Response

If the final transaction of locked transaction series receives a Split Response, the initiating bridge's secondary interface keeps LOCK# asserted until the end of the Split Completion transaction that terminates the Sequence (i.e., byte count for the request is satisfied or an error occurs). Although the spec permits the initiating bridge's secondary interface to deassert LOCK# in any clock after the Split Completion has completed, it recommends that the initiating bridge deassert LOCK# when it deasserts TRDY# at the end of the Split Completion.

The Unlocking of a Target Bridge

A target bridge unlocks itself whenever LOCK# and FRAME# are detected deasserted on its primary interface (on the same rising-edge of the clock). The target bridge deasserts LOCK# on its secondary bus in any clock after that, but the spec recommends that it do so as soon as possible to avoid subsequent transactions being terminated with Retry unnecessarily.

When Bridge Starts Second Series Immediately After First

If a bridge wants to perform two, back-to-back locked transaction series, it must ensure that both FRAME# and LOCK# are deasserted at the same time for at least one clock before initiating the second locked transaction series. This ensures that a target bridge locked by the first locked transaction series is unlocked prior to starting the second locked transaction series.

Retry Issued to Owner Not a Problem

After having established a lock on a bridge in the path to the Completer, a subsequent attempt to access the bridge by the locking agent may result in a Retry. This does not mean that the locked bridge is rejecting its owner. Rather, it has a temporary logic busy condition that prevents it from handling the access right now. The initiator merely retries the transaction at a later time and, if the locked bridge is no longer busy, it will accept the transaction.

DAC Command Lock Timing

In the First Access

When in the first transaction of a locked transaction series the initiating bridge is using the DAC command to address a memory location over the 4GB address boundary, LOCK# remains deasserted in the first Address Phase and is asserted in the clock immediately following the first Address Phase (in other words, it's asserted in the second Address Phase).

In Subsequent Accesses of Locked Series

If, in the subsequent transactions of a locked transaction series, the initiating bridge is using the DAC command to address a memory location over the 4GB address boundary, LOCK# is driven to the deasserted state in the first Address Phase and is then reasserted in the clock immediately following the first Address Phase (in other words, it's reasserted in the second Address Phase).

Part 6:
Error Detection and Handling

Previous Part

Part 5 covered the operation of PCIX-to-PCIX bridges as well as some operational aspects of Host/PCIX bridges. It consists of the following chapters:

- Chapter 24: PCIX-to-PCIX Bridges
- Chapter 25: Locked Transaction Series

This Part

Part 6 covers error detection and handling and consists of Chapter 26: Error Detection and Handling.

The Next Part

Part 7 highlights some of the more important aspects of the electrical portion of the PCI-X spec and consists of Chapter 27: Electrical Issues.

26 *Error Detection and Handling*

The Previous Chapter

The previous chapter described the locking mechanism that permits the processor, through the Host/PCIX bridge, to perform a series of transactions to a Completer with the guarantee that no PCI-X Requester upstream of the Completer will be able to access the Completer. In addition, no Requester other than the Host/PCIX bridge (in other words, the processor) will be able to access main memory.

This Chapter

This chapter provides a detailed description of error handling for non-bridge and bridge functions.

The Next Chapter

The next chapter highlights some of the more important aspects of the electrical portion of the PCI-X spec.

Handling of a Target Abort

Introduction

When an initiator starts a transaction, the target may respond by issuing a Target Abort. This is a fatal error and terminates the transaction. There are three scenarios:

- A **Requester may have initiated a transfer request**. The target that responds to the transaction (either the Completer, or a bridge residing in the path to the Completer) may issue a Target Abort to the Requester. This subject is covered in "Requester Receives Target Abort" on page 604.
- In the case of a transfer request that receives a Split Response, the Completer later initiates a Split Completion transaction to return the previously requested read data or a write completion notice. The **target** that responds (either the Requester or a bridge in the path back to the Requester) **may issue a Target Abort in response to the Completer's Split Completion** transaction. This subject is covered in "Completer Receives Target Abort on Split Completion" on page 606.
- A PCIX-to-PCIX **bridge may be re-initiating a transfer request** that was originated by a Requester residing on the other side of the bridge, and the target that responds may issue a Target Abort to the bridge. This subject is covered in "Handling Target Abort on Other Side of Bridge" on page 638.

A detailed description of Target Abort signaling may be found in "Target Abort" on page 290.

Requester Receives Target Abort

In this scenario, the Requester initiated a transfer request and the target that responds to the transaction (either the Completer, or a bridge residing in the path to the Completer) may issue a Target Abort to the Requester. The Target Abort may be issued in any Data Phase of the transaction. This is handled as follows:

- Due to the fatal nature of the error (a Target Abort), the Requester will not repeat the transaction and the Sequence ID is retired and may be reused in a future transaction request.
- The Requester sets the Received Target Abort bit in its PCI configuration Status register (see Figure 26-1 on page 605).
- The target that responded sets the Signaled Target Abort bit in its PCI configuration Status register.
- The Requester then generates an interrupt to invoke a handler to service the error:
  - Assuming that the Requester is capable of generating an interrupt, it will do so, causing an interrupt to the processor. The processor executes the interrupt handler within the Requester's driver and the handler checks the function's Status register to determine the reason for the interrupt. When it determines that the Requester received a Target Abort, it clears the Requester's Received Target Abort status bit. The

handler then checks the Status registers of each function on the Requester's bus to determine which function delivered the Target Abort. The handler clears the Signaled Target Abort bit in the offending target's Status register and then reports the problem back to the OS. The action taken by the OS is OS-specific.

- If the Requester is not capable of generating a function-specific interrupt (i.e., it implements neither an interrupt pin nor MSI capability), it will assert SERR# and set the Signaled System Error bit in its status register (if enabled to do so with the SERR# Enable bit in its Command register (see Figure 26-2 on page 606). Upon detecting the assertion of SERR#, the chipset will typically generate a fatal hardware interrupt (e.g., an NMI in an x86 processor environment), causing the processor to start execution of its fatal hardware error handler. The handler code scans the Status registers in all platform functions to determine which function(s) asserted SERR#. When it detects the Signaled System Error status bit set, it determines that the Received Target Abort status bit is also set. It clears the status bits and scans the bus for the offending target (the one with the Signaled Target Abort set to one in its status register).

Figure 26-1: PCI Configuration Status Register

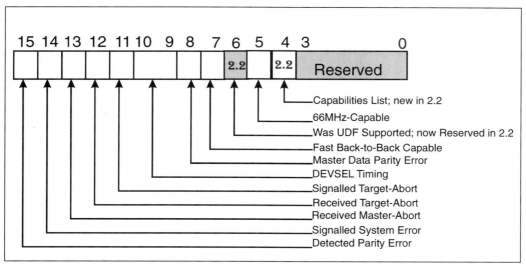

Figure 26-2: PCI Configuration Command Register

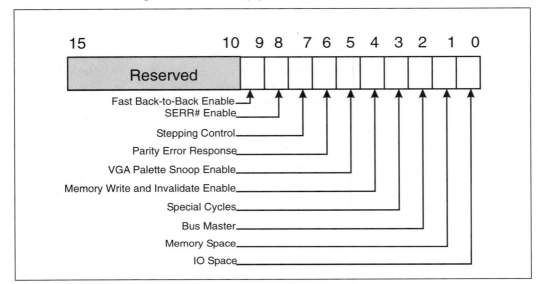

Completer Receives Target Abort on Split Completion

In the case of a transfer request that receives a Split Response, the Completer later initiates a Split Completion transaction to return the previously requested read data or a write completion notice. The target that responds to the Split Completion (either the Requester or a bridge in the path back to the Requester) may issue a Target Abort in response to the Completer's Split Completion transaction.

When Split Completion Target Abort Is Permissible

The Requester is permitted to signal Target Abort in response to a Split Completion only under error conditions in which the integrity of data in the system cannot be guaranteed. An example of such an error condition is a parity error in the Split Completion address. In that case, since the address consists of the bus, device and function number of the targeted Requester as well as its transaction tag, a Split Completion with a corrupted address is either trying to deliver read data or a Split Write completion message to the wrong Requester, or perhaps to

Chapter 26: Error Detection and Handling

the correct Requester, but for the wrong transaction number (i.e., tag). In this case, just as in the PCI environment, all targets that detect an Address Phase parity error must assert SERR# (if enabled to do so via the SERR# Enable bit in their respective Command registers). Also, targets that assert SERR# must set the Signaled System Error and Detected Parity Error bits in their respective Status registers. In addition, the target (i.e., Requester) that appears to be the target of the Split Completion might also assert DEVSEL# and generate a Target Abort.

The spec states the following regarding the target that appears to be addressed by the corrupted Split Completion address:

> "If the device asserts DEVSEL# prior to detecting a parity error in the address or Attribute Phase, the device has the option either to complete the transaction as if no error occurred or to signal Target Abort (even if the transaction is a Split Completion)."

Regarding this text, the author offers this caveat: as already noted, a corrupted Split Completion address is quite serious. If, in addition to asserting SERR#, the Requester chooses (as noted above) to complete the transaction as if no error occurred (i.e., it accepts all of the Split Completion data), it must discard the data (since it either wasn't meant for this Requester or is being supplied to fulfill a different request issued by this Requester).

Assuming that the Requester does signal Target Abort to a Split Completion, it is handled as indicated in the following two sections.

Discard of Completion for a Write or Non-Prefetchable Read

If the Split Request was a write (either IO or configuration) or if it addressed a memory location that has no read side effects (i.e., Prefetchable memory), the Completer must discard the Split Completion and take no further action (i.e., in the Completer no status bits are set, no interrupt is generated, and SERR# is not asserted). The Completer does not set the Received Target Abort bit in its Status register.

The Requester that issued the Target Abort may or may not take any additional action. If it has no outstanding Split requests, it almost certainly would take no additional action (aside from setting its Signaled System Error status bit if it asserted SERR#). If, for example, it were to generate an interrupt to invoke the handler within its driver, the driver would almost certainly be confused because it had not previously issued any transaction requests to its Requester.

Assuming that a Requester issued a Target Abort to the Completer due to a corrupted Split Completion address, there is another Requester somewhere in the system whose Split read or write request will never get a completion. It is expected that all Requesters start an internal timer upon issuing a request and, if a completion is not received within a reasonable amount of time (Requester design-specific as to what's considered to be reasonable), the Requester sets a status bit in a function-specific status register and generates an interrupt to invoke its driver to come check its status.

Discard of Completion for IO, Config, or Prefetchable Memory Read

If the Split Request was a read (IO, memory or configuration) and the location has read side effects (if it was a memory read request, it was from Non-Prefetchable memory), the Completer must discard the Split Completion, set the Split Completion Discarded bit in the PCI-X Status Register (see Figure 26-3 on page 608), and assert SERR# (if enabled via the SERR# Enable bit in the Completer's Command register). The Completer will, of course, also set the Signaled System Error bit in its Status register. The Completer does not set the Received Target Abort bit in its Status register.

Figure 26-3: PCI-X Status Register

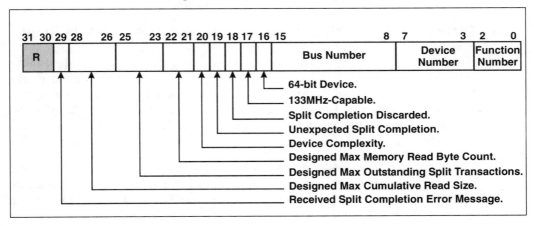

Handling of a Master Abort

Introduction

A Master Abort occurs because the initiator times out without successfully establishing a connection with a target. This is the normal end to a Special Cycle transaction (see "Special Cycle Command" on page 159), but is an bad end to any other transaction type. A detailed description of Master Abort signaling can be found in "Connection Timeout" on page 105. There are three cases:

1. The Requester experiences a Master Abort (see "Requester Handling of Master Abort" on page 609).
2. The Completer experiences a Master Abort when it initiates a Split Completion transaction (see "Completer Handling of Master Abort on a Split Completion" on page 610).
3. A bridge experiences a Master Abort when performing a transaction for an initiator on the other side of the bridge. A description of this scenario can be found in "Handling Master Abort on Other Side of a Bridge" on page 629.

The sections that follow describe the first two cases.

Requester Handling of Master Abort

This discussion assumes that a Requester has initiated a transaction other than a Special Cycle transaction (for more information on the Special Cycle transaction, refer to "Special Cycle Command" on page 159).

Upon sampling DEVSEL# in the deasserted state on four successive rising-edges of the clock, the Requester times out and returns the bus to the Idle state in a graceful manner with no data transferred.

If Host/PCI Bridge Type 0 Config Transaction

If the Requester was the Host/PCI bridge and it was performing a Type 0 Configuration transaction, it takes the actions defined in "Type 0 Configuration Transactions" on page 435.

If Not Host/PCIX Bridge Type 0 Config Transaction

If the Requester was not the Host/PCIX bridge or it was the Host/PCIX bridge but it was performing a transaction other than a Type 0 Configuration transaction, the Requester sets the Received Master Abort bit (see Figure 26-1 on page 605) in its Status register to one. Additional actions taken are specified in the next two sections.

If Requester Capable of Generating Interrupts. Assuming that the Requester is capable of generating an interrupt, it will do so, causing an interrupt to the processor. The processor executes the interrupt handler within the Requester's driver and the handler checks the function's Status register to determine the reason for the interrupt. When it determines that the Requester experienced a Master Abort, it clears the Requester's Received Master Abort status bit. Additional actions taken by the handler in response to the Master Abort are function-specific.

If Requester Can't Generate Interrupts. If the Requester is not capable of generating a Requester-specific interrupt (i.e., it implements neither an interrupt pin nor MSI capability), it will assert SERR# and set the Signaled System Error status bit (if enabled to do so with the SERR# Enable bit in its Command register; see Figure 26-2 on page 606). Upon detecting the assertion of SERR#, the chipset will typically generate a fatal hardware interrupt (e.g., an NMI in an x86 processor environment), causing the processor to start execution of its fatal hardware error handler within the OS. The handler code scans the Status registers in all platform functions to determine which function(s) asserted SERR#. The error is reported and/or logged and the processor is then typically halted or placed in a tight, do-nothing loop.

Completer Handling of Master Abort on a Split Completion

General

The Completer may experience a Master Abort when it initiates a Split Completion transaction. This means that no target will accept the Split Completion. The Completer therefore has an orphan Split Completion on its hands and it stands to reason that this is a very serious error.

A Completer may experience a Master Abort on a Split Completion for one of three reasons:

Chapter 26: Error Detection and Handling

- There is a parity error in the Address Phase of the transaction and no target recognizes the Sequence ID. All targets that detect the parity error will assert SERR# and set the Signaled System Error bits in their respective Status registers (SERR# is asserted assuming that the SERR# Enable bit in their respective Command registers is set to one).
- The Split Completion address has been corrupted in flight, but multiple bits have been affected and, although the address is therefore incorrect, no target detects a parity error. As a result, the Split Completion address is not recognized by any target and DEVSEL# is therefore not asserted in response to the transaction. Since there is no parity error, SERR# isn't asserted by any agent.
- A PCIX-to-PCIX bridge has erroneously passed the Split Completion onto the wrong bus (due to an internal bridge logic failure, or to the bridge's receipt of a Split Completion with a corrupted address but with good parity). As result, the Split Completion address is not recognized by any target and DEVSEL# is therefore not asserted in response to the transaction. Since there is no parity error, SERR# isn't asserted by any agent.

Discard of Completion for a Write or Non-Prefetchable Read

If the Split Request was a write (either IO or configuration) or if it addresses a memory location that has no read side effects (i.e., Prefetchable memory), the Completer must discard the Split Completion and take no further action (i.e., in the Completer no status bits are set, no interrupt is generated, and SERR# is not asserted). The Completer does not set the Received Master Abort bit in its Status register.

There is another Requester somewhere in the system whose Split read or write request will never get a completion. It is expected that all Requesters start an internal timer upon issuing a request and, if a completion is not received within a reasonable amount of time (Requester design-specific as to what's considered to be reasonable), that Requester sets a status bit in a function-specific status register and generates an interrupt to invoke its driver to come check its status.

Discard of Completion of IO, Config, or Prefetchable Memory Read

If the Split Request was a read (IO, memory or configuration) and the location has read side effects (if it was a memory read request, it was from Non-Prefetchable memory), the Completer must discard the Split Completion, set the Split Completion Discarded bit in the PCI-X Status Register (see Figure 26-3 on page 608), and assert SERR# (if enabled via the SERR# Enable bit in the Completer's Command register). The Completer will, of course, also set the Signaled System

Error bit in its Status register. The Completer does not set the Received Master Abort bit in its Status register.

Target Handling of Address or Attribute Phase Parity Error

Upon detecting a parity error in the Address or Attribute Phase of a transaction, a PCI-X target must:

- assert SERR# (if the SERR# Enable bit is set to one in its Command register).
- set the Detected Parity Error bit to one in its Status register.
- set the Signaled System Error bit to one in its Status register.

In addition, if the target appears to be the one addressed by the transaction, the target has the following options:

- If the target detects an Address Phase parity error, it may be designed not to assert DEVSEL#, thereby causing the initiator to experience a Master Abort.
- If the target decodes the address and command and asserts DEVSEL# prior to detecting a parity error in the Address or the Attribute Phase, aside from asserting SERR# and setting the appropriate status bits, the target could be designed to take one of the following actions:
  - complete the transaction in a normal manner.
  - signal Target Abort to the initiator.
- If the target has already issued a Split Response and then detects an Attribute Phase parity error, it must discard the transaction. If the Attribute Phase information has been corrupted, this means that the Requester ID and/or the Byte Transfer Count is incorrect. If the Requester ID is incorrect, the resulting Split Completion would not be recognized by the Requester. If the Byte Transfer Count is incorrect, then the Requester would accept the resulting Split Completion data, but would then discard it.

Data Phase Parity

PCI Chipset Typically Murders System on Data Parity Error

For a brief review of error handling in the PCI environment, refer to "Data Phase Parity Error Recovery Usually Not Possible" on page 21. For a more comprehensive discussion of PCI parity error handling, refer to the chapter entitled *Error Detection and Handling* in the MindShare book entitled *PCI System Architecture, Fourth Edition* or later (published by Addison-Wesley).

Chapter 26: Error Detection and Handling

The fatal flaw in the PCI environment is that most PCI chipsets are designed to monitor the PERR# signal and to issue a fatal hardware interrupt (e.g., an NMI interrupt in the x86 environment) to the processor when PERR# is asserted by any agent. The end result is that, although the PCI spec recommends that recovery from a parity error should be attempted, the generation of a fatal interrupt precludes any hope of error recovery by the bus master, its associated driver, or by the OS. All hope is lost. As an example, in Windows NT, it results in the Blue Screen of Death.

In PCI-X, Chipset Doesn't Monitor PERR#

General

Unlike the typical PCI chipset, the PCI-X chipset is never permitted to monitor PERR# (with murder on its mind) unless it is the initiator of a write transaction. In that case, it behaves like any initiator with respect to checking PERR# to verify that the target received the data without error.

Requester's Data Parity Error Recovery Enable Bit

Basic Description. The PCI-X Command register (Figure 26-4 on page 613) contains the Data Parity Error Recovery Enable bit. This bit is only implemented in a Requester and never in a function that never acts as a Requester. The bit is cleared by the assertion of RST#, so the default action on detection of a Data Phase parity error is to not attempt recovery. More information on the action(s) taken when the bit is cleared can be found in "If Not Set, PCI Compatibility Dictates Murdering System" on page 614.

Figure 26-4: PCI-X Command Register

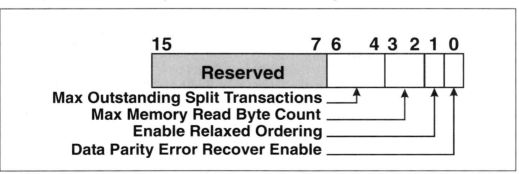

Set by OS or Driver's Initialization Code at Startup Time. During the OS boot process, the OS loads drivers from mass storage into memory for the devices that it or the BIOS have discovered in the system. Upon loading each driver into memory, the OS calls the driver's initialization code entry point. The initialization code within the driver is typically responsible for finishing the configuration and setup of its related device(s). Prior to this point in time, either the BIOS or the OS has already programmed each function's configuration registers with resources (e.g., memory and IO decoders have already been programmed with base address assignments). Some actions typically taken by the driver's initialization code include:

- The driver reads its function's Base Address registers (BARs) to obtain the base address of its application-specific register set (e.g., the base address of the Ethernet adapter's IO or memory-mapped IO register set). These base addresses are stored in the body of the driver to enable it to communicate with its device during run-time.
- The driver performs a series of IO writes or memory-mapped IO writes to its function's application-specific register set to get the function ready for run-time operation.
- If the function generates interrupts when it requires servicing, the driver reads its function's Interrupt Line register to determine what IRQ line its function asserts when it generates interrupt requests. The driver then places a pointer to its interrupt handler entry point in the associated entry in the Interrupt Table in main memory.
- If the driver's interrupt handler incorporates an event handler to deal with Data Phase parity errors, the driver either sets the Data Phase Parity Error Recovery Enable bit directly itself or issues a request to the OS to do so. If the driver does not incorporate such an event handler, the Data Parity Error Recovery Enable bit remains cleared to zero.
- Either the driver itself finally sets the Bus Master Enable, Memory Space, and IO Space bits in the function's Command register (see Figure 26-2 on page 606), or the OS will do so after the driver returns control to it.

If Not Set, PCI Compatibility Dictates Murdering System. During run-time, the Requester may detect a Data Phase parity error (when receiving data in a read, or the target may assert PERR# back to the Requester during a write).

- The Requester sets the Detected Parity Error bit in its Status register if it is a read parity error.

- The target sets the Detected Parity Error bit in its Status register if it is a write parity error.
- The Requester sets the Master Data Parity Error bit in its Status register.

Assume that the following conditions are true at the instant when the parity error is detected by the Requester:

- The Parity Error Response bit in the Requester's Command register is one.
- The Data Parity Error Recovery Enable bit is zero because the Requester's driver doesn't implement a Data Phase parity error handler.

In this case, the Requester will assert SERR# to the chipset and the chipset will generate a fatal hardware interrupt to the processor. In other words, because the driver doesn't implement a Data Phase parity error recovery handler, the action taken is backward-compatible with the typical action taken by PCI chipsets in the event of a Data Phase parity error.

Recovery Must Be Performed Under Software Guidance. The Requester hardware must never attempt Data Phase parity error recovery on its own. Rather, if enabled to do so (i.e., the Data Parity Error Recovery Enable bit is set to one), the Requester generates an interrupt and invokes its driver to service the error.

Driver Reports Error to OS. The intention of the PCI-X spec is that, upon being informed (via an interrupt) of a Data Phase parity error, the driver informs the OS and the OS then instructs the driver on the appropriate action to take in its handler (see next section).

OS Instructs Driver on Action(s) to Take. The OS usually provides an API used by the device driver to report Data Phase parity errors to the OS. The OS may specify that the device driver must perform certain actions to recover from the error. For example, the following is a partial list of actions that the OS might require the device driver to perform:

- Reschedule the failing transaction.
- Notify the user of the failing transaction.
- Re-initialize the card and continue.
- Take the card off-line.

OS Vendor Specifies Who Clears Parity Error Status Bits. When a Data Phase parity error has occurred, status bits are set in one or more devices:

- The Master Data Parity Error bit is set in the Requester's Status register.
- The Detected Parity Error bit is set in the Requester or target's Status register.
- Status bits may be set in the status registers of one or more bridges residing between the Requester and the Completer.

The OS vendor defines which software entity has the responsibility of clearing these bits after the error has been handled.

Requester Handling of PERR# With Split Response

Data Error Received With Split Response on Read

The target can issue a Split Response in response to any of the following read transactions:

- Memory Read Dword.
- IO Read.
- Configuration Read.
- Interrupt Acknowledge.
- Memory Read Block.

Refer to Figure 26-5 on page 618. When a target issues a Split Response in response to a read transaction, it is indicating that the read data will be returned later in a series of one or more Split Completion transactions. However, the spec does require the target to provide a data value of all ones (see clock five) along with the Split Response and it requires that the parity be correct for the all ones data pattern delivered in the clock that TRDY# is asserted (clock five in the figure) plus the state of the Byte Enables in the clock prior to the one in which the data is driven (clock four in the figure). Although not pictured in the figure, the parity bit must be driven to the appropriate value one clock after the data is driven.

When the Requester detects a parity error in the first Data Phase of a read and the target terminates the transaction with a Split Response, the Requester:

- Must (assuming that the Parity Error Response bit in its Command register is set to one) set the Master Data Parity Error bit in its Status register.
- Must set the Detected Parity Error bit in its Status register.
- Must (assuming that the Parity Error Response bit in its Command register is set to one) assert PERR#.

- If the Data Parity Error Recovery Enable bit is not set in the Requester's PCI-X Command register (see "Requester's Data Parity Error Recovery Enable Bit" on page 613), the Requester must also assert SERR# and set the Signaled System Error bit in its status register (assuming that its SERR# Enable bit is set to one in its Command register).

It should be noted that this is an interesting situation because the data parity error has nothing whatsoever to do with the requested read data. The target that issued the Split Response will subsequently initiate a Split Completion transaction to return the requested read data and the read data may be delivered without error.

Upon detecting the error in the Split Response data pattern, the Requester could be designed to set a bit in a device-specific status register to note the event, but the spec recommends that the Requester not generate an interrupt to report the error until after all of the requested read data has been returned by the Completer in a subsequent Split Completion transaction(s). The Requester then generates the interrupt to invoke its device driver. This avoids the possibility of the interrupt handler believing that the read data has arrived at the Requester before it actually has. Upon entry to the handler, the handler would check the status of the device and discover that there had been a parity error on the Split Response data pattern and the resulting actions (if any) taken by the handler are handler-specific.

Figure 26-5: Example Split Response on a Read

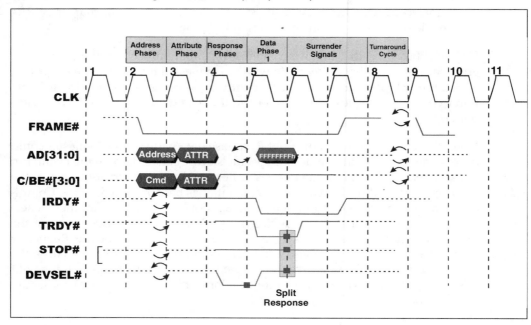

Data Error Received With Split Response on Dword Write

Refer to Figure 26-6 on page 619. When a dword write (an IO Write or a Configuration Write) is terminated by the target with a Split Response, the target snarfs (i.e., quietly latches) a copy of the write data as well as the Byte Enable settings. As in any other write transaction, the Requester must drive the parity bit (not shown in the figure) for the data and Byte Enables one clock after it drives the write data and asserts IRDY# (the data is driven in the fourth clock cycle of the transaction; the fifth if the Requester uses the Dual-Address Cycle command).

- The target checks the parity and asserts PERR# back to the Requester (assuming that its Parity Error Response bit is set to one in its Command register).
- The target also sets the Detected Parity Error bit to one in its Status register.
- The Completer will later perform a Split Completion transaction and will return a Split Completion Message (SCM) indicating that a Split Write Data Parity Error was detected.

When the Requester detects PERR# asserted, it means that the data item and/or Byte Enables were corrupted in flight and the target has received bad data and/or Byte Enables to deliver to the target location(s).

Upon detection of PERR#, the Requester will set the Master Data Parity Error bit in its Status register to one (assuming that the Parity Error Response bit in its Command register is set to one). The spec doesn't indicate what action the Requester will take when it detects PERR# asserted along with the receipt of the Split Response, but it is the author's opinion that it will not take any action at that time. Because the target issued a Split Response, it is required to return a subsequent SCM indicating (in this case) that a Split Write Data Parity Error was detected. Upon receipt of the SCM, the Requester will generate an interrupt to invoke the interrupt handler within its driver and deliver the error. At that point, it's interrupt handler/function-specific what action(s) will be taken.

Figure 26-6: Example Dword Write Receiving Split Response

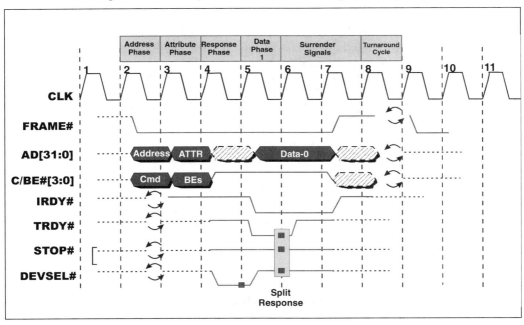

Requester/Completer Handling of Data Error During Split Completion

During a Split Completion transaction, the Completer is the source of the data, the Byte Enables and the parity bit. The Requester acts as the target and checks the parity for correctness immediately after it receives each data item. If the Requester detects a data parity error:

- The Requester sets the Detected Parity Error bit in its Status register.
- The Requester sets the Master Data Parity Error bit in its Status register. Though it is the target of the Split Completion, it was the originator of the request and is therefore responsible for reporting the error to software.

The author hasn't been able to find anywhere in the spec where it clearly says whether or not the Requester must accept all of the data in this case, but believes this to be the case. When all of the requested data (or the write completion message) has been received, the Requester will either:

- Assert SERR# if the Data Parity Error Recovery Enable bit in its PCI-X Command register is not set (assuming that the SERR# Enable bit in its Command register is set to one).
- If the Data Parity Error Recovery Enable bit in its PCI-X Command register is set, it generates an interrupt and reports the error to the interrupt handler within its device driver. For more information on the Data Parity Error Recovery Enable bit, refer to "Requester's Data Parity Error Recovery Enable Bit" on page 613.

Split Read Errors

General

A dword or burst read request may encounter an error at any of three stages:

- An error may be encountered **during** the **issuance of** the **read request**. The error can take one of three forms:

- An **Address Phase parity error**. This subject is covered in "Target Handling of Address or Attribute Phase Parity Error" on page 612.
- An **Attribute Phase parity error**. This subject is covered in "Target Handling of Address or Attribute Phase Parity Error" on page 612.
- A **data parity error** during the Data Phase. This subject is covered in "Data Error Received With Split Response on Read" on page 616.

- An error may be encountered after the **Completer** receives the request and **attempts** to **read** the data **from internal locations**. The sections that follow describe the actions taken in this situation.
- A data parity error may be encountered **during** the **delivery of** the **requested read data in a Split Completion** transaction. This subject is covered in "Requester/Completer Handling of Data Error During Split Completion" on page 620.

Read Data Returned in One or More Split Completions

This section assumes that the Completer has received the read request without error and is currently accumulating (i.e., reading) the requested read data from internal locations in order to fulfill the request. The Completer will return the requested read data in a series of one or more Split Completion transactions.

The Completer could accumulate all of the requested read data and then arbitrate for the bus to return it to the Requester. Although in this case it is the Completer's intention to perform a single Split Completion transaction to return all of the requested read data, the Split Completion transaction may have to traverse a PCIX-to-PCIX bridge to get to the Requester. The bridge may not currently have sufficient internal buffer space available to accept all of the requested read data. In this case, acting as the target of the Split Completion, the bridge will issue a Disconnect At Next ADB to the Completer as it approaches a buffer-full condition. The Completer is then obliged to end the transaction at the next block boundary and will have to rearbitrate for bus ownership and then must initiate another Split Completion to resume read data delivery at the point of disconnection. The point is, although the Completer has all of the requested read data ready to deliver in a single Split Completion transaction, it may be forced (by buffer-availability issues within a bridge) to perform a series of Split Completions to return all of the data to the Requester.

On the other hand, the Completer may start to accumulate the requested read data in an internal buffer and then arbitrate for bus ownership to start returning read data before it actually has all of the data ready to deliver. In this case, the

Completer may run out of data during the initial Split Completion transaction. As it approaches a temporary buffer-dry condition, the Completer would therefore issue a Disconnect At Next ADB to the target (the Requester or a bridge that resides between the Completer and the Requester). When it has more data buffered up for delivery, the Completer would re-arbitrate for bus ownership and initiate another Split Completion transaction to continue data delivery to the Requester.

Internal Completer Error Can Occur at Any Time

At any point during this process, the Completer may encounter an internal problem that will prevent it from returning all of the requested read data. It may have already performed a series of one or more Split Completions without error, or it may encounter an internal error that prevents it from returning any of the requested read data successfully.

At any point during the fulfillment of the read request, the Requester must therefore be prepared for the possible receipt of a Split Completion Message (SCM) indicating that the Completer has encountered a problem that prevents it from returning the remaining read data. It could occur in the very first Split Completion transaction or in any subsequent Split Completion associated with the original read request.

Receipt of SCM Terminates Read Sequence

Receipt of an SCM terminates a Sequence regardless of how many bytes remain to be sent. The presence of the error message is indicated by a one in the SCM Attribute bit (see Figure 26-7 on page 622), and a one in the SCE (Split Completion Error) bit. The message (SCM) is a 32-bit data value delivered in the one and only Data Phase of this Split Completion transaction. The two sections that follow define the effect of the SCM on both the Requester and any bridge residing between the Completer and the Requester.

Figure 26-7: Split Completion Attributes Format

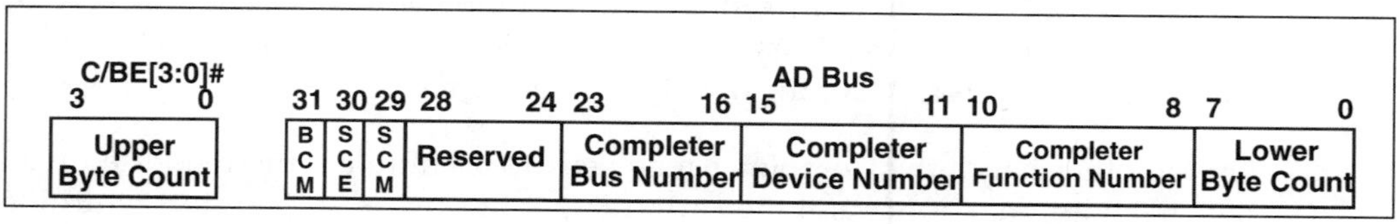

C/BE[3:0]#		AD Bus					
3 0	31 30 29 28 24	23 16	15 11	10 8	7 0
Upper Byte Count	B C M / S C E / S C M / Reserved	Completer Bus Number	Completer Device Number	Completer Function Number	Lower Byte Count

Effect of SCM on a Bridge

If the request was a burst read, the Byte Count field in the SCM (see Figure 26-8 on page 623) indicates the number of bytes that were not sent for this Sequence (due to the error), and the Remaining Lower Address field indicates the lower seven bits of the starting address of the remainder of the Sequence. A bridge uses this information to release buffer space that it may have reserved to hold the read data requested by the Requester (because the remaining read data will not be returned by the Completer due to the internal error).

If the Split Request was a dword transaction, the Completer sets the:

- Remaining Lower Address field to zero.
- 12-bit Upper and Lower Remaining Byte Count fields to a value of four.

Figure 26-8: SCM Format

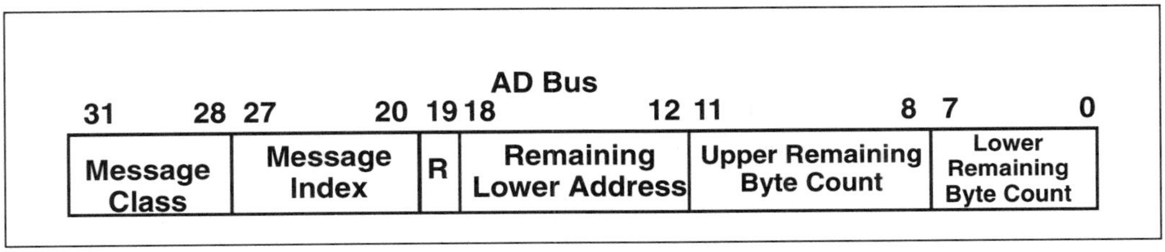

			AD Bus			
31 28	27 20	19 18	12	11	8	7 0
Message Class	**Message Index**	R	**Remaining Lower Address**	**Upper Remaining Byte Count**		**Lower Remaining Byte Count**

Effect of SCM on the Requester

Upon receipt of the SCM, the set state of the SCE bit informs the Requester that an error has occurred. The nature of the error is indicated by the Message Class and Message Index fields (see Figure 26-8 on page 623). In the case of an internal read error within the Completer, these field values are:

- Message Class = 2h (Completer Error Class). See Table 26-1 on page 624.
- Message Index = 8Xh (Device-Specific Error). See Table 26-2 on page 625.

Please note that the spec does not state that this is the class/index delivered on a read error, but there really are no other choices, so this has to be it. The request wasn't a write and the device reporting the error is the Completer, not a bridge. Furthermore, within the Completer Error Class, the only applicable choice is the Device-Specific Error index value.

The Requester will hold the least-significant nibble of the device-specific error code (the Xh portion of the 8Xh value) in an internal, device-specific register and generates an interrupt to invoke the interrupt handler within its device driver. The actions taken by the handler are device-specific and are outside the scope of the spec. For additional information regarding a device-specific Completer class error, refer to "Handling Completer Device-Specific Error" on page 629.

Table 26-1: Currently Defined Message Classes

Message Class	Description
0h	**Write Completion Class**.
1h	**PCI-X bridge Error Class**. An error was encountered on the other side of a bridge.
2h	**Completer Error Class**. An error was encountered within the Completer.
3h-Fh	Reserved for future assignment.

Table 26-2: Message Class 2h: Completer Error Message Class Index Values

Message Index Value	Description
00h	**Byte Count Out-of-Range**. This message can only occur for a burst memory read wherein the end address (as specified by the byte count) exceeds the end address of the Completer addressed in the Address Phase. • Prior to initiating the Split Completion containing this SCM, the Completer must return all data between the start address and the Completer's end address via one or more Split Completion transactions. • When the Requester receives this message, it generates an interrupt request to invoke the interrupt handler within its device driver. The driver then checks a device-specific status register to determine the nature of the problem. • The spec takes the point of view that a Requester attempting to perform a burst read beyond a target's address boundary is a rare case. The device driver may or may not implement an error handler for this condition. If it doesn't, the error is fatal. The driver may have a handler, however, that will issue another read request to its Requester, causing it to initiate another burst memory read starting at the next address.
01h	**Split Write Data Parity Error**. On an IO or Configuration Write, the Completer may signal a Split Response, but also detect corrupted write data. In this case, the Completer asserts PERR# to the initiator of the write when it issues the Split Response and subsequently sends it this SCM message in the Split Completion. The initiator of the write sets the Master Data Parity Error bit in its Status register. If the initiator of the write is a bridge, it sets the Master Data Parity Error bit in the status register associated with the destination bus (Status register if the parity error occurred on the bridge's primary side; Secondary Status register if it occurred on its secondary side).
02h-7Fh	Reserved for future assignment.

Table 26-2: Message Class 2h: Completer Error Message Class Index Values (Continued)

Message Index Value	Description
8Xh	**Device-Specific Error**. If the Completer detects an error other than Byte Count Out-of-Range or a Split Write Data Parity Error, it sends a device-specific error message back to the Requester. The message value is 8Xh, where "Xh" represents one of 16 possible device-specific error codes. Naturally, only device-specific software (such as the device's driver) would know how to interpret these error codes. Also refer to "Device-Specific Error Handling" on page 325.
90h-FFh	Reserved for future assignment.

Requester Handling of Unexpected Split Completion

Each Requester maintains a queue of one or more previously issued transactions that received Split Responses and were suspended to await fulfillment. This is referred to as its Split Transaction Queue.

When the Completer is ready to return a write completion message or the read data previously requested by a Split Transaction, the Completer initiates a Split Completion transaction. It uses the Sequence ID issued in the initial request as the address in the Split Completion transaction's Address Phase. A Requester with one or more outstanding requests in its Split Transaction queue uses the Sequence ID delivered in the Split Completion's Address Phase to determine whether or not to claim the transaction (i.e., assert DEVSEL#) and to identify which transaction is being addressed for fulfillment.

Upon latching and examining a Split Completion address, a Requester may experience a match on its Requester ID but determine that the Tag portion of the Sequence ID supplied in the Split Completion's Address Phase does not match any of its outstanding Split Transactions. In this case, the Requester has two options:

- It can ignore the transaction by not asserting DEVSEL#. In this case, the Completer will experience a Master Abort. This scenario is covered in "Completer Handling of Master Abort on a Split Completion" on page 610.
- It can claim the transaction (assert DEVSEL#). In this case, the Requester must accept all of the data supplied by the Completer and then discard it

(because the Requester did not request the data). The Requester also must set the Unexpected Split Completion bit in its PCI-X Status register (see "Unexpected Split Completion (this is also not a good thing!)" on page 480). It then generates an interrupt to invoke the interrupt handler within its driver. The handler checks its status and determines that its Requester has received an unexpected Split Completion. The resulting action(s) taken by the handler is device-specific.

Requester Handling of Split Completion Error Messages

Handling Completer Byte Count Out-of-Range Error

This error is Index 00h in the Completer Message Class (class 2h).

Memory Writes Never Split, so SCMs Don't Apply

This message (as well as any other SCM) does not apply to a burst memory write transaction because memory writes are always posted and are never Split.

Read Immediate Treated Same as Write at Device Boundary

Assume that a Requester issues a memory read burst transaction, that it is claimed by a target, and the target immediately starts supplying the requested read data to the Requester (as opposed to issuing a Split Response and returning the requested data in a later Split Completion transaction). It is possible that the byte transfer count issued in the Attribute Phase defines an end address that lies beyond the target's last location. In this case, the target continues to supply read data to the Requester until the transaction approaches its end address. It then issues a Disconnect At Next ADB to the Requester, forcing it to prematurely end the transaction before all of the requested read data has been received. If the Requester chooses to rearbitrate for bus ownership and resume the read at the point of disconnection, it does not have to use the same Sequence ID. This is a totally new transaction and is treated as such by the target that responds. That target may immediately start supplying read data or may issue a Split Response.

Split Read Straddling Device Boundary Causes SCM

If the target of a burst read issues a Split Response to the Requester, it has committed to return the requested read data in a series of one or more Split Completion transactions to be performed at a later time. Upon examining the end address defined by the start address and the specified byte transfer count, the Completer may discover that the end address lies beyond its last location.

In this case, the Completer must return all of the requested read data between the start address and its last location in a series of one or more Split Completion transactions. It must then issue a final Split Completion transaction to return a Split Completion error message. The transaction has the following characteristics:

- In the transaction's Attribute Phase, the SCM and SCE bits are set to one (see Figure 26-7 on page 622).
- The message (see Figure 26-8 on page 623) must indicate Message Class 2h (the Completer Message Class; see Table 26-1 on page 624).
- The Message Index must be 00h (Byte Count Out-of-Range; see Table 26-2 on page 625).

Read Burst Straddling Device Boundary Considered Rare Case

From the spec's point of view, a normally functioning Requester (or, more likely, its associated driver) understands the address range of the Completer it is attempting to read from and does not request read data that straddles the boundary between the targeted Completer and another device.

However, a Requester is permitted to initiate a burst read that crosses a device boundary only if:

- it knows the Completer will execute the transaction as an Immediate Transaction (because that means the Requester and its driver won't have to deal with the Byte Count Out-of-Range error message; see "Read Immediate Treated Same as Write at Device Boundary" on page 627), or
- the Requester is prepared for a Split Completion Message indicating the request is out of range. In other words, the Requester's interrupt handler within its driver includes an error handler that gracefully handles the error.

Upon receipt of this error message, the Requester will set a device-specific status bit to indicate the nature of the problem (byte count out-of-range) and generates an interrupt to invoke the interrupt handler within its driver. Upon determining the nature of the problem, the driver then instructs the Requester to perform another burst memory read starting where the previous one left off.

Handling Completer Split Write Data Parity Error

This error is Index 01h in the Completer Message Class (class 2h). By sending this message in response to an IO or Configuration Write request, the Completer is indicating that it detected a write data parity error when the initiator issued the original transaction request. For more information, refer to "Data Error Received With Split Response on Dword Write" on page 618.

Handling Completer Device-Specific Error

This error is Index 8Xh in the Completer Message Class (class 2h), where Xh represents the device-specific error code. The Completer returns this error code to the Requester if it encounters an internal error other than those represented by any of the other currently defined Completer Class errors (see Table 26-2 on page 625). For an example of a device-specific error, refer to "Split Read Errors" on page 620.

Handling Master Abort on Other Side of a Bridge

Error Description

This error is Index 00h in the Bridge Message Class (class 1h). A PCIX-to-PCIX bridge attempted to pass a Requester's transaction to the side of the bridge that the Completer resides on, but the transaction was not claimed by any target (i.e., DEVSEL# was sampled deasserted in the A, B, C, and Subtractive time slots).

The Master Abort affects status bits within the bridge (as defined in the next section) and, if the transaction it was forwarding was not a memory write, the bridge must send an SCM back to the Requester. If the transaction was a memory write, the bridge does not generate an SCM. Its actions are defined in "Bridge Memory Write Master Aborts" on page 632.

The sections that follow describe the effects of the Master Abort on both the bridge and on the Requester.

Effect of Master Abort on Bridge

The actions taken by the bridge depend on:

- the current state of the Master Abort Mode bit in the bridge's Bridge Control register (note that this bit only affects the bridge's behavior in the case of a memory write that results in a Master Abort; for all other transaction types, the state of this bit has no effect),
- the transaction type that was forwarded, and
- which side of the bridge the Master Abort was encountered on.

The sections that follow define the actions taken for each transaction type. The current state of the Master Abort Mode bit and the side of the bridge the abort occurred on are covered for each transaction case.

Bridge Interrupt Acknowledge Master Aborts. This case will never occur because PCIX-to-PCIX bridges do not pass an Interrupt Acknowledge transaction through in either direction. As in PCI, this means that the Interrupt Controller must reside on PCI-X bus 0 (i.e., the bus directly on the other side of the Host/PCI-X bridge).

Bridge Special Cycle Master Aborts. This case will never occur because PCIX-to-PCIX bridges do not pass a Special Cycle transaction through in either direction. As in PCI, this means that any logic responsible for observing processor-initiated Special Cycle transactions must reside on PCI-X bus 0 (i.e., the bus directly on the other side of the Host/PCI-X bridge).

However, it should be noted that a bridge could receive a Special Cycle Request on either interface (in the form of a Type 1 Configuration Write transaction), and the targeted bus is the one on the other side of the bridge. In that case, the bridge will experience a Master Abort when it performs the Special Cycle transaction, but Master Abort is the natural end to a Special Cycle transaction and is not an error. For a detailed description of the Special Cycle transaction, refer to "Special Cycle Command" on page 159, and "Special Cycle Command" on page 235. For a detailed discussion of the Special Cycle Request, refer to MindShare's book entitled *PCI System Architecture, Fourth Edition* or later (published by Addison-Wesley).

Bridge IO Read Master Aborts. IO Reads that traverse a PCIX-to-PCIX bridge are always treated as Split Transactions. When a bridge forwards an IO Read through and it ends in a Master Abort, the bridge takes the following actions:

Chapter 26: Error Detection and Handling

- It sets the Received Master Abort bit in either the Status register if the abort occurred on its primary side; or the Secondary Status register if the abort occurred on its secondary side.
- The bridge creates an SCM using the Bridge Message Class (1h) and an Index of 00h and initiates a Split Completion transaction on the Requester side of the bridge to return the SCM to the Requester. This transaction has the following characteristics:
  - In the Split Completion transaction, the Split Completion address (see Figure 26-9 on page 631) the bridge uses is created using the information originally supplied in the Requester's Address and Attribute Phases.
  - If the abort occurred on the bridge's primary side, in the Split Completion's Attribute Phase (see Figure 26-10 on page 631) the Completer ID consists of the Bus, Device and Function Number fields from the bridge's PCI-X Status register (see Figure 26-11 on page 632).
  - If the abort occurred on the bridge's secondary side, in the Split Completion's Attribute Phase the Completer ID consists of the bus number value copied from the bridge's Secondary Bus Number register, and the Device and Function Number fields are cleared to zero.
  - The SCM and SCE bits are set to one, the BCM bit is cleared to zero, and the byte count is set to four (as it is in all Split Completions that deliver a message).

Figure 26-9: Split Completion Address Format

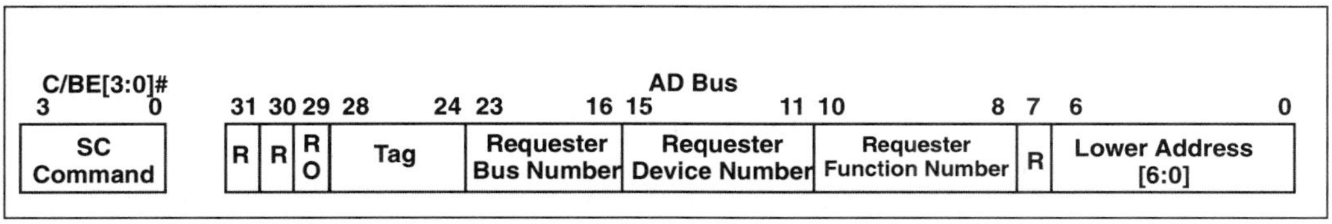

C/BE[3:0]# 3 0	31 30 29 28 24 23 16 15 11 10 8 7 6 0
SC Command	R	R	RO	Tag	Requester Bus Number	Requester Device Number	Requester Function Number	R	Lower Address [6:0]

Figure 26-10: Split Completion Attribute Format

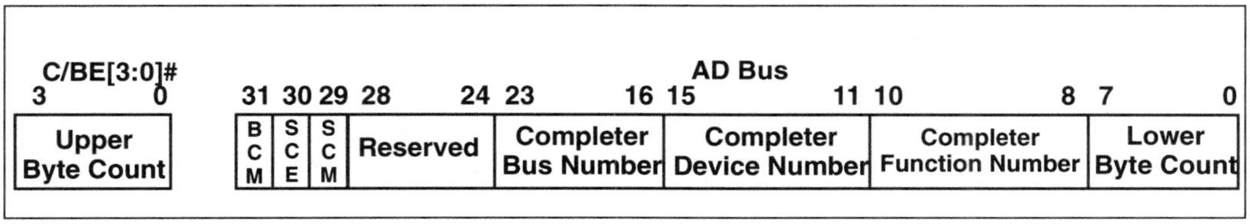

C/BE[3:0]# 3 0	31 30 29 28 24 23 16 15 11 10 8 7 0
Upper Byte Count	BCM	SCE	SCM	Reserved	Completer Bus Number	Completer Device Number	Completer Function Number	Lower Byte Count

Figure 26-11: PCI-X Bridge Status Register

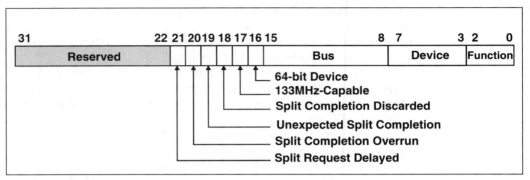

Bridge IO Write Master Aborts. An IO Write that traverses a PCIX-to-PCIX bridge is always treated as a Split Transaction. In the event of a Master Abort on the destination bus, the bridge behavior is identical to that described in "Bridge IO Read Master Aborts" on page 630.

Bridge Configuration Read Master Aborts. A Configuration Read (either Type 0 or Type 1) that traverses a PCIX-to-PCIX bridge is always treated as a Split Transaction. In the event of a Master Abort on the destination bus, the bridge behavior is identical to that described in "Bridge IO Read Master Aborts" on page 630.

Bridge Configuration Write Master Aborts. A Configuration Write (either Type 0 or Type 1) that traverses a PCIX-to-PCIX bridge is always treated as a Split Transaction. In the event of a Master Abort on the destination bus, the bridge behavior is identical to that described in "Bridge IO Read Master Aborts" on page 630.

Bridge Memory Read Dword Master Aborts. A Memory Read Dword that traverses a PCIX-to-PCIX bridge is always treated as a Split Transaction. In the event of a Master Abort on the destination bus, the bridge behavior is identical to that described in "Bridge IO Read Master Aborts" on page 630.

Bridge Memory Write Master Aborts. While all other transaction types that traverse a PCIX-to-PCIX bridge are handled as Split Transactions (with the exception of Split Completion transactions), a memory write that must traverse a bridge is always handled as a posted-write. How a bridge handles a Memory Write, Memory Write Block, or Alias to Memory Write Block transaction that ends in a Master Abort depends on the current state of the Master Abort Mode bit in the Bridge Control register. When the bridge is performing a memory write transaction to dump the contents of its posted-write buffer, it handles a Master Abort as follows:

- It sets the Received Master Abort bit in either the Status register if the abort occurred on its primary side; or the Secondary Status register if the abort occurred on its secondary side.
- If the bridge starts the memory write (that experiences the abort) while the originator of the write data is still performing the burst memory write on the other side of the bridge, the bridge, acting as the target of the burst memory write on the other bus, must issue a Disconnect At Next ADB. It must discard all of the write data associated with the disconnected write that is still residing in its posted-write buffer.
- If the initiator that originated the write data on the other side of the bridge has already ended its memory write burst transaction, the bridge must discard all of the write data associated with that write transaction that is still residing in its posted-write buffer.
- If the Master Abort Mode bit is cleared, the bridge takes no further action on the error.
- If the Master Abort Mode bit is set, the bridge asserts SERR# on the primary side and sets the Signaled System Error bit in its status register (if the SERR# Enable bit in its Command register is set to one).

Bridge Memory Read Ends in Master Abort. A Memory Read Block (or Alias) that traverses a PCIX-to-PCIX bridge is always treated as a Split Transaction. In the event of a Master Abort on the destination bus, the bridge behavior is identical to that described in "Bridge IO Read Master Aborts" on page 630.

Bridge Split Completion Ends in Master Abort. There are two possible scenarios wherein a PCIX-to-PCIX bridge performs a Split Completion transaction:

- The bridge forwards a Split Completion transaction generated by the Completer to return completion data (or a message) to the Requester.
- The bridge forwards a Split Completion transaction generated by another bridge further along the path to the Completer.

A bridge forwards a Split Completion transaction back to the Requester and, if no target claims the transaction, it results in a Master Abort on the destination bus. When this occurs, the bridge takes the following actions:

- If the abort occurs on the primary side of the bridge, the bridge sets the Received Master Abort bit in the Status register (see Figure 26-1 on page 605) and the Split Completion Discarded bit in the PCI-X Bridge Status register (see Figure 26-11 on page 632).
- If the abort occurs on the secondary side of the bridge, the bridge sets the Received Master Abort bit in the Secondary Status register (see Figure 26-12 on page 634) and the Split Completion Discarded bit in the PCI-X Secondary Status register (see Figure 26-13 on page 635).

In both cases, the bridge discards the Split Completion data and asserts SERR# on its primary side (assuming that the SERR# Enable bit is set to one in its Command register), regardless of the state of the Master Abort Mode bit in its Bridge Control register.

Figure 26-12: Bridge's Secondary Status Register

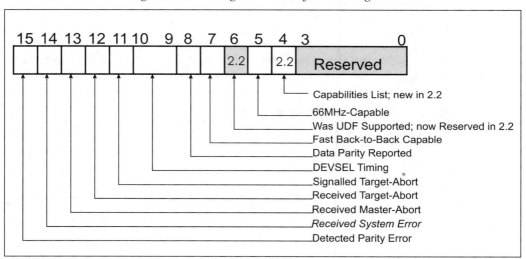

Figure 26-13: Bridge's PCI-X Secondary Status Register

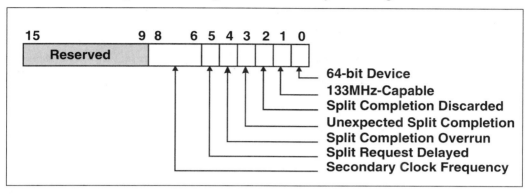

Effect of Master Abort SCM on Requester

When the Requester receives a Split Completion containing an error message indicating that a bridge on the path to the Completer experienced a Master Abort while performing a request issued by the Requester, the manner in which the Requester handles the error depends on the type of transaction as well as the nature of the Requester. The sections that follow describe how the Requester handles the error message for each transaction type.

Requester Interrupt Acknowledge Gets Master Abort SCM. The Host/PCI bridge is the only Requester that will perform the Interrupt Acknowledge transaction. When the processor is interrupted by an external hardware interrupt, it suspends execution of the currently executing program and performs an Interrupt Acknowledge on its Front Side Bus (FSB) to obtain the interrupt vector from the Interrupt Controller. The Host/PCI bridge in turn initiates an Interrupt Acknowledge transaction on the PCI-X bus to make the interrupt vector request visible to the Interrupt Controller (which resides within a device on PCI-X bus zero).

Since PCIX-to-PCIX bridges do not forward Interrupt Acknowledge transactions in either direction, there is no possibility that the Host/PCI bridge will receive an SCM indicating that a Master Abort occurred on the other side of a bridge.

Requester Special Cycle Gets Master Abort SCM. This transaction will never result in the Bridge Class Master Abort message. See "Bridge Special Cycle Master Aborts" on page 630.

Requester IO Read or IO Write Gets Master Abort SCM. When a Requester that had issued an IO Read or Write subsequently receives an SCM indicating that a bridge on the path to the Completer experienced a Master Abort while attempting the IO operation, this is a critical error (it's highly unlikely that a Requester would perform an IO operation and not care that it failed to connect with a target). In response to receipt of this message, the Requester would set the Received Split Completion Error Message bit in its PCI-X Status register (see Figure 26-3 on page 608). In addition, the Requester must also set the Received Master Abort bit in its Status register (see Figure 26-1 on page 605).

The Requester would then generate an interrupt to invoke the interrupt handler within its driver to service the error. Although the resulting actions taken by the driver are device-specific, the driver almost certainly would treat this as a critical error.

Requester Configuration Read Gets Master Abort SCM. Ultimately, the originator of all Configuration transactions is the Host/PCI-X bridge under the guidance of the configuration software being executed by the processor. When the Host/PCI-X bridge issues a Configuration Read request and receives a Split Response, it may subsequently receive an SCM indicating that a bridge on the path to the Completer experienced a Master Abort while attempting the Configuration Read. The Host/PCI-X bridge then takes the following actions:

- It sets the Received Split Completion Error Message bit in its PCI-X Status register (see Figure 26-3 on page 608).
- In addition, the bridge must also set the Received Master Abort bit in its Status register (see Figure 26-1 on page 605).

Just as in PCI, when the Host/PCIX bridge experiences a Master Abort on a Configuration Read, it must return read data of all ones to the processor. Therefore, upon receipt of the Bridge Class Master Abort SCM, the Host/PCIX bridge supplies read data of all ones to the processor. See additional information in the next section.

Requester Configuration Write Gets Master Abort SCM. The originator of all Configuration transactions is the Host/PCI-X bridge under the guidance of the configuration software being executed by the processor. After the Host/PCI-X bridge issues a Configuration Write request and receives a Split Response, it may subsequently receive an SCM indicating that a bridge on the path to the Completer experienced a Master Abort while attempting the Configuration Write. The Host/PCI-X bridge then takes the following actions:

- It sets the Received Split Completion Error Message bit in its PCI-X Status register (see Figure 26-3 on page 608).
- In addition, the bridge must also set the Received Master Abort bit in its Status register (see Figure 26-1 on page 605).

Just as in PCI, when the Host/PCI bridge experiences a Master Abort on a Configuration Write, it must tell the processor that the write completed without error. The PCI spec has always included this rule (mainly, for the sake of completeness). Therefore, upon receipt of the Bridge Class Master Abort SCM, the Host/PCI bridge permits the processor that initiated the write request to complete its write transaction without error.

It is the author's opinion, however, that writing to a function's configuration registers before discovering if the function exists is just plain silly. It has always been the intention of the PCI spec that the very first access to a PCI function's configuration space would read from its Vendor ID register. If a value of all ones is returned, it means that function does not exist within the targeted device. In that case, the programmer must remember to clear the Received Master Abort bit in the Host/PCIX bridge's Status register and, if the Received Split Completion Error Message bit is set in the Host/PCIX bridge's PCI-X Status register, this indicates that the Master Abort was actually experienced by a PCIX-to-PCIX bridge further out in the hierarchy. The error handler software scans all PCIX-to-PCIX bridges to determine which of them generated the error message and clears the Received Master Abort status bit in its Secondary Status register.

Requester Memory Read Dword Gets Master Abort SCM. The description in "Requester IO Read or IO Write Gets Master Abort SCM" on page 636 also holds true for a Memory Read Dword transaction that receives an SCM indicating that a bridge along the path to the Completer experienced a Master Abort.

Requester Memory Write Gets Master Abort SCM. Memory write transactions (Memory Write, Memory Write Block, and Alias) are always posted and are never Split. A Requester will therefore never receive an SCM related to a memory write.

Requester Memory Read Gets Master Abort SCM. The description in "Requester IO Read or IO Write Gets Master Abort SCM" on page 636 also holds true for a Memory Read Block (or Alias) transaction that receives an SCM indicating that a bridge along the path to the Completer experienced a Master Abort.

Requester Split Completion Gets Master Abort SCM. Split Completion transactions are generated by the Completer or by a bridge that resides between the Completer and Requester (when a bridge initiates the Requester's transaction on the Completer's bus and the Completer treats it as an immediate transaction). The Requester never initiates a Split Completion transaction and therefore will never receive an SCM in response to one.

For a discussion of the Completer's response when it experiences a Master Abort on a Split Completion transaction, refer to "Completer Handling of Master Abort on a Split Completion" on page 610. For a discussion of a PCIX-to-PCIX bridge's response when it experiences a Master Abort on a Split Completion transaction, refer to "Bridge Split Completion Ends in Master Abort" on page 633.

Handling Target Abort on Other Side of Bridge

Error Description

This error is Index 01h in the Bridge Message Class (class 1h). A PCIX-to-PCIX bridge attempted to pass a Requester's transaction to the side of the bridge that the Completer resides on. The transaction was claimed by a target (i.e., DEVSEL# was sampled asserted), but the target then issued a Target Abort to the bridge.

The Target Abort affects status bits within the bridge (as defined in the next section) and, if the transaction it was forwarding was not a memory write, the bridge must send an SCM back to the Requester. If the transaction was a memory write, the bridge does not generate an SCM. Its actions are defined in "Bridge Memory Write Master Aborts" on page 632.

The sections that follow describe the effects of the Target Abort on both the bridge and on the Requester.

Effect of Target Abort on Bridge

The actions taken by the bridge depend on:

* the transaction type that was forwarded, and
* which side of the bridge the Target Abort was encountered on.

The sections that follow define the actions taken for each transaction type. In each transaction case, the side of the bridge the abort occurred on affects the bridge's resulting actions.

Bridge Interrupt Acknowledge Target Aborts. This case will never occur because PCIX-to-PCIX bridges do not pass an Interrupt Acknowledge transaction through in either direction. As in PCI, this means that the Interrupt Controller must reside on PCI-X bus 0 (i.e., the bus directly on the other side of the Host/PCI-X bridge).

Bridge Special Cycle Target Aborts. This case will never occur because PCIX-to-PCIX bridges do not pass a Special Cycle transaction through in either direction. As in PCI, this means that any logic responsible for observing processor-initiated Special Cycle transactions must reside on PCI-X bus 0 (i.e., the bus directly on the other side of the Host/PCI-X bridge). Furthermore, it is illegal for any target to respond in any way (including Target Abort) to a Special Cycle transaction. Master Abort is the natural end to a Special Cycle transaction and is not an error.

For a detailed description of the Special Cycle transaction, refer to "Special Cycle Command" on page 159, and "Special Cycle Command" on page 235. For a detailed discussion of the Special Cycle Request, refer to MindShare's book entitled *PCI System Architecture*, *Fourth Edition* or later (published by Addison-Wesley).

Bridge IO Read Target Aborts. IO Reads that traverse a PCIX-to-PCIX bridge are always treated as Split Transactions. When a bridge forwards an IO Read through and it ends in a Target Abort, the bridge takes the following actions:

- It sets the Received Target Abort bit in either the Status register if the abort occurred on its primary side; or the Secondary Status register if the abort occurred on its secondary side.
- The bridge creates an SCM using the Bridge Message Class (1h) and an Index of 01h and initiates a Split Completion transaction on the Requester side of the bridge to return the SCM to the Requester. This transaction has the following characteristics:
  - In the Split Completion transaction, the Split Completion address (see Figure 26-9 on page 631) the bridge uses is created using the information originally supplied in the Requester's Address and Attribute Phases.
  - If the abort occurred on the bridge's primary side, in the Split Completion's Attribute Phase (see Figure 26-10 on page 631) the Completer ID consists of the Bus, Device and Function Number fields from the bridge's PCI-X Status register (see Figure 26-11 on page 632).

- If the abort occurred on the bridge's secondary side, in the Split Completion's Attribute Phase the Completer ID consists of the bus number value copied from the bridge's Secondary Bus Number register, and the Device and Function Number fields are cleared to zero.
- The SCM and SCE bits are set to one, the BCM bit is cleared to zero, and the byte count is set to four (as it is in all Split Completions that deliver a message).

Bridge IO Write Target Aborts. An IO Write that traverses a PCIX-to-PCIX bridge is always treated as a Split Transaction. In the event of a Target Abort on the destination bus, the bridge behavior is identical to that described in "Bridge IO Read Target Aborts" on page 639.

Bridge Configuration Read Target Aborts. A Configuration Read (either Type 0 or Type 1) that traverses a PCIX-to-PCIX bridge is always treated as a Split Transaction. In the event of a Target Abort on the destination bus, the bridge behavior is identical to that described in "Bridge IO Read Target Aborts" on page 639.

Bridge Configuration Write Target Aborts. A Configuration Write (either Type 0 or Type 1) that traverses a PCIX-to-PCIX bridge is always treated as a Split Transaction. In the event of a Target Abort on the destination bus, the bridge behavior is identical to that described in "Bridge IO Read Target Aborts" on page 639.

Bridge Memory Read Dword Target Aborts. A Memory Read Dword that traverses a PCIX-to-PCIX bridge is always treated as a Split Transaction. In the event of a Target Abort on the destination bus, the bridge behavior is identical to that described in "Bridge IO Read Target Aborts" on page 639.

Bridge Memory Write Target Aborts. While all other transaction types that traverse a PCIX-to-PCIX bridge are handled as Split Transactions (with the exception of Split Completion transactions), a memory write (Memory Write, Memory Write Block, and Alias) that must traverse a bridge is always handled as a posted-write. When the bridge is performing a memory write transaction to dump the contents of its posted-write buffer, it handles a Target Abort as follows:

- It sets the Received Target Abort bit in either the Status register if the abort occurred on its primary side; or the Secondary Status register if the abort occurred on its secondary side.

- If the bridge starts the memory write (that experiences the abort) while the originator of the write data is still performing the burst memory write on the other side of the bridge, the bridge, acting as the target of the burst memory write on the other bus, must issue a Disconnect At Next ADB. It must discard all of the write data associated with the disconnected write that is still residing in its posted-write buffer.
- If the initiator that originated the write data on the other side of the bridge has already ended its memory write burst transaction, the bridge must discard all of the write data associated with that write transaction that is still residing in its posted-write buffer.
- The bridge asserts SERR# on the primary side and sets the Signaled System Error bit in its status register (if the SERR# Enable bit in its Command register is set to one).

Bridge Memory Read Block Ends in Target Abort. A Memory Read Block (or Alias) that traverses a PCIX-to-PCIX bridge is always treated as a Split Transaction. In the event of a Target Abort on the destination bus, the bridge behavior is identical to that described in "Bridge IO Read Target Aborts" on page 639.

Bridge Split Completion Ends in Target Abort. There are two possible scenarios wherein a PCIX-to-PCIX bridge performs a Split Completion transaction:

- The bridge forwards a Split Completion transaction generated by the Completer to return completion data (or a message) to the Requester.
- The bridge forwards a Split Completion transaction generated by another bridge further back along the path to the Completer.

If a bridge forwards a Split Completion transaction back to the Requester and it results in a Target Abort on the destination bus, the bridge takes the following actions:

- If the abort occurs on the primary side of the bridge, the bridge sets the Received Target Abort bit in the Status register (see Figure 26-1 on page 605) and the Split Completion Discarded bit in the PCI-X Bridge Status register (see Figure 26-11 on page 632).
- If the abort occurs on the secondary side of the bridge, the bridge sets the Received Target Abort bit in the Secondary Status register (see Figure 26-12 on page 634) and the Split Completion Discarded bit in the PCI-X Secondary Status register (see Figure 26-13 on page 635).
- In both cases, the bridge discards the Split Completion data and asserts SERR# on its primary side and sets the Signaled System Error bit in its status register (if the SERR# Enable bit in its Command register is set to one).

Effect of Target Abort SCM on Requester

When the Requester receives a Split Completion containing an error message indicating that a bridge on the path to the Completer experienced a Target Abort while performing a request issued by the Requester, the manner in which the Requester handles the error depends on the type of transaction as well as the nature of the Requester. The sections that follow describe how the Requester handles the Bridge Class Target Abort error message for each transaction type.

Requester Interrupt Acknowledge Gets Target Abort SCM. The Host/PCIX bridge is the only Requester that will perform the Interrupt Acknowledge transaction. When the processor is interrupted by an external hardware interrupt, it suspends execution of the currently executing program and performs an Interrupt Acknowledge on its Front Side Bus (FSB) to obtain the interrupt vector from the Interrupt Controller. The Host/PCIX bridge in turn initiates an Interrupt Acknowledge transaction on the PCI-X bus to make the interrupt vector request visible to the Interrupt Controller (which resides within a device on PCI-X bus zero).

Since PCIX-to-PCIX bridges do not forward Interrupt Acknowledge transactions in either direction, there is no possibility that the Host/PCIX bridge will receive an SCM indicating that a Target Abort occurred on the other side of a bridge.

Requester Special Cycle Gets Target Abort SCM. It is illegal for any target to respond in any way to a Special Cycle transaction, so it is never split and therefore will never result in an SCM indicating a Bridge Class Target Abort message. See "Bridge Special Cycle Master Aborts" on page 630.

Requester IO Read or IO Write Gets Target Abort SCM. When a Requester that had issued an IO Read or Write subsequently receives an SCM indicating that a bridge on the path to the Completer experienced a Target Abort while attempting the IO operation, this is a critical error. In response to receipt of this message, the Requester would set the Received Split Completion Error Message bit in its PCI-X Status register (see Figure 26-3 on page 608). In addition, the Requester must also set the Received Target Abort bit in its Status register (see Figure 26-1 on page 605).

The Requester would then generate an interrupt to invoke the interrupt handler within its driver to service the error. Although the resulting actions taken by the driver are device-specific, the driver would treat this as a critical error.

Requester Configuration Read Gets Target Abort SCM. The originator of all Configuration transactions is the Host/PCI-X bridge under the guidance of the configuration software being executed by the processor. When the Host/PCI-X bridge issues a Configuration Read request and receives a Split Response, it may subsequently receive an SCM indicating that a bridge on the path to the Completer experienced a Target Abort while attempting the Configuration Read. The Host/PCI-X bridge then takes the following actions:

- It sets the Received Split Completion Error Message bit in its PCI-X Status register (see Figure 26-3 on page 608).
- In addition, the Host/PCIX bridge must also set the Received Target Abort bit in its Status register (see Figure 26-1 on page 605).

The Host/PCIX bridge would then generate an interrupt to invoke the interrupt handler within its driver. The driver would detect the bridge's Received Target Abort bit set to one in the bridge's Status register. It would also detect the Received Split Completion Error Message bit set in the bridge's PCI-X Status register. This means that the Target Abort was actually experienced by a PCIX-to-PCIX bridge further out in the hierarchy, so the driver would scan the system's PCI-X buses looking for the bridge that has the Received Target Abort bit set in either its Status or Secondary Status register. The driver would then scan all of the functions on the bridge's primary or secondary side looking for the culprit that issued the Target Abort (it will have the Signaled Target Abort bit set to one in its Status register). The driver would be responsible for clearing the error bits set in the Host/PCIX bridge as well as those set in the PCIX-to-PCIX bridge's and the target's status registers.

A Target Abort is a very serious error and the driver will most likely end up passing it to the OS. At that point, it's OS-specific what actions will be taken (but it won't be pretty).

Requester Configuration Write Gets Target Abort SCM. Same as previous section.

Requester Memory Read Dword Gets Target Abort SCM. The description in "Requester IO Read or IO Write Gets Target Abort SCM" on page 642 also holds true for a Memory Read Dword transaction that receives an SCM indicating that a bridge along the path to the Completer experienced a Target Abort.

PCI-X System Architecture

Requester Memory Write Gets Target Abort SCM. Memory write transactions (Memory Write, Memory Write Block, and Alias) are always posted and are never Split. A Requester will therefore never receive an SCM related to a memory write.

Requester Memory Read Gets Target Abort SCM. The description in "Requester IO Read or IO Write Gets Target Abort SCM" on page 642 also holds true for a Memory Read Block (or Alias) transaction that receives an SCM indicating that a bridge along the path to the Completer experienced a Target Abort.

Requester Split Completion Gets Target Abort SCM. Split Completion transactions are generated by the Completer or by a bridge that resides between the Requester and Completer (when a bridge initiates the Requester's transaction on the Completer's bus and the Completer treats it as an immediate transaction). The Requester never initiates a Split Completion transaction and therefore will never receive an SCM in response to one.

For a discussion of the Completer's response when it experiences a Target Abort on a Split Completion transaction, refer to "Completer Receives Target Abort on Split Completion" on page 606. For a discussion of a PCIX-to-PCIX bridge's response when it experiences a Master Abort on a Split Completion transaction, refer to "Bridge Split Completion Ends in Target Abort" on page 641.

Handling Split Write Data Parity Error on Other Side of Bridge

Error Description

This error is Index 02h in the Bridge Message Class (class 1h). A PCIX-to-PCIX bridge attempted to pass a Requester's IO Write or Configuration Write transaction to the side of the bridge that the Completer resides on. The bridge drives the write data and the Byte Enables to the target and the target detects a parity error and asserts PERR# to the bridge.

Bridge May Deliberately Forward a Bad Split Write...

If the bridge detects a data parity error on the originating bus for an IO Write or a Configuration Write that it must forward across the bridge, the bridge, acting as the target of the write, asserts PERR# on the originating bus. It sets the

Detected Parity Error bit in its status register for the originating bus (Status register for primary side; Secondary Status register for secondary side). Assuming that the bridge also issues a Split Response to the initiator, it is then obliged to forward the transaction, and must later perform a Split Completion transaction to communicate the success or failure of the write to the Requester. In forwarding the write, the bridge must be a faithful messenger and must therefore drive bad parity to the Completer.

...Or Split Write May Become Corrupted When Bridge Forwards It

In this case, the target on the destination bus asserts PERR# to the bridge's interface upon receipt of the corrupted data. There are two possible scenarios:

- The target asserts TRDY# to accept the data. In this case, the initiating bridge sets the Master Data Parity Error bit in the status register associated with the initiating bridge interface (Status register if it's the primary interface; Secondary Status register if it's the secondary interface). The bridge creates a Split Completion Error Message with the bridge error class (class 1h) and the index value for a corrupted write (index 02h).
- The target may issue a Split Response (as well as signaling PERR# back to the initiating bridge). In this case, the target will respond with a subsequent Split Completion transaction containing an error message.

Effect of Split Write Data Parity Error on Bridge

In either case (see previous two sections), when the bridge performs the write on the destination bus, the target will assert PERR# back to the bridge upon receipt of the bad data and/or Byte Enables. For a description of the bridge's handling of a Split Write data parity error, refer to "Scenario 2: Data Parity Error on Split Write" on page 551.

Effect of Split Write Data Parity Error on Requester

Upon receipt of a Split Completion Error Message indicating that a write Data Phase parity error occurred on the other side of a bridge (Index 02h in the Bridge Message Class), the Requester will:

- Set the Received Split Completion Error Message bit in its Status register,
- Set an error bit in a device-specific status register to indicate the nature of the error, and
- Generate an interrupt to invoke its driver.

The driver will then check its status to determine the nature of the error and will take a series of device-specific actions to handle the error.

Usage of SERR#

SERR# is asserted under the following circumstances (note that in each case, it is assumed that the device has been enabled to assert SERR# via the SERR# Enable bit in its Command register or, if it's a bridge, via the SERR# Enable bit in its Command register or Bridge Control register):

- Each device that detects an Address or Attribute Phase parity error will assert SERR#.
- If a Data Phase parity error is detected by the Requester and the Data Parity Error Recovery Enable bit in its PCI-X Command register is cleared to zero, it will assert SERR#.
- If a Requester detects a Master Abort or a Target Abort and it does not have the ability to generate an interrupt to invoke an error handler within its driver, then it will assert SERR#.
- If a Split Completion transaction initiated by a Completer or a bridge in the path between the Completer and the Requester terminates with a Master Abort or a Target Abort and if the original request was a read from an IO location or non-Prefetchable memory, the Completer or the bridge must discard the Split Completion, set the Split Completion Discarded bit in its PCI-X Status Register, and assert SERR#.
- If one of bridge's interfaces is operating in PCI mode and it is forced to discard a Delayed Read Completion (DRC) or a Delayed Write Completion (DWC) because the originating PCI master neglected to repeat the transaction on a timely basis (somewhere between 2^{10} and 2^{15} clocks after the bridge received the DRC or DWC), and the Discard Timer SERR# Enable bit is set to one in the Bridge Control register, then the bridge will assert SERR#.
- If a bridge initiates a Split Completion transaction containing a Split Completion Error Message and it detects a Data Phase Parity Error (i.e., the target asserts PERR# back to the bridge) when it sends the message to the Requester, then the bridge will assert SERR#.
- If a bridge accept a posted memory write without error and then detects PERR# asserted when it performs the posted write on the destination bus, the bridge will assert SERR#.
- If a bridge accept a posted memory write without error and then experiences a Master Abort when it performs the posted write on the destination bus, the bridge will assert SERR#. It also sets the Received Master Abort status bit to one in the appropriate status register (Status register if the abort

was detected on its primary interface; Secondary Status register if detected on its secondary interface). If the burst memory write transaction in still in progress on the originating bus, the bridge will disconnect it on an ADB.

In addition, a PCI-X device asserts SERR# under all of the same circumstances that are specified for PCI devices in the PCI 2.2 spec.

Part 7:
Electrical Issues

Previous Part

Part 6 covered error detection and handling and consists of Chapter 26: Error Detection and Handling.

This Part

Part 7 highlights some of the more important aspects of the electrical portion of the PCI-X spec and consists of Chapter 27: Electrical Issues.

27 *Electrical Issues*

The Previous Chapter

The previous chapter provided a detailed description of error handling for non-bridge and bridge functions.

This Chapter

This chapter highlights some of the more important aspects of the electrical portion of the PCI-X spec.

Introduction

It is not the author's intention to cut-and-paste all of the tables and notes from the electrical portion of the spec into this chapter. Rather, this chapter is intended to highlight some important issues related to the electrical design. The reader is urged to consult the electrical portion of the spec for a detailed description of the electrical aspects of PCI-X system and device design.

LVS Bus

As described in "PCI-X Is a Low-Voltage Swing (LVS) Bus" on page 83, the PCI-X bus runs at relatively high speeds and must be implemented as a 3.3 Volt signaling environment.

Attention to Detail

In any high-speed bus design, the system board designer must pay close attention to trace layout, impedance, crosstalk, and inductance. The device designer must pay close attention to trace layout on add-in cards as well as driver/receiver characteristics.

PCI-X System Architecture

Most Parameters Tighter Than PCI

Many of the timing and design parameters specified for 66 and 133MHz PCI-X operation are tighter than those specified for a PCI bus implementation. Rather than attempt to highlight all of those differences here, the reader is urged to study the comparison tables and figures in the electrical portion of the specification. The spec writers listed the 33MHz PCI, 66MHz PCI, 66MHz PCI-X, and 133MHz PCI-X characteristics in side-by-side comparison tables and also superimposed the PCI-X output high and output low driver I/V curves over the PCI curves.

Maximum Number of Loads and Connectors on Bus

As discussed in "Maximum Reliable Speed Verified by Design and Testing" on page 63, the system designer engages in strenuous testing to establish the maximum speed at which a bus may be reliably run.

Cards Keyed as 3.3 Volt or Universal Cards

PCI-X add-in cards must be keyed as 3.3V cards or as Universal cards. For detail on add-in card keying, refer to the chapter entitled *Add-In Cards and Connectors* in the MindShare book *PCI System Architecture, Fourth Edition* (published by Addison-Wesley).

133MHz PCI-X Device Must Support 66MHz PCI

The spec dictates that 133Mhz-capable PCI-X devices must support both 33 and 66MHz PCI operation. A 66MHz-capable PXI-X device must support 33MHz PCI, and may optionally support 66MHz PCI.

Add-In Card Trace Lengths

The add-in card trace length specifications in the PCI-X spec differ from those in the PCI 2.2 spec in the following manner:

- In the 2.2 PCI spec, no minimum trace length is specified for the signals associated with the lower half of the bus. The PCI-X spec calls out a minimum trace length of 0.75 inches. This was added to give the system board designer a more accurate idea of the minimum trace lengths on each card. To ensure proper operation of the reflective wave bus, this is important when performing trace length budgeting.

- The 2.2 PCI spec called out no minimum trace length and a maximum trace length of 2.0 inches for the 64-bit extension signals on an add-in card. PCI-X adds a minimum trace length of 1.75 inches (to facilitate system board trace length budgeting). It has also extended the maximum trace length to 2.75 inches. While this technically makes PCI-X non-compliant with the PCI spec, it was necessary because many designers found it difficult to impossible to meet the 2.0 inch maximum specified in the PCI spec.

- While the PCI spec does not specify a minimum or a maximum for the length of the RST# trace on the add-in card, the PCI-X spec dictates a minimum length of 0.75 inches and a maximum length of 3.0 inches. This was done to ensure that the initialization pattern and REQ64# remain stable for the appropriate time after the rising-edge of RST#.

Initialization Pattern Setup/Hold Time

General

The Source Bridge must ensure that the initialization pattern is stable for a minimum of 10 clock cycles prior to the removal of RST# and that the pattern is held on the bus for no longer than 50ns (it can be any value between 0 and 50ns).

Trhff Must Be Taken Into Account

The PCI 2.2 spec dictates that the Source Bridge must ensure that no initiator starts a transaction for a minimum of five clock cycles after the removal of RST#. This time interval is referred to as Trhff (Time from RST# high to first FRAME# assertion) and is guaranteed by designing the arbiter within the Source Bridge so that no initiator is granted ownership during this time interval.

At a clock speed of 133MHz, each clock cycle is 7.5ns in duration. Five clock cycles is therefore 37.5ns, while six clock cycles would be 40ns in duration. If the arbiter is designed to grant bus ownership to a requesting initiator within five or six clocks after RST# is removed, the Source Bridge must make sure that it limits the initialization pattern hold time to less than this period. The following must also be taken into account:

"Any signals in the initialization pattern asserted after the rising edge of RST# must be deasserted no later than two clocks before the first FRAME# and must be floated no later than one clock before FRAME# is asserted."

IDSEL Routing

General

As discussed in "Device Selection" on page 426, the Source Bridge routes the outputs of its Device decoder (i.e., the IDSEL signals) over the upper AD lines as shown in Table 27-1 on page 654. As shown, the spec dictates that the Source Bridge itself is always Device 0 on its secondary bus. The spec also recommends that in systems with add-in board connectors that route the IDSELs over AD bus, the first four add-in board connectors are recommended to be connected as shown in Table 27-1 on page 654 to minimize the length of the IDSEL traces. It's interesting to note that this is consistent with the slot numbering defined in the PCI spec. For more information, refer to the section entitled *Chassis/Slot Numbering* in the MindShare book *PCI System Architecture, Fourth Edition* (published by Addison-Wesley).

Table 27-1: Routing of IDSELs to Upper AD Lines

IDSEL for Device Number:	Is always routed to the Device over AD Line:
0	AD[16]. Note that Device 0 is always the Source Bridge for the bus.
1	AD[17]; recommended that it be connected to add-in card connector one.
2	AD[18]; recommended that it be connected to add-in card connector two.
3	AD[19]; recommended that it be connected to add-in card connector three.
4	AD[20]; recommended that it be connected to add-in card connector four.
5	AD[21]

Table 27-1: Routing of IDSELs to Upper AD Lines (Continued)

IDSEL for Device Number:	Is always routed to the Device over AD Line:
6	AD[22]
7	AD[23]
8	AD[24]
9	AD[25]
10	AD[26]
11	AD[27]
12	AD[28]
13	AD[29]
14	AD[30]
15	AD[31]

IDSEL Series Resistor Value

The PCI-X spec defines the value of the series resistors that connect the appropriate upper AD trace to the device's IDSEL pin as 2K Ohms +/-5%.

Appendix A

Protocol Rules

Protocol Rules

Introduction

This appendix is provided as a convenience for the reader and contains all of the protocol rules listed in the spec. The reader should note that all section references (e.g., "See Section 2.12.1 for dual address cycles") are references to sections within the PCI-X spec itself.

General Bus Rules

The following rules generally apply to all transactions:

1. As in conventional PCI, the first clock in which FRAME# is asserted is the Address Phase. In the Address Phase, the AD bus contains the starting address (except Split Completion, Interrupt Acknowledge, or Special Cycle) and the C/BE# bus contains the command. (See Section 2.12.1 for dual address cycles.)
2. Except as listed below, the starting address of all transactions is permitted to be aligned to any byte. As in conventional PCI, the starting address of Configuration Read and Configuration Write transactions is aligned to a DWORD boundary. Split Completion transactions use only a partial starting address as described in Section 2.10.3. As in conventional PCI, Interrupt Acknowledge and Special Cycle transactions have no address.
3. The Attribute Phase follows the Address Phase(s). C/BE[3::0]# and AD[31::00] contain the attributes. C/BE[7::4]# and AD[63::32] are reserved and driven high by 64-bit initiators. The attributes include additional information about the transaction.
4. The C/BE# bus is reserved (driven high) the clock after the Attribute Phase.
5. Burst transactions include the byte count in the attributes. The byte count indicates the number of bytes between the first byte of the transaction and the last byte of the Sequence, inclusive.
6. DWORD transactions do not use a byte count.
7. The target Response Phase is one or more clocks after the Attribute Phase and ends when the target asserts DEVSEL#.

8. As in conventional PCI, there are no Data Phases if the target does not assert DEVSEL#, resulting in a Master Abort. All other transactions have one or more Data Phases following the target Response Phase.

9. As in conventional PCI, transactions using the I/O Read, I/O Write, Configuration Read, Configuration Write, Interrupt Acknowledge, and Special Cycle commands are initiated only as 32-bit transactions (REQ64# deasserted). Memory Read DWORD commands also have the same restriction in PCI-X mode. In PCI-X, the length of all these transactions is limited to one Data Phase. Transactions using the Memory Write, Memory Read Block, Memory Write Block, Alias to Memory Read Block, Alias to Memory Write Block, and Split Completion are permitted by both 64- and 32-bit initiators and are permitted to have one or more Data Phases, up to the maximum required to satisfy the byte count.

10. As in conventional PCI, data is transferred on any clock in which both IRDY# and TRDY# are asserted.

11. The following rules apply to the use of byte enables:
    - a. Byte enables are included in the Requester Attributes for all DWORD transactions. Byte enables are included on the C/BE# bus during the Data Phases of all Memory Write burst transactions. Byte enables further qualify the bytes affected by the transaction. Only bytes for which the byte enable is asserted are affected by the transaction.
    - b. The C/BE# bus is reserved and driven high during the single Data Phase of all DWORD transactions and throughout all Data Phases of all burst transactions except Memory Write.
    - c. DWORD transactions are permitted to have any combination of byte enables, including no byte enables asserted. See Section 2.3 for restrictions on starting address and byte enables.
    - d. Memory Write transactions are permitted to have any combination of byte enables between the starting and ending addresses, inclusive. Byte enables must be deasserted for bytes before the starting address and after the ending address (if those addresses are not aligned to the width of the bus). See Section 2.12.3 for exceptions and additional requirements when a 64-bit initiator addresses a 32-bit target.
    - e. The byte count of Memory Write transactions is not adjusted for bytes whose byte enables are deasserted within the transaction. In other words, the byte count is the same whether all or none of the byte enables were asserted.

12. Device state machines must not be confused by target control signals (DEVSEL#, TRDY#, and STOP#) asserting while the bus is Idle (FRAME# and IRDY# both deasserted). (In some systems, the PCI-X initialization pattern appears on the bus when another device is being hot-inserted onto the bus. See Section 6.2.3.2.)

13. Like conventional PCI, no device is permitted to drive and receive a bus signal at the same time. (See Section 3.1.)

Initiator Rules

The following rules control the way a device initiates a transaction:

1. As in conventional PCI, a PCI-X initiator begins a transaction by asserting FRAME#. (See Section 2.7.2.1 for differences for configuration transactions.)
2. In most cases, the initiator asserts FRAME# within two clocks after GNT# is asserted and the bus is Idle. If the transaction uses a configuration command, the initiator must assert FRAME# six clocks after GNT# is asserted and the bus is Idle.
3. The initiator asserts and deasserts control signals as follows:
   - a. The initiator asserts FRAME# to signal the start of the transaction. It deasserts FRAME# on the later of the following two conditions:
     - 1) one clock before the last Data Phase.
     - 2) two clocks after the target asserts TRDY# (or terminates the transaction in some other way as described in Section 2.11.2).

     The two conditions for the deassertion of FRAME# cover two cases discussed in Section 2.11. The first case (1) is if the transaction has four or more Data Phases. The second case (2) is if the transaction has less than four Data Phases.
   - b. Initiator Wait States are not permitted. The initiator asserts IRDY# two clocks after the Attribute Phase. It deasserts it on the later of the following two conditions:
     - 1) one clock after the last Data Phase.
     - 2) two clocks after the target asserts TRDY# (or terminates the transaction in some other way as described in Section 2.11.2).

     The two conditions for the deassertion of IRDY# cover two cases discussed in Section 2.11. The first case (1) is if the transaction has three or more Data Phases. The second case (2) is if the transaction has less than three Data Phases.
4. If no target asserts DEVSEL# on or before the Subtractive decode time, the initiator ends the transaction as a Master Abort.
5. For write and Split Completion transactions, the initiator must drive data on the AD bus two clocks after the Attribute Phase. If the transaction is a burst with more than one Data Phase, the initiator advances to the second data value two clocks after the target asserts DEVSEL#, in anticipation of the target asserting TRDY#. If the target also inserts Wait States, the initiator must toggle between its first and second data values until the target asserts TRDY# (or terminates the transaction). See Section 2.12.3 for requirements for a 64-bit initiator writing to 32-bit targets.

6. The initiator is required to terminate the transaction when the byte count is satisfied.

7. The initiator is permitted to disconnect a burst transaction (before the byte count is satisfied) only on an ADB. If the initiator intends to disconnect the transaction on the first ADB, and the first ADB is less than four Data Phases from the starting address, the initiator must adjust the byte count to terminate the transaction on that ADB.

8. If a burst transaction would otherwise cross the next ADB, and the target signals Disconnect at Next ADB four Data Phases before an ADB or on the first Data Phase, the initiator deasserts FRAME# two clocks later and disconnects the transaction on the ADB. The initiator treats Disconnect at Next ADB the same as Data Transfer in all other Data Phases.

9. If the transaction has four or more data phases, the initiator floats the C/BE# bus on the clock it deasserts IRDY#. If the transaction has less than four data phases, the initiator floats the C/BE# bus either on the clock it deasserts IRDY# or one clock after that.

10. If the transaction is a write with four or more data phases, the initiator floats the AD bus on the clock it deasserts IRDY#. If the transaction is a write with less than four data phases, the initiator floats the AD bus either on the clock it deasserts IRDY# or one clock after that.

11. The default Latency Timer value for initiators in PCI-X mode is 64. Initiators must disconnect the current transaction on the next ADB if the Latency Timer expires and GNT# is deasserted.

Target Rules

The following rules apply to the way a target responds to a transaction:

1. Memory address ranges (including those assigned through Base Address registers) for all devices must be no smaller than 128 bytes. System configuration software assigns the memory range of each function of each device (that requests Memory Space) to different ranges aligned to ADBs. No two device-functions respond to addresses between the same two adjacent ADBs.

2. The target claims the transaction by asserting DEVSEL# using decodes A, B, C, or Subtractive, as given in Table 2-6.

3. After a target asserts DEVSEL#, it must complete the transaction with one or more Data Phases by signaling one or more of the following: Split Response, Target Abort, Single Data Phase Disconnect, Wait State, Data Transfer, Retry, or Disconnect at Next ADB. See Table 2-14.

4. The target is not permitted to signal Wait State after the first Data Phase. If the target signals Split Response, Target Abort, or Retry, the target must do

so within eight clocks of the assertion of FRAME#. If the target signals Single Data Phase Disconnect, Data Transfer, or Disconnect at Next ADB, the target must do so within 16 clocks of the assertion of FRAME#. All PCI-X targets (including the host bridge) are subject to the same target initial latency limits.

5. If a PCI-X target signals Data Transfer (with or without preceding Wait States), the target is limited to disconnecting the transaction only on an ADB (until the byte count is satisfied). To disconnect the transaction on an ADB, the target signals Disconnect at Next ADB on any Data Phase. Once the target has signaled Disconnect at Next ADB, it must continue to do so until the end of the transaction.

   If the target signals Disconnect at Next ADB four or more clocks before an ADB, the initiator disconnects the transaction on that ADB. If the transaction starting address is less than four Data Phases from an ADB and the target signals Disconnect at Next ADB on the first Data Phase (with or without preceding Wait States), the transaction ends on that ADB. (See Section 2.11.2.2.)

6. The target is permitted to signal Single Data Phase Disconnect only on the first Data Phase (with or without preceding Wait States). It is permitted to do so both on burst transactions (even if the byte count is small enough to limit the transaction to a single Data Phase) and DWORD transactions (which are always a single Data Phase). (See Section 2.11.2.1.)

7. The target is permitted to signal Target Abort on any Data Phase regardless of its relationship to an ADB.

8. The target deasserts DEVSEL#, STOP#, and TRDY# one clock after the last Data Phase (if they are not already deasserted) and floats them one clock after that.

9. If the transaction is a read, the target floats the AD bus on the clock after the last data phase, regardless of the number of data phases in the transaction or the type of termination. That is, the target floats the AD bus on the clock it deasserts DEVSEL#, STOP#, and/or TRDY# after signaling the last Data Transfer or target termination.

Bus Arbitration Rules

The following protocol rules apply to bus arbitration:

1. As in conventional PCI, the arbitration algorithm is not specified. The arbiter is required to be fair to all devices (see Section 4.1). If a device signals Split Response, arbitration within that device must fairly allow the initiation of the Split Completion (see Section 4.1.1).

2. All REQ# and GNT# signals are registered by the arbiter as well as by initiators. That is, they are clocked directly into and out of flip-flops at the arbiter and device interfaces.

3. An initiator is permitted to assert and deassert REQ# on any clock. Unlike conventional PCI, there is no requirement to deassert REQ# after a target termination (STOP# asserted). (The arbiter is assumed to monitor bus transactions to determine when a transaction has been target terminated if the arbiter uses this information in its arbitration algorithm.)

4. An initiator is permitted to deassert REQ# on any clock independent of whether GNT# is asserted. An initiator is permitted to deassert REQ# without initiating a transaction after GNT# is asserted.

5. If all the GNT# signals are deasserted, the arbiter is permitted to assert any GNT# on any clock. After the arbiter asserts GNT#, the arbiter must keep it asserted for a minimum of five clocks while the bus is Idle, or until the initiator asserts FRAME# or deasserts REQ#. (This provides the opportunities for all devices to execute configuration transactions.)

6. If only one REQ# is asserted, it is recommended that the arbiter keep GNT# asserted to that device.

7. If the arbiter deasserts GNT# to one device, it must wait until the next clock to assert GNT# to another device.

8. An initiator is permitted to start a new transaction (drive the AD bus, etc.) on any clock N in which the initiator's GNT# was asserted on clock N-2, and either the bus was Idle (FRAME# and IRDY# were both deasserted) on clock N-2 or FRAME# was deasserted and IRDY# was asserted on clock N-3 (see Section 4.1.1). An initiator is permitted to start a new transaction on clock N even if GNT# is deasserted on clock N-1.

9. All fast back-to-back transactions as defined in PCI 2.2 are not permitted in PCI-X mode.

10. In PCI hot-plug systems, the arbiter must coordinate with the Hot-Plug Controller to prevent hot-plug operations from interfering with other bus transactions. See Section 4.3.

Configuration Transaction Rules

The following protocol rules apply to configuration transactions:

1. PCI-X initiators must drive the address for four clocks before asserting FRAME# for configuration transactions when in PCI-X mode.

2. In addition to the information required in conventional PCI for a Type 0 configuration transaction, in PCI-X the transaction must include the target device number in AD[15::11] of the Address Phase. (See Section 2.7.2.2.) The target device bus number is provided in AD[7::0] of the Attribute Phase.

The target of a Type 0 Configuration Write transaction stores its device number and bus number in its internal registers.

3. Software is required to write to the Configuration Space of every device on a bridge's secondary bus after changing that bridge's secondary bus number. This occurs as part of the device enumeration process.

4. Type 1 configuration transactions flow through the bus hierarchy the same as in conventional PCI.

Parity Error Rules

The following rules apply to parity error conditions:

1. If a device receiving data (i.e., the target of a write or Split Completion and the initiator of a read) detects a data parity error, it must assert PERR# (if enabled) on the second clock after PAR64 and PAR are driven (one clock later than conventional PCI).

2. During read transactions, the target drives PAR64 (if responding as a 64-bit device) and PAR on clock N+1 for the read data it drives on clock N and the byte enables driven by the initiator on clock N-1. During write transactions, the initiator drives PAR64 (if responding as a 64-bit device) and PAR on clock N+1 for the write data and the byte enables it drives on clock N.

3. All PCI-X devices are required to service data parity error conditions for their transactions. See Section 5.4.1.

4. If a device detects a parity error on an Attribute Phase, the device asserts SERR# (if enabled), independent of whether the device decodes its address during the Address Phase.

5. For Split Transactions, the requester sets the Master Data Parity Error bit in the Status register for data parity errors on either the Split Request or the Split Completion.

6. If data parity error recovery is disabled, the device asserts SERR# when a data parity error occurs (see Section 5.4.1).

7. Other requirements for asserting SERR# and setting status bits for address-phase and data-phase errors are the same as for conventional PCI.

Bus Width Rules

The following rules apply to the width of the transaction:

1. As in conventional PCI, PCI-X devices are permitted to implement either a 64-bit or a 32-bit interface.

2. The width of the address is independent of the width of the data transfer.
3. All devices that initiate memory transactions must be capable of generating 64-bit memory addresses.
4. If a device requests a memory range through a Base Address register, that Base Address register must be 64 bits wide.
5. If an address is greater than 4 GB, all initiators (including 64-bit devices) generate a dual address cycle.
6. The Attribute Phase is always a single clock long for both 64-bit and 32-bit initiators.
7. Only burst transactions (memory commands other than Memory Read DWORD) use 64-bit data transfers. (This maximizes similarity with conventional PCI, in which only memory transactions use 64-bit data transfers.) The width of each transaction is determined with a handshake protocol on REQ64# and ACK64# that is similar to conventional PCI.

Split Transaction Rules

The following rules apply to Split Transactions:

1. Any transaction that is terminated with Split Response results in one or more Split Completion transactions.
2. Split Completions contain either read data or a Split Completion Message but not both.
3. If the completer returns read data, the Completer must return all the data (the full byte count) unless an error occurs. The read data is delivered in multiple Split Completion transactions if either the initiator or the target disconnects it at ADBs. The initiator (completer) is also permitted to adjust the byte count of the Split Completion to terminate it on the first ADB. Each time the Split Completion resumes after a disconnection, the initiator adjusts the byte count (and starting address) to indicate the number of bytes remaining in the Sequence.
4. The requester must accept all Data Phases of a Split Completion. The requester must terminate a Split Completion with Data Transfer or Target Abort. (Initial Wait States are permitted.) The requester must never terminate a Split Completion transaction with Split Response, Single Data Phase Disconnect, Retry, or Disconnect at Next ADB. A PCI-X bridge forwarding a Split Completion from one PCI bus to another (when both are operating in PCI-X mode) is permitted to disconnect the Split Completion or terminate it with Retry under certain conditions (see Section 8.4.5).
5. If the request is a write transaction, or if the completer encounters an error while executing the request, the completer sends a Split Completion Message to the requester. Although Split Completion transactions are consid-

ered burst transactions (i.e., they include the byte count), a Split Completion Message is always a single Data Phase. The Split Completion Message includes not only an indication of how the transaction completed, but if an error occurred during a read operation, the message includes an indication of the length of the Sequence that remains unsent. Intervening bridges optionally use this information to manage their internal buffers.

Appendix B

Glossary

Glossary

Table G-1: Glossary of Terms

Term	Definition
Address Order	The byte address is incremented sequentially beginning with the start address of the sequence. For example, Split Completions in the same sequence (i.e., resulting from a single Split Request) must be returned in address order.
Allowable Disconnect Boundary (ADB)	An **address divisible by 128**. The initiator and the target are only permitted to disconnect burst transactions on ADBs.
ADB Delimited Quanta (ADQ)	**An ADQ is the amount of data transferred within each ADB**. When a burst transaction starts, the byte-specific start address issued may or may not start on an ADB (i.e., an address divisible by 128). In addition, the burst may or may not continue across the next ADB. As an example, assume that a transaction starts at any address within an ADB, crosses two ADBs, and completes without transferring all of the data within the next ADB. This transaction includes three ADQs of data.
Application Bridge	A device that resides on a PCI or a PCI-X bus on one side and connects to a PCI-X bus on its other side, but it implements a Type 00 Configuration Header and a Class code that indicates its function as something other than a bridge.

Table G-1: Glossary of Terms (Continued)

Term	Definition
Attributes and the Attribute Phase	The Attributes consist of the 36-bits of additional transaction information provided by the initiator during the Attribute phase of the transaction. This information is provided on AD[31:0] and C/BE[3:0]#. The Attribute phase occurs in the clock immediately following the Address phase. C/BE[7:4]# and AD[63:32] are reserved and must be driven high by 64-bit initiators.
Burst Transaction	A burst transaction can be of any length from 1 to 4096 bytes and can be initiated as either a 32- or 64-bit transaction. In each Data Phase of a Memory Write burst transaction, the C/BE signals indicate the bytes to be transferred within the current dword (or quadword, if a 64-bit transaction). In all other burst transactions, the C/BE signals are reserved and must be driven high by the initiator in all Data Phases. The burst transaction types are: • Memory Read Block • Memory Write Block • Memory Write • Alias to Memory Read Block • Alias to Memory Write Block • Split Completion
Byte Count	The number of bytes to be transferred in a Sequence. In all burst transactions other than Memory Write, the number of bytes transferred is governed solely by the Byte Count, while the Byte Enables are not used. In the Memory Write Transaction, the Byte Count defines the overall span of memory locations within which bytes are to be written, while the Byte Enables in each Data Phase identify the bytes to be written within the current dword (or qword, if a 64-bit transfer).

Table G-1: Glossary of Terms (Continued)

Term	Definition
Completer	The device addressed by a transaction request. This is not necessarily the target that responds to the transaction request by asserting DEVSEL#. As an example, the initiator of the transaction request may reside on one bus while the addressed device resides on the other side of a PCI-X bridge. In this case, the completer is the device addressed by the requests, while the target that responds with DEVSEL# to the initiator is the bridge.
Completer Attributes	The target of a transaction request my respond with a Split Response to indicate that it will complete the transaction at a later time by initiating a Split Completion transaction. In the Attribute Phase of the subsequent Split Completion transaction, the Completer supplies an array of attributes referred to as the Completer Attributes. This includes the Completer's ID, the transfer count, the request completion status, etc.
Completer ID	The Completer's bus, device, and function number. This information is embedded within the attributes delivered in the Attribute Phase of each Split Completion transaction.
Complex device	See "Device Complexity" on page 481 and "Application Bridge" on page 564.
Configuration Attributes	The attribute information delivered in the Attribute Phase of a Type 0 configuration transaction. This includes the Requester ID, Secondary Bus Number, and the Sequence Tag. If the configuration transaction originated as a Type 1 configuration transaction on the primary side of a PCI-X bridge and was converted to a Type 0 configuration transaction when it was passed to the destination bus, the bridge inserts the number of its secondary bus in the Secondary Bus Number field.

Table G-1: Glossary of Terms (Continued)

Term	Definition
Data Phase	A Data Phase completes when the target signals the transfer of a data item or terminates the transaction. Transactions terminated by the target with a Split Response or a Retry have a single Data Phase. A Data Phase may consist of more than one clock cycle if the target inserts Wait States into the Data Phase.
Disconnection	Defined as the termination of a burst transaction after some but not all of the byte count has been satisfied. While it is the termination of the current transaction, it does not complete the Sequence. • Targets can disconnect any transaction after a single Data Phase by signaling Single Data Phase Disconnect. • Targets can also disconnect on any ADB by signaling Disconnect at Next ADB. • Initiators can disconnect on any ADB four or more Data Phases from the starting address by deasserting FRAME# two clocks before the ADB.
Device	A PCI or PCI-X compliant component or card. As defined in the PCI spec, the device may contain one or more functions.
Downstream	See "Definition of Downstream and Upstream" on page 579.
Dword	Four bytes of data aligned on address divisible by four.

Table G-1: Glossary of Terms (Continued)

Term	Definition
Dword Transaction	A transaction type (i.e., command) that is only permitted to have an Address Phase, an Attribute Phase, and a single Data Phase. A dword transaction is by definition initiated as a 32-bit transaction and is never initiated as a 64-bit transaction. The Byte Count field of the attributes is reserved (except in a configuration read or write transaction) and is not used. Rather, the Byte Enables, C/BE[3:0]#, issued in the Data Phase indicate the bytes to be read or written within the dword identified by AD[31:2] in the transaction's Address Phase. The dword transaction types are: • Interrupt Acknowledge • Special Cycle • IO Read • IO Write • Configuration Read • Configuration Write • Memory Read Dword
Ending Address	Last address included in the Sequence. For a burst transaction, it is calculated by adding the Byte Count to the Sequence start address and subtracting one. For a dword transaction, it is the last byte addressed (via the Byte Enables, C/BE[3:0]#) within the dword addressed by AD[31:2].
Full Lock	See "Sequence of Events" on page 583.
Function	As defined in the PCI spec, each device (i.e., component or card) can contain between one and eight functions. A function is a logical device that resides within a (physical) device. Each function has its own dedicated 64 dwords of configuration space for the implementation of its configuration registers.

Table G-1: Glossary of Terms (Continued)

Term	Definition
Immediate Transaction	Transactions terminated by the target with Retry or Split Response are not Immediate transactions. An Immediate transaction terminates in a way that includes transferring data or with an error that completes the Sequence. Transactions in which the target signals Data Transfer, Single Data Phase Disconnect, Disconnect at Next ADB, Master Abort, or Target Abort are Immediate transactions.
Initiator	A device that initiates a transaction by requesting bus ownership, asserting FRAME# and driving the command address. A bridge forwarding a transaction to the bus on its opposite side acts as the initiator of the transaction it initiates on the other side.
Initiator Lock	See "Sequence of Events" on page 583.
North Bridge (aka NB)	This is the slang name for the Host/PCI (or Host/PCI-X) bridge.
PCI-X Bridge	A bridge between two buses that are PCI-X capable. If a conventional PCI device is present on either side of the bridge, that interface of the bridge (primary or secondary) will operate in conventional PCI mode.
PCI-X Initialization Pattern	The pattern delivered to PCI-X devices by the bus's Source Bridge on the rising-edge of RST#. The pattern informs the PCI-capable devices of the bus clock frequency range as well as the bus protocol (conventional PCI or PCI-X). Refer to Chapter 4, entitled "Device Types and Bus Initialization," on page 55.
Primary Bus	The side of a PCIX-to-PCIX bridge that is closer to the processor and main memory.
Quadword or Qword	A group of eight contiguous memory or IO locations that starts on an address boundary divisible by eight.

Table G-1: Glossary of Terms (Continued)

Term	Definition
Requester	The requester is the initiator that originally issued a transaction request. The initial transaction request may receive a Split Response from the Completer (if they both reside on the same bus) or from a bridge that resides between the Requester and the Completer. In this case, the Requester will be the target of a subsequent Split Completion transaction issued by the Completer (if it resides on the same bus) or by a bridge (that resides between the Requester and the Completer).
Requester Attributes	Format of the attributes issued in all transactions other than Type 0 configuration transactions and Split Completion transactions. These attributes include information about the Requester and the Sequence.
Requester ID	When the Requester originates a transaction request, it includes its identity (i.e., Requester ID) by providing its Bus Number, Device Number and Function Number in the transaction's Attribute Phase. In Split Completion transactions, this information is provided in the Address Phase rather than the Attribute Phase and is used to identify the Requester that this Split Completion transaction wishes to reconnect with.
Secondary Bus	The side of a PCIX-to-PCIX bridge that is further away from the processor and main memory.

Table G-1: Glossary of Terms (Continued)

Term	Definition
Sequence	A Sequence is the series of one or more transactions performed to accomplish one overall transfer originally initiated by a Requester. The Sequence consists of one transaction if it doesn't receive a Split Response. Reception of a Split Response for the first transaction indicates that a subsequent series of one or more Split Completion transactions will be performed to transfer the remainder of the data. Each transaction associated with a specific Sequence uses the same, unique Sequence ID (i.e., Requester ID and Tag).
Sequence ID	Each transaction associated with a Sequence uses the same, unique Sequence ID. The ID consists of the Requester ID (i.e., the Bus Number, Device Number and Function Number of the Requester that initiated the Sequence) and Tag (a 5-bit number that is assigned to a Sequence by the Requester).
Sequence Size	The number of ADQs required to encompass all of the data to be transferred in a Sequence. Some examples: • The Sequence Size of dword transaction is one ADQ (because, by definition, a single dword resides within a single data block aligned on an address divisible by 128; in other words, within one ADB). • The Sequence Size of a burst that begins within the bounds of one ADB and ends within the bounds of the next, sequential ADB is two ADQs.
Sequence Termination	A Sequence is permanently terminated under two circumstances: • All of the data has been transferred successfully. • A fatal error has occurred. Examples would be a Master Abort and a Target Abort.
Simple Device	See "Device Complexity" on page 481.

Table G-1: Glossary of Terms (Continued)

Term	Definition
Source Bridge	The Source Bridge for a PCI-X bus is the one that senses the state of M66EN and PCIXCAP from devices on that bus and then issues the appropriate PCI-X initialization pattern to the PCI-X devices that reside on the bus. The Source Bridge must also be capable of initiating Type 0 configuration transactions on that PCI-X bus.
South Bridge (aka SB)	This is the slang name for the PCI-to-ISA, PCI-to-EISA, PCIX -to-ISA, or PCIX-to-EISA bridge.
Split Completion	A Split Completion transaction is issued by the Sequence Completer to reconnect with the Sequence Requester for the purpose of returning the results of a previously received read or write Sequence. If the Split Completion must cross a bridge to get to the Sequence Requester, the bridge initiates the Split Completion on the other side of the bridge to make it visible to the Requester (or another bridge that may be in the path to the Requester). Split Completion also refers to a queue entry associated with a Split Completion transaction within the Split Transaction queue of the Requester, the Completer, and within any bridges between the Requester and the Completer.
Split Completion Address	The Split Completion Address is placed on the AD bus during the Address Phase of a Split Completion transaction and consists of the Requester ID and the Sequence Tag.
Split Completion Message	This is a Split Completion transaction that notifies the Sequence Requester that a read or write request encountered an error, or that a write request completed without error. In a Split Completion transaction's Attribute Phase, the Split Completion Message bit that indicates (if set) that the Completion is a Message rather than one that is returning previously requested read data.

Table G-1: Glossary of Terms (Continued)

Term	Definition
Split Request	A transaction request that is terminated with a Split Response is transformed into a Split Request. This means that the transaction result will be returned by the Completer (or by the bridge) at a later time rather than immediately (in this transaction). Split Request also refers to a queue entry associated with a Split Request transaction within the Split Transaction queue of the Requester, the Completer, and within any bridges between the Requester and the Completer. When the Completer executes the Split Request, it is transformed into a Split Completion.
Split Response	If the target (the Completer or a bridge) of a transaction decides to memorize a transaction request and complete it at a later time, it indicates this to the transaction initiator by issuing a Split Response to the transaction initiator. This transforms the transaction request into a Split Request.
Split Transaction	When the original transaction request receives a Split Response from the target (the Completer or a bridge), the request is transformed into a Split Request. The target of the original transaction request (the Completer or a bridge) will return the transaction results at a later time as a series of one or more Split Completion transactions.
Starting Address	The address indicated in the Address Phase of all transaction types other than Split Completion, Interrupt Acknowledge, or Special Cycle transactions. While the start address of a configuration transaction must be dword-aligned, the start address of all other transaction types (with the exception of those noted earlier) is byte-aligned.

Table G-1: Glossary of Terms (Continued)

Term	Definition
Tag	A 5-bit number assigned by the originator of a Sequence. The Sequence originator assigns a unique Tag to each Sequence it originates and cannot reuse the Tag assigned to one of its Sequences until the Sequence has been retired (by a successful transfer of all of the requested data or by reception of an error).
Target	When an initiator starts a transaction, the device that responds by asserting DEVSEL#. This is either the Completer (if it resides on the same bus as the initiator) or a bridge that resides between the transaction originator and the Completer addressed by the request.
Target Data Phase Signaling	In each Data Phase, the target signals one of the following to the initiator: • Split Response • Target Abort • Single Data Phase Disconnect • Wait State • Data Transfer • Retry • Disconnect at Next ADB
Target Lock	See "Sequence of Events" on page 583.
Toggling, data	See "On Burst Writes, Insert Wait States in Pairs" on page 257.
Transaction	The combination of address, attribute, target response, data, and bus turn-around phases associated with a single assertion of FRAME#.
Transaction Termination	The protocol used by the initiator or the target to end a transaction.
Upstream	See "Definition of Downstream and Upstream" on page 579.

Index

Index

Index

Index

Stepping Control bit 468

T

TA# 159
Tag 34, 114, 500, 505, 542
Target Abort 107, 290, 320, 499, 580, 589, 603
Target Abort on Other Side of Bridge 638
Target Abort on Split Completion 606
Target Latency 191
target-lock state 584
termination, initiator 104, 280
termination, target 106, 290
timeslice 19
toggling data 257, 369, 384
Trace Length 379, 652
Transaction of Four or More Data Phases 281
Transaction of Less Than Four Data Phases 282
Transfer Acknowledge 159
Transfer Length 95, 166
translating PCI To PCI-X 536
Translating PCI-X to PCI 543
Trhfa 80, 191
Trhff 68, 653
Type 0 Configuration Read 439
Type 0 Configuration transaction 206, 207, 426, 436
Type 0 Configuration Write 430, 443, 477
Type 1 configuration access 206, 207, 430, 447

U

Unexpected Split Completion Bit 480, 500, 504, 626
Unlocking of a Target Bridge 599
upstream 331, 426, 507, 579

V

vector 154
Virtual Buffer Space mode 508
VPD 456

W

Wait State pairs 257, 384

Wait States 13, 31
width of a PCI-X function's connection 332
Write Completion Class 318, 624
Write Data Parity error 320

The PC System Architecture Series

The PC System Architecture Series is a crisply written and comprehensive set of guides to the most important PC hardware standards. Each title illustrates the relationship between the software and hardware, and thoroughly explains the architecture, features, and operation of systems built using one particular type of chip or hardware specification.

MindShare, Inc. is one of the leading technical training companies in the computer industry,

providing innovative courses for dozens of companies, including Intel, IBM, and Compaq.

> *"There is only one way to describe the series of PC hardware and architecture books written by Tom Shanley and Don Anderson: INVALUABLE."*
> —*PC Magazine*'s "Read Only" column

ISBN 0-201-40994-1

ISBN 0-201-70069-7

ISBN 0-201-40997-6

ISBN 0-201-40995-X

ISBN 0-201-48535-4

ISBN 0-201-40996-8

ISBN 0-201-30974-2

ISBN 0-201-72682-3

ISBN 0-201-40991-7

ISBN 0-201-30973-4

ISBN 0-201-40992-5

ISBN 0-201-41013-3

ISBN 0-201-40990-9

ISBN 0-201-55447-X

ISBN 0-201-46137-4

http://www.awl.com/cseng/series/mindshare/

♦ Addison-Wesley

These limitations or exclusions of warranties and liability do not affect or prejudice the statutory rights of a consumer; i.e., a person acquiring goods otherwise than in the course of a business.

6. LIMITATION OF DAMAGES:

MINDSHARE SHALL NOT BE LIABLE FOR ANY INDIRECT, SPECIAL, INCIDENTAL OR CONSEQUENTIAL DAMAGES OR LOSS (INCLUDING DAMAGES FOR LOSS OF BUSINESS, LOSS OF PROFITS, OR THE LIKE), WHETHER BASED ON BREACH OF CONTRACT, TORT (INCLUDING NEGLIGENCE), PRODUCT LIABILITY OR OTHERWISE, EVEN IF MINDSHARE OR ITS REPRESENTATIVES HAVE BEEN ADVISED OF THE POSSIBILITY OF SUCH DAMAGES. SOME STATES DO NOT ALLOW THE LIMITATION OR EXCLUSION OF LIABILITY FOR INCIDENTAL OR CONSEQUENTIAL DAMAGES, SO THIS LIMITATION OR EXCLUSION MAY NOT APPLY TO YOU. The limited warranty, exclusive remedies and limited liability set forth above are fundamental elements of the basis of the bargain between Mindshare and you. You agree that Mindshare would not be able to provide the CD on an economic basis without such limitations.

7. GOVERNMENT END USERS (USA only):

RESTRICTED RIGHTS LEGEND The CD is "Restricted Computer Software." Use, duplication, or disclosure by the U.S. Government is subject to restrictions as set forth in this Agreement and as provided in DFARS 227.7202-1(a) and 227.7202-3(a) (1995), DFARS 252.227-7013 (OCT 1988), FAR 12.212(a)(1995), FAR 52.227-19, or FAR 52.227-14, as applicable." Manufacturer: Mindshare, Inc., 4285 Slash Pine Drive, Colorado Springs, CO 80908.

8. GENERAL:

This Agreement shall be governed by the internal laws of the State of Colorado. This Agreement contains the complete agreement between the parties with respect to the subject matter hereof, and supersedes all prior or contemporaneous agreements or understandings, whether oral or written. All questions concerning this Agreement shall be directed to: Mindshare, Inc., 4285 Slash Pine Drive, Colorado Springs, CO 80908, Attention: Chief Financial Officer.

Mindshare is registered trademark of Mindshare, Inc.

Single-User License Agreement 9/4/00.